OREGON CAMPING

OREGON
CAMPING

The Complete Guide to
More Than 700 Campgrounds

FIRST EDITION

Tom Stienstra

AVALON
TRAVEL

FOGHORN OUTDOORS:
OREGON CAMPING
The Complete Guide to
More Than 700 Campgrounds

First Edition

Tom Stienstra

Published by
Avalon Travel Publishing
5855 Beaudry Street
Emeryville, CA 94608, USA

Please send all comments, corrections,
additions, amendments, and critiques to:

✒️FOGHORN OUTDOORS®
OREGON CAMPING
AVALON TRAVEL PUBLISHING
5855 BEAUDRY ST.
EMERYVILLE, CA 94608, USA
email: atpfeedback@avalonpub.com
website: www.foghorn.com

Printing History
First edition—April 2002
5 4 3 2 1

ISBN: 1-56691-470-1
ISSN: 1538-2745

Editor: Jeff Lupo
Series Manager: Marisa Solís
Copy Editor: Karen Bleske
Proofreader: Jeannie Trizzino
Researchers: Michelle Mauro, Ryan Bacchia, Stephani Cruickshank
Graphics: Susan Snyder
Illustrations: Bob Race
Cover Design: Jacob Goolkasian
Production: Darren Alessi, Patrick David Barber Design
Map Editor: Olivia Solís
Cartography: CHK America, Kat Kalamaras, Suzanne Service, Mike Morgenfeld
Index: Laura Welcome

Front cover photo: ©Terry Donnely, Deschutes National Forest, OR

Distributed by Publishers Group West

Printed in the USA by R.R. Donnelley

About the Author

Tom Stienstra has been a full-time outdoors writer for 25 years, spending 200 days afield each year, camping, hiking, fishing and boating, searching for the best of the outdoors and writing about it. Tom has been twice awarded the Presidents Award by the Outdoors Writers Association of America as the National Outdoor Writer of the Year, newspaper division. He is the nation's top-selling author of outdoor guidebooks. In 1999 and 2000, Amazon.com awarded his book *Foghorn Outdoors: California Camping* as the No. 1 outdoor book in the nation. He lives with his wife, Stephani, and two sons, Jeremy and Kris, in the "State of Jefferson." He has family and relatives in Lake Oswego, Springfield, Monroe, and Battle Ground, Washington. He can be reached directly on the Internet at www.TomStienstra.com, where his other current books are available, including:

Foghorn Outdoors: California Camping
Foghorn Outdoors: California Fishing
Foghorn Outdoors: California Hiking (with Ann Marie Brown)
Foghorn Outdoors: California Recreational Lakes & Rivers
Foghorn Outdoors: California Wildlife (with illustrator Paul Johnson)
Foghorn Outdoors: Northern California Cabins & Cottages
  (with Stephani Stienstra)
Foghorn Outdoors: Washington Camping (with Stephani Stienstra)

Contents

SPECIAL TOPICS

Keep It Wild 3

SPECIAL TOPICS

Our Commitment

We are committed to making *Foghorn Outdoors: Oregon Camping* the most accurate, thorough, and enjoyable camping guide to the state. Every camping spot in this book has been carefully reviewed and accompanied with the most up-to-date information available. It is possible, however, that some fees listed in this book have changed, or that certain camping destinations have opened, closed, or changed hands. If you have a specific need or concern, it's a good idea to call the campground ahead of time.

If you would like to comment on the book, whether it's to suggest a tent or RV spot we overlooked, or to let us know about any noteworthy experience—good or bad—that occurred while using *Foghorn Outdoors: Oregon Camping* as your guide, we would appreciate hearing from you. Please address correspondence to:

Foghorn Outdoors: Oregon Camping, 1st edition
Avalon Travel Publishing
5855 Beaudry Street
Emeryville, CA 94608
U.S.A.

email: atpfeedback@avalonpub.com

Maps

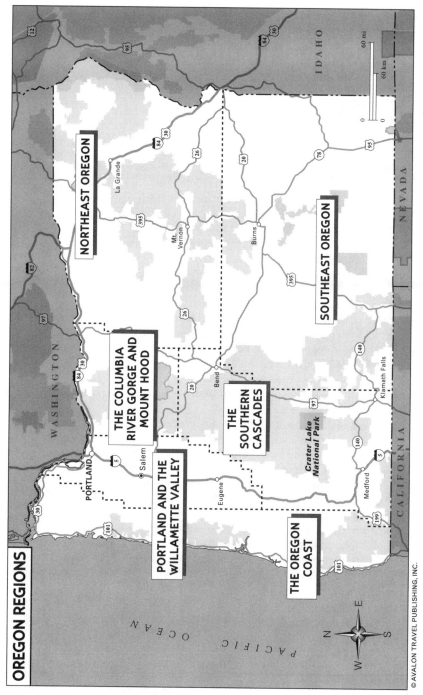

OREGON REGIONS

NORTHEAST OREGON

SOUTHEAST OREGON

THE COLUMBIA RIVER GORGE AND MOUNT HOOD

THE SOUTHERN CASCADES

PORTLAND AND THE WILLAMETTE VALLEY

THE OREGON COAST

Crater Lake National Park

WASHINGTON

IDAHO

NEVADA

CALIFORNIA

PACIFIC OCEAN

La Grande
Mt. Vernon
Burns
Bend
Salem
PORTLAND
Eugene
Medford
Klamath Falls

60 mi
60 km

© AVALON TRAVEL PUBLISHING, INC.

Credits and Acknowledgments

Michelle Mauro, Research Editor
Ryan Bacchia, Research Editor
Stephani Cruickshank, Research Editor

The following state and federal resource experts provided critical information and galley reviews regarding changes in reservations, fees, directions, and recreational opportunities. We are extremely grateful for their timely help and expert advice:

U. S. Forest Service
Daniel Harkenrider, Columbia River Gorge National Scenic Area
Barbara Smith, Crooked River National Grassland, Haystack Reservoir
Tina Smith, Deschutes National Forest, Crescent Ranger District
Bob Henning, Deschutes National Forest, Sisters Ranger District
Theresa Whitmire, Fremont National Forest, Bly Ranger District
Barry Schullanberger, Fremont National Forest, Lakeview Ranger District
Annette Montgomery, Fremont National Forest, Paisley Ranger District
Doug Ehran, Fremont National Forest, Silver Lake Ranger District
Charlie Krauss, Klamath National Forest, Scott River Ranger District
Amanda Vonwiller, Malheur National Forest
Shannon Winegar and Tracie Lieuallan, Malheur National Forest, Blue Mountain Ranger District
Joan Suther, Malheur National Forest, Emigrant Creek Ranger District
Carole Holly, Malheur National Forest, Prairie City Ranger District
Christine Hunt, Mount Hood National Forest, Barlow Ranger District
Glenda Woodcock, Mount Hood National Forest, Clackamas River Ranger District
Doug Jones, Mount Hood National Forest, Hood River Ranger District
Fran Lanagan, Mount Hood National Forest, Zigzag Ranger District
Linda Rock, Ochoco National Forest
John Zapell, Oregon Dunes National Recreation Area
John McKelligott, Rogue River National Forest, Applegate Ranger District
Bryce Leppek, Rogue River National Forest, Ashland Ranger District
Newell Schooler, Rogue River National Forest, Butte Falls and Prospect Ranger Districts
Linda Elfman, Siskiyou National Forest, Chetco Ranger District
Judith McHugh, Siskiyou National Forest, Galice and Illinois Valley Ranger Districts
Theresa Miller, Siskiyou National Forest, Gold Beach Ranger District
Reenay Stinson, Siskiyou National Forest, Powers Ranger District

Kathy Bailey, Siuslaw National Forest, Hebo Ranger District
John Zapell, Siuslaw National Forest, Mapleton Ranger District
Roxanne Lechner, Siuslaw National Forest, Waldport Ranger District
Sheri Gregory, Umatilla National Forest, Heppner Ranger District
Karen Kendall, Umatilla National Forest, North Fork John Day Ranger District
Jeff Bloom, Umatilla National Forest, Walla Walla Ranger District
Cindy Pack, Umpqua National Forest, Cottage Grove Ranger District
Terry Klingenberg, Umpqua National Forest, Diamond Lake Ranger District
Wayne Brady, Umpqua National Forest, North Umpqua Ranger District
Lori Depew, Umpqua National Forest, Tiller Ranger District
Angelica Johnson, Wallowa-Whitman National Forest
Tom Smit, Wallowa-Whitman National Forest, Pine Ranger District
Betty Duncan, Wallowa-Whitman National Forest, Unity Ranger District
Rick Thompson, Wallowa-Whitman National Forest
Rick Ley, Willamette National Forest, Blue River Ranger District
Ray Crist, Willamette National Forest, Detroit Ranger District
Dave Graham, Willamette National Forest, McKenzie Ranger District
Sherri Jensen, Willamette National Forest, Middle Fork Ranger District
Lupe Wilson, Willamette National Forest, Sweet Home Ranger District
Jeanie Sheehan, Winema National Forest
The publicity-shy staffs at Wallowa Mountains Visitor Center at Wallowa-Whitman National Forest, Eagle Cap, and Wallowa Valley Ranger Districts, Hells Canyon National Recreation Area

U.S. Army Corps of Engineers
Terry Green, Portland Ranger District

Bureau of Land Management
Fred McDonald and Evelyn Treiman, Burns District
Nancy Zepf, Coos Bay District
Doug Huntington, Eugene District
Grant Wiedenbach, Lakeview District
Jim Leffman, Medford District
Charlie Moon, Prineville District
Chuck White, Roseburg District
Tina Tyler, Salem District
Tom Christensen and Bob Alward, Vale District
Staff, Baker City Office

National Parks
Raven Balderas, Crater Lake National Park

National Wildlife Refuge
Tori Nunn, Hart Mountain National Antelope Refuge

Oregon State Parks

Debbie Lund, Ainsworth State Park
Greg Pelton, Beachside State Park
Patty Green, Beverly Beach State Park
Frank Arnold, Bullards Beach State Park
Pat Bry, Cape Blanco State Park and Humbug State Park
Brian Wais, Cape Lookout State Park
Bonnie Lee, Cascadia State Park
Sven Anderson, Cascara Campground
Jeff Powell, Champoeg State Heritage Area
Dennis Bradley, Clyde Holliday State Park and Unity Lake State Recreation Area
Barb Lakey, Collier Memorial State Park and Jackson F. Kimball State Park
Melanie Collins, Devil's Lake State Park
Bob Spratt, Deschutes River State Recreation Area
Mike Kuihuis, Detroit Lake State Park
Irene Fitzpatrick, Emigrant Springs State Heritage Area and Ukiah-Dale State
   Recreation Site
Bill Myers, Farewell Bend State Recreation Area
Macy Yates, Fort Stevens State Park
Wally Conklin, Goose Lake State Park
Fawn Gates, Jessie M. Honeyman Memorial State Park
Kelli Leiby, Joseph H. Stewart State Park
Ben Cox, Lake Owyhee State Park
Sue Gravin, LaPine State Park
Wanda Powell, Loeb State Park
Heidi Hansberger, Memaloose State Park
Eric Timmons, Milo McIver State Park
Randy Diestler, Minam State Park and Wallowa Lake State Park
Marsha Staben, Nehalem Bay State Park and Oswald West State Park
Arliss Perkins, Prineville Reservoir State Park
John Martin, Saddle Mountain State Park
Paul Lucas, Silver Falls State Park
Melanie Whisler, South Beach State Park
Celia Sheridan, Sunset Bay State Park
Lee Allen, Umpqua Lighthouse State Park
Donna Wilson, Valley of the Rogue State Park
Diane McClay, Viento State Park
Loretta Munsterman, William M. Tugman State Park

Oregon State Forest

Randy Peterson, Tillamook State Forest, Forest Grove District
Clyde Zeller, Tillamook State Forest, Tillamook District

Author's Note

If this book looks different from anything you have ever seen about Oregon, that is because it is.

I have made it a personal mission to win your trust and put the best of Oregon's great outdoors right in the palms of your hands in this book.

The reason I wrote the book was simple: I never wanted to get stuck again for the night without a spot. So I searched them out, primarily for myself. In the end, that is the best public value of the book: you will never get stuck for the night again. With this book, the days of being a prisoner of hope are over.

In this mission to make *Foghorn Outdoors: Oregon Camping* your book of choice, I have incorporated what I have learned in the past 25 years of roaming around the West as a full-time outdoors writer. I then hired three research editors to fact-check my work and review it with resource specialists. Together we faxed 700 pages of galley proofs to more than 100 rangers and recreation specialists at field offices and to the owners of each privately operated park. In the process, each word of every page has been reviewed by three or four specialists, with hundreds of people involved in polishing the final product.

When my publisher checked out the competition and compared the work with other books in the market, we discovered thousands of errors and listings that were outdated. We also discovered directions that were simply wrong or incoherent.

I have written every direction in the book so it is as if a person in the right seat is reading it to the person who is driving. Compare the directions and maps in this book with anything else out there and this alone can make it your book of choice.

Many of the most beautiful places on earth are in Oregon, and when my family and friends heard I was writing this book, they all instantly hated me! They figured all of their favorite spots would be revealed to all. But after reviewing the manuscript, they don't hate me anymore (except for this one cousin). That is because they have discovered, as I have, that Oregon is filled with beautiful, little-used campgrounds that are perfect jump-off points for adventures—and they represent hundreds of outstanding destinations, in addition to their sprinkling of favorites.

Some of the highlights of this book include:

- 750 campgrounds, featuring national forests, local, county, state and national parks, BLM land, land managed by the U.S. Army Corps of Engineers and Department of Forestry, and privately owned and operated parks.
- 10,000 updates and upgrades from anything previously published.
- 45 extremely detailed maps.
- Directions that are the easiest-to-use (and most-fact-checked) of any outdoor book in the state.
- Detailed and fact-checked information about each camp's facilities, fees, reservation policies, and nearby recreation.

- Helpful and anecdotal information about how to put the fun into every trip, including tips on catching fish, dealing with bears, and finding the best camp tents, bags, food, water purifiers, and more.
- Icons that quickly identify activities at each camp, and if pets are allowed.
- Every telephone number in the book has been phoned and reviewed.

I get tons of emails and letters, and I read each one carefully. These have been of great benefit. In the process, I have incorporated dozen of suggestions from readers to make this the book they want it to be. Your comments are always welcome and appreciated.

As you might figure, this is not a hobby for me, as it is for some part-time writers who publish books. This is my full-time job. Because I spend 200 days a year in the field, I understand how seriously people take their fun, what they need to know to make their trips work, as well as their underlying fears that they might get stuck for the night without a spot.

My advice is to never go anywhere without this book sitting on your front seat! See you out there!

—Tom Stienstra
website: www.TomStienstra.com

How to Use This Book

Foghorn Outdoors: Oregon Camping is divided into six chapters based on regional boundaries. Each chapter begins with a map of the area, which is further broken down into grid maps. These grid maps show the location of all the campgrounds in that chapter.

Despite the vast number of campgrounds featured in this guide, it's not difficult to navigate this book. In fact, it can be done easily in two ways:

1. If you know the name of the specific campground where you'd like to stay, or the name of the surrounding geographical area or nearby feature (town, national or state park or forest, mountain, lake, river, etc.), look it up in the index beginning on page 471 and turn to the corresponding page.

2. If you know the general area you want to visit, turn to the Oregon map and map list on pages x–xi. Find the region in which your destination lies, and turn to that map at the beginning of that chapter. You can then determine which campgrounds are in or near your destination by their corresponding numbers. Opposite the map will be a chapter table of contents listing each campground in the chapter by map number and the page number it's profiled on. Then turn to the corresponding page for the campground you're interested in.

About the Campground Profiles

Each campground in this book begins with a brief overview of its setting. Topics such as facilities, amenities, nearby or on-site recreation options, historical trivia, and ambience may also be addressed. The practical information you need to plan your trip is broken down further into the following categories:

- **Location** — This category provides the general location of the campground by naming its proximity to the nearest major town or landmark. Following this information is the name of the map that the campground can be found on. The entire entry will be written like this: "North of Portland; see Portland and the Willamette Valley map 1, grid a1."

- **Campsites, facilities** — This category provides the number of campsites for both tents and RVs and whether hookups are available. Facilities such as restrooms, picnic areas, recreation areas, laundry, and dump station will be addressed here, as well as the availability of piped water, showers, playground, stores, among others. The campground's pet policy is also mentioned here.

- **Reservations, fees** — This category notes whether reservations are accepted, and the rates for tent and RV sites. If there are additional fees for parking or pets, or discounted weekly or seasonal rates, that will also be noted here.

- **Directions** — This category provides mile-by-mile driving directions to the campground from the nearest major town.

- **Contact** — This category provides an address, phone number, and Internet address, if available, for the campground.

About the Icons
The icons in this book are designed to provide at-a-glance information on activities that are available on-site or nearby each campground. Some icons have been selected to also represent facilities available or services provided. They are not meant to represent every activity or service, but rather those that are most significant.

⚐ — Hiking trails are available.

⚐ — Biking trails or routes are available. This usually refers to mountain biking, although it may represent road cycling as well. Refer to the text for that campground for details.

⚐ — Swimming opportunities are available.

⚐ — Fishing opportunities are available.

⚐ — Boating opportunities are available. Various types of vessels apply under this umbrella activity, including motorboats and personal watercrafts (Jet Skis). Refer to the text for that campground for more detail, including mph restrictions and boat ramp availability.

⚐ — Winter sports are available. This general category may include activities such as downhill skiing, cross-country skiing, snowshoeing, snow mobiling, snowboarding, and ice skating. Refer to the text for that campground for more detail on which sports are available.

⚐ — Hot or cold springs are located nearby. Refer to the listing text for more information

⚐ — Pets are permitted. Campgrounds that allow pets may require an additional fee or that pets be leashed. Campgrounds may also restrict pet size or behavior. Refer to the text for that campground for specific instructions or call in advance.

⚐ — A playground is available. A campground with a playground can be desireable for campers traveling with children.

⚐ — Wheelchair access is provided, as advertised by campground managers. However, concerned persons are advised to call the contact number of a campground to be certain that their specific needs will be met.

 — RV sites are provided.

 — Tent sites are provided.

About the Ratings

Each campground in this book has been rated on a scale of **1** to **10** for scenic beauty. Ratings are based solely on scenic appeal and do not reflect quality issues such as the cleanliness of the camp or the temperament of the management, which can change from day to day.

About the Maps

The maps in this book are designed to show the general location of campgrounds and are not meant to substitute for more detailed road maps. Readers are advised to take additional maps when heading out to any campground, particularly when venturing into the wilderness.

INTRODUCTION

Introduction

Going on a camping trip can be like trying to put hiking boots on an octopus. You've tried it too, eh? Instead of the relaxing and fun trip full of adventure, it turns into a scenario called You against the World. You might as well try to fight a volcano.

But it doesn't have to be that way, and that's what this book is all about. If you give it a chance, it can put the mystery, excitement, and fun back into your camping vacations—and remove the fear of snarls, confusion, and occasional temper explosions of volcanic proportions that keep people at home, locked away from the action.

Mystery? There are hundreds of hidden, rarely used campgrounds listed and mapped in this book that you have never dreamed of. *Excitement?* At many of them you'll find the sizzle with the steak, the hike to a great lookout, the big fish at the end of the line. *Fun?* The how-to section of this book can help you take the futility out of your trips and put the fun back in. Add it up, put it in your cash register, and you can turn a camping trip into the satisfying adventure it's meant to be, whether it's just an overnight quicky or a monthlong expedition.

It has been documented that 95 percent of American vacationers use only 5 percent of the available recreation areas. With this book you can leave the herd, wander and be free, and join the inner circle, the Five Percenters who know the great hidden areas used by so few people. To join the Five Percent Club, you should take a hard look at the maps for the areas you wish to visit and the corresponding listings of campgrounds. As you study the camps, you'll start to feel a sense of excitement building, a feeling that you are about to unlock a door and venture into a world that is rarely viewed. When you feel that excitement, act on it. Parlay that energy into a great trip.

The campground maps and listings can serve in two ways: 1) If you're on the road late in the day and you're stuck for a spot for the night, you can likely find one nearby; or 2) if you are planning a trip, you can tailor a vacation to fit exactly into your plans rather than heading off and hoping—maybe praying—it turns out all right.

For the latter you may wish to obtain additional maps, particularly if you are venturing into areas governed by the U.S. Forest Service or Bureau of Land Management. Both are federal agencies that offer low-cost maps detailing all hiking trails, lakes, streams, and backcountry camps reached via logging roads. How to obtain these and other maps is described in the Resource Guide on pages 467 to 470.

Backcountry camps listed in this book are often in primitive and rugged settings but provide the sense of isolation that you may want from a trip. They also provide good jump-off points for backpacking trips, if that's your calling. These camps are often free, and we have listed hundreds of them.

At the other end of the spectrum are the developed parks for RVs. They offer a home away from home, with everything from full hookups to a grocery store and laundry room. These spots are just as important as the remote camps with no facilities. Instead of isolation, an RV park provides a place to shower and get outfitted for food and clean clothes. For RV cruisers, it's a place to stay in high style while touring the area. RV parks range in price from $12–25 per night, depending on location, and an advance deposit may be necessary in summer.

Somewhere between the two extremes—the remote, unimproved camps and the lavish RV parks—are hundreds and hundreds of campgrounds that provide a compromise: beautiful settings and some facilities, with a small overnight fee. Piped water, vault toilets, and picnic tables tend to come with the territory, along with a fee that usually ranges $6–15, with the higher-priced sites near population centers. Because they offer a bit of both worlds, they are in high demand. Reservations are usually advised, and at state parks, particularly during the summer season, you can expect company. This doesn't mean you need to abandon them in hopes of a less confined environment. For one thing, most state parks have set up quotas so that you don't feel as if you've been squeezed in with a shoehorn, and for another, the same parks are often uncrowded during the off-season or on weekdays.

Before your trip you'll want to get organized, and that's where you must start putting socks on that giant octopus. The trick to organization for any task is breaking it down to its key components, and then solving each element independent of the others. Remember the octopus. Grab a moving leg, jam on a boot, and make sure it's on tight before reaching for another leg. Do one thing at a time, in order, and all will get done quickly and efficiently.

In the stories that follow, we have isolated the different elements of camping, and you should do the same when planning for your trip. There are separate stories on each of the primary ingredients for a successful trip: 1) Food and cooking gear; 2) Clothing and weather protection; 3) Hiking and foot care and how to choose the right boots and socks; 4) Sleeping gear; 5) Combating bugs and some common sense first-aid; 6) Catching fish, avoiding bears, and camp fun; 7) Outdoors with kids; 8) Weather prediction; and 9) How to beat the time trap. We've also included sections on boat-in and desert camping, and ethics in the outdoors, as well as a camping gear checklist.

Keep It Wild

"Enjoy America's country and leave no trace." That's the motto of the Leave No Trace program, and we strongly support it. Promoting responsible outdoor recreation through education, research, and partnerships is its mission. Look for the **Keep It Wild Tips,** developed from the policies of Leave No Trace, sprinkled throughout the front of this book. For a free pocket-sized, weatherproof card printed with these policies, as well as information that details how to minimize human impact on wild areas, contact Leave No Trace at P.O. Box 997, Boulder CO, 80306; tel. 800/332-4100; website: www.lnt.org.

Now you can become completely organized for your trip in just one week, spending just a little time each evening. Getting organized is an unnatural act for many. By splitting up the tasks, you take the pressure out of planning and put the fun back in.

As a full-time outdoors writer, the question I am asked more than any other is: "Where are you going this week?" All of the answers are in this book.

Northwest Forest Pass

In some areas, the Northwest Forest Pass has been established to better fund recreation facilities in national forests. The pass costs $30 per year or $5 per day for parked vehicles in areas where the pass is being tested. At national forests where the permit is mandatory, it is required for parking at trailheads, and in effect, is thus often like a parking permit. The permit is also required at camps where otherwise no camping fee is charged. It is noted in each camp listing in this book where the Northwest Forest Pass is required, or if it is required at nearby trailheads.

It is required at a relative handful of camps, including in Mt. Hood National Forest and Deschutes National Forest (two camps). It is also required at a number of trailheads in many national forests: Mt. Hood, Rogue River, Siskiyou, Siuslaw, Wallowa-Whitman, Willamette, Winema, Deschutes, Umatilla and Umpqua; and at Columbia River Gorge National Scenic Area.

The permit was established as a pilot program. Federal legislation may make it a permanent feature across the state.

For more information, phone 800/270-7504; website: www.naturenw.org, or ask in person at the district ranger stations listed for each Forest Service camp in the book.

Camping Tips

Food and Cooking Gear

It was a warm, crystal-clear day, the kind of day when if you had ever wanted to go skydiving, you would go skydiving. That was exactly the case for my old pal Foonsky, who had never before tried the sport. But a funny thing happened after he jumped out of the plane and pulled on the rip cord: his parachute didn't open.

In total free fall, Foonsky watched the earth below getting closer and closer. Not one to panic, he calmly pulled the rip cord on the emergency parachute. Again nothing happened. No parachute, no nothing.

The ground was getting ever closer, and as he tried to search for a soft place to land, Foonsky detected a small object shooting up toward him, growing larger as it approached. It looked like a camper.

Figuring this was his last chance, Foonsky shouted as they passed in midair, "Hey, do you know anything about parachutes?"

The other fellow just yelled back as he headed off into space, "Do you know anything about lighting camping stoves?"

Well, Foonsky got lucky and his parachute opened. As for the other guy, well, he's probably in orbit like a NASA weather satellite. If you've ever had a mishap while lighting a camping stove, you know exactly what I'm talking about.

When it comes to camping, all gear is not created equal. Nothing is more important than lighting your stove easily and having it reach full heat without feeling as if you're playing with a short fuse to a miniature bomb. If your stove does not work right, your trip can turn into a disaster, regardless of how well you have planned the other elements. In addition, a bad stove will add an underlying sense of foreboding to your day. You will constantly have the inner suspicion that your darn stove is going to foul up again.

Camping Stoves

If you are buying a camping stove, remember this one critical rule: do not leave the store with a new stove unless you have been shown exactly how to use it.

Know what you are getting. Many stores that specialize in outdoor recreation equipment now provide experienced campers/employees who will demonstrate the use of every stove they sell and while they're at it, describe their respective strengths and weaknesses.

An innovation by Peak 1 is a two-burner backpacking stove that allows you to boil water and heat a pot of food simultaneously. While that has long been standard for car campers using Coleman's legendary camp stove, it was previously unheard of for wilderness campers in high-elevation areas. Another recent invention is the flameless stove (no kidding) that allows campers to cook in a tent safely for the first time.

A stove that has developed a cultlike following is the little Sierra, which burns small twigs and pinecones, then uses a tiny battery-driven fan to develop increased heat and cooking ability. It's an excellent alternative for long-distance backpacking trips, as it solves the problem of carrying a fuel bottle, especially on expeditions for which large quantities of fuel would otherwise be needed. Some tinkering with the flame (a very hot one) is required, and they are legal and functional only in the alpine zone where dry wood is available. Also note that in years with high fire danger, the U.S. Forest Service will enact rules prohibiting open flames, and fires are also often prohibited above an elevation of 10,000 feet.

I prefer a small, lightweight stove that uses white gas so I can closely gauge fuel consumption. My pal Foonsky uses one with a butane bottle because it lights so easily. We have contests to see who can boil a pot of water faster, and the difference is usually negligible. Thus, other factors are important when choosing a stove.

Of these, ease of cleaning the burner is the most important. If you camp often, especially with a smaller stove, the burner holes will eventually become clogged. Some stoves have a built-in cleaning needle; a quick twist of the knob and you're in business. Others require disassembly and a protracted session using special cleaning tools. If a stove is difficult to clean, you will tend to put off doing it, and your stove will sputter and pant while you feel humiliated watching the cold pot of water sitting there.

Before making a purchase, have the salesperson show you how to clean the burner head. Except in the case of large, multiburner family camping stoves, which rarely require cleaning, this test can do more to determine the long-term value of a stove than any other factor.

Fuels for Camping Stoves

White gas and butane have long been the most popular camp fuels, but a newly developed fuel could dramatically change that.

LPG (liquid petroleum gas) comes in cartridges for easy attachment to a stove or lantern. At room temperature, LPG is delivered in a combustible gaseous form. When you shake the cartridge, the contents sound liquid; that is because the gas liquefies under pressure, which is why it is so easy to use. Large amounts of fuel are compressed into small canisters.

While convenience has always been the calling card for LPG, recent innovations have allowed it to become a suitable choice for winter and high-altitude mountaineering expeditions, coming close to matching white gas performance specs. For several years now, MSR, Epi (Coleman), Coleman, Primus, Camping Gaz, Markill, and other makers have been mixing propane, butane, and isobutane to improve performance capabilities.

Two important hurdles that stood in the way of LPG's popularity have been leaped. Coleman, working in cooperation with the U.S. Postal Service, has developed a program in which three-packs of 170-gram Coleman Max fuel cartridges can be shipped by mail to any address or post office in the 50 states and Puerto Rico. Also, each Coleman Max fuel cartridge is now made of aluminum and comes with a special device that allows the consumer to puncture the cartridge safely once the fuel is gone and then toss it into any aluminum recycling container.

The following details the benefits and drawbacks of other available fuels.

White gas: White gas is the most popular camp fuel because it is sold at most outdoor recreation stores and many supermarkets and is inexpensive and effective. It burns hot, has virtually no smell, and evaporates quickly when spilled. If you are caught in wet, miserable weather and can't get a fire going, you can use white gas as an emergency fire starter; however, if you do so, use it sparingly and never on an open flame.

White gas is a popular fuel both for car campers, who use the large, two-burner stoves equipped with a fuel tank and a pump, and for hikers who carry a lightweight backpacking stove. On the latter, lighting can require priming with a gel called priming paste, which some people dislike. Another problem with white gas is that it can be extremely explosive.

As an example, I once almost burned my beard completely off in a mini-explosion while lighting one of the larger stoves designed for car camping. I was in the middle of cooking dinner when the flame suddenly shut down. Sure enough, the fuel tank was empty, and after refilling it, I pumped the tank 50 or 60 times to regain pressure. When I lit a match, the sucker ignited from three feet away. The resulting explosion was like a stick of dynamite going off, and immediately the smell of

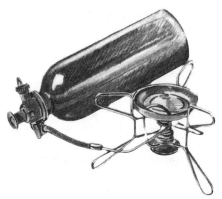

Stoves are available in many styles and burn a variety of fuels. These are three typical examples. Top: **White gas** *stoves are the most popular because they are inexpensive and easy to find; they do require priming and can be explosive. Middle:* **Gas canister** *stoves burn propane, butane, isobutane, and mixtures of the three. These are the easiest to use but have two disadvantages: 1) Because the fuel is bottled, determining how much fuel is left can be difficult. 2) The fuel is limited to above-freezing conditions. Bottom:* **Liquid fuel** *stoves burn Coleman fuel, denatured alcohol, kerosene, and even gasoline; these fuels are economical and have a high heat output, but most must be primed.*

burning beard was in the air. In a flash, my once thick, dark beard had been reduced to a mass of little yellow burned curlicues.

My error? After filling the tank, I forgot to shut the fuel cock off while pumping up the pressure in the tank. As a result, the stove burners were slowly producing the gas/air mixture as I pumped the tank, filling the air above the stove. Then strike a match from even a few feet away and ka-boom!

Butane: The explosive problem can be solved by using stoves that burn bottled butane fuel. Butane requires no pouring, pumping, or priming, and butane stoves are the easiest to light. Just turn a knob and light—that's it. On the minus side, because it comes in bottles, you never know precisely how much fuel you have left. And when a bottle is empty, you have a potential piece of litter. (Never litter. Ever.)

During high fire danger the U.S. Forest Service will enact rules prohibiting open flames. Fires are also often prohibited above an elevation of 10,000 feet.

The other problem with butane is that it just plain does not work well in cold weather or when there is little fuel left in the cartridge. Since you cannot predict mountain weather in spring or fall, you can wind up using more fuel than originally projected. That can be frustrating, particularly if your stove starts wheezing when there are still several days left to go. In addition, with most butane cartridges, if there is any chance of the temperature's falling below freezing, you often have to sleep with the cartridge to keep it warm or forget about using it come morning.

Coleman Max Performance Fuel: This new fuel offers a unique approach to solving the consistent burn challenge facing all pressurized gas cartridges: operating at temperatures at or below 0° F. Using a standard propane/butane blend for high-octane performance, Coleman gets around the drop-off in performance other cartridges experience by usng a version of fuel injection. A hose inside the cartridge pulls liquid fuel into the stove, where it vaporizes—a switch from the

---

Keep It Wild Tip 1: Campfires

1. Fire use can scar the backcountry. If a fire ring is not available, use a lightweight stove for cooking.
2. Where fires are permitted, use existing fire rings away from large rocks or overhangs.
3. Don't char rocks by building new rings.
4. Gather sticks from the ground that are no larger than the diameter of your wrist.
5. Don't snap branches of live, dead, or downed trees, which can cause personal injury and also scar the natural setting.
6. Put the fire "dead out" and make sure it's cold before departing. Remove all trash from the fire ring and sprinkle dirt over the site.
7. Remember that some forest fires can be started by a campfire that appears to be out. Hot embers burning deep in the pit can cause tree roots to catch fire and burn underground. If you ever see smoke rising from the ground, seemingly from nowhere, dig down and put the fire out.

standard approach of pulling only a gaseous form of the fuel into a stove. By drawing liquid out of the cartridge, Coleman gets around the tendency of propane to burn off first and allows each cartridge to deliver a consistent mix of propane and butane to the stove's burners throughout the cartridge's life.

Butane/Propane: This blend offers higher octane performance than butane alone, solving the cold temperature doldrums somewhat. However, propane burns off before butane, so there will be a performance drop as the fuel level in the cartridge lowers.

Propane: Now available for single-burner stoves using larger, heavier cartridges to accommodate higher pressures, propane offers the very best performance of any of the pressurized gas canister fuels.

Primus Tri-Blend: This blend is made up of 20 percent propane, 70 percent butane, and 10 percent isobutane and is designed to burn with more consistent heat and efficiency than standard propane/butane mixes.

Denatured alcohol: Though this fuel burns cleanly and quietly and is virtually explosion-proof, it generates much less heat than pressurized or liquid gas fuels.

Kerosene: Never buy a stove that uses kerosene for fuel. Kerosene is smelly and messy, generates low heat, needs priming, and is virtually obsolete as a camp fuel in the United States. As a test I once tried using a kerosene stove. I could scarcely boil a pot of water. In addition, some kerosene leaked out when the stove was packed, ruining everything it touched. The smell of kerosene never did go away. Kerosene remains popular in Europe only because most campers there haven't yet heard much about white gas. When they do, they will demand it.

Building Fires

One summer expedition took me to the Canadian wilderness in British Columbia for a 75-mile canoe trip on the Bowron Lake Circuit, a chain of 13 lakes, six rivers, and seven portages. It is one of the truly great canoe trips in the world, a loop that ends just a few hundred feet from its starting point. But at the first camp at Kibbee Lake, my stove developed a fuel leak at the base of the burner, and the nuclear-like blast that followed just about turned Canada into a giant crater.

As a result, the final 70 miles of the trip had to be completed without a stove, cooking done on open fires each night. The problem was compounded by the weather. It rained eight of the 10 days. Rain? In Canada, raindrops the size of silver dollars fall so hard they actually bounce on the lake surface. We had to stop paddling a few times to empty the rainwater out of the canoe. At the end of the day we'd make camp and then face the test: either make a fire or go to bed cold and hungry.

With an ax, at least we had a chance for success. As soaked as all the downed wood was, I was able to make my own fire-starting tinder from the chips of split logs; no matter how hard it rains, the inside of a log is always dry.

In miserable weather, matches don't stay lit long enough to get the tinder started. Instead we used either a candle or little waxlike fire-starter cubes that remain lit for several minutes. From those we could get the tinder going. Then we added small, slender strips of wood that had been axed from the interior of the logs. When the flame reached a foot high, we added the logs, their dry interiors facing in. By the time the inside of the logs had caught fire, the outside would be drying from the heat. It wasn't long before a royal blaze was brightening the rainy night.

That's a worst-case scenario, and I hope you will never face anything like it. Nevertheless, being able to build a good fire and cook on it can be one of the more satisfying elements of a camping trip. At times just looking into the flames can provide a special satisfaction at the end of a good day.

However, never expect to build a fire for every meal or in some cases even to build one at all. Many state and federal campgrounds have been picked clean of downed wood, or forest fire danger forces rangers to prohibit fires altogether during the fire season. In either case you must use your camp stove or go hungry.

But when you can build a fire and the resources for doing so are available, it will enhance the quality of your camping experience. Of the campgrounds listed in this book, those where you are permitted to build fires will usually have fire rings. In primitive areas where you can make your own fire, you should dig a ring eight inches deep, line the edges with rock, and clear all the needles and twigs in a five-foot radius. The next day, when the fire is dead, you can discard the rocks, fill over the black charcoal with dirt, and then scatter pine needles and twigs over it. Nobody will even know you camped there. That's the best way I know to keep a secret spot a real secret.

When you start to build a campfire, the first thing you will notice is that no matter how good your intentions, your fellow campers will not be able to resist moving the wood around. Watch. You'll be getting ready to add a key piece of wood at just the right spot, and your companion will stick his mitts in, confidently believing he has a better idea. He'll shift the fire around and undermine your best-thought-out plans.

So I enforce a rule on camping trips: one person makes the fire while everybody else stands clear or is involved with other camp tasks such as gathering wood, getting water, putting up tents, or planning dinner. Once the fire is going strong, then it's fair game; anyone adds logs at his or her discretion. But in the early, delicate stages of the campfire, it's best to leave the work to one person.

Before a match is ever struck, you should gather a complete pile of firewood. Then start small, with the tiniest twigs you can find, and slowly add larger twigs as you go, crisscrossing them like a miniature tepee. Eventually you will get to the big chunks that will produce high heat. The key is to get one piece of wood burning into another, which then burns into another, setting off what I call the chain of flame. Conversely, single pieces of wood set apart from each other will not burn.

On a dry summer evening at a campsite where plenty of wood is available, about the only way you can blow the deal is to get impatient and try to add the big pieces too quickly. Do that and you'll get smoke, not flames, and it won't be long before every one of your fellow campers is poking at your fire. It will drive you crazy, but they just won't be able to help it.

Cooking Gear

I like traveling light, and I've found that all I need for cooking is a pot, small frying pan, metal pot grabber, fork, knife, cup, and matches. If you want to keep the price of food low and also cook customized dinners each night, a small pressure cooker can be just the ticket. (See the Keeping the Price Down section). I store all my gear in one small bag that fits into my pack. If I'm camping out of my four-wheel-drive rig, the little bag of cooking gear is easy to keep track of. Going simple, not complicated, is the key to keeping a camping trip on the right track.

You can get more elaborate by buying complete kits with plates, a coffeepot, large pots, and other cookware, but what really counts is having a single pot that makes you happy. It needs to be just the right size, not too big or small, and stable enough so it won't tip over, even if it is at a slight angle on a fire, full of water at a full boil. Mine is just 6 inches wide and 4.5 inches deep. It holds better than a quart of water and has served me well for several hundred camp dinners.

The rest of your cook kit is easy to complete. The frying pan should be small, light-gauge aluminum, and Teflon-coated, with a fold-in handle so it's no hassle to store. A pot grabber is a great addition. It's a little aluminum gadget that clamps to the edge of pots and allows you to lift them and pour water with total control without burning your fingers. For cleanup take a plastic scrubber and a small bottle filled with dish cleaner, and you're in business.

A sierra cup, a wide aluminum cup with a wire handle, is an ideal item to carry because you can eat out of it as well as use it for drinking. This means no plates to scrub after dinner, so cleanup is quick and easy. In addition, if you go for a hike, you can clip it to your belt with its handle.

If you want a more formal setup complete with plates, glasses, silverware, and the like, you can end up spending more time preparing and cleaning up from meals than you do enjoying the country you are exploring. In addition, the more equipment you bring, the more loose ends you will have to deal with, and loose ends can cause plenty of frustration. If you have a choice, go simple.

And remember what Thoreau said: "A man is rich in proportion to what he can do without."

Food and Cooking Tricks

On a trip to the Bob Marshall Wilderness in western Montana, I woke up one morning, yawned, and said, "What've we got for breakfast?"

The silence was ominous. "Well," finally came the response, "we don't have any food left."

"What!?"

"Well, I figured we'd catch trout for meals every other night."

On the return trip, we ended up eating wild berries, buds, and, yes, even roots (not too tasty). When we finally landed the next day at a suburban pizza parlor, we nearly ate the wooden tables.

Running out of food on a camping trip can do more to turn reasonable people into violent grumps than any other event. There's no excuse for it, not when a system for figuring meals can be outlined with precision and little effort. You should not go out and buy a bunch of food, throw it in your rig, and head off for yonder. That leaves too much to chance. And if you've ever been in the woods and real hungry, you'll know it's worth taking a little effort to make sure a day or two of starvation will not occur. Here's a three-step solution:

1. Draw up a general meal-by-meal plan and make sure your companions like what's on it.
2. Tell your companions to buy any specialty items (such as a special brand of coffee) on their own and not to expect you to take care of everything.
3. Put all the food on your living room floor and literally plan out every day of your trip, meal by meal, putting the food in plastic bags as you go. That way you will know exact food quotas and will not go hungry.

Fish for your dinner? There's one guarantee as far as that goes: if you expect to catch fish for meals, you will most certainly get skunked. If you don't expect to catch fish for meals, you will probably catch so many they'll be coming out of your ears. I've seen it a hundred times.

Keeping the Price Down
"There must be some mistake," I said with a laugh. "Whoever paid $750 for camp food?"

But the amount was as clear as the digital numbers on the cash register: $753.27.

"How is this possible?" I asked the clerk.

"Just add it up," she responded, irritated.

Then I started figuring. The freeze-dried backpack dinners cost $6 apiece. A small pack of beef jerky went for $2, the beef sticks for $.75, granola bars for $.50. Multiply it all by four hungry men, including Foonsky, for 21 days. This food was to sustain us on a major expedition—four guys hiking 250 miles over three weeks from Mt. Whitney to Yosemite Valley.

The dinners alone cost close to $500. Add in the usual goodies—jerky, granola bars, soup, dried fruit, oatmeal, Tang, candy, and coffee—and I felt as if an earthquake had struck when I saw the tab.

A lot of campers have received similar shocks. In preparation for their trips, campers shop with enthusiasm. Then they pay the bill in horror.

Well, there are solutions, lots of them. You can eat gourmet style in the outback without having your wallet cleaned out. But it requires do-it-yourself cooking, more planning, and careful shopping. It also means transcending the push-button I-want-it-now attitude that so many people can't leave behind when they go to the mountains.

The secret is to bring along a small pressure cooker. A reader in San Francisco, Mike Bettinger, passed this tip on to me. Little pressure cookers weigh about two pounds, which may sound like a lot to backpackers and backcountry campers. But when three or four people are on a trip, it actually saves weight.

The key is that it allows campers to bring items that are difficult to cook at high

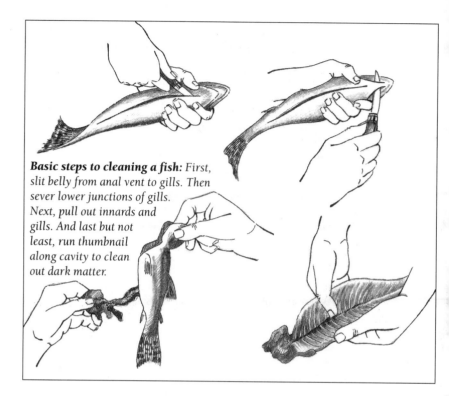

Basic steps to cleaning a fish: *First, slit belly from anal vent to gills. Then sever lower junctions of gills. Next, pull out innards and gills. And last but not least, run thumbnail along cavity to clean out dark matter.*

altitudes, such as brown and white rice; red, black, pinto, and lima beans; and lentils. You pick one or more for a basic staple and then add a variety of freeze-dried ingredients to make a complete dish. Available are packets of meat, vegetables, onions, shallots, and garlic. Sun-dried tomatoes, for instance, reconstitute wonderfully in a pressure cooker. Add herbs, spices, and maybe a few rainbow trout, and you will be eating better out of a backpack than most people do at home.

"In the morning, I have used the pressure cooker to turn dried apricots into apricot sauce to put on the pancakes we made with sourdough starter," Bettinger said. "The pressure cooker is also big enough for washing out cups and utensils. The days when backpacking meant eating terrible freeze-dried food are over. It doesn't take a gourmet cook to prepare these meals, only some thought beforehand."

Now when Foonsky, Mr. Furnai, Rambob, and I sit down to eat such a meal, we don't call it "eating." We call it "hodgepacking" or "time to pack your hodge." After a particularly long day on the trail, you can do some serious hodgepacking.

If your trip is a shorter one, say for a weekend, you can bring more fresh food to add some sizzle to the hodge. You can design a hot soup/stew mix that is good enough to eat at home.

Start by bringing a pot of water to a full boil, then adding pasta, ramen noodles, or macaroni. While it simmers, cut in a potato, carrot, onion, and garlic clove, and

How to Make Beef Jerky in Your Own Kitchen

Start with a couple pieces of meat: lean top round, sirloin, or tri-tip. Cut it into 3/16-inch strips across the grain, trimming out the membrane, gristle, and fat. Marinate the strips for 24 hours in a glass dish. The fun begins in picking a marinade. Try two-thirds teriyaki sauce, one-third Worcestershire sauce. You can customize the recipe by adding pepper, ground mustard, bay leaf, red wine vinegar, garlic, and, for the brave, Tabasco sauce.

After a day or so, squeeze out each strip of meat with a rolling pin, lay them in rows on a cooling rack over a cookie sheet, and dry them in the oven at 125 degrees for 12 hours. Thicker pieces can take as long as 18 to 24 hours.

That's it. The hardest part is cleaning the cookie sheet when you're done. The easiest part is eating your own homemade jerky while sitting at a lookout on a mountain ridge. The do-it-yourself method for jerky may take a day or so, but it is cheaper and can taste better than any store-bought jerky.

---

cook for about 10 minutes. When the vegetables have softened, add in a soup mix or two, maybe some cheese, and you are just about in business. But you can still ruin it and turn your hodge into slodge. Make sure you read the directions on the soup mix to determine cooking time. It can vary widely. In addition, make sure you stir the whole thing up; otherwise you will get these hidden dry clumps of soup mix that taste like garlic sawdust.

How do I know? Well, it was up near Kearsage Pass in the Sierra Nevada, where, feeling half-starved, I dug into our nightly hodge. I will never forget that first bite—I damn near gagged to death. Foonsky laughed at me, until he took his first bite (a nice big one) and then turned green.

Another way to trim food costs is to make your own beef jerky, the trademark staple of campers for more than 200 years. A tiny packet of beef jerky costs $2, and for that 250-mile expedition, I spent $150 on jerky alone. Never again. Now we make our own and get big strips of jerky that taste better than anything you can buy.

If all this still doesn't sound like your idea of a gourmet but low-cost camping meal, well, you are forgetting the main course: rainbow trout. Remember: if you don't plan on catching them for dinner, you'll probably snag more than you can finish in one night's hodgepacking.

Some campers go to great difficulties to cook their trout, bringing along frying pans, butter, grills, tinfoil, and more, but all you need is some seasoned salt and a campfire.

Rinse the gutted trout, and while it's still wet, sprinkle on a good dose of seasoned salt, both inside and out. Clear any burning logs to the side of the campfire, then lay the trout right on the coals, turning it once so both sides are cooked. Sound ridiculous? Sound like you are throwing the fish away? Sound like the fish will burn up? Sound like you will have to eat the campfire ash? Wrong on all counts. The fish cooks perfectly, the ash doesn't stick, and after cooking trout this way, you may never fry trout again.

But if you can't convince your buddies, who may insist the trout should be fried, then make sure you have butter to fry them in, not oil. Also make sure you cook them all the way through, so the meat strips off the backbone in two nice, clean fillets. The fish should end up looking like one that Sylvester the Cat just drew out of his mouth—only the head, tail, and a perfect skeleton.

You can supplement your eats with sweets, nuts, freeze-dried fruits, and drink mixes. In any case, make sure you keep the dinner menu varied. If you and your buddies look into your dinner cups and groan, "Ugh, not this again," you will soon start dreaming of cheeseburgers and french fries instead of hiking, fishing, and finding beautiful campsites.

If you are car camping and have a big ice chest, you can bring virtually anything to eat and drink. If you are on the trail and don't mind paying the price, the newest freeze-dried dinners provide another option.

Some of the biggest advances in the outdoors industry have come in the freeze-dried dinners now available to campers. Some of them are almost good enough to serve in restaurants. Sweet-and-sour pork over rice, tostadas, Burgundy chicken—it sure beats the poopy goop we used to eat, like the old soupy chili-mac dinners that tasted bad and looked so unlike food that consumption was near impossible, even for my dog, Rebel. Foonsky usually managed to get it down, but just barely.

To provide an idea of how to plan a menu, consider what my companions and I ate while hiking 250 miles on California's John Muir Trail:
- Breakfast: instant soup, oatmeal (never get plain), one beef or jerky stick, coffee or hot chocolate.
- Lunch: one beef stick, two jerky sticks, one granola bar, dried fruit, half cup of pistachio nuts, Tang, one small bag of M&Ms.
- Dinner: instant soup, one freeze-dried dinner, one milk bar, rainbow trout.

What was that last item? Rainbow trout? Right! Unless you plan on it, you can catch them every night.

Clothing and Weather Protection

What started as an innocent pursuit of a perfect campground evolved into one heck of a predicament for Foonsky and me.

We had parked at the end of a logging road and then bushwhacked our way down a canyon to a pristine trout stream. On my first cast—a little flip into the plunge pool of a waterfall—I caught a 16-inch rainbow trout, a real beauty that jumped three times. Magic stuff.

Then just across the stream, we saw it: The Perfect Camping Spot. On a sandbar on the edge of the forest, there lay a flat spot, high and dry above the river. Nearby was plenty of downed wood from past winter storms that we could use for firewood. And, of course, this beautiful trout stream was bubbling along just 40 yards from the site.

But nothing is perfect, right? To reach it, we had to wade across the river, although it didn't appear to be too difficult. The cold water tingled a bit, and the river came up surprisingly high, just above the belt. But it would be worth it to camp at The Perfect Spot.

Once across the river, we put on some dry clothes, set up camp, explored the woods, and fished the stream, catching several nice trout for dinner. But late that afternoon, it started raining. What? Rain in the summertime? Nature makes its own rules. By the next morning, it was still raining, pouring like a Yosemite waterfall from a solid gray sky.

That's when we noticed The Perfect Spot wasn't so perfect. The rain had raised the river level too high for us to wade back across. We were marooned, wet, and hungry.

"Now we're in a heck of a predicament," said Foonsky, the water streaming off him.

Getting cold and wet on a camping trip with no way to warm up is not only unnecessary and uncomfortable, it can be a fast ticket to hypothermia, the number one killer of campers in the woods. By definition, hypothermia is a condition in which body temperature is lowered to the point that it causes illness. It is particularly dangerous because the afflicted are usually unaware it is setting in. The first sign is a sense of apathy, then a state of confusion, which can lead eventually to collapse (or what appears to be sleep), then death.

You must always have a way to get warm and dry in short order, regardless of any conditions you may face. If you have no way of getting dry, then you must take emergency steps to prevent hypothermia. Those steps are detailed in the first-aid section.

But you should never reach that point. For starters, always have spare sets of clothing tucked away so no matter how cold and wet you might get, you have something dry to put on. On hiking trips I always carry a second set of clothes, sealed to stay dry, in a plastic garbage bag. I keep a third set waiting back at the truck.

If you are car camping, your vehicle can cause an illusory sense of security. But with an extra set of dry clothes stashed safely away, there is no illusion. The security is real. And remember, no matter how hot the weather is when you start your trip, always be prepared for the worst. Foonsky and I learned the hard way.

So both of us were soaking wet on that sandbar, and with no other choice we tried holing up in the tent for the night. A sleeping bag with Quallofil or another polyester fiberfill can retain warmth even when wet, because the fill is hollow and retains its loft. So as miserable as it was, we made it through the night.

The rain stopped the next day and the river dropped a bit, but it was still rolling big and angry. Using a stick as a wading staff, Foonsky crossed about 80 percent of the stream before he was dumped, but he made a jump for it and managed to scramble to the riverbank. He waved for me to follow. "No problem," I thought.

It took me 20 minutes to reach nearly the same spot where Foonsky had been dumped. The heavy river current was above my belt and pushing hard. Then in the flash of an instant, my wading staff slipped on a rock. I teetered in the river current and was knocked over like a bowling pin. I became completely submerged. I went tumbling down the river, heading right toward the waterfall. While underwater I looked up at the surface, and I can remember how close it seemed yet how out of control I was. Right then this giant hand appeared, and I grabbed it. It was Foonsky. If it weren't for that hand, I would have sailed right over the waterfall.

My momentum drew Foonsky right into the river, and we scrambled in the current, but I suddenly sensed the river bottom under my knees. On all fours, the two of us clambered ashore. We were safe.

"Thanks, ol' buddy," I said.

"Man, we're wet," he responded. "Let's get to the rig and get some dry clothes on."

The Art of Layering

The most important element in enjoying the outdoor experience in any condition is to stay dry and warm. There is no substitute. You must stay dry and you must stay warm.

Thus comes the theory behind layering, which suggests that as your body temperature fluctuates or the weather shifts, you simply peel off or add available layers as needed—and have a waterproof shell available in case of rain.

The introduction of a new era of outdoor clothing has made it possible for campers to turn choosing clothes into an art form. Like art, it comes much more expensive than throwing on a pair of blue jeans, a T-shirt, and some flannel, but for many it is worth the price.

In putting together your ideal layering system, there are some general considerations. What you need to do is create a system that effectively combines elements of breathability, wicking, rapid drying, insulation, durability, wind resistance, and water repellence while still being lightweight and offering the necessary freedom of movement, all with just a few garments.

The basic intent of a base layer is to manage moisture. Your base layer will be the first article of clothing you put on and the last to come off. Since your own skin will be churning out the perspiration, the goal of this second skin is to manage the moisture and move it away from you without trapping your body's heat. The only time that cotton should become a part of your base layer is if you wish to keep cool, not warm, such as in a hot desert climate where evaporative cooling becomes your friend, not your enemy.

That is why the best base layer available is from bicomponent knits, that is, blends of polyester and cotton, which work to provide wicking and insulating properties in one layer. The way it works is that the side facing your skin is water hating, while the side away from your skin is water loving; thus it pulls or "wicks" moisture through. You'll stay dry and happy, even with only one layer on, something not possible with old single-function weaves. The best include Thermax, Capilene, Driclime, Lifa, and Polartec 100.

Stretch fleece and microdenier pile also provide a good base layer, though they can be used as a second layer as well. Microdenier pile can be worn alone or layered under or over other pieces, and it has excellent wicking capability as well as more windproof potential.

The next layer should be a light cotton shirt or a long-sleeved cotton/wool shirt, or both, depending on the coolness of the day. For pants, many just wear blue jeans when camping, but blue jeans can be hot and tight, and once wet, they tend to stay that way. Putting on wet blue jeans on a cold morning is a torturous way to start the day. (I tell you this from experience, since I have suffered that fate a number of times.) A better choice is pants made from a cotton/canvas mix, which are available at outdoors stores. They are light, have a lot of give, and dry quickly. If the weather is quite warm, shorts that have some room to them can be the best choice.

Finally, you'll top the entire ensemble off with a thin windproof, water-resistant layer. You want this layer to breathe like crazy, yet not be so porous that rain runs through it like floodwaters through a leaking dike. Patagonia's Velocity shell is one of the best. Its outer fabric is DWR- (durable water-repellent) treated, and the coating is by Gore. Patagonia calls it Pneumatic (Gore now calls it Activent, while Marmot, Moonstone, and North Face all offer their own versions). Though condensation will still build up inside, it manages to get rid of enough moisture.

It is critical to know the difference between "water-resistant" and "waterproof." This is covered later in the chapter under the Rain Gear section.

But hey, why does anybody need all this fancy stuff just to go camping? Fair question. Like the introduction of Gore-Tex years ago, all this fabric and fiber mumbo jumbo has its skeptics, including me. You don't have to opt for this aerobic-function fashion statement; it is unnecessary on many camping trips. But the fact is you must be ready for anything when you venture into the outdoors. And the truth is that the new era of outdoor clothing works, and it works better than anything that has come before.

Regardless of what you choose, weather should never be a nuisance or cause discomfort, regardless of what you experience. Instead it should provide a welcome change of pace.

About Hats
One final word of advice: always pack along a warm hat for those times when you need to seal in warmth. You lose a large percentage of heat through your head. I almost always wear a wide-brimmed hat, something like the legendary outlaws

---

Keep It Wild Tip 2: Travel Lightly

1. Visit the backcountry in small groups.
2. Below tree line, always stay on designated trails.
3. Don't cut across switchbacks.
4. When traveling cross-country where no trails are available, follow animal trails or spread out with your group so no new routes are created.
5. Read your map and orient yourself with landmarks, a compass, and an altimeter. Try, if possible to avoid marking trails using rock cairns, and especially avoid using tree scars or ribbons. The one area where this be impossible is above tree line, where routes can seemingly disappear amid rock and ice.

---

wore 150 years ago. There's actually logic behind it: my hat is made of kangaroo skin (waterproof), is rigged with a lariat (it can be cinched down when it's windy), and has a wide brim that keeps the tops of my ears from being sun-burned (years ago they once were burned to a red crisp on a trip where I was wear-ing a baseball hat). But to be honest, I like how it looks, kind of like my pal Waylon Jennings.

Vests and Parkas

In cold weather you should take the layer system one step further with a warm vest and a parka jacket. Vests are especially useful because they provide warmth with-out the bulkiness of a parka. The warmest vests and parkas are either filled with down or Quallofil, or they are made with a cotton/wool mix. Each has its respective merits and problems. Down fill provides the most warmth for the amount of weight, but becomes useless when wet, closely resembling a wet dishrag. Quallofil keeps much of its heat-retaining quality even when wet, but it is expensive. Vests made of cotton/wool mixes are the most attractive and also are quite warm, but they can be as heavy as a ship's anchor when wet.

Sometimes the answer is combining the two. One of my best camping com-panions wears a good-looking cotton/wool vest and a parka filled with Quallofil. The vest never gets wet, so weight is not a factor.

Rain Gear

One of the most miserable nights I ever spent in my life was on a camping trip where I didn't bring my rain gear or a tent. Hey, it was early August, the temper-ature had been in the 90s for weeks, and if anybody had said it was going to rain, I would have told him to consult a brain doctor. But rain it did. And as I got wetter and wetter, I kept saying to myself, "Hey, it's summer, it's not supposed to rain." Then I remembered one of the 10 commandments of camping: forget your rain gear and you can guarantee it will rain.

To stay dry, you need some form of water-repellent shell. It can be as simple as a $5 poncho made out of plastic or as elaborate as a Gore-Tex rain jacket-and-pants set that costs $300. What counts is not how much you spend, but how dry you stay.

Waterproof: impervious to water. Though rain won't penetrate wa-terproof material, if you're at all mobile, you'll soon find yourself wet from perspiration that can't evaporate.

The most important thing to realize is that waterproof and water-resistant are completely different things. In ad-dition, there is no such thing as rain gear that is both wa-terproof and breathable. The more waterproof a jacket is, the less it breathes. Conversely, the more breathable a jacket is, the less waterproof it becomes.

Water-resistant: resistant but not impervious to water. You'll stay dry using water-resistant material only if it isn't pouring.

If you wear water-resistant rain gear in a downpour, you'll get soaked. Water-resistant rain gear is appealing because it breathes and will keep you dry in the light stuff, such as mist, fog, even a little splash from a canoe paddle. But in rain? Forget it.

So what is the solution?

I've decided that the best approach is a set of fairly light but 100 percent-waterproof rain gear. I recently bought a hooded jacket and pants from Coleman, and my assessment is that it is the most cost-efficient rain gear I've ever had. All I can say is, hey, it works: I stay dry, it doesn't weigh much, and it didn't cost a fortune.

You can also stay dry with any of the waterproof plastics and even heavy-duty rubber-coated outfits made for commercial fishermen. But these are uncomfortable during anything but a heavy rain. Because they are heavy and don't breathe, you'll likely get soaked anyway (that is, from your own sweat), even if it isn't raining hard.

On backpacking trips, I still stash a super lightweight water-repellent slicker for day hikes, and a poncho, which I throw over my pack at night to keep it dry. But otherwise I never go anywhere—*anywhere*—without my rain gear.

Some do just fine with a cheap poncho, and note that ponchos can serve other uses in addition to a raincoat. Ponchos can be used as a ground tarp, as a rain cover for supplies or a backpack, or can be roped up to trees in a pinch to provide a quick storm ceiling if you don't have a tent. The problem with ponchos is that in a hard rain, you just don't stay dry. First your legs get wet, then they get soaked. Then your arms follow the same pattern. If you're wearing cotton, you'll find that once part of the garment gets wet, the water will spread until, alas, you are dripping wet, poncho and all. Before long you start to feel like a walking refrigerator.

One high-cost option is buying a Gore-Tex rain jacket and pants. Gore-Tex is actually not a fabric as is commonly believed, but a laminated film that coats a breathable fabric. The result is lightweight, water-repellent, breathable jackets and pants. They are perfect for campers, but they cost a fortune.

Some hiking buddies of mine have complained that the older Gore-Tex rain gear loses its water-repellent quality over time. However, manufacturers insist that this is the result of water seeping through seams, not leaks in the jacket. At each seam, tiny needles have pierced the fabric, and as tiny as the holes are, water will find a way through. An application of Seam Lock, especially at major seams around the shoulders of a jacket, can usually fix the problem.

If you don't want to spend the big bucks for Gore-Tex rain gear but want more rain protection than a poncho affords, a coated nylon jacket is the compromise that many choose. They are inexpensive, have the highest water-repellency of any rain gear, and are warm, providing a good outer shell for your layers of clothing. But they are not without fault. These jackets don't breathe at all, and if you zip them up tight, you can sweat a river.

My brother Rambob gave me a nylon jacket before a mountain climbing expedition. I wore that $20 special all the way to the top with no complaints; it's warm and 100 percent waterproof. The one problem with nylon is when temperatures drop below freezing. It gets so stiff that it feels as if you are wearing a straitjacket. But at $20, it seems like a treasure, especially compared to a $180 Gore-Tex jacket.

There's one more jacket-construction term to know: DWR, or durable water-repellent finish. All of the top-quality jackets these days are DWR-treated. The

DWR causes water to bead up on the shell. When the DWR wears off, even a once-waterproof jacket will feel like a wet dishrag.

Also note that ventilation is the key to coolness. The only ventilation on most shells is often the zipper. But waterproof jackets need additional openings. Look for mesh-backed pockets and underarm zippers, as well as cuffs, waists, and hems that can be adjusted to open wide. Storm flaps (the baffle over the zipper) that close with hook-and-loop material or snaps let you leave the zipper open for airflow into the jacket.

Other Gear—and a Few Tips

What are the three items most commonly forgotten on a camping trip? A hat, sunglasses, and lip balm.

A hat is crucial, especially when you are visiting high elevations. Without one you are constantly exposed to everything nature can give you. The sun will dehydrate you, sap your energy, sunburn your head, and in worst cases, cause sunstroke. Start with a comfortable hat. Then finish with sunglasses, lip balm, and sunscreen for additional protection. They will help protect you from extreme heat.

To guard against extreme cold, it's a good idea to keep a pair of thin ski gloves stashed away with your emergency clothes, along with a wool ski cap. The gloves should be thick enough to keep your fingers from stiffening up, but pliable enough to allow full movement so you don't have to take them off to complete simple tasks, like lighting a stove. An alternative to gloves is glovelets, which look like gloves with no fingers. In any case, just because the weather turns cold doesn't mean that your hands have to.

And if you fall into a river as Foonsky and I did—well, I hope you have a set of dry clothes waiting back at your rig. Oh, and a hand reaching out to you.

Hiking and Foot Care

We had set up a nice little camp in the woods, and my buddy, Foonsky, was strapping on his hiking boots, sitting against a big Douglas fir.

"New boots," he said with a grin. "But they seem pretty stiff."

We decided to hoof it down the trail for a few hours, exploring the mountain wildlands that are said to hide Bigfoot and other strange creatures. After just a short while on the trail, a sense of peace and calm seemed to settle in. The forest provides the chance to be purified with clean air and the smell of trees, freeing you from all troubles.

But it wasn't long before a look of trouble was on Foonsky's face. And no, it wasn't from seeing Bigfoot.

"Got a hot spot on a toe," he said.

Immediately we stopped. He pulled off his right boot, then his socks, and inspected the left side of his big toe. Sure enough, a blister had bubbled up, filled with fluid, but hadn't popped. From his medical kit, Foonsky cut a small piece of moleskin to fit over the blister and taped it to hold it in place. In a few minutes we were back on the trail.

A half hour later, there was still no sign of Bigfoot. But Foonsky stopped again and pulled off his other boot. "Another hot spot." On the little toe of his left foot was another small blister, over which he taped a Band-Aid to keep it from further chafing against the inside of his new boot.

In just a few days, ol' Foonsky, a strong, 6-foot-5, 200-plus-pound guy, was walking around like a sore-hoofed horse that had been loaded with a month's worth of supplies and ridden over sharp rocks. Well, it wasn't the distance that had done Foonsky in; it was those blisters. He had them on eight of his 10 toes and was going through Band-Aids, moleskin, and tape like a walking emergency ward. If he used any more tape, he would've looked like a mummy from an Egyptian tomb.

If you've ever been in a similar predicament, you know the frustration of wanting to have a good time, wanting to hike and explore the area where you have set up a secluded camp, only to be turned gimp-legged by several blisters. No one is immune—all are created equal before the blister god. You can be forced to bow to it unless you get your act together.

That means wearing the right-style boots for what you have in mind and then protecting your feet with carefully selected socks. If you are still so unfortunate as to get a blister or two, it means knowing how to treat them fast so they don't turn your walk into a sore-footed endurance test.

What causes blisters? In almost all cases, it is the simple rubbing of a foot against the rugged interior of a boot. That can be worsened by several factors:

1. A very stiff boot or one in which your foot moves inside as you walk, instead of the boot flexing as if it were another layer of skin.

2. Thin, ragged, or dirty socks. This is the fastest route to blisters. Thin socks will allow your feet to move inside of your boots, ragged socks will allow your skin to chafe directly against the boot's interior, and dirty socks will wrinkle and fold, also rubbing against your feet instead of cushioning them.

3. Soft feet. By themselves, soft feet will not cause blisters, but in combination with a stiff boot or thin socks, they can cause terrible problems. The best way to toughen up your feet is to go barefoot. In fact, some of the biggest, toughest-looking guys you'll ever see, from Hell's Angels to pro football players, have feet that are as soft as a baby's butt. Why? Because they never go barefoot and don't hike much.

Selecting the Right Boots

One summer I hiked 400 miles, including 250 miles in three weeks, along the crest of California's Sierra Nevada, and another 150 miles over several months in an earlier general training program. In that span I got just one blister, suffered on the fourth day of the 250-miler. I treated it immediately and suffered no more. One key is wearing the right boot, and for me, that means a boot that acts as a thick layer of skin that is flexible and pliable to my foot. I want my feet to fit snugly in them, with no interior movement.

There are three kinds of boots: mountaineering boots, hiking (or backpacking) boots, and canvas walking shoes. Select the right one for you or pay the consequences.

Mountaineering boots

The stiffest of the lot is the mountaineering boot. These boots are often identified by midrange tops, laces that extend almost as far as the toe area, and ankle areas that are as stiff as a board. The lack of "give" is what endears them to mountaineers. Their stiffness is preferred when rock climbing, walking off-trail on craggy surfaces, or hiking down the edge of streambeds where walking across small rocks can cause you to turn your ankle. Because these boots don't give on rugged, craggy terrain, they reduce ankle injuries and provide better traction.

The drawback to stiff boots is that if you don't have the proper socks and your foot starts slipping around in the boot, you will get a set of blisters that would raise even Foonsky's eyebrows. But if you just want to go for a walk or a good tromp with a backpack, then hiking shoes or backpacking boots will serve you better.

Canvas walking shoes

Canvas walking shoes are the lightest of all boots, designed for day walks or short backpacking trips. Some of the newer models are like rugged tennis shoes, designed with a canvas top for lightness and a lug sole for traction. These are perfect for people who like to walk but rarely carry a backpack. Because they are flexible, they are easy to break in, and with fresh socks they rarely cause blister problems. Because they are light, general hiking fatigue is greatly reduced.

On the negative side, because canvas shoes have shallow lug soles, traction can be far from good on slippery surfaces. In addition, they provide less than ideal ankle support, which can be a problem in rocky areas, such as along a stream where you might want to go trout fishing. Turn your ankle and your trip can be ruined.

Backpacking boots

My preference is for a premium backpacking boot, the perfect medium between the stiff mountaineering boot and the soft canvas walking shoe. The deep lug bottom provides traction, the high ankle coverage provides support, yet the soft, waterproof leather body gives each foot a snug fit. Add it up and that means no blisters. On the negative side, they can be quite hot, weigh a ton, and if they get wet, take days to dry.

There are a zillion styles, brands, and price ranges to choose from. If you wander about comparing all their many features, you will get as confused as a kid in a toy store. Instead, go into the store with your mind clear about what you want, find it, and buy it. If you want the best, expect to spend $85–110 for canvas walking shoes, from $130–180 and sometimes more for hiking or mountaineering boots. I have spent as much as $250 for hiking boots that I have worn for close to 2,000 miles. Yet another time I spent $185, thinking I was getting stellar quality, but they turned out to be miserable blister makers, and even after a year of trying to get my money's worth, they never worked right on the trail and now occupy a dark place deep in my closet.

This is one area where you don't want to scrimp, so try not to yelp about the high cost. Instead, walk out of the store believing you deserve the best, and that's exactly what you just paid for. Another trick I have learned is to bring several pairs of different style hiking boots on adventures, then change them constantly according to the terrain. Use heavy boots for steep trails with loose footing, lightweight models for flat routes with a hard surface. This works wonders to avoid blisters and muscle soreness because you are constantly changing what I call "the point of attack."

If you plan on using the advice of a shoe salesperson, first look at what kind of boots he or she is wearing. If he or she isn't even wearing boots, then any advice the salesperson might tender may not be worth a plugged nickel. Most people I know who own quality boots, including salespeople, will wear them almost daily if their job allows, since boots are the best footwear available. However, even these well-meaning folks can offer sketchy advice. Every hiker I've ever met will tell you he wears the world's greatest boot.

Instead, enter the store with a precise use and style in mind. Rather than fish for suggestions, tell the salesperson exactly what you want, try two or three brands of the same style, and always try on both boots in a pair simultaneously so you know exactly how they'll feel. If possible, walk up and down stairs with them. Are they too stiff? Are your feet snug yet comfortable, or do they slip? Do they have that "right" kind of feel when you walk?

If you get the right answers to those questions, then you're on your way to blister-free, pleasure-filled days of walking.

Socks
The poor gent was scratching his feet as if ants were crawling over them. I looked closer. Huge yellow calluses covered the bottoms of his feet, and at the ball and heel, the calluses were about a quarter-inch thick, cracking and sore.

"I don't understand it," he said. "I'm on my feet a lot, so I bought a real good pair of hiking boots. But look what they've done to my feet. My feet itch so much I'm going crazy."

People can spend so much energy selecting the right kind of boot that they virtually overlook wearing the right kind of socks. One goes with the other.

Your socks should be thick enough to cushion your feet as well as fit snugly. Without good socks you might try to get the bootlaces too tight—and that's like putting a tourniquet on your feet. You should have plenty of clean socks on hand, or plan on washing what you have on your trip. As socks are worn, they become compressed, dirty, and damp. Any one of those factors can cause problems.

My camping companions believe I go overboard when it comes to socks, that I bring too many and wear too many. But it works, so that's where the complaints stop. So how many do I wear? Well, it varies. On day hikes, I have found a sock called a SmartWool that makes my size 13s feel as if I'm walking on pillows. But on long expeditions, the 200-milers, I sometimes wear three socks on each foot, believe it or not. It may sound like overkill, but each has its purpose, and as I said, it works.

The interior sock is thin, lightweight, and made of polypropylene or silk synthetic materials designed to transport moisture away from your skin. With a poly interior sock, your foot stays dry when it sweats. Without a poly sock, your foot can get damp and mix with dirt, which can cause a hot spot to start on your foot. Eventually you get blisters, lots of them.

The second sock is for comfort and can be cotton, but a thin wool-based composite is ideal. Some made of the latter can wick moisture away from the skin, much like polypropylene does. If wool itches your feet, a thick cotton sock can be suitable, though cotton collects moisture and compacts more quickly than other socks. If you're on a short hike, though, cotton will do just fine.

The exterior sock should be made of high-quality, thick wool—at least 80 percent wool. It will cushion your feet, provide that just-right snug fit in your boot, and give you some additional warmth and insulation in cold weather. It is critical to keep the wool sock clean. If you wear a dirty wool sock over and over again, it will compact and lose its cushion and start wrinkling while you hike, then your feet will catch on fire from the blisters that start popping up. Of course, when wearing multiple socks, especially a wool composite, you will likely need to go up a boot size so they fit comfortably.

A Few More Tips

If you are like most folks—that is, the bottoms of your feet are rarely exposed and quite soft—you can take additional steps in their care. The best tip is keeping a fresh foot pad made of sponge rubber in your boot. Another cure for soft feet is to get out and walk or jog on a regular basis before your camping trip.

If you plan to use a foot pad and wear three socks, you will need to use these items when sizing boots. It is an unforgiving error to wear thin cotton socks when buying boots and later try to squeeze all this stuff, plus your feet, into them. There just won't be enough room.

The key to treating blisters is fast work at the first sign of a hot spot. But before you remove your socks, check to see if the sock has a wrinkle in it, a likely cause of the problem. If so, either change socks or pull them tight, removing the tiny folds, after taking care of the blister. Cut a piece of moleskin to cover the offending toe, securing the moleskin with white medical tape. If moleskin is not available, small Band-Aids can do the job, but these have to be replaced daily, and sometimes with even more frequency. At night, clean your feet and sleep without socks.

Two other items that can help your walking is an Ace bandage and a pair of gaiters.

For sprained ankles and twisted knees, an Ace bandage can be like an insurance policy to get you back on the trail and out of trouble. Over the years I have had serious ankle problems and have relied on a good wrap with a four-inch bandage to get me home. The newer bandages come with the clips permanently attached, so you don't have to worry about losing them.

Gaiters are leggings made of plastic, nylon, or Gore-Tex that fit from just below your knees, over your calves, and attach under your boots. They are of particular help when walking in damp areas or in places where rain is common. As your legs brush against ferns or low-lying plants, gaiters will deflect the moisture. Without them, your pants will be soaking wet in short order.

Should your boots become wet, a good tip is never to try to force-dry them. Some well-meaning folks will try to dry them quickly at the edge of a campfire or actually put the boots in an oven. While this may dry the boots, it can also loosen the glue that holds them together, ultimately weakening them until one day they fall apart in a heap.

A better bet is to treat the leather so the boots become water-repellent. Silicone-based liquids are the easiest to use and least greasy of the treatments available.

A final tip is to have another pair of lightweight shoes or moccasins that you can wear around camp and in the process give your feet the rest they deserve.

Sleeping Gear

One mountain night in the pines on an eve long ago, my dad, brother, and I had rolled out our sleeping bags and were bedded down for the night. After the pre-trip excitement, a long drive, an evening of trout fishing, and a barbecue, we were like three tired doggies who had played too much.

But as I looked up at the stars, I was suddenly wide awake. This kid was still wired. A half hour later? No change—wide awake.

And as little kids can do, I had to wake up ol' dad to tell him about it. "Hey, Dad, I can't sleep."

"This is what you do," he said. "Watch the sky for a shooting star and tell yourself that you cannot go to sleep until you see at least one. As you wait and watch, you will start getting tired, and it will be difficult to keep your eyes open. But tell yourself you must keep watching. Then you'll start to really feel tired. When you finally see a shooting star, you'll go to sleep so fast you won't know what hit you."

Well, I tried it that night and I don't even remember seeing a shooting star, I went to sleep so fast.

It's a good trick, and along with having a good sleeping bag, ground insulation, maybe a tent, or a few tricks for bedding down in a pickup truck or motor home, you can get a good night's sleep on every camping trip.

More than 20 years after that camping episode with my dad and brother, we made a trip to the planetarium at the Academy of Sciences in San Francisco to see a show on Halley's Comet. The lights dimmed, and the ceiling turned into a night sky, filled with stars and a setting moon. A scientist began explaining phenomena of the heavens.

After a few minutes, I began to feel drowsy. Just then, a shooting star zipped across the planetarium ceiling. I went into a deep sleep so fast it was like I was in a coma. I didn't wake up until the show was over, the lights were turned back on, and the people were leaving.

Feeling drowsy, I turned to see if ol' Dad had liked the show. Oh yeah? Not only had he gone to sleep too, but he apparently had no intention of waking up, no matter what. Just like a camping trip.

Sleeping Bags

Question: What could be worse than trying to sleep in a cold, wet sleeping bag on a rainy night without a tent in the mountains?

Answer: Trying to sleep in a cold, wet sleeping bag on a rainy night without a tent in the mountains when your sleeping bag is filled with down.

Water will turn a down-filled sleeping bag into a mushy heap. Many campers do not like a high-tech approach, but the state-of-the-art polyfiber sleeping bags can keep you warm even when wet. That factor, along with temperature rating and weight, is key when selecting a sleeping bag.

A sleeping bag is a shell filled with heat-retaining insulation. By itself it is not warm. Your body provides the heat, and the sleeping bag's ability to retain that heat is what makes it warm or cold.

The old-style canvas bags are heavy, bulky, cold, and when wet, useless. With other options available, their use is limited. Anybody who sleeps outdoors or backpacks should choose otherwise. Buy and use a sleeping bag filled with down or one of the quality poly-fills. Down is light, warm, and aesthetically pleasing to those who don't think camping and technology mix. If you choose a down bag, be sure to keep it double wrapped in plastic garbage bags on your trip to keep it dry. Once it's wet, you'll spend your nights howling at the moon.

The polyfiber-filled bags are not necessarily better than those filled with down, but they can be. Their one key advantage is that even when wet, some poly-fills can retain up to 85 percent of your body heat. This allows you to sleep and get valuable rest even in miserable conditions. And my camping experience is that no matter how lucky you may be, there comes a time when you will get caught in an unexpected, violent storm and everything you've got will get wet, including your sleeping bag. That's when a poly-fill bag becomes priceless. You either have one and can sleep, or you don't have one and suffer. It is that simple. Of the synthetic fills, Quallofil made by DuPont is the industry leader.

But just because a sleeping bag uses a high-tech poly-fill doesn't necessarily make it a better bag. There are other factors.

The most important are a bag's temperature rating and weight. The temperature rating of a sleeping bag refers to how cold it can get before you start actually feeling cold. Many campers make the mistake of thinking, "I only camp in the summer, so a bag rated at 30 or 40 degrees should be fine." Later they find out it isn't so fine, and all it takes is one cold night to convince them of that. When selecting the right temperature rating, visualize the coldest weather you might ever confront, and then get a bag rated for even colder weather.

For instance, if you are a summer camper, you may rarely experience a night in the low 30s or high 20s. A sleeping bag rated at 20 degrees would be appropriate, keeping you snug, warm, and asleep. For most campers, I advise bags rated at 0 or 10 degrees.

If you buy a poly-filled sleeping bag, never leave it squished in your stuff sack between camping trips. Instead, keep it on a hanger in a closet or use it as a blanket. One thing that can reduce a poly-filled bag's heat-retaining qualities is if

Even with the warmest sleeping bag in the world, if you just lay it down on the ground and try to sleep, you will likely get as cold as a winter cucumber. That is because the cold ground will suck the warmth right out of your body. The solution? A sleeping pad.

you lose the loft out of the tiny hollow fibers that make up the fill. You can avoid this with proper storage.

The weight of a sleeping bag can also be a key factor, especially for backpackers. When you have to carry your gear on your back, every ounce becomes important. Sleeping bags that weigh just three pounds are available, although they are expensive. But if you hike much, it's worth the price to keep your weight to a minimum. For an overnighter, you can get away with a four- or 4.5-pound bag without much stress. However, bags weighing five pounds and up should be left back at the car.

I have two sleeping bags: a seven-pounder that feels like a giant sponge, and a little three-pounder. The heavy-duty model is for pickup truck camping in cold weather and doubles as a blanket at home. The lightweight bag is for hikes. Between the two, I'm set.

Insulation Pads

Even with the warmest sleeping bag in the world, if you just lay it down on the ground and try to sleep, you will likely get as cold as a winter cucumber. That is because the cold ground will suck the warmth right out of your body. The solution is to have a layer of insulation between you and the ground. For this you can use a thin Insulite pad, a lightweight Therm-a-Rest inflatable pad, a foam pad or mattress, air bed, or a cot. Here is a capsule summary of all three:

- **Insulite pads:** They are light, inexpensive, roll up quick for transport, and can double as a seat pad at your camp. The negative side is that in one night, they will compress, making you feel that you are sleeping on granite.
- **Therm-a-Rest pads:** These are a real luxury because they do everything an Insulite pad does, but also provide a cushion. The negative side is that they are expensive by comparison, and if they get a hole in them, they become worthless without a patch kit.
- **Air beds, foam mattresses, and cots:** These are excellent for car campers. The new line of air beds available are outstanding, especially the thicker ones, and inflate quickly with an electric motor inflator that plugs into a power plug or cigarette lighter in your vehicle. Foam mattresses are also excellent, in

fact, the most comfortable of all, but their size precludes many from considering them. I've found that cots work great, too. When I finally wore out my old wood one, I replaced it immediately with one of the new high-tech and light metal ones. For camping in the back of a pickup truck with a camper shell, the cots with three-inch legs are best, of course.

A Few Tricks

When surveying a camp area, the most important consideration should be to select a good spot to sleep. Everything else is secondary. Ideally, you want a flat spot that is wind-sheltered and on ground soft enough to drive stakes into. Yeah, and I want to win the lottery, too.

Sometimes that ground will have a slight slope to it. In that case, always sleep with your head on the uphill side. If you sleep parallel to the slope, every time you roll over, you'll find yourself rolling down the hill. If you sleep with your head on the downhill side, you'll get a headache that feels as if an ax is embedded in your brain.

When you've found a good spot, clear it of all branches, twigs, and rocks, of course. A good tip is to dig a slight indentation in the ground where your hip will fit. Since your body is not flat, but has curves and edges, it will not feel comfortable on flat ground. Some people even get severely bruised on the sides of their hips when sleeping on flat, hard ground. For that reason alone they learn to hate camping. What a shame, especially when solved so easily with a Therm-a-Rest pad, foam insulation, air bed, or a cot.

After the ground is prepared, throw a ground cloth over the spot, which will keep much of the morning dew off you. In some areas, particularly where fog is a problem, morning dew can be heavy and get the outside of your sleeping bag quite wet. In that case, you need overhead protection, such as a tent or some kind of roof, like a poncho or tarp with its ends tied to trees.

Tents and Weather Protection

All it takes is to get caught in the rain once without a tent and you will never go anywhere without one again. A tent provides protection from rain, wind, and mosquito attacks. In exchange, you can lose a starry night's view, though some tents now even provide moon roofs.

A tent can be as complex as a four-season, tubular-jointed dome with a rain fly or as simple as two ponchos snapped together and roped up to a tree. They can be as cheap as a $10 tube tent, which is nothing more than a hollow piece of plastic, or as expensive as a $500 five-person deluxe expedition dome model. They vary greatly in size, price, and put-up time. If you plan on getting a good one, plan on doing plenty of shopping and asking lots of questions. With a little bit of homework, you can get the right answers to these questions:

Will it keep me dry?

On many one-person and two-person tents, the rain fly does not extend far enough to keep water off the bottom sidewalls of the tent. In a driving rain, water can also drip from the rain fly and onto the bottom side-walls of the tent. Eventually the water can leak through to the inside, particularly through the seams where the tent has been sewn together.

You must be able to stake out your rain fly so it completely covers all of the tent. If you are tent shopping and this does not appear possible, then don't buy the tent. To prevent potential leaks, use a seam waterproofer such as Seam Lock, a gluelike substance, to close potential leak areas on tent seams. For large umbrella tents, keep a patch kit handy.

Another way to keep water out of your tent is to store all wet garments outside the tent, under a poncho. Moisture from wet clothes stashed in the tent will condense on the interior tent walls. If you bring enough wet clothes into the tent, by the next morning you can feel as if you're camping in a duck blind.

How hard is it to put up?

If a tent is difficult to erect in full sunlight, you can just about forget it at night. Some tents can go up in just a few minutes, without requiring help from another camper. This might be the kind of tent you want.

The way to compare put-up time of tents when shopping is to count the number of connecting points from the tent poles to the tent and the number of stakes required. The fewer the better. Think simple. My tent has seven connecting points and, minus the rain fly, requires no stakes. It goes up in a few minutes. If you need a lot of stakes, it is a sure tip-off to a long put-up time. Try it at night or in the rain, and you'll be ready to cash your chips and go for broke.

Another factor is the tent poles themselves. Some small tents have poles that are broken into small sections that are connected by bungee cords. It takes only an instant to convert them to a complete pole.

Some outdoor shops have tents on display on their showroom floors. Before buying the tent, have the salesperson take the tent down and put it back up. If it takes him more than five minutes, or he says he doesn't have time, then keep looking.

Is it roomy enough?

Don't judge the size of a tent on floor space alone. Some tents small on floor space can give the illusion of roominess with a high ceiling. You can be quite comfortable in them and snug.

But remember that a one- or two-person tent is just that. A two-person tent has room for two people plus gear. That's it. Don't buy a tent expecting it to hold more than it is intended to.

How much does it weigh?
If you're a hiker, this be-comes the preeminent ques-tion. If it's much more than six or seven pounds, forget it. A 12-pound tent is bad enough, but get it wet and it's like carrying a piano on your back. On the other hand, weight is scarcely a factor if you camp only where you can take your car. My dad, for instance, used to have this giant canvas umbrella tent that folded down to a neat little pack that weighed about 500 pounds.

Family Tents
It is always worth spending the time and money to buy a tent you and your fam-ily will be happy with.

Though many good family tents are available for $125–175, particularly from Coleman, Cabela's, and Remington, here is a synopsis of two of the best tents avail-able anywhere, without regard to cost, generally ranging from $350–600:

Sierra Designs Mondo 5CD
800/736-8551

10.14 pounds

82 square feet / 20-square-foot covered entry / Inside peak height: five feet, five inches

If you've got a family that likes to head for distant camps, then this is your tent. It's light enough to pack along, yet big enough to accommodate a family of four. Using speed clips, this tent is by far the easiest and quickest to set up of any family tent I've used. A generous rain fly and covered entry area (new adjustment features allow various awning configurations) mean more than adequate protection from the elements, no mat-ter how hard they are pelting down.

Kelty Domolite 6
800/423-2320

16.4 pounds

81.5 square feet / Inside peak height: five feet, seven inches

Using three 18-foot-long

A-frame style tents have gone the way of the dinosaur. With the world going high-tech, tents of today vary greatly in com-plexity, size, price, and put-up time. And they wouldn't be fit for this new millen-nium without offer-ing options such as moon roofs, rain flies, and tent wings. Be sure to buy the one that's right for your needs.

fiberglass poles, the Domolite boasts a sleek, low profile that slips the wind very nicely. Each pole slides easily through continuous pole sleeves, thanks to rubber-tipped ends, making set-up a snap. Kelty has an optional covered entry area, since without it, the tent is barely adequate shelter should you have to weather a deluge in cramped quarters. Floor seams are taped for added waterproofness. A great package.

Bivouac Bags

If you like going solo and choose not to own a tent at all, a bivy bag, short for bivouac bag, can provide the weather protection you require. A bivy bag is a water-repellent shell in which your sleeping bag fits. It is light and tough, and for some is the perfect alternative to a heavy tent. My own bivy weighs 31 ounces and cost me $240, made by OR (Outdoor Research), and I just plain love the thing on expeditions. On the downside, however, it can be a bit difficult getting settled just right in it, and some say they feel claustrophobic at the close quarters. My biggest fear was the idea of riding out a storm. You can hear the rain hitting you, and sometimes even feel the pounding of the drops through the bivy bag. For some, it can be unsettling to try and sleep under such circumstances. On the other hand, I've always looked forward to it. In cold weather, it also helps to keep you warm.

Pickup Truck Campers

If you own a pickup truck with a camper shell, you can turn it into a self-contained campground with a little work. This can be an ideal way to go: it's fast, portable, and you are guaranteed a dry environment.

But that does not necessarily mean it is a warm environment. In fact, without insulation from the metal truck bed, it can be like trying to sleep on an iceberg. That is because the metal truck bed will get as cold as the air temperature, which is often much colder than the ground temperature. Without insulation, it can be much colder in your camper shell than it would be on the open ground.

When I camp in my rig, I use a large piece of foam for a mattress and insulation. The foam measures four inches thick, 48 inches wide, and 76 inches long. It makes for a bed as comfortable as anything one might ask for. In fact, during the winter, if I don't go camping for a few weeks because of writing obligations, I sometimes will throw the foam on the floor, lay down the old sleeping bag, light a fire, and camp right in my living room. It's in my blood, I tell you. Air beds and cots are also extremely comfortable and I've used both many times. Whatever you choose, just make sure you have a comfortable sleeping unit. Good sleep makes for great camping trips.

RVs

The problems RVers encounter come from two primary sources: lack of privacy and light intrusion.

The lack of privacy stems from the natural restrictions of where a land yacht can go. Without careful use of the guide section of this book, motor-home owners can find themselves in parking lot settings, jammed in with plenty of neighbors. Because RVs often have large picture windows, you lose your privacy, causing some late nights; then, come daybreak, light intrusion forces an early wake up. The result is you get shorted on your sleep.

The answer is to carry inserts to fit over the inside of your windows. This closes off the outside and retains your privacy. And if you don't want to wake up with the sun at daybreak, you don't have to. It will still be dark.

First Aid and Insect Protection

The mountain night could not have been more perfect, I thought as I lay in my sleeping bag.

The sky looked like a mass of jewels and the air tasted sweet and smelled of pines. A shooting star fireballed across the sky, and I remember thinking, "It just doesn't get any better."

Just then, as I was drifting into sleep, a mysterious buzz appeared from nowhere and deposited itself inside my left ear. Suddenly awake, I whacked my ear with the palm of my hand, hard enough to cause a minor concussion. The buzz disappeared. I pulled out my flashlight and shined it on my palm, and there, lit in the blackness of night, lay the squished intruder: a mosquito, dead amid a stain of blood.

Satisfied, I turned off the light, closed my eyes, and thought of the fishing trip planned for the next day. Then I heard them. It was a squadron of mosquitoes flying landing patterns around my head. I tried to grab them with an open hand, but they dodged the assault and flew off. Just 30 seconds later another landed in my left ear. I promptly dispatched the invader with a rip of the palm.

Now I was completely awake, so I got out of my sleeping bag to retrieve some mosquito repellent. But en route, several of the buggers swarmed and nailed me in the back and arms. After I applied the repellent and settled snugly again in my sleeping bag, the mosquitoes would buzz a few inches from my ear. After getting a whiff of the poison, they would fly off. It was like sleeping in a sawmill.

The next day, drowsy from little sleep, I set out to fish. I'd walked but 15 minutes when I brushed against a bush and felt this stinging sensation on the inside of my arm, just above the wrist. I looked down: a tick had his clamps in me. I ripped it out before he could embed his head into my skin.

After catching a few fish, I sat down against a tree to eat lunch and just watch the water go by. My dog, Rebel, sat down next to me and stared at the beef jerky I was munching as if it were a T-bone steak. I finished eating, gave him a small piece, patted him on the head, and said, "Good dog." Right then, I noticed an itch on my arm where a mosquito had drilled me. I unconsciously scratched it. Two days later, in that exact spot, some nasty red splotches started popping up. Poison oak. By petting my dog and then scratching my arm, I had transferred the oil residue of the poison oak leaves from Rebel's fur to my arm.

When I returned home, Foonsky asked me about the trip.

"Great," I said. "Mosquitoes, ticks, poison oak. Can hardly wait to go back."

"Sorry I missed out," he answered.

Mosquitoes, No-See-Ums, Gnats, and Horseflies

On a trip to Canada, Foonsky and I were fishing a small lake from the shore when suddenly a black horde of mosquitoes could be seen moving across the lake toward us. It was like when the French army looked across the Rhine and saw the Wehrmacht coming. There was a buzz in the air. We fought them off for a few minutes, then made a fast retreat to the truck and jumped in, content the buggers had been fooled. But in some way still unknown to us, the mosquitoes gained entry to the truck. In 10 minutes, we squished 15 of them as they attempted to plant their oil drills into our skins. Just outside the truck, the black horde waited for us to make a tactical error such as rolling down a window. It finally took a miraculous hailstorm to foil the attack.

When it comes to mosquitoes, no-see-ums, gnats, and horseflies, there are times when there is nothing you can do. However, in most situations you can muster a defense to repel the attack.

The first key with mosquitoes is to wear clothing too heavy for them to drill through. Expose a minimum of skin, wear a hat, and tie a bandanna around your neck, preferably one that has been sprayed with repellent. If you try to get by with just a cotton T-shirt, you will be declared a federal mosquito sanctuary.

So first your skin must be well covered, exposing only your hands and face. Second, you should have your companion spray your clothes with repellent. Third, you should dab liquid repellent directly on your skin.

At night, the easiest way to get a good sleep without mosquitoes buzzing in your ear is to sleep in a bug-proof tent. If the nights are warm and you want to see the stars, new tent models are available that have a skylight covered with mosquito netting. If you don't like tents on summer evenings, mosquito netting rigged with an air space at your head can solve the problem. Otherwise prepare to get bitten, even with the use of mosquito repellent.

If your problems are with no-see-ums or biting horseflies, then you need a slightly different approach.

No-see-ums are tiny black insects that look like nothing more than a sliver of dirt on your skin. Then you notice something stinging, and when you rub the area, you scratch up a little no-see-um. The results are similar to mosquito bites, making your skin itch, splotch, and when you get them bad, swell. In addition to using the techniques described to repel mosquitoes, you should go one step further.

The problem is that no-see-ums are tricky little devils. Somehow they can actually get under your socks and around your ankles where they will bite to their hearts' content all night long while you sleep, itch, sleep, and itch some more. The best solution is to apply a liquid repellent to your ankles, then wear clean socks.

Horseflies are another story. They are rarely a problem, but when they get their dander up, they can cause trouble you'll never forget.

One such episode occurred when Foonsky and I were paddling a canoe along the shoreline of a large lake. This giant horsefly, about the size of a fingertip, started dive-bombing the canoe. After 20 minutes, it landed on Foonsky's thigh. He immediately slammed it with an open hand, then let out a blood-curdling "Yeeeee-ow!" that practically sent ripples across the lake. When Foonsky whacked it, the horsefly had somehow turned around and bit him on the hand, leaving a huge red welt.

> Mosquito Repellent: Taking vitamin B1 and eating garlic are reputed to act as natural insect repellents, but I've met a lot of mosquitoes that are not convinced. A better bet is to examine the label of the repellent in question for N,N diethyl-m-toluamide, commonly known as DEET. That is a poison, and the percentage of it in the container must be listed and will indicate that brand's effectiveness. Inert ingredients are mainly fluids used to fill the bottles.

In the next 10 minutes, that big fly strafed the canoe on more dive-bomb runs. I finally got my canoe paddle, swung it as if it were a baseball bat, and nailed that horsefly as if I'd hit a home run. It landed about 15 feet from the boat, still alive and buzzing in the water. While I was trying to figure what it would take to kill this bugger, a large rainbow trout surfaced and snatched it out of the water, finally avenging the assault.

If you have horsefly or yellow jacket problems, you'd best just leave the area. One, two, or a few can be dealt with. More than that and your fun camping trip will be about as fun as being roped to a tree and stung by an electric shock rod.

On most trips, you will spend time doing everything possible to keep from getting bitten by mosquitoes or no-see-ums. When that fails, you must know what to do next, and fast, if you are among those ill-fated campers who get big red lumps from a bite inflicted from even a microscopic mosquito.

A fluid called After Bite or a dab of ammonia should be applied immediately to the bite. To start the healing process, apply a first-aid gel (not a liquid), such as the one made by Campho-Phenique.

DEET Versus "Natural" Repellents
What is DEET? You're not likely to find the word DEET on any repellent label. That's because DEET stands for N,N diethyl-m-toluamide. If the label contains this scientific name, the repellent contains DEET. Despite fears of DEET-associated health risks and the increased attention given natural alternatives, DEET-based

repellents are still acknowledged as by far the best option when serious insect protection is required.

What are the health risks associated with using DEET? A number of deaths and a number of medical problems have been attributed in the press to DEET in recent years—events that those in the DEET community vehemently deny as being specifically DEET-related, pointing to reams of scientific documentation as evidence. It does seem logical to assume that if DEET can peel paint, melt nylon, destroy plastic, wreck wood finishes, and damage fishing line, then it must be hell on the skin—perhaps worse.

On one trip, I had a small bottle of mosquito repellent in the same pocket as a Swiss army knife. Guess what happened? The mosquito repellent leaked a bit and literally melted the insignia right off the knife. DEET will also melt synthetic clothes. That is why in bad mosquito country, I'll expose a minimum of skin, just hands and face (with full beard), and apply the repellent only to my cheeks and the back of my hands, perhaps wear a bandanna sprinkled with a few drops as well. That does the trick, with a minimum of exposure to the repellent.

Although nothing definitive has been published, there is a belief among a growing number in the scientific community that repeated applications of products containing low percentages of DEET can be potentially dangerous. It is theorized that this actually puts consumers at a greater risk for absorbing high levels of DEET into the body than if they had just used one application of a 30–50 percent DEET product with an efficacy of four to six hours. Also being studied is the possibility that low levels of DEET, which might not otherwise be of toxicological concern, may become hazardous if they are formulated with solvents or dilutents (considered inert ingredients) that may enhance the absorption rate.

Are natural alternatives a safer choice? To imply that essential oils are completely safe because they are a natural product is not altogether accurate. Essential oils, while derived from plants that grow naturally, are chemicals too. Some are potentially hazardous if ingested, and most are downright painful if they find their way into the eyes or onto mucus membranes. For example, pennyroyal is perhaps the most toxic of the essential oils used to repel insects and can be deadly if taken internally. Other oils used include citronella (perhaps the most common, it's extracted from an aromatic grass indigenous to Southern Asia), eucalyptus, cedarwood, and peppermint.

Three citronella-based products, Buzz Away (manufactured by Quantum), Avon's Skin-So-Soft, and Natrapel (manufactured by Tender), have received EPA registration and approval for sale as repellents for use in controlling mosquitoes, flies, gnats, and midges.

How effective are natural repellents? While there are numerous studies cited by those on the DEET and citronella sides of the fence, the average effective repelling time of a citronella product appears to range from 1.5 to two hours. Tests conducted at Cambridge University, England, comparing Natrapel to DEET-based Skintastic (a low-percentage DEET product) found citronella to be just as effective in repelling mosquitoes. The key here is effectiveness and the amount of time until reapplication.

Keep It Wild Tip 4: Sanitation

If no refuse facility is available:
1. Deposit human waste in "cat holes" dug six to eight inches deep. Cover and disguise the cat hole when finished.
2. Deposit human waste at least 75 paces (200 feet) from any water source or camp.
3. Use toilet paper sparingly. When finished, carefully burn it in the cat hole, then bury it.
4. If no appropriate burial locations are available, such as in popular wilderness camps above tree line in granite settings, then all human refuse should be double-bagged and packed out.
5. At boat-in campsites, chemical toilets are required. Chemical toilets can also solve the problem of larger groups camping for long stays at one location where no facilities are available.
6. To wash dishes or your body, carry water away from the source and use small amounts of biodegradable soap. Scatter dishwater after all food particles have been removed.
7. Scour your campsites for even the tiniest piece of trash and any other evidence of your stay. Pack out all the trash you can, even if it's not yours. Finding cigarette butts, for instance, provides special irritation for most campers. Pick them up and discard them properly.
8. Never litter. Never. Or you become the enemy of all others.

Citronella products work for up to two hours and then require reapplication (the same holds true for other natural formulations). Products using a low-percentage level of DEET also require reapplication every two hours to remain effective. So if you're going outside for only a short period in an environment where insect bites are more an irritant than a hazard, you would do just as well to go natural.

What other chemical alternatives are there? Another line of defense against insects is the chemical permethrin, used on clothing, not on skin. Permethrin-based products are designed to repel and kill arthropods or crawling insects, making them a preferred repellent for ticks. The currently available products will remain effective, repelling and killing mosquitoes, ticks, and chiggers, for two weeks and through two launderings.

Ticks

Ticks are nasty little vermin that will wait in ambush, jump on unsuspecting prey, and then crawl to a prime location before filling their bodies with their victim's blood.

I call them Dracula bugs, but by any name they can be a terrible camp pest. Ticks rest on grass and low plants and attach themselves to those who brush against the vegetation (dogs are particularly vulnerable). Typically they are no more than 18 inches above ground, and if you stay on the trails, you can usually avoid them.

There are two common species of ticks. The common coastal tick is larger, brownish in color, and prefers to crawl around before putting its clamps on you. The latter habit can be creepy, but when you feel it crawling, you can just pick it off and dispatch it. The coastal tick's preferred destination is usually the back of your neck, just where the hairline starts. The other species, the wood tick, is small and black, and when he puts his clamps in, it's immediately painful. When a wood tick gets into a dog for a few days, it can cause a large red welt. In either case, ticks should be removed as soon as possible.

If you have hiked in areas infested with ticks, it is advisable to shower as soon as possible, washing your clothes immediately. If you just leave your clothes in a heap, a tick can crawl out and invade your home. They like warmth, and one way or another, they can end up in your bed. Waking up in the middle of the night with a tick crawling across your chest can really give you the creeps.

Once a tick has its clampers in you, you must decide how long it has been there. If it has been a short time, the most painless and effective method for removal is to take a pair of sharp tweezers and grasp the little devil, making certain to isolate the mouth area, then pull him out. Reader Johvin Perry sent in the suggestion to coat the tick with Vaseline, which will cut off its oxygen supply, after which it may voluntarily give up the hunt.

If the tick has been in longer, you may wish to have a doctor extract it. Some people will burn a tick with a cigarette, or poison it with lighter fluid, but this is not advisable. No matter how you do it, you must take care to remove all of it, especially its clawlike mouth.

The wound, however small, should then be cleansed and dressed. This is done by applying liquid peroxide, which cleans and sterilizes, and then applying a dressing coated with a first-aid gel such as First-Aid Cream, Campho-Phenique, or Neosporin.

Lyme disease, which can be transmitted by the bite of the deer tick, is rare but common enough to warrant some attention. To prevent tick bites, some people tuck their pant legs into their hiking socks and spray tick repellent, called Permamone, on their pants.

The first symptom of Lyme disease is that the bite area will develop a bright red, splotchy rash. Other possible early symptoms include headache, nausea, fever, and/or a stiff neck. If this happens, or if you have any doubts, you should see your doctor immediately. If you do get Lyme disease, don't panic. Doctors say it is easily treated in the early stages with simple antibiotics. If you are nervous about getting Lyme disease, carry a small plastic bag with you when you hike. If a tick manages to get his clampers into you, put it in the plastic bag after you pull it out. Then give it to your doctor for analysis to see if the tick is a carrier of the disease.

During the course of my hiking and camping career, I have removed ticks from my skin hundreds of times without any problems. However, if you are worried about ticks, you can buy a tick removal kit from any outdoors store. These kits allow you to remove ticks in such a way that their toxins are guaranteed not to enter your bloodstream.

If you are particularly wary of ticks or perhaps even have nightmares of them, wear long pants that are tucked into the socks, as well as a long-sleeved shirt tucked securely into the pants and held with a belt. Clothing should be light in color, making it easier to see ticks, and tightly woven so ticks have trouble hanging on. On one hike with my mom, Eleanor, I brushed more than 100 ticks off my blue jeans in less than an hour, while she did not pick up a single one on her polyester pants.

Perform tick checks regularly, especially on the back of the neck. The combination of DEET insect repellents applied to the skin and permethrin repellents applied directly to clothing is considered to be the most effective line of defense against ticks.

Poison Oak

After a nice afternoon hike, about a five-miler, I was concerned about possible exposure to poison oak, so I immediately showered and put on clean clothes. Then I settled into a chair with my favorite foamy elixir to watch the end of a baseball game. The game went 18 innings; meanwhile, my dog, tired from the hike, went to sleep on my bare ankles.

A few days later I had a case of poison oak. My feet looked as though they had been on fire and put out with an ice pick. The lesson? Don't always trust your dog, give him a bath as well, and beware of extra-inning ball games.

You can get poison oak only from direct contact with the oil residue from the leaves. It can be passed in a variety of ways, as direct as skin-to-leaf contact or as indirect as leaf to dog, dog to sofa, sofa to skin. Once you have it, there is little you can do but itch yourself to death. Applying Caladryl lotion or its equivalent can help because it contains antihistamines, which attack and dry the itch.

A tip that may sound crazy but seems to work is advised by my pal Furniss. You should expose the afflicted area to the hottest water you can stand, then suddenly immerse it in cold water. The hot water opens the skin pores and gets the "itch" out, and the cold water then quickly seals the pores.

In any case, you're a lot better off if you don't get poison oak to begin with. Remember that poison oak can disguise itself. In the spring, it is green; then it gradually turns reddish in the summer. By fall, it becomes a bloody, ugly-looking red. In the winter, it loses its leaves altogether and appears to be nothing more than barren, brown sticks of a small plant. However, at any time and in any form, its contact with skin can quickly lead to infection.

Avoiding Poison Oak *Remember the old Boy Scout saying: "Leaves of three, let them be."*

Some people are more easily afflicted than others, but if you are one of the lucky few who aren't, don't cheer too loudly. While some people can be exposed to the oil residue of poison oak with little or no effect, the body's resistance can gradually be worn down with repeated exposure. At one time I could practically play in the stuff and the only symptom would be a few little bumps on the inside of my wrist. Now, more than 15 years later, my resistance has broken down. If I merely rub against poison oak now, in a few days the exposed area can look as if it were used for a track meet.

So regardless of whether you consider yourself vulnerable or not, you should take heed to reduce your exposure. That can be done by staying on trails when you hike and making sure your dog does the same. Remember, the worst stands of poison oak are usually brush-infested areas just off the trail. Protect yourself also by dressing so your skin is completely covered, wearing long-sleeved shirts, long pants, and boots. If you suspect you've been exposed, immediately wash your clothes and then wash yourself with aloe vera, rinsing with a cool shower.

And don't forget to give your dog a bath as well.

Sunburn

The most common injury suffered on camping trips is sunburn, yet some people wear it as a badge of honor, believing that it somehow enhances their virility. Well, it doesn't. Neither do suntans. And too much sun can lead to serious burns or sunstroke.

It is easy enough to avoid. Use a high-level sunscreen on your skin, apply lip balm with sunscreen, and wear sunglasses and a hat. If any area gets burned, apply First-Aid Cream, which will soothe and provide moisture for your parched, burned skin.

The best advice is not to get even a suntan. Those who do are involved in a practice that can be eventually ruinous to their skin and possibly lead to cancer.

A Word about Giardia and Cryptosporidium

You have just hiked in to your backwoods spot, you're thirsty and a bit tired, but you smile as you consider the prospects. Everything seems perfect—there's not a stranger in sight, and you have nothing to do but relax with your pals.

You toss down your gear, grab your cup, dip it into the stream, and take a long drink of that ice-cold mountain water. It seems crystal pure and sweeter than anything you've ever tasted. It's not till later that you find out it can be just like drinking a cup of poison.

Whether you camp in the wilderness or not, if you hike, you're going to get thirsty. And if your canteen runs dry, you'll start eyeing any water source. Stop! Do not pass Go. Do not drink.

By drinking what appears to be pure mountain water without first treating it, you can ingest a microscopic protozoan called *Giardia lamblia*. The pain of the ensuing abdominal cramps can make you feel that your stomach and intestinal tract are in a knot, ready to explode. With that comes long-term diarrhea that is worse than even a bear could imagine.

Doctors call the disease *giardiasis,* or giardia for short, but it is difficult to diagnose. One friend of mine who contracted giardia was told he might have stomach cancer before the proper diagnosis was made.

Drinking directly from a stream or lake does not mean you will get giardia, but you are taking a giant chance. There is no reason to assume such a risk, potentially ruining your trip and enduring weeks of misery.

A lot of people are taking that risk. I made a personal survey of campers in the Yosemite National Park wilderness, and found that roughly only one in 20 was equipped with some kind of water-purification system. The result, according to the Public Health Service, is that an average of 4 percent of all backpackers and campers suffer giardiasis. According to the Parasitic Diseases Division of the Center for Infectious Diseases, the rates range from 1 percent to 20 percent across the country.

But if you get giardia, you are not going to care about the statistics. "When I got giardia, I just about wanted to die," said Henry McCarthy, a California camper. "For about 10 days, it was the most terrible thing I have ever experienced. And through the whole thing, I kept thinking, 'I shouldn't have drunk that water, but it seemed all right at the time.'"

That is the mistake most campers make. The stream might be running free, gurgling over boulders in the high country, tumbling into deep, oxygenated pools. It looks pure. Then in a few days, the problems suddenly start. Drinking untreated water from mountain streams is a lot like playing Russian roulette. Sooner or later the gun goes off.

Filters

There's really no excuse for going without a water filter: handheld filters are getting more compact, lighter, easier to use, and often less expensive. Having to boil water or endure chemicals that leave a bad taste in the mouth has been all but eliminated.

With a filter, you just pump and drink. Filtering strains out microscopic contaminants, rendering the water clear and somewhat pure. How pure? That depends on the size of the filter's pores—what manufacturers call pore-size efficiency. A filter with a pore-size efficiency of one micron or smaller will remove protozoa such as *Giardia lamblia* and cryptosporidium, as well as parasitic eggs and larva, but it takes a pore-size efficiency of less than 0.4 microns to remove bacteria. All but one of the filters recommended here do that.

A good backcountry water filter weighs less than 20 ounces, is easy to grasp, simple to use, and a snap to clean and maintain. At the very least, buy one that will remove protozoa and bacteria. (A number of cheap, pocket-size filters remove only *Giardia lamblia* and cryptosporidium. That, in my book, is risking your health to save money.) Consider the flow rate, too: a liter per minute is good.

Treating Your Water Means Avoiding Diarrhea: The only sure way to beat giardia and other water-borne diseases is to filter or boil your water before drinking, eating, or brushing your teeth. And the best way to prevent the spread of giardia is to bury your waste products at least eight inches deep and 100 feet away from natural waters.

All filters will eventually clog—it's a sign that they've been doing their job. If you force water through a filter that's becoming difficult to pump, you risk injecting a load of microbial nasties into your bottle. Some models can be backwashed, brushed, or, as with ceramic elements, scrubbed to extend their useful lives. And if the filter has a prefilter to screen out the big stuff, use it: it will give your filter a boost in mileage, which can then top out at about 100 gallons per disposable element. Any of the filters reviewed here will serve well on an outing into the wilds, providing you always play by the manufacturer's rules. They cost about $35–75, up to more than $200, depending on the volume of water they are constructed to filter.

- **First Need Deluxe:** The 15-ounce First Need Deluxe from General Ecology does something no other handheld filter will do: it removes protozoa, bacteria, and viruses without using chemicals. Such effectiveness is the result of a fancy three-stage matrix system. Unfortunately, if you drop the filter and unknowingly crack the cartridge, all the little nasties can get through. General Ecology's solution is to include a bottle of blue dye that indicates breaks. The issue hasn't scared off too many folks, though: the First Need has been around since 1982. Additional cartridges cost $30. A final note: the filter pumps smoothly and puts out more than a liter per minute. A favorite of mine.

Water filters are a wise investment since all wilderness water should be considered contaminated. Make sure the filter can be easily cleaned or has a replaceable cartridge. The filter pores must be 0.4 microns or less to remove bacteria.

- **PentaPure Oasis:** The PentaPure Oasis Water Purification System from WTC/Ecomaster offers drinkable water with a twist: you squeeze and sip instead of pumping. Weighing 6.5 ounces, the system packages a three-stage filter inside a 21-ounce-capacity sport bottle with an angled and sealing drinking nozzle, ideal for mountain bikers. The filter removes and/or kills protozoa, bacteria, and viruses, so it's also suitable for world travel. It's certainly convenient: just fill the bottle with untreated water, screw on the cap, give it a firm squeeze (don't expect the easy flow of a normal sport bottle; there's more work being done), and sip. The Oasis only runs into trouble if the water source is shallow; you'll need a cup for scooping.

- **Basic Designs Ceramic:** The Basic Designs Ceramic Filter Pump weighs eight ounces and is as stripped-down a filter as you'll find. The pump is simple, easy to use, and quite reliable. The ceramic filter effectively removes protozoa and bacteria, making it ideal and cost effective for backpacking—but it won't protect against viruses. Also, the filter element is too bulbous to work directly from a shallow water source; like the PentaPure, you'll have to decontaminate a pot, cup, or bottle to transfer your unfiltered water. It's a great buy, though, for anyone worried only about *Giardia lamblia* and cryptosporidium.

- **SweetWater WalkAbout:** The WalkAbout is perfect for the day hiker or backpacker who obsesses on lightening the load. The filter weighs just 8.5 ounces, is easily cleaned in the field, and removes both protozoa and bacteria: a genuine bargain. There are some trade-offs, however, for its diminutiveness. Water delivery is a tad slow at just under a liter per minute, but redesigned filter cartridges ($12.50) are now good for up to 100 gallons.

- **MSR MiniWorks:** Like the WalkAbout, the bargain-priced MiniWorks has a bigger and more expensive water-filtering brother. But in this case the differences are harder to discern: the new 14.3-ounce MiniWorks looks similar to the $140 WaterWorks II, and like the WaterWorks is fully field-maintainable, while guarding against protozoa, bacteria, and chemicals. But the Mini is the best-executed, easiest-to-use ceramic filter on the market, and it attaches directly to a standard one-quart Nalgene water bottle. Too bad it takes 90 seconds to filter that quart.

- **PUR Explorer:** The Explorer offers protection from all the bad guys—viruses as well as protozoa and bacteria—by incorporating an iodine matrix into the filtration process. An optional carbon cartridge ($20) neutralizes the iodine's noxious taste. The Explorer is also considered a trusty veteran among water filters because of its smooth pumping action and nifty back-washing feature: with a quick twist, the device switches from filtering mode to self-cleaning mode. It may be on the heavy side (20 ounces) and somewhat pricey, but the Explorer works very well on iffy water anywhere.

- **Katadyn U.S.A. Mini Filter:** The Mini Filter is a much more compact version of Katadyn's venerable Pocket Filter. This one weighs just eight ounces, ideal for the minimalist backcountry traveler, and it effectively removes protozoa and bacteria. A palm-of-the-hand-size filter, however, makes it challenging to put any kind of power behind the pump's tiny handle, and the filtered water comes through at a paltry half-liter per minute. It also requires more cleaning than most filters—though the good news is that the element is made of long-lasting ceramic. Ironically, one option lets you buy the Mini Filter with a carbon element instead of the ceramic. The pumping is easier, the flow rate is better, and the price is way down ($99), but I'd only go that route if you'll be pumping from clear mountain streams.

- **MSR WaterWorks II Ceramic:** At 17.4 ounces the WaterWorks II isn't light, but for the same price as the Katadyn you get a better flow rate (90 seconds per liter), an easy pumping action, and—like the original Mini Filter—a long-lasting ceramic cartridge. This filter is a good match for the person who encounters a lot of dirty water—its three-stage filter weeds out protozoa, bacteria, and chemicals—and is mechanically inclined. The MSR can be completely disassembled afield for troubleshooting and cleaning. (If you're not so endowed, take the filter apart at home only, as the potential for confusion is somewhat high.) By the way, the company has corrected the clogging problem that plagued a previous version of the WaterWorks.

The big drawback with filters is that if you pump water from a mucky lake, the filter can clog in a few days. Therein lies the weakness. Once plugged up, it is useless, and you have to replace it or take your chances.

One trick to extend the filter life is to fill your cook pot with water, let the sediment settle, then pump from there. As an insurance policy, always have a spare filter canister on hand.

Boiling water

Except for water filtration, this is the only treatment that you can use with complete confidence. According to the federal Parasitic Diseases Division, it takes a few minutes at a rolling boil to be certain you've killed *Giardia lamblia*. At high elevations, boil for three to five minutes. A side benefit is that you'll also kill other dangerous bacteria that live undetected in natural waters.

But to be honest, boiling water is a thorn for most people on backcountry trips. For one thing, if you boil water on an open fire, what should taste like crystal-pure mountain water tastes instead like a mouthful of warm ashes. If you don't have a campfire, it wastes stove fuel. And if you are thirsty *now*, forget it. The water takes hours to cool.

The only time boiling always makes sense, however, is when you are preparing dinner. The ash taste will disappear in whatever freeze-dried dinner, soup, or hot drink you make.

Water-purification pills

Pills are the preference for most backcountry campers, and this can get them in trouble. At just $3–8 per bottle, which can figure up to just a few cents per canteen, they do come cheap. In addition, they kill most of the bacteria, regardless of whether you use iodine crystals or potable aqua iodine tablets.

The problem is they just don't always kill *Giardia lamblia,* and that is the one critter worth worrying about on your trip. That makes water-treatment pills unreliable and dangerous.

Another key element is the time factor. Depending on the water's temperature, organic content, and pH level, these pills can take a long time to do the job. A minimum wait of 20 minutes is advised. Most people don't like waiting that long, especially when they're hot and thirsty after a hike and thinking, "What the heck, the water looks fine."

And then there is the taste. On one trip, my water filter clogged and we had to use the iodine pills instead. It doesn't take long to get tired of the iodine-tinged taste of the water. Mountain water should be one of the greatest tasting beverages of the world, but the iodine kills that.

No treatment
This is your last resort and, using extreme care, can be executed with success. One of my best hiking buddies, Michael Furniss, is a nationally renowned hydrologist, and on wilderness trips he has shown me the difference between safe and dangerous water sources.

Long ago, people believed that just finding water running over a rock was a guarantee of its purity. Imagine that. What we've learned is that the safe water sources are almost always small springs in high, craggy mountain areas. The key is making sure no one has been upstream from where you drink.

Furniss mentioned that another potential problem in bypassing water treatment is that even in settings free of *Giardia lamblia,* you can still ingest other bacteria that cause stomach problems.

Hypothermia
No matter how well planned your trip might be, a sudden change in weather can turn it into a puzzle for which there are few answers. Bad weather or an accident can set in motion a dangerous chain of events.

Such a chain of episodes occurred for my brother Rambob and me on a fishing trip one fall day just below the snow line. The weather had suddenly turned very cold, and ice was forming along the shore of the lake. Suddenly, the canoe became terribly imbalanced, and just that quick it flipped. The little life vest seat cushions were useless, so using the canoe as a paddleboard, we tried to kick our way back to shore where my dad was going crazy at the thought of his two sons drowning before his eyes.

It took 17 minutes in that 38-degree water, but we finally made it to shore. When they pulled me out of the water, my legs were dead, not strong enough even to hold up my weight. In fact, I didn't feel so much cold as tired, and I just wanted to lie down and go to sleep.

I closed my eyes, and my brother-in-law, Lloyd Angal, slapped me in the face several times, then got me on my feet and pushed and pulled me about.

In the celebration over our making it to shore, only Lloyd had realized that hypothermia was setting in. Hypothermia is the condition in which the temperature of the body is lowered to the point that it causes poor reasoning, apathy, and collapse. It can look like the afflicted person is just tired and needs to sleep, but that sleep can be the first step toward a coma.

Ultimately my brother and I shared what little dry clothing remained. Then we began hiking around to get muscle movement, creating internal warmth. We ate whatever munchies were available because the body produces heat by digestion. But most important, we got our heads as dry as possible. More body heat is lost through wet hair than any other single factor.

A few hours later, we were in a pizza parlor replaying the incident, talking about how only a life vest can do the job of a life vest. We decided never again to rely on those little flotation seat cushions that disappear when the boat flips.

Almost by instinct we had done everything right to prevent hypothermia: don't go to sleep, start a physical activity, induce shivering, put dry clothes on, dry your head, and eat something. That's how you fight hypothermia. In a dangerous situation, whether you fall in a lake or a stream or get caught unprepared in a storm, that's how you can stay alive.

After being in that ice-bordered lake for almost 20 minutes and then finally pulling ourselves to the shoreline, we discovered a strange thing. My canoe was flipped right-side up and almost all of its contents were lost: tackle box, flotation cushions, and cooler. But remaining were one paddle and one fishing rod, the trout rod my grandfather had given me for my 12th birthday.

Lloyd gave me a smile. "This means that you are meant to paddle and fish again," he said with a laugh.

Getting Unlost

You could not have been more lost. But there I was, a guy who is supposed to know about these things, transfixed by confusion, snow, and hoofprints from a big deer.

I discovered it is actually quite easy to get lost. If you don't get your bearings, getting found is the difficult part. This occurred on a wilderness trip where I'd hiked in to a remote lake and then set up a base camp for a deer hunt.

"There are some giant bucks up on that rim," confided Mr. Furnai, who lives near the area. "But it takes a mountain man to even get close to them."

That was a challenge I answered. After four-wheeling it to the trailhead, I tromped off with pack and rifle, gut-thumped it up 100 switchbacks over the rim, then followed a creek drainage up to a small but beautiful lake. The area was stark and nearly treeless, with bald granite broken only by large boulders. To keep from getting lost, I marked my route with piles of small rocks to act as directional signs for the return trip.

But at daybreak the next day, I stuck my head out of my tent and found eight inches of snow on the ground. I looked up into a gray sky filled by huge, cascading snowflakes. Visibility was about 50 yards, with fog on the mountain rim. "I better get out of here and get back to my truck," I said to myself. "If my truck gets buried at the trailhead, I'll never get out."

After packing quickly, I started down the mountain. But after 20 minutes, I began to get disoriented. You see, all the little piles of rocks I'd stacked to mark the way were now buried in snow, and I had only a smooth white blanket of snow to guide me. Everything looked the same, and it was snowing even harder now.

Five minutes later I started chewing on some jerky to keep warm, then suddenly stopped. Where was I? Where was the creek drainage? Isn't this where I was supposed to cross over a creek and start the switchbacks down the mountain?

Right then I looked down and saw the tracks of a huge deer, the kind Mr. Furnai had talked about. What a predicament: I was lost and snowed in and seeing big hoof-

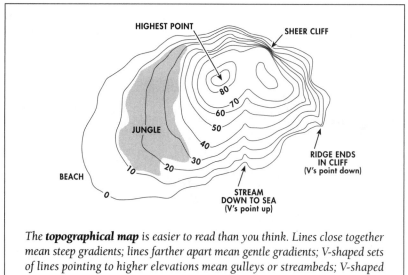

HIGHEST POINT

SHEER CLIFF

80
70
60
50
40
30
20
10
0

JUNGLE

BEACH

RIDGE ENDS
IN CLIFF
(V's point down)

STREAM
DOWN TO SEA
(V's point up)

*The **topographical map** is easier to read than you think. Lines close together mean steep gradients; lines farther apart mean gentle gradients; V-shaped sets of lines pointing to higher elevations mean gulleys or streambeds; V-shaped sets of lines pointing to lower elevations mean ridges.*

prints in the snow. Part of me wanted to abandon all safety and go after that deer, but a little voice in the back of my head won out. "Treat this as an emergency," it said.

The first step in any predicament is to secure your present situation, that is, to make sure it does not get any worse. I unloaded my rifle (too easy to slip, fall, and have a misfire), took stock of my food (three days' worth), camp fuel (plenty), and clothes (rain gear keeping me dry). Then I wondered, "Where the hell am I?"

I took out my map, compass, and altimeter, then opened the map and laid it on the snow. It immediately began collecting snowflakes. I set the compass atop the map and oriented it to north. Because of the fog, there was no way to spot landmarks, such as prominent mountaintops, to verify my position. Then I checked the altimeter, which read 4,900 feet. Well, the elevation at my lake was 5,320 feet. That was critical information.

I scanned the elevation lines on the map and was able to trace the approximate area of my position, somewhere downstream from the lake, yet close to a 4,900-foot elevation. "Right here," I said, pointing to a spot on the map with a finger. "I should pick up the switchback trail down the mountain somewhere off to the left, maybe just 40 or 50 yards away."

Slowly and deliberately, I pushed through the light, powdered snow. In five minutes, I suddenly stopped. To the left, across a 10-foot depression in the snow, appeared a flat spot that veered off to the right. "That's it! That's the crossing."

In minutes, I was working down the switchbacks, on my way, no longer lost. I thought of the hoofprints I had seen, and now that I knew my position, I wanted to head back and spend the day hunting. Then I looked up at the sky, saw it filled with

falling snowflakes, and envisioned my truck buried deep in snow. Alas, this time logic won out over dreams.

In a few hours, now trudging through more than a foot of snow, I was at my truck at a spot called Doe Flat, and next to it was a giant, all-terrain U.S. Forest Service vehicle and two rangers.

"Need any help?" I asked them.

They just laughed. "We're here to help you," one answered. "It's a good thing you filed a trip plan with our district office in Gasquet. We wouldn't have known you were out here."

To keep from getting lost (above tree line or in sparse vegetation), mark your route with **trail ducks,** *small piles of rock which act as directional signs for the return trip.*

"Winter has arrived," said the other. "If we don't get your truck out now, it will be stuck here until next spring. If we hadn't found you, you might have been here until the end of time."

They connected a chain from the rear axle of their giant rig to the front axle of my truck and started towing me out, back to civilization. On the way to pavement, I figured I had gotten some of the more important lessons of my life. Always file a trip plan and have plenty of food, fuel, and a camp stove you can rely on. Make sure your clothes, weather gear, sleeping bag, and tent will keep you dry and warm. Always carry a compass, altimeter, and map with elevation lines, and know how to use them, practicing in good weather to get the feel of it. It is almost never necessary to mark your path, and this should be a last reosrt to minimize impact to wild places. The one exception can be above tree line, where it can occasionally be difficult to find trails amid nothing but rock and ice, and small rock cairns placed sparingly can guide the way.

And if you get lost and see the hoofprints of a giant deer, well, there are times when it is best to pass them by.

Catching Fish, Avoiding Bears, and Having Fun

Feet tired and hot, stomachs hungry, we stopped our hike for lunch beside a beautiful little river pool that was catching the flows from a long but gentle waterfall. My brother Rambob passed me a piece of jerky. I took my boots off, then slowly dunked my feet into the cool, foaming water.

I was gazing at a towering peak across a canyon when suddenly, wham! There was a quick jolt at the heel of my right foot. I pulled my foot out of the water to find that, incredibly, a trout had bitten it.

My brother looked at me as if I had antlers growing out of my head. "Wow!" he exclaimed. "That trout almost caught himself an outdoors writer!"

It's true that in remote areas trout sometimes bite on almost anything, even feet. On one high-country trip I caught limits of trout using nothing but a bare hook. The only problem is that the fish will often hit the splitshot sinker instead of the hook. Of course, fishing isn't usually that easy. But it gives you an idea of what is possible.

America's wildlands are home to a remarkable abundance of fish and wildlife. Deer browse with little fear of man, bears keep an eye out for your food, and little critters such as squirrels and chipmunks are daily companions. Add in the fishing, and you've got yourself a camping trip.

Your camping adventures will evolve into premium outdoor experiences if you can work in a few good fishing trips, avoid bear problems, and occasionally add a little offbeat fun with some camp games.

Trout and Bass

He creeps up on the stream as quiet as an Indian scout, keeping his shadow off the water. With his little spinning rod he'll zip his lure within an inch or two of its desired mark, probing along rocks, the edges of riffles, pocket water, or wherever he can find a change in river habitat. Rambob is trout fishing, and he's a master at it.

Why We Fish: Fishing can give you a sense of exhilaration, like taking a hot shower after being coated with dust. On your walk back to camp, the steps come easy. You suddenly understand what John Muir meant when he talked of developing a oneness with nature, because you have it. That's what fishing can provide.

In most cases he'll catch a trout on his first or second cast. After that it's time to move up the river, giving no spot much more than five minutes' due. Stick and move, stick and move, stalking the stream like a bobcat zeroing in on an unsuspecting rabbit. He might keep a few trout for dinner, but mostly he releases what he catches. Rambob doesn't necessarily fish for food. It's the feeling that comes with it.

You don't need a million dollars' worth of fancy gear to catch fish. What you need is the right outlook, and that can be learned. That goes regardless of whether you are fishing for trout or bass, the two most popular fisheries in the United States. Your fishing tackle selection should be as simple and clutter free as possible.

At home I've got every piece of fishing tackle you might imagine, more than 30 rods and many tackle boxes, racks, and cabinets filled with all kinds of stuff. I've got one lure that looks like a chipmunk and another that resembles a miniature can of beer with hooks. If I hear of something new, I want to try it and usually do. It's a result of my lifelong fascination with the sport.

But if you just want to catch fish, there's an easier way to go. And when I go fishing, I take that path. I don't try to bring everything. It would be impossible. Instead I bring a relatively small amount of gear. At home I will scan my tackle boxes for equipment and artificial lures, make my selections, and bring just the essentials. Rod, reel, and tackle will fit into a side pocket of my backpack or a small carrying bag.

So what kind of rod should be used on an outdoor trip? For most camper/anglers, I suggest the use of a light, multipiece spinning rod that will break down to

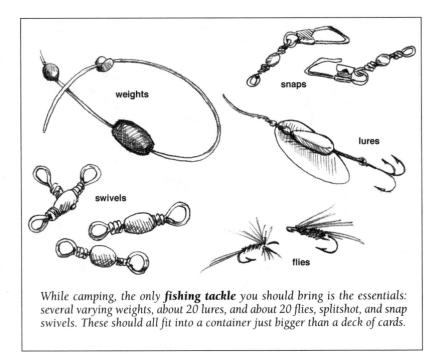

*While camping, the only **fishing tackle** you should bring is the essentials: several varying weights, about 20 lures, and about 20 flies, splitshot, and snap swivels. These should all fit into a container just bigger than a deck of cards.*

a small size. The lowest-priced, quality six-piece rod on the market is the Daiwa 6.5-foot pack rod, No. 6752, which is made of a graphite/glass composite that gives it the quality of a much more expensive model. And it comes in a hard plastic carrying tube for protection. Other major rod manufacturers, such as Fenwick, offer similar premium rods. It's tough to miss with any of them.

The use of graphite/glass composites in fishing rods has made them lighter and more sensitive, yet stronger. The only downside to graphite as a rod material is that it can be brittle. If you rap your rod against something, it can crack or cause a weak spot. That weak spot can eventually snap under even light pressure, like setting a hook or casting. Of course, a bit of care will prevent that from ever occurring.

If you haven't bought a fishing reel in some time, you will be surprised at the quality and price of micro spinning reels on the market. The reels come tiny and strong, with rear-control drag systems. Sigma, Shimano, Cardinal, Abu, and others all make premium reels. They're worth it. With your purchase, you've just bought a reel that will last for years and years.

The one downside to spinning reels is that after long-term use, the bail spring will weaken. The result is that after casting and beginning to reel, the bail will sometimes not flip over and allow the reel to retrieve the line. Then you have to do it by hand. This can be incredibly frustrating, particularly when stream fishing, where instant line pickup is essential. The solution is to have a new bail spring installed every few years. This is a cheap, quick operation for a tackle expert.

You might own a giant tackle box filled with artificial lures, but on your fishing trip you are better off to fit just the essentials into a small container. One of the best ways to do that is to use the Plano Micro-Magnum 3414, a tiny two-sided tackle box for trout anglers that fits into a shirt pocket. In mine, I can fit 20 lures in one side of the box and 20 flies, splitshot, and snap swivels in the other. For bass lures, which are bigger, you need a slightly larger box, but the same principle applies.

There are more fishing lures on the market than you can imagine, but a few special ones can do the job. I make sure these are in my box on every trip. For trout, I carry a small black Panther Martin spinner with yellow spots, a small gold Kastmaster, a yellow Roostertail, a gold Z-Ray with red spots, a Super Duper, and a Mepps Lightning spinner.

You can take it a step further using insider's wisdom. My old pal Ed "the Dunk" showed me his trick of taking a tiny Dardevle spoon, spray painting it flat black, and dabbing five tiny red dots on it. It's a real killer, particularly in tiny streams where the trout are spooky.

The best trout catcher I've ever used on rivers is a small metal lure called a Met-L Fly. On days when nothing else works, it can be like going to a shooting gallery. The problem is that the lure is nearly impossible to find. Rambob and I consider the few we have remaining so valuable that if the lure is snagged on a rock, a cold swim is deemed mandatory for its retrieval. These lures are as hard to find in tackle shops as trout can be to catch without one.

For bass, you can also fit all you need into a small plastic tackle box. I have fished with many bass pros, and all of them actually use just a few lures: a white spinner bait, a small jig called a Gits-It, a surface plug called a Zara Spook, and plastic worms. At times, as when the bass move into shoreline areas during the spring, shad minnow imitations like those made by Rebel or Rapala can be dynamite. My favorite is the one-inch, blue-silver Rapala. Every spring as the lakes begin to warm and the fish snap out of their winter doldrums, I like to float and paddle around in my small raft. I'll cast that little Rapala along the shoreline and catch and release hundreds of bass, bluegill, and sunfish. The fish are usually sitting close to the shoreline, awaiting my offering.

Fishing Tips

There's an old angler's joke about how you need to think like a fish. But if you're the one getting zilched, you may not think it's so funny.

The irony is that it is your mental approach, what you see and what you miss, that often determines your fishing luck. Some people will spend a lot of money on tackle, lures, and fishing clothes, and that done, just saunter up to a stream or lake, cast out, and wonder why they are not catching fish. The answer is their mental outlook. They are not attuning themselves to their surroundings.

You must live on nature's level, not your own. Try this and you will become aware of things you never believed even existed. Soon you will see things that will allow you to catch fish. You can get a head start by reading about fishing, but to get your degree in fishing, you must attend the University of Nature.

On every fishing trip, regardless what you fish for, try to follow three hard-and-fast rules:
1. Always approach the fishing spot so you will be undetected.
2. Present your lure, fly, or bait in a manner so it appears completely natural, as if no line was attached.
3. Stick and move, hitting one spot, working it the best you can, then move to the next.

Approach

No one can just walk up to a stream or lake, cast out, and start catching fish as if someone had waved a magic wand. Instead, give the fish credit for being smart. After all, they live there.

Your approach must be completely undetected by the fish. Fish can sense your presence through sight and sound, though this is misinterpreted by most people. By sight, this rarely means the fish actually see you; more likely they will see your shadow on the water or the movement of your arm or rod while casting. By sound, it doesn't mean they hear you talking, but that they will detect the vibrations of your footsteps along the shore, kicking a rock, or the unnatural plunking sound of a heavy cast hitting the water. Any of these elements can spook them off the bite. In order to fish undetected, you must walk softly, keep your shadow off the water, and keep your casting motion low. All of these keys become easier at sunrise or sunset, when shadows are on the water. At midday a high sun causes a high level of light penetration in the water, which can make the fish skittish to any foreign presence.

Like hunting, you must stalk the spots. When my brother Rambob sneaks up on a fishing spot, he is like a burglar sneaking through an unlocked window.

Presentation

Your lure, fly, or bait must appear in the water as if no line were attached, so it looks as natural as possible. My pal Mo Furniss has skin-dived in rivers to watch what the fish see when somebody is fishing.

"You wouldn't believe it," he said. "When the lure hits the water, every trout within 40 feet, like 15, 20 trout, will do a little zigzag. They all see the lure and are aware something is going on. Meanwhile, onshore the guy casting doesn't get a bite and thinks there aren't any fish in the river."

If your offering is aimed at fooling a fish into striking, it must appear as part of its natural habitat, like an insect just hatched or a small fish looking for a spot to hide. That's where you come in.

After you have sneaked up on a fishing spot, you should zip your cast upstream and start your retrieval as soon as it hits the water. If you let the lure sink to the bottom and then start the retrieval, you have no chance. A minnow, for instance, does not sink to the bottom, then start swimming. On rivers, the retrieval should be more of a drift, as if the "minnow" is in trouble and the current is sweeping it downstream.

The rule of the wild is that wildlife will congregate wherever there is a distinct change in habitat. To find **where fish are hiding,** look where a riffle pours into a small pond, where a rapid plunges into a deep hole and flattens, and around submerged trees, rock piles, and boulders in the middle of a long riffle.

When fishing on trout streams, always hike and cast upriver and retrieve as the offering drifts downstream in the current. This is effective because trout will sit almost motionless, pointed upstream, finning against the current. This way they can see anything coming their direction, and if a potential food morsel arrives, all they need to do is move over a few inches, open their mouths, and they've got an easy lunch. Thus you must cast upstream.

Conversely, if you cast downstream, your retrieval will bring the lure from behind the fish, where he cannot see it approaching. And I've never seen a trout that had eyes in its tail. In addition, when retrieving a downstream lure, the river current will tend to sweep your lure inshore to the rocks.

Finding Spots

A lot of anglers don't catch fish, and a lot of hikers never see any wildlife. The key is where they are looking.

The rule of the wild is that fish and wildlife will congregate wherever there is a distinct change in the habitat. This is where you should begin your search. To find deer, for instance, forget probing a thick forest, but look for where it breaks into a meadow or a clear-cut has splayed a stand of trees. That's where the deer will be.

In a river, it can be where a riffle pours into a small pool, a rapid that plunges into a deep hole and flattens, a big boulder in the middle of a long riffle, a shoreline point, a rock pile, a submerged tree. Look for the changes. Conversely, long, straight stretches of shoreline will not hold fish—the habitat is lousy.

On rivers, the most productive areas are often where short riffles tumble into small oxygenated pools. After sneaking up from the downstream side and staying low, you should zip your cast so the lure plops gently into the white water just above the pool. Start your retrieval instantly; the lure will drift downstream and plunk into the pool. Bang! That's where the trout will hit. Take a few more casts and then head upstream to the next spot.

With a careful approach and lure presentation and by fishing in the right spots, you have the ticket to many exciting days on the water.

Of Bears and Food

The first time you come nose-to-nose with a bear can make your skin quiver.

Even the sight of mild-mannered black bears, the most common bear in America, can send shock waves through your body. They weigh 250–400 pounds and have large claws and teeth that are made to scare campers. When they bound, the muscles on their shoulders roll like ocean breakers.

Bears in camping areas are accustomed to sharing the mountains with hikers and campers. They have become specialists in the food-raiding business. As a result, you must be able to make a bear-proof food hang or be able to scare the fellow off. Many campgrounds provide bear- and raccoon-proof food lockers. You can also stash your food in your vehicle, but that limits the range of your trip.

If you are staying at one of the easy backpack sites listed in this book, there will be no food lockers available. Your car will not be there, either. The solution is to make a bear-proof food hang, suspending all of your food wrapped in a plastic garbage bag from a rope in midair, 10 feet from the trunk of a tree and 20 feet off the ground. (Counterbalancing two bags with a rope thrown over a tree limb is very effective, but finding an appropriate limb can be difficult.)

This is accomplished by tying a rock to a rope, then throwing it over a high but sturdy tree limb. Next, tie your food bag to the rope and hoist it in the air. When you are satisfied with the position of the food bag, tie off the end of the rope to another tree. In an area frequented by bears, a good food bag is a necessity—nothing else will do.

I've been there. On one trip my pal Foonsky and my brother Rambob left to fish, and I was stoking up an evening campfire when I felt the eyes of an intruder on my back. I turned around and saw a big bear heading straight for our camp. In the next half hour I scared the bear off twice, but then he got a whiff of something sweet in my brother's pack.

The bear rolled into camp like a truck, grabbed the pack, ripped it open, and plucked out the Tang and the Swiss Miss. The 350-pounder then sat astride a nearby log and lapped at the goodies like a thirsty dog drinking water.

Once a bear gets his mitts on your gear, he considers it his. I took two steps toward the pack, and that bear jumped off the log and galloped across the camp right at me. Scientists say a man can't outrun a bear, but they've never seen how fast I can go up a granite block with a bear on my tail.

Shortly thereafter, Foonsky returned to find me perched on top of the rock and demanded to know how I could let a bear get our Tang. It took all three of us, Foonsky, Rambob, and me, charging at once and shouting like madmen, to clear the bear out of camp and send him off over the ridge. We learned never to let food sit unattended.

Fun and Games

"Now what are we supposed to do?" the young boy asked his dad.

"Yeah, Dad, think of something," said another son.

Well, Dad thought hard. This was one of the first camping trips he'd taken with

---

Bear Territory

If you are hiking in a wilderness area that may have bears, it becomes a necessity to wear bells on your pack. That way the bear will hear you coming and likely get out of your way. Keep talking, singing, or maybe even debating the country's foreign policy, but do not fall into a silent hiking vigil. And if a breeze is blowing in your face, you must make even more noise (a good excuse to rant and rave about the government's domestic affairs). Noise is important, because your smell will not be carried in the direction you are hiking. As a result the bear will not smell you coming.

If a bear can hear you and smell you, it will tend to get out of the way and let you pass without your knowing it was even close by. The exceptions are if you are carrying fish or lots of sweets in your pack or if you are wearing heavy, sweet deodorants or makeup. All of these are bear attractants.

minimum 10 feet

maximum diameter
1 inch

minimum diameter
4 inch

heavy stick

minimum 22 feet to ground

minimum 20 feet to food bags

food wrapped in
plastic bags

*In an area frequented by bears, a good **bear-proof food hang** is a must. Food should be stored in a plastic bag 10 feet from the trunk of the tree and at least 20 feet from the ground.*

his sons and one of the first lessons he received was that kids don't appreciate the philosophic release of mountain quiet. They want action and lots of it. With a glint in his eye, Dad searched around the camp and picked up 15 twigs, breaking them so each was four inches long. He laid them in three separate rows, three twigs in one row, five twigs in another, and seven in the other.

"OK, this game is called 3-5-7," said Dad. "You each take turns picking up sticks. You are allowed to remove all or as few as one twig from a row, but here's the catch: you can pick only from one row per turn. Whoever picks up the last stick left is the loser."

I remember this episode well because those two little boys were my brother Bobby, as in Rambobby, and me. And to this day, we still play 3-5-7 on campouts, with the winner getting to watch the loser clean the dishes. What I have learned in the span of time since that original episode is that it does not matter what your age is: campers need options for camp fun.

Some evenings, after a long hike or ride, you are likely to feel too worn out to take on a serious romp downstream to fish, or a climb up to a ridge for a view. That is especially true if you have been in the outback for a week or more. At that point a lot of campers will spend their time resting and gazing at a map of the area, dreaming of the next day's adventure, or just take a seat against a rock, watching the colors of the sky and mountain panorama change minute by minute. But kids in the push-button video era, and a lot of adults too, want more. After all, "I'm on vacation; I want some fun."

There are several options, such as the 3-5-7 twig game, and they should be just as much a part of your trip planning as arranging your gear.

For kids, plan on games, the more physically challenging the competition, the better. One of the best games is to throw a chunk of wood into a lake and challenge the kids to hit it by throwing rocks. It wreaks havoc on the fishing, but it can keep kids totally absorbed for some time. Target practice with a wrist-rocket slingshot is also all consuming for kids, firing rocks away at small targets like pinecones set on a log.

You can also set kids off on little missions near camp, such as looking for the footprints of wildlife, searching out good places to have a "snipe hunt," picking up twigs to get the evening fire started, or having them take the water purifier to a stream to pump some drinking water into a canteen. The latter is an easy, fun, yet important task that will allow kids to feel a sense of equality they often don't get at home.

For adults, the appeal should be more to the intellect. A good example is star and planet identification, and while you are staring into space, you're bound to spot a few asteroids or shooting stars. A star chart can make it easy to find and identify many distinctive stars and constellations, such as Pleiades (the Seven Sisters), Orion, and others from the zodiac, depending on the time of year. With a little research, this can add a unique perspective to your trip. You could point to Polaris, one of the most easily identified of all stars, and note that navigators in the 1400s used it to find their way. Polaris, of course, is the North Star and is at the end of the handle of the Little Dipper. Pinpointing Polaris is quite easy. First find the Big Dipper and then find the outside stars of the ladle of the Big Dipper. They are called the "pointer stars" because they point right at Polaris.

A tree identification book can teach you a few things about your surroundings. It is also a good idea for one member of the party to research the history of the area you have chosen and another to research the geology. With shared knowledge, you end up with a deeper love of wild places.

Another way to add some recreation into your trip is to bring a board game, a number of which have been miniaturized for campers. The most popular are chess, checkers, and cribbage. The latter comes with an equally miniature set of playing cards. And if you bring those little cards, that opens a vast set of other possibilities. With kids along, for instance, just take three queens out of the deck and you can play Old Maid.

But there are more serious card games, and they come with high stakes. Such occurred on one high-country trip where Foonsky, Rambob, and I sat down for a late-afternoon game of poker. In a game of seven-card stud, I caught a straight on the sixth card and felt like a dog licking on a T-bone. Already I had bet several Skittles and peanut M&Ms on this promising hand.

Then I examined the cards Foonsky had face up. He was showing three sevens, and acting as happy as a grizzly with a pork chop—or a full house. He matched my bet of two peanut M&Ms, then raised me three SweetTarts, one Starburst, and one sour apple Jolly Rancher. Rambob folded, but I matched Foonsky's bet and hoped for the best as the seventh and final card was dealt.

Just after Foonsky glanced at that last card, I saw him sneak a look at my grape stick and beef jerky stash.

"I raise you a grape stick," he said.

Rambob and I both gasped. It was the highest bet ever made, equivalent to a million dollars laid down in Las Vegas. Cannons were going off in my chest. I looked hard at my cards. They looked good, but were they good enough?

Even with a great hand like I had, a grape stick was too much to gamble, my last one with 10 days of trail ahead of us. I shook my head and folded my cards. Foonsky smiled at his victory.

But I still had my grape stick.

Old Tricks Don't Always Work

Most people are born honest, but after a few camping trips, they usually get over it.

I remember some advice I got from Rambob, normally an honest soul, on one camping trip. A giant mosquito had landed on my arm and he alerted me to some expert advice.

"Flex your arm muscles," he commanded, watching the mosquito fill with my blood. "He'll get stuck in your arm, then he'll explode."

For some reason, I believed him. We both proceeded to watch the mosquito drill countless holes in my arm.

Alas, the unknowing face sabotage from their most trusted companions on camping trips. It can arise at any time, usually in the form of advice from a friendly, honest-looking face, as if to say, "What? How can you doubt me?" After that mosquito episode, I was a little more skeptical of my dear old brother. Then the next day, when another mosquito was nailing me in the back of the neck, out came this gem:

"Hold your breath," he commanded. I instinctively obeyed. "That will freeze the mosquito," he said, "then you can squish him."

But in the time I wasted holding my breath, the little bugger was able to fly off without my having the satisfaction of squishing him. When he got home, he probably told his family, "What a dummy I got to drill today!"

Over the years, I have been duped numerous times with dubious advice:

On a grizzly bear attack: "If he grabs you, tuck your head under the grizzly's chin; then he won't be able to bite you in the head." This made sense to me until the first time I came face-to-face with a nine-foot grizzly 40 yards away. In seconds, I was at the top of a tree, which suddenly seemed to make the most sense.

On coping with animal bites: "If a bear bites you in the arm, don't try to jerk it away. That will just rip up your arm. Instead force your arm deeper into his mouth. He'll lose his grip and will have to open it to get a firmer hold, and right then you can get away." I was told this in the Boy Scouts, and when I was 14, I had a chance to try it out when a friend's dog bit me as I tried to pet it. What happened? When I shoved my arm deeper into his mouth, he bit me three more times.

On cooking breakfast: "The bacon will curl up every time in a camp frying pan. So make sure you have a bacon stretcher to keep it flat." As a 12-year-old Tenderfoot, I spent two hours looking for the bacon stretcher until I figured out the camp leader had forgotten it. It wasn't for several years that I learned that there is no such thing.

On preventing sore muscles: "If you haven't hiked for a long time and you are facing a rough climb, you can keep from getting sore muscles in your legs, back, and shoulders by practicing the 'Dead Man's Walk.' Simply let your entire body go slack, and then take slow, wobbling steps. This will clear your muscles of lactic acid, which causes them to be so sore after a rough hike." Foonsky pulled this one on me. Rambob and I both bought it and tried it while we were hiking up Mt. Whitney, which requires a 6,000-foot elevation gain in six miles. In one 45-minute period, about 30 other hikers passed us and looked at us as if we were suffering from some rare form of mental aberration.

Fish won't bite? No problem: "If the fish are not feeding or will not bite, persistent anglers can still catch dinner with little problem. Keep casting across the current, and eventually, as they hover in the stream, the line will feed across their open mouths. Keep reeling and you will hook the fish right in the side of the mouth. This technique is called 'lining.' Never worry if the fish will not bite, because you can always line 'em." Of course, heh, heh, heh, that explains why so many fish get hooked in the side of the mouth.

How to keep bears away: "To keep bears away, urinate around the borders of your campground. If there are a lot of bears in the area, it is advisable to go right on your sleeping bag." Yeah, surrrrrre.

What to do with trash: "Don't worry about packing out trash. Just bury it. It will regenerate into the earth and add valuable minerals." Bears, raccoons, skunks, and other critters will dig up your trash as soon as you depart, leaving one huge mess for the next camper. Always pack out everything.

Often the advice comes without warning. That was the case after a fishing trip with a female companion, when she outcaught me two to one, the third such trip in a row. I explained this to a shopkeeper, and he nodded, then explained why.

"The male fish are able to detect the female scent on the lure, and thus become aroused into striking."

Of course! That explains everything!

Getting Revenge

I was just a lad when Foonsky pulled the old snipe-hunt trick on me. It took nearly 30 years to get revenge.

You probably know about snipe hunting. The victim is led out at night in the woods by a group, and then is left holding a bag.

"Stay perfectly still and quiet," Foonsky explained. "You don't want to scare the snipe. The rest of us will go back to camp and let the woods settle down. Then when the snipe are least expecting it, we'll form a line and charge through the forest with sticks, beating bushes and trees, and we'll flush the snipe out right to you. Be ready with the bag. When we flush the snipe out, bag it. But until we start our charge, make sure you don't move or make a sound or you will spook the snipe and ruin everything."

I sat out there in the woods with my bag for hours, waiting for the charge. I waited, waited, and waited. Nothing happened. No charge, no snipe. It wasn't until well past midnight that I figured something was wrong. When I finally returned to camp, everybody was sleeping.

Well, I tell ya, don't get mad at your pals for the tricks they pull on you. Get revenge. About 25 years later, on the last day of a camping trip, the time finally came.

"Let's break camp early," Foonsky suggested to Mr. Furnai and me. "Get up before dawn, eat breakfast, pack up, and be on the ridge to watch the sun come up. It will be a fantastic way to end the trip."

"Sounds great to me," I replied. But when Foonsky wasn't looking, I turned his alarm clock ahead three hours. So when the alarm sounded at the appointed 4:30 A.M. wake-up time, Mr. Furnai and I knew it was actually only 1:30 A.M.

Foonsky clambered out of his sleeping bag and whistled with a grin. "Time to break camp."

"You go ahead," I answered. "I'll skip breakfast so I can get a little more sleep. At the first sign of dawn, wake me up, and I'll break camp."

"Me, too," said Mr. Furnai.

Foonsky then proceeded to make some coffee, cook a breakfast, and eat it, sitting on a log in the black darkness of the forest, waiting for the sun to come up.

An hour later, with still no sign of dawn, he checked his clock. It now read 5:30 A.M. "Any minute now we should start seeing some light," he said.

He made another cup of coffee, packed his gear, and sat there in the middle of the night, looking up at the stars, waiting for dawn. "Anytime now," he said. He ended up sitting there all night long.

Revenge is sweet. Before a fishing trip at a lake, I took Foonsky aside and explained that the third member of the party, Jimbobo, was hard of hearing and very sensitive about it. "Don't mention it to him," I advised. "Just talk real loud."

Meanwhile, I had already told Jimbobo the same thing. "Foonsky just can't hear very good."

We had fished less than 20 minutes when Foonsky got a nibble.

"GET A BITE?" shouted Jimbobo.

"YEAH!" yelled back Foonsky, smiling. "BUT I DIDN'T HOOK HIM!"

"MAYBE NEXT TIME!" shouted Jimbobo with a friendly grin.

Well, they spent the entire day yelling at each other from the distance of a few feet. They never did figure it out. Heh, heh, heh.

That is, I thought so, until we made a trip salmon fishing. I got a strike that almost knocked my fishing rod out of the boat. When I grabbed the rod, it felt as if Moby Dick were on the other end. "At least a 25-pounder," I said. "Maybe bigger."

The fish dove, ripped off line, and then bulldogged. "It's acting like a 40-pounder," I announced, "Huge, just huge. It's going deep. That's how the big ones fight."

Some 15 minutes later, I finally got the "salmon" to the surface. It turned out to be a coffee can that Foonsky had clipped on the line with a snap swivel. By maneuvering the boat, he made the coffee can fight like a big fish.

This all started with a little old snipe hunt years ago. You never know what your pals will try next. Don't get mad. Get revenge.

Camping Options
Boat-in Seclusion

Most campers would never think of trading in their cars, pickup trucks, or RVs for a boat, but people who go by boat on a camping trip enjoy virtually guaranteed seclusion and top-quality outdoor experiences.

Camping with a boat is a do-it-yourself venture in living under primitive circumstances. Yet at the same time you can bring along any luxury item you wish, from giant coolers, stoves, and lanterns to portable gasoline generators. Weight is almost never an issue.

Many outstanding boat-in campgrounds in beautiful surroundings are available in Oregon. The best are on the shores of lakes accessible by canoe or skiff, and at offshore islands reached by saltwater cruisers. Several boat-in camps are detailed in this book.

If you want to take the adventure a step further and create your own boat-in camp, perhaps near a special fishing spot, this is a go-for-it deal that provides the best way possible to establish your own secret campsite. But most people who set out freelance style forget three critical items for boat-in camping: a shovel, a sunshade, and an ax. Here is why these items can make a key difference in your trip:

Shovel: Many lakes and virtually all reservoirs have steep, sloping banks. At reservoirs subject to drawdowns, what was lake bottom in the spring can be a campsite in late summer. If you want a flat area for a tent site, the only answer is to dig one out yourself. A shovel gives you that option.

Sunshade: The flattest spots to camp along lakes often have a tendency to support only sparse tree growth. As a result, a natural shield from sun and rain is rarely available. What? Rain in the summer? Oh yeah, don't get me started. A light tarp, set up with poles and staked ropes, solves the problem.

Ax: Unless you bring your own firewood, which is necessary at some sparsely wooded reservoirs, there is no substitute for a good, sharp ax. With an ax, you can almost always find dry firewood, since the interior of an otherwise wet log will be dry. When the weather turns bad is precisely when you will most want a fire. You may need an ax to get one going.

In the search to create your own personal boat-in campsite, you will find that the flattest areas are usually the tips of peninsulas and points, while the protected back ends of coves are often steeply sloped. At reservoirs, the flattest areas are usually near the mouths of the feeder streams and the points are quite steep. On rivers, there are usually sandbars on the inside of tight bends that make for ideal campsites.

Almost all boat-in campsites developed by government agencies are free of charge, but you are on your own. Only in extremely rare cases is piped water available.

Any way you go, by canoe, skiff, or power cruiser, you end up with a one-in-a-million campsite you can call your own.

Desert Outings

It was a cold, snowy day in Missouri when 10-year-old Rusty Ballinger started dreaming about the vast deserts of the West.

"My dad was reading aloud from a Zane Grey book called *Riders of the Purple Sage*," Ballinger said. "He would get animated when he got to the passages about the desert. It wasn't long before I started to have the same feelings."

That was in 1947. Ballinger, now in his 60s, has spent a good part of his life exploring the West, camping along the way. "The deserts are the best part. There's something about the uniqueness of each little area you see," Ballinger said. "You're constantly surprised. Just the time of day and the way the sun casts a different color. It's like the lady you care about. One time she smiles, the next time she's pensive. The desert is like that. If you love nature, you can love the desert. After awhile, you can't help but love it."

A desert adventure is not just an antidote for a case of cabin fever in the winter. Whether you go by RV, pickup truck, car, or on foot, it provides its own special qualities.

If you go camping in the desert, your approach has to be as unique as the setting. For starters, don't plan on any campfires, but bring a camp stove instead. And unlike in the mountains, do not camp near a water hole. That's because an animal such as a badger, coyote, or desert bighorn might be desperate for water, and if you set up camp in the animal's way, you may be forcing a confrontation.

In some areas, there is a danger of flash floods. An intense rain can fall in one area, collect in a pool, then suddenly burst through a narrow canyon. If you are in its path, you could be injured or drowned. The lesson? Never camp in a gully.

"Some people might wonder, 'What good is this place?'" Ballinger said. "The answer is that it is good for looking at. It is one of the world's unique places."

Camp Ethics and Politics

The perfect place to set up a base camp turned out to be not so perfect. In fact, according to Doug Williams of California, it did not even exist.

Williams and his son, James, had driven deep into Angeles National Forest, prepared to set up camp and then explore the surrounding area on foot. But when they reached their destination, no campground existed.

"I wanted a primitive camp in a national forest where I could teach my son some basics," said the senior Williams. "But when we got there, there wasn't much left of the camp, and it had been closed. It was obvious that the area had been vandalized."

It turned out not to be an isolated incident. A lack of outdoor ethics practiced by a few people using the unsupervised campgrounds available on national forestland has caused the U.S. Forest Service to close a few of them and make extensive repairs to others.

"There have been sites closed, especially in Angeles and San Bernardino National Forests in Southern California," said David Flohr, regional campground coordinator for the U.S. Forest Service. "It's an urban type of thing, affecting forests near urban areas, and not just Los Angeles. They get a lot of urban users and they bring with them a lot of the same ethics they have in the city. They get drinking and

---

Keep It Wild Tip 6: Respect Other Users

1. Horseback riders have priority over hikers. Step to the downhill side of the trail and talk softly when encountering horseback riders.
2. Hikers and horseback riders have priority over mountain bikers. When mountain bikers encounter other users even on wide trails, they should pass at an extremely slow speed. On very narrow trails they should dismount and get off to the side so hikers or horseback riders can pass without having their trip disrupted.
3. Mountain bikes aren't permitted on most single-track trails and are expressly prohibited in designated wilderness areas and all sections of the Pacific Crest Trail. Mountain bikers breaking these rules should be confronted and told to dismount and walk their bikes until they reach a legal area.
4. It's illegal for horseback riders to break off branches that may be in the path of wilderness trails.
5. Horseback riders on overnight trips are prohibited from camping in many areas and are usually required to keep stock animals in specific areas where they can do no damage to the landscape.

they're not afraid to do things. They vandalize and run. Of course, it is a public facility, so they think nobody is getting hurt."

But somebody is getting hurt, starting with the next person who wants to use the campground. And if the ranger district budget doesn't have enough money to pay for repairs, the campground is then closed for the next arrivals. Just ask Doug and James Williams.

In an era of considerable fiscal restraint for the U.S. Forest Service, vandalized campgrounds could face closure instead of repair in the next few years. Williams had just a taste of it, but Flohr, as camping coordinator, gets a steady diet.

"It starts with behavior," Flohr said. "General rowdiness, drinking, partying, and then vandalism. It goes all the way from the felt tip pen things (graffiti) to total destruction, blowing up toilet buildings with dynamite. I have seen toilets destroyed totally with shotguns. They burn up tables, burn barriers. They'll burn up signs for firewood, even the shingles right off the roofs of the bathrooms. They'll shoot anything, garbage cans, signs. It can get a little hairy. A favorite is to remove the stool out of a toilet building. We've had people fall in the open hole."

The National Park Service had a similar problem some years back, especially with rampant littering. Park Director Bill Mott responded by creating an interpretive program that attempts to teach visitors the wise use of natural areas, and to have all park workers set examples by picking up litter and reminding others to do the same.

The U.S. Forest Service has responded with a similar program, making brochures available that detail the wise use of national forests. The four most popular brochures are titled: "Rules for Visitors to the National Forest," "Recreation in the National Forests," "Is the Water Safe?" and "Backcountry Safety Tips." These include details on campfires, drinking water from lakes or streams, hypothermia, safety, and outdoor ethics. They are available free by writing U.S. Forest Service, Pacific Northwest Region 6, 333 S.W. First Avenue, Portland, OR 97204-3440; or P.O. Box 3623, Portland, OR 97208-3623; (503) 808-2651; website: www.fs.fed.us/r6.

Flohr said even experienced campers sometimes cross over the ethics line unintentionally. The most common example, he said, is when campers toss garbage into the outhouse toilet, rather than packing it out in a plastic garbage bag.

"They throw it in the vault toilet bowls, which just fills them up," Flohr said. "That creates an extremely high cost to pump it. You know why? Because some poor guy has to pick that stuff out piece by piece. It can't be pumped."

At most backcountry sites, the U.S. Forest Service has implemented a program called "Pack it in, pack it out," even posting signs that remind all visitors to do so. But a lot of people don't do it, and others may even uproot the sign and burn it for firewood.

On a trip to a secluded lake near Carson Pass in the Sierra Nevada, I arrived at a small, little-known camp where the picnic table had been spray painted and garbage had been strewn about. A pristine place, the true temple of God, had been defiled.

In setting up camp, always be mindful of potential ecological disturbances. Pitch tents and dispose of human waste at least 200 feet from the water's edge. In grizzly bear territory, increase the distance between your tent and your cooking area, food-hang, and the water's edge threefold. In other words, if you're in grizzly country, do all your cooking 100 yards (not feet) downwind of your sleeping area. If you can establish an escape tree nearby, all the better.

Getting Along with Fellow Campers

The most important thing about a camping, fishing, or hunting trip is not where you go, how many fish you catch, or how many shots you fire. It often has little to do with how beautiful the view is, how easily the campfire lights, or how sunny the days are.

Oh yeah? Then what is the most important factor? The answer: the people you are with. It is that simple.

Who would you rather camp with? Your enemy at work or your dream mate in a good mood? Heh, heh. You get the idea. A camping trip is a fairly close-knit experience, and you can make lifetime friends or lifelong enemies in the process. That is why your choice of companions is so important. Your own behavior is equally consequential.

Yet most people spend more time putting together their camping gear than considering why they enjoy or hate the company of their chosen companions. Here are 10 rules of behavior for good camping mates:

1. **No whining:** Nothing is more irritating than being around a whiner. It goes right to the heart of adventure, since often the only difference be-

tween a hardship and an escapade is simply whether or not an individual has the spirit for it. The people who do can turn a rugged day in the outdoors into a cherished memory. Those who don't can ruin it with their incessant sniveling.

2. **Activities must be agreed upon:** Always have a meeting of the minds with your companions over the general game plan. Then everybody will possess an equal stake in the outcome of the trip. This is absolutely critical. Otherwise they will feel like merely an addendum to your trip, not an equal participant, and a whiner will be born (see No. 1).

3. **Nobody's in charge:** It is impossible to be genuine friends if one person is always telling another what to do, especially if the orders involve simple camp tasks. You need to share the space on the same emotional plane, and the only way to do that is to have a semblance of equality, regardless of differences in experience. Just try ordering your mate around at home for a few days. You'll quickly see the results, and they aren't pretty.

4. **Equal chances at the fun stuff:** It's fun to build the fire, fun to get the first cast at the best fishing spot, and fun to hoist the bagged food for a bear-proof food hang. It is not fun to clean the dishes, collect firewood, or cook every night. So obviously there must be an equal distribution of the fun stuff and the not-fun stuff, and everybody on the trip must get a shot at the good and the bad.

5. **No heroes:** No awards are bestowed for achievement in the outdoors, yet some guys treat mountain peaks, big fish, and big game as if they are prizes in a trophy competition. Actually, nobody cares how wonderful you are, which is always a surprise to trophy chasers. What people care about is the heart of the adventure, the gut-level stuff.

6. **Agree on a wake-up time:** It is a good idea to agree on a general wake-up time before closing your eyes for the night, and that goes regardless of whether you want to sleep in late or get up at dawn. Then you can proceed on course regardless of what time you crawl out of your sleeping bag in the morning, without the risk of whining (see No. 1).

7. **Think of the other guy:** Be self-aware instead of self-absorbed. A good test is to count the number of times you say, "What do you think?" A lot of potential problems can be solved quickly by actually listening to the answer.

8. **Solo responsibilities:** There are a number of essential camp duties on all trips, and while they should be shared equally, most should be completed solo. That means that when it is time for you to cook, you don't have to worry about me changing the recipe on you. It means that when it is my turn to make the fire, you keep your mitts out of it.

9. **Don't let money get in the way:** Of course everybody should share equally in trip expenses, such as the cost of food, and it should be split up before you head out yonder. Don't let somebody pay extra, because that person will likely try to control the trip. Conversely, don't let somebody weasel out of paying a fair share.

10. **Accordance on the food plan:** Always have complete agreement on what you plan to eat each day. Don't figure that just because you like Steamboat's Sludge, everybody else will, too, especially youngsters. Always, always, always check for food allergies such as nuts, onions, or cheese, and make sure each person brings his or her own personal coffee brand. Some people drink only decaffeinated; others might gag on anything but Burma monkey beans.

Obviously, it is difficult to find companions who will agree on all of these elements. This is why many campers say that the best camping buddies they'll ever have are their mates, those who know all about them and like them anyway.

Outdoors with Kids

How do you get a boy or girl excited about the outdoors? How do you compete with the television and remote control? How do you prove to a kid that success comes from persistence, spirit, and logic, which the outdoors teaches, and not from pushing buttons?

The answer is in the **Ten Camping Commandments for Kids.** These are lessons that will get youngsters excited about the outdoors, and that will make sure adults help the process along, not kill it. I've put this list together with the help of my own kids, Jeremy and Kris, and their mother, Stephani. Some of the commandments are obvious, some are not, but all are important:

> Two Dogs: "There are two dogs inside of you," my dad once said, "a good one, and a bad one. The one you feed is the one that will grow. Always try to feed the good dog."

1. Take children to places where there is a guarantee of action. A good example is camping in a park where large numbers of wildlife can be viewed, such as squirrels, chipmunks, deer, and even bears. Other good choices are fishing at a small pond loaded with bluegill, or hunting in a spot where a kid can shoot a .22 at pinecones all day. Boys and girls want action, not solitude.

2. Enthusiasm is contagious. If you aren't excited about an adventure, you can't expect a child to be. Show a genuine zest for life in the outdoors, and point out everything as if it is the first time you have ever seen it.

3. Always, always, always be seated when talking to someone small. This allows the adult and child to be on the same level. That is why fishing in a small boat is perfect for adults and kids. Nothing is worse for youngsters than having a big person look down at them and give them orders. What fun is that?

4. Always *show* how to do something, whether it is gathering sticks for a campfire, cleaning a trout, or tying a knot. Never tell—always show. A button usually clicks to "off" when a kid is lectured. But kids can learn behavior patterns and outdoor skills by watching adults, even when the adults are not aware they are being watched.

5. Let kids be kids. Let the adventure happen, rather than trying to force it within some preconceived plan. If they get sidetracked watching pollywogs, chasing butterflies, or sneaking up on chipmunks, let them be. A youngster can have more fun turning over rocks and looking at different kinds of bugs than sitting in one spot, waiting for a fish to bite.

6. Expect short attention spans. Instead of getting frustrated about it, use it to your advantage. How? By bringing along a bag of candy and snacks. Where there is a lull in the camp activity, out comes the bag. Don't let them know what goodies await, so each one becomes a surprise.

7. Make absolutely certain the child's sleeping bag is clean, dry, and warm. Nothing is worse than discomfort when trying to sleep, but a refreshing sleep makes for a positive attitude the next day. In addition, kids can become quite scared of animals at night. A parent should not wait for any signs of this, but always play the part of the outdoor guardian, the one who will take care of everything.

8. Kids quickly relate to outdoor ethics. They will enjoy eating everything they cook, building a safe campfire, and picking up all their litter, and they will develop a sense of pride that goes with it. A good idea is to bring extra plastic garbage bags to pick up any trash you come across. Kids long remember when they do something right that somebody else has done wrong.

9. If you want youngsters hooked on the outdoors for life, take a close-up photograph of them holding up fish they have caught, blowing on the campfire, or completing other camp tasks. Young children can forget how much fun they had, but they never forget if they have a picture of it.

10. The least important word you can ever say to a kid is "I." Keep track of how often you are saying "Thank you" and "What do you think?" If you don't say them very often, you'll lose out. Finally, the most important words of all are: "I am proud of you."

Predicting Weather

Foonsky climbed out of his sleeping bag, glanced at the nearby meadow, and scowled hard.

"It doesn't look good," he said. "Doesn't look good at all."

I looked at my adventure companion of 20 years, noting his discontent. Then I looked at the meadow and immediately understood why: *"When the grass is dry at morning light, look for rain before the night."*

"How bad you figure?" I asked him.

"We'll know soon enough, I reckon," Foonsky answered. "Short notice, soon to pass. Long notice, long it will last."

When you are out in the wild, spending your days fishing and your nights camping, you learn to rely on yourself to predict the weather. It can make or break you. If a storm hits the unprepared, it can quash the trip and possibly endanger the

---

Keep It Wild Tip 7: Plan Ahead and Prepare

1. Learn about the regulations and issues that apply to the area you're visiting.
2. Avoid heavy-use areas.
3. Obtain all maps and permits.
4. Bring extra garbage bags to pack out any refuse you come across.

participants. But if you are ready, a potential hardship can be an adventure.

You can't rely on TV weather forecasters, people who don't even know that when all the cows on a hill are facing north, it will rain that night for sure. God forbid if the cows are all sitting. But what do you expect from TV's talking heads?

Foonsky made a campfire, started boiling some water for coffee and soup, and we started to plan the day. In the process, I noticed the smoke of the campfire: it was sluggish, drifting and hovering.

"You notice the smoke?" I asked, chewing on a piece of homemade jerky.

"Not good," Foonsky said. "Not good." He knew that sluggish, hovering smoke indicates rain.

"You'd think we'd have been smart enough to know last night that this was coming," Foonsky said. "Did you take a look at the moon or the clouds?"

"I didn't look at either," I answered. "Too busy eating the trout we caught." You see, if the moon is clear and white, the weather will be good the next day. But if there is a ring around the moon, the number of stars you can count inside the ring equals the number of days until the next rain. As for clouds, the high, thin clouds called cirrus indicate a change in the weather.

We were quiet for a while, planning our strategy, but as we did so, some terrible things happened: a chipmunk scampered past with his tail high, a small flock of geese flew by very low, and a little sparrow perched on a tree limb quite close to the trunk.

"We're in for trouble," I told Foonsky.

"I know, I know," he answered. "I saw 'em, too. And come to think of it, no crickets were chirping last night either."

"Damn, that's right!"

These are all signs of an approaching storm. Foonsky pointed at the smoke of the campfire and shook his head as if he had just been condemned. Sure enough, now the smoke was blowing toward the north, a sign of a south wind. *"When the wind is from the south, the rain is in its mouth."*

"We'd best stay hunkered down until it passes," Foonsky said.

I nodded. "Let's gather as much firewood now as we can, get our gear covered up, then plan our meals."

"Then we'll get a poker game going."

As we accomplished these camp tasks, the sky clouded up, then darkened. Within an hour we had gathered enough firewood to make a large pile, enough wood to keep a fire going no matter how hard it rained. The day's meals had been separated out of the food bag so it wouldn't have to be retrieved during the storm. We buttoned two ponchos together, staked two of the corners with ropes to the ground, and tied the other two with ropes to different tree limbs to create a slanted roof/shelter.

As the first raindrop fell with that magic sound on our poncho roof, Foonsky was just starting to shuffle the cards.

"Cut for deal," he said.

Just as I did so, it started to rain a bit harder. I pulled out another piece of beef jerky and started chewing on it. It was just another day in paradise.

Weather lore can be valuable. Small signs provided by nature and wildlife can be translated to provide a variety of weather information. Here is the list I have compiled over the years:

When the grass is dry at morning light,
Look for rain before the night.

Short notice, soon to pass.
Long notice, long it will last.

When the wind is from the east,
`Tis fit for neither man nor beast.

When the wind is from the south,
The rain is in its mouth.

When the wind is from the west,
Then it is the very best.

Red sky at night, sailors' delight.
Red sky in the morning, sailors take warning.

When all the cows are pointed north,
Within a day rain will come forth.

Onion skins very thin, mild winter coming in.
Onion skins very tough, winter's going to be very rough.

When your boots make the squeak of snow,
Then very cold temperatures will surely show.

If a goose flies high, fair weather ahead.
If a goose flies low, foul weather will come instead.

A thick coat on a woolly caterpillar means a big, early snow is coming.

Chipmunks will run with their tails up before a rain.

Bees always stay near their hives before a rainstorm.

When the birds are perched on large limbs near tree trunks, an intense but short storm will arrive.

On the coast, if groups of seabirds are flying a mile inland, look for major winds.

If crickets are chirping very loud during the evening, the next day will be clear and warm.

If the smoke of a campfire at night rises in a thin spiral, good weather is assured for the next day.

If the smoke of a campfire at night is sluggish, drifting and hovering, it will rain the next day.

If there is a ring around the moon, count the number of stars inside the ring, and that is how many days until the next rain.

If the moon is clear and white, the weather will be good the next day.

High, thin clouds, or cirrus, indicate a change in the weather.

Oval-shaped lenticular clouds indicate high winds.

Two levels of clouds moving in different directions indicate changing weather soon.

Huge, dark, billowing clouds, called cumulonimbus, suddenly forming on warm afternoons in the mountains mean that a short but intense thunderstorm with lightning can be expected.

When squirrels are busy gathering food for extended periods, it means good weather is ahead in the short term, but a hard winter is ahead in the long term.

And God forbid if all the cows are sitting down. . . .

Beating the Time Trap

If the great outdoors is so great, then why don't people enjoy it more? The answer is because of the time trap, and I will tell you exactly how to beat it.

For many, the biggest problem is finding the time to go, whether it is camping, hiking, fishing, boating, backpacking, biking, or even just for a good drive in the country. The solution? Well, believe it or not, the answer is to treat your fun just as you treat your work, and I'll tell you how.

Consider how you treat your job: Always on time? Go there every day you are scheduled? Do whatever it takes to get there and get it done? Right? No foolin' that's right. Now imagine if you took the same approach to the outdoors.

Suddenly your life would be a heck of a lot better.

The secret is to schedule all of your outdoor activities. For instance, I go fishing every Thursday evening, hiking every Sunday morning, and on an overnight trip every new moon (when stargazing is best). No matter what, I'm going. Just like going to work, I've scheduled it. The same approach works with longer adventures. The only reason I have been able to complete hikes ranging from 200 to 300 miles was that I scheduled the time to do it. The reason I spend so many days a year in the field is that I schedule them. In my top year, I had nearly 200 days where at least part of the day was enjoyed taking part in outdoor recreation.

If you get out your calendar and write in the exact dates you are going, then you'll go. If you don't, you won't. Suddenly, with only a minor change in your life plan, you can be living the life you were previously dreaming about.

See you out there.
—Tom Stienstra

Camping Gear Checklist

Cooking Gear

- Camp fuel
- Camp stove
- Dish soap and scrubber
- Fire-starter cubes or candle
- Itemized food
- Knife, fork
- Matches stored in resealable (such as Ziploc) bags
- Plastic spade
- Pot, pan, cup
- Pot grabber
- Salt, pepper, spices

Optional Cooking Gear

- Ax or hatchet
- Can opener
- Clothespins
- Dustpan
- Grill
- Ice chest
- Spatula
- Tablecloth
- Tinfoil
- Whisk broom
- Wood or charcoal for barbecue

Camping Clothes

- Cotton/canvas pants
- Cotton shirt
- Hat
- Long-sleeved cotton/ wool shirt
- Parka
- Polypropylene underwear
- Rain jacket, pants, or poncho
- Sunglasses
- Vest

Optional Clothing

- Gloves
- Seam Lock
- Shorts
- Ski cap
- Swimsuit

Hiking Gear

- Backup lightweight shoes
- 80% wool socks
- Gaiters
- Innersole or foot cushion
- Moleskin and medical tape
- Polypropylene socks
- Quality hiking boots
- Strong bootlaces
- Thick cotton socks
- Water-repellent boot treatment

Sleeping Gear

- Sleeping bag
- Insulite or Therm-a-Rest pad
- Ground tarp
- Tent

Optional Sleeping Gear

- Air pillow
- Catalytic heater
- Foam pad for truck bed
- Mosquito netting
- RV Windshield light screen

First Aid

- Ace bandage
- Adhesive bandages
- After-Bite or ammonia
- Aspirin
- Athletic tape
- Biodegradable soap
- Caladryl or Tecnu
- Campho-Phenique gel
- First-aid cream
- Moleskin
- Mosquito repellent
- Neosporin
- Roller gauze
- Sterile gauze pads
- Sunscreen
- Thermometer
- Towelettes
- Tweezers

Optional First Aid
- Coins for emergency phone calls
- Extra set of matches
- Mirror for signaling
- Water purification system

Fishing/Recreation Gear

- Fishing reel with fish-line splitshot, snap swivels
- Fishing rod
- Knife
- Pliers

Optional Recreation Gear
- Backpacking cribbage board
- Deck of cards
- Knapsack for each person
- Stargazing chart
- Tree identification handbook

Miscellaneous

- Camera and film
- Compass
- Feminine hygiene products
- Flashlight
- Handkerchief
- Lantern and fuel
- Lip balm
- Maps
- Nylon rope for food hang
- Plastic garbage bags
- Toilet paper
- Toothbrush and toothpaste
- Watch

Optional Miscellaneous
- Binoculars
- Notebook and pen
- Towel

The Oregon Coast

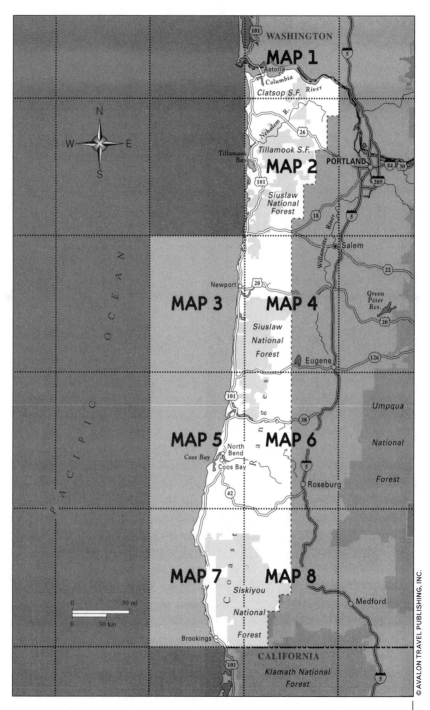

Map 1

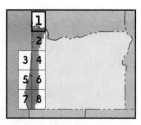

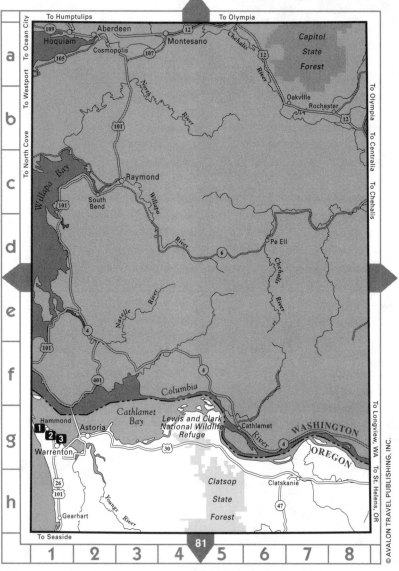

Map 2

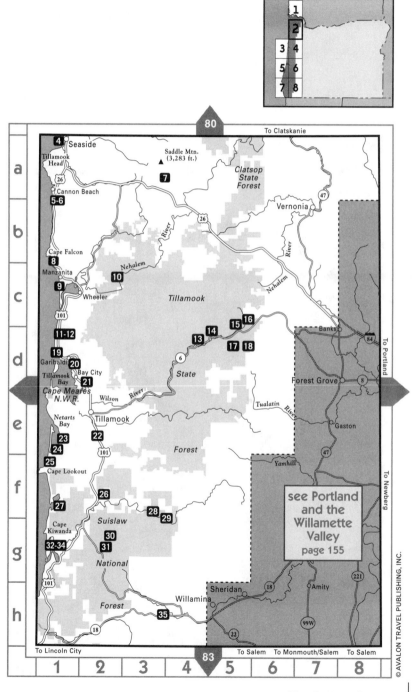

© AVALON TRAVEL PUBLISHING, INC.

Map 3

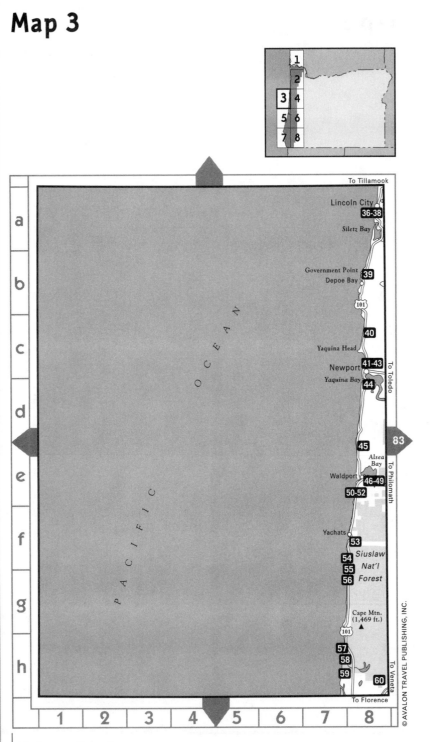

To Tillamook

Lincoln City
36-38

Siletz Bay

Government Point 39
Depoe Bay

101

40

Yaquina Head

Newport 41-43

Yaquina Bay 44

45

Alsea Bay

Waldport 46-49

50-52

Yachats 53

54 Siuslaw
55 Nat'l
56 Forest

Cape Mtn.
(1,469 ft.)
▲

101

57

58

59 60

To Florence

To Toledo

To Philomath 83

To Veneta

O C E A N

P A C I F I C

© AVALON TRAVEL PUBLISHING, INC.

Map 4

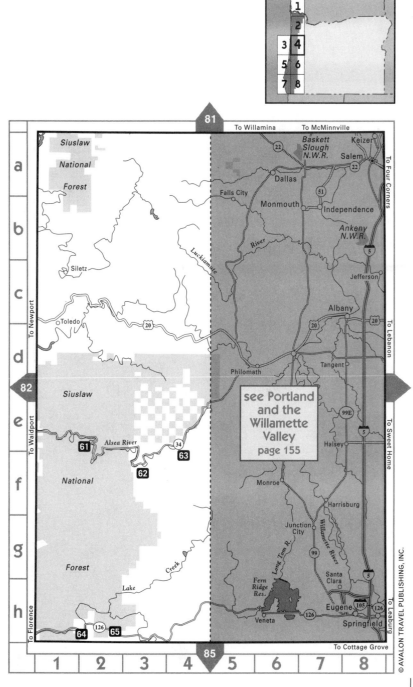

Siuslaw National Forest

To Willamina   To McMinnville

Baskett Slough N.W.R.   Keizer

Salem

22

Dallas

Falls City

Monmouth   Independence

51

Ankeny N.W.R.

Luckiamute   River

Siletz

Jefferson

Albany

20

Toledo

20

Philomath   Tangent

Siuslaw

99E

see Portland and the Willamette Valley page 155

Alsea River

61

34

63

Halsey

62

National

Monroe

Harrisburg

Forest

Junction City

99

Creek

Long Tom R.

Santa Clara

Willamette River

Lake

Fern Ridge Res.

Eugene

105

64   126   65

126

Veneta

Springfield

To Florence   To Waldport   To Newport

To Four Corners   To Lebanon   To Sweet Home   To Leaburg

To Cottage Grove

81

82

85

1   2   3   4   5   6   7   8

© AVALON TRAVEL PUBLISHING, INC.

Map 5

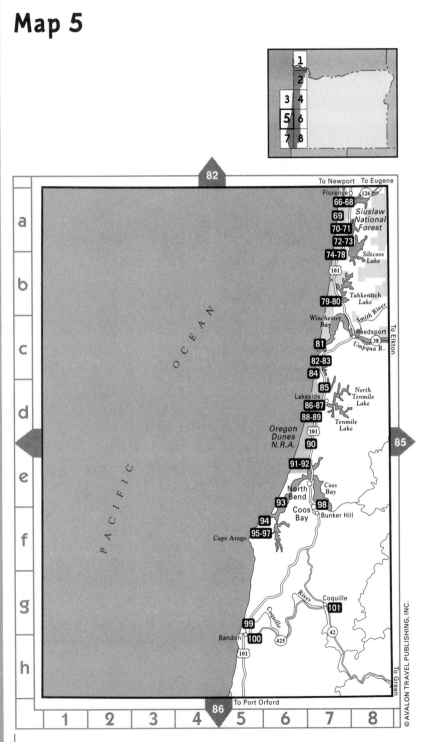

Map 6

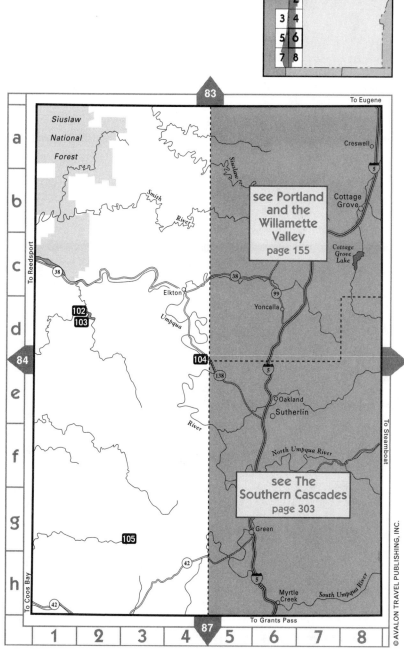

To Eugene

Siuslaw
National
Forest

Creswell

see Portland
and the
Willamette
Valley
page 155

Cottage
Grove

Smith
River

Cottage
Grove
Lake

To Reedsport

38

38

99

Elkton

102
103

Umpqua

Yoncalla

84

104

138

5

Oakland

River

Sutherlin

North Umpqua River

see The
Southern Cascades
page 303

105

Green

To Steamboat

42

5

To Coos Bay

Myrtle
Creek

South Umpqua River

42

To Grants Pass

87

© AVALON TRAVEL PUBLISHING, INC.

1 2 3 4 5 6 7 8

a b c d e f g h

Map 7

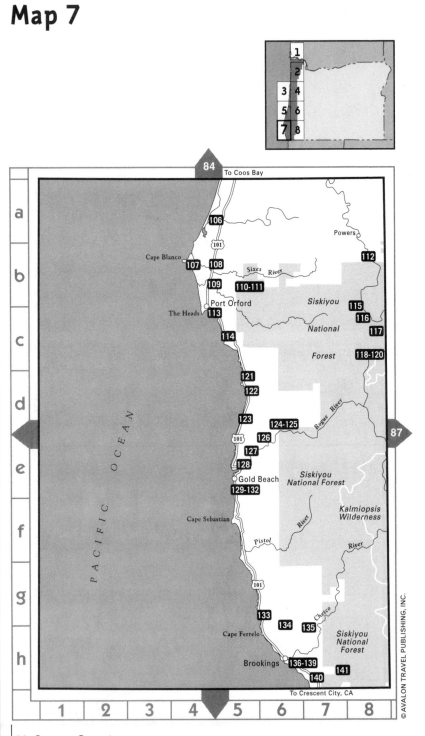

Map 8

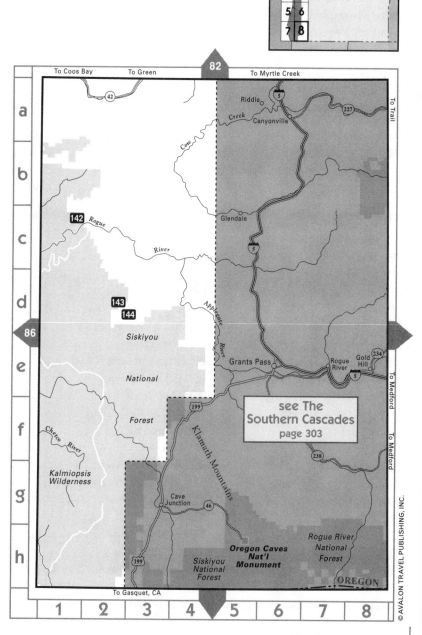

To Coos Bay To Green 82 To Myrtle Creek

42 Riddle 5 227 To Trail

a

Cow Creek Canyonville

b

142 Rogue Glendale

c

River 5

d

143 Applegate

144

86 Siskiyou River

e

National Grants Pass Rogue River Gold Hill 234

5 To Medford

199

f

Chetco River Forest Klamath Mountains 238

To Medford

g

Kalmiopsis Wilderness Cave Junction 46

see The
Southern Cascades
page 303

h

199 Siskiyou National Forest Oregon Caves Nat'l Monument Rogue River National Forest

OREGON

To Gasquet, CA

1 2 3 4 5 6 7 8

The Oregon Coast

(CONTINUED ON NEXT PAGE)

(CONTINUED)

◼ Fort Stevens State Park

This is a classic spot, set at the northern tip of Oregon, right where the Columbia River enters the Pacific Ocean. A historical military area, freshwater lake, swimming, beachcombing, trails, wildlife viewing, and a historic shipwreck site make Fort Stevens a uniquely diversified park. This 3,700-acre park has nine miles of bike trails and six miles of hiking trails, allowing exploration of the park through spruce and hemlock forests, wetlands, dunes, and shore pines. The trailhead for the Oregon Coast Trail is here as well. History buffs will find a museum, tours of the fort and artillery batteries, and the remains of the *Peter Iredale* shipwreck.

Location: At the mouth of the Columbia River; The Oregon Coast Map 1, grid g1.

Campsites, facilities: There are 40 tent sites, 170 sites for trailers or RVs up to 50 feet with full hookups, and 320 sites with partial hookups, and a special camping area for hikers and bicyclists; 15 yurts and four group tent areas are also available. Picnic tables and fire grills are provided. Drinking water, flush toilets, a sanitary disposal station, transfer and recycling station, showers, firewood, and a playground are available. Some facilities are wheelchair-accessible. Boat docks and launching facilities are nearby. Leashed pets are permitted.

Reservations, fees: Reservations recommended ($6 reservation fee). Sites are $18–22 per night, and $4.50 for hikers/bikers. Yurts are $30 per night. Open year-round.

Directions: From Portland turn west on U.S. 26 and drive 73 miles to the junction with U.S. 101. Turn right (north) on U.S. 101 and drive about 15 miles (about one-quarter mile past the Camp Rilea Army Base). Turn west on Perkins Road/Highway 104 at the sign for Fort Stevens State Park and drive about one mile to Ocean View Cemetery Road. Turn left and drive about 2.5 miles (Ocean View Cemetery Road becomes Ridge Road) to the park entrance.

Contact: Fort Stevens State Park, Ridge Road, Hammond, OR 97121; 800/551-6949 or 503/861-1671, reservations 800/452-5687.

◼ Astoria/Warrenton Seaside KOA

This campground is nestled in a wooded area adjacent to Fort Stevens State Park, and tours of that historical military site can be arranged. This is an excellent option if the state park campground is full. A host of activities are available in the immediate area, including bicycling, hiking, deep-sea fishing, and beachcombing. Horse stables are within 10 miles. See the description of Fort Stevens State Park for further details about the area.

Location: Near Fort Stevens State Park; The Oregon Coast Map 1, grid g1.

Campsites, facilities: There are 311 sites for tents, trailers, or RVs up to 80 feet, and 54 one- and two-bedroom cabins. Cable TV, restrooms, showers, security, a public phone, a laundry room, limited groceries, ice, snacks, RV supplies, LP gas, and a barbecue are available. Recreational facilities include a playground, a game room, a recreation field, horseshoes, a spa, and a heated swimming pool. Some facilities are wheelchair-accessible. Leashed pets are permitted.

Reservations, fees: Reservations recommended. Sites are $23–55 per night. Major credit cards accepted. Open year-round.

Directions: From Portland turn west on U.S. 26 and drive 73 miles to the junction with U.S. 101. Turn right (north) on U.S. 101 and drive about 15 miles (about one-quarter mile past the Camp Rilea Army Base). Turn west on Perkins Road/Highway 104 at the sign for Fort Stevens State Park and drive about one mile to Ocean View Cemetery Road. Turn left and drive about 2.5 miles (Ocean View Cemetery Road becomes Ridge Road) to the campground directly across from the state park.

Contact: Astoria/Warrenton Seaside KOA, 1100 Ridge Rd., Hammond, OR 97121; 800/562-8506 or 503/861-2606; fax 503/861-3209; website: www.koa.com.

🔟 Kampers West Campground

🏃 🚴 🏊 🎣
🚗 🐕 🚐 ⛺ 7

Just four miles from Fort Stevens State Park, this privately run site offers full RV services. Nearby recreation possibilities include an 18-hole golf course, hiking trails, marked bike trails, and a riding stable.

Location: Near Fort Stevens State Park; The Oregon Coast Map 1, grid g1.

Campsites, facilities: There are 180 sites for trailers or RVs of any length, including a small area for tents only. Electricity, drinking water, and picnic tables are provided. Flush toilets, bottled gas, sanitary services, showers, laundry facilities, and ice are available. A store and a café are within one mile. Leashed pets and motorbikes are permitted.

Reservations, fees: Reservations accepted. Sites are $19–24.61 per night. Senior discount available. Open year-round.

Directions: From Portland turn west on U.S. 30 and drive 105 miles north and west to Astoria and the junction of U.S. 101. Turn south and drive 6.5 miles to the Warrenton/Hammond Junction. Turn west on Warrenton and drive 1.5 miles to the campground on the right.

Contact: Kampers West Campground, 1140 N.W. Warrenton Dr., Warrenton, OR 97146; 503/861-1814; fax 503/861-3620.

🔟 Venice RV Park

🏃 🚴 🏊
🎣 🛶 🐕 🚐 3

This park along the Neawanna River—one of two rivers running through Seaside—is less than a mile from the beach. Crab pot rentals are available, a great bonus. Seaside offers beautiful ocean beaches for fishing and surfing, moped and bike rentals, shops, and a theater. The city provides swings and volleyball nets on the beach. An 18-hole golf course is nearby.

Location: On the Neawanna River; The Oregon Coast Map 2, grid a1.

Campsites, facilities: There are 31 sites for trailers or RVs of any length; 13 are pull-through sites. Electricity, drinking water, sewer, cable TV, and picnic tables are provided. Flush toilets, showers, a laundry room, and ice are available. A store and a café are within one mile. Leashed pets are permitted.

Reservations, fees: Reservations preferred. Sites are $22 per night. Senior discount available. Open year-round.

Directions: From Portland on I-5, turn west on U.S. 26 and drive 73 miles to the junction with U.S. 101. Turn north on U.S. 101 and drive four miles to Seaside. Continue to the north end of town and turn left (west) on 24th Avenue. The campground is on the corner at 1032 24th Avenue.

Contact: Venice RV Park, 1032 24th Ave., Seaside, OR 97138; 541/779-7096.

🔟 Sea Ranch RV Park

🏃 🚴 🏊
🎣 🐕 🚐 ⛺ 9

This resort is in a wooded area with nearby access to the beach. Activities at the camp include stream fishing, horseback riding, and swimming on the seashore. A golf course is six miles away, and the historical

Lewis and Clark Trail is nearby. Elk hunters camp here in season. The beach and the town of Cannon Beach are within walking distance of the resort.

Location: Near the Pacific Ocean; The Oregon Coast Map 2, grid a1.

Campsites, facilities: There are 80 sites for tents, trailers, and RVs, and three cabins with fireplace and porch that sleep four. Restrooms, showers, a sanitary dump, and a public phone are available. Supplies are available within two miles. Leashed pets are permitted.

Reservations, fees: Reservations recommended. Sites are $19–22 per night, $5 per person per night for more than two people. Cabins are $65 per night. Major credit cards accepted. Open year-round.

Directions: From Portland on I-5, turn west on U.S. 26 and drive 73 miles to the junction with U.S. 101. Turn south on U.S. 101 and drive three miles to the Cannon Beach exit. The park is south 0.3 mile on the left.

Contact: Sea Ranch RV Park, P.O. Box 214, 415 Fir St., Cannon Beach, OR 97110; 503/436-2815; website: www.cannon-beach.net/searanch.

6 RV Resort at Cannon Beach

9

This private resort is about seven blocks from one of the nicest beaches in the region. From the town of Cannon Beach you can walk for miles in either direction. Ecola State Park is just two miles north. Nearby recreational facilities include marked bike trails, a riding stable, and tennis courts.

Location: Near Ecola State Park; The Oregon Coast Map 2, grid a1.

Campsites, facilities: There are 100 sites for trailers or RVs of any length; 11 are drive-through sites. Electricity, drinking water, sewer hookups, and picnic tables are pro-vided. Flush toilets, bottled gas, showers, firewood, a recreation hall, a store, a spa, a laundry room, ice, a playground, and a swimming pool are available. Leashed pets are permitted.

Reservations, fees: Reservations accepted. Sites are $23–37 per night. Open year-round.

Directions: From Portland on I-5, turn west on U.S. 26 and drive 73 miles to the junction with U.S. 101. Turn south on U.S. 101 and drive four miles to the Cannon Beach exit at milepost 29.5. Turn left (east) and drive 200 feet to the campground.

Contact: RV Resort at Cannon Beach, P.O. Box 219, 345 Elk Creek Rd., Cannon Beach, OR 97110; 503/436-2231; fax 503/436-1527.

7 Saddle Mountain State Park

7

This camp is set inland and is a good alternative to the many beachfront parks. A 2.5-mile trail climbs to the top of Saddle Mountain, a great lookout on clear days. This park is a real find for the naturalist interested in rare and unusual varieties of plants, many of which have established themselves along the slopes of this isolated mountain.

Location: On Saddle Mountain; The Oregon Coast Map 2, grid a3.

Campsites, facilities: There are 10 primitive tent sites. Drinking water, garbage bins, picnic tables, and fire grills are provided. Flush toilets and firewood are available. Leashed pets are permitted.

Reservations, fees: No reservations accepted. Sites are $7–10 per night, $7 for an additional vehicle. Open March through October.

Directions: From Portland turn west on U.S. 26 and drive about 63 miles to Necanicum Junction and Saddle Mountain Road. Turn north on Saddle Mountain Road and drive seven miles to the park. The road dead-ends at the park.

Contact: Saddle Mountain State Park, P.O. Box 681, Cannon Beach, OR 97110; 800/551-6949 or 503/436-2844 (this phone number reaches Ecola State Park, which manages Saddle Mountain).

8 Oswald West State Park

8

This state park is set along a dramatic section of the Oregon coast with rugged cliffs rising high above the ocean. You can't see the beach from the campsites, but you can hear the ocean. The park does offer 15 miles of hiking trails, including the Oregon Coast Trail and a trail to the point of Cape Falcon, where campers can enjoy scenic views. A small beach attracts windsurfers and boogie boarders and several fishing streams are nearby. The park is in a beautiful rainforest setting, with gigantic spruce and cedar trees.

Location: On the Pacific Ocean; The Oregon Coast Map 2, grid b1.

Campsites, facilities: There are 36 primitive walk-in tent sites. Wheelbarrows are available for campers to transport their supplies. Picnic tables and fire grills are provided. Drinking water, flush toilets, garbage bins, and firewood are available. Leashed pets are permitted.

Reservations, fees: No reservations accepted. Sites are $10–14 per night. Major credit cards accepted. Open March through October.

Directions: From Portland turn west on U.S. 26 and drive 73 miles to the junction with U.S. 101. Turn south on U.S. 101 and drive four miles to Cannon Beach. Continue 10 miles south on U.S. 101 to the parking area. Walk one-quarter mile to the campground.

Contact: Oswald West State Park, 9500 Sandpiper Lane, Nehalem, OR 97131; 800/452-5687 or 503/368-5943.

9 Nehalem Bay State Park

7

This state park on a sandy point separating the Pacific Ocean and Nehalem Bay offers six miles of beach frontage. Crabbing and fishing on the bay are popular. The neighboring towns of Manzanita and Nehalem offer fine dining and shopping. The Oregon Coast Trail passes through the park. A horse camp with corrals and a 7.5-mile equestrian trail are available. There is also a 1.75-mile bike trail. An airport is adjacent to the park, and there are airstrip fly-in campsites.

Location: On the Pacific Ocean; The Oregon Coast Map 2, grid c1.

Campsites, facilities: There are 277 sites for trailers or RVs up to 60 feet long, a special camping area for hikers and bicyclists, and six primitive fly-in sites next to the airport. There are also 16 yurts and 17 sites with stock corrals. Electricity, drinking water, picnic tables, and fire grills are provided. Flush toilets, a sanitary disposal station, showers, and firewood are available. Some facilities are wheelchair-accessible. Boat-launching facilities are nearby on Nehalem Bay, and an airstrip is adjacent to the park. Leashed pets are permitted.

Reservations, fees: Reservations accepted ($6 reservation fee). Sites are $10–19 per night, and $4 for hikers/bikers. Yurts are $27 per night; horse sites are $10–14 per night and $1.50 per horse per night. There is a charge of $7 per night for an additional vehicle. Fly-in sites are $10–14 per night, not including tie-down. Major credit cards accepted. Open year-round.

Directions: From Portland drive west on U.S. 26 for 73 miles to the junction with U.S. 101. Turn south on U.S. 101 and drive 19 miles to Manzanita. Turn right (west) on the park entrance road and drive 1.5 miles to the campground.

Contact: Nehalem Bay State Park, 9500 Sandpiper Ln., Nehalem, OR 97131; 503/368-5154, reservations 800/452-5687.

10 Nehalem Falls

10

This beautiful campground, among old-growth hemlock and spruce, is within a two-minute walk of lovely Nehalem Falls. A one-half-mile loop trail follows the adjacent Nehalem River, where fishing and swimming are options.

Location: In Tillamook State Forest; The Oregon Coast Map 2, grid c2.

Campsites, facilities: There are 14 sites for tents, trailers, or RVs up to 40 feet long, four walk-in tent sites, and one group site. Drinking water, picnic tables, garbage dumpsters, fire grills, and vault toilets are available. Some facilities are wheelchair-accessible. Leashed pets are permitted.

Reservations, fees: Reservations accepted for the group site only. Sites are $10 per night, walk-in sites are $5 per night, and the group site is $25 per night; $2 per night for an additional vehicle. Open Memorial Day weekend through October.

Directions: From Tillamook on U.S. 101 northbound, drive 22 miles to Highway 53. Turn right (east) and drive 1.3 miles to Miami Foley Road. Turn right (south) and drive one mile to Foss Road (narrow and rough). Turn left and drive seven miles to the campground on the left.

Contact: Tillamook State Forest, Tillamook District, 4907 E. 3rd St., Tillamook, OR 97141;

503/842-2545; fax 503/842-3143; website: www.odf.state.or.us.

11 Jetty Fishery RV Park

7

This small park is at the base of a mile-long jetty that extends into Nehalem Bay and the ocean. Fishing and crabbing are good off the jetty, but sometimes the snags bite well, too. The small beach on the bay side of the jetty is a popular spot for kids. For boaters there is an adjacent full-service marina. Live crab is often for sale—and that says it all.

Location: On Nehalem Bay; The Oregon Coast Map 2, grid d1.

Campsites, facilities: There are 10 tent sites and 14 sites for trailers or RVs of any length. Electricity, drinking water, and picnic tables are provided. Flush toilets, bottled gas, firewood, a store, showers, a café, ice, boat docks, launching facilities, and boat rentals are available. Leashed pets are permitted.

Reservations, fees: Reservations accepted. Sites are $18 per night. Open year-round.

Directions: From Portland on I-5, turn west on U.S. 26 and drive 73 miles to the junction with U.S. 101. Turn south on U.S. 101 and drive 27 miles to the park entrance.

Contact: Jetty Fishery RV Park, 27550 U.S. Hwy. 101 N, Rockaway, OR 97136; 503/368-5746; fax 503/568-5748.

12 Shorewood Travel Trailer Village

7

This park is on an ideal beach for surf fishing for perch or beachcombing during low tides. The 1.5-mile hike to the Tillamook Bay jetty is a good side trip. An 18-hole golf course is a short drive from the park.

Location: On the Pacific Ocean; The Oregon Coast Map 2, grid d1.

Campsites, facilities: There are 105 sites for trailers or RVs of any length. No tents are allowed. Electricity, drinking water, and picnic tables are provided. Flush toilets, sanitary services, cable TV, showers, a laundry room, and ice are available. A store and a café are within one mile. Leashed pets are permitted.

Reservations, fees: Reservations accepted. Sites are $21 per night. Open year-round.

Directions: From Portland on I-5, turn west on U.S. 26 and drive 73 miles to the junction with U.S. 101. Turn south on U.S. 101 and drive 30 miles to the town of Rockaway Beach. Continue on U.S. 101 to about one mile south of town to the Shorewood sign; then turn west and drive three blocks to the park.

Contact: Shorewood Travel Trailer Village, 17600 Ocean Blvd., Rockaway Beach, OR 97136; 503/355-2278.

13 Jones Creek

 7

Set in a forest of fir, hemlock, spruce, and alder, campsites here are spacious and private. The adjacent Wilson River provides opportunities for steelhead and salmon fishing (artificial lures only). There's a scenic 3.8-mile trail along the riverfront. The camp fills up on holiday weekends.

Location: On the Wilson River in Tillamook State Forest; The Oregon Coast Map 2, grid d4.

Campsites, facilities: There are 28 sites for tents, trailers, or RVs (27 are 50 feet long and one is 72 feet long and pull-through), nine walk-in tent sites, and one group site. A camp host is on-site, and drinking water, picnic tables, fire grills, vault toilets, garbage dumpsters, and a horseshoe pit are available. Some facilities are wheelchair-accessible. Leashed pets are permitted.

Reservations, fees: Reservations required for the group site only. Sites are $10 per night, walk-in sites are $5 per night, and the group site is $25 per night; an additional vehicle is $2 per night, with a two-vehicle limit. Open Memorial Day weekend through October.

Directions: From Portland turn west on U.S. 26 and drive 24 miles to Highway 6. Turn west on Highway 6 and drive 28 miles to milepost 22.7 and North Fork Road. Turn right and drive one-quarter mile to the campground on the left.

Contact: Tillamook State Forest, Tillamook District, 4907 E. 3rd St., Tillamook, OR 97141; 503/842-2545; fax 503/842-3143; website: www.odf.state.or.us.

14 Elk Creek Walk-In

7

This small campground is set among fir, alder, and maple on Elk Creek and borders the Wilson River. Elk Creek is closed to fishing. For fishing information on Wilson River, call first as regulations often change here each year.

Location: On Elk Creek in Tillamook State Forest; The Oregon Coast Map 2, grid d5.

Campsites, facilities: There are 15 walk-in tent sites. Drinking water, picnic tables, fire grills, and vault toilets are available. Pack out all garbage. Some facilities are wheelchair-accessible. Leashed pets are permitted.

Reservations, fees: No reservations accepted. Sites are $5 per night, $2 per night for an additional vehicle. Open Memorial Day weekend through October.

Directions: From Portland turn west on U.S. 26 and drive 24 miles to Highway 6. Turn west on Highway 6 and drive 23 miles to milepost 28 and the campground entrance road on the right. Turn right on Elk Creek Road and drive one-half mile to the campground on the left.

Contact: Tillamook State Forest, Forest Grove District, 801 Gales Creek Rd., Forest Grove, OR 97116; 503/357-2191; website: www.odf.state.or.us

15 Jordan Creek OHV Staging Area

6

This is an Off-Highway Vehicle camp at the bottom of a scenic, steep canyon next to Jordan Creek. Wooded campsites are clustered around a central parking area, and the park caters to OHV campers. There are almost 40 miles of OHV trails, varying from moderate to difficult. There's no fishing in Jordan Creek.
Location: Near Jordan Creek in Tillamook State Forest; The Oregon Coast Map 2, grid c5.
Campsites, facilities: There are six sites for tents, trailers, or RVs of any length. No drinking water, but picnic tables, fire grills, garbage bins, and vault toilets are available. Some facilities are wheelchair-accessible. Leashed pets are permitted.
Reservations, fees: No reservations accepted. Sites are $5 per night, $2 per night for an additional vehicle. Open March through November.
Directions: From Tillamook on U.S. 101, turn east on Highway 6 and drive 17.9 miles to Jordan Creek Road. Turn right and drive 2.2 miles to the campground on the right.
Contact: Tillamook State Forest, Tillamook District, 4907 E. 3rd St., Tillamook, OR 97141; 503/842-2545; fax 503/842-3143; website: www.odf.state.or.us.

16 Gales Creek

7

Gales Creek runs through this heavily forested camp. The Gales Creek Trailhead is accessible from camp, providing hiking and mountain

biking opportunities. A day-use picnic area is also available.
Location: On Gales Creek in Tillamook State Forest; The Oregon Coast Map 2, grid c5.
Campsites, facilities: There are 19 sites for tents, trailers, or RVs up to 35 feet long, and four walk-in tent sites. Drinking water, picnic tables, fire grills, garbage bins, and vault toilets are available. Some facilities are wheelchair-accessible. Leashed pets are permitted.
Reservations, fees: No reservations accepted. Family sites are $10 per night; walk-in sites are $5 per night; an additional vehicle is $2 per night. Open Memorial Day weekend through October.
Directions: From Portland turn west on U.S. 26 and drive 24 miles to Highway 6. Turn west on Highway 6 and drive 17 miles to the campground entrance road (Rogers Road) on the right at milepost 35. Turn right on Rogers Road and drive one mile to the campground.
Contact: Tillamook State Forest, Forest Grove District, 801 Gales Creek Rd., Forest Grove, OR 97116; 503/357-2191; website: www.odf.state.or.us.

17 Stagecoach Horse Camp

6

This camp is for horse camping only. There's a small seasonal stream through the camp. Two-hour and four-hour loop trails are accessible from the camp.
Location: In Tillamook State Forest; The Oregon Coast Map 2, grid d5.
Campsites, facilities: There are 11 sites for tents, trailers, or RVs up to 30 feet long. No drinking water, but picnic tables, fire grills, a picnic shelter, and vault toilets are available. Pack out all garbage. Stock facilities include corrals at each site and stock water. Some facilities are

wheelchair-accessible. Leashed pets are permitted.

Reservations, fees: No reservations accepted. Sites are $5 per night, $2 per night for an additional vehicle. Open year-round.

Directions: From Portland turn west on U.S. 26 and drive 24 miles to Highway 6. Turn west on Highway 6 and drive 19 miles to Beaver Dam Road. Turn left (south) and drive one mile to University Falls Road. Turn right and drive 3.5 miles to Rutherford Road. Turn right again and drive a short distance to the first gravel road on the left. Turn left and drive one-half mile to the campground on the left.

Contact: Tillamook State Forest, Forest Grove District, 801 Gales Creek Rd., Forest Grove, OR 97116; 503/357-2191; website: www.odf.state.or.us.

18 Browns Camp

6

This camp is next to the Devil's Lake Fork of the Wilson River and has sites with and without tree cover. It is surrounded by miles of OHV trails and caters to off-highway vehicle campers. Don't expect peace and quiet. No fishing is allowed here.

Location: In Tillamook State Forest; The Oregon Coast Map 2, grid d5.

Campsites, facilities: There are 29 sites for tents, trailers, or RVs up to 45 feet long. Drinking water, picnic tables, fire grills, garbage bins, and vault toilets are available. Some facilities are wheelchair-accessible. Leashed pets are permitted.

Reservations, fees: No reservations accepted. Sites are $10 per night, $2 per night for an additional vehicle. Open March through November.

Directions: From Portland turn west on U.S. 26 and drive 24 miles to Highway 6. Turn west on Highway 6 and drive 19 miles to Beaver Dam Toad. Turn left (south) and drive 2.5

miles to Scoggins Road. Turn left (southeast) and drive one-half mile to the campground.

Contact: Tillamook State Forest, Forest Grove District, 801 Gales Creek Rd., Forest Grove, OR 97116; 503/357-2191; website: www.odf.state.or.us.

19 Barview Jetty County Park

7

This park covering 160 acres is near the beach, adjacent to Tillamook Bay in a wooded area. The sites are set on grassy hills. Nearby recreation options include an 18-hole golf course, hiking trails, bike trails, surf and scuba fishing, and a full-service marina.

Location: Near Garibaldi; The Oregon Coast Map 2, grid d1.

Campsites, facilities: There are 249 sites for tents or RVs of any length, 60 with full hookups. Electricity, drinking water, sewer hookups, and picnic tables are provided. Flush toilets, a dump station, showers, and a playground are available. Bottled gas, a store, a café, and ice are within one mile. Leashed pets are permitted.

Reservations, fees: Reservations accepted. Sites are $15–30 per night, plus $5 for each additional vehicle or tents, a $2 dump station fee, a $2 shower fee for nonregistered guests (free for registered campers), and $5 for firewood. Open year-round.

Directions: From Portland on I-5, turn west on U.S. 26 and drive 24 miles to Highway 6. Turn left on Highway 6 and drive 44 miles to Tillamook. Turn north on U.S. 101 and drive 12 miles to the park on the left (two miles north of the town of Garibaldi).

Contact: Barview Jetty County Park, P.O. Box 633, Garibaldi, OR 97118; 503/322-3522; fax 503/842-2721; website: www.co.tilla mook.or.us.

20 Biak-by-the-Sea RV Park

7

This park along the shore of Tillamook Bay is a prime retreat for deep-sea fishing, crabbing, clamming, surf fishing, scuba diving, and beachcombing. The nearby town of Tillamook is home to a cheese factory and a historical museum. A good side trip is Cape Meares State Park, where you can hike through the national wildlife preserve and see how the seabirds nest along the cliffs. There is also a golf course nearby.

Location: On Tillamook Bay; The Oregon Coast Map 2, grid d1.

Campsites, facilities: There are 45 drive-through sites for trailers or RVs of any length. Electricity, drinking water, sewer hookups, and cable TV are provided. Flush toilets, coin-operated showers, and laundry facilities are available. Bottled gas, a store, a café, and ice are within one mile. Boat docks, launching facilities, and rentals are nearby. Leashed pets and motorbikes are permitted.

Reservations, fees: Reservations recommended. Sites are $20 per night. Major credit cards accepted. Open year-round.

Directions: From Portland turn west on U.S. 26 and drive 24 miles to Highway 6. Turn west on Highway 6 and drive 44 miles to Tillamook and U.S. 101. Turn north and drive 10 miles to 7th Street. Turn left on 7th Street and drive to the park on the left (just over the tracks).

Contact: Biak-by-the-Sea RV Park, P.O. Box 396, Garibaldi, OR 97118; 503/322-2111.

21 Pacific Campground

6

This campground is at the southern end of Tillamook Bay, not far from the Wilson River. The Tillamook Cheese Factory—the place for cheese tours, is just south of the park. An 18-hole golf course is also nearby. See the description of Biak-by-the-Sea RV Park for more information about the area.

Location: On Tillamook Bay; The Oregon Coast Map 2, grid d2.

Campsites, facilities: There are 20 tent sites and 31 drive-through sites for trailers or RVs of any length. Electricity, drinking water, sewer hookups, and picnic tables are provided. Flush toilets, cable TV, showers, firewood, and ice are available. A store and a café are within one mile. Leashed pets (except in the tent area) and motorbikes are permitted.

Reservations, fees: Reservations accepted. Sites are $13–23 per night for two people, plus $1 for each additional person. Open year-round.

Directions: From Portland turn west on U.S. 26 and drive 24 miles to Highway 6. Turn west on Highway 6 and drive 44 miles to Tillamook. Turn north on U.S. 101 and drive 1.5 miles to the campground entrance across from the Tillamook Cheese Factory.

Contact: Pacific Campground, 1950 Suppress Rd. N, Tillamook, OR 97141; 503/842-5201; fax 503/842-0588.

22 Pleasant Valley RV Park

8

This campground along the Tillamook River is very clean, with many recreation options in the immediate area.

Location: On the Tillamook River; The Oregon Coast Map 2, grid e2.

Campsites, facilities: There are 10 tent sites and 74 sites for trailers or RVs of any length, plus two cabins. Drinking water and picnic tables are provided. Flush toilets, bottled gas, sanitary services, showers, firewood, a recreation hall, electricity, sewer hookups, cable TV, a store, a laundry room, ice, and a playground are available. Boat-launching facilities are nearby. Leashed pets are permitted.

Reservations, fees: Reservations accepted. Sites are $16–21.50 per night; cabins are $27 per night. Senior discount available. Open year-round.

Directions: From Portland turn west on U.S. 26 and drive 24 miles to Highway 6. Turn west on Highway 6 and drive 44 miles to Tillamook and U.S. 101. Turn south on U.S. 101 and drive six miles to the campground entrance on the right.

Contact: Pleasant Valley RV Park, 11880 U.S. Hwy. 101 S, Tillamook, OR 97141; 503/842-4779; fax 503/842-2293.

23 Bay Shore RV Park

8

This is one of three camps on the east shore of Netarts Bay. A golf course is eight miles away. Sunsets and wildlife watching are notable here.

Location: On Netarts Bay; The Oregon Coast Map 2, grid e1.

Campsites, facilities: There are 53 sites for trailers or RVs of any length; 11 are drive-through sites. Electricity, drinking water, sewer hookups, and picnic tables are provided. Flush toilets, bottled gas, coin-operated showers, a meeting room, a laundry room, crab-cooking facilities, crab bait, and ice are available. Boat docks, launching facilities, and rentals are available on-site. A store and a café are within one mile. Leashed pets are permitted.

Reservations, fees: Reservations recommended. Sites are $23–25 per night. Major credit cards accepted. Open year-round.

Directions: From Portland turn west on U.S. 26 and drive 24 miles to Highway 6. Turn west on Highway 6 and drive 44 miles to Tillamook

and Netarts Highway. Turn west on Netarts Highway and drive six miles to the campground entrance.

Contact: Bay Shore RV Park, P.O. Box 218, Netarts, OR 97413; 503/842-7774.

24 Big Spruce RV Park

8

This trailer park is one block from the boat launch on Netarts Bay. It is a short drive from Cape Lookout State Park, Cape Meares State Park, and the national wildlife refuge. Netarts Bay offers sheltered waters, perfect for small boaters to take advantage of the excellent crabbing. Riding stables are also nearby.

Location: On Netarts Bay; The Oregon Coast Map 2, grid e1.

Campsites, facilities: There are 23 sites for trailers or RVs of any length; seven are drive-through sites. Electricity, drinking water, sewer hookups, and picnic tables are provided. Flush toilets, bottled gas, cable TV, showers, a crab cooker, fish-cleaning station, and a laundry room are available. Boat docks, launching facilities, and boat rentals are available on-site. A store, ice, clamming and crabbing gear, a café, and ice are within one mile. Leashed pets are permitted.

Reservations, fees: Reservations accepted. Sites are $20 per night for two campers and two vehicles, $2 additional for each additional camper or vehicle. Open year-round.

Directions: From Portland turn west on U.S. 26 and drive 24 miles to Highway 6. Turn west on Highway 6 and drive 44 miles to Tillamook and Netarts Highway. Turn west on Netarts Highway and drive 6.5 miles to the campground entrance.

Contact: Big Spruce RV Park, 4850 Netarts Hwy. W, Tillamook, OR 97141; 503/842-7443; fax 503/815-1641.

25 Cape Lookout State Park

🚶 🎣 🐕 ♿ 🚐 ⛺ 8

On a sand spit between Netarts Bay and the ocean, Cape Lookout has more than eight miles of hiking and walking trails that wind through old-growth forest. The Cape Lookout Trail follows the headland for more than two miles. Another walk will take you out through a variety of estuarine habitats along the five-mile sand spit that extends between the ocean and Netarts Bay. This is a paradise for bird-watchers, with many species to view. You might also catch the local hang-gliders and paragliders that frequent the park. Fishing is another option here.

Location: Near Netarts Bay; The Oregon Coast Map 2, grid f1.

Campsites, facilities: There are 177 tent sites, 35 sites with full or partial hookups for trailers or RVs up to 60 feet long, and a special tent camping area for hikers and bicyclists. There are also four group tent areas and 10 yurts. Picnic tables and fire grills are provided. Flush toilets, sanitary services, showers, garbage bins, and firewood are available. A restaurant is within one mile. Some facilities are wheelchair-accessible. Leashed pets are permitted.

Reservations, fees: Reservations accepted ($6 reservation fee). Sites are $16–20 per night, $4 per night for hikers/bikers, and yurts are $27 per night; an additional vehicle is $7 per night. Open year-round.

Directions: From Portland turn west on U.S. 26 and drive 24 miles to Highway 6. Turn west on Highway 6 and drive 44 miles to Tillamook. Turn southwest on Netarts Road and drive 11 miles to the park entrance on the right.

Contact: Cape Lookout State Park, 13000 Whiskey Creek Rd. W, Tillamook, OR 97141; 800/452-5687 or 503/842-4981.

26 Camper Cove RV Park and Campground

🎣 🐕 🚐 ⛺ 6

This small, wooded campground along Beaver Creek is just far enough off the highway to provide quiet. The park can be used as a base camp for anglers, with steelhead and salmon fishing in season in the nearby Nestucca River. It gets crowded here, especially in the summer, so be sure to make a reservation whenever possible. Ocean beaches are four miles away.

Location: On Beaver Creek; The Oregon Coast Map 2, grid f2.

Campsites, facilities: There are five tent sites and 17 sites for RVs up to 40 feet long, plus two cabins. Electricity, drinking water, sewer hookups, and picnic tables are provided. Flush toilets, fire pits, a dump station, showers, firewood, a recreation hall, laundry facilities, and ice are available. Leashed pets are permitted.

Reservations, fees: Reservations accepted. Sites are $13.50–17.50 and cabin rentals are $30 per night. Senior discount available. Open year-round.

Directions: From Portland, turn west on U.S. 26 and drive 24 miles to Highway 6. Turn west on Highway 6 and drive 44 miles to Tillamook and U.S. 101. Turn south on U.S. 101 and drive 11.5 miles to the park entrance on the right (2.5 miles north of Beaver).

Contact: Camper Cove RV Park and Campground, P.O. Box 42, Beaver, OR 97108; 503/398-5334.

27 Sand Beach

🏊 🎣 🐕 🚐 ⛺ 5

This area is known for its beach area with large sand dunes, which are popular with off-road vehicle enthusiasts. It's noisy and can be windy. The campground is set along the shore of Sand Lake, which is actually more like an estuary since the ocean is just around the bend. This is the only coastal U.S. Forest Service campground for many miles, and it's quite popular. If you're planning a trip for midsummer, be sure to reserve far in advance. Entry permits are required for three-day holiday weekends.

Location: In Siuslaw National Forest; The Oregon Coast Map 2, grid f1.

Campsites, facilities: There are 101 sites for tents, trailers, or RVs up to 30 feet long. (If filled, the east and west parking lots provide additional sites for trailers or RVs.) Picnic tables and fire pits are provided. Drinking water, garbage bins, and flush toilets are available. Leashed pets are permitted.

Reservations, fees: Reservations accepted ($8.65 reservation fee) and a good idea in midsummer. Sites are $12 per night, $6 for an additional vehicle. The east and west parking lots are $6 per night. Senior discount available. Open late April to late September.

Directions: From Tillamook on U.S. 101, drive south for 11 miles to County Road 8. Turn west on County Road 8 and follow the signs to the campground.

Contact: Siuslaw National Forest, Hebo Ranger District, 31525 Hwy. 22, Hebo, OR 97122; 503/392-3161, reservations 877/444-6777; fax 503/392-4203; website (for reservations): www.reserveusa.com.

28 Rocky Bend

🐕 🏕 5

This campground along the Nestucca River is a little-known, secluded spot that provides guaranteed peace and quiet. There isn't much in the way of recreational activities out here, but hiking, fishing, clamming, and swimming are available along the coast, a relatively short drive away.

Location: On the Nestucca River in Siuslaw National Forest; The Oregon Coast Map 2, grid f3.

Campsites, facilities: There are six tent sites. Picnic tables and fire pits are provided, but there is no drinking water. Vault toilets are available. No garbage service is provided, so you must pack out what you bring in. Leashed pets are permitted.

Reservations, fees: No reservations; no fee. Open year-round.

Directions: On U.S. 101 southwest of Portland, drive to the tiny town of Beaver and Blaine Road. Turn east on Blaine Road (keep right; Blaine Road turns into Nestucca River Access Road) and drive 15.5 miles to the campground.

Contact: Siuslaw National Forest, Hebo Ranger District, 31525 Hwy. 22, Hebo, OR 97122; 503/392-3161; fax 503/392-4203.

29 Dovre, Fan Creek, Alder Glen

🐟 🐕 ♿ 🚐 🏕 5

This is a series of three BLM campgrounds set along the Nestucca River. The camps are near the river, with alder trees and shrubs between sites, and some have river views. Tourists don't know about these spots. The Nestucca is a gentle river, with the water not deep enough for swimming.

Location: On the Nestucca River; The Oregon Coast Map 2, grid g3.

Campsites, facilities: Dovre has nine sites, Fan Creek has 11 sites, and Alder Glen has 10 sites for tents or small RVs or trailers. Picnic tables and fire grills are provided. Drinking water, fire grills, and vault toilets are available. Garbage must be packed out. Some facilities are wheelchair-accessible, including a fishing pier at Alder Glen. Leashed pets are permitted.

Reservations, fees: No reservations. Sites are $6 per night, with a limit of two vehicles per site. Senior discount available. Open year-round.

Directions: On U.S. 101 southwest of Portland, drive to the tiny town of Beaver and Blaine Road. Turn east on Blaine Road (keep right; Blaine Road turns into Nestucca River Access Road) and drive 17.5 miles to Alder Glen. Continue east for seven more miles to reach Fan Creek and nine more miles to reach Dovre.

Contact: Bureau of Land Management, Salem District, 1717 Fabry Rd. SE, Salem, OR 97306; 503/375-5646; fax 503/375-5622.

30 Hebo Lake

7

This U.S. Forest Service campground along the shore of Hebo Lake is a secluded spot with sites nestled under trees. The trailhead for the eight-mile-long Pioneer-Indian Trail is in the campground. The trail around the lake is wheelchair-accessible.

Location: On Hebo Lake in Siuslaw National Forest; The Oregon Coast Map 2, grid g2.

Campsites, facilities: There are 15 sites for tents, trailers, or RVs up to 18 feet long. Picnic tables and fire pits are provided. Drinking water, garbage bins, and vault toilets are available. Boats without motors are allowed on the lake. Some facilities are wheelchair-accessible. Leashed pets are permitted.

Reservations, fees: No reservations accepted. Sites are $6 per night, $3 for an additional vehicle. Senior discount available. Open May to mid-October.

Directions: On U.S. 101 southwest of Portland, drive to the town of Hebo and Highway 22. Turn east on Highway 22 and drive one-quarter mile to Forest Road 14. Turn left (east) and drive five miles to the campground.

Contact: Siuslaw National Forest, Hebo Ranger District, 31525 Hwy. 22, Hebo, OR 97122; 503/392-3161; fax 503/392-4203.

31 Castle Rock

4

This tiny spot along Three Rivers provides an inland alternative for tent campers to the large beachfront RV parks popular on the Oregon coast. Fishing can be good here. Though primitive, this camp is along the edge of the highway and can fill up quickly.

Location: On Three Rivers in Siuslaw National Forest; The Oregon Coast Map 2, grid g2.

Campsites, facilities: There are four tent sites. Drinking water, picnic tables, garbage bins, and a vault toilet are provided. Leashed pets are permitted.

Reservations, fees: No reservations; no fee. Open year-round.

Directions: On U.S. 101 southwest of Portland, drive to the town of Hebo and Highway 22. Turn east on Highway 22 and drive five miles to the campground.

Contact: Siuslaw National Forest, Hebo Ranger District, 31525 Hwy. 22, Hebo, OR 97122; 503/392-3161; fax 503/392-4203.

32 Cape Kiwanda RV Park

8

This park is a short distance from Cape Kiwanda State Park, which is open for day use only. Highlights at the park include a boat launch and hiking trails that lead out to the cape. A recreation option is four miles south at Nestucca Spit, where there is another day-use park. The point extends about three miles and is a good spot for bird-watching. The campsites do not have ocean views.

Location: On the Pacific Ocean; The Oregon Coast Map 2, grid g1.

Campsites, facilities: There are 25 tent sites, 150 sites for trailers or RVs of any length, and three camping cabins. Electricity, drinking water, sewer hookups, and picnic tables are provided. Flush toilets, sanitary services, showers, firewood, a recreation hall, laundry facilities, propane, a seafood market, a gift shop, an automatic teller machine, and a playground are available. Bottled gas, a store, a café, and ice are within one mile. Boat docks, launching facilities, and rentals are nearby. Leashed pets and motorbikes are permitted.

Reservations, fees: Reservations accepted. Sites are $16–25 per night, camping cabins $45 per night. Open year-round.

Directions: From Portland, turn west on U.S. 26 and drive 24 miles to Highway 6. Turn west on Highway 6 and drive 44 miles to Tillamook and U.S. 101. Turn south on U.S. 101 and drive 25 miles to the Pacific City exit and Brooten Road. Turn right and drive three miles toward Pacific City and Three Capes Drive. Turn left, cross the bridge, and bear right on Three Capes Drive. Continue one mile north to the park on the right.

Contact: Cape Kiwanda RV Park, P.O. Box 129, Pacific City, OR 97135; 503/965-6230; fax 503/965-6235; email: capekiwanda@oregoncoast.com.

33 Webb Park

7

This public campground is an excellent alternative to the more crowded commercial RV parks off U.S. 101. It's not as developed, but it offers a quiet, private setting and access to the ocean. Fishing and swimming are among your options here. The camp is just behind the new inn at Cape Kiwanda.

Location: Near the Pacific Ocean; The Oregon Coast Map 2, grid g1.

Campsites, facilities: There are 30 sites for tents, trailers, or RVs; six have partial hookups. Drinking water, a dump station, showers, flush toilets, and beach launching are available. Leashed pets are permitted.

Reservations, fees: Reservations accepted. Sites are $14–16 per night. Open year-round.

Directions: From Portland turn west on U.S. 26 and drive 24 miles to Highway 6. Turn west on Highway 6 and drive 44 miles to Tillamook and U.S. 101. Turn south on U.S. 101 and drive about 25 miles to the Pacific City exit and Highway 30. From Pacific City, turn right (north) and drive to the four-way stop at McPhillips Drive. Turn left and drive one-half mile to Cape Kiwanda and the park on the right.

Contact: Tillamook County Parks, P.O. Box 1072, Pacific City, OR 97135; 503/965-5001; fax 503/842-2721; website: www.co.tillamook.or.us.

34 Raines Resort and RV Park

6

This campground is on the Nestucca River, which attracts a king salmon run from late August through Thanksgiving. A full-service marina is close by. This is a good camp for watching wildlife.

Location: On the Nestucca River; The Oregon Coast Map 2, grid g1.

Campsites, facilities: There are 12 sites for tents, trailers, or RVs up to 30 feet. Electricity, drinking water, sewer hookups, and picnic tables are provided. Flush toilets, sanitary services, showers, and a laundry room are available. Bottled gas, a café, a store, and ice are within one mile. Boat docks and launching facilities are at the resort. Leashed dogs are permitted.

Reservations, fees: Reservations accepted. Sites are $15–20 per night, $7–10 per night for tents. Open year-round.

Directions: From Portland, drive west on U.S. 26 for 24 miles to Highway 6. Turn west on Highway 6 and drive 44 miles to Tillamook at U.S. 101. Turn south on U.S. 101 and drive 25 miles to the Pacific City exit. Turn right on Brooten Road and drive six miles to the Woods Bridge. Turn left on Ferry Street and cross Woods Bridge. After you cross the bridge, the park entrance is immediately to the right.

Contact: Raines Resort and RV Park, P.O. Box 777, Pacific City, OR 97135; 503/965-6371.

35 Wandering Spirit RV Park

6

The major draw here is the nearby casino, but there is the added benefit of shaded sites next to the Yamhill River, providing fishing and swimming options. Fishing is good for steelhead and salmon in season. Golf courses and wineries are available within 10 miles.

Location: On the Yamhill River; The Oregon Coast Map 2, grid h3.

Campsites, facilities: There are 105 sites for trailers and RVs up to 45 feet long, and 10 tent sites. Drinking water, electricity, sewer hookups, cable TV, telephone service, restrooms, showers, a sanitary disposal station, laundry facilities, and a minimart are available. Propane, a clubhouse, a basketball hoop, an exercise room, and game room are also available on-site. A 24-hour free bus shuttles campers to and from the Spirit Mountain Casino, restaurants, and shops less than two miles away. Some facilities are wheelchair-accessible. Leashed pets are permitted.

Reservations, fees: Reservations recommended. Sites are $12 for tents, $22 for RVs per night. Senior discount available. Open year-round.

Directions: From Salem drive west on Highway 22 about 25 miles to Highway 18. Turn west on Highway 18 and drive about nine miles to the park on the left.

Contact: Wandering Spirit RV Park, 28800 Salmon River Hwy., Grand Ronde, OR 97347; 800/390-6980; fax 503/879-5171; website: www.wanderingspiritrvpark.com.

36 Devil's Lake State Park

7

The only coastal camp in Oregon in the midst of a city, Devil's Lake is a center of summertime activity, a take-your-pick deal. You can boat, canoe, kayak, fish, or water-ski. An alternative is to head west and explore the seven miles of beaches. Lincoln City also has a number of arts and crafts galleries in town. East Devil's Lake is two miles east with a boat ramp and picnic facilities.

Location: On Devil's Lake; The Oregon Coast Map 3, grid a8.

Campsites, facilities: There are 54 tent sites and 31 sites with full hookups for trailers or RVs up to 60 feet long. There are also 10 yurts and a separate area for hikers and bikers. Picnic tables and fire grills are provided. Drinking water, garbage bins, flush toilets, showers, and firewood are available. Some facilities are wheelchair-accessible. Boat docks and launching facilities are nearby. Leashed pets are permitted.

Reservations, fees: Reservations accepted ($6 reservation fee). Sites are $17–22 per night, $4.85 for hikers/bikers, and yurts are $30 per night; an additional vehicle is $7 per night. Boat mooring $7 per night. Major credit cards accepted. Open year-round.

Directions: From Portland drive south on Highway 99

West to Highway 18. Turn west on Highway 18 and drive 47 miles to U.S. 101. Turn south on U.S. 101 and drive five miles to Lincoln City. Follow the signs to the park in town.

Contact: Devil's Lake State Park, 1452 N.E. 6th St., Lincoln City, OR 97367; 503/994-2002, reservations 800/452-5687.

37 Tree N' Sea Trailer Park

 5

This quiet campground on the ocean in Lincoln City is a pleasant RV park that makes an adequate layover spot. Crabbing is a popular activity here. See the descriptions of KOA Lincoln City and Devil's Lake State Park for recreation.

Location: On the Pacific Ocean; The Oregon Coast Map 3, grid a8.

Campsites, facilities: There are 42 sites for trailers or RVs up to 32 feet. Electricity, drinking water, cable TV, and sewer hookups are provided. Flush toilets and showers are available. A store, a café, and coin-operated laundry are within one mile. Small, leashed pets are permitted.

Reservations, fees: Reservations recommended. Sites are $20–24 per night. Open year-round.

Directions: From Portland drive south on Highway 99 West to Highway 18. Turn west on Highway 18 and drive 47 miles to U.S. 101. Turn south on U.S. 101 and drive five miles to Lincoln City. Turn west on Southwest 51st Street and drive one block to the park.

Contact: Tree N' Sea Trailer Park, 1015 S.W. 51st St., Lincoln City, OR 97367; 541/996-3801.

38 KOA Lincoln City

7

This area offers opportunities for beachcombing, tide pooling, and fishing along a seven-mile stretch of beach. Two stops to consider if you're going into Lincoln City for supplies: the Premier Market, which has smoked salmon, and the Colonial Bakery, which carries the best pastries west of Paris. Nearby recreation options include an 18-hole golf course and tennis courts.

Location: Near the Pacific Ocean; The Oregon Coast Map 3, grid a8.

Campsites, facilities: There are 15 tent sites and 52 sites for trailers or RVs up to 60 feet long; 13 are drive-through sites. There are also one-room camping cabins. Electricity, drinking water, cable TV, modem access, flush toilets, a dump station, public phones, showers, a store, a café, a gift shop, LP gas, ice, RV supplies, video rentals, a game room, coin-operated laundry facilities, and a playground are available. Firewood is available for purchase. Leashed pets are permitted.

Reservations, fees: Reservations accepted. Sites are $20–25 per night, double-occupancy; cabins are $37 per night. Open year-round.

Directions: From Portland drive south on Highway 99 West to Highway 18. Turn west on Highway 18 and drive 47 miles to U.S. 101. Turn south on U.S. 101 and drive 1.5 miles to East Devil's Lake Road. Turn east on East Devil's Lake Road and drive one mile to the park.

Contact: KOA Lincoln City, 5298 N.E. Park Ln., Otis, OR 97368; 541/994-2961; fax 541/994-9454.

39 Sea and Sand RV Park

9

Beachcombing for fossils and agates is popular at this oceanfront park near Gleneden Beach on Siletz Bay. The sites have ocean views and pleasant terraces. The Siletz River and numerous small creeks are in the area.

Location: Near Siletz Bay; The Oregon Coast Map 3, grid b8.

Campsites, facilities: There are 85 sites for trailers or RVs up to 35 feet long. Electricity, drinking water, sewer hookups, cable TV, and picnic tables are provided. Flush toilets, showers, sanitary services, firewood, and a laundry room are available. A store, a café, and ice are within one mile. Leashed pets are permitted.

Reservations, fees: Reservations accepted. Sites are $21–25 per night. Open year-round.

Directions: From Portland turn south on Highway 99 West and drive southwest to Highway 18. Turn west on Highway 18 and drive 47 miles to U.S. 101. Turn south on U.S. 101 and drive five miles to Lincoln City. Continue another nine miles south on U.S. 101 to the campground entrance (on the beach side of the highway).

Contact: Sea and Sand RV Park, 4985 U.S. Hwy. 101 N, Depoe Bay, OR 97341; 541/764-2313.

40 Beverly Beach State Park

7

This beautiful campground is in a wooded, grassy area on the east side of U.S. 101. Giant, wind-sculpted trees surround the campsites along Spencer Creek. Like magic, you walk through a tunnel under the roadway and emerge on a beach that extends from Yaguna Head to the headlands of Otter Rock and from which a lighthouse is visible. A one-mile hiking trail is available. Just a mile to the north is a small day-use state park called Devil's Punchbowl, named for an unusual bowl-shaped rock formation with caverns under it where the waves rumble about. For some great ocean views, head north one more mile to the Otter Crest Wayside. The Oregon Coast Aquarium i[s] drive.

Location: On the [Ore]gon Coast Map 3, grid c8.

Campsites, facilities: There are 129 tent sites, 129 sites with full or partial hookups for trailers or RVs of any length, a special camping area for hikers and bicyclists, and a reserved group area. There is also a village of 21 yurts. Picnic tables and fire grills are provided. Drinking water, flush toilets, showers, garbage bins, and a sanitary disposal station are available. Some facilities are wheelchair-accessible. Leashed pets are permitted.

Reservations, fees: Reservations accepted ($6 reservation fee). Sites are $11–21 per night, $4 for hikers/bikers, and yurts are $30 per night; $7 per night for an additional vehicle. Major credit cards accepted. Open year-round.

Directions: From I-5 at Albany, turn west on U.S. 20 and drive 66 miles to Newport and U.S. 101. Turn north on U.S. 101 and drive seven miles to the park entrance.

Contact: Beverly Beach State Park, 198 N.E. 123rd St., Newport, OR 97365; 800/551-6949 or 541/265-9278, reservations 800/452-5687.

41 Agate Beach RV Park

6

This park is a short distance from Agate Beach Wayside, a small state park with beach access. Agate hunting can be good. Sometimes the agates are covered by a layer of sand, and you have to dig a bit. But other times wave action will clear the sand, unveiling the agates at low tides. Beverly Beach State Park is 4.5 miles north.

Location: Near the Pacific Ocean; The Oregon Coast Map 3, grid c8.

Campsites, facilities: There are 32 sites for trailers or up to 40 feet long. Electricity, drinking water, sewer hookups, cable TV, and picnic tables are provided. Flush toilets, sanitary services, showers, and a laundry room are available. A store and ice are within one mile. Leashed pets are permitted.

Reservations, fees: Reservations accepted. Sites are $21.50–22.50 per night. Open year-round.

Directions: From Albany drive west on U.S. 20 for 66 miles to Newport and U.S. 101. Turn north on U.S. 101 and drive three miles to the park on the north end of town.

Contact: Agate Beach RV Park, 6138 N. Coast Hwy., Newport, OR 97365; 541/265-7670.

42 Harbor Village RV Park

 6

This wooded and landscaped park is near the shore of Yaquina Bay. See the description of Port of Newport Marina and RV Park for information on attractions in Newport. Nearby recreation options include clamming, crabbing, deep-sea fishing, an 18-hole golf course, hiking trails, and a full-service marina.

Location: On Yaquina Bay; The Oregon Coast Map 3, grid c8.

Campsites, facilities: There are 40 sites for trailers or RVs. Electricity, drinking water, sewer hookups, cable TV, and picnic tables are provided. Flush toilets, showers, and a laundry room are available. Bottled gas, a store, and a café are within one mile. Boat docks, launching facilities, and rentals are nearby. One leashed pet per site is permitted.

Reservations, fees: Reservations accepted. Sites are $17 for two people per night. Open year-round.

Directions: From Albany drive west on U.S. 20 for 65.5 miles into Newport and John Moore Road (lighted intersection). Turn left (south) on John Moore Road and drive one-

half mile to the bay and Bay Boulevard. Bear left and drive a short distance to the park entrance on the left.

Contact: Harbor Village RV Park, 923 S.E. Bay Blvd., Newport, OR 97365; 541/265-5088; fax 541/265-5895.

43 Port of Newport Marina and RV Park

7

This public park is set along the shore of Yaquina Bay near Newport, a resort town that offers a variety of attractions. Among them are ocean fishing, a museum and aquarium at the nearby Hatfield Marine Science Center, the Undersea Garden, the Waxworks, Ripley's Believe It or Not, and the Lincoln County Historical Society Museum. Nearby recreation options include an 18-hole golf course, hiking trails, and full-service marina.

Location: On Yaquina Bay; The Oregon Coast Map 3, grid c8.

Campsites, facilities: There are 115 sites for trailers or RVs. Electricity, drinking water, and sewer hookups are provided. Flush toilets, showers, cable TV, a store, a laundry room, and ice are available. A marina with boat docks and launching facilities is available on-site. Leashed pets are permitted.

Reservations, fees: Reservations accepted. Sites are $23.54 per night. Open year-round.

Directions: From Albany drive west on U.S. 20 for 66 miles to Newport and U.S. 101. Turn south on U.S. 101 and drive one-half mile (over the bridge) to Marine Science Drive. Turn right (east) and drive a half mile to the park entrance on the left.

Contact: Port of Newport Marina and RV Park, 600 S.E. Bay Blvd., Newport, OR 97365 (physical address: 2301 S.E. O.S.U. Dr., Newport, OR 97365); 541/867-3321; fax 541/867-3352; website: www.portofnewport.com.

44 South Beach State Park

 7

This park along the beach offers opportunities for beachcombing, fishing, crabbing, windsurfing, boating, and hiking. In fact, the Oregon Coast Trail passes right through the park. A primitive hike-in campground is also available. The park is within walking distance of Oregon Aquarium. A nice plus is that an on-duty full-time naturalist provides campground talks. For information on attractions in Newport, see the description of Port of Newport Marina and RV Park

Location: On the Pacific Ocean; The Oregon Coast Map 3, grid d8.

Campsites, facilities: There are 244 sites for trailers or RVs of any length, and an area of six primitive tent sites for hikers and bicyclists. There are also three group sites and 22 yurts. Picnic tables, electricity, and fire grills are provided. Drinking water, restroom with flush toilets and showers, garbage bins, recycling, a sanitary disposal station, and firewood are available. Some facilities are wheelchair-accessible. Leashed pets are permitted.

Reservations, fees: Reservations accepted ($6 reservation fee). Sites are $13–27 per night; yurts are $27 per night; the group fee is $65 per night; and the fee for hikers/bicyclists is $4. Major credit cards accepted. Open year-round.

Directions: From Albany drive west on U.S. 20 for 66 miles to Newport and U.S. 101. Turn south and drive three miles to the park entrance on the right.

Contact: South Beach State Park, 5580 S. Coast Hwy., South Beach, OR 97366; 541/867-4715, reservations 800/452-5687.

45 Seal Rock RV Cove

 8

This RV park is on the rugged coastline near Seal Rock State Park (open for day use only), where you may find seals, sea lions, and a variety of birds. The ocean views are stunning.

Location: Near Seal Rock State Park; The Oregon Coast Map 3, grid e8.

Campsites, facilities: There are 26 sites for trailers or RVs of any length—two are drive-through sites—and 15 tent sites. Electricity, drinking water, sewer hookups, picnic tables, and fire ring are provided. Flush toilets, showers, and firewood are available. A store, a café, and ice are within one mile.

Reservations, fees: Reservations accepted. Sites are $15–30 per night. Senior discount available. Open year-round.

Directions: From Albany drive west on U.S. 20 for 66 miles to Newport and U.S. 101. Turn south and drive 10 miles to the town of Seal Rock. Continue south on U.S. 101 for one-quarter mile to the park entrance on the left.

Contact: Seal Rock Trailer and RV Cove, P.O. Box 71, Seal Rock, OR 97376; 541/563-3955.

46 Drift Creek Landing

6

This campground is along the shore of the Alsea River in a heavily treed and mountainous area. The Oregon Coast Aquarium is 15 miles away, and an 18-hole golf course is nearby. For more information on the area, see the description of Waldport/Newport KOA.

Location: On the Alsea River; The Oregon Coast Map 3, grid e8.

Campsites, facilities: There are 49 sites for trailers or RVs of any length, and 10 mobile home sites. Electricity, drinking water, and sewer hookups are provided. Flush toilets, private telephone service, cable TV, bottled gas, showers, a recreation hall, a store, a café, a laundry room, boat docks, boat rentals, and launching facilities are available. Leashed pets are permitted.

Reservations, fees: Reservations accepted. Sites are $20 per night. Open year-round.
Directions: From Albany drive west on U.S. 20 for 66 miles to Newport and U.S. 101. Turn south and drive 14 miles to Waldport and Highway 24. Turn east on Highway 34 and drive 3.5 miles to the campground.
Contact: Drift Creek Landing, 3851 Hwy. 34, Waldport, OR 97394; 541/563-3610; fax 541/563-2612.

47 Fishin' Hole Trailer Park

6

This is one of several campgrounds along the shore of the Alsea River. For information on the area, see the description of Waldport/Newport KOA.
Location: On the Alsea River; The Oregon Coast Map 3, grid e8.
Campsites, facilities: There are 16 tent sites and 20 sites for trailers or RVs of any length. Electricity, drinking water, sewer hookups (10 sites only), picnic tables, flush toilets, showers, a laundry room, boat docks, boat rentals, and launching facilities are available. Leashed pets are permitted.
Reservations, fees: Reservations accepted. Tent sites $12 per night, RV sites $15-18, with $1 additional fee for cable TV. Open year-round.
Directions: From Albany drive west on U.S. 20 for 66 miles to Newport and U.S. 101. Turn south and drive 14 miles to Waldport and Highway 34. Turn east on Highway 34 and drive four miles to the entrance on the left.
Contact: Fishin' Hole Trailer Park, 3911 Hwy. 34, Waldport, OR 97394; 541/563-3401, reservations 877/770-6137.

48 Chinook Trailer Park

7

This trailer park is along the shore of the Alsea River, about 3.5 miles from the ocean. For more information on the area, see the description of Waldport/Newport KOA.
Location: On the Alsea River; The Oregon Coast Map 3, grid e8.
Campsites, facilities: There are six sites for tents and 22 sites with full hookups for trailers or RVs of any length. Electricity, drinking water, cable TV, sewer hookups, flush toilets, showers, and a laundry room are available. A store, a café, and ice are within one mile. Boat docks are nearby. Bottled gas is available 3.5 miles away. Leashed pets and motorbikes are permitted.
Reservations, fees: Reservations accepted. Sites are $10-16 per night. Open year-round.
Directions: From Albany drive west on U.S. 20 for 66 miles to Newport and U.S. 101. Turn south and drive 14 miles to Waldport and Highway 34. Turn east on Highway 34 and drive 3.5 miles to the park entrance.
Contact: Chinook Trailer Park, 3299 Hwy. 34, Waldport, OR 97394; 541/563-3485.

49 Taylor's Landing

9

This campground is along the Alsea River. For more information on the area, see the description of Waldport/Newport KOA.
Location: On the Alsea River; The Oregon Coast Map 3, grid e8.
Campsites, facilities: There are six tent sites and 28 sites for trailers or RVs. Electricity, drinking water, cable TV, sewer hookups, and picnic tables are provided. Flush toilets, bottled gas, showers, a café, and a laundry room are available. Boat docks, launching facilities, and rentals are nearby. Leashed pets are permitted.

Reservations, fees: Reservations accepted. Sites are $19–22 per night. Open year-round.

Directions: From Albany drive west on U.S. 20 for 66 miles to Newport and U.S. 101. Turn south and drive 14 miles to Waldport and Highway 34. Turn east on Highway 34 and drive seven miles to the entrance on the right.

Contact: Taylor's Landing, 7164 Alsea Hwy. 34, Waldport, OR 97394; tel./fax 541/528-3388.

50 Waldport/Newport KOA

8

This pretty park set amid some of the oldest pine trees in Oregon is within walking distance of the beach, the bay, and downtown Waldport—and to top it off, the campsites have beautiful ocean views. Alsea Bay's sandy and rocky shorelines make this area a favorite with anglers. The crabbing and clamming can also be quite good. Ona Beach State Park, about five miles north on U.S. 101, offers more fishing and a boat ramp along Beaver Creek. It's open for day use only. Other nearby recreation options include hiking trails, marked bike trails, the Oregon Coast Aquarium, and a marina.

Location: On Alsea Bay; The Oregon Coast Map 3, grid e8.

Campsites, facilities: There are 12 tent sites and 75 sites for trailers or RVs of any length, plus 15 cabins. Electricity, drinking water, cable TV, and sewer hookups are provided. Flush toilets, showers, and a recreation hall are available. Bottled gas, sanitary services, a store, a café, a coin laundry, and ice are within one mile. Boat docks, launching facilities, and boat rentals are nearby. Leashed pets are permitted.

Reservations, fees: Reservations accepted. Sites are $18–23 per night. Open year-round.

Directions: From Albany drive west on U.S. 20 for 66 miles to Newport and U.S. 101. Turn south and drive to milepost 155 at the north

end of the Alsea Bay Bridge. The park is on the west side of the bridge.

Contact: Waldport/Newport KOA, P.O. Box 397, Waldport, OR 97394; 541/563-2250; fax 541/563-4098; website: www.koa.com.

51 Beachside State Park

7

This state park offers about nine miles of beach and is not far from Alsea Bay and the Alsea River. Every site is seconds from the beach. This is a popular winter camping park. Within 30 miles in either direction, you'll find visitor centers, tide pools, hiking and driving tours, three lighthouses, crabbing, clamming, fishing, an aquarium, and science centers. See the description of Waldport/Newport KOA for more information on the fishing opportunities in the area.

Location: Near Alsea Bay; The Oregon Coast Map 3, grid e8.

Campsites, facilities: There are 28 sites for tents, 33 sites with water and electrical hookups for trailers or RVs up to 30 feet long, two yurts, and a special camping area for hikers and bicyclists. Picnic tables and fire grills are provided. Drinking water, garbage bins, flush toilets, showers, recycling, and firewood are available. A horseshoe pit is available nearby. Some facilities are wheelchair-accessible. Leashed pets are permitted.

Reservations, fees: Reservations accepted ($6 reservation fee). Sites are $17–21.20 per night and yurts are $28.62 per night; the fee is $4 per night for hikers/bicyclists and $7 per night for an additional vehicle. Major credit cards accepted. Open mid-March through October, weather permitting.

Directions: From Albany drive west on U.S. 20 for 66 miles to Newport and U.S. 101. Turn south on U.S. 101 and drive 16 miles to Waldport. Continue south on U.S. 101 for four miles to the park entrance.

Contact: Beachside State Park, P.O. Box 693, Waldport, OR 97973; 541/563-3220, reservations 800/452-5687; fax 541/563-3657.

52 Tillicum Beach

8

Ocean-view campsites are a big draw at this campground along the water just south of Beachside State Park. Nearby forest roads provide access to streams in the mountains east of the beach area. A U.S. Forest Service map details the possibilities. Since it's just off the highway, this camp fills up very quickly in the summer, so expect crowds.

Location: On the Pacific Ocean in Siuslaw National Forest; The Oregon Coast Map 3, grid e8.

Campsites, facilities: There are 61 sites for tents, trailers, or RVs up to 40 feet long. Picnic tables and fire grills are provided. Flush toilets, garbage bins, and drinking water are available. Leashed pets are permitted.

Reservations, fees: No reservations accepted. Sites are $14 per night, $5 for an additional vehicle. Senior discount available. Open year-round.

Directions: From Albany drive west on U.S. 20 for 66 miles to Newport and U.S. 101. Turn south on U.S. 101 and drive 14 miles to Waldport. Continue south on U.S. 101 for 4.5 miles to the campground entrance on the right.

Contact: Siuslaw National Forest, Waldport Ranger District, P.O. Box 400, Waldport, OR 97394; 541/563-3211; fax 541/563-3124; concessionaire, American Land and Leisure, 541/547-3679.

53 Cape Perpetua

8

This U.S. Forest Service campground is set along Cape Creek in the Cape Perpetua Scenic Area. The visitor information center provides hiking and driving maps to guide you through this spectacular region, and you can also watch a movie about the area. Maps highlight the tide-pool and picnic spots. The coastal cliffs are perfect for whale-watching from December through March. Neptune State Park is just south and offers additional rugged coastline vistas.

Location: On Cape Creek in Siuslaw National Forest; The Oregon Coast Map 3, grid f8.

Campsites, facilities: There are 37 sites for tents, trailers, or RVs up to 22 feet long, plus one group site that can accommodate 100 campers. Picnic tables and fire grills are provided. Flush toilets, drinking water, and garbage bins are available. Leashed pets are permitted.

Reservations, fees: Reservations required for the group site. Individual sites are $14 per night, $5 for an additional vehicle; call for group site rates. Senior discount available. Open year-round.

Directions: From Albany drive west on U.S. 20 for 66 miles to Newport and U.S. 101. Turn south and drive 23 miles to Yachats. Continue three miles south on U.S. 101 to the entrance on the left.

Contact: Siuslaw National Forest, Waldport Ranger District, P.O. Box 400, Waldport, OR 97394; 541/563-3211; fax 541/563-3124; concessionaire, 541/822-3799; make group-site reservations through the concessionaire, American Land and Leisure, 541/547-3679.

54 Sea Perch

8

Sea Perch is right in the middle of one of the most scenic areas on the Oregon coast. This private camp just south of Cape Perpetua has sites on the beach and lawn areas, plus its own shell museum and gift shop. Big rigs are welcome here. For more information on the area, see the description of Cape Perpetua.

Location: Near Cape Perpetua; The Oregon Coast Map 3, grid f8.

Campsites, facilities: There are 18 back-up sites with full hookups and 17 pull-through sites for RVs or trailers of any length. Electricity, drinking water, sewer hookups, and picnic tables are provided. Flush toilets, sanitary services, showers, firewood, a recreation hall, a laundry room, ice, store, modem hookups, and a beach are available. Leashed pets and motorbikes are permitted.

Reservations, fees: Reservations accepted. Sites are $28 per night June through October, $24 in off-season. Open year-round.

Directions: From Albany drive west on U.S. 20 for 66 miles to Newport and U.S. 101. Turn south and drive 23 miles to Yachats. Continue south on U.S. 101 for 6.5 miles to the campground at milepost 171 on the right.

Contact: Sea Perch, 95480 U.S. Hwy. 101, Yachats, OR 97498; 541/547-3505.

55 Rock Creek

7

This little campground is set along Rock Creek just one-quarter mile from the ocean. It's a premium spot for coastal-highway travelers, although it can get packed very quickly. An excellent side trip is Cape Perpetua, a designated scenic area a few miles up the coast. The cape offers beautiful ocean views and a visitor center that will supply you with information on nature trails, picnic spots, tide pools, and where to find the best viewpoints in the area.

Location: On Rock Creek in Siuslaw National Forest; The Oregon Coast Map 3, grid f8.

Campsites, facilities: There are 16 sites for tents, trailers, or RVs up to 22 feet long. Fire grills and picnic tables are provided. Flush toilets, garbage bins, and drinking water are available. Leashed pets are permitted.

Reservations, fees: No reservations accepted. Sites are $14 per night, $5 for an additional vehicle. Major credit cards accepted. Senior discount available. Open year-round.

Directions: From Albany drive west on U.S. 20 for 66 miles to Newport and U.S. 101. Turn south and drive 23 miles to Yachats. Continue south on U.S. 101 for 10 miles to the campground entrance on the left.

Contact: Siuslaw National Forest, Waldport Ranger District, P.O. Box 400, Waldport, OR 97394; 541/563-3211; fax 541/563-3124; concessionaire, American Land and Leisure, 541/547-3679.

56 Lanham Bike-In Camp

7

This very primitive camp is a good layover spot for cyclists working their way along the coast highway—and you can't beat the price. See the description of Rock Creek for area information.

Location: In Siuslaw National Forest; The Oregon Coast Map 3, grid g8.

Campsites, facilities: There are six primitive hike-in/bike-in tent sites. Picnic tables and fire grills are provided. Garbage bins are available, but there is no drinking water here; it can be obtained at Rock Creek. Leashed pets are permitted.

Reservations, fees: No reservations accepted. There is no fee. Open year-round.

Directions: From Albany drive west on U.S. 20 for 66 miles to Newport and U.S. 101. Turn south and drive 23 miles to Yachats. Continue south on U.S. 101 for 10 miles (just past Rock Creek Campground) to the campground entrance. Hike or bike in from there.

Contact: Siuslaw National Forest, Waldport Ranger District, P.O. Box 400, Waldport, OR 97394; 541/563-3211; fax 541/563-3124.

57 Carl G. Washburne State Park

🚶 🚴 🐕 🚐 ⛺ 7

These are spacious campsites with a buffer of native plants between you and the highway. At night you can hear the pounding surf. There is a creek running through the campground, and elk have been known to wander through. Short hikes lead from the campground to a two-mile-long beach, extensive tide pools along the base of the cliffs, and a three-mile trail to Heceta Head Lighthouse. Just three miles south of the park are the Sea Lion Caves, where an elevator takes visitors down into the cavern for an insider's view of the life of a sea lion.

Location: On the Pacific Ocean; The Oregon Coast Map 3, grid h8.

Campsites, facilities: There are seven primitive walk-in sites, 58 sites with full hookups for trailers or RVs up to 45 feet long, and two yurts. A special area is available for hikers and bicyclists. Drinking water, garbage bins, a sanitary disposal station, and picnic tables are provided. Flush toilets, showers, and firewood are available. Leashed pets are permitted.

Reservations, fees: No reservations accepted. Sites are $16.05–20.33 per night, $4 per night for hikers/bicyclists; yurts are $30 per night; an additional vehicle is $7 per night. Open year-round.

Directions: From Eugene drive west on Highway 126 for 61 miles to Florence and U.S. 101. Turn north on U.S. 101 and drive 12.5 miles to the park entrance road (well signed, 10 miles south of the town of Yachats). Turn west and drive a short distance to the park.

Contact: Carl G. Washburne State Park, 93111 U.S. Hwy. 101 N, Florence, OR 97439; 800/452-5687 or 541/547-3416.

58 Alder Dune

🚶 🎣 🚤 🐕 🚐 ⛺ 7

This wooded campground is near four lakes—Alder Lake, Sutton Lake, Dune Lake, and Mercer Lake (the largest). A boat launch is available at Sutton Lake. An option is exploring the expansive sand dunes in the area by foot. There is no off-road-vehicle access here. See the description of Harbor Vista Park for other information on the area.

Location: Near Alder Lake in Siuslaw National Forest; The Oregon Coast Map 3, grid h8.

Campsites, facilities: There are 39 sites for tents, trailers, or RVs up to 30 feet long. Picnic tables and fire grills are provided. Flush toilets, garbage bins, and drinking water are available. Leashed pets are permitted.

Reservations, fees: No reservations accepted. Sites are $12 per night, $10 for an additional vehicle. Senior discount available. Open mid-May through mid-September.

Directions: From Eugene drive west on Highway 126 for 61 miles to Florence and U.S. 101. Turn north on U.S. 101 and drive eight miles to the campground on the left.

Contact: Siuslaw National Forest, Mapleton Ranger District, 4480 U.S. Hwy. 101, Building G, Florence, OR 97439; 541/902-8526; fax 541/902-6946.

59 Sutton

🚶 🎣 🐕 🚐 ⛺ 7

This campground is adjacent to Sutton Creek not far from Sutton Lake. Holman Vista on Sutton Beach Road provides a beautiful view of the dunes and ocean, and vegetation provides some privacy between sites. Wading and fishing are both popular. A hiking trail system leads from the camp out to the dunes. There is no off-road-vehicle access here. An alternative camp is Alder Dune to the north.

Location: Near Sutton Lake in Siuslaw National Forest; The Oregon Coast Map 3, grid h8.

Campsites, facilities: There are 80 sites for tents, trailers, or RVs up to 30 feet long, 20 with partial hookups. There are also group sites. Picnic tables and fire grills are provided. Flush toilets, garbage bins, and drinking water are available. A boat ramp is nearby. Leashed pets are permitted.

Reservations, fees: Reservations necessary for group sites only. Rates are $12–15 per night for single sites, $7 for an additional vehicle; call for group camp rates. Senior discount available. Open year-round.

Directions: From Eugene drive west on Highway 126 for 61 miles to Florence and U.S. 101. Turn north on U.S. 101 and drive six miles to Sutton Beach Road (Forest Road 794). Turn northwest and drive 1.5 miles to the campground entrance.

Contact: Siuslaw National Forest, Mapleton Ranger District, 4480 U.S. Hwy. 101, Building G, Florence, OR 97439; 541/902-8526; fax 541/902-6946.

60 North Fork Siuslaw

6

Little known and little used, this wooded camp along the North Fork of the Siuslaw River is the ideal hideaway. A dirt road opposite the camp follows Wilhelm Creek for about two miles. A newly constructed trail through old-growth forest is nearby. See a U.S. Forest Service map for other side-trip possibilities.

Location: On the North Fork of the Siuslaw River in Siuslaw National Forest; The Oregon Coast Map 3, grid h8.

Campsites, facilities: There are six tent sites. Picnic tables and fire grills are provided. Chemical toilets and garbage bins are available. No drinking water is available. Leashed pets are permitted.

Reservations, fees: No reservations accepted; sites are $5 per night in summer, $2.50 for an additional vehicle. Senior discount available. Open May through October.

Directions: From Eugene drive west on Highway 126 for 50 miles to County Road 5070/North Fork (one mile east of Florence). Turn right and drive 12 miles northeast to the campground.

Contact: Siuslaw National Forest, Mapleton Ranger District, 4480 U.S. Hwy. 101, Building G, Florence, OR 97439; 541/902-8526; fax 541/902-6946.

61 Canal Creek

5

This pleasant little campground is just off the beaten path in a large, wooded, open area along Canal Creek. It feels remote because a creek runs through the campground and there are also historic homesites nearby, with old fruit trees on the grounds. Yet it has easy access and is close to the coast and all the amenities. The climate here is relatively mild, but on the other hand, there is the rain in winter—lots of it.

Location: On Canal Creek in Siuslaw National Forest; The Oregon Coast Map 4, grid e1.

Campsites, facilities: There are 11 sites for tents only and 10 sites for tents or small RVs, plus a group area. Picnic tables and fire grills are provided. Drinking water, garbage bins, and vault toilets are available. The group site has a picnic shelter and a play area. Leashed pets are permitted.

Reservations, fees: Group reservations required; individual sites are $6 per night, $3 for an additional vehicle. Senior discount available. Open year-round.

Directions: From Albany drive west on U.S. 20 for 15 miles to Philomath and Highway 34. Turn south on Highway 34 and drive 52 miles to Forest Road 3462. Turn south and drive four miles to the camp.

Contact: Siuslaw National Forest, Waldport Ranger District, P.O. Box 400, Waldport, OR 97394; 541/563-3211; fax 541/563-3124; make group-site reservations through the concessionaire, American Land and Leisure, 541/547-3679.

62 Blackberry

 7

This is a good base camp for a fishing trip on the Alsea River. The U.S. Forest Service provides boat launches and picnic areas at several spots along this stretch of river. Often there will be a camp host, who can give you inside information on nearby recreational opportunities. Large fir trees and lawn separate the sites.

Location: On the Alsea River in Siuslaw National Forest; The Oregon Coast Map 4, grid f3.

Campsites, facilities: There are 32 sites for tents, trailers, or RVs. Picnic tables and fire grills are provided. Drinking water, garbage bins, and flush toilets are available. There is no firewood. A boat ramp is on-site. Leashed pets are permitted.

Reservations, fees: No reservations accepted. Sites are $9 per night, $5 for an additional vehicle. Senior discount available. Open year-round.

Directions: From Albany drive west on U.S. 20 for 15 miles to Philomath and Highway 34. Turn south on Highway 34 and drive 41 miles to the campground entrance.

Contact: Siuslaw National Forest, Waldport Ranger District, P.O. Box 400, Waldport, OR 97394; 541/563-3211; fax 541/563-3124; concessionaire, American Land and Leisure, 541/547-3679.

63 Alsea Falls

8

The beautiful surroundings of Alsea Falls can be enjoyed by exploring the trails that wander through the park and lead to the picnic area down near the falls. Trails to McBee Park and Green Peak Falls are accessible from the campground along the South Fork of the river. The campsites are situated in a 40-year-old forest of Douglas fir and vine maple. On a warm day Alsea Falls offers cool relief along the river. The area was named after its original inhabitants, the Alsea Indians.

Location: Adjacent to the South Fork of the Alsea River; The Oregon Coast Map 4, grid f4.

Campsites, facilities: There are 22 sites for tents, trailers, or RVs up to 30 feet long. Fire pits are provided. Drinking water, vault toilets, garbage bins, and fireplaces for wood and charcoal are available. Leashed pets are permitted.

Reservations, fees: No reservations accepted. Sites are $6 per night, with an additional charge of $4 per each additional vehicle. Senior discount available. Open mid-May to late September.

Directions: From Albany drive west on U.S. 20 for nine miles to Corvallis. Turn south (left) onto Highway 99 and drive 15 miles to County Road 45120. Turn west (right) and drive five miles to Alpine Junction. Continue along the South Fork Alsea Access Road nine miles to the campground on the right.

Contact: Bureau of Land Management, Salem District Office, 1717 Fabry Rd. SE, Salem, OR 97306; 503/375-5646; fax 503/375-5622.

64 Maple Lane Trailer Park-Marina

 5

This park along the shore of the Siuslaw River in Mapleton is close to hiking trails. The general area is surrounded by Siuslaw National Forest land. A U.S. Forest Service map details nearby backcountry side-trip options.

Location: On the Siuslaw River; The Oregon Coast Map 4, grid h2.

Campsites, facilities: There are two tent sites and 46 sites with full hookups for trailers or RVs up to 35 feet. Electricity, drinking water, and sewer hookups are provided. Flush toilets, bottled gas, sanitary services, and showers are available. A store, a café, and ice are behind the park. A bait and tackle shop is open during the fishing season. Boat docks and launching facilities are on-site. Small pets (under 15 pounds) are permitted.

Reservations, fees: Reservations accepted. Sites are $7–14 per night. Open year-round.

Directions: From Eugene drive west on Highway 126 for 47 miles to Mapleton. Continue on Highway 126 for one-quarter mile past the business district to the park entrance on the left.

Contact: Maple Lane Trailer Park-Marina, 10730 Hwy. 126, Mapleton, OR 97453; 541/268-4822.

65 Archie Knowles

5

This little campground along Knowles Creek about three miles east of Mapleton is rustic with mixed forested and lawn areas, yet it offers easy proximity to the highway.

Location: On Knowles Creek in Siuslaw National Forest; The Oregon Coast Map 4, grid h2.

Campsites, facilities: There are nine sites for tents, trailers, or RVs up to 16 feet long. Picnic tables and fire grills are provided. Chemical toilets, garbage bins, and drinking water are available. Leashed pets are permitted.

Reservations, fees: No reservations accepted. Sites are $10 per night, $7 for an additional vehicle. Senior discount available. Open May to late September.

Directions: From Eugene drive west on Highway 126 44 miles to the campground entrance (three miles east of Mapleton).

Contact: Siuslaw National Forest, Mapleton Ranger District, 4480 U.S. Hwy. 101, Building G, Florence, OR 97439; 541/902-8526; fax 541/902-6946.

66 Harbor Vista County Park

6

This county park out among the dunes near the entrance to the harbor offers a great lookout point from the observation deck. A number of side trips are available, including the Sea Lion Caves, Darlington State Park, Jessie M. Honeyman Memorial State Park (see the description of Jessie M. Honeyman), and the Indian Forest, just four miles north of Florence. Florence also has displays of Native American dwellings and crafts.

Location: Near Florence; The Oregon Coast Map 5, grid a7.

Campsites, facilities: There are 38 sites for tents, trailers, or RVs up to 60 feet long. Picnic tables and garbage bins are provided. Electricity, flush toilets, fire rings, sanitary disposal station, coin-operated showers, drinking water, a pay phone, and a playground are available. Pets and motorbikes are permitted.

Reservations, fees: Reservations accepted ($10 fee).

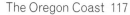

Sites are $11–16 per night, $5 per night for a third vehicle. Open year-round.

Directions: From Eugene drive west on Highway 126 for 61 miles to Florence and U.S. 101. Turn right (north) and drive four miles to 35th Street. Turn left and drive to where it dead-ends into Rhododendron Drive. Turn right and drive 1.4 miles to North Jetty Road. Turn left and drive one-half block to Harbor Vista Road. Turn left and continue to the campground at 87658 Harbor Vista Road.

Note: Follow these exact directions. Previous visitors to this park taking a different route will discover part of Harbor Vista Road is now gated.

Contact: Harbor Vista County Park, Harbor Vista Road, Florence, OR 97439; 541/997-5987; website: www.co.lane.or.us/park.

67 B and E Wayside Mobile and RV Park

5

This landscaped park is beautifully maintained, clean, and quiet. See the descriptions of Lane County Harbor Vista Park and Port of Siuslaw RV and Marina for side-trip ideas. Nearby recreation options include two golf courses and a riding stable (two miles away).

Location: Near Florence; The Oregon Coast Map 5, grid a8.

Campsites, facilities: There are 24 sites for trailers or RVs of any length. Electricity, drinking water, sewer hookups, and picnic tables are provided. Flush toilets, sanitary services, showers, and a laundry room are available. Bottled gas, a store, ice, a café, and restaurant are within two miles. Boat-launching facilities are nearby. Small leashed pets are permitted.

Reservations, fees: Reservations accepted. Sites are $20 per night. Open year-round.

Directions: From Eugene drive west on Highway 126 for 61 miles to Florence and U.S. 101.

Turn north on U.S. 101 and drive 1.8 miles to the park on the right.

Contact: B and E Wayside Mobile and RV Park, 3760 U.S. Hwy. 101 N, Florence, OR 97439; 541/997-6451.

68 Port of Siuslaw RV and Marina

8

This public resort can be found along the Siuslaw River in a grassy, urban setting. Anglers with boats will find that the U.S. 101 bridge support pilings make good spots for crabbing and fishing for perch and flounder. A new set of docks with drinking water, electricity, gasoline, security, and a fish-cleaning station are available. The sea lion caves and estuary are a bonus for wildlife lovers, and nearby lakes make swimming and water-skiing a possibility. Golf is within driving distance, and horses can be rented about nine miles away.

Location: On the Siuslaw River; The Oregon Coast Map 5, grid a8.

Campsites, facilities: There are 84 sites for tents, trailers, or RVs of any length. Electricity, drinking water, sewer hookups, cable TV and picnic tables are provided. Flush toilets, sanitary services, showers, a laundry room, and boat docks are available. A café and ice are within one mile. Leashed pets are permitted.

Reservations, fees: Reservations accepted. Sites are $16–18 per night. Open year-round.

Directions: From Eugene drive west on Highway 126 for 61 miles to Florence and U.S. 101. Turn south on U.S. 101 and drive to Harbor Street. Turn left (east) on Harbor Street and drive about three blocks to the park and marina.

Contact: Port of Siuslaw RV and Marina, P.O. Box 1638, Florence, OR 97439; 541/997-3040.

69 Jessie M. Honeyman Memorial State Park

🚶 🚲 ⛵ 🎣
🚗 🐕 ♿ 🚐 ⛺ 7

This popular state park is within walking distance of the shore of Cleowax Lake and adjacent to the dunes of the Oregon Dunes National Recreation Area. There are two miles of dunes between the park and the ocean. The dunes here are quite impressive, with some reaching to 500 feet. In the winter, it is open to OHV use. For thrill seekers, sand boards are available to rent in nearby Florence for sandboarding on the dunes. The two lakes in the park offer facilities for boating, fishing, and swimming. A one-mile hiking trail with access to the dunes is available in the park and off-road vehicle trails are nearby in the sand dunes.

Location: Near Cleowax Lake; The Oregon Coast Map 5, grid a8.

Campsites, facilities: There are 237 sites for tents and 141 sites for trailers or RVs up to 60 feet long (with full or partial hookups), a special camping area for hikers and bicyclists, six group tent areas, and 10 yurts. Picnic tables, garbage bins, and fire grills are provided. Drinking water, flush toilets, sanitary services, showers, evening interpretive programs and events, and firewood are available. Some facilities are wheelchair-accessible. Boat docks and launching facilities are nearby. Leashed pets are permitted.

Reservations, fees: Reservations accepted ($6 reservation fee). Sites are $13–22 per night, $4 for hikers/bicyclists; group areas are $64 per night, yurts are $30 per night; an additional vehicle is $7 per night. Open year-round.

Directions: From Eugene drive west on Highway 126 for 61 miles to Florence and U.S. 101. Turn south on U.S. 101 and drive three miles to the park entrance.

Contact: Jessie M. Honeyman Memorial State Park, 84505 U.S. Hwy. 101, Florence, OR 97439; 800/551-6949 or 541/997-3641, reservations 800/452-5687.

70 Lakeshore RV Park

⛵ 🎣 🚤 🐕 🚐 5

Here's a prime area for vacationers. This park is set along the shore of Woahink Lake, a popular spot to fish for trout, perch, catfish, crappie, bluegill, and bass. It's adjacent to Jessie M. Honeyman Memorial State Park and the Oregon Dunes National Recreation Area. Off-road-vehicle access to the dunes is four miles northeast of the park. Hiking trails through the dunes can be found at Honeyman Memorial State Park. If you set out across the dunes off the trail, note your path. People hiking off-trail commonly get lost here.

Location: On Woahink Lake; The Oregon Coast Map 5, grid a8.

Campsites, facilities: There are 20 sites for trailers or RVs of any length; six are drive-through sites. Electricity, drinking water, cable TV, and sewer hookups are provided. Flush toilets, showers, and a laundry room are available. A café is within three miles. Boat docks are nearby. Leashed pets are permitted.

Reservations, fees: Reservations accepted. Sites are $18 per night. Open year-round.

Directions: From Eugene drive west on Highway 126 for 61 miles to Florence and U.S. 101. Turn south on U.S. 101 and drive four miles to milepost 195 and the park on the left.

Contact: Lakeshore RV Park, 83763 U.S. Hwy. 101, Florence, OR 97439; 541/997-2741; website: www.lakeshorerv.com.

71 Woahink Lake RV Resort

🥾 🎣 🚤 🐕 🚐 7

One of several RV parks in the Florence area, this quiet, clean camp is across from Woahink Lake, where trout fishing is an option. Nearby Oregon Dunes National Recreation Area is a good side trip.

Location: On Woahink Lake; The Oregon Coast Map 5, grid a8.

Campsites, facilities: There are 76 sites for trailers or RVs of any length. No tent camping is allowed. Electricity, drinking water, sewer hookups, restrooms, showers, cable TV, a public phone, and a laundry room are available. Recreational facilities include horseshoe pits, a recreation hall, a game room, and a boat dock. One large or two small leashed pets per site are permitted.

Reservations, fees: Reservations recommended. Sites are $23.50 per night. Senior discount available. Open year-round.

Directions: From Eugene drive west on Highway 126 for 61 miles to Florence and U.S. 101. Turn south on U.S. 101 and drive 5.1 miles to the camp on the right.

Contact: Woahink Lake RV Resort, 83570 U.S. Hwy. 101 S, Florence, OR 97439; 541/997-6454, reservations 800/659-6454; fax 541/902-0481; email (for reservations): wohink@presys.com.

72 Mercer Lake Resort

🏊 🎣 🚤 🐕 🚐 7

This resort is set along the shore of Mercer Lake, one of a number of lakes that have formed among the ancient dunes in this area.

Location: On Mercer Lake; The Oregon Coast Map 5, grid a8.

Campsites, facilities: There are 13 sites for trailers or RVs of any length; four are drive-through sites. Electricity, drinking water, cable TV, sewer hookups, and picnic tables are provided. Flush toilets, sanitary services,

showers, a store, a laundry room, and ice are available. Boat docks, launching facilities, and fishing boat rentals are on-site. Leashed pets are permitted.

Reservations, fees: Reservations recommended. Sites are $15–19 per night. Open year-round.

Directions: From Eugene drive west on Highway 126 for 61 miles to Florence and U.S. 101. Turn north on U.S. 101 and drive five miles to Mercer Lake Road. Turn east and drive just under one mile to Bay Berry Lane. Turn left and drive to the campground.

Contact: Mercer Lake Resort, 88875 Bay Berry Ln., Florence, OR 97439; 800/355-3633 or 541/997-3633; fax 541/997-5096.

73 Carter Lake

🥾 🏊 🎣 🚤 🐕 ♿ 🚐 ⛺ 9

This campground is on the north shore of Carter Lake, where you can fish almost right from your campsite. Boating, swimming, and fishing are permitted on this long, narrow lake, which is set among dunes overgrown with vegetation. The nearby Taylor Dunes Trail is an easy half-mile wheelchair-accessible trail to the dunes past Taylor Lake. Hiking is allowed in the dunes, but there is no off-road-vehicle access here. If you want off-road access, head north one mile to Siltcoos Road, turn west, and drive 1.3 miles to Driftwood II.

Location: On Carter Lake in Oregon Dunes National Recreation Area; The Oregon Coast Map 5, grid a8.

Campsites, facilities: There are 23 sites for tents, trailers, or RVs up to 35 feet long. Picnic tables, garbage service, and fire grills are provided. Drinking water and flush toilets are available. Leashed pets are permitted.

Reservations, fees: Reservations accepted ($8.65 reservation fee). Sites are $13 per night, $7 per night for an additional vehicle. Senior discount available. Open April through September.

Directions: From Eugene drive west on Highway 126 for 61 miles to Florence and U.S. 101. Turn south on U.S. 101 and drive 8.5 miles to Forest Road 1084. Turn right on Forest Road 1084 and drive west 200 yards to the camp.

Contact: Oregon Dunes National Recreation Area, 855 U.S. Hwy. 101, Reedsport, OR 97467; 541/271-3611, reservations 877/444-6777; fax 541/750-7244; website (for reservations): www.reserveusa.com.

74 Driftwood II

6

This is primarily a campground for off-road vehicles. It's set near the ocean, but without an ocean view, in Oregon Dunes National Recreation Area and has off-road-vehicle access. Several small lakes, the Siltcoos River, and Siltcoos Lake are nearby. Note that ATV use is prohibited between 10 P.M. and 6 A.M.

Location: Near Siltcoos Lake in Oregon Dunes National Recreation Area; The Oregon Coast Map 5, grid b7.

Campsites, facilities: There are 69 sites for tents, trailers, or RVs up to 50 feet long. Picnic tables, garbage service, and fire grills are provided. Drinking water and flush and vault toilets are available. A sanitary disposal station is within five miles. Some facilities are wheelchair-accessible. Boat docks, launching facilities, and rentals can be found about four miles away on Siltcoos Lake. Leashed pets are permitted.

Reservations, fees: Reservations accepted ($8.65 reservation fee). Sites are $13 per night, $7 per night for each additional vehicle. Senior discount available. Open year-round.

Directions: From Eugene drive west on Highway 126 for 61 miles to Florence and U.S. 101. Turn south on U.S. 101 and drive seven miles to Siltcoos Beach Road. Turn right and drive 1.5 miles west to the campground.

Contact: Oregon Dunes National Recreation Area, 855 U.S. Hwy. 101, Reedsport, OR 97467; 541/271-3611, reservations 877/444-6777; fax 541/750-7244; website (for reservations): www.reserveusa.com.

75 Lagoon

9

One of several campgrounds in the area, this one is along the lagoon about one mile from Siltcoos Lake and set one-half mile inland. The Lagoon Trail is a prime spot for wildlife viewing for marine birds and other aquatic species.

Location: Near Siltcoos Lake in Oregon Dunes National Recreation Area; The Oregon Coast Map 5, grid b7.

Campsites, facilities: There are 39 sites for tents, trailers, or RVs up to 35 feet long. Picnic tables, garbage service, and fire grills are provided. Drinking water and flush and vault toilets are available. A telephone and sanitary services are within five miles. Boat docks, launching facilities, and rentals are nearby on Siltcoos Lake. Leashed pets are permitted.

Reservations, fees: No reservations accepted. Sites are $13 per night, $7 per night for an additional vehicle. Senior discount available. Open year-round.

Directions: From Eugene drive west on Highway 126 for 61 miles to Florence and U.S. 101. Turn south on U.S. 101 and drive seven miles to Siltcoos Beach Road. Turn right on Siltcoos Beach Road and drive west for 1.2 miles to the campground.

Contact: Oregon Dunes National Recreation Area, 855

U.S. Hwy. 101, Reedsport, OR 97467; 541/271-3611; fax 541/750-7244.

76 Darlings Resort

 7

This park can be found in a rural area along the north shore of Siltcoos Lake, adjacent to the extensive Oregon Dunes National Recreation Area. Sites are right on the lake; fish from your picnic table. An access point to the dunes for hikers and off-road vehicles is just across the highway. The lake has a full-service marina.

Location: On Siltcoos Lake; The Oregon Coast Map 5, grid b7.

Campsites, facilities: There are 42 sites for trailers or RVs of any length; 18 have full hookups. Electricity, cable TV, drinking water, sewer hookups, and picnic tables are provided. Flush toilets, showers, firewood, a store, a tavern, a deli, boat docks, boat rentals, launching facilities, and a laundry room are available. Leashed pets are permitted.

Reservations, fees: Reservations accepted. Sites are $14–22.50 per night. Open year-round.

Directions: From Eugene drive west on Highway 126 for 61 miles to Florence and U.S. 101. Turn south on U.S. 101 and drive five miles to North Beach Road. Turn east and drive one-half mile to the resort.

Contact: Darlings Resort, 4879 Darling Loop, Florence, OR 97439; 541/997-2841; website: www.darlingsresort.com.

77 Tyee

6

This wooded campground along the shore of the Siltcoos River is an option to Driftwood II and Lagoon. Swimming, fishing, and water-skiing are permitted at the nearby lake, where there is a canoe portage trail and a boat ramp. Off-road-vehicle access to the dunes is available from Driftwood II, and there are hiking trails in the area.

Location: On the Siltcoos River in Oregon Dunes National Recreation Area; The Oregon Coast Map 5, grid b7.

Campsites, facilities: There are 16 sites for tents, trailers, or RVs up to 30 feet long. Picnic tables, garbage service, and fire grills are provided. Drinking water, vault toilets, and a day-use area (with horseshoe pits, electricity, and 10 tables) are available. A store, boat docks, launching facilities, and rentals are nearby. Some facilities are wheelchair-accessible. Leashed pets are permitted.

Reservations, fees: Reservations accepted ($8.65 reservation fee). Sites are $13 per night, $7 per night for an additional vehicle. Senior discount available. Open year-round.

Directions: From Eugene drive west on Highway 126 for 61 miles to Florence and U.S. 101. Turn south on U.S. 101 and drive six miles to the Westlake turnoff. Turn and you'll see the campground.

Contact: Oregon Dunes National Recreation Area, 855 U.S. Hwy. 101, Reedsport, OR 97467; 541/271-3611, reservations 877/444-6777; fax 541/750-7244; website (for reservations): www.reserveusa.com.

78 Waxmyrtle

7

One of three camps in the immediate vicinity, Waxmyrtle is adjacent to Lagoon and less than a mile from Driftwood II. The camp is near the Siltcoos River and a couple of miles from Siltcoos Lake, a good-sized lake with boating facilities where you can water-ski, fish, and swim. A pleasant hiking trail is available that meanders through the dunes and along the estuary.

Location: Near Siltcoos Lake in Oregon Dunes National Recreation Area; The Oregon Coast Map 5, grid b7.

Campsites, facilities: There are 54 sites for tents, trailers, or RVs up to 35 feet long. Picnic tables, garbage service, and fire grills are provided. Drinking water and flush toilets are available. Boat docks, launching facilities, and rentals are nearby on Siltcoos Lake. Leashed pets are permitted.

Reservations, fees: No reservations accepted. Sites are $13 per night, $7 per night for an additional vehicle. Senior discount available. Open late May to mid-October.

Directions: From Eugene drive west on Highway 126 for 61 miles to Florence and U.S. 101. Turn south on U.S. 101 and drive seven miles to Siltcoos Beach Road. Turn right and drive 1.3 miles west to the campground.

Contact: Oregon Dunes National Recreation Area, 855 U.S. Hwy. 101, Reedsport, OR 97467; 541/271-3611; fax 541/750-7244.

79 Tahkenitch Landing

6

This camp overlooking Tahkenitch Lake has easy access for fishing and swimming. Fishing is excellent on Tahkenitch, which means "a lake with many fingers." There is no drinking water here, but water, a boat ramp, and a dock are available nearby at Tahkenitch Lake.

Location: Near Tahkenitch Lake in Oregon Dunes National Recreation Area; The Oregon Coast Map 5, grid b7.

Campsites, facilities: There are 27 sites for tents, trailers, or RVs up to 30 feet long. Picnic tables and garbage service are provided. Vault toilets, boat-launching facilities, and a floating dock are available, but there is no drinking water. Leashed pets are permitted.

Reservations, fees: No reservations accepted. Sites are $12 per night, $7 per night

for an additional vehicle. Senior discount available. Open year-round.

Directions: From Eugene drive west on Highway 126 for 61 miles to Florence and U.S. 101. Turn south on U.S. 101 and drive 14 miles to the campground on the east side of the road.

Contact: Oregon Dunes National Recreation Area, 855 U.S. Hwy. 101, Reedsport, OR 97467; 541/271-3611; fax 541/750-7244.

80 Tahkenitch

7

This very pretty campground is in a wooded area across the highway from Tahkenitch Lake, which has numerous coves and backwater areas for fishing and swimming. A hiking trail close to the camp goes through the dunes out to the beach, as well as to Threemile Lake. If this camp is filled, Tahkenitch Landing provides nearby space.

Location: Near Tahkenitch Lake in Oregon Dunes National Recreation Area; The Oregon Coast Map 5, grid b7.

Campsites, facilities: There are 25 sites for tents, trailers, or RVs up to 30 feet long. Picnic tables, garbage service, and fire grills are provided. Drinking water and flush and vault toilets are available. Boat docks and launching facilities are on the lake across the highway. Leashed pets are permitted.

Reservations, fees: Reservations accepted ($8.65 reservation fee). Sites are $13 per night, $7 per night for an additional vehicle. Senior discount available. Open mid-May through Labor Day weekend.

Directions: From Eugene drive west on Highway 126 for 61 miles to Florence and U.S. 101. Turn south on U.S. 101 and drive 14 miles. The campground entrance is on the right.

Contact: Oregon Dunes National Recreation Area, 855 U.S. Hwy. 101, Reedsport, OR

97467; 541/271-3611, reservations 877/444-6777; fax 541/750-7244; website (for reservations): www.reserveusa.com.

81 Surfwood Campground and RV Park

 6

Fishing is the focal point at this park half a mile from the marina at Winchester Bay. Hiking is another option, with trails heading west across the dunes to the ocean and east to lakes in wooded areas. An elk preserve can be found adjacent to Highway 38 about 10 miles to the east. The campground itself has pull-through sites separated by shrubs that create privacy.

Location: On Winchester Bay; The Oregon Coast Map 5, grid c7.

Campsites, facilities: There are 22 tent sites and 141 sites for trailers or RVs; 64 are drive-through sites. Electricity, drinking water, sewer hookups, picnic tables, and fire pits are provided. Flush toilets, showers, sanitary services, firewood, a store, a laundry room, ice, cable TV, tennis courts, a playground, modem access, and a seasonal pool and sauna are available. Boat docks and launching facilities are within a half mile. Leashed pets and motorbikes are permitted.

Reservations, fees: Reservations accepted. Sites are $12–17 per night. Open year-round.

Directions: From Eugene drive south on I-5 about 35 miles to Exit 162 and Highway 38. Turn west on Highway 38 and drive 64 miles to Reedsport and U.S. 101. Turn south and drive to milepost 215 (2.5 miles south of the last stoplight in Reedsport) and the park (one-half mile north of Winchester Bay).

Contact: Surfwood Campground and RV Park, 75381 U.S. Hwy. 101, Reedsport, OR 97467; tel./fax 541/271-4020; website: www .rvrschoice.com/surfwood.

82 Discovery Point RV Park

7

This resort is on the shore of Winchester Bay in a fishing village near the mouth of the Umpqua River. For details on nearby recreation options, see the description of Surfwood Campground and RV Park.

Location: On Winchester Bay; The Oregon Coast Map 5, grid c7.

Campsites, facilities: There are 15 tent sites and 50 sites for trailers or RVs of any length; 14 are drive-through sites. Electricity, drinking water, sewer hookups, and picnic tables are provided. Flush toilets, showers, a store, a laundry room, and ice are available. Sanitary services and bottled gas are within one mile. Boat docks and launching facilities are nearby. Leashed pets and motorbikes are permitted.

Reservations, fees: Reservations accepted. Sites are $18–20 per night. Open year-round.

Directions: From Eugene drive south on I-5 for about 35 miles to Exit 162 and Highway 38. Turn west on Highway 38 and drive 64 miles to Reedsport and U.S. 101. Turn south on U.S. 101 and drive three miles to the Windy Cove exit near Winchester Bay. Take that exit and drive west 1.5 miles to the resort.

Contact: Discovery Point RV Park, HC 81, P.O. Box 242, Reedsport, OR 97467; 541/271-3443; fax 541/271-9285.

83 Windy Cove County Park

7

This county park actually comprises two parks, Windy Cove A and B. Set near ocean beaches and sand dunes, both offer other nearby recreational facilities, including an 18-hole golf course, hiking trails, and a lighthouse.

Location: On the Pacific Ocean; The Oregon Coast Map 5, grid c7.

Campsites, facilities: There are 29 tent sites and 63 sites with full hookups for trailers or RVs up to 60 feet long, and four sites with partial hookups. Electricity, drinking water, sewer hookups, and picnic tables are provided. Flush toilets, showers, and cable TV are available. Bottled gas, sanitary services, a store, a café, a coin laundry, and ice are within one mile. Boat docks, launching facilities, boat charters, and rentals are nearby. Leashed pets are permitted.

Reservations, fees: No reservations accepted. Sites are $12–15 per night. Open year-round.

Directions: From Eugene drive south on I-5 to Exit 162 and Highway 38. Turn west on Highway 38 and drive 64 miles to Reedsport and U.S. 101. Turn south on U.S. 101 and drive three miles to the Windy Cove exit near Winchester Bay. Take that exit and drive west to the park on the left.

Contact: Windy Cove County Park, 684 Salmon Harbor, Reedsport, OR 97467; 541/271-5634 or 541/271-4138.

84 Umpqua Lighthouse State Park

7

This park is near Lake Marie and less than a mile from Salmon Harbor on Winchester Bay. Near the mouth of the Umpqua River, this unusual area has dunes as high as 500 feet. Hiking trails lead out from the park and into the Oregon Dunes National Recreation Area. The park offers more than two miles of beach access on the ocean and half a mile along the Umpqua River. The adjacent lighthouse is still in operation and tours are available during the summer season.

Location: On the Umpqua River; The Oregon Coast Map 5, grid c7.

Campsites, facilities: There are 24 tent sites, 20 sites with full hookups for trailers or RVs up to 45 feet long, two cabins, and six deluxe yurts. Drinking water, garbage bins, and picnic tables are provided. Flush toilets, showers, and firewood are available. Boat docks and launching facilities are on the Umpqua River. Leashed pets are permitted.

Reservations, fees: Reservations accepted ($6 reservation fee). Sites are $13–17 per night, cabins are $35 per night, yurts are $50–60 per night; an additional vehicle is $7 per night. Major credit cards accepted. Open year-round.

Directions: From Eugene drive south on I-5 to Exit 162 and Highway 38. Turn west on Highway 38 and drive 64 miles to Reedsport and U.S. 101. Turn south on U.S. 101 and drive six miles to Umpqua Lighthouse Road. Turn right and drive one mile to the park.

Contact: Umpqua Lighthouse State Park, c/o Sunset Bay State Park, 10965 Cape Arago Hwy., Coos Bay, OR 97420; 800/551-6949 or 541/271-4118, reservations 800/452-5687.

85 William M. Tugman State Park

7

This campground is set along the shore of Eel Lake, which offers almost five miles of shoreline for swimming, fishing, boating, and sailing. It's perfect for bass fishing. A boat ramp is available, but there is a 10 mph speed limit for boats. Oregon Dunes National Recreation Area is across the highway. Hiking is available just a few miles north at Umpqua Lighthouse State Park. A trail along the south end of the lake allows hikers to get away from the developed areas of the park and explore the lake's many outlets. This camp has gone from 3 to 13 yurts, and they are almost always booked up.

Location: On Eel Lake; The Oregon Coast Map 5, grid d7.

Campsites, facilities: There are 99 sites with water and electrical hookups for trailers or RVs up to 50 feet long, a special camping area for hikers, and 13 yurts. Electricity, drinking water, and picnic tables are provided. Flush toilets, sanitary services, showers, firewood, and a picnic shelter are available. Some facilities are wheelchair-accessible. Boat docks and launching facilities are nearby. Leashed pets are permitted.

Reservations, fees: Reservations accepted. Sites are $15 per night, $4 per night for hikers/bicyclists; yurts are $27 per night; $7 per night for an additional vehicle. Major credit cards accepted. Open year-round.

Directions: From Eugene drive south on I-5 to Exit 162 and Highway 38. Turn west on Highway 38 and drive 64 miles to Reedsport and U.S. 101. Turn south on U.S. 101 and drive eight miles to the park entrance on the left.

Contact: Sunset Bay State Park, 10965 Cape Arago Hwy., Coos Bay, OR 97420; 541/759-3604 or 800/551-6949, reservations 800/452-5687.

86 North Lake Resort and Marina

8

This 40-acre resort along the shore of Tenmile Lake is wooded and secluded, with a private beach, a perfect layover spot for U.S. 101 travelers. The lake has a full-service marina, and bass fishing can be good here.

Location: On Tenmile Lake; The Oregon Coast Map 5, grid d7.

Campsites, facilities: There are 40 tent sites and 60 RV sites, some with full hookups. Picnic tables are provided. Flush toilets, sanitary services, showers, firewood, a store, ice,

electricity, phone/modem hookups, cable TV, drinking water, coin-operated laundry facilities, horseshoe pits, a volleyball court, and sewer hookups are available. A café, boat docks, launching facilities, and rentals are nearby. Leashed pets are permitted.

Reservations, fees: Reservations accepted. Tent sites are $18 per night, RV sites are $23 per night. Senior discount available. Open March through October.

Directions: From Eugene drive south on I-5 to Exit 162 and Highway 38. Turn west on Highway 38 and drive 64 miles to Reedsport and U.S. 101. Turn south on U.S. 101 and drive 11 miles to the Lakeside exit. Take that exit and drive east on North Lake Avenue for three-quarters of a mile, then continue on North Lake Road for one-half mile to the resort on the left.

Contact: North Lake Resort and Marina, 2090 North Lake Ave., Lakeside, OR 97449; 541/759-3515; fax 541/759-3515.

87 Osprey Point RV Resort

7

This is one of Oregon's premier bass fishing lakes and yet only three miles from the ocean. The resort is situated in a large open area adjacent to Tenmile Lake and a half mile from North Lake. The lakes are connected by a navigable canal. Nearby hiking trails are in the Oregon Dunes National Recreation Area, and wooded trails are in Elliot State Forest. This is a destination resort more than an overnight stop, with weekend barbecues and occasional live entertainment.

Location: On Tenmile Lake; The Oregon Coast Map 5, grid d7.

Campsites, facilities: There are 20 tent sites, and 132 sites for tents, trailers, or RVs of any size. RV sites have electricity, drinking water, sewer, picnic tables, fire pits, phone, and cable TV provided. The park is also modem friendly. Drinking water, restrooms with flush toilets and showers, garbage bins, dump station, coin-operated laundry facilities, restaurant, cocktail lounge, grocery store, full service marina with boat docks, launch, fishing pier, fish-cleaning station, horseshoe pits, volleyball, tether ball, a recreation hall, video arcade, beauty and barber shops, and pizza parlor are available. Leashed pets are permitted.

Reservations, fees: Reservations accepted. Sites are $17–30 per night, $2.50 per each additional vehicle; winter rates are $16–28 per night. Major credit cards accepted. Open year-round.

Directions: From Coos Bay, drive north on U.S. 101 for 13 miles to the Lakeside exit. Take that exit east into town (across the railroad tracks) to North Lake Road. Turn left (north) on North Lake Road and drive one-half mile to the resort on the right.

Contact: Osprey Point RV Resort, 1505 North Lake Rd., Lakeside, OR 97449; 541/759-2801; fax 541/759-3198; website: www.osprey point.net.

88 Eel Creek

8

This campground along Eel Creek is near both Eel and Tenmile Lakes. Water skiing is allowed on Tenmile Lake but not at Eel Lake. Nearby trails offer access to the Umpqua Dunes Scenic Area, where you'll find spectacular scenery in an area closed to off-road vehicles. Off-road access is available at Spinreel.

Location: Near Eel Lake in Oregon Dunes National Recreation Area; The Oregon Coast Map 5, grid d7.

Campsites, facilities: There are 52 sites for tents, trailers, or RVs up to 35 feet long. Picnic tables, garbage service, and fire grills

are provided. Drinking water and flush and vault toilets are available. Boat docks, launching facilities, and rentals are nearby. Leashed pets are permitted.

Reservations, fees: No reservations accepted. Sites are $13 per night, $7 per night for an additional vehicle. Senior discount available. Open year-round.

Directions: From Eugene drive south on I-5 to Exit 162 and Highway 38. Turn west on Highway 38 and drive 64 miles to Reedsport and U.S. 101. Turn south on U.S. 101 and drive 10.5 miles to the park entrance.

Contact: Oregon Dunes National Recreation Area, 855 U.S. Hwy. 101, Reedsport, OR 97467; 541/271-3611; fax 541/750-7244.

89 Spinreel

6

This campground, primarily for off-road-vehicle enthusiasts, is several miles inland at the outlet of Tenmile Lake in the Oregon Dunes National Recreation Area. A boat launch is near the camp. Other recreational opportunities include hiking trails and off-road-vehicle access to the dunes. Off-road-vehicle rentals are available adjacent to the camp.

Location: On Tenmile Creek in Oregon Dunes National Recreation Area; The Oregon Coast Map 5, grid d7.

Campsites, facilities: There are 36 sites for tents, trailers, or RVs up to 40 feet long. Drinking water, garbage service, and flush toilets are available. Picnic tables and fire grills are provided. Firewood, a store, and a coin laundry are nearby. Boat docks, launching facilities, and rentals are on Tenmile Lake. Leashed pets are permitted.

Reservations, fees: No reservations accepted. Sites are $13 per night. Senior discount available. Open year-round.

Directions: From Coos Bay drive north on U.S. 101 for 10 miles to the campground entrance road (well signed). Turn northwest and drive one mile to the campground.

Contact: Oregon Dunes National Recreation Area, 855 U.S. Hwy. 101, Reedsport, OR 97467; 541/271-3611; fax 541/750-7244.

90 Oregon Dunes KOA

5

This ATV-friendly park has direct access to Oregon Dunes National Recreation Area with miles of ATV trails. It is a fairly open campground with grass and young trees. A small lake is on the premises, and the ocean is a 15-minute drive away. Mill Casino is about six miles south on U.S. 101. Freshwater and ocean fishing are nearby. A golf course is about five miles away.

Location: Six miles north of North Bend, next to the Oregon Dunes National Recreation Area; The Oregon Coast Map 5, grid d7.

Campsites, facilities: There are 10 tent sites, 63 sites for tents, trailers, or RVs of any size, and three cabins. RV sites have electricity, drinking water, sewer, picnic tables, fire pits, and satellite TV provided. There is a data port on-site for computers. Drinking water, restrooms with flush toilets and showers, garbage bins, wheelchair facilities, coin-operated laundry, minimart, horseshoe pits, volleyball, and a picnic shelter with electricity, sink, and electric cooktops are available. ORV rentals are nearby. Leashed pets are permitted, except in cabins.

Reservations, fees: Reservations accepted. Sites are $19–46 per night, $2 per each additional vehicle. Major credit cards accepted. Open year-round.

Directions: From Coos Bay drive north on U.S. 101 past North Bend for six miles to milepost 229 and the campground entrance road on the left.

Contact: Oregon Dunes KOA, 68632 U.S. Hwy. 101, North Bend, OR 97459; 541/756-4851; fax 541/756-8838.

91 Wild Mare Horse Camp

7

This horse camp has paved parking, with single and double corrals. No off-road vehicles are allowed within the campground. Horses can be ridden straight out into the dunes—they cannot be ridden on the developed trails. The heavily treed shoreline gives rise to treed sites, with some bushes.

Location: Oregon Dunes National Recreation Area; The Oregon Coast Map 5, grid e6.

Campsites, facilities: There are 12 horse campsites for tents, trailers, or RVs up to 50 feet long. There is a maximum of two vehicles per site. Picnic tables and fire pits are provided. Drinking water, vault toilets, and garbage bins are available. Leashed pets are permitted.

Reservations, fees: Reservations accepted ($8.65 reservation fee). Sites are $12 per night, $7 per each additional vehicle. Major credit cards accepted. Senior discount available. Open year-round.

Directions: From Coos Bay drive north on U.S. 101 for 1.5 miles to Horsfall Dunes and Beach Access Road. Turn left and drive west for one mile to the campground access road. Turn right and drive three-quarters of a mile to the campground on the left.

Contact: Oregon Dunes National Recreation Area, 855 U.S. Hwy. 101, Reedsport, OR 97467; 541/271-3611, reservations 877/444-6777; fax 541/750-7244.

92 Bluebill

 6

This campground gets very little camping pressure although there are some good hiking trails available. It's next to little Bluebill Lake, which sometimes dries up during the summer. A one-mile trail goes around the lake bed. The camp is a short distance from Horsfall Lake, which is surrounded by private property. If you continue west on the forest road, you'll come to a picnicking and parking area near the beach that has off-road-vehicle access to the dunes at the Horsfall day-use area or Horsfall Beach.

Location: On Bluebill Lake in Oregon Dunes National Recreation Area; The Oregon Coast Map 5, grid e6.

Campsites, facilities: There are 18 sites for tents, trailers, or RVs up to 30 feet long. Picnic tables, garbage service, and fire grills are provided. Flush toilets and drinking water are available. Leashed pets are permitted.

Reservations, fees: No reservations accepted. Sites are $13 per night, and $7 per night for each additional vehicle. Senior discount available. Open May through November.

Directions: From Coos Bay drive north on U.S. 101 for 1.5 miles north to Horsfall Dunes and Beach Access Road. Turn west and drive one mile to Horsfall Road. Turn northwest and drive two miles to the campground entrance.

Contact: Oregon Dunes National Recreation Area, 855 U.S. Hwy. 101, Reedsport, OR 97467; 541/271-3611; fax 541/750-7244.

93 Horsfall

 4

This campground is actually a nice, large paved area for parking RVs. It's the staging area for off-road-vehicle access into the southern section of Oregon Dunes National Recreation Area. If Horsfall is full, try Horsfall Beach nearby, an overflow area with 34 tent and RV sites.

Location: In Oregon Dunes National Recreation Area; The Oregon Coast Map 5, grid e6.

Campsites, facilities: There are 70 sites for trailers or RVs up to 50 feet in length. Drinking water, garbage service, coin-operated showers, a pay phone, and flush toilets are available. Leashed pets are permitted.

Reservations, fees: Reservations accepted ($8.65 reservation fee). Sites are $13 per night, $7 per night for an additional vehicle. Senior discount available. Open year-round.

Directions: From Coos Bay drive north on U.S. 101 for 1.5 miles to Horsfall Road. Turn west on Horsfall Road and drive about one mile to the campground access road. Turn on the campground access road (well signed) and drive one-half mile to the campground.

Contact: Oregon Dunes National Recreation Area, 855 U.S. Hwy. 101, Reedsport, OR 97467; 541/271-3611, reservations 877/444-6777; fax 541/750-7244; website (for reservations): www.reserveusa.com.

94 Sunset Bay State Park

8

Situated in one of the most scenic areas on the Oregon Coast, this park features beautiful, sandy beaches protected by towering sea cliffs. A network of hiking trails connects Sunset Bay with nearby Shore Acres and Cape Arago Parks. Swimming, boating, fishing, clamming, and golfing are some of the options here.

Location: Near Sunset Bay; The Oregon Coast Map 5, grid f5.

Campsites facilities: There are 66 sites for tents or self-contained RVs, 29 sites with full hookups for trailers or RVs up to 47 feet long, a separate area for hikers and bicyclists, eight yurts, and two group camps. Drinking water, picnic tables, garbage bins, and fire grills are provided. Flush toilets, showers, a meeting hall, a boat ramp, and firewood are available. A restaurant is within three miles. Some facilities are wheelchair-accessible. Leashed pets are permitted.

Reservations, fees: Reservations accepted ($6 reservation fee). Sites are $16–19 per night, sites for hikers/bicyclists are $4 per night, yurts are $27 per night, the group camp is $60 per night for up to 25 people; $7 per night for an additional vehicle. Major credit cards accepted. Open year-round.

Directions: In Coos Bay, take the Charleston Ocean Beaches exit to Newmark Avenue and drive west for three miles to Cape Arago Highway. Turn left and drive about five miles south to Charleston and cross the South Slough Bridge. Continue on Cape Arago Highway about three miles to the park entrance on the left.

Contact: Sunset Bay State Park, 10965 Cape Arago Hwy., Coos Bay, OR 97420; 541/888-4902, reservations 800/452-5687.

95 Bastendorff Beach Park

🚶 🚴 🏊 🎣 🚗
🐕 🍴 ♿ 🚐 ⛺ 8

This campground provides access to the ocean and a small lake. Nearby activities include sand-dune buggy riding, golfing, clamming, crabbing, fishing, swimming, whale-watching, and boating. Horses may be rented near Bandon. A nice side trip is to Shore Acres State Park and Botanical Gardens, about 2.5 miles away.

Location: Near Cape Arago State Park; The Oregon Coast Map 5, grid f5.

Campsites, facilities: There are 25 tent sites, 56 sites for trailers or RVs with partial

hookups, and two cabins. Drinking water, picnic tables, restrooms, coin-operated showers, a sanitary dump, a public phone, and a fireplace are provided. A fish-cleaning station, horseshoe pits, a playground, basketball courts, and a picnic area with shelter and barbecue are also available. The facilities are wheelchair-accessible. Leashed pets are permitted.

Reservations, fees: Reservations accepted for the shelter and cabins only. Sites are $15–18 per night, $10–14 in offseason. Open year-round.

Directions: In Coos Bay, take the Charleston Ocean Beaches exit to Newmark Avenue and drive west for three miles to Cape Arago Highway. Turn left and drive about five miles south to Charleston and cross the South Slough Bridge. Continue on Cape Arago Highway about two miles to the park entrance.

Contact: Coos County Parks, Coos County Courthouse, 250 N. Baxter St., Coquille, OR 97423, or Bastendorff Beach Park, 4250 Bastendorff Beach Rd., Coos Bay, OR 97420; 541/888-5353, reservations (shelter and cabin only) 541/396-3121, ext. 354; website: www.cooscountyparks.com.

96 Charleston Marina RV Park

🚶 🏊 🎣 🚗
🐕 🍴 ♿ 🚐 ⛺ 7

This large, developed park and marina is near Charleston on the Pacific Ocean. Recreational activities in and near the campground include hiking, swimming, clamming, crabbing, boating, huckleberry and blackberry picking, and fishing for tuna, salmon, and halibut.

Location: On Coos Bay; The Oregon Coast Map 5, grid f5.

Campsites, facilities: There are 108 sites for tents, trailers, or RVs up to 50 feet, and two yurts. Drinking water, cable TV, restrooms, showers, a sanitary dump, a public phone, a laundry room, a playground, and LP gas are available. A marina with a boarding dock and launch ramp are on-site. The facilities are wheelchair-accessible. Leashed pets are permitted.

Reservations, fees: Reservations recommended. Sites are $10–19 per night, $30 per night for yurts. Open year-round.

Directions: In Coos Bay take the Charleston Ocean Beaches exit to Newmark Avenue and drive west for three miles to Cape Arago Highway. Turn left and drive about five miles south to Charleston and cross the South Slough Bridge; continue to Boat Basin Drive. Turn right and drive one-quarter mile to Kingfisher Drive. Turn right and drive 200 feet to the campground on the left.

Contact: Charleston Marina RV Park, P.O. Box 5409, Charleston, OR 97420-0607; 541/888-9512; fax 541/888-6111; website: www.charlestonmarina.com.

97 Oceanside RV Park

 7

This is one of several private, developed parks in the Charleston area. The park is within walking distance of the Pacific Ocean, with opportunities for swimming, fishing, clamming, crabbing, and boating. A marina is 1.5 miles away.

Location: Near the Pacific Ocean; The Oregon Coast Map 5, grid f5.

Campsites, facilities: There are 10 tent sites and 70 full-hookup sites (30- or 50-amp) for trailers or RVs. Restrooms, showers, a public phone, modem hookups, a fish-cleaning station, and LP gas are available. Equipment for crabbing and clamming is also available. The facilities are wheelchair-accessible. Leashed pets are permitted.

Reservations, fees: Reservations recommended. Sites are $15–22 per night in summer, $9–16 in offseason. Open year-round.

Directions: In Coos Bay, take the Charleston Ocean Beaches exit to Newmark Avenue and drive west for three miles to Cape Arago Highway. Turn left and drive about five miles south to Charleston and cross the South Slough Bridge. Continue on Cape Arago Highway for 1.8 miles to the park entrance on the right.

Contact: Oceanside RV Park, 9838 Cape Arago Hwy., Charleston, OR 97420; 541/888-2598 or 800/570-2598; email: oceanside@harborside.com; website: www.harborside.com/~oceanside.

98 Kelley's RV Park

5

This is a clean, well-maintained RV park in the town of Coos Bay, well known for its fishing for salmon and rockfish and for its lumber industry. A shaded picnic area here overlooks the bay. A full-service marina is a giant plus.

Location: Near Coos Bay; The Oregon Coast Map 5, grid f7.

Campsites, facilities: There are 38 sites for tents, trailers, or RVs of any length; three are drive-through sites. Electricity, drinking water, sewer hookups, and picnic tables are provided. Flush toilets and a laundry room are available. Boat docks and launching facilities are nearby. Bottled gas, a store, and café are available within a mile. Leashed pets are permitted.

Reservations, fees: Reservations accepted. Sites are $15–16 per night. Open year-round.

Directions: In Coos Bay on U.S. 101, drive to the Charleston exit. Take that exit to South Empire

Boulevard and drive 4.5 miles to the park at 555 S. Empire Boulevard.

Contact: Kelley's RV Park, 555 S. Empire Blvd., Coos Bay, OR 97420; 541/888-6531.

99 Bullards Beach State Park

7

The Coquille River is the centerpiece of this park, which has good fishing in season for both boaters and crabbers, with four miles of shore access. If fishing is not your thing, the park also has several hiking trails. The Coquille River Lighthouse is at the end of the road that wanders through the park. During the summer there are tours to the tower. Equestrians can explore the seven-mile horse trail.

Location: On the Coquille River; The Oregon Coast Map 5, grid g5.

Campsites, facilities: There are 185 sites with full or partial hookups for trailers or RVs up to 64 feet long; 13 yurts are also available, including three that are wheelchair-accessible. Each yurt can sleep five people. A special area for horses and an area reserved for hikers and bicyclists are also available. Drinking water, garbage bins, picnic tables, and fire grills are provided. Flush toilets, a sanitary disposal station, showers, firewood, a yurt meeting hall, and a loading ramp for horses are available. Some facilities are wheelchair-accessible. Boat docks and launching facilities are in the park on the Coquille River. Leashed pets are permitted.

Reservations, fees: Reservations accepted ($6 reservation fee). Sites are $15–19 per night, yurts are $27 per night, and sites for hikers/bicyclists are $4 per night; additional vehicles are $7 per night. Horse camping is $13 per night and $1.50 per night per horse. Major credit cards accepted. Open year-round.

Directions: In Coos Bay drive south on U.S. 101 for about 22 miles to the park on the right (two miles north of Bandon).

Contact: Bullards Beach State Park, P.O. Box 569, Bandon, OR 97411; 800/452-5687 or 541/347-2209.

100 Bandon RV Park

4

This in-town RV park is a good base for many adventures. Rock hounds will enjoy combing for agates and other semiprecious stones hidden along the beaches, while kids can explore the West Coast Game Park Walk-Through Safari petting zoo seven miles south of town. Bandon State Park, four miles south of town, has a nice wading spot in the creek at the north end of the park. Nearby recreation opportunities include two 18-hole golf courses, a riding stable, and tennis courts. Bullards State Beach is about 2.5 miles north.

Location: Near Bullards Beach State Park; The Oregon Coast Map 5, grid h5.

Campsites, facilities: There are 44 sites for trailers or RVs of any length; some are drive-through sites. Electricity, drinking water, cable TV, and sewer hookups are provided. Flush toilets, sanitary services, showers, and a laundry room are available. Bottled gas and a store are within two blocks. Boat docks and launching facilities are nearby. Leashed pets are permitted.

Reservations, fees: Reservations accepted. Sites are $18–20 per night. Major credit cards accepted. Open year-round.

Directions: From Coos Bay drive south on U.S. 101 for 26 miles to Bandon and the Highway 42S junction. Continue south on U.S. 101 for one block to the park.

Contact: Bandon RV Park, 935 2nd Street SE, Bandon, OR 97411; 541/347-4122, reservations 800/393-4122.

101 Laverne County Park

🚶 🚴 🏊 🎣 🛶
🐕 ⛺ ♿ 🚐 ⛺ **9**

This beautiful park is on the river with a small falls and many trees, including a myrtlewood grove and old-growth Douglas fir. Mountain bikers can take an old wagon road, and golfers can enjoy any of several courses. There are a few hiking trails and a very popular swimming hole. Fishing includes salmon, steelhead, and trout, and the wildlife includes deer, elk, bear, raccoons, and cougar. Side trips include the museums at Myrtle Point and Coos Bay, local Indian items, and an old stagecoach house in Dora.

Location: In Fairview on the North Fork of the Coquille River; The Oregon Coast Map 5, grid g7.

Campsites, facilities: There are 76 sites for tents, trailers, or RVs of any size. There is also a large group site at West Laverne B with 22 RV hookups. One cabin is also available. Drinking water, electricity, picnic tables, and fire pits are provided. Restrooms with flush toilets and showers (two barrier-free), garbage bins, dump station, playground, four cooking shelters with barbecue, a swimming hole (unsupervised), horseshoe pits, volleyball and baseball areas are available. Ice and a restaurant are within 1.5 miles. Propane, bottled gas, a store, and gasoline are within five miles. Leashed pets are permitted, and there is a pet area.

Reservations, fees: Reservations for group site and cabin ($5 reservation fee). Family sites are $10–15 per night, with an additional charge of $5 per each additional vehicle. Cabin is $25–30 per night. Senior discount available for Coos County residents. Open year-round.

Directions: From Coos Bay drive south on U.S. 101 for six miles to the junction with Highway 42. Turn east and drive 11 miles to Coquille and West Central. Turn left and drive a half mile to Fairview McKinley Road. Turn right and drive eight miles to the Fairview Store. Continue east another five miles (past the store) to the park on the right.

Contact: Laverne County Park, Coos County, 61217 Fairview McKinley Rd., Coquille, OR 97423; 541/396-2344; website: www.co.coos.or.us.

102 Loon Lake Recreation Area Campground

🚶 🏊 🚐 🏠 🐕 🚐 ⛺ **8**

Loon Lake was created 1,400 years ago when a nearby mountain crumbled and slid downhill, damming the creek with house-sized boulders. Today the lake is a half mile wide and nearly two miles long, covers 260 acres, and is more than 100 feet deep in places. It is ideally located to provide a warm, wind-sheltered summer climate for various water activities. A nature trail leads to a waterfall about a half mile away. Evening interpretive programs are held during summer weekends.

Location: On Loon Lake; The Oregon Coast Map 6, grid d2.

Campsites, facilities: There are 61 sites for tents, trailers, or RVs of any size. There are also five group sites for up to 15 people per site. Picnic tables and fire pits are provided. Drinking water, restrooms with flush toilets and showers, garbage bins, dump station, a sand beach, boat ramp and moorings, and gasoline are available. Leashed pets are permitted.

Reservations, fees: Reservations required for group sites only ($6 reservation fee). Family sites are $12–13 per night, with an additional charge of $7 per each additional vehicle. Group sites are $35 per night. Senior discount available. Open late May through mid-September, weather permitting.

Directions: From Eugene drive south on I-5 to Exit 162 and Highway 38. Turn west on Highway 38 and drive 43 miles to milepost 13.5 and County Road 3 exit. Turn south and drive 7.5 miles to the campground.

Contact: Bureau of Land Management, Coos Bay District Office, 1300 Airport Ln., North Bend, OR 97459; 541/756-0100, reservations 800/452-5687; fax 541/751-4303.

103 Loon Lake Lodge Resort

8

This resort has one mile of lake frontage and is nestled among the tall trees on pretty Loon Lake. It's not a long drive from either U.S. 101 or I-5, making it an ideal layover spot for travelers eager to get off the highway. The lake offers good bass fishing, swimming, boating, and water-skiing.

Location: On Loon Lake; The Oregon Coast Map 6, grid d2.

Campsites, facilities: There are 100 sites for tents, trailers, or RVs up to 32 feet—50 are partial hookups; group sites and cabins are also available. Electricity, drinking water, a public phone, security, a game room, restaurant, bar, grocery store, ice, gas, and a beach are available. A boat ramp, dock, marina, and rentals are also available. Leashed pets are permitted.

Reservations, fees: Reservations recommended. Sites are $16–19 per night. Cabins are $54–69 per night. Major credit cards accepted. Open year-round.

Directions: From Eugene drive south on I-5 to Exit 162 and Highway 38. Turn west on Highway 38 and drive 43 miles to milepost 13.5 and County Road 3 exit. Turn south and drive 8.2 miles to the resort on the right.

Contact: Loon Lake Lodge Resort, 9011 Loon Lake Rd., Reedsport, OR 97467; 541/599-2244; fax 541/599-2274.

104 Tyee

 7

Here's a classic spot, set along the Umpqua River with great steelhead, salmon, and small mouth bass fishing in season. Boat launches are available a few miles upstream and downstream of the campground. The camp isn't far from I-5, and it's the only campground in the immediate vicinity. Another plus: this campground was renovated in 2001. Because this camp has become popular, another camp will be constructed 2.5 miles down the road, likely available starting 2002.

Location: On the Umpqua River; The Oregon Coast Map 6, grid d4.

Campsites, facilities: There are 15 sites for tents, trailers, or RVs up to 25 feet long. Drinking water, garbage service, fire grills, and picnic tables are provided. Vault toilets and a day-use area with horseshoe pits, and a pavilion with barbecue, water, electricity, and 10 tables are available. A camp host is on-site. A store is within one mile. Some facilities are wheelchair-accessible. Leashed pets are permitted.

Reservations, fees: No reservations accepted. Sites are $8 per night, $3 for each additional vehicle. Senior discount available. Open year-round.

Directions: From Roseburg drive north on I-5 to Exit 136 and Highway 138. Take that exit and drive west on Highway 138 for 12 miles. Cross Bullock Bridge and continue to County Road 57. Turn right and drive one-half mile to the campground entrance.

Contact: Bureau of Land Management, Roseburg District, 777 Garden Valley Blvd., Roseburg, OR 97470; 541/440-4930; fax 541/440-4948.

105 Park Creek

🐕 🏕 7

Want to be by yourself? You came to the right place. This pretty little campground offers peaceful, shady campsites under an old-growth canopy of Douglas fir, western hemlock, red cedar, and myrtlewood. Relax and enjoy nearby Park Creek and Middle Creeks.

Location: Near Coquille; The Oregon Coast Map 6, grid g3.

Campsites, facilities: There are 15 sites for tents, small trailers, or camping vans. Picnic tables and fire grills are provided. Vault toilets and garbage bins are available. There is no drinking water. Leashed pets are permitted.

Reservations, fees: No reservations accepted. There is no fee, but the stay limit is 14 days. Open year-round.

Directions: From Coos Bay drive south on U.S. 101 for six miles to the junction with Highway 42. Turn east and drive 11 miles to Coquille and Coquille Fairview Road. Turn east on Coquille Fairview Road and drive 7.5 miles to Fairview and Coos Bay Wagon Road. Turn right and drive four miles to Middle Creek Access Road. Turn east (left) and drive nine miles to the campground.

Contact: Bureau of Land Management, Coos Bay District, 1300 Airport Ln., North Bend, OR 97459; 541/756-0100; fax 541/751-4303; website: www.co.coos.or.us.

106 KOA Bandon-Port Orford

🚶 🏊 🐕 🛶 🚐 🏕 7

This spot is considered to be just a layover camp, but it offers large, secluded sites nestled among big trees and coastal ferns. A new pool and spa is now open. The Elk and Sixes Rivers, where the fishing can be good, are minutes away, and Cape Blanco State Park is just a few miles down the road.

Location: Near the Elk River; The Oregon Coast Map 7, grid a5.

Campsites, facilities: There are 46 tent sites and 26 drive-through sites for trailers or RVs of any length. Six cabins are also available. Picnic tables are provided. Flush toilets, bottled gas, sanitary services, showers, firewood, a recreation hall, a store, a laundry room, ice, a playground, electricity, drinking water, and sewer hookups are available. Pets and motorbikes are permitted.

Reservations, fees: Reservations accepted. Sites are $22–28 per night; cabins are $40 per night. The park is open year-round.

Directions: From Coos Bay drive south on U.S. 101 for 50 miles to the campground at milepost 286 near Langlois, on the west side of the highway.

Contact: KOA Bandon-Port Orford, 46612 U.S. Hwy. 101, Langlois, OR 97450; 541/348-2358.

107 Cape Blanco State Park

🚶 🚴 🐟 🛶
🐕 ♿ 🚐 🏕 8

This large park is named for the white *(blanco)* chalk appearance of the sea cliffs, which rise 200 feet above the ocean. Sea lions inhabit the offshore rocks, and trails and a road lead to the black sand beach below the cliffs. Another highlight is the good access to the Sixes River, which runs for more than two miles through the meadows and forests of the park. Trails for horseback riding are also available and there are more than eight miles of trails with many spectacular ocean vistas, woodland and wetland settings. Lighthouse and historic Hughes House tours are nearby.

Location: Between the Sixes and Elk Rivers; The Oregon Coast Map 7, grid b4.

Campsites, facilities: There are 54 sites with water and electrical hookups for tents, trailers, or RVs up to 65 feet long. Other options are a special camp for horses, a camping area reserved for hikers and bicyclists, four cabins, and one primitive group site that can accommodate 25 people. Garbage bins, picnic tables, drinking water, electrical hookups, and fire grills are provided. Firewood, flush toilets, showers, and a sanitary disposal station are available. Some facilities are wheelchair-accessible. Leashed pets are permitted.

Reservations, fees: Reservations accepted for cabins, group site, and horse camp ($6 reservation fee). Sites are $18 per night; cabins are $35 per night; and sites for hikers/bicyclists are $4 per night; $7 per night for all additional vehicles. Horse camping is $13 per night, plus $1.50 per horse per night. Major credit cards accepted. Open year-round.

Directions: From Coos Bay, turn south on U.S. 101 and drive approximately 46 miles (south of Sixes, five miles north of Port Orford) to Cape Blanco Road. Turn right (northwest) and drive five miles to the campground on the left.

Contact: Humbug Mountain State Park, P.O. Box 1345, Port Orford, OR 97465; 541/332-6774, reservations 800/452-5687. This park is under the same management as Humbug Mountain State Park.

108 Sixes River

🐟 🐕 🚐 ⛺ 6

Set along the banks of the Sixes River at an elevation of 4,303 feet, this site is a favorite of miners, fishermen, and nature lovers. There are opportunities to pan or sluice for gold year-round or through a special limited permit. Dredging is permitted from July 15 through September. The camp roads are paved.

Location: On the Sixes River; The Oregon Coast Map 7, grid b5.

Campsites, facilities: There are 19 sites for tents, trailers, or RVs up to 30 feet long. Picnic tables, garbage service, and fire grills are provided. Drinking water and vault toilets are available. Leashed pets are permitted.

Reservations, fees: No reservations accepted. Sites are $5 per night, plus $3 for each additional vehicle, with a 14-day stay limit. Senior discount available. Open year-round.

Directions: From Coos Bay drive south on U.S. 101 for 40 miles to Sixes and Sixes River Road. Turn left (east) on Sixes River Road and drive 12 miles to the campground. The last half mile is an unpaved road.

Contact: Bureau of Land Management, Coos Bay District, 1300 Airport Ln., North Bend, OR 97459; 541/756-0100; fax 541/751-4303; website: www.or.blm.gov/coosbay.

109 Elk River Campground

🐟 🚤 🐕 ♿ 🚐 ⛺ 7

This quiet and restful camp is an excellent base for fall and winter fishing on the Elk River, which is known for its premier salmon fishing. A one-mile private access road goes to the river, so guests get their personal fishing holes.

Location: Near the Elk River; The Oregon Coast Map 7, grid b5.

Campsites, facilities: There are 50 sites for tents, trailers, or RVs up to 40 feet long, all with full hookups. Picnic tables are provided. Drinking water, restrooms, showers, a sanitary dump station, a public phone, modem hookups, cable TV, and a laundry room are available. Recreational facilities include a sports field, horseshoes, a recreation hall, and a boat ramp. Some facilities are wheelchair-accessible. Leashed pets are permitted.

Reservations, fees: Reservations recommended. Sites are $11–15 per night. Weekly and monthly rates are available. Senior discount available. Open year-round.

Directions: From Port Orford drive north on U.S. 101 for 1.5 miles to Elk River Road (milepost 297). Turn right (east) on Elk River Road and drive 1.8 miles to the campground on the left.

Contact: Elk River Campground, 93363 Elk River Rd., Port Orford, OR 97465; 541/332-2255; fax 541/332-6033.

110 Laird Lake

8

This secluded campground is set at 1,600 feet elevation, along the shore of pretty Laird Lake (six feet at its deepest point) in a very private and scenic spot. Some old-growth cedar logs are in the lake. Most campers have no idea such a place exists in the area. This can be just what you're looking for if you're tired of fighting the crowds at the more developed camps along U.S. 101.

Location: On Laird Lake in Siskiyou National Forest; The Oregon Coast Map 7, grid b5.

Campsites, facilities: There are four tent sites, with additional dispersed space for camping. There is no drinking water, and all garbage must be packed out. Leashed pets are permitted.

Reservations, fees: No reservations; no fee. Open year-round.

Directions: From Port Orford drive north on U.S. 101 for three miles to County Road 208. Turn right and drive 7.5 miles southeast to Forest Road 5325. Turn southeast and drive 15.5 miles to the campground. The road is paved for 11 miles and rock surfaced for the last 4.5 miles to the campground.

Contact: Siskiyou National Forest, Powers Ranger District, Powers, OR 97466; 541/439-6200; fax 541/439-6217.

111 Butler Bar

6

This campground at an elevation of 800 feet is set back from the shore of the Elk River and surrounded by old-growth, hardwood forest, with some reforested areas nearby. Across the river is the Grassy Knob Wilderness, but it has no trails and is generally too rugged to hike. No fishing for steelhead or salmon is permitted here on the Elk River.

Location: On the Elk River in Siskiyou National Forest; The Oregon Coast Map 7, grid b5.

Campsites, facilities: There are seven sites for tents. Picnic tables and fire grills are provided. Drinking water and pit toilets are available, but all garbage must be packed out. Leashed pets are permitted.

Reservations, fees: No reservations; no fee. Open year-round.

Directions: From Port Orford drive north on U.S. 101 for three miles to County Road 208. Turn right and drive 7.5 miles southeast to Forest Road 5325. Turn southeast and drive 11 miles to the campground. The road is paved.

Contact: Siskiyou National Forest, Powers Ranger District, Powers, OR 97466; 541/439-6200; fax 541/439-6217.

112 Powers County Park

9

This private and secluded public park in a wooded, mountainous area is a great stop for travelers going between I-5 and the coast. A small lake at the park provides a spot for visitors to boat, swim, and fish for trout. Only nonmotorized boats allowed. On display at the park are an old steam donkey and a hand-carved totem pole. This park is reputed to have the biggest cedar tree in Oregon.

Location: Near the South Fork of the Coquille River; The Oregon Coast Map 7, grid b8.

Campsites, facilities: There are 40 sites for tents, trailers, or RVs. One cabin is also available. Drinking water, restrooms, showers, a sanitary dump, and a public phone are provided. Other facilities include a boat ramp, horseshoes, a playground, three large picnic shelters, tennis courts, and a recreation field. Supplies are available within one mile. Some facilities are wheelchair-accessible. Leashed pets are permitted.

Reservations, fees: No reservations for sites. Picnic shelters may be reserved. Sites are $10–15 per night, cabin is $25–30 per night. Senior discount available. Open year-round.

Directions: From Coos Bay drive south on U.S. 101 for six miles to the junction with Highway 42. Turn east and drive 20 miles to Myrtle Point. Continue on Highway 42 to the Powers Highway (Highway 242) exit. Turn southwest (right) and drive 19 miles to the park on the right.

Contact: Coos County Parks, Coos County Courthouse, 250 N. Baxter St., Coquille, OR 97423; 541/439-2791, reservations (for picnic shelters) 541/396-3121; website: www.co.coos.or.us.

113 Port Orford Trailer Village

5

The hosts make you feel at home at this friendly mom-and-pop campground in Port Orford. An informal group campfire and happy hour is scheduled each evening. Other nice touches include a small gazebo where you can get coffee each morning and a patio where you can sit. Fishing is good during the fall and winter on the nearby Elk and Sixes Rivers, and the campground has a smokehouse, a freezer, and a cleaning table.

Location: Near the Elk and Sixes Rivers; The Oregon Coast Map 7, grid c5.

Campsites, facilities: There are seven tent sites and 49 sites for trailers or RVs of any length; two are drive-through sites. Electricity, drinking water, sewer hookups, and picnic tables are provided. Flush toilets, bottled gas, sanitary services, showers, a recreation hall, and a laundry room are available. Boat docks and launching facilities are nearby. Lake, river, and ocean are all within 1.5 miles. Pets and motorbikes are permitted.

Reservations, fees: Reservations accepted. Sites are $18 per night. Senior discount available. Open year-round.

Directions: In Port Orford on U.S. 101, drive to Madrona Avenue. Turn east and drive one block to Port Orford Loop. Turn north and drive one-half mile to the camp on the left side.

Contact: Port Orford Trailer Village, P.O. Box 697, Port Orford, OR 97465; 541/332-1041.

114 Humbug Mountain State Park

7

The park and campground are dominated by Humbug Mountain (1,756 feet elevation) and surrounded by forested hills. The campground enjoys some of the warmest weather on the Oregon coast. Windsurfing and scuba diving are popular, as is hiking the three-mile trail to Humbug Peak. Both ocean and freshwater fishing are accessible nearby.

Location: Near the Pacific Ocean; The Oregon Coast Map 7, grid c5.

Campsites, facilities: There are 63 tent sites and 35 sites with full hookups for trailers or RVs up to 55 feet long. A special camping area is provided for hikers and bicyclists. Fire grills, picnic tables, garbage bins, and drinking water are provided. Flush toilets, showers, and firewood are available. Leashed pets are permitted.

Reservations, fees: No reservations. Sites are $16–18 per night; $7 per night for all additional vehicles. The camping area for hikers/bicyclists is $4 per night. Open year-round.

Directions: From Port Orford drive south on U.S. 101 for six miles to the park entrance on the left.

Contact: Humbug Mountain State Park, P.O. Box 1345, Port Orford, OR 97465; 541/332-6774.

115 Daphne Grove

🐕 ♿ 🚐 ⛺ 7

This prime spot (at 1,000 feet elevation) along the South Fork of the Coquille River, surrounded by old-growth Douglas fir, cedar, and maple, is far enough out of the way to attract little attention. No fishing is allowed. The road is paved all the way to, and in, the campground, a plus for RVs and "city cars."

Location: On the South Fork of the Coquille River in Siskiyou National Forest; The Oregon Coast Map 7, grid c8.

Campsites, facilities: There are 15 sites for tents, trailers, or RVs up to 35 feet long. There is one group site that can accommodate up to 25 people. Picnic tables, garbage bins, and fire grills are provided. Vault toilets and drinking water are available. Some facilities are wheelchair-accessible. Leashed pets are permitted.

Reservations, fees: No reservations accepted. Sites are $8 per night from late May to late September, senior discount available; free the rest of the year. Phone the Powers Ranger District for current group rates. Open year-round, with limited winter facilities.

Directions: From Coos Bay drive south on U.S. 101 for six miles to the junction with Highway 42. Turn east and drive 20 miles to Myrtle Point. Continue on Highway 42 to

Powers Highway (Highway 242). Turn southwest (right) and drive 18 miles to Powers and County Road 90. Turn south and drive 4.3 miles to Forest Road 33. Turn south and drive 10.5 miles to the campground entrance.

Contact: Siskiyou National Forest, Powers Ranger District, Powers, OR 97466; 541/439-6200; fax 541/439-6217.

116 Myrtle Grove

🏃 🐕 ⛺ 6

This U.S. Forest Service campground is along the South Fork of the Coquille River, a little downstream from Daphne Grove, at an elevation of 500 feet. No fishing is allowed. Campsites are set under a canopy of big leaf maple and Douglas fir in a narrow, steep canyon. The Big Tree Recreation Site, home to a huge Port Orford cedar, is a few miles away. A prime hike can be made on the trail that runs adjacent to Elk Creek. (The road to Big Tree may be closed because of slides, so be sure to check with the ranger district in advance.)

Location: On the South Fork of the Coquille River in Siskiyou National Forest; The Oregon Coast Map 7, grid c8.

Campsites, facilities: There are five tent sites. Picnic tables and fire grills are provided. Pit toilets are available. There is no drinking water, and all garbage must be packed out. Leashed pets are permitted.

Reservations, fees: No reservations; no fee. Open year-round.

Directions: From Coos Bay drive south on U.S. 101 for six miles to the junction with Highway 42. Turn east and drive 20 miles to Myrtle Point. Continue on Highway 42 to Powers Highway (Highway 242). Turn southwest (right) and drive 18 miles to Powers and County Road 90. Turn south and drive 4.3 miles to Forest Road 33. Turn south to the camp. The road is paved all the way to the camp.

Contact: Siskiyou National Forest, Powers Ranger District, 42861 Highway 242, Powers, OR 96466; 541/ 439-6200; 541/ 439-6217.

117 Squaw Lake

8

This campground (at 2,200 feet elevation) along the shore of one-acre Squaw Lake is set in rich, old-growth forest. Squaw is more of a pond than a lake, but it is stocked with trout in the spring. Get there early; the fish are generally gone by midsummer. The trailheads for the Panther Ridge Trail and Coquille River Falls Trail are a 10-minute drive from the campground. It's strongly advised that you obtain a U.S. Forest Service map detailing the backcountry roads and trails.

Location: On Squaw Lake in Siskiyou National Forest; The Oregon Coast Map 7, grid c8.

Campsites, facilities: There are seven partially developed sites for tents, trailers, or RVs up to 21 feet. Pit toilets are available. There is no drinking water, and all garbage must be packed out. Leashed pets are permitted.

Reservations, fees: No reservations; no fee. Open year-round.

Directions: From Coos Bay drive south on U.S. 101 for six miles to the junction with Highway 42. Turn east and drive 20 miles to Myrtle Point. Continue on Highway 42 to Powers Highway (Highway 242). Turn southwest (right) and drive 18 miles to Powers and County Road 90. Turn south and drive 4.3 miles to Forest Road 33. Turn south and drive 12.5 miles to Forest Road 3348. Turn southeast and drive 4.5 miles to the campground entrance road. Turn east and drive one mile to the campground. The road is paved for all but the last half mile.

Contact: Siskiyou National Forest, Powers Ranger District, Powers, OR 97466; 541/439-6200; fax 541/439-6217.

118 Rock Creek

6

This little-known camp (elevation 1,400 feet) in a tree-shaded canyon is surrounded by old-growth forest and some reforested areas. It is set near Rock Creek, just upstream from its confluence with the South Fork of the Coquille River. No fishing is allowed. A good side trip here is the one-mile climb to Azalea Lake, which is stocked with trout. There are some hike-in campsites at the lake, but they have no piped drinking water. In July the azaleas are spectacular.

Location: Near the South Fork of the Coquille River in Siskiyou National Forest; The Oregon Coast Map 7, grid c8.

Campsites, facilities: There are seven sites for tents, trailers, or RVs. Picnic tables, drinking water, and fire grills are provided; all garbage must be packed out. Vault toilets and firewood are available. Leashed pets are permitted.

Reservations, fees: No reservations accepted. Sites are $8 per night from late May to late September, senior discount available; free the rest of the year. Open year-round, with limited winter facilities.

Directions: From Coos Bay drive south on U.S. 101 for six miles to the junction with Highway 42. Turn east and drive 20 miles to Myrtle Point. Continue on Highway 42 to Powers Highway (Highway 242). Turn southwest (right) and drive 18 miles to Powers and County Road 90. Turn south and drive 4.3 miles to Forest Road 33. Turn south and drive for 13 miles to the campground entrance road. Turn southwest and drive 1.5 miles to the campground. The road is paved all the way.

Contact: Siskiyou National Forest, Powers Ranger District, Powers, OR 97466; 541/439-6200; fax 541/439-6217.

119 Illahe

 7

This quiet and isolated camping area has great hiking opportunities, beginning at the nearby Upper Rogue River Trail. Boating and fishing are just a mile away at Foster Bar Campground. It's a pretty spot with privacy between sites and hidden from the majority of tourists. Deer are in abundance here.

Location: On the Rogue River in Siskiyou National Forest; The Oregon Coast Map 7, grid c8.

Campsites, facilities: There are 14 sites for tents, trailers, or RVs up to 21 feet long. Drinking water, fire rings, garbage bins, and picnic tables are provided. Flush toilets are available. A store is within five miles. Boat docks are nearby. Leashed pets are permitted.

Reservations, fees: No reservations accepted. Sites are $5 per night, plus $3 for each additional vehicle. Senior discount available. Open mid-May to mid-October.

Directions: From Gold Beach on U.S. 101, turn east on County Road 595. Drive east for 35 miles (it becomes Forest Road 33) to a junction for Illahe, Illahe Campground, and Foster Bar. Turn right on County Road 375 and drive five miles to the campground.

Contact: Siskiyou National Forest, Gold Beach Ranger District, 29279 Ellensburg Ave., Gold Beach, OR 97444; 541/247-3600; fax 541/247-3617.

120 Foster Bar

This camping area is on the banks of the Rogue River. At the nearby Rogue River Trail, there's a takeout point for rafters. Hiking op-

portunities are good and you can also fish from the river bar. Illahe Campground and Agness RV Park provide nearby camping options.

Location: On the Rogue River in Siskiyou National Forest; The Oregon Coast Map 7, grid d8.

Campsites, facilities: There are several dispersed sites for tents, trailers, or RVs up to 16 feet long, though access is difficult for RVs and trailers. Flush toilets, garbage bins, and boat-launching facilities are available, but there is no drinking water. Leashed pets are permitted.

Reservations, fees: No reservations; no fee. Open year-round.

Directions: From Gold Beach on U.S. 101, turn east on County Road 595 and drive 35 miles (it becomes Forest Road 33) to the junction for Illahe, Illahe Campground, and Foster Bar. Turn right on County Road 375 and drive five miles to the campground.

Contact: Siskiyou National Forest, Gold Beach Ranger District, 29279 Ellensburg Ave., Gold Beach, OR 97444; 541/247-3600; fax 541/247-3617.

121 Arizona Beach Campground

7

This pleasant campground offers grassy, tree-lined sites along half a mile of ocean beach frontage. Many of the RV sites provide ocean frontage. A creek runs through the campground, and you can swim at the mouth of it in the summer. Elk and deer roam nearby. A small lake is available for fishing.

Location: Near Gold Beach; The Oregon Coast Map 7, grid d5.

Campsites, facilities: There are 150 sites, including 48 tent sites, 78 sites for trailers or RVs of any length, including seven drive-through sites, and trailer rentals. Electricity, drinking water, sewer hookups, and picnic tables are provided. Flush toilets, bottled gas, sanitary services, showers, firewood, a store, a laundry room, recreation room, gold panning, and a playground are available. Leashed pets and motorbikes are permitted.

Reservations, fees: Reservations accepted. Tents sites are $16 per night, RV sites are $23–26 per night, trailer rentals are $60–90. Open year-round.

Directions: From Gold Beach drive north on U.S. 101 for 14 miles to the campground on the right.

Contact: Arizona Beach Campground, 36939 U.S. Hwy. 101, Gold Beach, OR 97444; 541/332-6491.

122 Honeybear Campground

🥾 🚲 🎣 🐕 🧺 🚐 ⛺ 10

This campground offers wooded sites with ocean views. The owners have built a huge, authentic chalet that contains a German deli, a recreation area, and a big dance floor. On summer nights they hold dances with live music. A restaurant is available on-site with authentic German food.

Location: Near Gold Beach; The Oregon Coast Map 7, grid d5.

Campsites, facilities: There are 20 tent sites and 65 sites for trailers or RVs of any length; 30 are drive-through sites with full hookups, 15 with patios. Picnic tables are provided. Flush toilets, electricity, drinking water, cable TV, sanitary services, showers, firewood, a recreation hall, a restaurant, a store, a laundry room, ice, and a playground are available. Leashed pets and motorbikes are permitted.

Reservations, fees: Reservations accepted. Sites are $14.95–25 per night. Open year-round, weather permitting.

Directions: From Gold Beach drive north on U.S. 101 for nine miles to Ophir Road near milepost 321. Turn north and drive two miles to the campground on the right side of the road.

Contact: Honeybear Campground, P.O. Box 97, Ophir, OR 97464; 541/247-2765 or 800/822-4444; website: www.honeybearrv.com.

123 Nesika Beach Trailer Park

🥾 🚲 🎣 🐕 🚐 ⛺ 7

This campground next to Nesika Beach is a good layover spot for U.S. 101 cruisers. An 18-hole golf course is close by.

Location: Near Gold Beach; The Oregon Coast Map 7, grid d5.

Campsites, facilities: There are six tent sites and 32 sites for trailers or RVs of any length. Electricity, drinking water, cable TV, sewer hookups, and picnic tables are provided. Flush toilets, sanitary services, showers, a store, a laundry room, and ice are available. Pets and motorbikes are permitted.

Reservations, fees: Reservations accepted. Sites are $12–19 per night. Senior discount available. Open year-round.

Directions: From Gold Beach drive north on U.S. 101 for six miles to Nesika Road. Turn left and drive three-quarters of a mile west to the campground on the right.

Contact: Nesika Beach Trailer Park, 32887 Nesika Rd., Gold Beach, OR 97444; 541/247-6077.

124 Quosatana

🥾 🚲 🎣 🛥 🐕 ♿ 🚐 ⛺ 6

This campground is set along the banks of the Rogue River upstream from the much smaller Lobster Creek Campground. In the campground are a large, grassy area and a barrier-free trail with interpretive signs.

Ocean access is just a short drive away, and the quaint town of Gold Beach offers a decent side trip. Nearby Otter Point State Park (day use only) has further recreation options. The Shrader Old-Growth Trail and Myrtle Tree Trail are nearby hiking opportunities. This is a good base camp for a hiking or fishing trip.

Location: On the Rogue River in Siskiyou National Forest; The Oregon Coast Map 7, grid e6.

Campsites, facilities: There are 42 sites for tents, trailers, or RVs up to 32 feet long. Drinking water, fire grills, garbage bins, and picnic tables are provided. Flush toilets, a sanitary disposal station, a fish-cleaning station, and a boat ramp are available. Some facilities are wheelchair-accessible. Leashed pets are permitted.

Reservations, fees: No reservations accepted. Sites are $8 per night, plus $3 for each additional vehicle. Senior discount available. Open year-round.

Directions: From Gold Beach on U.S. 101, turn east on County Road 595 and drive 13 miles (it becomes Forest Road 33) to the campground on the left.

Contact: Siskiyou National Forest, Gold Beach Ranger District, 29279 Ellensburg Ave., Gold Beach, OR 97444; 541/247-3600; fax 541/247-3617.

125 Lobster Creek

 6

This small campground on a river bar along the Rogue River is about a 15-minute drive from Gold Beach, and it makes a good base for a fishing trip. It's heavily forested with myrtles and Douglas fir, and the Shrader Old-Growth Trail and Myrtle Tree Trail are nearby.

Location: On the Rogue River in Siskiyou National Forest; The Oregon Coast Map 7, grid e6.

Campsites, facilities: There are six sites for tents, trailers, or RVs up to 21 feet long.

Fire rings and picnic tables are provided. Flush toilets are available, but there is no drinking water and all garbage must be packed out. A boat launch is also available. Leashed pets are permitted.

Reservations, fees: No reservations accepted. Sites are $5 per night, plus $3 for each additional vehicle. Camping is also permitted on a gravel bar area for $3 per night. Senior discount available. Open mid-May to mid-October.

Directions: From Gold Beach on U.S. 101, turn east on County Road 595 and drive 10 miles (it becomes Forest Road 33) to the campground on the left.

Contact: Siskiyou National Forest, Gold Beach Ranger District, 29279 Ellensburg Ave., Gold Beach, OR 97444; 541/247-3600; fax 541/247-3617.

126 Kimball Creek Bend

 6

This campground on the scenic Rogue River is just far enough from the coast to provide quiet and its own distinct character. Nearby recreation options include an 18-hole golf course, hiking trails, and boating facilities.

Location: On the Rogue River; The Oregon Coast Map 7, grid e5.

Campsites, facilities: There are 13 tent sites and 56 sites for trailers or RVs of any length; 18 are drive-through sites. Electricity, drinking water, sewer hookups, and picnic tables are provided. Flush toilets, bottled gas, sanitary services, showers, a recreation hall, a store, a laundry room, ice, and a playground are available. Boat docks and launching facilities are nearby. Leashed pets are permitted.

Reservations, fees: Reservations accepted. Sites are $20–29.50 per night. Open year-round.

Directions: From Gold Beach drive north on U.S. 101 for one mile (on the north side of the Rogue River) to Rogue River Road. Turn east and drive about eight miles to the campground.

Contact: Kimball Creek Bend, 97136 North Bank Rogue, Gold Beach, OR 97444; 541/247-7580, reservations 888/814-0633.

127 Lucky Lodge RV Park

6

This is a good layover spot for U.S. 101 travelers who want to get off the highway circuit. It is set on the shore of the Rogue River and offers opportunities for fishing, boating, and swimming. Most sites have a view of the river. Nearby recreation options include hiking trails.

Location: On the Rogue River; The Oregon Coast Map 7, grid e5.

Campsites, facilities: There are four tent sites and 32 full-hookup sites for trailers or RVs of any length; most are drive-through sites. Electricity, drinking water, sewer hookups, and picnic tables are provided. Flush toilets, bottled gas, sanitary services, showers, firewood, a recreation hall, and a laundry room are available. Boat docks and rentals are within eight miles. Leashed pets are permitted.

Reservations, fees: Reservations accepted. Sites are $19 per night. Open year-round.

Directions: From Gold Beach drive north on U.S. 101 for four miles (on the north side of the Rogue River) to Rogue River Road. Turn east and drive one-quarter mile to the campground.

Contact: Lucky Lodge RV Park, 32040 Watson Ln., Gold Beach, OR 97444; 541/247-7618.

128 Indian Creek Recreation Park

7

This campground is along the Rogue River on the outskirts of the town of Gold Beach. Nearby recreation options include a riding stable, riding trails, and boat trips on the Rogue.

Location: On the Rogue River; The Oregon Coast Map 7, grid e5.

Campsites, facilities: There are 25 tent sites and 100 sites for trailers or RVs of any length. Electricity, drinking water, sewer and cable TV hookups, and picnic tables are provided. Flush toilets, showers, firewood, a recreation hall, a store, a sauna, a café, a laundry room, ice, and a playground are available. Bottled gas is within two miles. Boat docks, launching facilities, and rentals are nearby. Leashed pets and motorbikes are permitted.

Reservations, fees: Reservations accepted. Sites are $15–24 per night. Senior discount available. Open year-round.

Directions: On U.S. 101, drive to the northern end of Gold Beach to Jerry's Flat Road (just south of the Patterson Bridge). Turn east on Jerry's Flat Road and drive one-half mile to the campground.

Contact: Indian Creek Recreation Park, 94680 Jerry's Flat Rd., Gold Beach, OR 97444; 541/247-7704.

129 Ireland's Ocean View RV Park

8

One of the newest RV parks in the area, this spot is on the beach in the quaint little town of Gold Beach, only one mile from the famous Rogue River. This park is very clean with blacktop roads and grass beside each site.

Recreation options include beachcombing, fishing, and boating. Great ocean views are possible from the observatory/lighthouse.

Location: On the Pacific Ocean; The Oregon Coast Map 7, grid e5.

Campsites, facilities: There are 33 sites for trailers or RVs up to 40 feet. Tent camping is permitted only in combination with an RV. Cable TV, phones, showers, restrooms, a laundry room, a recreation room, horseshoe pits, and picnic areas are available. Leashed pets are permitted.

Reservations, fees: Reservations recommended. Sites are $15–22 per night. Open year-round.

Directions: On U.S. 101, drive to the southern end of Gold Beach (U.S. 101 becomes Ellensburg Avenue) and look for the camp at 20272 Ellensburg Avenue (across from the U.S. Forest Service office).

Contact: Ireland's Ocean View RV Park, 29272 Ellensburg Ave., P.O. Box 727, Gold Beach, OR 97444; 541/247-0148; website: www.irelandsrvpark.com.

130 Oceanside RV Park

5

Set 100 yards from the ocean, this park is close to beachcombing terrain, marked bike trails, and boating facilities. The park is also adjacent to the mouth of the Rogue River, in the Port of Gold Beach.

Location: On the Pacific Ocean; The Oregon Coast Map 7, grid e5.

Campsites, facilities: There are 80 sites for trailers or RVs of any length; 20 are drive-through sites. Electricity, drinking water, sewer hookups, and picnic tables are provided. Flush toilets, showers, a coin-operated laundry, cable TV, a small store, and ice are available. Bottled gas, sanitary services, a store, and a café are within two miles. Boat docks, launching facilities, and rentals

are nearby. Leashed pets and motorbikes are permitted.

Reservations, fees: Reservations recommended in the summer. Sites are $10–15 for camping per night, $13–20 for partial hookups, and $15–22 for full hookups. Open year-round.

Directions: On U.S. 101, drive to central Gold Beach and the intersection with Moore Street. Turn west and drive two blocks to Airport Way. Turn right and drive three blocks to South Jetty Road. Turn left and look for the park on the left.

Contact: Oceanside RV Park, P.O. Box 1107, Gold Beach, OR 97444; 541/247-2301.

131 Hunter Creek RV Park

7

This camp set amid wooded mountains on a small stream in the town of Gold Beach is preferred by tent campers over the other camps in town since it's a bit more private and secluded. For anglers, steelhead fishing can be excellent from January through March.

Location: On Hunter Creek; The Oregon Coast Map 7, grid e5.

Campsites, facilities: There are 60 sites for tents, trailers, or RVs. Restrooms, showers, drinking water, a public phone, a laundry room, a playground, and a game room are available.

Reservations, fees: Reservations recommended. Sites are $13–16 per night. Senior discount available. Open year-round.

Directions: In Gold Beach drive on U.S. 101 to the southern end of town to Hunter Creek Road. Turn east and drive three-quarters of a mile to the campground on the left side of the road.

Contact: Hunter Creek RV Park, P.O. Box 1227, 28555

Hunter Creek Loop, Gold Beach, OR 97444; 541/247-2322; fax 541/247-0578.

132 Agness RV Park

🚶 🚴 🏊

🛶 🚗 🐕 🚐   7

This is a destination campground on the scenic Rogue River in the middle of the Siskiyou National Forest. Fishing is the main focus here. Boating is sharply limited because the nearest pullout is 12 miles downstream. It's advisable to obtain a U.S. Forest Service map detailing the backcountry.

Location: On the Rogue River; The Oregon Coast Map 7, grid e5.

Campsites, facilities: There are 81 sites for trailers or RVs of any length; 43 are drive-through sites. Electricity, drinking water, sewer hookups, and picnic tables are provided. Flush toilets, sanitary services, showers, and a laundry room are available. A store, a café, bottled gas, and ice are within 100 yards. Boat-launching facilities are nearby. Pets are permitted.

Reservations, fees: Reservations accepted. Sites are $17 per night. The RV park is open year-round.

Directions: In Gold Beach drive on U.S. 101 to the southern end of the Rogue River Bridge and Jerry's Flat Road. Turn east on Jerry's Flat Road and you'll see the entrance to the campground on the left.

Contact: Agness RV Park, 4215 Agness Rd., Agness, OR 97406; 541/247-2813; website: www.agnessrv.com.

133 Whaleshead Beach Resort

🚶 🚴 🏊

🐕 ♿ 🚐 🏕   7

This resort, about a quarter of a mile from the beach, is set in a forested area with a small stream nearby. Activities at and around the camp include ocean and river fishing, jet boat trips, whale-watching excursions, and a golf course (13 miles away). Each campsite has a deck, and all cabins have an ocean view. What makes this camp unique is a tunnel that connects the campground to a trail to the beach.

Location: Near the Pacific Ocean; The Oregon Coast Map 7, grid h6.

Campsites, facilities: There are 115 sites for tents, trailers, or RVs of any length; 15 cabins are also available. Cable TV, restrooms, showers, drinking water, a public phone, a laundry room, limited groceries, ice, snacks, RV supplies, LP gas, horseshoe pits, and a restaurant are available. There is a sanitary dump station six miles away. Some facilities are wheelchair-accessible. Leashed pets are permitted.

Reservations, fees: Reservations recommended. Sites are $15–25 per night. Cabins are $65–140 per night. Open year-round.

Directions: From Brookings drive 6.5 miles north on U.S. 101 to milepost 349.5 and look for the park on the right.

Contact: Whaleshead Beach Resort, 19921 Whaleshead Rd., Brookings, OR 97415; 541/469-7446; fax 541/469-7447; website: www.whalesheadresort.com.

134 Loeb State Park

🚶 🏊 🎣 🐕 🚐 🏕   8

This park is in a canyon formed by the Chetco River. The campsites are nestled in a beautiful old myrtlewood grove. The northernmost redwood grove in the United States can be reached by a three-quarter-mile self-guided River View Trail adjacent to the Chetco River. Nature programs and interpretive tours are available.

Location: Near the Chetco River; The Oregon Coast Map 7, grid h7.

Campsites, facilities: There are 50 sites with partial hookups (water and electricity) for tents, trailers, or RVs up to 50 feet long, and three log cabins. Picnic tables, drinking water, garbage bins, and fire grills are provided. Flush toilets and firewood are available. Leashed pets are permitted.

Reservations, fees: Reservations accepted for cabins. Sites are $12–16 per night, $7 per night for all additional vehicles, $35 per night for cabins. Open year-round.

Directions: On U.S. 101, drive to south Brookings and County Road 784 (North Bank Chetco River Road). Turn northeast and drive 10 miles northeast on North Bank Road to the park entrance on the right.

Contact: Harris Beach State Park, 1655 U.S. Hwy. 101, Brookings, OR 97415; 541/469-2021 or 800/551-6949.

135 Little Redwood

7

This campground is set among old-growth fir trees near the banks of the Chetco River. This is an official put-in spot for rafting and river boats. The camp is also on the main western access route to the Kalmiopsis Wilderness, which is about 20 miles away. Campsites are fairly private, though close together.

Location: On the Chetco River in Siskiyou National Forest; The Oregon Coast Map 7, grid h7.

Campsites, facilities: There are 11 sites for tents, trailers, or RVs up to 16 feet long,. Picnic tables, garbage containers, and fire grills are provided. Drinking water and vault toilets are available. Leashed pets are permitted.

Reservations, fees: No reservations accepted. Sites are $10 per night, plus $3 for each additional nontowed vehicle. Senior discount available. Open late May to mid-September.

Directions: On U.S. 101, drive to south Brookings and County Road 784 (North Bank Chetco River Road). Turn northeast on North Bank Chetco River Road and drive 13.5 miles (the road becomes Forest Road 1376) to the campground.

Contact: Siskiyou National Forest, Chetco Ranger District, 555 5th St., Brookings, OR 97415; 541/469-2196; fax 541/469-2196.

136 Harris Beach State Park

8

The park boasts the largest island off the Oregon coast. Bird Island (also called Goat Island) is a breeding site for such rare birds as the tufted puffin. This park has sandy beaches interspersed with eroded sea stacks. The park's beauty changes with the seasons. Wildlife viewing opportunities are abundant (gray whales, harbor seals, and sea lions). In the fall and winter the nearby Chetco River attracts good runs of salmon and steelhead, respectively.

Location: On the Pacific Ocean; The Oregon Coast Map 7, grid h6.

Campsites, facilities: There are 63 sites for tents or self-contained RVs, and 86 sites with full or partial hookups for trailers or RVs up to 50 feet long. There are six yurts, each accommodating five people, and a special camping area for hikers and bicyclists. Picnic tables, garbage bins, and fire grills are provided. Electricity, drinking water, sewer and cable TV hookups, flush toilets, sanitary services, showers, laundry room, and firewood are available. Some facilities are wheelchair-accessible. Leashed pets are permitted.

Reservations, fees: Reservations accepted ($6 reservation fee). Sites are $13–19 per night; yurts are $27 per night, and all additional vehicles are $7 per night; sites for hikers/bikers are $4 per night.

Major credit cards accepted.

Open year-round.

Directions: From Brookings drive north on U.S. 101 for two miles to the park entrance on the left.

Contact: Harris Beach State Park, 1655 U.S. Hwy. 101, Brookings, OR 97415; 541/469-2021, reservations 800/452-5687.

137 Port of Brookings Harbor Beachfront RV Park

8

This park is a great layover spot just past the Oregon/California border on the Pacific Ocean. Oceanfront sites are available, and recreational activities include boating, fishing, and swimming. Nearby Harris Beach State Park makes a good side trip, with beach access and hiking trails.

Location: On the Pacific Ocean; The Oregon Coast Map 7, grid h6.

Campsites, facilities: There are 25 tent sites and 138 spaces for trailers or RVs of any length. Restrooms, showers, a sanitary dump, a public phone, a laundry room, ice, and a marina with a boat ramp, a boat dock, and snacks are available nearby. The facilities are wheelchair-accessible. Leashed pets are permitted.

Reservations, fees: Reservations recommended. Sites are $13–21 per night. Open year-round.

Directions: From Brookings drive south on U.S. 101 for 2.5 miles to Benham Lane. Turn west on Benham Lane and drive a half mile (it becomes Lower Harbor Road) to Boat Basin Road. Turn left and drive two blocks to the park on the right.

Contact: Port of Brookings Harbor Beachfront RV Park, 16035 Boat Basin Rd., Brookings, OR 97415; 541/469-5867 or 800/441-0856 in Oregon; website: www.port/brookings/harbor.org.

138 At Rivers Edge RV Resort

7

This campground lies along the banks of the Chetco River, just upstream from Brookings Harbor. It is a favorite spot for fishermen, with salmon and steelhead trips on the Chetco in the fall and winter. Deep-sea trips for salmon or rockfish are available nearby in the summer. This resort looks like the Rhine Valley in Germany, a pretty canyon between the trees and the river. A golf course is nearby.

Location: On the Chetco River; The Oregon Coast Map 7, grid h6.

Campsites, facilities: There are 110 sites for trailers or RVs of any length, including 15 drive-through sites, and two cabins. Electricity, drinking water, and sewer hookups are provided. Flush toilets, bottled gas, sanitary services, showers, a recreation hall with exercise equipment, a laundry room, recycling station, a small boat launch, and cable TV are available. Leashed pets are permitted.

Reservations, fees: Reservations recommended in fall. Sites are $20–25 per night. Open year-round.

Directions: On U.S. 101, drive to the southern end of Brookings (harbor side) and to South Bank Chetco River Road (a cloverleaf exit). Turn east on South Bank Chetco River Road and drive 1.5 miles to the park entrance on the left (a slanted left turn, through the pillars, well signed).

Contact: At Rivers Edge RV Resort, 98203 South Bank Chetco Rd., Brookings, OR 97415; 888/295-1441 or 541/469-3356; fax 541/412-0466; website: www.atriversedge.com.

139 Chetco RV Park

7

This park is near both the Chetco River, known for its winter steelhead run, and the beach. Whale-watching is good from January through May. The nature trails a short drive up the river road are a nice side trip.

Location: Near the Chetco River; The Oregon Coast Map 7, grid h6.

Campsites, facilities: There are 117 drive-through sites for trailers or RVs of any length. Electricity, drinking water, sewer hookups, and picnic tables are provided. Flush toilets, sanitary services, showers, a recreation hall, a laundry room, and ice are available. Boat docks, launching facilities, and rentals are nearby. Small pets are permitted.

Reservations, fees: Reservations accepted. Sites are $15–18 per night. Open year-round.

Directions: In Brookings drive south on U.S. 101 to the Chetco River Bridge. Continue one mile south on U.S. 101 to the park entrance on the east side (left) of the road.

Contact: Chetco RV Park, 16117 U.S. Hwy. 101 S, Brookings, OR 97415; 541/469-3863; fax 541/469-4025.

140 Sea Bird RV

 5

This is one of several campgrounds in the area. Nearby recreation options include marked bike trails, a full-service marina, and tennis courts. This park has paved roads and granite sites. It is a nice, neat park. There is also a beach for surfing near the park.

Location: On the Pacific Ocean; The Oregon Coast Map 7, grid h6.

Campsites, facilities: There are 60 sites for trailers or RVs of any length; nine are drive-through sites. Electricity, drinking water, sewer hookups, and picnic tables are provided. Flush toilets, sanitary services, showers, a recreation hall, and a laundry room are available. Boat docks, launching facilities,

and rentals are nearby. Leashed pets and motorbikes are permitted.

Reservations, fees: Reservations accepted. Sites are $16 per night. Senior discount available. Open year-round.

Directions: In Brookings drive south on U.S. 101 to the Chetco River Bridge. Continue one-quarter mile south on U.S. 101 to the park entrance on the left.

Contact: Sea Bird RV, P.O. Box 1026, Brookings, OR 97415; 541/469-3512.

141 Winchuck

6

This forested campground is on the banks of the Winchuck River, an out-of-the-way stream that out-of-towners don't know exists. It's quiet, remote, and not that far from the coast, although it feels like an inland spot. If this is full, Ludlum Campground is about two miles away on Forest Road 1108.

Location: On the Winchuck River in Siskiyou National Forest; The Oregon Coast Map 7, grid h7.

Campsites, facilities: There are 15 sites for tents, trailers, or RVs up to 30 feet. Picnic tables, garbage bins, and fire grills are provided. Vault toilets and drinking water are available. Leashed pets are permitted.

Reservations, fees: No reservations accepted. Sites are $10 per night, plus $3 for each additional nontowed vehicle. Senior discount available. Open late May to mid-September.

Directions: From Brookings drive south on U.S. 101 for 5.5 miles to County Road 896. Turn east and drive six miles to Forest Road 1107. Turn east and drive one mile to the campground.

Contact: Siskiyou National Forest, Chetco Ranger District, 555 5th St., Brookings, OR 97415; tel./fax 541/469-2196.

142 Tucker Flat

🏃 🏊 🐕 ⛺ 7

Above the clear waters of Mule Creek, this campground borders the Wild Rogue Wilderness. Tucker Flat offers a trailhead into the Wild Rogue Wilderness and lots of evidence of historic mining. Mosquitoes can be a problem, and bears occasionally wander through. The historic Rogue River Ranch is just one-quarter mile away, and the museum and other buildings are open during the summer. The Rogue River Ranch is on the National Register of Historic Places. Tucker Flat campground can also be reached by hiking the Rogue River Trail or by floating the Rogue River and hiking up past the Rogue River Ranch. There are also scenic bridges along Mule Creek. Campers and hikers are advised to stop by the Medford BLM office for maps.

Location: On the Rogue River; The Oregon Coast Map 8, grid c2.

Campsites, facilities: There are eight primitive tent sites. Picnic tables and fire grills are provided. Vault toilets and bear-proof trash cans are available. There is no drinking water. Leashed pets are permitted.

Reservations, fees: No reservations; no fee. Open year-round, weather permitting.

Directions: From Grants Pass drive one mile north on I-5 to Exit 61. Take that exit and drive west on Merlin-Galice Access Road for 20 miles to the Grave Creek Bridge (the second bridge over the Rogue River). Cross the bridge and drive a short distance to BLM Road 34-8-1. Turn left and drive 16 miles to BLM Road 32-8-31. Turn left and drive seven miles to BLM Road 32-9-14.2. Turn left and drive 15 miles to the campground (around the bend from the Rogue River Ranch).

Contact: Bureau of Land Management, Medford District, 3040 Biddle Rd., Medford, OR 97504; 541/618-2200; fax 541/618-2400; website: www.or.blm.gov/medford.

143 Big Pine

🏃 🐕 ♿ ⛺ 8

This little campground (elevation 2,400 feet) is near the banks of Myers Creek in a valley of large pine and Douglas fir. Many sites are right on the creek, and all are shaded. One of the world's tallest ponderosa pine trees grows near the campground. A 1.1-mile barrier-free, interpretive trail starts at the campground and a day-use area is available.

Location: On Myers Creek in Siskiyou National Forest; The Oregon Coast Map 8, grid d2.

Campsites, facilities: There are 14 tent sites. Picnic tables and fire grills are provided. Vault toilets, drinking water, and garbage bins are available. The facilities are wheelchair-accessible. Leashed pets are permitted.

Reservations, fees: No reservations accepted. Sites are $5 per night, $2 per night for an additional vehicle. Senior discount available. Open late May to mid-October.

Directions: From Grants Pass drive north on I-5 for 3.5 miles to Exit 61 (Merlin-Galice Road). Take that exit and drive northwest for 12.5 miles to Forest Road 25. Turn left on Forest Road 25 and head southwest for 12.8 miles to the campground on the right.

Contact: Siskiyou National Forest, Galice Ranger District, 200 N.E. Greenfield Rd., Grants Pass, OR 97526; 541/471-6500; fax 541/471-6514.

144 Sam Brown and Sam Brown Horse Camp

🏃 ♿ 🚐 ⛺ 8

This campground is in an isolated area near Grants Pass along Briggs Creek in a valley of pine and Douglas fir. It is set at an elevation of 2,500 feet. Many sites lie in the shade of trees, and a creek runs along one side of the campground. Taylor Creek Trail, Briggs Creek Trail, and Dutchy Creek Trail are nearby and popular for hiking and horseback riding. An amphitheater is available for small group presentations.

Location: Near Grants Pass in Siskiyou National Forest; Oregon Coast map 8, grid d2.

Campsites, facilities: There are 37 sites for tents, trailers, or RVs of any length at Sam Brown and seven equestrian tent sites with small corrals across the road at Sam Brown Horse Camp. At Sam Brown, picnic tables and fire rings or grills are provided and drinking water and vault toilets are available. A picnic shelter, solar shower, and an amphitheater are available. Many sites are wheelchair-accessible.

Reservations, fees: No reservations accepted. Sites are $5 per night. There is a $2 charge for each additional vehicle at both camps. Senior discount available. Open late May to mid-October.

Directions: From Grants Pass drive north on I-5 for 3.5 miles to Exit 61 (Merlin-Galice Road). Take that exit and drive northwest for 12.5 miles to Forest Road 25. Turn left on Forest Road 25 and head southwest for 13.5 miles to the campground.

Contact: Siskiyou National Forest, Galice Ranger District, 200 N.E. Greenfield Rd., Grants Pass, OR 97526; 541/471-6500; fax 541/471-6514.

PORTLAND AND THE WILLAMETTE VALLEY

Portland and the Willamette Valley

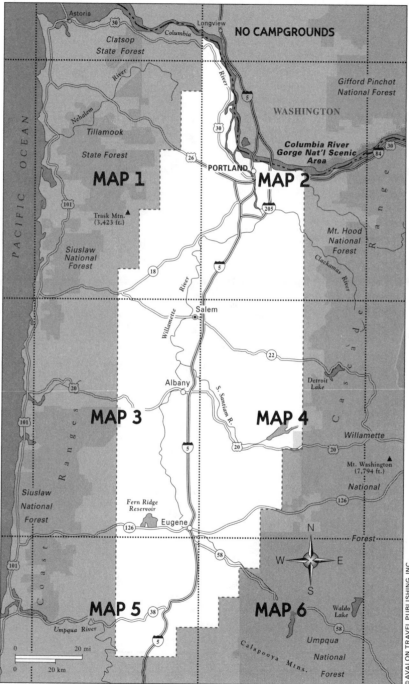

Map 1

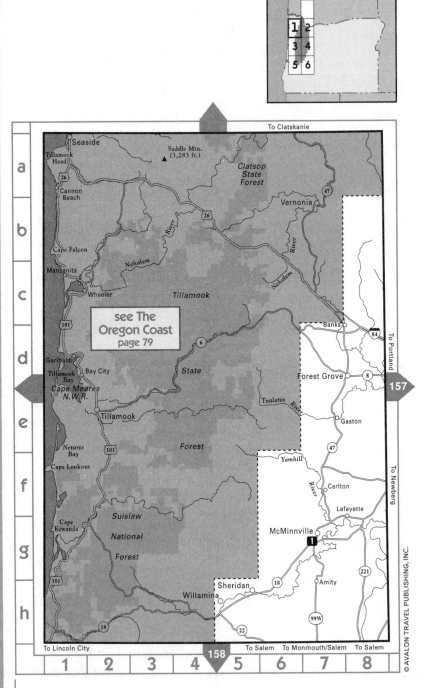

see The Oregon Coast page 79

157

158

To Clatskanie

Seaside

Tillamook Head

Saddle Mtn. (3,283 ft.)

Clatsop State Forest

Cannon Beach

Vernonia

Cape Falcon

River

Nehalem

Manzanita

Nehalem

Wheeler

Tillamook

Banks

To Portland

State

Garibaldi

Bay City

Forest Grove

Tillamook Bay

Cape Meares N.W.R.

Tualatin River

Tillamook

Gaston

Netarts Bay

Forest

Yamhill

To Newberg

Cape Lookout

River

Carlton

Lafayette

Suislaw

McMinnville

National

Cape Kiwanda

Forest

Sheridan

Amity

Willamina

To Lincoln City

To Salem   To Monmouth/Salem   To Salem

© AVALON TRAVEL PUBLISHING, INC.

Map 2

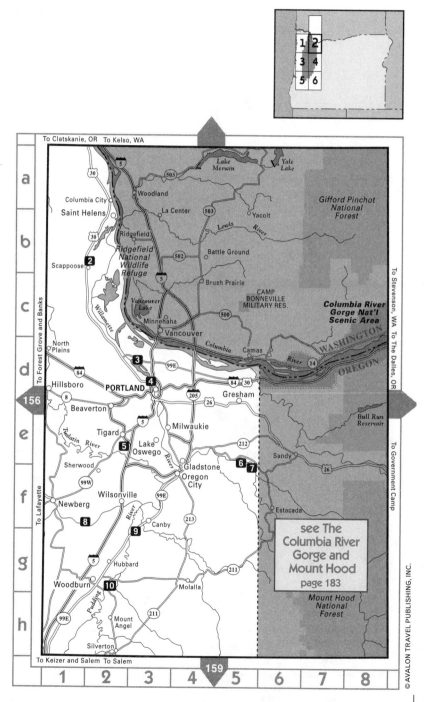

To Clatskanie, OR   To Kelso, WA

Lake Merwin

Yale Lake

30

5

503

Woodland

Columbia City

Saint Helens

La Center

503

Yacolt

Gifford Pinchot National Forest

30

Ridgefield

Scappoose

2

Ridgefield National Wildlife Refuge

502

Battle Ground

5

Lewis River

Brush Prairie

CAMP BONNEVILLE MILITARY RES.

Columbia River Gorge Nat'l Scenic Area

To Stevenson, WA

To The Dalles, OR

Willamette

Vancouver Lake

500

North Plains

Minnehaha

Vancouver

Columbia River

Camas

WASHINGTON

OREGON

14

I-84

3

99E

Hillsboro

PORTLAND

4

84

30

8

205

26

Gresham

Bull Run Reservoir

Beaverton

Tualatin River

5

Tigard

5

Lake Oswego

River

Milwaukie

212

Sandy

To Government Camp

26

Sherwood

99W

Gladstone

6

7

Oregon City

Wilsonville

99E

Estacada

Newberg

8

River

213

Canby

9

211

Hubbard

5

see The **Columbia River Gorge and Mount Hood** page 183

Woodburn

10

Molalla

Paudling River

211

Mount Hood National Forest

99E

Mount Angel

Silverton

To Keizer and Salem   To Salem

156

159

1   2   3   4   5   6   7   8

Map 3

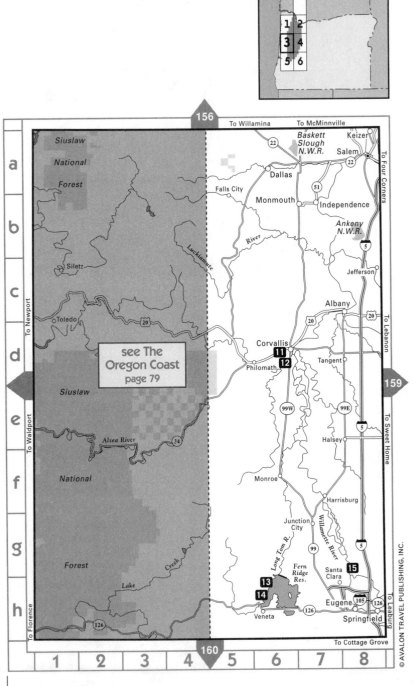

Map 4

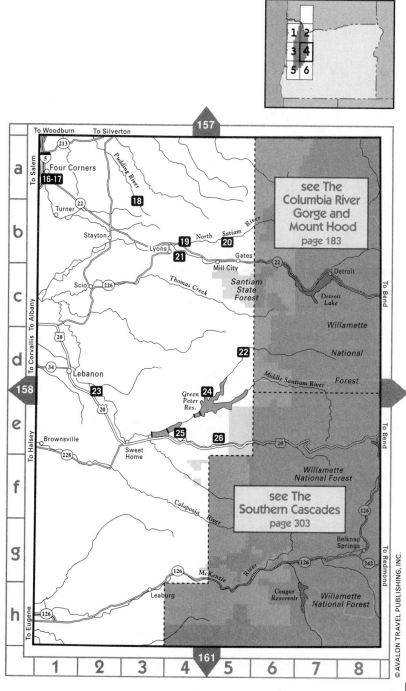

© AVALON TRAVEL PUBLISHING, INC.

Map 5

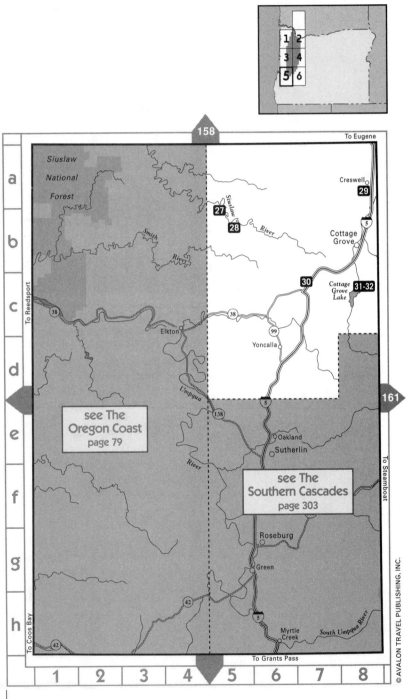

158

To Eugene

Siuslaw
National
Forest

Creswell
29

27
Siuslaw
28
River

5

Cottage
Grove

Smith
River

30
Cottage
Grove
Lake
31-32

To Reedsport

38

38

99

Elkton

Yoncalla

Umpqua

161

138

**see The
Oregon Coast
page 79**

Oakland
Sutherlin

To Steamboat

River

**see The
Southern Cascades
page 303**

Roseburg

Green

To Coos Bay

42

42

5

Myrtle
Creek

South Umpqua River

To Grants Pass

© AVALON TRAVEL PUBLISHING, INC.

Map 6

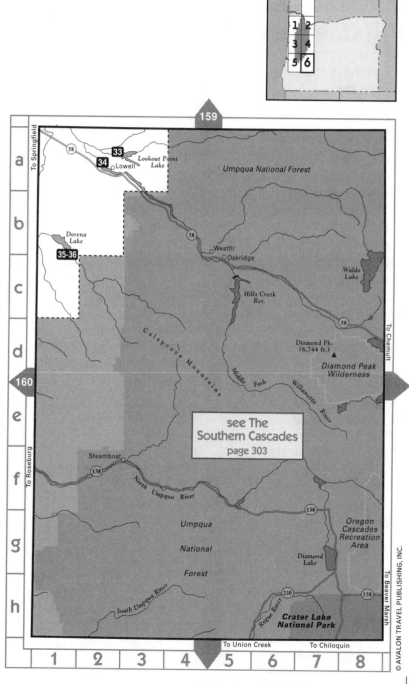

To Springfield

58
33
34
Lowell
Lookout Point Lake

Umpqua National Forest

a

58
Westfir
Oakridge

Waldo Lake

Dorena Lake

35-36

b

Hills Creek Res.

58

c

To Chemult

Calapooya Mountains

Diamond Pk. (8,744 ft.)

Diamond Peak Wilderness

d

160

Middle Fork

Willamette River

see The
Southern Cascades
page 303

e

To Roseburg

Steamboat

138

North Umpqua River

f

138

Umpqua

National

Forest

Oregon Cascades Recreation Area

Diamond Lake

g

To Beaver Marsh

South Umpqua River

230

Rogue River

138

h

Crater Lake National Park

To Union Creek   To Chiloquin

1   2   3   4   5   6   7   8

© AVALON TRAVEL PUBLISHING, INC.

Portland and the Willamette Valley

■ Mulkey RV Park

🐟 🐕 🚴 🚐 ⛺ 7

If you're in the area and looking for a camping spot, you'd best stop here—there are no other campgrounds within 30 miles. This wooded park is set near the South Yamhill River. Nearby recreation options include an 18-hole golf course, tennis courts, and the Western Deer Park and Arboretum, which has a playground.

Location: Near the South Yamhill River; Portland and the Willamette Valley map 1, grid g7.

Campsites, facilities: There are 70 sites for tents, trailers, or RVs of any length. Electricity, drinking water, sewer hookups, and picnic tables are provided. Flush toilets, showers, a store, bottled gas, and a laundry are available. Leashed pets and motorbikes are permitted.

Reservations, fees: Reservations recommended. Sites are $15–20 per night. Major credit cards accepted. Open year-round.

Directions: From Portland turn south on Highway 99 and drive about 31 miles to McMinnville and Highway 18. Turn southwest on Highway 18 and drive 3.5 miles to the park entrance.

Contact: Mulkey RV Park, 14325 S.W. Hwy. 18, McMinnville, OR 97128; 877/472-2475, 503/472-2475; fax 503/472-0718.

■ Scappoose RV Park

🐕 🚴 ♿ 🚐 ⛺ 6

This is a county-operated RV park. It is set next to the rural Scappoose airport, making it a convenient spot for private pilots. The sites are partially shaded, with spruce, oak, and maple trees. It is less than a mile from the Columbia River, set on the edge of a dike. It is about a 30-minute drive from Portland.

Location: In Scappoose; Portland and the Willamette Valley map 2, grid b1.

Campsites, facilities: There are several tent sites in dispersed areas, seven sites for trailers or RVs, six with full hookups. Picnic tables and fire grills are provided. Drinking water, a restroom with flush toilets and showers, sanitary disposal station, firewood, and a playground with equipment and horseshoe pits is available. Leashed pets are permitted.

Reservations, fees: Reservations are accepted. Sites are $12–18 per night, $7 for each additional vehicle. Senior discount available. Open year-round.

Directions: From Portland turn west on U.S. 30 and drive to Scappoose. Continue one mile north on U.S. 30 to West Lane Road. Turn east (right) and drive three-quarters mile to Honeyman Road. Turn left and drive one block to the park on the right.

Contact: Columbia County Forest, Parks and Recreation, 34038 N. Honeyman Rd., Scappoose, OR 97056; 503/543-3225, reservations 503/397-2353.

■ Jantzen Beach RV Park

🚶 🚲 🏊 🚐 🐕 🚴 🚐 6

This RV campground is near the banks of the Columbia River on the outskirts of Portland. Options include seasonal swimming. An 18-hole golf course and tennis courts are close by. Many recreation opportunities are available in the Portland area. Numerous marinas on the Willamette and Columbia Rivers offer boat trips and rentals, and the city parks and nearby state parks have hiking, bicycling, and horseback riding possibilities. The Columbia River Highway (U.S. 30) is a scenic drive. If golf is your game, Portland has 18 public golf courses. The winter ski areas at Mount Hood are within an hour's drive.

Location: Near the Columbia River; Portland and the Willamette Valley map 2, grid d3.

Campsites, facilities: There are 169 sites for trailers or RVs of any length. Electricity, drinking water, sewer hookups, cable TV, modem access, and picnic tables are provided. Flush toilets, showers, a recreation hall, a laundry room, a playground, and a swimming pool (seasonal) are available. Bottled gas, a store, ice, and a café are within one mile. Boat docks, launching facilities, and rentals are nearby. Leashed pets are permitted.

Reservations, fees: Reservations accepted. Sites are $24–26 per night. Senior discount available. Major credit cards accepted. Open year-round.

Directions: From Portland on I-5 drive four miles north to the Jantzen Beach exit (Exit 308) and take Hayden Island Drive. Turn west on Hayden Island Drive and drive one-half mile to the park on the right.

Contact: Jantzen Beach RV Park, 1503 N. Hayden Island Dr., Portland, OR 97217; 503/289-7626; fax 503/289-9220.

4 Fir Grove RV and Trailer Park

7

This park is near the banks of the Columbia River in the outskirts of Portland. See previous listing for information about the nearby recreation opportunities.

Location: Near the Columbia River; Portland and the Willamette Valley map 2, grid d3.

Campsites, facilities: There are six sites for trailers or RVs of any length. Electricity, drinking water, and sewer hookups are provided. Flush toilets, laundry facilities, and showers are available. Bottled gas, sanitary services, a store, a café, and a playground are within one mile. Leashed pets and motorbikes are permitted.

Reservations, fees: Reservations accepted. Sites are $22–25 per night. Open year-round.

Directions: In Portland on I-205, take Exit 23B onto Columbia Boulevard and drive about 400 yards northeast to Northeast Killingsworth. Drive about one mile west on Northeast Killingsworth to the park entrance.

Contact: Fir Grove RV and Trailer Park, 5541 N.E. 72nd St., Portland, OR 97218; 503/252-9993.

5 RV Park of Portland

6

This park just south of Portland in a wooded setting has spacious sites, all with access to lawn areas.

Location: In Tualatin; Portland and the Willamette Valley map 2, grid e2.

Campsites, facilities: There are 100 sites, most of them drive-through sites for trailers or RVs of any length. Electricity, drinking water, sewer hookups, and picnic tables are provided. Flush toilets, sanitary services, showers, a laundry room, and a playground are available. Bottled gas, a store, a café, and ice are within one mile. Leashed pets and motorbikes are permitted.

Reservations, fees: Reservations accepted. Sites are $22.99 per night. Open year-round.

Directions: From Portland drive south on I-5 to Tualatin and Exit 289. Take Exit 289, turn east on Highway 212, and drive one-half mile to the campground on the left.

Contact: RV Park of Portland, 6645 S.W. Nyberg Rd., Tualatin, OR 97062; 503/692-0225; website: www.rvparkofportland.com.

6 Barton Park

6

Getting here may seem a bit of a maze, but the trip is well worth it. This camp on the Clackamas River is surrounded by woods and tall trees. The nearby Clackamas River can provide good salmon fishing.

Location: Near the Clackamas River; Portland and the Willamette Valley map 2, grid e5.

Campsites, facilities: There are 99 sites for tents, trailers, and RVs of any length. Restrooms, showers, a sanitary dump, a public phone, and a barbecue are available. Recreational facilities include horseshoe pits, a playground, volleyball, baseball, and a boat ramp. Supplies are available within one mile. Leashed pets are permitted.

Reservations, fees: Reservations recommended. Sites are $12–16 per night. Open May through October.

Directions: From Portland drive south on I-5 to I-205. Turn east and drive about 20 miles to the Clackamas/Estacada exit (Highway 212). Turn east on Highway 212 and drive about five miles to the Carver exit (Highway 224). Turn right on Highway 224 and drive about 6.5 miles to the town of Barton and Baker's Ferry Road. Turn right and drive one-quarter mile to Barton Park Road. Turn left and drive to the park on the left.

Contact: Clackamas County Parks Department, 9101 S.E. Sunnybrook Blvd., Clackamas, OR 97015; 503/353-4414; fax 503/353-4420; website: www.co.clackamas.or.us.

7 Metzler Park

8

This county campground on a small stream not far from the Clackamas River is a hot spot for fishing, swimming, and picnicking.

Be sure to make your reservation early at this very popular park.

Location: On Clear Creek; Portland and the Willamette Valley map 2, grid f5.

Campsites, facilities: There are 70 sites for tents, trailers, and RVs. Electricity, restrooms, showers, a sanitary dump, a public phone, a playground, and a recreation field with basketball, volleyball, and baseball are available. Propane, ice, and laundry facilities are within five miles. Leashed pets are permitted.

Reservations, fees: Reservations recommended. Sites are $12–16 per night. Open May through September.

Directions: From Portland drive east on U.S. 26 from Gresham 11 miles to Sandy and Highway 211. Turn right (south) and drive six miles to a junction. Turn south (still Highway 211) and drive over the bridge to South Springwater Road. Turn right on South Springwater Road and drive about one-quarter mile to Metzler Park Road. Turn left on Metzler Park Road and drive three-quarters of a mile to the park.

Contact: Clackamas County Parks Department, S.E. Sunnybrook Blvd., Clackamas, OR 97015; 503/353-4414; fax 503/353-4420; website: www.co.clackamas.or.us.

8 Champoeg State Heritage Area

7

Situated on the south bank of the Willamette River, this state park has an interpretive center, a botanical garden featuring native plants, and hiking and bike trails. In July a pageant reenacting the early history of the area is staged Thursday through Sunday evenings. There are also a log cabin museum, the historic

Newell House, and a visitor center worth a tour.

Location: On the Willamette River; Portland and the Willamette Valley map 2, grid f1.

Campsites, facilities: There are six tent sites and 84 sites for trailers or RVs up to 50 feet, eight with full hookups, the rest with partial hookups. There are also three group areas that accommodate a maximum of 25 people each, six walk-in sites, six cabins, six yurts, a hiker/biker camp, an RV group area with 10 sites with electric hook-ups only. Picnic tables and fire grills are provided. Drinking water, garbage bins, flush toilets, a sanitary disposal station, showers, a group recreation hall for up to 55 people, and firewood are available. Some facilities are wheelchair-accessible. Boat docking facilities are nearby. Leashed pets are permitted.

Reservations, fees: Reservations accepted ($6 reservation fee). Sites are $15–20 per night, $4 per night for hiker/biker sites; yurts are $27 per night and cabins are $35 per night; $7 per night for an additional vehicle. Major credit cards accepted. Open year-round, with limited winter facilities in day-use areas.

Directions: From Portland drive south on I-5 to Exit 278, the Donald/Aurora exit. Take that exit and turn west (right) on Ehlen Road and drive three miles to Case Road. Turn north and drive 5.5 miles (the road becomes Champoeg Road) to the park on the right.

Contact: Champoeg State Heritage Area, 7679 Champoeg Rd. NE, Saint Paul, OR 97137; 503/678-1251, extension 225, reservations 800/452-5687.

9 Isberg RV Park

7

This RV campground is in a rural area just off the main highway. The setting is very pretty, thanks to lots of evergreen trees that shelter the camp from the highway. Portland and Salem are just 20 minutes away.

Location: Near Aurora; Portland and the Willamette Valley map 2, grid g3.

Campsites, facilities: There are 148 sites for trailers or RVs of any length. Electricity, drinking water, and sewer hookups are provided. Flush toilets, bottled gas, showers, a recreation hall, cable TV, a store, a swimming pool, a laundry room, and ice are available. Leashed pets are permitted.

Reservations, fees: Reservations accepted. Sites are $21.50–24 per night. Open year-round.

Directions: From Portland drive south on I-5 to Exit 278, the Donald/Aurora exit. Take that exit and turn left (east) on Ehlen Road and drive to Dolores Way. Turn right on Dolores Way and drive a quarter mile to the park on the right.

Contact: Isberg RV Park, 21599 Dolores Way NE, Aurora, OR 97002; 503/678-2646; fax 503/678-2724.

10 Feyrer Memorial Park

5

On the scenic Molalla River, this county park offers swimming and excellent salmon fishing. This is a superb option for weary I-5 cruisers; the park is only 30 minutes off the highway and provides a peaceful, serene environment.

Location: On the Molalla River; Portland and the Willamette Valley map 2, grid g2.

Campsites, facilities: There are 19 sites for tents, trailers, and RVs. Electricity, drinking water, restrooms, showers, a sanitary dump, and a public phone are provided. There are also a playground and recreation field. Some facilities are wheelchair-accessible. Supplies are available within three miles. Leashed pets are permitted.

Reservations, fees: Reservations recommended. Sites are $12–16 per night. Open May through September.

Directions: From Portland drive south on I-5 to Woodburn and Exit 271. Take that exit and drive east on Highway 214 and continue (the road changes to Highway 211 at the crossing with Highway 99E) to Molalla and Feyrer Park Road. Turn right and drive three miles to the park on the left.

Contact: Clackamas County Parks Department, S.E. Sunnybrook Blvd., Clackamas, OR 97015; 503/353-4414; fax 503/353-4420; website: www.co.clackamas.or.us.

⓫ Corvallis Mobile Home Park

 5

This is a decent layover spot on your way to and from the coast. It's in a bucolic setting, across the way from Oregon State University's cow and llama grazing land. Nearby recreation options include an 18-hole golf course, hiking trails, and a riding stable.

Location: In Corvallis; Portland and the Willamette Valley map 3, grid d6.

Campsites, facilities: There are 18 sites for trailers or RVs. Electricity, drinking water, and hookups for sewer and basic cable are provided. Flush toilets, showers, a store, a deli, a laundry room, and ice are available. Bottled gas and sanitary services are within one mile. Pets are permitted.

Reservations, fees: Sites are $15 per night. Open year-round.

Directions: In Corvallis drive west on U.S. 20 for 2.5 miles to 53rd Street. Turn north and drive 1.3 miles to the park on the right.

Contact: Corvallis Mobile Home Park, 200 N.W. 53rd St., Corvallis, OR 97330; tel./fax 541/752-2334.

⓬ Willamette City Park

8

This 40-acre city park is on the banks of the Willamette River just outside Corvallis. The camping area is actually a large clearing near the entrance to the park, which has been left in its natural state. There are trails leading down to the river, and the bird-watching is good here.

Location: On the Willamette River; Portland and the Willamette Valley map 3, grid d6.

Campsites, facilities: There are 13 sites for tents, trailers, or RVs of any length. Vault toilets, drinking water, a covered outdoor kitchen area, picnic tables, and a small playground are available. Bottled gas, a store, a café, a coin laundry, and ice are within one mile. There is a dump station in the center of town, three miles away. Boat docks and launching facilities are within one mile. Leashed pets are permitted.

Reservations, fees: No reservations accepted. Sites are $9 per night. Open April to mid-November to self-contained RVs and from March through October to tents, trailers, and RVs.

Directions: On I-5, take Exit 228 (five miles south of Albany) to Highway 34. Turn west and drive nine miles to Corvallis and Highway 99W. Turn left (south) and drive one mile to Southeast Goodnight Road. Turn left (east) and drive a half mile to the park.

Contact: Corvallis Department of Parks and Recreation, P.O. Box 1083, Corvallis, OR 97339; 541/766-6918; fax 541/754-1701; website: www.ci.corvallis.or.us/pr/prhome.html.

⓭ Richardson Park

🚶 🚴 🏊 🎣 🛶
🏕 ⛹ ♿ 🚐 ⛺ 7

This pretty Lane County park is a favorite for sailing and sailboards, as the wind is consistent. Boating and water-skiing are also popular. A walking trail around the reservoir doubles as a bike trail, with swimming, fishing, and watching wildlife as optional activities. The Corps of Engineers has wildlife areas nearby. The historic Applegate Trail is featured in a kiosk display in the park.

Location: On Fern Ridge Reservoir; Portland and the Willamette Valley map 3, grid h6.

Campsites, facilities: There are 88 partial hookup sites for tents, trailers, or RVs up to 60 feet long, and seven group sites (maximum 16 people per site). Three sites are wheelchair-accessible, as are the restrooms. Electricity, drinking water, picnic tables, and fire pits are provided. Restrooms with flush toilets, sinks, and hot showers, a dump station, and garbage bins are available. Group sites are double campsites. A part-time attended marina with minimal supplies, including ice, a boat launch and transient boat docks, unsupervised swimming, and a playground are available in the park. There is a small town within 10 miles. Leashed pets are permitted.

Reservations, fees: Reservations accepted ($10 reservation fee); they're required at least two weeks before visit. Sites are $16 per night, with a charge of $5 per additional vehicle. Call for group site fees. Maximum stay is 14 days in a 30-day period. Open mid-April through mid-October.

Directions: In Eugene on I-5, drive to Exit 195B and Belt Line Road. Turn west on Belt Line Road and drive 6.5 miles to Junction City Airport exit and Highway 99. Turn right on Highway 99 and drive north for two blocks to Clear Lake Road. Turn left and drive 8.5 miles to the campground on the left.

Contact: Richardson Park, 25950 Richardson Park Rd., Junction City, OR 97448; 541/935-2005; website: www.co.lane.or.us/park.

⓮ Fern Ridge Shores

🚴 🏊 🎣
🚐 🏕 ♿ 🚐 7

This camp is in a wooded area along the shore of Fern Ridge Reservoir, where swimming, boating, and bass fishing are among the pastimes. You might catch a glimpse of an egret, heron, osprey, deer, or red fox—or even an eagle; there are three nesting pairs of eagles in the park. This is a friendly, family-oriented park that makes a great vacation destination, as well as an excellent layover for travelers cruising I-5.

Location: On Fern Ridge Reservoir; Portland and the Willamette Valley map 3, grid h6.

Campsites, facilities: There are 61 sites with full hookups for trailers and RVs up to 40 feet long. Restrooms, showers, security, and a public phone are available. Horseshoes, a field, a boat ramp, and a dock are available nearby. Some facilities are wheelchair-accessible. Two leashed pets per site are permitted.

Reservations, fees: Reservations recommended. Sites are $20–25 per night. Open year-round.

Directions: From Eugene drive west on Highway 126 for 10 miles to Ellmaker Road (just before Venta). Turn right (north) on Ellmaker Road and drive 1.1 miles to Jeans Road. Turn right (east) and drive 1.3 miles to the park on the right.

Contact: Fern Ridge Shores, 29652 Jeans Rd., Veneta, OR 97487; 541/935-2335; fax 541/935-5417.

15 Eugene Kamping World

🥾 🐕 🏕️ ♿ 🚐 ⛺ 5

Eugene is one of Oregon's major cities, but it offers many riverside parks and hiking opportunities. Both the Willamette and McKenzie Rivers run right through town. The McKenzie, in particular, can provide good trout fishing. A golf course is nearby.

Location: Near the Willamette River; Portland and the Willamette Valley map 3, grid g8.

Campsites, facilities: There are 30 tent sites and 114 drive-through sites for trailers or RVs of any length. Electricity, drinking water, sewer hookups, and picnic tables are provided. Flush toilets, bottled gas, sanitary services, showers, a recreation hall, cable TV, a miniature golf course, a store, a laundry room, ice, and a playground are available. A café is within one mile. Small leashed pets are permitted.

Reservations, fees: Reservations accepted. Sites are $16–21 per night. Open year-round.

Directions: From Eugene drive north on I-5 for seven miles to Coburg and Exit 199. Take that exit and drive west for a quarter mile to South Stewart Way (the campground access road). Turn left and drive up the driveway.

Note: As of 2002, this RV park's phone and fax number were disconnected with no referral. Do not plan on staying here unless you have independent verification that the park is open.

Contact: Eugene Kamping World, 90932 S. Stewart Way, Coburg, OR 97408; 541/343-4832; fax 541/343-3008.

16 Forest Glen RV Resort

🎣 🐕 🏕️ ♿ 🚐 6

This RV resort is directly behind ThrillVille USA, an amusement park with rides, miniature golf, Go-Karts, waterslides, and a snack bar. ThrillVille is open during the summer. Another bonus is that the campground has a fishing pond with bass and trout, along with paddleboats. A winery tour at Willamette Vineyards is available just one mile south via I-5, and a golf course is one mile to the north. Campsites here are often more private and shaded than many RV parks. Additions to the park include weekly activities, including Bingo and meals served on weekends.

Location: South of Salem; Portland and the Willamette Valley map 4, grid a1.

Campsites, facilities: There are 70 sites for trailers or RVs of any length, some with picnic tables and fire pits. Electricity, drinking water, and sewer hookups are provided. Flush toilets, showers, and a laundry room are available. A clubhouse with exercise equipment and games and a playground are available nearby. A store, a café, and ice are within two miles. Leashed pets are permitted. Some facilities are wheelchair-accessible.

Reservations, fees: No reservations. Sites are $25.50 per night. Open year-round.

Directions: From Salem drive south on I-5 for one mile to Exit 248. Take that exit and turn left on Delaney Road and drive 100 yards to Enchanted Way. Turn right and drive a quarter mile to the park on the left.

Contact: Forest Glen RV Resort, 8372 Enchanted Way, Turner, OR 97392; 503/363-7616.

17 Salem Campground and RVs

🥾 🚲 🏊 🎣 🐕 🏕️ 🚐 ⛺ 5

This park with shaded sites is just off I-5 in Salem. A picnic area and a lake for swimming are within walking distance, and a nine-hole golf course, hiking trails, a riding stable, and tennis courts are nearby.

Location: In Salem; Portland and the Willamette Valley map 4, grid a1.

Campsites, facilities: There are 30 tent sites and 190 sites with full hookups for trailers or RVs of any length, most of which are drive-through sites. Picnic tables are provided. Flush toilets, bottled gas, sanitary services, showers, a recreation hall with a game room, a store, a laundry room, ice, a playground, electricity, drinking water, and sewer hookups are available. A café is within one mile. Leashed pets and motorbikes are permitted.

Reservations, fees: Reservations accepted. Sites are $14–21 per night. Senior discount available. Open year-round.

Directions: From Salem on I-5, take Exit 253 to Highway 22. Turn east and drive east for one-quarter mile to Lancaster Drive. Turn right on Lancaster Drive and drive to Hagers Grove Road. Turn right on Hagers Grove Road and drive to the park.

Contact: Salem Campground and RVs, 3700 Hagers Grove Rd. SE, Salem, OR 97301; 800/826-9605 or 503/581-6736; fax 888/827-9605; website: www.salemrv.com.

18 Silver Falls State Park

🚶 🚲 🏊 🐎
⛺ ♿ 🚐 △ 8

This is Oregon's largest state park, covering more than 8,700 acres. Numerous trails crisscross the area, including a seven-mile jaunt that meanders past 10 majestic waterfalls (some more than 100 feet high) in the rainforest of Silver Creek Canyon. Four of these falls have an amphitheater-like surrounding where you can walk behind the falls and feel the misty spray. A horse camp and a 14-mile equestrian trail are available in the park. Fitness-conscious campers can check out the three-mile jogging trail or the four-mile bike trail. There are also a rustic nature lodge and group lodging facilities.

Location: Near Salem; Portland and the Willamette Valley map 4, grid b3.

Campsites, facilities: There are 51 tent sites and 54 sites with water and electrical hookups for trailers or RVs up to 60 feet long, and 14 cabins. Picnic tables and fire grills are provided. There are also a group site, cabins, and a designated horse camp. Drinking water, garbage bins, flush toilets, sanitary services, showers, firewood, and a playground are available. Some facilities are wheelchair-accessible. Leashed pets are permitted.

Reservations, fees: Reservations accepted. Sites are $13–20 per night, the group site is $60 per night, cabins are $35 per night, and horse campsites are $13 per night with a $1.50 fee per horse. There is a $7 per night charge for an additional vehicle. Major credit cards accepted. Open year-round.

Directions: From Salem on I-5, take Exit 253 to Highway 22. Turn east and drive five miles to Highway 214. Turn left (east) and drive 15 miles to the park.

Contact: Silver Falls State Park, 20024 Silver Falls Hwy. SE, Sublimity, OR 97385; 503/873-8681 or 800/452-5687; fax 503/873-8925.

19 Fishermen's Bend

🚶 🚲 🛶 🚗
🐎 ⛺ ♿ 🚐 △ 7

Fishermen's Bend is a popular site for anglers of all ages, and the sites are spacious. A barrier-free fishing and river viewing area and a network of trails provide access to more than a mile of river. There's a one-mile, self-guided nature trail, and the nature center has a variety of displays. The amphitheater has films and activities on weekends. The front gate closes at 10 P.M.

Location: On the North Santiam River; Portland and the Willamette Valley map 4, grid b4.

Campsites, facilities: There are 39 sites for tents, trailers, or RVs; 21 are pull-through with water hookups, and 18 are tent/camper sites with water spigots nearby. There are also three group sites available for up to 60 people each, and two cabins. Drinking water, picnic tables, and fire pits are provided. Restrooms with flush toilets, sinks, and hot showers are available, with wheelchair facilities, as well as a dump station and garbage containers. A boat ramp, day-use area with playgrounds, baseball, volleyball, and basketball courts and fields, horseshoe pits, firewood for sale, and a picnic shelter are also available. Leashed pets are permitted.

Reservations, fees: Reservations accepted for group sites only ($6 reservation fee). Sites are $12–18 per night, $5 per night for an additional vehicle. Group sites are $60–90 per night. Cabins are $35 per night. Senior discount available. Open mid-May to mid-October.

Directions: From Salem on I-5, take Exit 253 to Highway 22. Turn east and drive 32 miles to the campground on the right.

Contact: Bureau of Land Management, Salem District Office, 1717 Fabry Rd. SE, Salem, OR 97306; 503/375-5646; reservations 888/242-4256; fax 503/375-5622; website: www.or.blm.gov/salem.

20 Elkhorn Valley

🏞️ 🏊 🎣 🐕 🚐 🏕️   7

This pretty campground along the Little North Santiam River, not far from the North Fork of the Santiam River, has easy access, an on-site host, and is only a short drive away from a major metropolitan area. The front gate is locked from 10 P.M. to 7 A.M. daily. This is an alternative to Shady Cove, which is about 10 miles to the east.

Location: On the Little North Santiam River; Portland and the Willamette Valley map 4, grid b5.

Campsites, facilities: There are 24 sites for tents, trailers, or RVs up to 18 feet long. Picnic tables, garbage bins, fire grills, vault toilets, and drinking water are available. Firewood is available for purchase. Leashed pets are permitted.

Reservations, fees: No reservations accepted. Sites are $10 per night, $5 per night for an additional vehicle. There is a 14-day stay limit. Senior discount available. Open mid-May to late September.

Directions: From Salem on I-5, take Exit 253 to Highway 22. Turn east and drive 25 miles to Elkhorn Road (North Fork Road). Turn left (northeast) and drive nine miles to the campground on the left.

Contact: Bureau of Land Management, Salem District Office, 1717 Fabry Rd. SE, Salem, OR 97306; 503/375-5646; fax 503/375-5622; website: www.or.blm.gov/salem.

21 John Neal Memorial Park

🏞️ 🎣 🚗 🐕 🛶 🚐 🏕️   6

This camp is set on the banks of the North Santiam River, offering good boating and trout fishing possibilities. Other options include exploring lakes and trails in the adjacent national forest land or visiting Silver Falls State Park.

Location: On the North Santiam River; Portland and the Willamette Valley map 4, grid b4.

Campsites, facilities: There are 40 sites for tents, trailers, and self-contained RVs. Restrooms, garbage bins, and drinking water are available. Recreational facilities include a boat ramp, a playground, horseshoes, a barbecue, and a recreation field. Ice and a grocery are within one mile. Leashed pets are permitted.

Reservations, fees: No reservations. Sites are $11 per night. Open May through October, depending on weather.

Directions: From Salem drive east on Highway 22 for about 20 miles to Highway 226. Turn right and drive south for two miles to Lyons and John Neal Park Road. Turn east and drive a short distance to the campground on the left.

Contact: Linn County Parks Department, 3010 Ferry St. SW, Albany, OR 97321; 541/ 967-3917; fax 541/924-0202; website: www .co.linn.or.us.

22 Yellowbottom

7

This campground is across the road from Quartzville Creek and is always missed by out-of-town visitors. It's nestled under a canopy of old-growth forest. The Rhododendron Trail, which is just under a mile, provides a challenging hike through forest and patches of rhododendrons. Some folks gold-pan here. Though primitive, the camp is ideal for a quiet getaway weekend.

Location: On Quartzville Creek; Portland and the Willamette Valley map 4, grid d5.

Campsites, facilities: There are 21 sites for tents, trailers, or RVs up to 28 feet; 10 are drive-through. Picnic tables, garbage bins, and fire grills are provided. Drinking water and vault toilets are available. Firewood is available for purchase. Some facilities are wheelchair-accessible. Leashed pets are permitted. There is a camp host.

Reservations, fees: No reservations. Sites are $8 per night, with a 14-day stay limit, $5 per night for an additional vehicle. Senior discount available. Open mid-May to late September.

Directions: From Albany drive east on U.S. 20 for about 35 miles (through Sweet Home) to Quartzville Road. Turn left (northeast) on Quartzville Road and drive 24 miles to the campground on the left.

Contact: Bureau of Land Management, Salem District, 1717 Fabry Rd. SE, Salem, OR 97306; 503/375-5646; fax 503/375-5622.

23 Waterloo County Campground

8

There is more than a mile of South Santiam River frontage in this campground. Swimming, fishing, picnicking, and field sports are options here. Small boats with trolling motors are the only boats usable here.

Location: On the South Santiam River; Portland and the Willamette Valley map 4, grid e2.

Campsites, facilities: There are 121 sites for tents, trailers, or RVs; 101 have partial hookups. Drinking water, fire pits, and picnic tables are provided. Restrooms with showers are available. Boat ramps and a playground are in the surrounding day-use area. A small grocery is within one mile. Leashed pets are permitted.

Reservations, fees: Reservations accepted ($11 reservation fee). Sites are $13–16 per night; there is a $5 fee for one additional vehicle. Senior discounts are available. Open year-round.

Directions: From Albany drive east on U.S. 20 for about 20 miles through Lebanon to the Waterloo exit. Turn north at the Waterloo exit and drive approximately two miles to the camp on the right. The camp is on the south side of the South Santiam River.

Contact: Linn County Parks Department, 3010 Ferry St. SW, Albany, OR 97321; 541/967-3917; fax 541/924-0202; website: www.co .linn.or.us.

24 Whitcomb Creek County Park

🏃 ⛱ 🏊 🚤
🐕 ♿ 🚐 ⛺ 8

This camp is on the north shore of Green Peter Reservoir in a wooded area with lots of ferns, which gives it a rainforest feel. Recreation options include swimming, sailing, hiking, and picnicking. Two boat ramps are on the reservoir about a mile from camp.

Location: On Green Peter Reservoir; Portland and the Willamette Valley map 4, grid e4.

Campsites, facilities: There are 39 tent, trailer, or RV sites. Picnic tables are provided. Drinking water is available to haul; vault toilets and garbage bins are available. Facilities are within 15 miles. Leashed pets are permitted.

Reservations, fees: Reservations accepted ($11 reservation fee). Sites are $11 per night. Open April through October.

Directions: From Albany drive east on U.S. 20 for about 35 miles (through Lebanon and Sweet Home) to the Quartzville Road exit (near Foster Reservoir). Turn north on Quartzville Road and drive 10 miles to the campground.

Contact: Linn County Parks Department, 3010 Ferry St. SW, Albany, OR 97321; 541/967-3917; fax 541/924-0202; website: www.co .linn.or.us.

25 Sunnyside County Park

This is Linn County's most popular park. Recreation options include boating, fishing, water-skiing, and swimming. A golf course is within 15 miles.

Location: On Foster Reservoir; Portland and the Willamette Valley map 4, grid e4.

Campsites, facilities: There are 165 sites for tents, trailers, or RVs. Electricity and drinking water are available at 133 sites; 27 sites are reserved for groups, who must take a minimum of eight sites, with a maximum of eight people per site. Drinking water, flush toilets, showers, a sanitary dump station, picnic areas, volleyball courts, a boat ramp, and moorage are available. Firewood can be obtained for a fee. Additional facilities are within two miles. Leashed pets are permitted.

Reservations, fees: Reservations accepted ($11 reservation fee). Sites are $13–16 per night; there is a $5 fee for one additional vehicle. Senior discounts are available. Open April through October.

Directions: From Albany drive east on U.S. 20 for about 35 miles (through Lebanon and Sweet Home) to the Quartzville Road exit (near Foster Reservoir). Turn north on Quartzville Road and drive one mile to the campground on the right. The camp is on the south side of Foster Reservoir.

Contact: Linn County Parks Department, 3010 Ferry St. SW, Albany, OR 97321; 541/967-3917; fax 541/924-0202; website: www.co .linn.or.us.

26 Cascadia State Park

🏃 ⛱ 🐟
🐕 ♿ 🚐 ⛺ 7

The highlight of this 258-acre park is Soda Creek Falls, with a fun three-quarter-mile hike to reach it. The park is set along the banks of the Santiam River. A newer trail ushers you through Douglas fir trees along the river, a good place to fish and swim. It's a great spot for a more intimate getaway for hikers, and also for reunions and meets for families, Boy Scouts, and other groups.

Location: On the Santiam River; Portland and the Willamette Valley map 4, grid e5.

Campsites, facilities: There are 25 primitive sites for tents, trailers, or self-contained RVs up to 35 feet long, and two group areas for tents. Picnic tables, garbage bins, and fire grills are provided. Drinking water, vault toilets, firewood, and ice are available. Some facilities are wheelchair-accessible. Leashed pets are permitted.

Reservations, fees: Reservations accepted for group areas only. Sites are $7–12 per night, $5 per night for an additional vehicle. Group sites are $60 for up to 25 people and $2.40 for each addtional person. Major credit cards accepted. Open March through October, weather permitting.

Directions: From Albany drive east on U.S. 20 for 40 miles to the park on the left (14 miles east of the town of Sweet Home).

Contact: Cascadia State Park, P.O. Box 736, Cascadia, OR 97329; 800/551-6949 or 541/367-6021, reservations 503/854-3406.

27 Whittaker Creek

7

This campground is home to one of the area's premier salmon spawning grounds, where annual runs of chinook, coho salmon, and steelhead can be viewed from the campground. The Old Growth Ridge Trail is accessible from the campground. This moderately difficult trail ascends 1,000 feet above the Siuslaw River through a stand of old-growth Douglas fir. Fishing is for trout and crayfish.

Location: Near the Siuslaw River; Portland and the Willamette Valley map 5, grid b5.

Campsites, facilities: There are 31 sites for tents, trailers, or RVs up to 35 feet long. Picnic tables and fire pits are provided. A camp host is on-site, and drinking water, vault toilets (wheelchair-accessible), garbage bins,

boat ramp, swimming beach, playground, and a picnic shelter are available. Leashed pets are permitted. One campsite is wheelchair-accessible.

Reservations, fees: No reservations accepted. Sites are $8 per night, with a charge of $5 per each additional vehicle. Senior discount available. Open mid-May through mid-October, weather permitting.

Directions: From Eugene drive west on Highway 126 for 33 miles to Siuslaw River Road. Turn left (south) and drive two miles to the campground on the right.

Contact: Bureau of Land Management, Eugene District Office, P.O. Box 10226, Eugene, OR 97440-2226; 541/683-6600; fax 541/683-6981.

28 Clay Creek

7

Clay Creek Trail, a two-mile loop, takes you to a ridge overlooking the river valley and is well worth the walk. Fishing for trout and crayfish is popular. Sites are situated in a forest of cedars, Douglas fir, and maple trees. The campground gets a medium amount of use.

Location: Near the Siuslaw River; Portland and the Willamette Valley map 5, grid b5.

Campsites, facilities: There are 21 sites for tents, trailers, or RVs up to 35 feet long. Picnic tables and fire pits are provided. Drinking water, vault toilets (one is wheelchair-accessible), garbage bins, a swimming beach with changing rooms, softball field, horseshoe pits, playground, and two group picnic shelters with fireplaces are available. There is a camp host. Leashed pets are permitted. One campsite is wheelchair-accessible.

Reservations, fees: No reservations accepted. Sites are $8 per night, with a charge of $5 per each additional vehicle. Senior discount available. Open mid-May through mid-October, depending on the weather.

Directions: From Eugene drive west on Highway 126 for 33 miles to Siuslaw River Road. Turn left (south) and drive 9.7 miles to Siuslaw River Access Road. Bear left and continue six miles to the campground on the right.

Contact: Bureau of Land Management, Eugene District Office, P.O. Box 10226, Eugene, OR 97440-2226; 541/683-6600; fax 541/683-6981.

29 KOA Sherwood Forest

5

Seven miles south of Eugene, this is an easy-to-reach layover for RV travelers heading up and down on I-5. Nearby recreational facilities include a golf course and tennis courts.

Location: Near Eugene; Portland and the Willamette Valley map 5, grid a8.

Campsites, facilities: There are 20 tent sites and 100 sites for trailers or RVs of any length. Electricity, drinking water, sewer hookups, and picnic tables are provided. Flush toilets, sanitary services, showers, a recreation hall, a store, a laundry room, ice, a playground, and a swimming pool are available. Bottled gas and a café are within one mile. Pets and motorbikes are permitted.

Reservations, fees: Reservations accepted. Sites are $17–23 per night. Open year-round.

Directions: From Eugene drive south on I-5 for seven miles to the Creswell exit. Take that exit and turn west on Oregon Avenue and drive one half block to the campground at 298 E. Oregon Avenue.

Contact: KOA Sherwood Forest, 298 E. Oregon Ave., Creswell, OR 97426; 541/895-4110; fax 541/895-5037; website: skydesigns.com/koa.

30 Pass Creek County Park

7

This decent layover spot for travelers on I-5 can be found in a wooded, hilly area with many shaded sites. View of the mountains give the park scenic value. There is a covered pavilion and gazebo with barbecue grills for get-togethers. You can find fishing and other water activities 11 miles away, and there is a covered bridge eight miles away for the history seekers. There are no other campgrounds in the immediate area, so if it's late and you need a place to stay, grab this one.

Location: Near Cottage Grove; Portland and the Willamette Valley map 5, grid c7.

Campsites, facilities: There are 30 tent sites and 30 sites for trailers or RVs up to 30 feet long. Electricity, drinking water, sewer hookups, and picnic tables are provided. Flush toilets, showers, and a playground are available. A store, a café, and ice are within one mile. Leashed pets are permitted.

Reservations, fees: No reservations accepted. Sites are $11–14 per night. Senior discount available for Douglas County residents. Open year-round.

Directions: On I-5 drive to Exit 163 (between Roseburg and Eugene). Take Exit 163 and turn west on Curtain Park Road. Drive west (under the freeway) for a very short distance to the park entrance.

Contact: Pass Creek County Park, P.O. Box 81, Curtin, OR 97428; 541/942-3281; website: www.co.douglas.or.us/parks.

31 Pine Meadows

6

This campground is surrounded by a varied landscape—marshland, grassland, and forest—near the banks of Cottage Grove

Reservoir. Boating, fishing, water-skiing, and swimming are among the recreation options. It's an easy hop from I-5.

Location: On Cottage Grove Reservoir; Portland and the Willamette Valley map 5, grid c8.

Campsites, facilities: There are 92 sites for tents, trailers, or RVs of any length, with some drive-through sites. Drinking water, picnic tables, garbage bins, and fire rings are provided. Flush toilets, sanitary disposal station, showers, children's play area, an amphitheater, interpretive displays, and a swimming area are available. A boat dock, launching facilities, and a minimarket are nearby. Leashed pets and street-legal motorbikes are permitted.

Reservations, fees: Reservations accepted ($8.65 reservation fee). Sites are $12 per night, $4 per night for an additional vehicle. Senior discount available. Open mid-May to mid-September.

Directions: From Eugene drive south on I-5 past Cottage Grove to Exit 172. Take that exit to London Road and drive south for 4.5 miles to Reservoir Road. Turn left and drive three miles to the camp entrance on the right.

Contact: U.S. Army Corps of Engineers, Recreation Information, Cottage Grove, OR 97424; 541/942-8657 or 541/942-5631, reservations 877/444-6777; fax 541/942-1305; website: www.nwp.usace.army.mil, for reservations: www.reserveusa.com.

32 Cottage Grove Lake/ Primitive

6

This campground on Cottage Grove Reservoir is open to boating, fishing, water-skiing, and swimming. See the description of neighboring Pine Meadows for more information.

Location: On Cottage Grove Reservoir; Portland and the Willamette Valley map 5, grid c8.

Campsites, facilities: There are 15 primitive sites for tents, or small, self-contained trailers or RVs. Picnic tables, vault toilets, drinking water, garbage bins, and fire rings are provided. Boat docks, launching facilities, and a minimarket are nearby. Leashed pets and street-legal motorbikes are permitted.

Reservations, fees: Reservations accepted ($8.65 reservation fee). Sites are $6 per night, $4 per night for an additional vehicle. Senior discount available. Open late May to early September.

Directions: From Eugene drive south on I-5 past Cottage Grove to Exit 172. Take that exit to London Road and drive south for 4.5 miles to Reservoir Road. Turn left and drive three miles to the camp entrance.

Contact: U.S. Army Corps of Engineers, Recreation Information, Cottage Grove, OR 97424; 541/942-8657 or 541/942-5631, reservations 877/444-6777; fax 541/942-1305; website: www.nwp.usace.army.mil, for reservations: www.reserveusa.com.

33 Cascara Campground

7

Campsites are set back and across the road from the reservoir, but you still get a lake view. Most sites have Douglas fir and white fir tree cover. These are spacious campsites. Water recreation is the primary activity here. Personal watercraft and water-skiing are allowed. Lake level drops in August. Water temperature is ideal for summer swimming.

Location: Fall Creek Reservoir State Recreation Area; Portland and the Willamette Valley map 6, grid a2.

Campsites, facilities: There are five walk-in sites for tents and 42 sites for trailers or RVs; no pull-through sites. Picnic tables, garbage service, and fire grills are provided. Drinking water, vault toilets, pay phone, and firewood are available, and there is a camp host.

A boat launch, dock, and swimming area are also available. Leashed pets are permitted.

Reservations, fees: No reservations. Sites are $11 per night, plus $5 for each additional vehicle. Major credit cards accepted. Open May through September.

Directions: From south Eugene on I-5, take Exit 188 to Highway 58. Drive 11 miles south to Lowell and Pioneer Street (at the covered bridge). Turn left and drive less than a quarter mile to West Boundary Road. Turn left and drive one block to Lowell Jasper Road. Turn right and drive 1.5 miles to Unity and Place Road. Turn right and drive about one mile to a fork with North Shore Road (Big Fall Creek Road). Bear left onto Big Fall Creek Road and drive about eight miles to the head of Fall Creek Reservoir and Peninsula Road (Forest Road 6250). Turn right and drive a half mile to the campground.

Contact: Fall Creek Reservoir State Recreation Area, P.O. Box 511, Lowell, OR 97452; 541/937-1173; or Oregon Parks and Recreation Department, P.O. Box 500, 97207 Portland, OR; 800/551-6949; website: www .Oregonstateparks.org.

34 Dexter Shores Motorhome and RV Park

7

If you're driving on I-5, this RV park is well worth the 15-minute drive out of Springfield. It's across the street from Dexter Point Reservoir, where fishing and boating are permitted. Swimming, sailing, windsurfing, and water-skiing are allowed on nearby Dexter and Fall Creek Lakes. There are three authentic Sioux tepees on the property in the summer, and three cabins.

Location: Near Dexter Point Reservoir; Portland and the Willamette Valley map 6, grid a2.

Campsites, facilities: There are five tent sites and 56 sites for trailers or RVs up to 40 feet in length, three tepees, and three one-bedroom cabins. Electricity, drinking water, sewer, cable TV and telephone hookups, picnic tables, and fire pits are provided. Flush toilets, sanitary services, showers, firewood, laundry room, and a playground are available. Bottled gas, a café, a restaurant, and ice are within one mile. Boat docks and launching facilities are nearby. Leashed pets and motorbikes permitted. No pets or smoking in vacation rentals.

Reservations, fees: Reservations accepted. Sites are $18–22 per night, tepees are $35, $40, and $45 per night; cabins are $85 on weekends, $65 on weekdays. Pet fee is $1 per pet per night. Open year-round.

Directions: From south Eugene on I-5, drive to Exit 188A and Highway 58. Take Highway 58 east and drive 11.5 miles to Lost Creek Road. Turn right (south) and drive to Dexter Road. Turn left (in front of the café) and drive east for one half block to the park on the right.

Contact: Dexter Shores Motorhome and RV Park, P.O. Box 70, Dexter, OR 97431; 541/937-3711, reservations 866/558-9777; fax 541/937-1724; website:dextershoresrvpark.com.

35 Baker Bay County Park

6

This campground is along the shore of Dorena Lake, where fishing, sailing, water-skiing, canoeing, swimming, and boating are among the recreation options. Row River Trail follows around part of the lake for a hike or bike ride, and there are covered bridges in the area. Golf can be pursued in Cottage Grove.

Location: On Dorena Lake; Portland and the Willamette Valley map 6, grid b1.

Campsites, facilities: There are 49 sites for tents, trailers, or self-contained RVs up to 35 feet long, plus two group sites for up to 25 people per group. Picnic tables and fire grills are provided. Drinking water, flush toilets, coin-operated showers, firewood, garbage bins, and a dump station are available. Some facilities are wheelchair-accessible. A concession stand with ice is in the park. A store is within two miles. Boat docks and launching facilities are nearby, with seasonal on-shore facilities for catamarans. Leashed pets are permitted.

Reservations, fees: Reservations accepted for group sites only, with a $40 deposit. Single sites are $12 per night, with an additional fee of $5 for additional vehicles, and group sites are $40 per night. Open mid-April through mid-October.

Directions: From Eugene drive south on I-5 for 22 miles to Cottage Grove and Exit 174 (Dorena Lake exit). Take that exit to Row Road and drive east for 4.4 miles (the road becomes Government Road). Bear right and drive 2.8 miles to the campground entrance on the left.

Contact: Baker Bay, 356 Government Rd., Dorena, OR 97434; 541/942-7669; website: www.co.lane.or.us/park.

36 Schwarz Park

7

This large campground is set below Dorena Lake on the Row River, where fishing, swimming, boating, and water-skiing are among the nearby recreation options. Note that chances of rain are high from May through mid-June and that there is a posted warning for consumption of fish from Dorena Lake. The Row River Trail parallels Dorena Lake's north shoreline for 6.2 miles. This paved trail is excellent for walking, bike riding, and shoreline access.

Location: On Dorena Lake; Portland and the Willamette Valley map 6, grid b1.

Campsites, facilities: There are 72 sites for trailers or RVs of any length, and six group sites. Drinking water, garbage bins, picnic tables and fire rings are provided. Flush toilets, a sanitary disposal station, and showers are available. Boat-launching facilities are on the lake about two miles upstream. Three sites are wheelchair-accessible. Leashed pets and street-legal motorbikes are permitted.

Reservations, fees: Reservations accepted. Sites are $10 per night, group sites are $90 per night; an additional vehicle is $4 per night. Senior discount available. Open late April to late September.

Directions: From Eugene drive south on I-5 for 22 miles to Cottage Grove and Exit 174. Take that exit to Shoreview Drive and continue (past Row Road) four miles east to the campground entrance.

Contact: U.S. Army Corps of Engineers, Recreation Information, Cottage Grove, OR 97424; 541/942-8657 or 541/942-5631, reservations 877/444-6777; fax 541/942-1305; website: www.nwp.usace.army.mil, for reservations: www.reserveusa.com.

THE COLUMBIA RIVER GORGE AND MOUNT HOOD

The Columbia River Gorge and Mount Hood

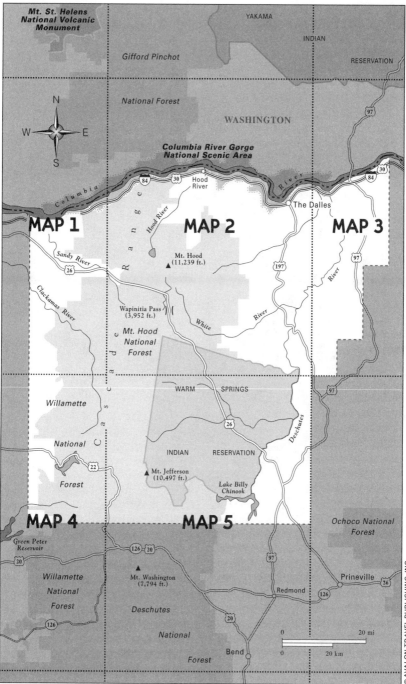

Mt. St. Helens
National Volcanic
Monument

Gifford Pinchot

National Forest

YAKAMA

INDIAN

RESERVATION

WASHINGTON

97

Columbia River Gorge
National Scenic Area

N
W   E
S

Columbia

84 30

Hood
River

Hood River

Range

Cascade

Sandy River

26

Clackamas River

Wapinitia Pass
(3,952 ft.)

White

River

River

Mt. Hood
(11,239 ft.)

MAP 1

MAP 2

MAP 3

Hood River

197

River

97

The Dalles

84 30

River

97

Mt. Hood
National
Forest

WARM   SPRINGS

Willamette

National

22

Forest

MAP 4

Green Peter
Reservoir

20

Willamette
National

Forest

126

INDIAN   RESERVATION

Mt. Jefferson
(10,497 ft.)

Lake Billy
Chinook

26

Deschutes

97

MAP 5

126 20

Mt. Washington
(7,794 ft.)

Deschutes

National

Forest

20

Bend

Redmond

126

97

Ochoco National
Forest

Prineville

26

126

0   20 mi

0   20 km

Map 1

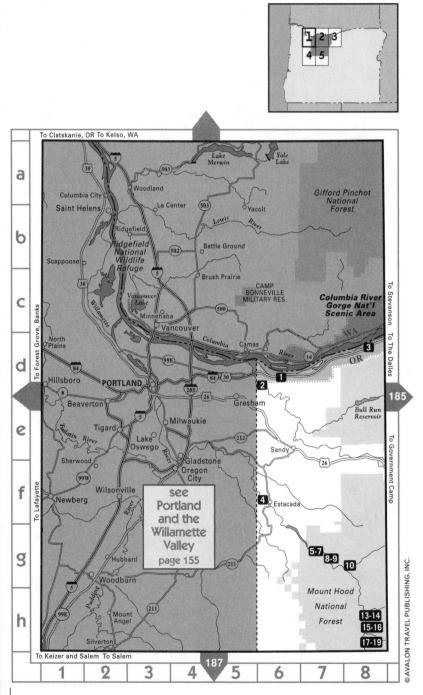

To Clatskanie, OR To Kelso, WA

a

Lake Merwin
Yale Lake
Woodland
Columbia City
Saint Helens
La Center
Yacolt
Gifford Pinchot National Forest

b

Ridgefield
Ridgefield National Wildlife Refuge
Scappoose
Battle Ground
Lewis River

c

Vancouver Lake
Minnehaha
Vancouver
CAMP BONNEVILLE MILITARY RES.
Columbia River Gorge Nat'l Scenic Area
To Stevenson To The Dalles

d

North Plains
Hillsboro
PORTLAND
Columbia River
Camas
WA
OR
3
1
2

185

e

Beaverton
Tigard
Lake Oswego
Milwaukie
Gresham
Bull Run Reservoir
Sandy
To Government Camp

f

Sherwood
Wilsonville
Newberg
Gladstone
Oregon City
4 Estacada

see Portland and the Willamette Valley page 155

g

Hubbard
Woodburn
5-7
8-9
10

h

Mount Angel
Silverton
Mount Hood National Forest
13-14
15-16
17-19

To Keizer and Salem To Salem

To Forest Grove, Banks
To Lafayette

187

1 2 3 4 5 6 7 8

© AVALON TRAVEL PUBLISHING, INC.

Map 2

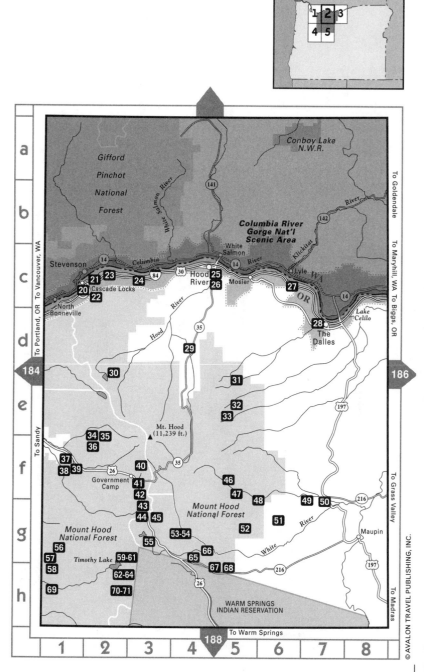

Conboy Lake N.W.R.

Gifford Pinchot National Forest

Columbia River Gorge Nat'l Scenic Area

To Goldendale

River

141

142

White Salmon River

White Salmon

Stevenson

14

Columbia

84

30

14

River

WA

OR

Lyle

Klickitat

To Maryhill, WA To Biggs, OR

Hood River

25

26

Mosier

27

14

21 23

24

20

22

Cascade Locks

North Bonneville

To Portland, OR To Vancouver, WA

Hood

River

35

29

28

The Dalles

Lake Celilo

184

30

31

186

197

32

33

Mt. Hood
(11,239 ft.)

34 35

36

37

38 39

40

35

To Sandy

Government Camp

41

42

43

44 45

46

47

48

49 50

216

To Grass Valley

51

52

53-54

55

Mount Hood National Forest

River

Maupin

56

57

58

69

Mount Hood National Forest

Timothy Lake

59-61

62-64

70-71

65

66

67 68

White

216

197

To Madras

WARM SPRINGS INDIAN RESERVATION

To Warm Springs

184 186 188

© AVALON TRAVEL PUBLISHING, INC.

The Columbia River Gorge and Mount Hood 185

Map 3

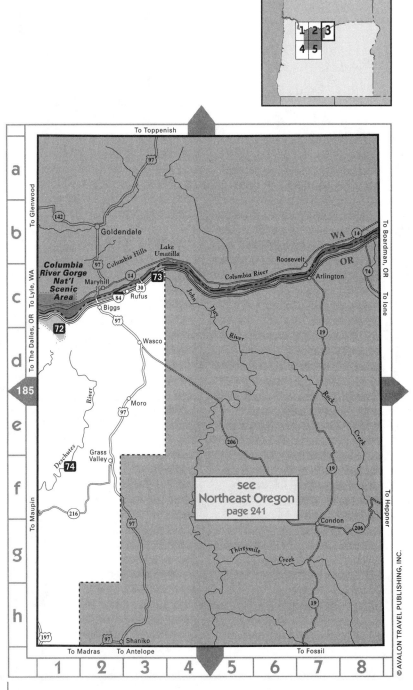

To Toppenish

To Glenwood

To Lyle, WA

To The Dalles, OR

To Maupin

Goldendale

Columbia River Gorge Nat'l Scenic Area

Columbia Hills

Lake Umatilla

Maryhill

Rufus

Biggs

Wasco

Moro

Grass Valley

Deschutes River

Columbia River

WA
OR

Roosevelt

Arlington

John Day River

Rock Creek

Thirtymile Creek

Condon

To Boardman, OR

To Ione

To Heppner

see
Northeast Oregon
page 241

Shaniko

To Madras   To Antelope

To Fossil

© AVALON TRAVEL PUBLISHING, INC.

Map 4

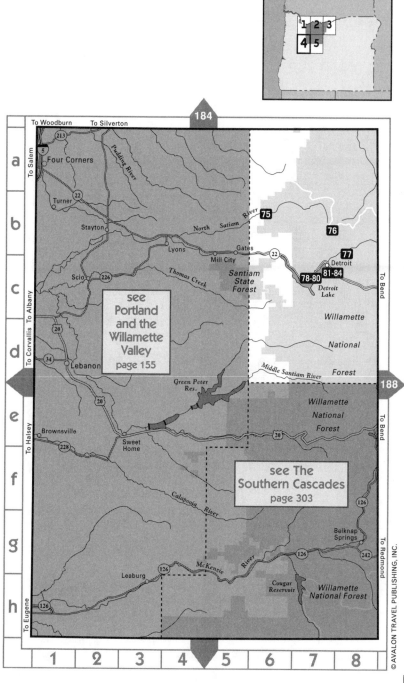

To Woodburn   To Silverton

184

To Salem

213

Four Corners

To Corvallis   To Albany

To Halsey

To Eugene

Turner

22

Stayton

Lyons

Scio

226

Thomas Creek

Lebanon

20

34

Green Peter
Res.

Brownsville

228

Sweet
Home

Calapooia River

Leaburg

126

McKenzie River

North Santiam River

Gates

Mill City

22

Santiam
State
Forest

75

76

77

Detroit

78-80

81-84

Detroit
Lake

Willamette

National

Forest

Middle Santiam River

Willamette

National

Forest

20

To Bend

To Bend

188

see
Portland
and the
Willamette
Valley
page 155

see The
Southern Cascades
page 303

126

Belknap
Springs

126

242

To Redmond

Cougar
Reservoir

Willamette
National Forest

© AVALON TRAVEL PUBLISHING, INC.

1   2   3   4   5   6   7   8

Map 5

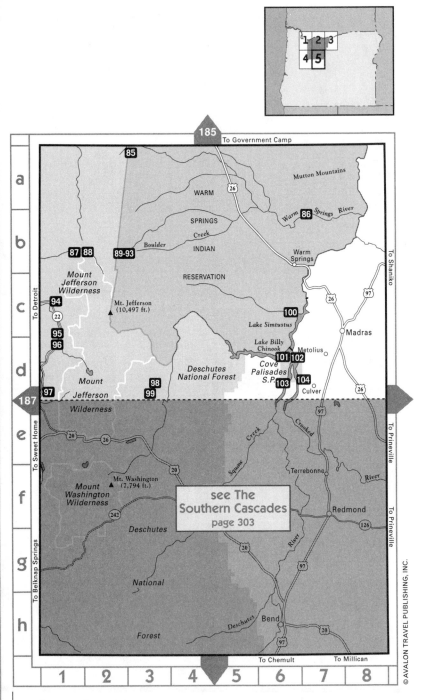

To Government Camp

85

Mutton Mountains

WARM

26

Warm 86 Springs River

SPRINGS

Creek

Boulder

Warm
Springs

87 88 89-93

INDIAN

Mount
Jefferson
Wilderness

RESERVATION

To Detroit

94

22

Mt. Jefferson
(10,497 ft.)

100

To Shaniko

97

26

Lake Simtustus

Madras

95
96

Lake Billy
Chinook

Metolius

97

Mount

101 102

Cove
Palisades
S.P.

98
99

Deschutes
National Forest

To Sweet Home

Jefferson

103 104

Culver

26

187

Wilderness

97

To Prineville

20

26

Squaw

Creek

Crooked

Mount
Washington
Wilderness

Mt. Washington
(7,794 ft.)

20

Terrebonne

River

To Prineville

242

Deschutes

**see The
Southern Cascades
page 303**

Redmond

126

To Belknap Springs

National

20

River

97

Forest

Deschutes

Bend

20

97

To Chemult

To Millican

© AVALON TRAVEL PUBLISHING, INC.

188 Oregon Camping

The Columbia River Gorge and Mount Hood

(CONTINUED ON NEXT PAGE)

🚹 Crown Point RV Park

🚶 🚲 🚗 🐴 🚐 ⛺ 6

This little park is near the Columbia River along scenic U.S. 30. Crown Point State Park is nearby and is open during the day. It offers views of the Columbia River Gorge and the historic Vista House, a memorial built in 1918 to honor Oregon's pioneers. Multnomah Falls offers another possible side trip.

Location: Near the Columbia River; The Columbia River Gorge and Mount Hood map 1, grid d6.

Campsites, facilities: There are five tent sites and 21 sites for trailers or RVs of any length. Electricity, drinking water, and picnic tables are provided. Flush toilets, bottled gas, sanitary services, coin-operated showers, a beauty shop, and a laundry room are available. There is a store and ice within walking distance. Leashed pets are permitted.

Reservations, fees: Reservations accepted. Sites are $15–22 per night. Senior discount available. Open year-round.

Directions: From Portland on I-84 eastbound, drive 16 miles to Exit 22 and Corbett. Take that exit and turn right on Corbett Hill Road and drive 1.5 miles to a Y with East Historic Columbia River Highway. Bear left and drive one-quarter mile to the park on the right.

Note: The recommended route has a 10 percent grade for 1.5 miles. An alternate route: from Portland on I-84 eastbound, drive to Exit 18/Lewis and Clark State Park. Take that exit to East Historic Columbia River Highway and drive seven miles to the park on the right.

Contact: Crown Point RV Park, 37000 E. Historic Columbia River Hwy., Corbett, OR 97019; 503/695-5207; fax 503/695-3217.

🛆 Oxbow Regional Park

🚶 🚲 🏊 🎣
🚗 🛶 🚐 ⛺ 7

This 1,000-acre park along the Sandy River, a short distance from the Columbia River Gorge, is a designated natural preservation area. Fishing, swimming, and nonmotorized boating are permitted here.

Location: On the Sandy River; The Columbia River Gorge and Mount Hood map 1, grid e6.

Campsites, facilities: There are 67 sites for tents, trailers, or RVs up to 35 feet long. Picnic tables are provided. Drinking water, flush and vault toilets, coin-operated showers, firewood, barbecues, and a playground are available. Boat-launching facilities are nearby. Gates lock at sunset and open at 6:30 A.M. No pets are permitted.

Reservations, fees: No reservations accepted. Sites are $10–15 per night. Open year-round, but subject to periodic closure; call for current status.

Directions: From Portland on I-84, drive to Exit 17. Turn south on Highway 257 and drive three miles to Division Street. Turn left and drive seven miles to the park.

Contact: Oxbow Regional Park, 3010 S.E. Oxbow Pkwy., Gresham, OR 97080; 503/663-4708. The park is managed by Metro-Region Parks and Green Spaces.

🛆 Ainsworth State Park

🚶 🐴 🚐 ⛺ 8

This state park is set along the scenic Columbia River Gorge, where the world's greatest concentration of high waterfalls, including famous Multnomah Falls, is on view. From the Nesmith Point Trail, there's a great view of St. Peter's Dome. A two-mile section of the Columbia River Gorge Trail connects this park with John Yeon State Park, which is open during the day. Anglers should check out the Bonneville Fish Hatchery.

Location: Along the Columbia River Gorge; The Columbia River Gorge and Mount Hood map 1, grid d8.

Campsites, facilities: There are 50 sites with full hookups for trailers or RVs up to 60 feet long, and five hiker/biker sites for tent camping. Picnic tables and fire grills are provided. Drinking water, flush toilets, showers, garbage bins, sanitary disposal station, and firewood are available. Leashed pets are permitted.

Reservations, fees: No reservations accepted. Sites are $13–20 per night, $5 per night for hiker/biker sites; $7 per night for an additional vehicle. Major credit cards accepted. Open March through October, weather permitting.

Directions: From Portland on I-84 eastbound, drive 37 miles to Exit 35. Turn southwest on the Columbia River Scenic Highway and continue a short distance to the park. An alternate route is to take the historic Columbia River Highway, a designated scenic highway, all the way from Portland (37 miles).

Contact: Columbia River Gorge District, P.O. Box 100, Corbett, OR 97019; 800/551-6949 or 503/695-2301.

❹ Milo McIver State Park

7

Though only 45 minutes from Portland, this park is far enough off the beaten track to provide a feeling of separation from the metropolitan area. It's set along the banks of the Clackamas River and has a boat ramp. Trails for hiking are available, and a 4.5-mile equestrian trail is also accessible. A fish hatchery is a nearby point of interest. Every April, 300 actors participate in a Civil War re-enactment here.

Location: On the Clackamas River; The Columbia River Gorge and Mount Hood map 1, grid f6.

Campsites, facilities: There are nine primitive tent sites and 44 sites with water and electrical hookups for trailers or RVs up to 50 feet long, one hiker/biker site, and three group tent areas. Picnic tables and fire grills are provided. Drinking water, garbage bins, flush toilets, sanitary disposal station, showers, picnic shelters, and firewood are available. Most facilities are wheelchair-accessible. Boat-launching facilities and an 18-hole disc golf course ("Frisbee golf") are nearby. Group facilities are available. Leashed pets are permitted.

Reservations, fees: Reservations accepted ($6 reservation fee). Sites are $10–16 per night, $7 per night for an additional vehicle; group sites are $60 per night. Major credit cards accepted. Open mid-March through October.

Directions: From Portland drive east on U.S. 26 from Gresham 11 miles to Sandy and Highway 211. Turn right (south) and drive six miles to a junction. Turn south (still Highway 211) and drive five miles to the park entrance road on the right.

Contact: Milo McIver State Park, 24101 South Entrance Road, Estacada, OR 97023; 503/630-7150 or 800/551-6949, reservations 800/452-5687.

❺ Promontory

7

This Portland General Electric camp on North Fork Reservoir is part of a large recreation area and park. The water is calm and ideal for boating, and the trout fishing is excellent. This reservoir is actually a dammed-up overflow on the Clackamas River. A trail travels along about one mile of the lake shoreline.

Location: On North Fork Reservoir; The Columbia River Gorge and Mount Hood map 1, grid g7.

Campsites, facilities: There are 47 sites for tents, trailers, or RVs up to 35 feet long, and one group site that can accommodate up to 35 people. There are no RV hookups. Restrooms, garbage bins, showers, limited groceries, ice, a playground, horseshoes, covered picnic shelters with sinks and electric stoves, and snacks are available. A fish-cleaning station, a fishing pier, a children's fishing pond, a boat ramp, a dock, and boat rentals are also on-site. Some facilities are wheelchair-accessible, including restrooms, some sites, the boat ramp, and the fishing pier. Leashed pets are permitted.

Reservations, fees: Reservations recommended. Sites are $14.50 per night. Open May 15 to October 1.

Directions: From Portland drive east on U.S. 26 from Gresham 11 miles to Sandy and Highway 211. Turn right (south) and drive six miles to a junction. Turn south (still Highway 211) and drive six miles to Estacada. Continue south on Highway 224 and drive seven miles to the campground on the right. The route is well signed.

Contact: Portland General Electric, 121 S.W. Salmon St., Portland, OR 97204; 503/464-8515, reservations 503/630-7229; fax 503/464-2944; website: www.portlandgeneral.com/parks.

6 Lazy Bend

8

This campground is set at 800 feet elevation along the banks of the Clackamas River near the large North Fork Reservoir. It's far enough off the highway to provide a secluded, primitive feeling, though it fills quickly on weekends and holidays. There's catch-and-release fishing only in the Clackamas.

Location: On the Clackamas River in Mount Hood National Forest; The Columbia River Gorge and Mount Hood map 1, grid g7.

Campsites, facilities: There are 21 sites for tents, trailers, or RVs up to 16 feet long. Picnic tables, garbage service, and fireplaces are provided. Drinking water and flush toilets are available. Leashed pets are permitted.

Reservations, fees: Reservations accepted for some sites ($8.65 reservation fee). Sites are $12 per night, $6 per night for an additional vehicle. Senior discount available. Open late April through Labor Day.

Directions: From Portland drive east on U.S. 26 from Gresham 11 miles to Sandy and Highway 211. Turn right (south) and drive six miles to a junction. Turn south (still Highway 211) and drive six miles to Estacada. Continue south on Highway 224 and drive 10.5 miles to the campground on the right.

Contact: Mount Hood National Forest, Clackamas River Ranger District, 595 N.W. Industrial Way, Estacada, OR 97023; 503/630-6861, reservations 877/444-6777; fax 503/630-2299; website (for reservations): www.reserve usa.com.

7 Armstrong

5

This campground is set at an elevation of 900 feet along the banks of the Clackamas River and offers good fishing access. Fishing is catch-and-release only.

Location: On the Clackamas River in Mount Hood National Forest; The Columbia River Gorge and Mount Hood map 1, grid g7.

Campsites, facilities: There are 12 sites for tents, trailers, or RVs up to 16 feet long. Picnic tables and fire rings are provided. Vault toilets and drinking water are available. Garbage service is available in the summer only. Some facilities are wheelchair-accessible. Leashed pets are permitted.

Reservations, fees: Reservations accepted ($8.65 reservation fee). Sites are $12 per night, $6 per night for an additional vehicle. Senior discount available. Open year-round, with limited winter services.

Directions: From Portland drive east on U.S. 26 from Gresham 11 miles to Sandy and Highway 211. Turn right (south) and drive six miles to a junction. Turn south (still Highway 211) and drive six miles to Estacada. Continue south on Highway 224 and drive 15 miles to the campground on the right.

Contact: Mount Hood National Forest, Clackamas River Ranger District, 595 N.W. Industrial Way, Estacada, OR 97023; 503/630-6861, reservations 877/444-6777; fax 503/630-2299; website (for reservations): www.reserve usa.com.

8 Carter Bridge

 5

This is a small, flat campground popular with anglers. The Clackamas River flows along one end, and the other borders the highway, with the attendant traffic noise.

Location: On the Clackamas River in Mount Hood National Forest; The Columbia River Gorge and Mount Hood map 1, grid g7.

Campsites, facilities: There are 15 sites for tents, trailers, or RVs up to 28 feet long. Picnic tables and fire pits are provided. Drinking water, vault toilets, and garbage bins are available. One toilet is wheelchair-accessible. Leashed pets are permitted.

Reservations, fees: No reservations accepted. Sites are $10 per night, $5 per night for an additional vehicle. Senior discount available. Open late May to early September, weather permitting.

Directions: From Portland drive east on U.S. 26 from Gresham 11 miles to Sandy and Highway 211. Turn right (south) and drive six miles to a junction. Turn south (still Highway 211) and drive six miles to Estacada.

Continue south on Highway 224 and drive 15.2 miles to the campground on the left.

Contact: Mount Hood National Forest, Clackamas River Ranger District, 595 N.W. Industrial Way, Estacada, OR 97023; 503/630-6861; fax 503/630-2299.

9 Lockaby

 6

This campground is set at an elevation of 900 feet, along the banks of the Clackamas River, next to Armstrong. Fishing in the Clackamas River is catch-and-release only.

Location: On the Clackamas River in Mount Hood National Forest; The Columbia River Gorge and Mount Hood map 1, grid g7.

Campsites, facilities: There are 30 sites for tents, trailers, or RVs up to 16 feet long. Picnic tables, fireplaces, drinking water, garbage service, and vault toilets are available. Leashed pets are permitted.

Reservations, fees: Reservations accepted ($8.65 reservation fee). Sites are $6 per night, $3 per night for an additional vehicle. Senior discount available. Open late May to early September.

Directions: From Portland drive east on U.S. 26 from Gresham 11 miles to Sandy and Highway 211. Turn right (south) and drive six miles to a junction. Turn south (still Highway 211) and drive six miles to Estacada. Continue south on Highway 224 and drive 15.3 miles to the campground on the left.

Contact: Mount Hood National Forest, Estacada Ranger District, 595 N.W. Industrial Way, Estacada, OR 97023; 503/630-6861, reservations 877/444-6777; fax 503/630-2299; website (for reservations): www.reserveusa.com.

10 Roaring River

 8

This campground, set among old-growth cedars at the confluence of the Roaring and Clackamas Rivers at an elevation of 1,000 feet, has access to the Dry Ridge Trail. The trail starts in camp, and it's a butt-kicker of an uphill climb. Several other trails into the adjacent roadless area are accessible from camp. See a U.S. Forest Service map for details.

Location: On the Roaring River in Mount Hood National Forest; The Columbia River Gorge and Mount Hood map 1, grid h8.

Campsites, facilities: There are 19 sites for tents, trailers, or RVs up to 16 feet long. Picnic tables, garbage service, fireplaces, drinking water, and vault toilets are available. Leashed pets are permitted.

Reservations, fees: Reservations accepted ($8.65 reservation fee). Sites are $12 per night, $6 per night for an additional vehicle. Senior discount available. Open mid-May to mid-September.

Directions: From Portland drive east on U.S. 26 from Gresham 11 miles to Sandy and Highway 211. Turn right (south) and drive six miles to a junction. Turn south (still Highway 211) and drive six miles to Estacada and Highway 224. Bear south on Highway 224 and drive 18 miles to the campground on the left.

Contact: Mount Hood National Forest, Clackamas River Ranger District, 595 N.W. Industrial Way, Estacada, OR 97023; 503/630-6861, reservations 877/444-6777; fax 503/630-2299; website (for reservations): www.reserveusa.com.

11 Sunstrip

3

This campground on the banks of the Clackamas River offers fishing and rafting access. One of several camps along the Highway 224 corridor, Sunstrip is a favorite with rafting enthusiasts and can fill up quickly on weekends. For those wanting another kind of experience, however, the fact that the campground is squeezed between the river and the highway, with power lines traversing the site, may be a turn-off.

Location: On the Clackamas River in Mount Hood National Forest; The Columbia River Gorge and Mount Hood map 1, grid h8.

Campsites, facilities: There are nine sites for tents, trailers, or RVs up to 18 feet long. Picnic tables, garbage service, fireplaces, drinking water, and vault toilets are available. Leashed pets are permitted.

Reservations, fees: Reservations accepted ($8.65 reservation fee). Sites are $12 per night, $6 per night for an additional vehicle. Senior discount available. Open year-round, with limited winter services.

Directions: From Portland drive east on U.S. 26 from Gresham 11 miles to Sandy and Highway 211. Turn right (south) and drive six miles to a junction. Turn south (still Highway 211) and drive six miles to Estacada and Highway 224. Bear south on Highway 224 and drive 19 miles to the campground.

Contact: Mount Hood National Forest, Clackamas River Ranger District, 595 N.W. Industrial Way, Estacada, OR 97023; 503/630-6861, reservations 877/444-6777; fax 503/630-2299; website (for reservations): www.reserveusa.com.

12 Rainbow

6

This campground is set at an elevation of 1,400 feet along the banks of the Oak Grove Fork of the Clackamas River, not far from where it empties into the Clackamas River. The camp is less than a quarter mile from Ripplebrook Campground.

Location: On the Oak Grove Fork of the Clackamas River in Mount Hood National Forest; The Columbia River Gorge and Mount Hood map 1, grid h8.

Campsites, facilities: There are 17 sites for tents, trailers, or RVs up to 16 feet long. There is no drinking water. Garbage service is provided during the summer. Fire grills and picnic tables are provided. Vault toilets are available. Leashed pets are permitted.

Reservations, fees: Reservations accepted ($8.65 reservation fee). Sites are $10 per night, $5 per night for an additional vehicle. Senior discount available. Open year-round, with limited winter services.

Directions: From Portland drive east on U.S. 26 from Gresham 11 miles to Sandy and Highway 211. Turn right (south) and drive six miles to a junction. Turn south (still Highway 211) and drive six miles to Estacada and Highway 224. Bear south on Highway 224 and drive 27 miles in national forest (the road becomes Forest Road 46). Continue south and drive about 100 yards to the campground on the right.

Contact: Mount Hood National Forest, Clackamas River Ranger District, 595 N.W. Industrial Way, Estacada, OR 97023; 503/630-6861, reservations 877/444-6777; fax 503/630-2299; website (for reservations): www.reserve usa.com.

13 Indian Henry

🚶 🎣 🐕 ♿ 🚐 ⛺ 8

One of the most popular campgrounds in the Clackamas River Ranger District, Indian Henry is along the banks of the Clackamas River at an elevation of 1,250 feet and has a wheelchair-accessible trail. Group campsites and an amphitheater are available. The nearby Clackamas River Trail has fishing access.

Location: On the Clackamas River in Mount Hood National Forest; The Columbia River Gorge and Mount Hood map 1, grid h8.

Campsites, facilities: There are 86 sites for tents, trailers, or RVs up to 22 feet long, and eight group tent sites. Picnic tables, garbage service, and fire grills are provided. Flush toilets, a sanitary dump station, and drinking water are available. Some facilities are wheelchair-accessible. Leashed pets are permitted.

Reservations, fees: Reservations accepted ($8.65 reservation fee). Sites are $12 per night, $6 per night for an additional vehicle. Senior discount available. Call for group site rates. Open late May to early September.

Directions: From Portland drive east on U.S. 26 from Gresham 11 miles to Sandy and Highway 211. Turn right (south) and drive six miles to a junction. Turn south (still Highway 211) and drive six miles to Estacada and Highway 224. Bear south on Highway 224 and drive 23 miles to Forest Road 4620. Turn right and drive one-half mile southeast to the campground on the left.

Contact: Mount Hood National Forest, Clackamas River Ranger District, 595 N.W. Industrial Way, Estacada, OR 97023; 503/630-6861, reservations 877/444-6777; fax 503/630-2299; website (for reservations): www.reserve usa.com.

14 Ripplebrook

🚶 🎣 🐕 🚐 7

Shaded sites with river views are a highlight at this campground along the banks of the Oak Grove Fork of the Clackamas River, where fishing is artificial lures and catch-and-release only. Note that the road to this camp was closed for two years in the late 1990s, and only recently have campers begun to return.

Location: On the Oak Grove Fork of the Clackamas River in Mount Hood National Forest; The Columbia River Gorge and Mount Hood map 1, grid h8.

Campsites, facilities: There are 13 sites for trailers or RVs up to 16 feet long. Picnic tables, garbage service, and fire grills are provided. Vault toilets are available, but there is no drinking water. Leashed pets are permitted; horses are not allowed in the campground.

Reservations, fees: Reservations accepted ($8.65 reservation fee). Sites are $10 per night, $6 per night for an additional vehicle. Senior discount available. Open late April to late September.

Directions: From Portland drive east on U.S. 26 from Gresham 11 miles to Sandy and Highway 211. Turn right (south) and drive six miles to a junction. Turn south (still Highway 211) and drive six miles to Estacada and Highway 224. Bear south on Highway 224 and drive 26.5 miles to the campground entrance on the left.

Contact: Mount Hood National Forest, Clackamas River Ranger District, 595 N.W. Industrial Way, Estacada, OR 97023; 503/630-6861, reservations 877/444-6777; fax 503/630-2299; website (for reservations): www.reserve usa.com.

15 Alder Flat Hike-In

9

This secluded hike-in campground is set along the banks of the Clackamas River in old-growth forest. If you want peace and quiet and don't mind the short walk to get it, this is the spot. Be sure to pack out whatever you bring in and remember that fishing in the Clackamas River is catch-and-release only.

Location: On the Clackamas River in Mount Hood National Forest; The Columbia River Gorge and Mount Hood map 1, grid h8.

Campsites, facilities: There are six tent sites at this hike-in campground. Picnic tables and fire grills are provided. There is no drinking water, no toilet, and no garbage service; pack out all garbage. Leashed pets are permitted.

Reservations, fees: No reservations; no fee. Open year-round.

Directions: From Portland drive east on U.S. 26 from Gresham 11 miles to Sandy and Highway 211. Turn right (south) and drive six miles to a junction. Turn south (still Highway 211) and drive six miles to Estacada and Highway 224. Bear south on Highway 224 and drive 26 miles to the Ripplebrook Ranger Station. Parking for the camp is about one-half mile west of the ranger station at the Alder Flat Trailhead. Hike one mile to the campground.

Contact: Mount Hood National Forest, Clackamas Ranger District, 61431 E. Hwy. 224, Estacada, OR 97023; 503/630-4256.

16 Riverside

8

The banks of the Clackamas River are home to this campground set at an elevation of 1,400 feet. A trail worth hiking leaves the camp and follows the river for four miles north. Fishing is another option here, and several old forest roads in the vicinity make excellent mountain biking trails.

Location: On the Clackamas River in Mount Hood National Forest; The Columbia River Gorge and Mount Hood map 1, grid h8.

Campsites, facilities: There are 16 sites for tents, trailers, or RVs up to 22 feet long. Picnic tables, garbage service, and fire grills are provided. Vault toilets and drinking water are available. Leashed pets are permitted; no horses are allowed in the campground.

Reservations, fees: Reservations accepted ($8.65 reservation fee). Sites are $12 per night, $6 per night for an additional vehicle. Senior discount available. Open mid-May to late September.

Directions: From Portland drive east on U.S. 26 from Gresham 11 miles to Sandy and Highway 211. Turn right (south) and drive six miles to a junction. Turn south (still Highway 211) and drive six miles to Estacada and Highway 224. Bear south on Highway 224 and drive 27 miles and into national forest (Highway 224 becomes Forest Road 46). Continue 2.5 miles south on Forest Road 46 to the campground on the right.

Contact: Mount Hood National Forest, Clackamas River Ranger District, 595 N.W. Industrial Way, Estacada, OR 97023; 503/630-6861, reservations 877/444-6777; fax 503/630-2299; website (for reservations): www.reserve usa.com.

17 Riverford

![icons] 4

Good fishing is a bonus around this campground at the confluence of the Clackamas and Collawash Rivers, a two-minute walk from the campground. It's small, and the sites provide little privacy. It is set at an elevation of 1,500 feet.

Location: On the Clackamas and Collawash Rivers in Mount Hood National Forest; The Columbia River Gorge and Mount Hood map 1, grid h8.

Campsites, facilities: There are 10 sites for tents. Picnic tables and fire grills are provided. Vault toilets are available. Garbage service is provided in the summer. There is no drinking water at the campground; water is available at nearby Two Rivers Picnic Area. Leashed pets are permitted.

Reservations, fees: No reservations accepted. Sites are $10 per night, $5 per night

for an additional vehicle. Senior discount available. Open year-round, with limited winter services.

Directions: From Portland drive east on U.S. 26 from Gresham 11 miles to Sandy and Highway 211. Turn right (south) and drive six miles to a junction. Turn south (still Highway 211) and drive six miles to Estacada and Highway 224. Bear south on Highway 224 and drive 27 miles in national forest (the road becomes Forest Road 46). Continue south on Forest Road 46 for 3.5 miles to the campground on the right.

Contact: Mount Hood National Forest, Clackamas River Ranger District, 595 N.W. Industrial Way, Estacada, OR 97023; 503/630-6861; fax 503/630-2299.

18 Raab

![icons] 7

This camp is set at an elevation of 1,500 feet along the banks of the Collawash River about a mile from its confluence with the Clackamas River. It gets moderate use, but it's usually quiet and has a nice, secluded atmosphere with lots of privacy among the sites.

Location: On the Collawash River in Mount Hood National Forest; The Columbia River Gorge and Mount Hood map 1, grid h8.

Campsites, facilities: There are 27 sites for tents, trailers, or RVs up to 22 feet long. Picnic tables, garbage service, and fire grills are provided. Vault toilets are available. There is no drinking water in the campground; water is available one mile away at Two Rivers Picnic Area. Leashed pets are permitted.

Reservations, fees: Reservations accepted ($8.65 reservation fee). Sites are $10 per night, $5 per night for an additional vehicle. Senior discount available. Open late May to early September.

Directions: From Portland drive east on U.S. 26 from Gresham 11 miles to Sandy and Highway 211. Turn right (south) and drive six miles to a junction. Turn south (still Highway 211) and drive six miles to Estacada and Highway 224. Bear south on Highway 224 and drive 27 miles in national forest (the road becomes Forest Road 46). Continue south on Forest Road 46 for 2.5 miles to Forest Road 63. Turn right and drive 1.5 miles to the campground on the right.

Contact: Mount Hood National Forest, Clackamas River Ranger District, 595 N.W. Industrial Way, Estacada, OR 97023; 503/630-6861, reservations 877/444-6777; fax 503/630-2299; website (for reservations): www.reserve usa.com.

Directions: From Portland drive east on U.S. 26 from Gresham 11 miles to Sandy and Highway 211. Turn right (south) and drive six miles to a junction. Turn south (still Highway 211) and drive six miles to Estacada and Highway 224. Bear south on Highway 224 and drive 27 miles in national forest (the road becomes Forest Road 46). Continue south on Forest Road 46 for 3.5 miles to Forest Road 63. Turn right and drive three miles to Forest Road 70. Turn right again and drive one mile to the campground on the left.

Contact: Mount Hood National Forest, Clackamas River Ranger District, 595 N.W. Industrial Way, Estacada, OR 97023; 503/630-6861, reservations 877/444-6777; fax 503/630-2299; website (for reservations): www.reserveusa.com.

🔢19 Kingfisher

🚶 🎣 〰️ 🐴 🚐 🏕️ 7

This pretty campground set at an elevation of 1,250 feet among old-growth forest is situated along the banks of the Hot Springs Fork of the Collawash River, and it is about three miles from Bagby Hot Springs, a U.S. Forest Service day-use area. It's an easy 1.5-mile hike to the hot springs from the day-use area. Fishing access is near the camp.

Location: On the Hot Springs Fork of the Collawash River in Mount Hood National Forest; The Columbia River Gorge and Mount Hood map 1, grid h8.

Campsites, facilities: There are 23 sites for tents, trailers, or RVs up to 16 feet long. Picnic tables and fireplaces are provided. Garbage service is provided during the summer. Vault toilets and drinking water are available. Leashed pets are permitted.

Reservations, fees: Reservations accepted ($8.65 reservation fee). Sites are $12 per night, $6 per night for an additional vehicle. Senior discount available. Open year-round, with limited winter facilities.

🔢20 Eagle Creek

🚶 🎣 🐴 🚐 🏕️ 8

This is the oldest Forest Service Camp in America. It is a good base camp for a hiking trip. The camp is set at 400 feet elevation among old-growth Douglas fir and hemlock. The Eagle Creek Trail leaves the campground and goes 13 miles to Wahtum Lake, where it intersects with the Pacific Crest Trail. There is a primitive campground at the 7.5-mile point. The upper seven miles of the trail pass through the Hatfield Wilderness.

Location: Near the Columbia Wilderness in Mount Hood National Forest; The Columbia River Gorge and Mount Hood map 2, grid c1.

Campsites, facilities: There are 20 sites for tents, trailers, or RVs up to 22 feet long. Picnic tables and fire grills are provided. Drinking water, garbage bins, and flush toilets are available. Boat docks and launching facilities are nearby on the Columbia River. Leashed pets are permitted.

Reservations, fees: Reservations required for groups. Sites are $10 per night, $5 per night for an additional vehicle. Open mid-May to October.

Directions: From Portland drive east on I-84 for 40 miles to Bonneville. Continue east for two miles to the campground.

Contact: Columbia River Gorge National Scenic Area, 902 Wasco Ave., Suite 200, Hood River, OR 97031; 541/386-2333; fax 541/386-1916.

21 Cascade Locks Marine Park

8

This public riverfront park covers 200 acres and offers a museum and boat rides. The salmon fishing is excellent here. Stern-wheeler dinner cruises are available. A new bike-in provides a recreation option, along with nearby hiking trails and tennis courts.

Location: In Cascade Locks; The Columbia River Gorge and Mount Hood map 2, grid c2.

Campsites, facilities: There are 35 sites for tents, trailers, and RVs of any length. Picnic tables are provided. Drinking water, flush toilets, sanitary services, showers, boat docks, launching facilities, and a playground are available. Bottled gas, a store, a café, a coin laundry, and ice are within one mile. Leashed pets and motorbikes are permitted.

Reservations, fees: No reservations accepted. Sites are $15 per night. Open year-round, with limited winter facilities.

Directions: From Portland drive east on I-84 for 44 miles to Cascade Locks. Take Exit 44 to Wanapa Street and drive one-half mile to the sign for the park on the left. Turn left and drive to the park (well signed).

Contact: Cascade Locks Marine Park, P.O. Box 307, 355 Wanapa St., Cascade Locks, OR 97014; 541/374-8619; fax 541/374-8428.

22 KOA Cascade Locks

5

This is a good layover spot for RVers touring the Columbia River corridor. The campground offers level, shaded RV sites and grassy tent sites. Nearby recreation options include bike trails, hiking trails, and tennis courts. The 200-acre Cascade Locks Marine Park is nearby and offers everything from museums to boat trips.

Location: Near the Columbia River; The Columbia River Gorge and Mount Hood map 2, grid c2.

Campsites, facilities: There are 78 sites for tents, trailers, or RVs of any length, plus nine cabins. Electricity, drinking water, sewer hookups, and picnic tables are provided. Flush toilets, bottled gas, sanitary services, showers, firewood, a hot tub, cable TV hookups, modem, a recreation hall, a store, a laundry room, ice, a playground, and a heated swimming pool are available. A café is within one mile. Leashed pets and motorbikes are permitted.

Reservations, fees: Reservations accepted. Sites are $19–26 per night; cabins are $36–42 per night for two people. Major credit cards accepted. Open February through November.

Directions: From Portland drive east on I-84 for 44 miles to Cascade Locks and Exit 44. Turn east on Forest Lane and drive one mile to the campground.

Contact: KOA Cascade Locks, 841 N.W. Forest Ln., Cascade Locks, OR 97014; 541/374-8668, reservations 800/KOA-8698 (562-8698); website: www.koa.com.

23 Herman Creek Horse Camp

5

This rustic campground with spacious sites is set at 1,000 feet elevation and is about one-half mile from Herman Creek, not far from the Pacific Crest Trail. This is a particularly beautiful area, separated from Washington by the Columbia River. There are many recreation options here, including biking, hiking, fishing, and boat trips.

Location: Near the Pacific Crest Trail in Mount Hood National Forest; The Columbia River Gorge and Mount Hood map 2, grid c2.

Campsites, facilities: There are seven sites for tents, trailers, or RVs up to 24 feet long. Drinking water, garbage bins, fire grills, and picnic tables are provided. Stock handling facilities are available. Sanitary services, showers, a store, a café, a coin laundry, and ice are nearby. Leashed pets are permitted.

Reservations, fees: No reservations accepted. Sites are $8 per night, $5 per night for an additional vehicle. Senior discount available. Open mid-May to October.

Directions: From Portland drive east on I-84 for 44 miles to Cascade Locks and Exit 44. Take that exit and drive straight ahead to the frontage road (Wanapa Street). Continue 1.5 miles (the road becomes Herman Creek Road) to the campground on the right.

Contact: Columbia River Gorge National Scenic Area, 902 Wasco Ave., Suite 200, Hood River, OR 97031; 541/386-2333; fax 541/386-1916.

24 Wyeth

5

This is a good layover spot for Columbia River corridor cruisers. The camp is set at 400 feet elevation along Gordon Creek, near the Columbia. See the description of Herman Creek Horse Camp for recreation details.

Location: On Gordon Creek in Mount Hood National Forest; The Columbia River Gorge and Mount Hood map 2, grid c2.

Campsites, facilities: There are 16 sites for tents, trailers, or RVs up to 32 feet long, and three group sites. Fire grills and picnic tables are provided. Drinking water and flush toilets are available. Leashed pets are permitted.

Reservations, fees: No reservations accepted. Sites are $10 per night, $5 per night for an additional vehicle. Senior discount available. Open mid-May to October.

Directions: From Portland drive east on I-84 for 44 miles to Cascade Locks. Continue east on I-84 for seven miles to Wyeth and Exit 51. Turn right and drive a quarter mile to the campground entrance.

Contact: Columbia River Gorge National Scenic Area, 902 Wasco Ave., Suite 200, Hood River, OR 97031; 541/386-2333; fax 541/386-1916.

25 Viento State Park

8

This park along the Columbia River Gorge offers scenic hiking trails and some of the best windsurfing in the Gorge. A picturesque drive is available 12 miles to the east along old U.S. 30, which skirts the Columbia River. Viento has a day-use picnic area right next to a babbling creek. Weekend interpretive programs are offered during the summer. There are several other day-use state parks along I-84 just west of Viento, including Wygant, Vinzenz Lausmann, and Seneca Fouts. All offer quality hiking trails and scenic views.

Location: Along the Columbia River Gorge; The Columbia River Gorge and Mount Hood map 2, grid c4.

Campsites, facilities: There are 17 tent sites and 58 sites with water and electrical hookups for trailers or RVs up to 30 feet long, with some sites accessible for RVs up to 40 feet long. Picnic tables and fire grills are provided. Drinking water, garbage bins, flush toilets, showers, firewood, and a playground are available. Leashed pets are permitted (six-foot maximum length leash).

Reservations, fees: No reservations. Sites are $13–20 per night, $7 per night for an additional vehicle. Major credit cards accepted. Open March through October, weather permitting.

Directions: From Portland drive east on I-84 for 56 miles to Exit 56 (eight miles west of Hood River). Take Exit 56 and drive to the park entrance. The park is set on both sides of I-84.

Contact: Columbia River Gorge District, P.O. Box 126, Hood River, OR 97019; 541/374-8811 or 800/551-6949.

26 Tucker County Park

🐟 🚗 🐕
🛶 ♿ 🚐 ⛺   6

This county park along the banks of the Hood River is just far enough out of the way to be missed by most of the tourist traffic. Many people who choose this county park come for the windsurfing. Other recreation includes trout fishing, rafting, and kayaking.

Location: On the Hood River; The Columbia River Gorge and Mount Hood map 2, grid c4.

Campsites, facilities: There are 80 tent sites and 13 sites for tents, trailers, or RVs up to 30 feet long. Picnic tables and fire rings are provided. Electricity, drinking water, flush toilets, showers, firewood, and a playground are available. A store, a café, coin-operated laundry facilities, and ice are within two miles. Leashed pets are permitted. Most facilities are wheelchair-accessible.

Reservations, fees: No reservations accepted. Sites are $13–14 per night. Open April through October.

Directions: From Portland turn east on I-84 and drive about 65 miles to the town of Hood River to Exit 62. Take the exit and drive east on Cascade Street and continue to 13th Street (first light). Turn right (south) and drive through and out of town; 13th Street becomes Tucker Road and then Dee Highway (Highway 281). Follow the signs to Park-

dale. The park is four miles out of town on the right.

Contact: Hood River County Parks, 918 18th St., Hood River, OR 97031; 541/387-6889; fax 541/386-6325.

27 Memaloose State Park

🐕 🚐 ⛺   7

This park borrows its name from ancient Native Americans who used nearby Memaloose Island as a sacred burial ground. Set along the hottest part of the scenic Columbia River Gorge, it makes a prime layover spot for campers cruising the Oregon-Washington border. Nature programs and interpretive events are also held here. This popular camp receives a good deal of traffic, so plan on arriving early to claim a spot even if you have a reservation.

Location: In the Columbia River Gorge; The Columbia River Gorge and Mount Hood map 2, grid c6.

Campsites, facilities: There are 67 tent sites and 43 sites with full hookups for trailers or RVs up to 60 feet long. Picnic tables and fire grills are provided. Drinking water, garbage bins, flush toilets, sanitary disposal station, showers, and firewood are available. Leashed pets and motorbikes are permitted.

Reservations, fees: Reservations accepted ($6 reservation fee). Sites are $11–19 per night, $7 per night for an additional vehicle. Major credit cards accepted. Open mid-March to late October.

Directions: This park is accessible only to westbound traffic on I-84. From The Dalles drive west on I-84 for 11 miles to the signed turnoff. (The park is about 75 miles east of Portland.)

Contact: Columbia River Gorge District, P.O. Box 100, Corbett, OR 97019; 541/478-3008 or 800/551-6949, reservations 800/452-5687.

28 Lone Pine RV Park

7

This private park isn't far from the Columbia River, where fishing, boating, and swimming are options. The area gets hot weather and occasional winds shooting through the river canyon during summer. Nearby recreation possibilities include an 18-hole golf course and tennis courts.

Location: Near the Columbia River; The Columbia River Gorge and Mount Hood map 2, grid d7.

Campsites, facilities: There are 22 drive-through sites for trailers or RVs of any length. Electricity, drinking water, and sewer hookups are provided. Flush toilets, showers, a café, a laundry room, ice, and a playground are available. Bottled gas and sanitary services are within one mile. Boat docks and launching facilities are nearby. Leashed pets are permitted.

Reservations, fees: Reservations accepted. Sites are $22–25 per night. Open mid-April through September.

Directions: From Portland turn east on I-84 and drive about 90 miles to The Dalles and Exit 87. Take Exit 87 to U.S. 197 and drive less than a quarter mile to the park.

Contact: Lone Pine RV Park, 335 U.S. Hwy. 197, The Dalles, OR 97058; 541/506-3755.

29 Kinnickkinnick

5

The campground is on a peninsula that juts into Laurence Lake. Only nonmotorized boats are allowed on this lake. Tree cover is fairly sparse, so campsite privacy varies. More than half of the sites are a short walk in from your vehicle.

Location: On Laurence Lake in Mount Hood National Forest; The Columbia River Gorge and Mount Hood map 2, grid d4.

Campsites, facilities: There are 20 sites for tents, trailers, or RVs up to 16 feet long. No drinking water is available, but picnic tables and fire rings with fire grills are provided. Vault toilets, garbage bins, and a boat ramp are available. Some sites are wheelchair-accessible. Leashed pets are permitted.

Reservations, fees: No reservations accepted. Sites are $10 per night. Senior discount available. Open May through September, weather permitting.

Directions: From Portland drive 62 miles west on I-84 to the city of Hood River. Take Exit 64 and drive about 14 miles south on Highway 35 to the town of Mount Hood and Cooper Spur Road. Turn right and drive three miles to Parkdale and Clear Creek Road. Turn left (south) and drive three miles to the Laurence Lake turnoff. Turn right on Forest Road 2840 (Laurence Lake Road) and drive four miles to the campground on the right.

Contact: Mount Hood National Forest, Hood River Ranger District, 6780 Hwy. 35, Mount Hood, OR 97041; 541/352-6002; fax 541/352-7365.

30 Lost Lake

9

Only nonmotorized boats are allowed on this 240-acre clear lake set against the Cascade Range. This campground is nestled in an old-growth forest of cedar, Douglas fir, and hemlock trees at 3,200 feet. Many sites have a lake view, and there is a great view of Mount Hood from the campground. Significant improvements to this campground were completed in late 1999.

Location: On Lost Lake, Mount Hood National Forest, Hood River District; The Columbia River Gorge and Mount Hood map 2, grid e2.

Campsites, facilities: There are 125 sites for tents, trailers, or RVs up to 32 feet long, and there is one large, separate group site. A horse camp with a corral is also available. Picnic tables and fire rings with grills are provided. Drinking water, vault toilets, garbage containers, a dump station, and a covered picnic shelter are available. Cabins, a grocery store, showers, beach picnic areas, a boat launch, and boat rentals are nearby. Many sites are wheelchair-accessible, and there is barrier-free boating and fishing, as well as 3.5 miles of barrier-free trails. Leashed pets are permitted.

Reservations, fees: Reservations accepted for group sites only. Major credit cards accepted. Sites are $15–20 per night, with an additional $5 per extra vehicle. Group sites are $40 per night. Senior discount available. The campground is open from mid-May to mid-October, weather permitting.

Directions: From Portland drive 62 miles east on I-84 to the city of Hood River. Take Exit 62/Westcliff exit to Cascade Road and drive east on Cascade Road to 13th Street. Turn right on 13th Street and drive through Hood River Heights. The road turns into Dee Highway. Continue seven miles, then turn right onto Lost Lake Road (Forest Road 13). Continue seven miles to the campground.

Contact: Mount Hood National Forest, Hood River Ranger District, 6780 Hwy. 35, Mount Hood, OR 97041; 541/352-6002; fax 541/352-7365; for reservations (group sites only) call Lost Lake Resort at 541/386-6366.

31 Knebal Springs

6

This spot is in a semi-primitive area near Knebal Springs, an ephemeral water source. The Knebal Springs Trailhead is at the campground. A level family bike trail is available here, a nice plus. A trail from the camp provides access to a network of other trails in the area. A U.S. Forest Service map is advised.

Location: Near Knebal Springs in Mount Hood National Forest; The Columbia River Gorge and Mount Hood map 2, grid e5.

Campsites, facilities: There are eight sites for tents and small trailers or RVs up to 22 feet long. Drinking water, picnic tables, and fire grills are provided. Vault toilets and horse loading and tending facilities are available. Leashed pets are permitted. All garbage must be packed out.

Reservations, fees: No reservations accepted. Northwest Forest Pass ($30 annual fee) or $5 daily fee per parked vehicle is required. Senior discount available. Open June to early October, weather permitting.

Directions: From Portland turn east on I-84 and drive about 90 miles to Exit 87. Take Exit 87 and turn south on U.S. 197 and drive 13 miles to Dufur and Dufur Valley Road. Turn right on Dufur Valley Road and drive west for 12 miles to Forest Road 44. Continue west on Forest Road 44 for four miles to Forest Road 4430. Turn north and drive four miles to Forest Road 1720. Turn southwest and drive one mile to the campground.

Contact: Mount Hood National Forest, Barlow Ranger District, 780 N.E. Court St., Dufur, OR 97021; 541/467-2291; fax 541/467-2271.

32 Eightmile Crossing

7

This campground is set at an elevation of 4,200 feet along Eightmile Creek. It gets relatively little camping pressure. It's pretty and shaded, with sites scattered along the banks of the creek. From the day-use area you have access to a nice hiking trail that runs along Eightmile Creek. There is also a three-quarter-mile wheelchair-accessible trail that links

Eightmile Campground to Lower Crossing Campground. The fishing can be good here, so bring your gear.

Location: On Eightmile Creek in Mount Hood National Forest; The Columbia River Gorge and Mount Hood map 2, grid e5.

Campsites, facilities: There are 24 sites for tents, trailers, or RVs up to 30 feet long. No drinking water is available, and all garbage must be packed out. Picnic tables and fire grills are provided. Vault toilets are available. Leashed pets are permitted.

Reservations, fees: No reservations accepted. Northwest Forest Pass ($30 annual fee) or $5 daily fee per parked vehicle is required. Senior discount available. Open June to mid-October.

Directions: From Portland turn east on I-84 and drive about 90 miles to Exit 87. Take Exit 87 and turn south on U.S. 197 and drive 13 miles to Dufur and Dufur Valley Road. Turn right on Dufur Valley Road and drive west for 12 miles to Forest Road 44. Continue west on Forest Road 44 for four miles to Forest Road 4430. Turn right and drive a short distance to the campground.

Contact: Mount Hood National Forest, Barlow Ranger District, 780 N.E. Court St., Dufur, OR 97021; 541/467-2291; fax 541/467-2271.

33 Pebble Ford

[icons] 6

This is just a little camping spot by the side of the gravel forest road. Primitive and quiet, it's an alternative to the better-known Eightmile Crossing. There are some quality hiking trails in the area if you're willing to drive two or three miles.

Location: In Mount Hood National Forest; The Columbia River Gorge and Mount Hood map 2, grid e5.

Campsites, facilities: There are three sites for tents, trailers, or RVs up to 16 feet long.

Picnic tables and fire grills are provided. Vault toilets are available. There is no drinking water. Leashed pets are permitted.

Reservations, fees: No reservations accepted. Northwest Forest Pass ($30 annual fee) or $5 daily fee per parked vehicle is required. Senior discount available. Open July to early October.

Directions: From Portland turn east on I-84 and drive about 90 miles to Exit 87. Take Exit 87 and turn south on U.S. 197 and drive 13 miles to Dufur and Dufur Valley Road. Turn right on Dufur Valley Road and drive west for 12 miles to Forest Road 44. Continue west on Forest Road 44 for five miles to Forest Road 130. Turn left (south) and drive a short distance to the campground on the left.

Contact: Mount Hood National Forest, Barlow Ranger District, 780 N.E. Court St., Dufur, OR 97021; 541/467-2291; fax 541/467-2271.

34 McNeil

[icons] 5

This campground is set at an elevation of 2,040 feet in Old Maid Flat, a special geological area along the Clear Fork of the Sandy River. There's a good view of Mount Hood from the campground entrance. Several trails nearby provide access to the wilderness backcountry. See a U.S. Forest Service map for details.

Location: On the Clear Fork of the Sandy River in Mount Hood National Forest; The Columbia River Gorge and Mount Hood map 2, grid e2.

Campsites, facilities: There are 34 sites for tents, trailers, or RVs up to 22 feet long. Picnic tables and vault toilets are provided. There is no drinking water. Leashed pets are permitted.

Reservations, fees: Reservations accepted ($8.65 reservation fee). Sites are

$10 per night, $5 per night for an additional vehicle. Senior discount available. Open May to late September.

Directions: From Portland drive 40 miles east on U.S. 26 to Zigzag. Turn left on County Road 18/East Lolo Pass Road and drive 4.5 miles to Forest Road 1825. Turn right on Forest Road 1825, drive less than one mile, bear right onto a bridge to stay on Forest Road 1825, and drive one-quarter mile to the campground on the left.

Contact: Mount Hood National Forest, Zigzag Ranger District, 65000 E. Hwy. 26, Welches, OR 97067; 503/622-7674, reservations 877/444-6777; fax 503/622-3163; website (for reservations): www.reserveusa.com.

35 Riley Horse Camp

6

Riley Horse Camp is close to McNeil and offers the same opportunities, except Riley provides stock facilities and is reserved for horse camping only on holidays. Secluded in an area of Douglas fir and lodgepole pine at 2,100 feet elevation, this is a popular base camp for horse packing trips.

Location: Near the Clear Fork of the Sandy River in Mount Hood National Forest; The Columbia River Gorge and Mount Hood map 2, grid e2.

Campsites, facilities: There are 14 sites for tents, trailers, or RVs up to 16 feet long. Drinking water, fire grills, vault toilets, and picnic tables are provided. Facilities for horses are available. Leashed pets are permitted.

Reservations, fees: Reservations accepted for some sites ($8.65 reservation fee). Sites are $12 per night, $6 per night for an additional vehicle. Senior discount available. Open May to late September.

Directions: From Portland drive 40 miles east on U.S. 26 to Zigzag. Turn right (north

east) on County Road 18/East Lolo Pass Road and drive 4.5 miles to Forest Road 1825. Turn right and drive one-half mile to Forest Road 380. Turn right and drive 100 yards to the camp.

Contact: Mount Hood National Forest, Zigzag Ranger District, 65000 E. Hwy. 26, Welches, OR 97067; 503/622-7674, reservations 877/444-6777; fax 503/622-3163; website (for reservations): www.reserveusa.com.

36 Lost Creek

8

This campground near McNeil and Riley has some of the same opportunities. Set in a cool, lush area on a creek at 2,600 feet elevation, it's barrier-free and offers an interpretive nature trail about one mile long and a wheelchair-accessible fishing pier.

Location: On Lost Creek in Mount Hood National Forest; The Columbia River Gorge and Mount Hood map 2, grid f2.

Campsites, facilities: There are five walk-in sites for tents and nine sites for trailers or RVs up to 22 feet long. Facilities are wheelchair-accessible. Drinking water, garbage service, fire grills, vault toilets, and picnic tables are provided. Leashed pets are permitted.

Reservations, fees: Reservations accepted ($8.65 reservation fee). Sites are $12–14 per night, $6 per night for an additional vehicle. Senior discount available. Open May to late September.

Directions: From Portland drive 40 miles east on U.S. 26 to Zigzag. Turn north on County Road 18/East Lolo Pass Road and drive 4.5 miles to Forest Road 1825. Turn right and drive two miles to a fork. Bear right and drive one-quarter mile to the campground on the right.

Contact: Mount Hood National Forest, Zigzag Ranger District, 65000 E. Hwy. 26, Welches, OR 97067; 503/622-7674, reservations 877/444-6777; fax 503/622-3163; website (for reservations): www.reserveusa.com.

37 Toll Gate

🚶 🐟 🐕 🚐 ⛺   8

This shady campground along the banks of the Zigzag River near Rhododendron is extremely popular, and finding a site on a summer weekend can be next to impossible. Luckily you can get a reservation. There are numerous hiking trails in the area. The nearest one to this campground leads east for several miles along the river. A historic Civilian Conservation Corps shelter from the 1930s is in the campground and can be used by campers.

Location: On the Zigzag River in Mount Hood National Forest; The Columbia River Gorge and Mount Hood map 2, grid f1.

Campsites, facilities: There are 14 tent sites and nine sites for trailers or RVs up to 16 feet long. Picnic tables and fire grills are provided. Drinking water, garbage service, and pit toilets are available. Leashed pets are permitted.

Reservations, fees: Reservations accepted for some sites ($8.65 reservation fee). Single sites are $12–14 per night, $5 per night for an additional vehicle. Double sites are $24 per night, $5 per night for an additional vehicle. Senior discount available. Open late May to late September.

Directions: From Portland drive east on U.S. 26 and drive 40 miles to Zigzag. Continue 2.5 miles southeast on U.S. 26 to the campground entrance.

Contact: Mount Hood National Forest, Zigzag Ranger District, 65000 E. Hwy. 26, Welches, OR 97067; 503/622-7674, reservations 877/444-6777; fax 503/622-3163; website (for reservations): www.reserveusa.com.

38 Green Canyon

🚶 🚲 🏊
🐕 ♿ 🚐 ⛺   8

Few out-of-towners know about this winner. But the locals do, and they keep the place hopping in the summer. The camp is at 1,600 feet elevation along the banks of the Salmon River. A long trail cuts through the site and parallels the river, passing through a magnificent old-growth forest. See a U.S. Forest Service map for details.

Location: On the Salmon River in Mount Hood National Forest; The Columbia River Gorge and Mount Hood map 2, grid f1.

Campsites, facilities: There are 15 sites for tents, trailers, or RVs up to 22 feet long. Picnic tables, garbage service, and fire grills are provided. Pit toilets are available. Drinking water is intermittently available. A store, a café, and ice are within five miles. Some facilities are wheelchair-accessible. Leashed pets are permitted.

Reservations, fees: No reservations accepted. Sites are $12–14 per night, $6 per night for an additional vehicle. Senior discount available. Open May to late September.

Directions: From Portland drive east on U.S. 26 for 39 miles to Forest Road 2618 (Salmon River Road) near Zigzag. Turn right and drive 4.5 miles to the campground on the right.

Contact: Mount Hood National Forest, Zigzag Ranger District, 65000 E. Hwy. 26, Welches, OR 97067; 503/622-7674; fax 503/622-3163.

39 Camp Creek

🚶 🐟 🐕 🚐 ⛺   8

This campground is set at 2,200 feet elevation, along Camp Creek, not far from the Zigzag River and it looks similar to Toll Gate, but larger and farther from the road.

A hiking trail runs through camp and along the river, and another leads south to Still Creek. This campground, along with Toll Gate to the west, is very popular and you'll probably need a reservation.

Location: Near the Zigzag River in Mount Hood National Forest; The Columbia River Gorge and Mount Hood map 2, grid f1.

Campsites, facilities: There are 24 sites for tents, trailers, or RVs up to 22 feet long. Drinking water, garbage bins, fire grills, and picnic tables are provided. Vault toilets are available. Leashed pets are permitted.

Reservations, fees: Reservations accepted for some sites ($8.65 reservation fee). Sites are $12–14 per night, $6 per night for an additional vehicle. Senior discount available. Open late May to late September.

Directions: From Portland drive east on U.S. 26 and drive 40 miles to Zigzag. Continue southeast on U.S. 26 for about four miles to the camp on the right.

Contact: Mount Hood National Forest, Zigzag Ranger District, 65000 E. Hwy. 26, Welches, OR 97067; 503/622-7674, reservations 877/444-6777; fax 503/622-3163; website (for reservations): www.reserveusa.com.

40 Alpine

🚶 🐕 ⛺ 8

This small campground is one mile from the Timberline Ski Area lodge at 5,400 feet elevation on the south slopes of Mount Hood. It can get quite crowded here on weekends. In spite of some traffic noise, the big trees lend a mountain feel and year-round snow skiing and boarding are less than one mile away. The Pacific Crest Trail is accessible from the Timberline Lodge. Be sure to come prepared for very cold nights.

Location: Near the Pacific Crest Trail in Mount Hood National Forest; The Columbia River Gorge and Mount Hood map 2, grid f3.

Campsites, facilities: There are 16 tent sites. Drinking water, fire grills, vault toilets, garbage service, and picnic tables are provided. Leashed pets are permitted.

Reservations, fees: No reservations accepted. Sites are $12 per night, $6 per night for an additional vehicle. Senior discount available. Open July to late September.

Directions: From Portland drive east on U.S. 26 and drive 55 miles to the small town of Government Camp. Continue east for one mile to Timberline Road (Forest Road 173). Turn left and drive 4.5 miles to the campground on the left.

Contact: Mount Hood National Forest, Zigzag Ranger District, 65000 E. Hwy. 26, Welches, OR 97067; 503/622-7674; fax 503/622-3163.

41 Still Creek

🚶 🚲 🎣 🐕 🚐 ⛺ 6

This primitive camp at 3,600 feet elevation, shaded primarily by fir and hemlock, sits along Still Creek where it pours off the south slope of Mount Hood. Adjacent to Summit Meadows, site of a pioneer gravesite from Oregon Trail days, it's a great place for views of mountains, sunsets, and wildlife. Anglers should bring along their rods: the fishing in Still Creek can be excellent.

Location: On Still Creek in Mount Hood National Forest; The Columbia River Gorge and Mount Hood map 2, grid f3.

Campsites, facilities: There are 27 sites for tents or self-contained trailers or RVs up to 16 feet long. Picnic tables, garbage service, and fire grills are provided. Pit toilets and drinking water are available. Leashed pets are permitted.

Reservations, fees: Reservations accepted ($8.65 reservation fee). Sites are $12 per night, $6 per night for an additional vehicle. Senior discount available. Open mid-June to late September.

Directions: From Portland drive 55 miles east on U.S. 26 to Government Camp. Continue east on U.S. 26 for one mile to Forest Road 2650. Turn right and drive south for 500 yards to the campground.

Contact: Mount Hood National Forest, Zigzag Ranger District, 65000 E. Hwy. 26, Welches, OR 97067; 503/622-7674, reservations 877/444-6777; fax 503/622-3163; website (for reservations): www.reserveusa.com.

42 Grindstone

7

This tiny campground, set at 3,400 feet elevation in a meadow along Barlow Creek, is a little-known and little-used spot. You won't find much out here but wind, water, and trees—but sometimes that's all you need. High-clearance vehicles recommended. This camp was a site first used by the pioneers.

Location: Near Barlow Creek in Mount Hood National Forest; The Columbia River Gorge and Mount Hood map 2, grid f3.

Campsites, facilities: There are three primitive sites for tents. Picnic tables and fire grills are provided. Vault toilets are available, but there is no drinking water and no garbage service; pack out all garbage. Leashed pets are permitted.

Reservations, fees: No reservations. Northwest Forest Pass ($30 annual fee) or $5 daily fee per parked vehicle is required. Senior discount available. Open May through September.

Directions: From Portland turn east on U.S. 26 and drive 57 miles (just past the town of Government Camp) to the junction with Highway 35. Turn right (southeast) on U.S. 26 and drive 4.5 miles to Forest Road 3530. Turn right and drive two miles to the campground on the right.

Contact: Mount Hood National Forest, Hood River Ranger District, 6780 Hwy. 35, Mount Hood, OR 97041; 541/352-6002; fax 541/352-7365.

43 Devil's Half Acre Meadow

8

Used by the pioneers, this campground is set at 3,600 feet elevation a few miles upstream on Barlow Creek from Grindstone Campground. Several hiking trails close to camp, including the Pacific Crest Trail, provide access to small lakes in the area. There are many historic points of interest in the vicinity. High-clearance vehicles recommended.

Location: On Barlow Creek in Mount Hood National Forest; The Columbia River Gorge and Mount Hood map 2, grid g3.

Campsites, facilities: There are five sites for tents, trailers, or RVs up to 16 feet long. Picnic tables and fire grills are provided. Firewood and pit toilets are available, but there is no drinking water and no garbage service; pack out all garbage. Leashed pets are permitted.

Reservations, fees: No reservations. Northwest Forest Pass ($30 annual fee) or $5 daily fee per parked vehicle is required. Senior discount available. Open May to October.

Directions: From Portland turn east on U.S. 26 and drive 57 miles (just past the town of Government Camp) to the junction with Highway 35. Turn right (southeast) on U.S. 26 and drive 4.5 miles to Forest Road 3530. Turn southeast and drive one mile to the campground.

Contact: Mount Hood National Forest, Hood River Ranger District, 6780 Hwy. 35, Mount Hood, OR 97041; 541/352-6002; fax 541/352-7365.

44 Trillium Lake

9

This campground is set at 3,600 feet elevation along the shores of Trillium Lake, which is about one-half mile long and one-quarter mile wide. Fishing is good in the evening here, and the nearby boat ramp makes this an ideal camp for anglers. The lake is great for canoes, rafts, and small rowboats. Trillium Lake is an extremely popular vacation destination, so expect plenty of company. Reservations highly recommended.

Location: On Trillium Lake in Mount Hood National Forest; The Columbia River Gorge and Mount Hood map 2, grid g3.

Campsites, facilities: There are 55 sites for tents, trailers, or RVs up to 40 feet long. Picnic tables and fire grills are provided. Pit toilets and drinking water are available. Some sites are wheelchair-accessible. Boat docks and launching facilities are available on the lake, but no motors are allowed. Leashed pets are permitted.

Reservations, fees: Reservations recommended ($8.65 reservation fee). Sites are $12–14 per night, multifamily sites are $24 per night, and an additional vehicle is $6. Senior discount available. Open late May to late September.

Directions: From Portland drive east on U.S. 26 and drive 55 miles to the small town of Government Camp. Continue east on U.S. 26 for 1.5 miles to Forest Road 2656. Turn right and drive 1.3 miles to the campground on the right.

Contact: Mount Hood National Forest, Zigzag Ranger District, 65000 E. Hwy. 26, Welches, OR 97067; 503/622-7674, reservations 877/444-6777; fax 503/622-3163; website (for reservations): www.reserveusa.com.

45 Frog Lake
🏃 🎣 🐕 ♿ 🚐 ⛺ 6

This classic spot in the Cascade Range is on the shore of little Frog Lake (more of a pond than a lake), at an elevation of 3,800 feet and a short distance from the Pacific Crest Trail. Several other trails lead to nearby lakes. A possible day trip is Clear Lake to the south, which offers more recreation options.

Location: Near the Pacific Crest Trail in Mount Hood National Forest; The Columbia River Gorge and Mount Hood map 2, grid g3.

Campsites, facilities: There are 33 sites for tents, trailers, or RVs up to 22 feet long. Drinking water, garbage bins, and picnic tables are provided. Vault toilets and firewood are available. Boat-launching facilities are nearby. No motorized boats are allowed. Leashed pets are permitted. Some barrier-free facilities are available.

Reservations, fees: Reservations accepted for some sites ($8.65 reservation fee). Sites are $8–14 per night, $6 per night for an additional vehicle. Senior discount available. Open mid-June to mid-September.

Directions: From Portland drive east on U.S. 26 and drive 57 miles to the junction with Highway 35 (two miles past Government Camp). Turn right (southeast) on U.S. 26 and drive seven miles to Forest Road 2610. Turn southeast and drive one-half mile to the campground.

Contact: Mount Hood National Forest, Hood River Ranger District, 6780 Hwy. 35, Mount Hood, OR 97041; 541/352-6002, reservations 877/444-6777; fax 541/352-7365; website (for reservations): www.reserveusa.com.

46 Badger Lake
🏃 🎣 🚐 🐕 ⛺ 8

This campground is set at an elevation of 4,400 feet, along the shore of Badger Lake. Nonmotorized boating is permitted if you can manage to get a boat in here over the rough roads. No trailers are allowed on campground roads. The camp is adjacent to the Badger Creek Wilderness, and numerous trails provide access to the backcountry. Badger Creek Trail heads out of camp northeast along Badger Creek for several miles.

Location: On Badger Lake in Mount Hood National Forest; The Columbia River Gorge and Mount Hood map 2, grid f5.

Campsites, facilities: There are four sites for tents only, accessible only by high-clearance vehicles. Picnic tables and fire grills are provided. Vault toilets are available. There is no drinking water and all garbage must be packed out. Leashed pets are permitted.

Reservations, fees: No reservations accepted. Northwest Forest Pass ($30 annual fee) or $5 daily fee per parked vehicle is required. Senior discount available. Open July to early October.

Directions: From Portland drive east on I-84 for 65 miles to Hood River, Exit 64 and Highway 35. Turn south and drive 37 miles to Forest Road 48. Turn left and drive 16 miles to Forest Road 4860. Turn left (north) and drive eight miles to Forest Road 140. Bear right and drive four miles to the lake. The last two miles on this primitive road require a high-clearance vehicle.

Contact: Mount Hood National Forest, Barlow Ranger District, 780 N.E. Court St., Dufur, OR 97021; 541/467-2291; fax 541/467-2271.

47 Bonney Meadow

9

At 4,800 feet of elevation, this primitive campground is on the east side of the Cascade Range. As a result, there is little water in the area—and also very few people, so you're liable to have the place all to yourself. Bonney Meadow Trail leaves from the campground and travels 1.5 miles up to a group of small lakes. There are great mountain views from this trail. See a U.S. Forest Service map for details.

Location: In Mount Hood National Forest; The Columbia River Gorge and Mount Hood map 2, grid g5.

Campsites, facilities: There are eight sites for tents and small trailers or RVs up to 16 feet long. Picnic tables and fire grills are provided. Vault toilets are available. There is no drinking water. Leashed pets are permitted.

Reservations, fees: No reservations accepted. Northwest Forest Pass ($30 annual fee) or $5 daily fee per parked vehicle is required. Senior discount available. Open July to early October.

Directions: From Portland turn east on I-84 and drive 65 miles to the town of Hood River, Exit 64 and Highway 35. Turn south on Highway 35 and drive 37 miles to Forest Road 48. Turn left and drive 14 miles to Forest Road 4890. Turn left and drive four miles north to Forest Road 4891. Turn right and drive a short distance to the campground.

Contact: Mount Hood National Forest, Barlow Ranger District, 780 N.E. Court St., Dufur, OR 97021; 541/467-2291; fax 541/467-2271.

48 Bonney Crossing

7

This campground at 2,200 feet elevation along Badger Creek is the trailhead for the Badger Creek Trail, which provides access to the Badger Creek Wilderness. The camp gets fairly light use and is usually very quiet. Fishing is available in the creek and is usually pretty good. Horse campers are welcome here.

Location: On Badger Creek in Mount Hood National Forest; The Columbia River Gorge and Mount Hood map 2, grid g5.

Campsites, facilities: There are eight sites for tents, trailers, or RVs up to 16 feet long. Picnic tables and fire grills are provided. Vault toilets are available. Stock facilities include horse corrals. There is no drinking water. Leashed pets are permitted. Pack out all garbage.

Reservations, fees: No reservations accepted. Northwest Forest Pass ($30 annual fee) or $5 daily fee per parked vehicle is required. Senior discount available. Open mid-April to mid-October.

Directions: From The Dalles drive south on U.S. 197 for 32 miles to Tygh Valley. Take the Tygh Valley exit to Tygh Valley Road. Turn west and drive one-fourth mile to Wamic Market Road (County Road 226). Turn west (right) and drive eight miles to Wamic. Continue through Wamic and drive seven miles to Forest Road 4810. Bear right and drive three miles to Forest Road 4811. Turn right and drive two miles to a junction with Forest Road 2710. Turn right and drive three miles to the campground on the right.

Contact: Mount Hood National Forest, Barlow Ranger District, 780 N.E. Court St., Dufur, OR 97021; 541/467-2291; fax 541/467-2271.

49 Pine Hollow Lakeside Resort

8

This resort on the shore of Pine Hollow Reservoir is the best game in town for RV campers, with some shaded lakefront sites and scenic views. Year-round fishing, boating, swimming, and water-skiing are some recreation options here.

Location: On Pine Hollow Reservoir; The Columbia River Gorge and Mount Hood map 2, grid g7.

Campsites, facilities: There are 35 tent sites and 75 sites for trailers or RVs. Electricity, drinking water, and picnic tables are provided. Flush toilets, bottled gas, sanitary services, showers, firewood, a store, a café, a laundry room, and ice are available. Boat docks, launching facilities, and rentals are nearby. Leashed pets are permitted.

Reservations, fees: Reservations accepted. Sites are $17–24 per night. Open mid-March through October.

Directions: From Portland turn east on I-84 and drive 91 miles to The Dalles, Exit 87, and Highway 197. Turn south and drive 31 miles to Tygh Valley and Wamic Market Road. Turn west and drive 4.5 miles to Ross Road. Turn north and drive 3.5 miles to the campground.

Contact: Pine Hollow Lakeside Resort, 34 N. Mariposa Dr., Wamic, OR 97063; 541/544-2271; website: www.pinehollowlakeside.com.

50 Wasco County Fairgrounds

6

This county campground is set near the confluence of Badger and Tygh Creeks. Hiking trails, marked bike trails, and tennis courts are nearby.

Location: Near Badger Creek; map The Columbia River Gorge and Mount Hood map 2, grid g7.

Campsites, facilities: There are 50 tent sites and 100 drive-through sites for trailers or RVs of any length. Electricity, drinking water, and picnic tables are provided. Flush toilets, a dump station, garbage bins, and coin-operated showers are available. Two community kitchens are available for a fee. A store, a café, and ice are within one mile. Leashed pets are permitted. Some facilities are wheelchair-accessible. Horse facilities are available, including stalls and an arena.

Reservations, fees: Reservations accepted. Sites are $10–12 per night. Open May through October.

Directions: From Portland turn east on I-84 and drive 91 miles to The Dalles, Exit 87, and Highway 197. Turn south and drive 31 miles to Tygh Valley and Main Street. Turn right at Main Street and drive two blocks to Fairgrounds Road. Turn right and drive one mile to the fairgrounds on the right.

Contact: Wasco County, 81849 Fairgrounds Rd., Tygh Valley, OR 97063; 541/483-2288.

51 Rock Creek Reservoir

🥾 🚲 🚣

🐕 ♿ 🚐 ⛺ 7

Fishing is excellent, and the environment is perfect for canoes or rafts at this campground along the shore of Rock Creek Reservoir at 2,200 feet elevation. There are views of Mount Hood from the day-use area. No hiking trails are in the immediate vicinity, but there are many old forest roads that are ideal for walking or mountain biking.

Location: On Rock Creek Reservoir in Mount Hood National Forest; The Columbia River Gorge and Mount Hood map 2, grid g6.

Campsites, facilities: There are 33 sites for tents, trailers, or RVs up to 18 feet long. Picnic tables, garbage service, and fire grills are provided. Vault toilets, drinking water, and firewood are available. Some of the facilities are wheelchair-accessible. There are boat docks nearby, but no motorboats are allowed on the reservoir. Leashed pets are permitted.

Reservations, fees: Reservations accepted ($8.65 reservation fee). Sites are $12 per night, $6 per night for an additional vehicle. Senior discount available. Open mid-April to early October.

Directions: From Portland turn east on I-84 and drive 91 miles to The Dalles, Exit 87, and Highway 197. Turn south and drive 31 miles to Tygh Valley and Wamic Market Road. Turn right and drive west for six miles to Forest Road 48. Turn west and drive one mile to Forest Road 4820. Turn west and drive a short distance to the campground.

Contact: Mount Hood National Forest, Barlow Ranger District, 780 N.E. Court St., Dufur, OR 97021; 541/467-2291, reservations 877/444-6777; fax 541/467-2271; website (for reservations): www.reserveusa.com.

52 Forest Creek

🥾 🎣 🐕 🚐 ⛺ 6

The elevation here is 3,000 feet. This very old camp along Forest Creek on the original Barlow Trail was once used by early settlers. Shaded by old-growth Douglas fir and ponderosa pine forest, you'll find solitude here. See a U.S. Forest Service map for specific roads and trails.

Location: On Forest Creek in Mount Hood National Forest; The Columbia River Gorge and Mount Hood map 2, grid g5.

Campsites, facilities: There are eight sites for tents, trailers, or RVs up to 16 feet long. No drinking water is available. Picnic tables and fire grills are provided. Vault toilets are available. Leashed pets are permitted. Pack out all garbage.

Reservations, fees: No reservations accepted. Northwest Forest Pass ($30 annual fee) or $5 daily fee per parked vehicle is required. Senior discount available. Open July to early October.

Directions: From Portland turn east on I-84 and drive 91 miles to The Dalles, Exit 87, and Highway 197. Turn south and drive 31 miles to Tygh Valley and Wamic Market Road. Turn right and drive west for six miles to Forest Road 48. Continue west and drive 12.5 miles southwest to Forest Road 4885. Turn left and drive one mile to Forest Road 3530. Turn left to the campground.

Contact: Mount Hood National Forest, Barlow Ranger District, 780 N.E. Court St., Dufur, OR 97021; 541/467-2291; fax 541/467-2271.

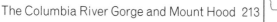

53 Barlow Creek

🚶 🎣 🐕 ⛺ 7

This campground is set along Barlow Creek at an elevation of 3,100 feet. It is on Old Barlow Road, which was the wagon trail for early settlers in this area. It is one of several primitive U.S. Forest Service camps in the immediate vicinity. There may not be much to do in these parts, but you sure can't beat the price. If this campground is full, Barlow Crossing Campground is one mile southeast on Forest Road 3530.

Location: On Barlow Creek in Mount Hood National Forest; The Columbia River Gorge and Mount Hood map 2, grid g4.

Campsites, facilities: There are five sites for tents. Picnic tables and fire grills are provided. Vault toilets are available, but there is no drinking water and no garbage service; pack out all garbage. Leashed pets are permitted.

Reservations, fees: No reservations. Northwest Forest Pass ($30 annual fee) or $5 daily fee per parked vehicle is required. Senior discount available. Open May through September.

Directions: From Portland drive east on U.S. 26 and drive 57 miles to the junction with Highway 35 (two miles past Government Camp). Turn right (southeast) on U.S. 26 and drive 12 miles to Forest Road 43. Turn left and drive five miles to Forest Road 3530. Turn north (left) and drive 1.5 miles to the campground on the left.

Contact: Mount Hood National Forest, Hood River Ranger District, 6780 Hwy. 35, Mount Hood, OR 97041; 541/352-6002; fax 541/352-7365.

54 White River Station

🚶 🚲 🛶 🐕 🚐 ⛺ 9

This tiny campground is set along the White River at an elevation of 3,000 feet. It is on Old Barlow Road, an original wagon trail used by early settlers. One of several small, secluded camps in the area, White River Station is quiet and private, but with poor fishing prospects.

Location: On the White River in Mount Hood National Forest; The Columbia River Gorge and Mount Hood map 2, grid g4.

Campsites, facilities: There are five sites for tents and RVs up to 32 feet long. Picnic tables and fire grills are provided. Vault toilets are available, but there is no drinking water and no garbage service; pack out all garbage. Leashed pets are permitted.

Reservations, fees: No reservations. Northwest Forest Pass ($30 annual fee) or $5 daily fee per parked vehicle is required. Senior discount available. Open May through September.

Directions: From Portland drive east on U.S. 26 and drive 57 miles to the junction with Highway 35 (two miles past Government Camp). Turn left on Highway 35 and drive two miles east to Forest Road 48. Turn right (south) and drive nine miles southeast to Forest Road 43. Turn right and drive one-quarter mile to Forest Road 3530. Turn left and drive 1.5 miles to the campground on the left.

Contact: Mount Hood National Forest, Barlow Ranger District, 780 N.E. Court St., Dufur, OR 97021; 541/467-2291; fax 541/467-2271.

55 Clear Lake

🚶 🏊 🛶 🛥️
🐕 ♿ 🚐 ⛺ 4

This campground is along the shore of Clear Lake, a spot favored by anglers, swimmers, and windsurfers, but it is a reservoir and subject to water-level fluctuations. The camp is wooded, with shady sites and is set at 3,600 feet elevation. The camp is sometimes noisy from the revels of the party set. If you want quiet, this camp is probably not for you. A nearby trail heads north from the lake and provides access to the Pacific Crest Trail and Frog Lake, both good recreation options.

Location: Near the Pacific Crest Trail in Mount Hood National Forest; The Columbia River Gorge and Mount Hood map 2, grid g3.

Campsites, facilities: There are 28 sites for tents, trailers, or RVs up to 32 feet long. Picnic tables, fire grills, drinking water, garbage bins, firewood, and vault toilets are available. Some facilities are wheelchair-accessible. Boat-launching facilities are nearby and motorboats are allowed, but the speed limit is 10 mph. Leashed pets are permitted.

Reservations, fees: Reservations accepted for some sites ($8.65 reservation fee). Sites are $8–14 per night, $6 per night for an additional vehicle. Senior discount available. Open late May to early September.

Directions: From Portland drive east on U.S. 26 and drive 57 miles to the junction with Highway 35 (two miles past Government Camp). Turn right (southeast) on U.S. 26 and drive nine miles to Forest Road 2630. Turn south and drive one mile to the campground on the right.

Contact: Mount Hood National Forest, Hood River Ranger District, 6780 Hwy. 35, Mount Hood, OR 97041; 541/352-6002, reservations 877/444-6777; fax 541/352-7365; website (for reservations): www.reserveusa.com.

56 Hideaway Lake

🚶🏊🎣 🚤🐕🚐🏕️ 9

This is a jewel of a spot—a small, deep lake where nonmotorized boats are allowed, but they must be carried about 100 yards to the lake. The campsites are separate and scattered around the water. At the north end of the lake, an 8.5-mile loop trail goes past a number of lakes in the Rock Lakes Basin, all of which support populations of rainbow and

brook trout. If you don't want to make the whole trip in a day, you can camp overnight at Serene Lake. See a U.S. Forest Service map for information.

Location: Near the Rock Lakes Basin in Mount Hood National Forest; The Columbia River Gorge and Mount Hood map 2, grid h1.

Campsites, facilities: There are nine sites for tents, small trailers, or camper vans up to 16 feet long. Picnic tables and fire grills are provided. Pit toilets are available. There is no drinking water. Leashed pets are permitted.

Reservations, fees: No reservations accepted. Sites are $10 per night, $5 per night for an additional vehicle. Open mid-June to late September, weather permitting.

Directions: From Portland drive east on U.S. 26 from Gresham 11 miles to Sandy and Highway 211. Turn right (south) and drive six miles to a junction. Turn south (still Highway 211) and drive six miles to Estacada and Highway 224. Bear south on Highway 224 and drive 27 miles to Forest Road 57. Turn east and drive 7.5 miles to Forest Road 58. Turn left and drive three miles north to Forest Road 5830. Turn left (northwest) and drive 5.5 miles to the campground on the left.

Contact: Mount Hood National Forest, Clackamas River Ranger District, 595 N.W. Industrial Way, Estacada, OR 97023; 503/630-6861; fax 503/630-2299.

57 High Rock Springs

🚶🐕🏕️ 7

This small, remote campground is set at 5,200 feet elevation within two miles of Stet Mountain. A half-mile climb earns a tremendous view of the surrounding area, including Mount Hood. About four miles east of the camp are trails that lead to some of the fishing lakes in the Rock Lakes Basin. In August and

September ripe huckleberries are yours for the picking.

Location: Near the Rock Lakes Basin in Mount Hood National Forest; The Columbia River Gorge and Mount Hood map 2, grid g1.

Campsites, facilities: There are six tent sites. Picnic tables and fire grills are provided. Drinking water and a pit toilet are available. Garbage must be packed out. Leashed pets are permitted.

Reservations, fees: No reservations; no fee. Open mid-June to late September, weather permitting.

Directions: From Portland drive east on U.S. 26 from Gresham 11 miles to Sandy and Highway 211. Turn right (south) and drive six miles to a junction. Turn south (still Highway 211) and drive six miles to Estacada and Highway 224. Bear south on Highway 224 and drive 27 miles to Forest Road 57. Turn east and drive 7.5 miles to Forest Road 58. Turn left and drive nine miles to Forest Road 58-190. Turn left and drive 1.5 miles to the campground.

Contact: Mount Hood National Forest, Clackamas River Ranger District, 595 N.W. Industrial Way, Estacada, OR 97023; 503/630-6861; fax 503/630-2299.

58 Lake Harriet

5

Formed by a dam on the Oak Grove Fork of the Clackamas River, this little lake is a popular spot during the summer. Rowboats and boats with small motors are permitted, but only nonmotorized boats are encouraged. The lake is stocked regularly and can provide good fishing for a variety of trout, including brown, brook, rainbow, and cutthroat. Anglers often stand shoulder-to-shoulder in summer.

Location: On Lake Harriet in Mount Hood National Forest; The Columbia River Gorge and Mount Hood map 2, grid g1.

Campsites, facilities: There are 13 sites for tents, trailers, or RVs up to 30 feet long. Picnic tables and fire grills are provided. Drinking water and vault toilets are available. Garbage service is provided in the summer. Some facilities are wheelchair-accessible. A fishing pier and boat-launching facilities are on the lake. Leashed pets are permitted.

Reservations, fees: Sites are $12 per night, $6 per night for an additional vehicle. Senior discount available. Open year-round, with limited winter services.

Directions: From Portland drive east on U.S. 26 from Gresham 11 miles to Sandy and Highway 211. Turn right (south) and drive six miles to a junction. Turn south (still Highway 211) and drive six miles to Estacada and Highway 224. Bear south on Highway 224 and drive 27 miles to Forest Road 57. Turn east and drive 7.5 miles to Forest Road 58. Turn left and drive 7.5 miles to Forest Road 4630. Turn left and drive two miles to the campground on the left.

Contact: Mount Hood National Forest, Clackamas River Ranger District, 595 N.W. Industrial Way, Estacada, OR 97023; 503/630-6861; fax 503/630-2299.

59 Gone Creek

8

This campground set along the south shore of Timothy Lake at 3,200 feet is one of four camps at the lake. Timothy Lake provides good fishing for brook trout, cutthroat trout, rainbow trout, and kokanee salmon. Boats with motors are allowed, but a 10 mph speed limit keeps it quiet. Several trails in the area—including the Pacific Crest Trail—provide access to several small mountain lakes.

Location: On Timothy Lake in Mount Hood National Forest; The Columbia River Gorge and Mount Hood map 2, grid h2.

Campsites, facilities: There are 45 sites for tents, trailers, or RVs up to 31 feet long. Drinking water, fire grills, garbage service, and picnic tables are provided. Vault toilets and firewood are available. A boat ramp is nearby. Leashed pets are permitted.

Reservations, fees: Reservations accepted ($8.65 reservation fee). Sites are $12–14 per night, $6 per night for an additional vehicle. Senior discount available. Open mid-May to mid-September.

Directions: From Portland turn east on U.S. 26 and drive 57 miles (just past the town of Government Camp) to the junction with Highway 35. Turn southeast on U.S. 26 and drive 15 miles to Forest Road 42 (Skyline Road). Turn right and drive eight miles to Forest Road 57. Turn right and drive one mile west to the campground on the right.

Contact: Mount Hood National Forest, Zigzag Ranger District, 65000 E. Hwy. 26, Welches, OR 97067; 503/622-7674, reservations 877/444-6777; fax 503/622-3163; website (for reservations): www.reserveusa.com.

60 Oak Fork

8

This forested camp is set in heavy timber and bear grass along the south shore of Timothy Lake, just east of Hoodview and Gone Creek campgrounds. Refer to these camps for more details.

Location: On Timothy Lake in Mount Hood National Forest; The Columbia River Gorge and Mount Hood map 2, grid h2.

Campsites, facilities: There are 47 sites for tents, trailers, or RVs up to 32 feet long. Picnic tables and fire grills are provided. Drinking water, firewood, and vault toilets are available. A boat ramp and launching facilities are nearby; the speed limit on the lake is 10 mph. Leashed pets are permitted.

Reservations, fees: Reservations accepted ($8.65 reservation fee). Sites are $12–14 per night, $6 per night for an additional vehicle. Senior discount available. Open June through mid-September.

Directions: From Portland turn east on U.S. 26 and drive 57 miles (just past the town of Government Camp) to the junction with Highway 35. Turn southeast on U.S. 26 and drive 15 miles to Forest Road 42 (Skyline Road). Turn right and drive eight miles to Forest Road 57. Turn right and drive three miles to the camp on the right.

Contact: Mount Hood National Forest, Zigzag Ranger District, 65000 E. Hwy. 26, Welches, OR 97067; 503/622-7674, reservations 877/444-6777; fax 503/622-3163; website (for reservations): www.reserveusa.com.

61 Pine Point

8

One of five camps on Timothy Lake, this spot is at an elevation of 3,200 feet on the southwest shore and has lake access and more open vegetation than the other Timothy Lake campgrounds. The trail that leads around the lake and to the Pacific Crest Trail passes along the campground. See the description of Gone Creek for boating and fishing details.

Location: On Timothy Lake in Mount Hood National Forest; The Columbia River Gorge and Mount Hood map 2, grid h2.

Campsites, facilities: There are 25 sites for tents, trailers, or RVs up to 31 feet long (10 single sites, 10 double sites, and five group sites). Picnic tables, garbage service, and fire grills are provided. Drinking water, firewood, a wheelchair-accessible fishing pier, and vault toilets are available.

A boat ramp and launching facilities are nearby; the

speed limit on the lake is 10 mph. Leashed pets are permitted.

Reservations, fees: Reservations accepted ($8.65 reservation fee). Sites are $12–14 per night, group sites are $24–30 per night; $6 per night for an additional vehicle. Senior discount available. Open late May to mid-September.

Directions: From Portland turn east on U.S. 26 and drive 57 miles (just past the town of Government Camp) to the junction with Highway 35. Turn southeast on U.S. 26 and drive 15 miles to Forest Road 42 (Skyline Road). Turn right and drive eight miles to Forest Road 57. Turn right and drive four miles to the park on the right.

Contact: Mount Hood National Forest, Zigzag Ranger District, 65000 E. Hwy. 26, Welches, OR 97067; 503/622-7674, reservations 877/444-6777; fax 503/622-3163; website (for reservations): www.reserveusa.com.

62 Hoodview

9

Here's another camp along the south shore of Timothy Lake; this one is set at 3,200 feet elevation. A trail out of camp branches south for a few miles, and if followed to the east, eventually leads to the Pacific Crest Trail. See the description of Gone Creek for boating and fishing information.

Location: On Timothy Lake in Mount Hood National Forest; The Columbia River Gorge and Mount Hood map 2, grid h2.

Campsites, facilities: There are 43 sites for tents, trailers, or RVs up to 31 feet long. Picnic tables, garbage service, and fire grills are provided. Drinking water, firewood, and vault toilets are available. A boat ramp is nearby and motorized boats are allowed but are limited to a speed of 10 mph. Leashed pets are permitted.

Reservations, fees: Reservations accepted ($8.65 reservation fee). Sites are $12–14 per night, $6 per night for an additional vehicle. Senior discount available. Open mid-May to mid-September.

Directions: From Portland turn east on U.S. 26 and drive 57 miles (just past the town of Government Camp) to the junction with Highway 35. Turn southeast on U.S. 26 and drive 15 miles to Forest Road 42 (Skyline Road). Turn right and drive eight miles to Forest Road 57. Turn right and drive three miles to the campground on the right.

Contact: Mount Hood National Forest, Zigzag Ranger District, 65000 E. Hwy. 26, Welches, OR 97067; 503/622-7674, reservations 877/444-6777; fax 503/622-3163; website (for reservations): www.reserveusa.com.

63 Meditation Point Walk-In/Boat-In

9

Accessible only by foot or boat, this remote and rustic camp set at 3,200 feet elevation offers the most secluded location along Timothy Lake. It's the only campground on the north shore of the lake, which means you'll get a quieter, less crowded environment, though you'll have to bring your own water. There is a 10 mph speed limit for boaters. Timothy Lake Trail makes a 14-mile loop around the lake.

Location: On Timothy Lake in Mount Hood National Forest; The Columbia River Gorge and Mount Hood map 2, grid h2.

Campsites, facilities: There are four boat-in or walk-in tent sites. Picnic tables and fire grills are provided. Vault toilets are available. There is no drinking water, and garbage must be packed out. Boat docks and launching facilities are nearby. Leashed pets are permitted.

Reservations, fees: No reservations; no fee. Open late May to mid-September.

Directions: From Portland drive east on U.S. 26 and drive 57 miles to the junction with Highway 35 (two miles past Government Camp). Turn right (southeast) on U.S. 26 for 15 miles to Forest Road 42/Skyline Road. Turn right and drive eight miles south to Forest Road 57. Turn right and drive five miles to Pine Point Campground. Park and hike one mile or take a boat to the north shore of the lake.

Contact: Mount Hood National Forest, Zigzag Ranger District, 65000 E. Hwy. 26, Welches, OR 97067; 503/622-7674; fax 503/622-3163.

64 Little Crater

5

This camp is set at 3,200 feet elevation next to Crater Creek and scenic Little Crater Lake. This camp is popular with hunters in the fall. Both the drinking water and the lake water flow from an artesian well, and the water is numbing cold. The Pacific Crest Trail is set near camp, providing hiking trail access. Fishing is poor at Little Crater lake. It is about a mile to little Timothy Lake, where a 10 mph speed limit is enforced. Bring your mosquito repellent; you'll need it.

Location: On Little Crater Lake in Mount Hood National Forest; The Columbia River Gorge and Mount Hood map 2, grid h2.

Campsites, facilities: There are 16 sites for tents, trailers, or RVs up to 22 feet long. Picnic tables, garbage bins, and fire grills are provided. Vault toilets, firewood, and drinking water are available. Leashed pets are permitted.

Reservations, fees: Reservations accepted for some sites ($8.65 reservation fee). Sites are $12 per night, $6 per night for an additional vehicle. Senior discount available. Open June to mid-September.

Directions: From Portland drive east on U.S. 26 and drive 57 miles to the junction with Highway 35 (two miles past Government Camp). Turn right (southeast) on U.S. 26 and drive 15 miles to Forest Road 42 (Skyline Road). Turn right and drive about six miles to Forest Road 58. Turn right and drive about 2.5 miles to the campground on the left.

Contact: Mount Hood National Forest, Zigzag Ranger District, 65000 E. Hwy. 26, Welches, OR 97067; 503/622-7674, reservations 877/444-6777; fax 503/622-3163; website (for reservations): www.reserveusa.com.

65 Clear Creek Crossing

7

This campground along the banks of Clear Creek is a secluded, little-known spot set at an elevation of 3,600 feet. Clear Creek Trail begins at the campground and is a very pretty walk. Fishing and hiking are two recreation options here.

Location: On Clear Creek in Mount Hood National Forest; The Columbia River Gorge and Mount Hood map 2, grid g4.

Campsites, facilities: There are seven sites for tents, trailers, or RVs up to 16 feet long. Picnic tables and fire grills are provided. Vault toilets are available. There is no drinking water, and all garbage must be packed out. Leashed pets are permitted.

Reservations, fees: No reservations accepted. Northwest Forest Pass ($30 annual fee) or $5 daily fee per parked vehicle is required. Senior discount available. Open May through September.

Directions: From Portland drive east on U.S. 26 for 55 miles to Government Camp. Continue three miles to a junction, turn right on U.S. 26, and drive south for 12 miles to Highway 216. Turn left (east) on Highway 216 and drive seven miles to Forest Road 2130. Turn left (north) on Forest Road 2130 and drive three miles to the campground.

Contact: Mount Hood National Forest, Barlow Ranger District, 780 N.E. Court St., Dufur, OR 97021; 541/467-2291; fax 541/467-2271.

66 Keeps Mill

9

This small, pretty campground is at the confluence of Clear Creek and the White River. No RVs are permitted. The elevation is 2,600 feet. Many hiking trails are in the area, some with awesome views of the White River Canyon, but be warned. These are butt-kicking canyon climbs.

Location: On Clear Creek in Mount Hood National Forest; The Columbia River Gorge and Mount Hood map 2, grid g4.

Campsites, facilities: There are five sites for tents only. The road to the campground is not good for trailers. Picnic tables and fire grills are provided. Vault toilets are available. There is no drinking water. Leashed pets are permitted.

Reservations, fees: No reservations accepted. Northwest Forest Pass ($30 annual fee) or $5 daily fee per parked vehicle is required. Senior discount available. Open May through September.

Directions: From Portland drive east on U.S. 26 for 55 miles to Government Camp. Continue three miles to a junction and turn right on U.S. 26 and drive south for 12 miles to Highway 216. Turn left (east) Highway 216 and drive three miles to Forest Road 2120. Turn left (north) on Forest Road 2120 and drive three miles to the campground.

Contact: Mount Hood National Forest, Barlow Ranger District, 780 N.E. Court St., Dufur, OR 97021; 541/467-2291; fax 541/467-2271.

67 Bear Springs

6

This campground is set along the banks of Indian Creek on the border of the Warm Springs Indian Reservation. The Bear Springs Work Center is near the camp, and rangers will be happy to supply maps and answer your questions about the area. There are both secluded and open sites set in old-growth forest.

Location: On Indian Creek in Mount Hood National Forest; The Columbia River Gorge and Mount Hood map 2, grid h5.

Campsites, facilities: There are 21 sites for tents, trailers, or RVs up to 32 feet long. Drinking water, fire grills, garbage bins, and picnic tables are provided. Vault toilets and firewood are available. Leashed pets are permitted.

Reservations, fees: Reservations accepted ($8.65 reservation fee). Sites are $10 per night, plus $6 for each additional vehicle. Senior discount available. Open June through September.

Directions: From Portland drive east on U.S. 26 for 55 miles to Government Camp. Continue three miles to a junction, turn right on U.S. 26, and drive south for 12 miles to Highway 216. Turn left (east) on Highway 216 and drive five miles to Reservation Road. Turn east (right) on Reservation Road and look for the campground on the right.

Contact: Mount Hood National Forest, Barlow Ranger District, 780 N.E. Court St., Dufur, OR 97021; 541/467-2291, reservations 877/444-6777; fax 541/467-2271; website (for reservations): www.reserveusa.com.

68 McCubbins Gulch

5

This is a small, primitive camp along a small creek that offers decent fishing and OHV recreation. There is a 40-mile network of OHV trails in the surrounding forest, with access right from camp. So though out of the way, this camp is heavily used; claim a spot early in the day. To the south is the Warm Springs Indian Reservation; do not trespass, as large fines are assessed those prosecuted. A nearby camping option is Bear Springs.

Location: In Mount Hood National Forest; The Columbia River Gorge and Mount Hood map 2, grid h5.

Campsites, facilities: There are 18 sites for tents and RVs up to 25 feet long. Picnic tables and fire grills are provided. Vault toilets are available. There is no drinking water and all garbage must be packed out. Leashed pets are permitted.

Reservations, fees: No reservations accepted. Northwest Forest Pass ($30 annual fee) or $5 daily fee per parked vehicle is required. Senior discount available. Open May through September.

Directions: From Portland drive east on U.S. 26 for 55 miles to Government Camp. Continue three miles to a junction and turn right on U.S. 26 and drive south for 12 miles to Highway 216. Turn left (east) on Highway 216 and drive six miles to Forest Road 2110. Turn a sharp left and drive 1.5 miles to the campground entrance on the right.

Contact: Mount Hood National Forest, Barlow Ranger District, 780 N.E. Court St., Dufur, OR 97021; 541/467-2291; fax 541/467-2271.

69 Shellrock Creek

🎣 🏠 🚐 ⛺   6

Used primarily as an overflow area for Lake Harriet campground, this quiet little campground is set at an elevation of 2,200 feet at a nice spot on Shellrock Creek. Small trout can be caught here, but remember that on the Clackamas River it's catch-and-release only. It's advisable to obtain a U.S. Forest

Service map that details the backcountry roads and trails.

Location: On Shellrock Creek in Mount Hood National Forest; The Columbia River Gorge and Mount Hood map 2, grid h1.

Campsites, facilities: There are eight sites for tents, trailers, or RVs up to 16 feet long. Picnic tables and fire grills are provided. Garbage service is provided during the summer. Vault toilets are available. There is no drinking water. Leashed pets are permitted.

Reservations, fees: No reservations accepted. Sites are $10 per night, $5 per night for an additional vehicle. Senior discount available. Open year-round, with limited winter services.

Directions: From Portland drive east on U.S. 26 from Gresham 11 miles to Sandy and Highway 211. Turn right (south) and drive six miles to a junction. Turn south (still Highway 211) and drive six miles to Estacada and Highway 224. Bear south on Highway 224 and drive 27 miles in national forest (the road becomes Forest Road 46) to Forest Road 57. Turn left (east) and drive 7.5 miles to Forest Road 58. Turn left and drive north one mile to the campground on the left.

Contact: Mount Hood National Forest, Estacada Ranger District, 595 N.W. Industrial Way, Estacada, OR 97023; 503/630-6861; fax 503/630-2299.

70 Joe Graham Horse Camp

🚶 🎣 🏠 🐕 🚐 ⛺   8

This campground is named for a forest ranger and is set at 3,250 feet elevation among majestic Douglas fir and hemlock, just north of tiny Clackamas Lake. It's one of two campgrounds in the area that allows horses; see the description of Clackamas Lake for additional information. Timothy Lake (the setting for the Gone Creek, Hoodview, Oak

Fork, Pine Point, and Meditation Point sites) provides a nearby alternative to the northwest. The Pacific Crest Trail is just east of camp.

Location: Near Clackamas Lake in Mount Hood National Forest; The Columbia River Gorge and Mount Hood map 2, grid h2.

Campsites, facilities: There are 14 sites for tents, trailers, horse trailers, or RVs up to 28 feet long; 11 have corrals and two have hitching rails. Picnic tables, hitching posts, garbage service, and fire grills are provided. Drinking water, vault toilets, and firewood are available. Leashed pets are permitted.

Reservations, fees: Reservations accepted ($8.65 reservation fee). Sites are $12 per night, $6 per night for an additional vehicle. Senior discount available. Open mid-May to mid-September.

Directions: From Portland turn east on U.S. 26 and drive 57 miles (just past the town of Government Camp) to the junction with Highway 35. Turn southeast on U.S. 26 and drive 15 miles to Forest Road 42 (Skyline Road). Turn right and drive eight miles to the campground on the left.

Contact: Mount Hood National Forest, Zigzag Ranger District, 65000 E. Hwy. 26, Welches, OR 97067; 503/622-7674, reservations 877/444-6777; fax 503/622-3163; website (for reservations): www.reserveusa.com.

71 Clackamas Lake

 7

This camp set at 3,400 feet elevation is a good place to go to escape the hordes of people at the lakeside sites at neighboring camps. The Pacific Crest Trail passes nearby, and Timothy Lake is little more than a one-mile hike from camp. See the description of Gone Creek for information on Timothy Lake. This is popuar spot for campers with horses.

Location: Near the Clackamas River in Mount Hood National Forest; The Columbia River Gorge and Mount Hood map 2, grid h2.

Campsites, facilities: There are 46 sites for tents, trailers, horse trailers, or RVs up to 16 feet long. Some sites have hitch rails and horses are permitted at the first 19 sites. Drinking water, garbage service, fire grills, and picnic tables are provided. Vault toilets and firewood are available. Boat docks and launching facilities are nearby at Timothy Lake, but only nonmotorized boats are allowed. Leashed pets are permitted.

Reservations, fees: Reservations accepted for some sites ($8.65 reservation fee). Sites are $12 per night, $6 per night for an additional vehicle. Senior discount available. Open June to mid-September.

Directions: From Portland turn east on U.S. 26 and drive 57 miles (just past the town of Government Camp) to the junction with Highway 35. Turn southeast on U.S. 26 and drive 15 miles to Forest Road 42 (Skyline Road). Turn right and drive eight miles to Forest Road 57. Continue 500 feet (on Forest Road 42) past the Clackamas Lake Historic Ranger Station to Forest Road 4270. Turn left and drive one-half mile to the campground on the left.

Contact: Mount Hood National Forest, Zigzag Ranger District, 65000 E. Hwy. 26, Welches, OR 97067; 503/622-7674, reservations 877/444-6777; fax 503/622-3163; website (for reservations): www.reserveusa.com.

72 Deschutes River State Recreation Area

This tree-shaded park in the Deschutes Canyon along the Deschutes River offers bicycling and hiking trails and good steelhead fishing in season. The Atiyeh Deschutes River Trail at river level is a favorite jaunt for hikers; be sure to look for the basketlike hanging nests of the orioles. There's a small day-use state park called Heritage Landing across the river, which has a boat ramp and restroom facilities. The U.S. Army Corps of Engineers offers a free train ride and tour of the dam at The Dalles during the summer. Good rafting is a bonus here. For 25 miles upstream the river is mostly inaccessible by car. Many fishermen launch boats here and then go upstream to the fishing grounds for steelhead. Note that no fishing is allowed from a boat here; you must wade into the river or fish from shore.

Location: On the Deschutes River; The Columbia River Gorge and Mount Hood map 3, grid c1.

Campsites, facilities: There are 35 primitive sites for tents, trailers, or self-contained RVs up to 30 feet long, 34 electric sites, and one covered camper wagon. There is also a group area for RVs and tents. Picnic tables and fire grills are provided. Drinking water, garbage bins, and flush toilets are available. Leashed pets are permitted.

Reservations, fees: Group reservations accepted ($6 reservation fee). Sites are $13–19 per night; the covered wagon fee is $27 per night; an additional vehicle is $5 per night. Major credit cards accepted. Open late April to October.

Directions: From Portland turn east on I-84 and drive about 90 miles to The Dalles. Continue east on I-84 for 12 miles to Exit 97, turn right, and drive 50 feet to Biggs-Rufus Highway. Turn left and drive about one mile, cross the Deschutes River, and turn right to the campground entrance.

Contact: Deschutes River State Recreation Area, 89600 Biggs-Rufus Hwy., Wasco, OR 97065; 541/739-2322 or 800/452-5687, reservations 800/452-5682.

73 Le Page Park

6

One half of the campsites are adjacent to the John Day River and the other half are on the other side of the road. The John Day River feeds into the Columbia just one-eighth mile north of the campground. The campground is partially shaded. Rattlesnakes are occasionally seen in the area, but are not abundant. Fishing includes smallmouth bass and catfish during the summer. The day-use area has a swimming beach, lawn, a boat launch, and boat docks. There are several other campgrounds nearby.

Location: On the John Day River; The Columbia River Gorge and Mount Hood map 3, grid c3.

Campsites, facilities: There are five tent sites and 22 partial hookup sites for tents, trailers, or RVs up to 40 feet long. Picnic tables and fire pits are provided. Drinking water and electricity, restrooms with flush toilets, sinks, and hot showers are available, as well as a boat ramp, docks, a dump station, and garbage containers. Food and laundry services are available five miles away in the town of Rufus. Leashed pets are permitted.

Reservations, fees: Reservations recommended ($8.65 reservation fee). Sites are $10–16 per night, $3 per night for an additional vehicle. Senior discount available. Open April through October.

Directions: From Portland on I-84, drive east 120 miles (30 miles past The Dalles) to Exit 114, the John Day River Recreation Area. The campground is just off I-84.

Contact: Army Corps of Engineers, Portland District, P.O. Box 2946, Portland, OR 97208-2946; 503/808-5150, reservations 877/444-6777; fax 503/808-4515; website (for reservations): www.reserveusa.com.

74 Beavertail

🎣 🚗 🐕 ♿ 🚐 ⛺ 6

This isolated campground is set at an elevation of 2,900 feet along the banks of the Deschutes River, with fishing and rafting options. The Deschutes is one of the classic steelhead streams in the Pacific Northwest. The landscape is open with canyon views. This is my favorite put-in spot for a drift boat for fishing float trips on the Deschutes. I've made the trip from Beavertail to the mouth of the Deschutes, ideal in four days, camping at BLM boat-in sites along the river, fly-fishing for steelhead. A boating pass is required to float the river. There are 12 other BLM campgrounds along upper and lower Deschutes River Road. The hardest part is getting used to the freight trains that rumble through the canyon at night.

Location: On the Deschutes River; The Columbia River Gorge and Mount Hood map 3, grid f1.

Campsites, facilities: There are 17 sites for tents, trailers, or RVs up to 30 feet long, and two group sites. Picnic tables, garbage bins, and fire grills are provided. Drinking water and vault toilets are available. Some facilities are wheelchair-accessible. Boat-launching facilities are nearby. Leashed pets are permitted.

Reservations, fees: No reservations accepted. Sites are $5–10 per night, with a 14-day stay limit. Senior discount available. Open year-round.

Directions: From Portland drive east on U.S. 84 to The Dalles and Highway 197. Turn south and drive to Maupin. Continue through Maupin, cross the bridge, and within a mile look for Deschutes River Road on your left. Turn left on Deschutes River Road and drive 21 miles northeast to the campground.

Contact: Bureau of Land Management, Prineville District, P.O. Box 550, Prineville, OR 97754; 541/416-6700; fax 541/416-6798.

75 Shady Cove

🥾 🎣 🐕 ⛺ 7

This campground is on the Little North Santiam River in the recently designated Opal Creek Scenic Recreation Area. Little North Santiam Trail is adjacent to the campground.

Location: On the Little North Santiam River in Willamette National Forest; The Columbia River Gorge and Mount Hood map 4, grid b6.

Campsites, facilities: There are 12 sites for tents or self-contained trailers or RVs up to 16 feet long. Picnic tables, garbage service (summer only), fire grills, and vault toilets are available. There is no drinking water. Leashed pets are permitted.

Reservations, fees: No reservations accepted. Sites are $5–10 per night, $3 per night for an additional vehicle. Senior discount available. Open year-round, weather permitting.

Directions: From Salem on I-5, take Exit 253 to Highway 22. Turn east and drive 23 miles to Mehama and North Fork Road (Marion County Road). Turn left and drive 17 miles northeast to the fork. Bear right on Forest Road 2207 and continue for two miles to the campground on the right.

Contact: Willamette National Forest, Detroit Ranger District, HC 73, P.O. Box 320, Mill City, OR 97360; 503/854-3366; fax 503/854-4239.

76 Elk Lake

🥾 🎣 🚗 🐕 ⛺ 9

This remote and primitive campground is on the shore of Elk Lake, where boating, fishing and swimming can be quite good in the summer. Wildflowers blooms can be beautiful in the nearby meadows. Several trails in the area provide access to the Bull of the Woods Wilderness (operated by Mount Hood National Forest) and the newly designated Opal

Creek Wilderness. There are also beautiful views of Battle Ax Mountain.

Location: Near Bull of the Woods Wilderness; The Columbia River Gorge and Mount Hood map 4, grid b8.

Campsites, facilities: There are 14 primitive tent sites. No drinking water is available. Garbage must be packed out. Primitive boat-launching facilities are available. Pets are permitted.

Reservations, fees: No reservations, no fee. Open July to mid-September.

Directions: From Salem on I-5, take Exit 253, turn east on Highway 22 and drive 52 miles to Detroit. Turn left on Forest Road 46/Breitenbush Road and drive 4.5 miles to Forest Road 4696/Elk Lake Road. Turn left and drive less than one mile to Forest Road 4697. Turn left and drive 9.5 miles to the campground on the left. The road is extremely rough for the last two miles. High-clearance vehicles recommended.

Contact: Willamette National Forest, Detroit Ranger District, HC 73, P.O. Box 320, Mill City, OR 97360; 503/854-3366; fax 503/854-4239.

77 Humbug

9

Fishing and hiking are popular at this campground along the banks of the Breitenbush River about four miles from where it empties into Detroit Lake. The lake offers many other recreation opportunities. The Humbug Flat Trailhead is behind Sites 9 and 10, and a scenic stroll through an old-growth forest follows the Breitenbush River. The rhododendrons put on a spectacular show from May through July.

Location: On the Breitenbush River in Willamette National Forest; The Columbia River Gorge and Mount Hood map 4, grid b8.

Campsites, facilities: There are 21 sites for tents, trailers, or RVs up to 22 feet long. Picnic

tables, garbage service (summer only), fire grills, drinking water, and vault toilets are available. Leashed pets are permitted.

Reservations, fees: No reservations accepted. Sites are $8 per night, $5 per night for an additional vehicle. Senior discount available. Open year-round, weather permitting, with limited winter facilities.

Directions: From Salem on I-5, take Exit 253, turn east on Highway 22 and drive 52 miles to Detroit. Turn left on Forest Road 46/Breitenbush Road and drive five miles northeast to the campground on the right.

Contact: Willamette National Forest, Detroit Ranger District, HC 73, P.O. Box 320, Mill City, OR 97360; 503/854-3366; fax 503/854-4239.

78 Detroit Lake State Park

7

This campground is set at 1,600 feet along the shore of Detroit Lake, which is 400 feet deep, nine miles long, and has more than 32 miles of shoreline. The park offers a fishing dock and a moorage area, and a boat ramp and bathhouse are available nearby at the Mongold Day Use Area. The lake is crowded on the opening day of trout season in late April because it's heavily stocked.

Location: On Detroit Lake; The Columbia River Gorge and Mount Hood map 4, grid c7.

Campsites, facilities: There are 132 tent sites and 179 sites with full or partial hookups for trailers or RVs up to 60 feet long, and 82 boat slips. Drinking water, garbage bins, fire grills, and picnic tables are provided. Flush toilets, showers, two playgrounds, swimming areas, a store, a visitor center, and firewood are available. Two boat docks and launching facilities are nearby. Leashed pets are permitted.

Reservations, fees: Reservations accepted ($6 reservation fee). Sites are $13–22 per night, $7 per night for an additional vehicle. Boating moorage is $7 per night. Major credit cards accepted. Open March through November, weather permitting.

Directions: From Salem drive east on Highway 22 for 50 miles to the park entrance on the right (located two miles west of Detroit).

Contact: Detroit Lake State Park, P.O. Box 549, Detroit, OR 97342; 503/854-3346, reservations 800/452-5687.

79 Piety Island Boat-In

10

This island gets crowded and has a reputation for sometimes attracting rowdy groups. Other campgrounds along the shore have drinking water. Piety Island Trail is a 1.5-mile climb to the top of the island. You'll find great vistas on this island.

Location: On Detroit Lake in Willamette National Forest; The Columbia River Gorge and Mount Hood map 4, grid c7.

Campsites, facilities: There are 12 tent sites on this island campground, which is accessible by boat only. Picnic tables and fire grills are provided. Pit toilets are available, but there is no drinking water, and all garbage must be packed out. Boat docks, launching facilities, and rentals are nearby. Leashed pets are permitted.

Reservations, fees: No reservations; no fee. Open May to late September.

Directions: From Salem drive east on Highway 22 for 45 miles to Detroit Lake. Continue east on Highway 22 along the north side of the lake to the boat ramp (a boat ramp is three miles west of the town of Detroit). Launch your boat and head southeast to the island in the middle of the lake. The campground is on the east side of the island.

Contact: Willamette National Forest, Detroit Ranger District, HC 73, Box 320, Mill City, OR 97360; 503/854-3366; fax 503/854-4239.

80 Southshore

9

This popular camp is along the south shore of Detroit Lake, where fishing, swimming, and water-skiing are some of the recreation options. The Stahlman Point Trailhead is about one-half mile from camp. There's a day-use area for picnicking and swimming. The views of the lake and surrounding mountains are outstanding.

Location: On Detroit Lake in Willamette National Forest; The Columbia River Gorge and Mount Hood map 4, grid c7.

Campsites, facilities: There are eight walk-in tent sites and 24 sites for tents, trailers, or RVs up to 22 feet long. Fire grills, garbage service, and picnic tables are provided. Vault toilets and drinking water are available. Boat-launching facilities are nearby at a day-use area. Leashed pets are permitted.

Reservations, fees: No reservations. Sites are $12–24 per night, $5 per night for an additional vehicle. Open mid-April to late September, with a gate preventing access during the off-season.

Directions: From Salem drive east on Highway 22 for 52 miles to Detroit. Continue southeast on Highway 22 for 2.5 miles to Forest Road 10 (Blowout Road). Turn right and drive four miles to the campground on the right.

Contact: Willamette National Forest, Detroit Ranger District, HC 73, Box 320, Mill City, OR 97360; 503/854-3366; fax 503/854-4239.

81 Cove Creek

10

See the description of Southshore and Hoover for recreation options.

Location: On Detroit Lake in Willamette National Forest; The Columbia River Gorge and Mount Hood map 4, grid c7.

Campsites, facilities: There are 63 sites for tents, trailers, or RVs, and one group site for up to 70 people. Picnic tables, garbage service, and fire rings are provided. Drinking water, restrooms with flush toilets and coin-operated showers, garbage bins, and a boat ramp are available. Some facilities are wheelchair-accessible. Leashed pets are permitted.

Reservations, fees: Reservations for group site only. Sites are $16 per night, $32 for double sites, $5 per night for an additional vehicle. Group sites are $150 per night. Senior discount available. Open late May to late September.

Directions: From Salem drive east on Highway 22 for 52 miles to Detroit. Continue southeast on Highway 22 for 2.5 miles to Forest Road 10 (Blowout Road). Turn right and drive three miles to the campground on the right.

Contact: Willamette National Forest, Detroit Ranger District, HC 73, Box 320, Mill City, OR 97360; 503/854-3366, reservations (group site only) 877/444-6777; fax 503/854-4239.

82 Hoover

9

This campground is along the eastern arm of Detroit Lake, near the mouth of the Santiam River. There is a wheelchair-accessible fishing area and nature trail. You're likely to see osprey fishing during the day, a truly special sight. See the description of Southshore for other recreation options.

Location: On Detroit Lake in Willamette National Forest; The Columbia River Gorge and Mount Hood map 4, grid c7.

Campsites, facilities: There are 37 sites for tents, trailers, or RVs up to 32 feet long. Picnic tables, garbage service, and fire grills

are provided. Flush toilets and drinking water are available. Some facilities are wheelchair-accessible. Boat docks and launching facilities are nearby. Leashed pets are permitted.

Reservations, fees: No reservations. Sites are $12–24 per night, $5 per night for an additional vehicle. Senior discount available. Open mid-April to late September; a gate prevents access in the off-season.

Directions: From Salem drive east on Highway 22 for 52 miles to Detroit. Continue southeast on Highway 22 for 2.5 miles to Forest Road 10 (Blowout Road). Turn right and drive one mile to the campground on the right.

Contact: Willamette National Forest, Detroit Ranger District, HC 73, Box 320, Mill City, OR 97360; 503/854-3366; fax 503/854-4239.

83 Upper Arm

7

This little campground is set along the shore of the narrow upper arm of Detroit Lake, close to where the Breitenbush River empties into it. It's the smallest and most primitive camp in the area with a large day-use area.

Location: On Detroit Lake in Willamette National Forest; The Columbia River Gorge and Mount Hood map 4, grid c8.

Campsites, facilities: There are five tent sites. Fire grills and picnic tables are provided. Pit toilets and garbage service (summer only) are available. There is no drinking water. Boat docks, launching facilities, and rentals are nearby. Leashed pets are permitted.

Reservations, fees: No reservations; no fee. Open year-round.

Directions: From Salem drive east on Highway 22 for 52 miles to Detroit and Forest Road 46 (Breitenbush Road). Turn left and drive one mile northeast to the campground on the left.

Contact: Willamette National Forest, Detroit Ranger

District, HC 73, Box 320, Mill City, OR 97360; 503/854-3366; fax 503/854-4239.

84 Hoover Group Camp

9

This is a perfect spot for a family reunion or club trip. Detroit Lake offers a myriad of activities, including hiking, fishing, swimming, and boating, just to name a few. The campground has nice, open sites and direct access to the lake. See descriptions of Hoover and Southshore Campgrounds.

Location: On Detroit Lake in Willamette National Forest; The Columbia River Gorge and Mount Hood map 4, grid c8.

Campsites, facilities: There are nine sites for tents, trailers, or RVs up to 15 feet long. This is a group camp that will accommodate up to 70 people. Drinking water and picnic tables are provided. Vault toilets and a group picnic shelter are available. Boat docks, launching facilities, and rentals are nearby. Leashed pets are permitted.

Reservations, fees: Reservations accepted ($8.65 reservation fee). Group sites are $120 per night, with a two-night minimum for weekend reservations. Open mid-April to late September.

Directions: From Salem drive east on Highway 22 for 52 miles to Detroit. Continue southeast on Highway 22 for 2.5 miles to Forest Road 10 (Blowout Road). Turn right and drive one-half mile to the campground on the right.

Contact: Willamette National Forest, Detroit Ranger District, HC 73, Box 320, Mill City, OR 97360; 503/854-3366, reservations 877/444-6777; fax 503/854-4239; website (for reservations): www.reserveusa.com.

85 Summit Lake

6

This is an idyllic setting in a remote area along the western slopes of the Cascade Range at an elevation of 4,200 feet. On the shore of little Summit Lake, the camp is primitive but a jewel. It's a perfect alternative to the more crowded camps at Timothy Lake, and you have access to all the same recreation options by driving just a short distance north.

Location: On Summit Lake in Mount Hood National Forest; The Columbia River Gorge and Mount Hood map 5, grid a3.

Campsites, facilities: There are six tent sites. Fire grills, garbage service, and picnic tables are provided. Vault toilets and drinking water are available. There is no drinking water. Nonmotorized boats are allowed. Leashed pets are permitted.

Reservations, fees: No reservations accepted. Sites are $8 per night. Senior discount available. Open late May through September, weather permitting.

Directions: From Portland turn east on U.S. 26 and drive 57 miles (just past the town of Government Camp) to the junction with Highway 35. Turn southeast on U.S. 26 and drive 15 miles to Forest Road 42 (Skyline Road). Turn right and drive 12 miles south to Forest Road 141 (a dirt road). Turn right and drive west about one mile to the campground on the left.

Contact: Mount Hood National Forest, Zigzag Ranger District, 65000 E. Hwy. 26, Welches, OR 97067; 503/622-7674; fax 503/622-3163.

86 Kah-Nee-Ta Resort

7

This resort features a full-concept spa that is stellar-rated. It is also the only public camp on the east side of the Warm Springs Indian Reservation; there are no other camps within 30 miles. The Warm Springs River runs nearby. Recreation options in the area include an 18-hole golf course, miniature golf, biking and hiking trails, a riding stable, and tennis courts.

Location: On the Warm Springs Indian Reservation; The Columbia River Gorge and Mount Hood map 5, grid b7.

Campsites, facilities: There are 50 drive-through sites for trailers or RVs of any length. Electricity, drinking water, cable TV, and sewer hookups are provided. Flush toilets, bottled gas, sanitary services, showers, a concession stand, laundry facilities, ice, a playground, a spa with a therapist, mineral baths, and an Olympic-sized, spring-fed swimming pool with a 140-foot water slide are available. Some facilities are wheelchair-accessible. Leashed pets and motorbikes are permitted, but some areas are restricted.

Reservations, fees: Reservations accepted. Sites are $38 per night; two-night minimum on weekends, three-night minimum on holiday weekends. Off-season discounts available. Open year-round.

Directions: From Portland turn east on U.S. 26 and drive about 105 miles to Warm Springs and Agency Hot Springs Road on the left. Turn left and drive 11 miles northeast to Kah-Nee-Ta and the resort on the right.

Contact: Kah-Nee-Ta Resort, P.O. Box K, Warm Springs, OR 97761; 541/553-1112; fax 541/302-6622; website: www.kahneeta resort.com.

87 Cleater Bend

Creek views are a highlight of this camp on the banks of the Breitenbush River with pretty, shaded sites. The camp is one-quarter mile from Breitenbush; see the description of Breitenbush for area details.

Location: Near the Breitenbush River in Willamette National Forest; The Columbia River Gorge and Mount Hood map 5, grid b1.

Campsites, facilities: There are nine sites for tents, trailers, or RVs up to 16 feet long. Picnic tables, garbage service (summer only), fire grills, drinking water, and vault toilets are available. Leashed pets are permitted.

Reservations, fees: No reservations accepted. Sites are $8 per night, $5 per night for an additional vehicle. Senior discount available. Open year-round, weather permitting.

Directions: From Salem on I-5, take Exit 253, turn east on Highway 22, and drive 50 miles to Detroit. Turn left on Forest Road 46/Breitenbush Road and drive nine miles to the campground on the right.

Contact: Willamette National Forest, Detroit Ranger District, HC 73, Box 320, Mill City, OR 97360; 503/854-3366; fax 503/854-4239.

88 Breitenbush

Fishing access is a plus at this campground along the Breitenbush River. The South Breitenbush Gorge National Recreation Trail is three miles away. Breitenbush Hot Springs is just over a mile away. If this campground is crowded, try nearby Cleater Bend.

Location: On the Breitenbush River in Willamette National Forest; The Columbia River Gorge and Mount Hood map 5, grid b1.

Campsites, facilities: There are 29 sites for tents, trailers, or RVs up to 22 feet long (longer trailers may be difficult to park and turn). Picnic tables, garbage service (summer only), and fire grills are provided. Drinking water and vault toilets are available. Leashed pets are permitted.

Reservations, fees: No reservations accepted. Sites

are $8–16 per night, $5 per night for an additional vehicle. Senior discount available. Open year-round, weather permitting, with limited winter facilities.

Directions: From Salem on I-5, take Exit 253, turn east on Highway 22, and drive 50 miles to Detroit. Turn left (north) on Forest Road 46/Breitenbush Road and drive 10 miles to the campground on the right.

Contact: Willamette National Forest, Detroit Ranger District, HC 73, Box 320, Mill City, OR 97360; 503/854-3366; fax 503/854-4239.

89 Lower Lake

7

This sunny, open campground is set at an elevation of 4,600 feet about three-quarters of a mile from Lower Lake, a small, deep lake that's perfect for fishing and swimming. The camp is less than a mile from Olallie Lake and near a network of trails that provide access to other nearby lakes. It's advisable to obtain a U.S. Forest Service map that details the backcountry roads and trails.

Location: Near Olallie Lake in Mount Hood National Forest; The Columbia River Gorge and Mount Hood map 5, grid b2.

Campsites, facilities: There are eight walk-in tent sites. Picnic tables and fire grills are provided. Pit toilets and garbage service are available. There is no drinking water. Boat docks, launching facilities, and rentals are nearby at Olallie Lake. Leashed pets are permitted.

Reservations, fees: No reservations accepted. Sites are $6 per night, $3 per night for an additional vehicle. Senior discount available. Open mid-June to late September.

Directions: From Portland drive east on U.S. 26 from Gresham 11 miles to Sandy and Highway 211. Turn right (south) and drive six miles to a junction. Turn south (still Highway

211) and drive six miles to Estacada and Highway 224. Bear south on Highway 224 and drive 27 miles in national forest (the road becomes Forest Road 46). Continue south on Forest Road 46 for 20 miles to Forest Road 4690. Turn left on Forest Road 4690 and drive southeast for 8.2 miles to Forest Road 4220. Turn right (south) and drive about 4.5 miles of rough road to the campground on the right.

Contact: Mount Hood National Forest, Clackamas River Ranger District, 595 N.W. Industrial Way, Estacada, OR 97023; 503/630-6861; fax 503/630-2299.

90 Camp Ten

9

Here's a camp along the shore of Olallie Lake, a popular area. This one is set at an elevation of 5,000 feet on the western shore in the midst of the Olallie Lake Scenic Area, which is home to a number of pristine mountain lakes and a network of hiking trails. See a U.S. Forest Service map for trail locations. Boats without motors—including canoes, kayaks, and rafts—are permitted on the lake.

Location: On Olallie Lake in Mount Hood National Forest; The Columbia River Gorge and Mount Hood map 5, grid b2.

Campsites, facilities: There are 10 sites for tents, trailers, or RVs up to 16 feet long. Picnic tables, garbage service, and fire grills are provided. Pit toilets are available. There is no drinking water. Boat docks, launching facilities, boat rentals, and a store that sells fishing tackle and other supplies are nearby. Leashed pets are permitted.

Reservations, fees: No reservations accepted. Sites are $6 per night, $3 per night for an additional vehicle. Senior discount available. Open mid-June to late September, weather permitting.

Directions: From Portland drive east on U.S. 26 from Gresham 11 miles to Sandy and Highway 211. Turn right (south) and drive six miles to a junction. Turn south (still Highway 211) and drive six miles to Estacada and Highway 224. Bear south on Highway 224 and drive 27 miles in national forest (the road becomes Forest Road 46). Continue south on Forest Road 46 for 20 miles to Forest Road 4690. Turn left on Forest Road 4690 and drive southeast for 8.2 miles to Forest Road 4220. Turn right (south) and drive about six miles of rough road to the campground.

Contact: Mount Hood National Forest, Clackamas River Ranger District, 595 N.W. Industrial Way, Estacada, OR 97023; 503/630-6861; fax 503/630-2299.

91 Paul Dennis

 10

This campground is set at an elevation of 5,000 feet along the north shore of Olallie Lake. From here you can see the reflection of Mt. Jefferson (10,497 feet). Boats with motors are not permitted on the lake. A trail from camp leads to Nep-Te-Pa Lake, Monon Lake, and Long Lake, which lies just east of the border of the Warm Springs Indian Reservation. It's advisable to obtain a U.S. Forest Service map.

Location: On Olallie Lake in Mount Hood National Forest; The Columbia River Gorge and Mount Hood map 5, grid b2.

Campsites, facilities: There are 17 sites for tents or small campers up to 16 feet long (trailers not recommended) and three hike-in tent sites. Picnic tables, garbage service, and fire grills are provided. Pit toilets are available. There is no drinking water. A store and ice are nearby. Boat docks, launching facilities, and rentals are on Olallie Lake. Leashed pets are permitted.

Reservations, fees: Reservations accepted. Sites are $9 per night, $4.50 for each additional vehicle. Open mid-June to late September.

Directions: From Portland drive east on U.S. 26 from Gresham 11 miles to Sandy and Highway 211. Turn right (south) and drive six miles to a junction. Turn south (still Highway 211) and drive six miles to Estacada and Highway 224. Bear south on Highway 224 and drive 27 miles in national forest (the road becomes Forest Road 46). Continue south on Forest Road 46 for 20 miles to Forest Road 4690. Turn left and drive southeast for 8.2 miles to Forest Road 4220. Turn right (south) and drive 6.2 miles to Forest Road 4220-170. Turn left and drive one-eighth mile to the campground.

Contact: Mount Hood National Forest, Clackamas River Ranger District, 595 N.W. Industrial Way, Estacada, OR 97023; 503/630-6861, reservations 503/557-1010; fax 503/630-2299.

92 Peninsula

10

Peninsula, the largest of several campgrounds along Olallie Lake, is set at an elevation of 4,900 feet on the south shore. The amphitheater is near camp, and during the summer rangers present campfire programs. Boats without motors are permitted on the lake. Numerous smaller lakes in the area can be reached from trails nearby. See the description of Paul Dennis for details.

Location: On Olallie Lake in Mount Hood National Forest; The Columbia River Gorge and Mount Hood map 5, grid b2.

Campsites, facilities: There are 35 sites for tents, trailers, or RVs up to 24 feet long, and six walk-in tent sites. Picnic tables, garbage service, and fire grills are provided. Vault toilets are available. There is no drinking water. Some facilities are wheelchair-accessible. Boat docks, launching facilities, and rentals are nearby. Leashed pets are permitted.

Reservations, fees: Reservations accepted. Sites are $12 per night, $6 per night for an additional vehicle, $6 for walk-in sites. Senior discount available. Open mid-June to late September.

Directions: From Portland drive east on U.S. 26 from Gresham 11 miles to Sandy and Highway 211. Turn right (south) and drive six miles to a junction. Turn south (still Highway 211) and drive six miles to Estacada and Highway 224. Bear south on Highway 224 and drive 27 miles in national forest (the road becomes Forest Road 46). Continue south on Forest Road 46 for 20 miles to Forest Road 4690. Turn left and drive southeast for 8.2 miles to Forest Road 4220. Turn right (south) and drive 6.5 miles of rough road to the campground.

Contact: Mount Hood National Forest, Clackamas River Ranger District, 595 N.W. Industrial Way, Estacada, OR 97023; 503/630-6861, reservations 503/557-1010; fax 503/630-2299.

93 Olallie Meadows

🥾 🎣 🐕 🚐 ⛺   8

This campground is set at 4,500 feet along a large and peaceful alpine meadow about three miles from Olallie Lake. The Pacific Crest Trail passes very close to camp. See the description of Paul Dennis for area details.

Location: Near Olallie Lake in Mount Hood National Forest; The Columbia River Gorge and Mount Hood map 5, grid b3.

Campsites, facilities: There are seven sites for tents, trailers, or RVs up to 16 feet long. Picnic tables, garbage service, and fire grills are provided. Pit toilets are available. There is no drinking water. Boat docks, launching facilities, and rentals are about

three miles away on Olallie Lake. Leashed pets are permitted.

Reservations, fees: No reservations accepted. Sites are $6 per night, $3 per night for an additional vehicle. Senior discount available. Open mid-June to late September.

Directions: From Portland drive east on U.S. 26 from Gresham 11 miles to Sandy and Highway 211. Turn right (south) and drive six miles to a junction. Turn south (still Highway 211) and drive six miles to Estacada and Highway 224. Bear south on Highway 224 and drive 27 miles in national forest (the road becomes Forest Road 46). Continue south on Forest Road 46 for 20 miles to Forest Road 4690. Turn left and drive southeast for 8.2 miles to Forest Road 4220. Turn right (south) and drive 1.5 miles to the campground on the left.

Contact: Mount Hood National Forest, Clackamas River Ranger District, 595 N.W. Industrial Way, Estacada, OR 97023; 503/630-6861; fax 503/630-2299.

94 Whispering Falls

🥾 🎣 🐕 🚐 ⛺   10

This popular campground is on the banks of the North Santiam River, where you can fish. If the campsites at Detroit Lake are crowded, this provides a more secluded option, and it's only about a 10-minute drive from the lake. Ospreys sometimes nest near the campground.

Location: On the North Santiam River near Detroit Lake in Willamette National Forest; The Columbia River Gorge and Mount Hood map 5, grid c1.

Campsites, facilities: There are 16 sites for tents, trailers, or RVs up to 22 feet long. Picnic tables, garbage service, and fire grills are provided. Drinking water and flush toilets are available. Leashed pets are permitted.

Reservations, fees: No reservations. Sites are $10 per night, $5 per night for an additional vehicle. Senior discount available. Open mid-April to late September; a gate prevents access in the off-season.

Directions: From Salem drive east on Highway 22 for 50 miles to Detroit. Continue east on Highway 22 for eight miles to the campground on the right.

Contact: Willamette National Forest, Detroit Ranger District, HC 73, Box 320, Mill City, OR 97360; 503/854-3366; fax 503/854-4239.

95 Riverside

7

This campground is set at an elevation of 2,400 feet along the banks of the North Santiam River, where the fishing can be good. A point of interest is the Marion Forks Fish Hatchery and interpretive site, 2.5 miles south. The Mt. Jefferson Wilderness is directly to the east in Willamette National Forest, and Minto Mountain Trail is three miles to the east.

Location: On the North Santiam River in Willamette National Forest; The Columbia River Gorge and Mount Hood map 5, grid c1.

Campsites, facilities: There are 37 sites for tents, trailers, or RVs up to 21 feet long. Picnic tables and fire grills are provided. Drinking water and pit toilets are available. Leashed pets are permitted.

Reservations, fees: No reservations. Sites are $8 per night, $5 per night for an additional vehicle. Senior discount available. Open late April to late September; a gate prevents access during the off-season.

Directions: From Salem drive east on Highway 22 for 50 miles to Detroit. Continue southeast on Highway 22 for 14 miles to the campground on the right.

Contact: Willamette National Forest, Detroit Ranger District, HC 73, Box 320, Mill City, OR 97360; 503/854-3366; fax 503/854-4239.

96 Marion Forks

8

This campground is along Marion Creek, adjacent to the Marion Forks Fish Hatchery. A U.S. Forest Service guard station and a restaurant are across Highway 22. There are some quality hiking trails in the area; the nearest is Independence Rock Trail, one-quarter mile north of the campground.

Location: On the Santiam River in Willamette National Forest; The Columbia River Gorge and Mount Hood map 5, grid d1.

Campsites, facilities: There are 15 sites for tents, trailers, or RVs up to 22 feet long. Picnic tables, fire grills, and garbage containers are provided. Pit toilets and drinking water are available. Leashed pets are permitted.

Reservations, fees: No reservations. Sites are $8 per night, $5 per night for an additional vehicle. Senior discount available. Open year-round, weather permitting, with no winter services.

Directions: From Salem drive east on Highway 22 for 50 miles to Detroit. Continue southeast on Highway 22 for 16 miles to the campground on the left.

Contact: Willamette National Forest, Detroit Ranger District, HC 73, Box 320, Mill City, OR 97360; 503/854-3366; fax 503/854-4239.

97 Big Meadows Horse Camp

10

Built by the U.S. Forest Service with the support of a horse club, this camp is used heavily by equestrians riding into the Big Meadows area and the adjacent Mt. Jefferson Wilderness. If you're not a horse lover, you may want to stick with Riverside or Marion Forks.

Location: Near Mt. Jefferson Wilderness in Willamette National Forest; The Columbia River Gorge and Mount Hood map 5, grid d1.

Campsites, facilities: There are nine sites for tents, trailers, or RVs. Picnic tables, garbage service, fire grills, and enclosed four-horse corrals are provided at each site. Drinking water and vault toilets are available. Leashed pets are permitted.

Reservations, fees: No reservations. Sites are $9 per night, $5 per night for an additional vehicle. Senior discount available. Open mid-April to mid-September, weather permitting.

Directions: From Salem drive east on Highway 22 for 50 miles to Detroit. Continue southeast on Highway 22 for 27 miles to Big Meadows Road (Forest Road 2267). Turn left and drive one mile to Forest Road 2257. Turn left and drive one-half mile to the campground on the left.

Contact: Willamette National Forest, Detroit Ranger District, HC 73, Box 320, Mill City, OR 97360; 503/854-3366; fax 503/854-4239.

98 Sheep Springs Horse Camp

7

This well-shaded equestrian camp with privacy screening between sites is near the trailhead for the Metolius-Windigo Horse Trail, which heads northeast into the Mt. Jefferson Wilderness and south to Black Butte. Contact the U.S. Forest Service for details and maps of the backcountry. The camp is set at an elevation of 3,200 feet.

Location: Near the Mt. Jefferson Wilderness in Deschutes National Forest; The Columbia River Gorge and Mount Hood map 5, grid d3.

Campsites, facilities: There are 11 sites for tents, trailers, or RVs up to 30 feet long. Drinking water and fire grills are provided. Vault toilets and box stalls for horses are available.

Reservations, fees: Reservations accepted ($8.65 reservation fee). Sites are $12 per night, $6 per night for an additional vehicle.

Senior discount available. Open late May to mid-October.

Directions: From Albany drive east on U.S. 20 for 87 miles to the sign for Jack Lake (located one mile east of Suttle Lake) and Suttle-Sherman Road. Turn left on Forest Road 12 and drive eight miles to Forest Road 1260. Turn left and drive 1.5 miles to Forest Road 1260-200. Turn right and drive 1.5 miles to the campground on the right.

Contact: Deschutes National Forest, Sisters Ranger District, P.O. Box 249, Sisters, OR 97759; 541/549-7700, reservations 877/444-6777; fax 541/549-7746; website (for reservations): www.reserveusa.com.

99 Jack Creek

5

A more primitive alternative to the other camps in the area, this campground is set along the banks of Jack Creek in an open setting among ponderosa pine. To protect the bull trout habitat, no fishing is permitted here.

Location: Near Mt. Jefferson Wilderness in Deschutes National Forest; The Columbia River Gorge and Mount Hood map 5, grid d3.

Campsites, facilities: There is an area for dispersed tent, trailer, or RV camping with access to some picnic tables and fire grills. Vault toilets are available. There is no drinking water, and all garbage must be packed out. Leashed pets are permitted.

Reservations, fees: No reservations; no fee. Open mid-April to mid-October.

Directions: From Albany drive east on U.S. 20 for 87 miles to the sign for Jack Lake (located one mile east of Suttle Lake) and Suttle-Sherman Road. Turn left on Forest Road 12 and drive five miles to Forest Road 1230. Turn left and drive three-quarters of a mile to Forest Road 1232. Turn left and drive one-quarter mile to the campground on the left.

Contact: Deschutes National Forest, Sisters Ranger District, P.O. Box 249, Sisters, OR 97759; 541/549-7700; fax 541/549-7746.

100 Pelton

8

This campground claims one-half mile of shoreline along the north side of Lake Simtustus. Campsites here are shaded with juniper in an area of rolling hills and sagebrush. One section of the lake is accessible for water-skiing and personal watercraft. It's a trophy fishing lake for kokanee and rainbow, brown, and bull trout. Cove Palisades State Park is about 15 miles south, providing additional recreational opportunities. Watch for osprey and bald and golden eagles.

Location: On Lake Simtustus in Deschutes National Forest; The Columbia River Gorge and Mount Hood map 5, grid c6.

Campsites, facilities: There are 75 sites for tents, trailers, or RVs up to 40 feet long, 30 with partial hook-ups, and one group site that can accommodate up to 50 campers. Drinking water, picnic tables, garbage service, and fire grills are provided. Restrooms, a restaurant, snack bar, minimart, gasoline, and a picnic shelter with sinks and electric stoves are available. Also, a full-service marina with boat rentals, a boat launch, boat dock, fishing pier, swimming beach, volleyball courts, horseshoe pits, and a playground are available. Leashed pets are permitted.

Reservations, fees: Reservations recommended. Sites are $14.50–20 per night; the group site is $65 per night. Major credit cards accepted. Open mid-April through October.

Directions: From Portland drive south on U.S. 26 for 108 miles to the town of Warm Springs. Continue south two miles to Pelton Dam Road. Turn right and drive three miles to the campground on the right.

Contact: Portland General Electric, 121 S.W. Salmon St., Portland, OR 97204; 503/464-8515, reservations 541/475-0517; fax 503/464-2944; website: www.portlandgeneral.rom/parks.

101 Perry South

6

This campground is set near the shore of the Metolius arm of Lake Billy Chinook. The lake can get very crowded and noisy; it attracts the powerboat/water-ski enthusiasts. See the description of KOA Madras/ Culver (in this chapter) and Crooked River Ranch RV Park (see the Southern Cascades chapter) for recreation details. The lake borders the Warm Springs Indian Reservation.

Location: On Lake Billy Chinook in Deschutes National Forest; The Columbia River Gorge and Mount Hood map 5, grid d6.

Campsites, facilities: There are four tent sites and 59 sites for tents, trailers, or RVs up to 40 feet long. Picnic tables, garbage service, and fire grills are provided. Drinking water, wheelchair-accessible vault toilets, fish-cleaning station, boat docks, and launching facilities are available. Leashed pets are permitted.

Reservations, fees: No reservations. Sites are $12 per night, plus $6 for each additional vehicle. Senior discount available. Open May through September.

Directions: From Bend drive north on U.S. 97 to Redmond, then continue north for 15 miles to the Culver Highway. Take the Culver Highway north to Culver, and continue two miles to Gem Lane. Turn left and drive two miles to Frazier Drive. Turn left and drive a short distance to Peck Road. Turn right and drive through Cove Palisades State Park to Jordan Road at the shore of Lake Billy Chinook. Turn left on Jordan Road and drive about 10 miles (over the bridge) to County Road 64. Continue (bearing left) and drive about eight miles to the campground entrance on the left (on the upper end of the Metolius Fork of Lake Billy Chinook).

Contact: Deschutes National Forest, Sisters Ranger District, P.O. Box 249, Sisters, OR 97759; 541/549-7700; fax 541/549-7746.

102 Monty

 5

Trout fishing can be good at this remote campground along the banks of the Metolius River near where it empties into Lake Billy Chinook. It gets light use. Warm Springs Indian Reservation is across the river.

Location: On the Metolius River in Deschutes National Forest; The Columbia River Gorge and Mount Hood map 5, grid d6.

Campsites, facilities: There are 20 sites for tents, trailers, or RVs up to 22 feet long. Picnic tables, garbage service, and fire grills are provided. Firewood and vault toilets are available. There is no drinking water. Boat docks and launching facilities are nearby at Perry South. Leashed pets are permitted.

Reservations, fees: No reservations. Sites are $10 per night, $5 per night for an additional vehicle. Senior discount available. Open May through September.

Directions: From Bend drive north on U.S. 97 to Redmond and continue north for 15 miles to the Culver Highway. Take the Culver Highway north to Culver and continue two miles to Gem Lane. Turn left and drive two miles to Frazier Drive. Turn left and drive a short distance to Peck Road. Turn right and drive through Cove Palisades State Park to Jordan Road at the shore of Lake Billy Chinook. Turn left on Jordan Road and drive about 10 miles (over the bridge) to County Road 64. Turn left and drive about 13 miles to the campground entrance (on the Metolius River above the headwaters of Lake Billy Chinook). The last five miles are very rough.

Contact: Deschutes National Forest, Sisters Ranger District, P.O. Box 249, Sisters, OR 97759; 541/549-7700; fax 541/549-7746.

103 Cove Palisades State Park

7

This park is a mile away from the shore of Lake Billy Chinook, where some lakeshore cabins are available. In Oregon's high desert region, its weather is sunny and warm in the summer and chilly but generally mild in the winter. Towering cliffs surround the lake and there are about 10 miles of hiking trails. Two popular special events are held here annually: Lake Billy Chinook Day in September and the Eagle Watch in February.

Location: On Lake Billy Chinook; The Columbia River Gorge and Mount Hood map 5, grid d6.

Campsites, facilities: There are 94 tent sites and 178 sites with full or partial hookups for trailers or RVs up to 60 feet long, plus three cabins and a group area. Picnic tables and fire grills are provided. Drinking water, garbage bins, flush toilets, sanitary disposal station, showers, firewood, a store, a restaurant, and ice are available. Some facilities are wheelchair-accessible. Boat docks, launching facilities, a marina, and boat rentals are nearby. Leashed pets are permitted.

Reservations, fees: Reservations accepted ($6 reservation fee). Sites are $13–20 per night, cabins are $45–65 per night, the group area is $60 per night, and there is a fee of $7 per night for an additional vehicle. Major credit cards accepted. Open year-round.

Directions: From Bend drive north on U.S. 97 for 13 miles to Redmond and continue north for 15 miles to the Culver Highway. Take the Culver Highway north to Culver and continue two miles to Gem Lane. Turn left and drive two miles to Frazier Drive. Turn left and drive a short distance to Peck Road. Turn right and drive to the park entrance.

Contact: Cove Palisades State Park, 7300 Jordan Rd., Culver, OR 97734; 800/551-6949 or 541/546-3412, reservations 800/452-5687.

104 KOA Madras/Culver

This campground has a relaxing atmosphere, with some mountain views, and is about three miles from Lake Billy Chinook, a steep-sided reservoir formed where the Crooked River, Metolius River, Deschutes River, and Squaw Creek all merge. Like much of the country east of the Cascades, this is a high desert area.

Location: Near Lake Billy Chinook; The Columbia River Gorge and Mount Hood map 5, grid d7.

Campsites, facilities: There are 31 tent sites and 68 drive-through sites for trailers or RVs of any length. Electricity, drinking water, sewer hookups, and picnic tables are provided. Flush toilets, bottled gas, sanitary services, showers, firewood, a recreation hall, a store, a laundry room, ice, a playground, and a swimming pool are available. Boat docks and launching facilities are nearby. Leashed pets and motorbikes are permitted.

Reservations, fees: Reservations accepted. Sites are $17–22 per night. Open year-round.

Directions: From Madras drive south on U.S. 97 for nine miles to Jericho Lane. Turn east and drive a half mile to the campground.

Contact: KOA Madras/Culver, S.W. Jericho Ln., Culver, OR 97734; 541/546-3046, reservations 800/563-1992; fax 541/546-7972.

NORTHEAST OREGON

Northeast Oregon

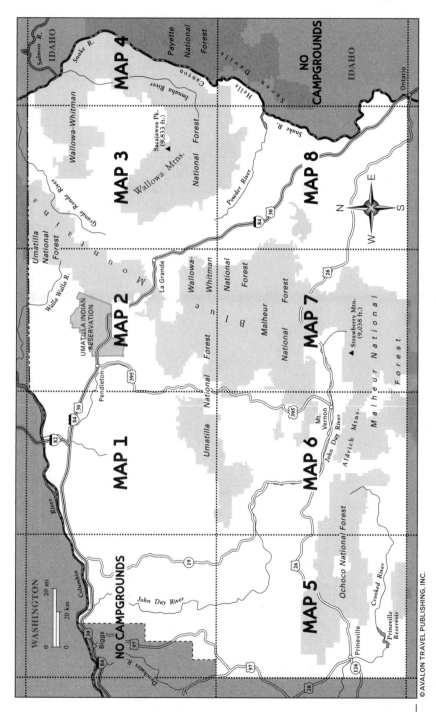

© AVALON TRAVEL PUBLISHING, INC.

Map 1

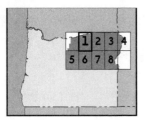

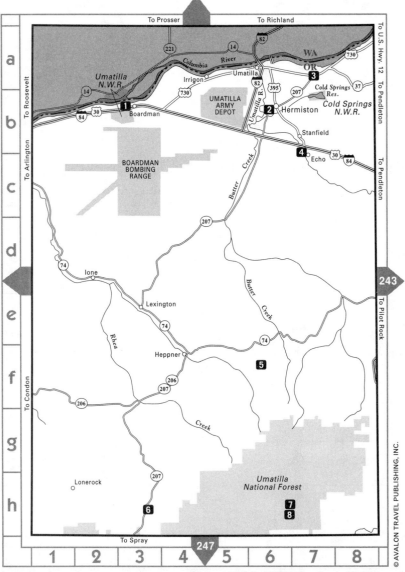

© AVALON TRAVEL PUBLISHING, INC.

Map 2

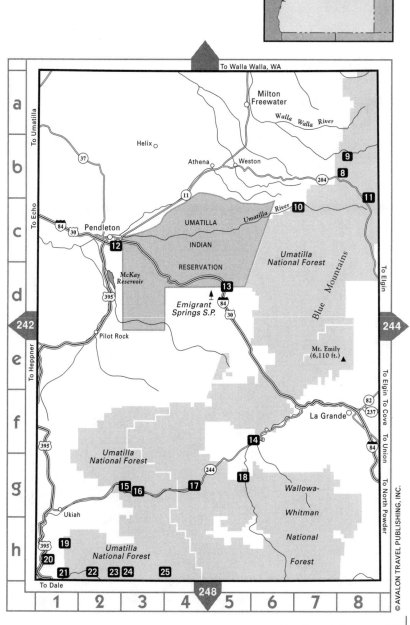

To Walla Walla, WA

Milton Freewater

Walla Walla River

Helix

Athena   Weston

To Umatilla

37

To Echo

11

Pendleton

84
30

12

UMATILLA

INDIAN

RESERVATION

Umatilla River

10

9

8

204

11

Umatilla
National Forest

Blue Mountains

McKay
Reservoir

395

Emigrant
Springs S.P.

13

84
30

242

Pilot Rock

244

Mt. Emily
(6,110 ft.)

To Heppner

To Elgin

82
237

La Grande

To Elgin To Cove

395

Umatilla
National Forest

244

14

18

To Union

84

To North Powder

15 16

17

Wallowa-

Ukiah

Whitman

19

National

Umatilla
National Forest

395

20

Forest

21   22   23 24   25

To Dale

248

© AVALON TRAVEL PUBLISHING, INC.

1 2 3 4
5 6 7 8

Map 3

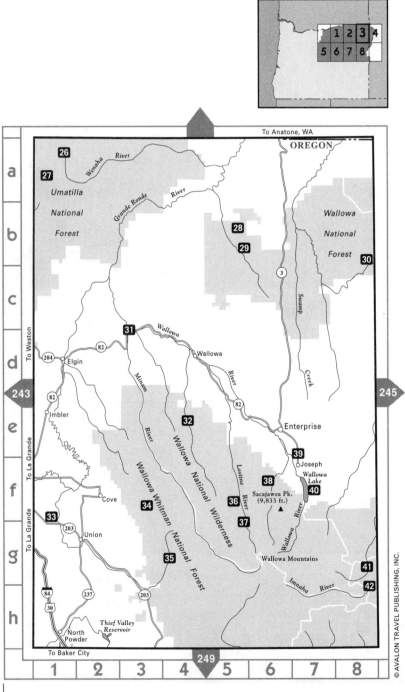

To Anatone, WA

OREGON

26

27

Wenaha River

Umatilla National Forest

Grande Ronde River

28

29

Wallowa National Forest

3

30

Swamp

To Weston

31

Wallowa

204

82

Elgin

Wallowa

River

82

Minam

Imbler

River

Creek

Enterprise

32

39

Joseph

To La Grande

Wallowa National Wilderness

38

Sacajawea Pk. (9,833 ft.)

Wallowa Lake

40

Cove

34

Lostine River

36

To La Grande

33

203

Union

Wallowa Whitman National Forest

37

Wallowa River

35

Wallowa Mountains

41

84

237

203

Imnaha River

42

30

Thief Valley Reservoir

North Powder

To Baker City

249

© AVALON TRAVEL PUBLISHING, INC.

243

245

Map 4

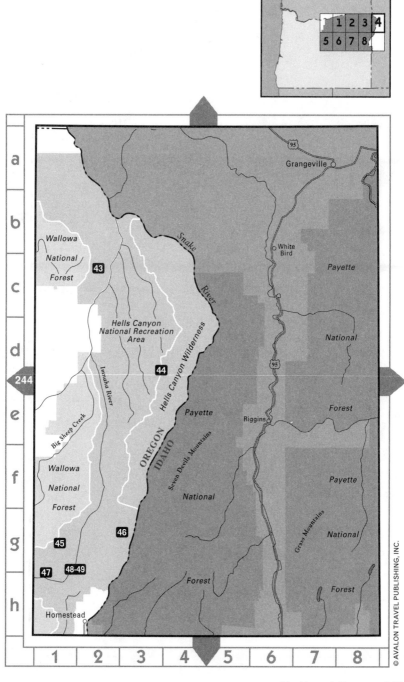

© AVALON TRAVEL PUBLISHING, INC.

Map 5

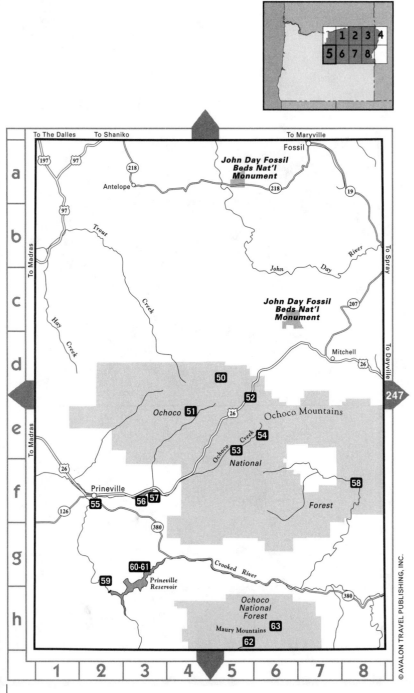

To The Dalles · To Shaniko · To Maryville

Fossil

John Day Fossil Beds Nat'l Monument

Antelope

Trout

Creek

Hay

Creek

John Day River

To Madras

To Spray

John Day Fossil Beds Nat'l Monument

Mitchell

To Dayville

247

50

52

Ochoco **51**

53 **54**

Ochoco Creek

Ochoco Mountains

National

To Madras

Prineville

55

56 **57**

Forest

58

380

Crooked River

60-61

59

Prineville Reservoir

Ochoco National Forest

Maury Mountains **63**

62

380

© AVALON TRAVEL PUBLISHING, INC.

Map 6

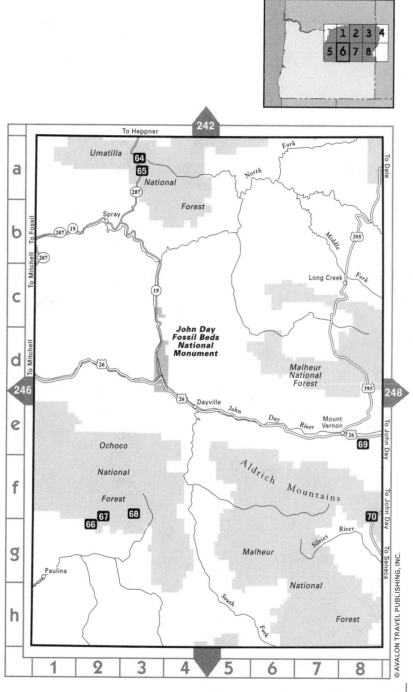

To Heppner

242

a
Umatilla
64
65
Fork
To Dale
207
North
National
Forest

To Fossil
b
207
19
Spray
Middle
395
To Mitchell
207

Long Creek
Fork
c
19

d
26
John Day
Fossil Beds
National
Monument
Malheur
National
Forest
To Mitchell
246
248
395
26
Dayville
John
Day
River
Mount
Vernon
To John Day
e
Ochoco
26
69

f
National
Aldrich
Mountains
To John Day
Forest
67
68
70
66
g
Paulina
Malheur
Sitkies
River
To Seneca

National
h
Forest

© AVALON TRAVEL PUBLISHING, INC.

1   2   3   4   5   6   7   8

Map 7

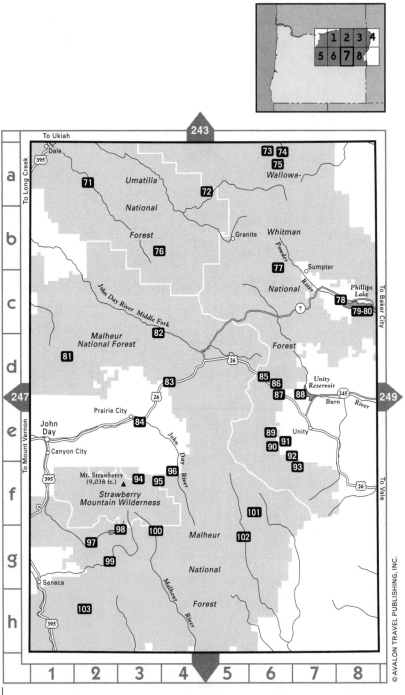

To Ukiah
Dale
To Long Creek
395
Umatilla
71
National
Forest
76
John Day River Middle Fork
Malheur
National Forest
81
82
83
26
Prairie City
84
John
Day
Canyon City
395
Mt. Strawberry
(9,038 ft.)
Strawberry
Mountain Wilderness
98
97
100
99
Seneca
103
395
To Mount Vernon

247

243

73 74
75
Wallowa-
72
Granite
Whitman
77
Sumpter
National
Phillips
Lake
78
To Baker City
79-80
7
Forest
85 86
Unity
87 Reservoir
88
245
Burn
River
Unity
89
90 91
92
93
To Vale
94 96
95
John Day River
101
102
Malheur
National
Forest
Malheur River
26

249

© AVALON TRAVEL PUBLISHING, INC.

Map 8

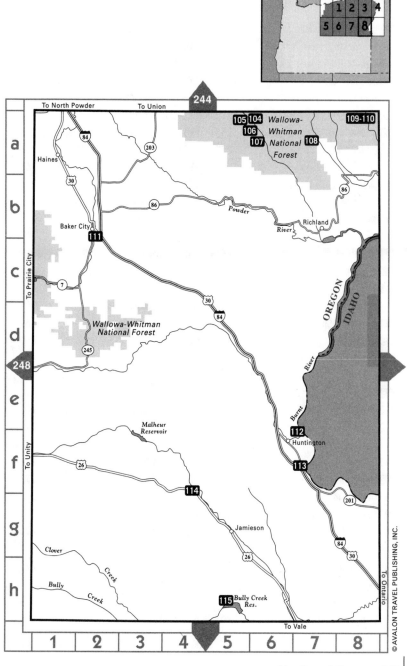

To North Powder   To Union

105 104 Wallowa-
106   Whitman
107   National
108   Forest

109-110

a

Haines

84

30

203

b

86

Powder

River   Richland

86

Baker City

111

To Prairie City

c

7

30

84

d

Wallowa-Whitman
National Forest

245

OREGON

IDAHO

248

River

e

Malheur
Reservoir

Burnt

112
Huntington

To Unity

f

26

113

114

201

Jamieson

g

Clover

26

84
30

To Omaha

Creek

h

Bully   Creek

115   Bully Creek
Res.

To Vale

1   2   3   4   5   6   7   8

© AVALON TRAVEL PUBLISHING, INC.

1 2 3 4
5 6 7 8

Northeast Oregon

1 Boardman Marina Park

🚴 🏊 🎣
� 🐕 🚐 ⛺ 7

This campground is near the Columbia River among maple, sycamore, and linden trees. In addition to fishing for bass, walleye, and crappie, nearby recreation options include a golf course, a marina, and tennis courts.

Location: On the Columbia River; Northeast Oregon map 1, grid b3.

Campsites, facilities: There are 63 sites for tents, trailers, or RVs of any length. Electricity, drinking water, and sewer hookups are available. Flush toilets, showers, fire grills, a sanitary disposal station, garbage bins, coin-operated laundry facilities, a day-use area with picnic shelters, a pay phone, firewood, and a boat dock are available. A boat marina, gasoline, propane, ice, and a grocery store are available within one mile. Leashed pets are permitted.

Reservations, fees: Reservations accepted by phone or fax. Tent sites are $10 per night, RV sites are $16–18 per night, $2 per night for a third vehicle. Senior discount available. Open year-round.

Directions: From Portland on Highway 84 eastbound, drive 164 miles to Boardman and Exit 164. Take that exit and turn north on Main Street and drive one-half mile to the park.

Contact: Boardman Marina Park, P.O. Box 8, Boardman, OR 97818; 541/481-7217, reservations 888/481-7217; fax 541/481-2828.

2 Dun-Rollin Trailer Park

🚶 🚴 🏊 🎣
� 🐕 🚣 🚐 8

This RV park is not far from the Columbia River and the Cold Springs National Wildlife Refuge. A golf course, bike paths, a marina, and tennis courts are close by.

Location: Near the Columbia River; Northeast Oregon map 1, grid b6.

Campsites, facilities: There are 15 sites for trailers or RVs of any length. Electricity, drinking water, and sewer hookups are provided. Flush toilets, sanitary disposal services, showers, laundry facilities, and a playground are available. Bottled gas, a store, a café, and ice are within one mile. Leashed pets and motorbikes are permitted.

Reservations, fees: Reservations accepted. Sites are $15 per night. Open year-round.

Directions: From Pendleton, drive west on U.S. 84 for 25 miles to Stanfield. Turn north on U.S. 395 and drive seven miles to Hermiston and Jennie Avenue. Turn right and drive a half mile to the park on the left.

Contact: Dun-Rollin Trailer Park, 445 E. Jennie, Hermiston, OR 97838; 541/567-6918.

3 Hat Rock Campground

🚶 🚴 🏊 🎣
� 🐕 🚐 ⛺ 7

This campground is not far from Hat Rock State Park, a day-use area with a boat launch along the banks of the Columbia River. The campground itself is very pretty, with lots of trees and close access to the river and fishing.

Location: Near the Columbia River; Northeast Oregon map 1, grid a7.

Campsites, facilities: There are eight tent sites and 60 sites for trailers or RVs of any length, 30 with full and 30 with partial hookups. Electricity, drinking water, sewer hookups, and picnic tables are provided. Flush toilets, sanitary disposal services, showers, a store, a café, a laundry room, a swimming pool, and ice are available. Boat docks and launching facilities are nearby. Leashed pets are permitted.

Reservations, fees: Reservations accepted. Sites are $14–15 per night, $8 per night on Tuesday and Wednesday. Senior discount available. Open year-round.

Directions: From Portland drive east on U.S. 84 for roughly 170 miles past Boardman to the junction of U.S. 84 and U.S. 730. Turn northeast on U.S. 730 and drive 18 miles to the junction with I-82. Continue east on U.S. 730 for one mile to the state park access road. Turn left (north) and drive one-half mile to the park on the left.

Contact: Hat Rock Campground, 82280 Hatrock Rd., Hermiston, OR 97838; 541/567-4188, or the Hat Rock Store, 541/567-0917.

4 Fort Henrietta RV Park

 7

The park is in the historic community of Echo along the Umatilla River. The river provides some good trout fishing. This is a quiet, pleasant layover spot for travelers cruising I-84.

Location: On the Umatilla River; Northeast Oregon map 1, grid c7.

Campsites, facilities: There are seven sites for trailers or RVs and an area for dispersed tent camping. Drinking water, restrooms, showers, and a sanitary dump station are provided. Some of the facilities are wheelchair-accessible. The camp is within walking distance of two restaurants. Licensed, leashed pets are permitted.

Reservations, fees: No reservations accepted. Sites are $15 per night. Open year-round.

Directions: From Pendleton drive west on I-84 to Exit 188 and the Echo Highway. Take the exit and turn southeast and drive one mile; cross the railroad tracks and drive to Dupont Street. Turn south and drive 0.3 mile to Main Street. Turn west and drive one block to the park on the left.

Contact: Echo City Hall, P.O. Box 9, Echo, OR 97826; 541/376-8675; fax 541/376-8218.

5 Cutsforth Forest Park

 8

This county park is secluded and private. It's set beside a small, wheelchair-accessible pond in a quiet, wooded area. Trout fishing is available in the stocked ponds. See the description of Anson Wright County Park for details on the area.

Location: On Willow Creek; Northeast Oregon map 1, grid f6.

Campsites, facilities: There are 35 sites for tents, trailers, or RVs up to 30 feet, including 22 sites with full hookups. Restrooms, showers, horseshoes, firewood, ice, and a playground are provided. Some facilities are wheelchair-accessible. Supplies are available in Heppner (22 miles away). Leashed pets are permitted.

Reservations, fees: No reservations accepted. Sites are $6–12 per night. Open May 15 to November 20, weather permitting.

Directions: From Pendleton on I-84, drive west for 27 miles to Exit 182 and Highway 207 (Heppner Highway). Turn south and drive 32 miles to Lexington and Highway 74. Turn left (southeast) on Highway 74 and drive 10 miles to Heppner. Continue south on Highway 207 for one-half mile to Willow Creek Road. Turn left on Willow Creek Road and drive for 23 miles to the park.

Contact: Morrow County Public Works, P.O. Box 428, Lexington, OR 97839; 541/989-9500; fax 541/989-8352.

6 Anson Wright County Park

 7

Set within wooded hills on a small stream, this county park offers visitors prime trout fishing in several stocked ponds as well as hiking opportunities. There is a wheelchair-accessible fishing pond. Attractions in the area include the Pendleton Mills, Emigrant Springs State Park, Hardman Ghost Town (10 miles away), and the Columbia River. There's also a nearby opal mine.

Location: On Rock Creek; Northeast Oregon map 1, grid h3.

Campsites, facilities: There are 34 sites for tents, trailers, or RVs up to 30 feet, including 24 sites with full hookups. Restrooms, showers, a barbecue, firewood, ice, and a playground are provided. Some facilities are wheelchair-accessible. Leashed pets are permitted.

Reservations, fees: No reservations accepted. Tent sites are $6, RV sites are $12 per night. Open late spring to early fall.

Directions: From Pendleton, drive west on I-84 for 27 miles to Exit 182 and Highway 207 (Heppner Highway). Turn south and drive 32 miles to Lexington and Highway 74. Turn south (left) and drive 10 miles to Heppner. Continue south on Highway 207 for 11 miles to Ruggs and a fork. Bear left at the fork (still Highway 207) and drive 12 miles to the park on the right.

Contact: Morrow County Public Works, P.O. Box 428, Lexington, OR 97839; 541/989-9500.

⛺ Divide Well

🐕 ⛺ 5

This is a primitive campground, but it is busy in the summer, even occasionally used for reunions. It is set at 4,700 feet and can serve as a good base camp for a hunting trip. Mule deer and Rocky Mountain elk can be spotted in the surrounding ponderosa pine and fir forest. Potamus Point Scenic Overlook, offering a spectacular view of the John Day River drainage, is 11 miles south of the camp on Forest Road 5316.

Location: In Umatilla National Forest; Northeast Oregon map 1, grid h7.

Campsites, facilities: There are 11 primitive tent sites and three primitive group sites. Picnic tables and a vault toilet are provided, but there is no drinking water. Pack out all garbage. Leashed pets are permitted.

Reservations, fees: No reservations; no fee. Open March through November.

Directions: From Pendleton drive south on U.S. 395 for 48 miles to Ukiah and Highway 244. Turn right (the road becomes Forest Road 53) and drive west on Forest Road 53 for about 14 miles to Forest Road 5327. Turn south and drive seven miles to the campground. A U.S. Forest Service map is recommended.

Contact: Umatilla National Forest, North Fork John Day Ranger District, P.O. Box 158, Ukiah, OR 97880; 541/427-3231; fax 541/276-5026.

⑧ Target Meadows

🥾 🚲 🐕 🚐 ⛺ 6

This quiet campground with shady sites and a sunny meadow is set at 4,800 feet, adjacent to the Burnt Cabin Trailhead, which leads to the South Fork of the Walla Walla River. An old military site can be viewed here.

Location: Near the South Fork of the Walla Walla River in Umatilla National Forest; Northeast Oregon map 2, grid b8.

Campsites, facilities: There are 19 sites for tents, trailers, or RVs. Drinking water, picnic tables, and fire grills are provided. Garbage bins and vault toilets are available. Leashed pets are permitted.

Reservations, fees: No reservations accepted. Sites are $10 per night, $5 per night for an additional vehicle. Senior discount available. Open mid-June to mid-November, weather permitting.

Directions: From Pendleton drive north on Highway 11 and drive 16 miles to Highway 204 near Weston. Turn east on Highway 204 and drive 17.5 miles to Forest Road 64. Turn left and drive one-half mile to Forest Road 6401. Turn left (north) and drive two miles to Road 6401-050. Turn right (north) and drive a half mile to the camp.

Contact: Umatilla National Forest, Walla Walla Ranger District, 1415 W. Rose St., Walla Walla, WA 99362; 509/522-6290; fax 509/522-6000.

9 Woodward

7

Nestled among the trees at an elevation of 4,950 feet, with some privacy screening between campsites, this popular campground has a view of Langdon Lake (though campers do not have access to the private lake). A flat trail circles the camp.

Location: Near Langdon Lake in Umatilla National Forest; Northeast Oregon map 2, grid b8.

Campsites, facilities: There are 18 sites for tents, trailers, or RVs. Drinking water, picnic tables, garbage bins, fire grills, and wheelchair-accessible vault toilets are provided. A picnic shelter is available. Leashed pets are permitted.

Reservations, fees: No reservations accepted. Sites are $10 per night, $5 per night for an additional vehicle. Open mid-June to mid-September.

Directions: From Pendleton on I-84, turn north on Highway 11 and drive approximately 27 miles to Weston and Highway 204. Turn east on Highway 204 and drive 17 miles to the campground along the highway (near Langdon Lake).

Contact: Umatilla National Forest, Walla Walla Ranger District, 1415 W. Rose St., Walla Walla, WA 99362; 509/525-6290; fax 509/522-6000.

10 Umatilla Forks

3

From mid- to late summer, it can get very warm at this camp. It is set in a canyon between the South and North Forks of the Umatilla River at an elevation of 2,400 feet. It has some tree cover, but little privacy between sites. Fishing (catch-and-release only) and hiking in the North Fork Umatilla Wilderness are popular nearby activities from early spring to late fall.

Location: Along the Umatilla River in Umatilla National Forest; Northeast Oregon map 2, grid c7.

Campsites, facilities: There are nine tent sites and five sites that can accommodate tents, trailers, or RVs. Drinking water, picnic tables, fire grills, and vault toilets are provided. No garbage service provided. Leashed pets are permitted.

Reservations, fees: No reservations. Sites are $5 per night, $5 per night for an additional vehicle. Senior discount available. Open April to October.

Directions: From Pendleton drive north on Highway 11 and drive about 25 miles to Athena and Pambrun Road. Turn right on Pambrun Road and drive five miles to Spring Hollow Road. Turn left on Spring Hollow Road (it becomes Thorn Hollow Road) and drive about 6.5 miles to Bingham Road (River Road). Turn left on Bingham Road (River Road), cross the railroad tracks, and follow signs for about five miles to Gibbon. Cross the railroad tracks at Gibbon and continue on Bingham Road (it becomes Forest Road 32) about 11 miles to the campground on the right.

Contact: Umatilla National Forest, Walla Walla Ranger District, 1415 W. Rose St., Walla Walla, WA 99362; 509/522-6290; fax 509/522-6000.

🔢11 Woodland

🚶 🚲 🐕 🚐 ⛺   4

This primitive camp with easy highway access and related road noise can be a perfect spot for I-84 cruisers looking for a short detour. Both shaded and sunny sites are available. It is popular with hunters during the fall. See a U.S. Forest Service map for details about the recreation options within driving distance.

Location: In Umatilla National Forest; Northeast Oregon map 2, grid c8.

Campsites, facilities: There are six sites for tents, trailers, or RVs. Picnic tables, fire grills, and vault toilets are provided, but there is no drinking water. No garbage facilities are provided, so campers must pack out their own trash. Leashed pets are permitted.

Reservations, fees: No reservations accepted. Sites are $5 per night. Open mid-June to mid-November, weather permitting.

Directions: From Pendleton drive north on Highway 11 and drive 16 miles to Highway 204 near Weston. Turn east on Highway 204 and drive 23 miles. The campground is just off the highway on the left.

Contact: Umatilla National Forest, Walla Walla Ranger District, 1415 W. Rose St., Walla Walla, WA 99362; 509/522-6290; fax 509/522-6000.

🔢12 Brook RV Park

🚶 🚲 🎣 🐕 🚐   5

This pleasant, riverside suburban park in Pendleton is on the historic Oregon Trail. There is also a Native American Cultural Center. This is a good waterfowl area, including on-site fishing along the Umatilla River, and at the McKay Creek National Wildlife Refuge seven miles south of Pendleton. The Pendleton Mills and outlet are in town. Other nearby recreation

opportunities include a golf course, bike paths, and tennis courts.

Location: Near the McKay Creek National Wildlife Refuge; Northeast Oregon map 2, grid c2.

Campsites, facilities: There are 43 sites for trailers or RVs. Electricity, drinking water, sewer hookups, and picnic tables are provided. Flush toilets, cable TV, showers, and a laundry room are available. Bottled gas, sanitary disposal services, a store, and a café are within one mile. Small leashed pets are permitted.

Reservations, fees: Reservations accepted. Sites are $18 per night. Open year-round.

Directions: From Pendleton on I-84, drive east for three miles to Exit 213. Take that exit and drive 2.3 miles to Southeast 8th Street. Turn right and drive two blocks. Cross the bridge at road's end and enter the park.

Contact: Brook RV Park, Northeast 8th Street, Pendleton, OR 97801; 541/276-5353.

🔢13 Emigrant Springs State Heritage Area

🚶 🐕 🚐 ⛺   7

Perched near the summit of the Blue Mountains, Emigrant Springs provides an opportunity to explore a popular pioneer stopover along the Oregon Trail. The park is nestled in an old-growth forest, lush with flora and teeming with native wildlife. You can explore nearby attractions such as the Blue Mountain Crossing Oregon Trail interpretive park or the Pendleton Woolen Mills and underground tours.

Location: Near the Umatilla Indian Reservation; Northeast Oregon map 2, grid d5.

Campsites, facilities: There are 33 tent sites, 18 sites with full hookups for trailers or RVs up to 60 feet long, a designated horse camp, and eight cabins. Picnic tables and fire grills are provided. Drinking water, garbage bins, flush toilets, showers, firewood, a laundry room, some horse facilities, a community building with a kitchen, a basketball court, an amphitheater, and a baseball field are available. Leashed pets are permitted.

Reservations, fees: Reservations accepted for cabins, horse camp, baseball field and community building ($6 reservation fee). Sites are $15–17 per night, cabins are $20–35 per night, and horse campsites are $7 per night and $1.50 per horse; each additional vehicle is $7 per night. Major credit cards accepted. Open year-round for cabins and four tent sites. Full operations are open mid-April through October.

Directions: From Pendleton drive southeast on I-84 for 26 miles to Exit 234. Take that exit to Old Oregon Trail Road (frontage road) and drive one-half mile to the park on the right.

Contact: Emigrant Springs State Heritage Area, P.O. Box 85, Meacham, OR 97859; 541/983-2277, reservations 800/452-5687.

14 Bird Track Springs

7

Set at an elevation of 3,100 feet about a five-minute walk from the Grande Ronde River, this campground has open, spacious sites right off the highway. Surrounding woods are primarily Douglas and white fir. The Bird Track Springs Interpretive Springs Trail provides a hiking option.

Location: Near the Grande Ronde River in Wallowa-Whitman National Forest; Northeast Oregon map 2, grid f5.

Campsites, facilities: There are 16 sites for tents. Picnic tables, garbage service (summer only), and fire rings are provided. Drinking water and wheelchair-accessible vault toilets are available. A camp host is on-site. Leashed pets are permitted.

Reservations, fees: No reservations. Sites are $8 per night. Senior discount available.

Open mid-May through November, weather permitting.

Directions: From Pendleton drive southeast on U.S. 84 for 42 miles to Highway 244. Turn southwest and drive 13 miles to the campground on the left.

Contact: Wallowa-Whitman National Forest, LaGrande Ranger District, 3502 Hwy. 30, LaGrande, OR 97850; 541/963-7186; fax 541/962-8580.

15 Lane Creek

4

This campground is set at 3,850 feet along Camas Creek and Lane Creek, just inside the forest boundary, with easy access to all the amenities of town. It's a popular stop for overnighters passing through. Some of the sites are close enough to the highway to get the noise. Highlights include a hot springs (privately owned) and good hunting and fishing. A U.S. Forest Service map details the back roads.

Location: On Camas Creek in Umatilla National Forest; Northeast Oregon map 2, grid g2.

Campsites, facilities: There are eight sites for tents, trailers, or RVs up to 45 feet long. Picnic tables, garbage bins, and fire grills are provided. Vault toilets are available. No drinking water is provided. Leashed pets are permitted.

Reservations, fees: No reservations accepted. Sites are $5 per night, $10 for group site. Senior discount available. Open May 1 through November.

Directions: From Pendleton drive south on U.S. 395 for 50 miles to Ukiah and Highway 244. Turn east on Highway 244 and drive nine miles to the campground.

Contact: Umatilla National Forest, North Fork John Day Ranger District, P.O. Box

158, Ukiah, OR 97880; 541/427-3231; fax 541/276-5026.

16 Bear Wallow Creek

 5

Set near the confluence of Bear Wallow and Camus Creeks at an elevation of 3,900 feet, this is one of three camps off Highway 244. The others are Lane Creek and Frazier. It's quiet, primitive, and used primarily in the summer. A three-quarter-mile interpretive trail highlighting steelhead habitat meanders next to Bear Wallow Creek. The trail is wheelchair-accessible.

Location: On Bear Wallow Creek in Umatilla National Forest; Northeast Oregon map 2, grid g3.

Campsites, facilities: There are eight sites for tents, trailers, or RVs up to 30 feet long. No drinking water is available, and garbage bins are provided in the summer only. Picnic tables and fire grills are provided. Vault toilets are available. Some facilities are wheelchair-accessible. Leashed pets are permitted.

Reservations, fees: No reservations accepted. Sites are $5 per night with a 14-day stay limit, group site $10 per night. Senior discount available. Open March through November.

Directions: From Pendleton drive south on U.S. 395 for 50 miles to Ukiah and Highway 244. Turn east on Highway 244 and drive 10 miles to the camp.

Contact: Umatilla National Forest, North Fork John Day Ranger District, P.O. Box 158, Ukiah, OR 97880; 541/427-3231; fax 541/276-5026.

17 Frazier

This campground set at 4,300 feet along the banks of Frazier Creek is a popular hunting area that also has some fishing. It's advisable to obtain a map of Umatilla National Forest. This campground is popular in the summer with the ATV crowd. There are nearly 100 miles of ATV and motorcycle trails at the nearby Winom-Frazier Off-Highway-Vehicle Complex. On weekends it's not a good spot for the traditional camper looking for quiet and solitude. Lehman Hot Springs, one mile away, provides a side trip option.

Location: On Frazier Creek in Umatilla National Forest; Northeast Oregon map 2, grid g4.

Campsites, facilities: There are 18 sites for tents, trailers, or RVs up to 30 feet long and some group sites. Picnic tables, fire grills, a picnic shelter, and vault toilets are available. There is no drinking water and no garbage bins except in summer. Some facilities are wheelchair-accessible. An ATV loading ramp is available. Leashed pets are permitted.

Reservations, fees: No reservations accepted. Sites are $5 per night; group sites are $10 per night. Senior discount available. Open May 1 through November.

Directions: From Pendleton drive south on U.S. 395 for 50 miles to Ukiah and Highway 244. Turn east on Highway 244 and drive 18 miles to Forest Road 5226. Turn south and drive a half mile to the campground.

Contact: Umatilla National Forest, North Fork John Day Ranger District, P.O. Box 158, Ukiah, OR 97880; 541/427-3231; fax 541/276-5026.

18 Spool Cart

This campground set at 3,500 feet elevation on the banks of the Grande Ronde River gets its name from the large cable spools that were left on a cart at the site for some years. The sites are fully wheelchair-accessible. Hilgard

Junction State Park to the north provides numerous recreation options, and the Oregon Trail Interpretive Park is nearby. This camp is popular with hunters in the fall. It's advisable to obtain a map of Wallowa-Whitman National Forest that details the back roads and other side trips.

Location: On the Grande Ronde River in Wallowa-Whitman National Forest; Northeast Oregon map 2, grid g5.

Campsites, facilities: There are 16 sites for tents, trailers, or RVs up to 22 feet long. Picnic tables and fire grills are provided. Firewood and vault toilets are available. There is no drinking water, and all garbage must be packed out. Leashed pets are permitted.

Reservations, fees: No reservations. Sites are $8 per night. Senior discount available. Open late May to late November.

Directions: From Pendleton drive southeast on U.S. 84 for 42 miles to Highway 244. Turn southwest and drive 13 miles to Forest Road 51. Turn south and drive seven miles to the campground on the right.

Contact: Wallowa-Whitman National Forest, LaGrande Ranger District, 3502 Hwy. 30, LaGrande, OR 97850; 541/963-7186; fax 541/962-8580.

19 Drift Fence

🥾 🐕 🚐 ⛺   5

Get this: it's not marked on the Umatilla National Forest Map. Hunting is a highlight at this campground set at 4,250 feet, with some elk and deer in the area. The camp is adjacent to Blue Mountain National Forest Scenic Byway. The Bridge Creek Interpretive Trail, three miles northwest of the campground off Forest Road 52, leads to a beautiful view of open meadow with various wildflowers and wildlife. Elk may be seen roaming in the Bridge Creek area.

Location: Near Ross Springs in Umatilla National Forest; Northeast Oregon map 2, grid h1.

Campsites, facilities: There are six sites for tents, trailers, or RVs up to 16 feet long. There is no drinking water, and all garbage must be packed out. A vault toilet and picnic tables are available. Leashed pets are permitted.

Reservations, fees: No reservations; no fee. Open May 1 to November.

Directions: From Pendleton drive south on U.S. 395 for 50 miles to Highway 244. Turn east on Highway 244 and drive one mile to Ukiah and Forest Road 52. Turn south on Forest Road 52 and drive eight miles to the campground on the right.

Contact: Umatilla National Forest, North Fork John Day Ranger District, P.O. Box 158, Ukiah, OR 97880; 541/427-3231; fax 541/276-5026.

20 Ukiah-Dale Forest State Recreation Site

🎣 🐕 🚐 ⛺   7

Fishing is a prime activity at this campground on Camas Creek, set at an elevation of 3,140 feet near the banks of the North Fork of the John Day River. It's a good layover for visitors cruising U.S. 395 looking for a spot for the night. Emigrant Springs State Park near Pendleton is a possible side trip.

Location: Near the North Fork of the John Day River; Northeast Oregon map 2, grid h1.

Campsites, facilities: There are 28 primitive sites for tents, trailers, or self-contained RVs up to 50 feet long. Picnic tables and fire pits are provided. Drinking water, firewood, and flush toilets are available. Leashed pets are permitted.

Reservations, fees: No reservations accepted. Sites are $10 per night, $7 per additional vehicle. Open mid-April to late October.

Directions: From Pendleton drive south on U.S. 395 for 50 miles to Highway 244 (near Ukiah). Continue south on U.S. 395 for three miles to the park.

Contact: Ukiah-Dale Forest State Recreation Site, P.O. Box 85, Meacham, OR 97859; 800/551-6949 or 541/983-2277.

21 Tollbridge

4

This small, secluded campground (elevation 3,800 feet) lies at the confluence of Desolation Creek and the North Fork of the John Day River and is adjacent to the Bridge Creek Wildlife Area. It can be beautiful or ugly, depending upon which direction you look. It's dusty in the summer, and there's sparse tree cover. Hunting and fishing are two options here. There's a geological interpretive sign in the camp.

Location: On the North Fork of the John Day River in Umatilla National Forest; Northeast Oregon map 2, grid h1.

Campsites, facilities: There are seven sites for tents, trailers, or RVs up to 31 feet long. Picnic tables and fire grills are provided. Drinking water and a vault toilet are available, but all garbage must be packed out. Leashed pets are permitted.

Reservations, fees: No reservations. Sites are $5 per night, with a 14-day stay limit. Senior discount available. Open May 1 to November.

Directions: From Pendleton drive south on U.S. 395 for 50 miles to the intersection with Highway 244. Continue south on U.S. 395 for 18 miles to Forest Road 55 (one mile north of Dale). Turn left and drive one-half mile southeast to Forest Road 10 and the campground access road. Drive a short distance to the campground.

Contact: Umatilla National Forest, North Fork John Day Ranger District, P.O. Box

158, Ukiah, OR 97880; 541/427-3231; fax 541/276-5026.

22 Gold Dredge Camp

7

Hunting and fishing are among the possibilities at this campground along the banks of the North Fork of the John Day River, a federally certified Wild and Scenic river. Dredge tailings from old mining activity are visible from the camp. By traveling to the end of Forest Road 5506, you have access to a trail that heads into the adjacent North Fork John Day Wilderness.

Location: On the North Fork of the John Day River in Umatilla National Forest; Northeast Oregon map 2, grid h2.

Campsites, facilities: There are six sites for tents, trailers, or RVs. No drinking water or fire grills are provided, but vault toilets and picnic tables are available. All garbage must be packed out. Leashed pets are permitted.

Reservations, fees: No reservations; no fee. Open May 1 to November.

Directions: From Pendleton drive south on U.S. 395 for 62 miles to Forest Road 55 (one mile north of Dale). Turn left and drive six miles to the crossroads. Continue east on Forest Road 5506 for 2.5 miles to the campground.

Note: The last two miles of road are very rough.

Contact: Umatilla National Forest, North Fork John Day Ranger District, P.O. Box 158, Ukiah, OR 97880; 541/427-3231; fax 541/276-5026.

23 Driftwood

6

This tiny campground with ponderosa pine and Douglas fir cover is on the banks of the North Fork of the John Day River at an elevation of 3,855 feet. Recreational opportunities include hunting, fishing, swimming, rafting, and float tubing. It is similar to Gold Dredge Campground.

Location: On the North Fork of the John Day River in Umatilla National Forest; Northeast Oregon map 2, grid h2.

Campsites, facilities: There are five sites for tents and trailers. Fire grills and picnic tables are provided. A vault toilet is available. No drinking water is available. All garbage must be packed out. Leashed pets are permitted.

Reservations, fees: No reservations; no fee. Open March through November.

Directions: From Pendleton drive south on U.S. 395 for 62 miles to Forest Road 55 (one mile north of Dale; it's easier to find if you know the marker, Texas Bar Road). Turn left and drive six miles to the crossroads. Continue east on Forest Road 5506 for one mile to the campground.

Note: the last two miles of road are very rough.

Contact: Umatilla National Forest, North Fork John Day Ranger District, P.O. Box 158, Ukiah, OR 97880; 541/427-3231; fax 541/276-5026.

24 Oriental Creek

4

This campground is set in a stand of mixed conifer at 3,500 feet along the banks of the North Fork of the John Day River and is popular with horse campers. Evidence of old mining activity is visible here. Nearby trails provide access to the North Fork John Day Wilderness. Hunting and fishing are two possible activities here. No motorbikes are permitted in the wilderness area. Be advised that the road in to this campground is rough and narrow in places.

Location: On the North Fork of the John Day River in Umatilla National Forest; Northeast Oregon map 2, grid h3.

Campsites, facilities: There are seven primitive tent sites. Pit toilets and picnic tables are available, but there is no drinking water. All garbage must be packed out. One toilet is wheelchair-accessible. Leashed pets are permitted.

Reservations, fees: No reservations; no fee. Open May 1 to November.

Directions: From Pendleton drive south on U.S. 395 for 62 miles to Forest Road 55 (one mile north of Dale; it's easier to find if you know the marker, Texas Bar Road). Turn left and drive six miles to the crossroads. Continue east on Forest Road 5506 for six miles to the campground. This road is rough and not recommended for trailers.

Contact: Umatilla National Forest, North Fork John Day Ranger District, P.O. Box 158, Ukiah, OR 97880; 541/427-3231; fax 541/276-5026.

25 Winom Creek

2

This campground has access to the Winom-Frazier ATV Trail Complex, 140 miles of ATV trails of varying difficulty. It was developed in the late 1980s for ATV enthusiasts. Check the campground bulletin boards for detailed maps of the terrain. The camp is also near the North Fork John Day Wilderness. Note that a fire during the 1990s burned part of the campground and surrounding area, but with the arrival of the new century, it is beginning to green up again.

Location: On Winom Creek in Umatilla National Forest; Northeast Oregon map 2, grid h4.

Campsites, facilities: There are five sites for tents, trailers, or RVs, and three group sites. Picnic tables and fire rings are provided. Vault toilets and an ATV loading ramp are available. There is no drinking water, and garbage must be packed out. Two of the group sites have picnic shelters. Some facilities are wheelchair-accessible.

Reservations, fees: No reservations; no fee. Open May 1 through November, weather permitting.

Directions: From Pendleton drive south on U.S. 395 for 50 miles to Highway 244. Turn east on Highway 244 and drive one mile to Ukiah and Forest Road 52. Turn south on Forest Road 52 and drive 20 miles to Forest Road 440. Turn right and drive one mile to the campground on the right. The last mile of the access road is narrow and steep.

Contact: Umatilla National Forest, North Fork John Day Ranger District, P.O. Box 158, Ukiah, OR 97880; 541/427-3231; fax 541/276-5026.

26 Mottet

🏃🐕🚐🏕️ 6

This campground is set at 5,200 feet along a ridgetop in a heavily timbered forest. A trailhead leads down to the South Fork of the Walla Walla River. Far from the beaten path, it's quite primitive and relatively unknown, so you're almost guaranteed privacy.

Location: Near the South Fork of the Walla Walla River in Umatilla National Forest; Northeast Oregon map 3, grid a1.

Campsites, facilities: There is one site for tents and five sites for trailers or RVs. Picnic tables and fire grills are provided. Spring water and vault toilets are available. Trash must be packed out; no garbage facilities are provided. Leashed pets are permitted.

Reservations, fees: No reservations. Sites are $5 per night. Senior discount available. Open late June to November, weather permitting.

Directions: From Pendleton drive north on Highway 11 and drive 16 miles to Highway 204 near Weston. Turn east on Highway 204 and drive 17.5 miles to Forest Road 64. Turn left and drive about 15 miles on Forest Road 64 to Forest Road 6403. Turn left and drive about two miles to the campground on the left. The road is rough for the last 1.5 miles.

Contact: Umatilla National Forest, Walla Walla Ranger District, 1415 W. Rose St., Walla Walla, WA 99362; 509/522-6290; fax 509/522-6000.

27 Jubilee Lake

🏃🏊🎣🚤
🐕♿🚐🏕️ 8

This campground along the shore of 90-acre Jubilee Lake (elevation 4,800 feet) is a good area for swimming, fishing, and hiking. This is the largest and most popular campground in Umatilla National Forest, and it fills up on weekends and holidays. Nonmotorized boats are permitted. A 2.8-mile trail loops around the lake and provides different levels of accessibility for people with disabilities. Fishing access is available along the trail.

Location: On Jubilee Lake in Umatilla National Forest; Northeast Oregon map 3, grid a1.

Campsites, facilities: There are four sites for tents and 47 sites for tents, trailers, or RVs up to 27 feet long, with some drive-through sites. Picnic tables and fire grills are provided. Drinking water, firewood, four picnic areas, and flush toilets are available. Some facilities are barrier-free. Boat docks and launching facilities are nearby. Leashed pets are permitted. Garbage service is provided during the summer.

Reservations, fees: No reservations accepted. Sites are $14 per night, plus $5 for each additional vehicle. Senior discount available. Open mid-June through mid-October.

Directions: From Pendleton drive north on Highway 11 and drive 16 miles to Highway 204 near Weston. Turn east on Highway 204 and drive 17.5 miles to Forest Road 64. Turn left and drive 12 miles northeast to Forest Road 250. Turn south and drive less than a half mile to the camp.

Contact: Umatilla National Forest, Walla Walla Ranger District, 1415 W. Rose St., Walla Walla, WA 99362; 509/522-6290; fax 509/522-6000.

28 Dougherty Springs

5

This wooded, primitive campground (elevation 5,100 feet) adjacent to Dougherty Springs is one in a series of remote camps set near natural springs. This camp is in an open area in sparse Douglas and white fir. Deer, elk, birds, and small mammals can be seen in the area. Hells Canyon National Recreation Area to the east provides many recreation options.

Location: Near Dougherty Springs in Wallowa-Whitman National Forest; Northeast Oregon map 3, grid b5.

Campsites, facilities: There are 12 sites for tents, trailers, or RVs up to 22 feet long. Picnic tables and fire grills are provided. Vault toilets are available, but there is no drinking water, and all garbage must be packed out. Pets are permitted.

Reservations, fees: No reservations; no fee. Open June to late November.

Directions: From LaGrande drive northeast on Highway 82 for 62 miles to Enterprise and Highway 3. Turn north on Highway 3 and drive 15 miles to Forest Road 46. Turn northeast and drive 30 miles to the campground.

Contact: Hells Canyon National Recreation Area, Wallowa Mountains Visitor Center, 88401 Hwy. 82, Enterprise, OR 97828; 541/426-5546.

29 Coyote

4

This campground set at 4,800 feet adjacent to Coyote Springs is the largest of the three primitive camps in the vicinity, offering open sites and privacy.

Location: Near Coyote Springs in Wallowa-Whitman National Forest; Northeast Oregon map 3, grid b5.

Campsites, facilities: There are 12 sites for tents, trailers, or RVs up to 22 feet long. Picnic tables and fire grills are provided. Vault toilets are available, but there is no drinking water, and all garbage must be packed out. A spring is within one-quarter mile. Pets are permitted.

Reservations, fees: No reservations; no fee. Open mid-May to December.

Directions: From LaGrande drive northeast on Highway 82 for 62 miles to Enterprise and Highway 3. Turn north on Highway 3 and drive 15 miles to Forest Road 46. Turn northeast and drive 25 miles to the campground.

Contact: Wallowa-Whitman National Forest, Wallowa Valley Ranger District, Wallowa Mountains Visitor Center, 88401 Hwy. 82, Enterprise, OR 97828; 541/426-5546.

30 Vigne

5

This campground, at 3,500 feet elevation along the banks of Chesnimnus Creek, has pretty, shaded riverside sites among Douglas and white fir. Fishing is a recreation possibility here, along with exploring a few of the many hiking trails in the area. See a U.S. Forest Service map for details.

Location: On Chesnimnus Creek in Wallowa-Whitman National Forest; Northeast Oregon map 3, grid b8.

Campsites, facilities: There are seven sites for tents,

trailers, or RVs up to 22 feet long. Picnic tables and fire grills are provided. Drinking water and vault toilets are available. All garbage must be packed out. Pets are permitted.

Reservations, fees: No reservations. Sites are $5 per night. Senior discount available. Open mid-April to late November.

Directions: From LaGrande drive northeast on Highway 82 for 62 miles to Enterprise and Highway 3. Turn north on Highway 3 and drive 15 miles to Forest Road 46. Turn northeast and drive 10 miles to Forest Road 4625. Turn east and drive 10 miles to the campground.

Contact: Wallowa-Whitman National Forest, Wallowa Valley Ranger District, Wallowa Mountains Visitor Center, 88401 Hwy. 82, Enterprise, OR 97828; 541/426-5546.

31 Minam State Park

7

In a remote, steep valley, large pine trees dominate the landscape of this park. The Wallowa River flows through the park and is noted for fishing and rafting, especially for spring and fall steelhead fishing. Wildlife is abundant, including deer, elk, bear, cougar, and occasionally, mountain sheep downriver. The park is small and pretty, well worth the detour off I-84.

Location: Near the Grande Ronde River; Northeast Oregon map 3, grid c3.

Campsites, facilities: There are 12 primitive sites for tents, trailers, or self-contained RVs up to 71 feet long. Picnic tables and fire grills are provided. Drinking water is available May 1–Oct. 15. Garbage bins and vault toilets are available. Raft rentals are available nearby. Leashed pets are permitted.

Reservations, fees: No reservations accepted. Sites are $7–10 per night, $7 per night for an additional vehicle. Open year-round.

Directions: From LaGrande drive northeast on Highway 82 for 18 miles to Elgin, then continue 14 miles to the park entrance road. Turn left (north) and drive two miles to the park.

Contact: Minam State Park, 72214 Marina Ln., Minan, OR 97846; 541/432-8855 or 800/551-6949.

32 Boundary

6

This pretty and primitive campground is set 100 yards from the banks of Bear Creek at 3,600 feet elevation and is heavily wooded with tamarack, Douglas, red, and white fir. Nearby trails provide access to the Eagle Cap Wilderness. This is another in a series of little-known primitive sites in the area.

Location: Near the Eagle Cap Wilderness in Wallowa-Whitman National Forest; Northeast Oregon map 3, grid e4.

Campsites, facilities: There are eight primitive tent sites. Picnic tables and fire rings are provided. Vault toilets are available. There is no drinking water and all garbage must be packed out. Pets are permitted.

Reservations, fees: No reservations; no fee. Open mid-June to November.

Directions: From LaGrande drive north on Highway 82 for 46 miles to Wallowa and Forest Road 8250. Turn south and drive eight miles to Forest Road 8250-040. Turn south and drive three-quarters of a mile to the camp.

Contact: Wallowa-Whitman National Forest, Eagle Cap Ranger District, Wallowa Mountains Visitor Center, 88401 Hwy. 82, Enterprise, OR 97828; 541/426-5546.

33 Hot Lake RV Resort

8

This camp is near Hot Lake, a small, hot spring-fed pond about one foot deep. While you can't soak in Hot Lake, you can soak in the spa at the resort. It's also on the historic Old Oregon Trail. Attractions in the area include Hilgard Junction State Park and Wallowa-Whitman National Forest.

Location: On Hot Lake; Northeast Oregon map 3, grid f1.

Campsites, facilities: There are 100 wide sites for tents, trailers, or RVs. Drinking water, restrooms, showers, laundry facilities, groceries, a sanitary dump station, a public phone, a swimming pool, a hot spa, ice, and RV supplies are available. Some facilities are wheelchair-accessible. Leashed pets are permitted.

Reservations, fees: Reservations recommended. Sites are $23.70 per night. Senior discount available. Open year-round.

Directions: At the junction of I-84 and Highway 203 one mile south of La Grande drive southeast on Highway 203 for five miles to Foothill Road. Turn left and drive 0.3 miles to the resort.

Contact: Hot Lake RV Resort, 65182 Hot Lake Ln., LaGrande, OR 97850; 541/963-5253; fax 541/663-0723.

34 Moss Springs

7

At 5,400 feet, this campground provides good views of the Grande Ronde Valley. A trailhead at this camp provides access to the Eagle Cap Wilderness, a good jump-off point for a multiday backpacking trip. Obtain a map of Wallowa-Whitman National Forest for detailed trail information. This camp is also a popular spot with horse packers. A loading ramp is provided. The Bieshears OHV Trail and the Mt. Fanny Mountain Bike Trail are just north of the camp.

Location: Near the Eagle Cap Wilderness in Wallowa-Whitman National Forest; Northeast Oregon map 3, grid f3.

Campsites, facilities: There are 12 tent and trailer sites. Picnic tables and fire grills are provided. No drinking water is provided, but water is available for stock. Horse facilities and wheelchair-accessible vault toilets are available. All garbage must be packed out. A camp host is on-site. Leashed pets are permitted.

Reservations, fees: No reservations. Sites are $8 per night. Senior discount available. Open June to mid-October.

Directions: From LaGrande drive east on Highway 237 for 15 miles to Cove and County Road 237. Turn southeast and drive 1.5 miles to Forest Road 6220. Turn east and drive eight miles to the camp entrance. The last 9.5 miles are on a steep gravel road.

Contact: Wallowa-Whitman National Forest, LaGrande Ranger District, 3502 Hwy. 30, LaGrande, OR 97850; 541/963-7186; fax 541/962-8580.

35 North Fork Catherine Creek

5

This campground along the North Fork of Catherine Creek is near a trailhead that provides access to various lakes and streams in the Eagle Cap Wilderness. The elevation here is 4,400 feet. It's a good starting point for a hiking trip. The camp is popular with hunters in the fall. A U.S. Forest Service map details the possibilities.

Location: Near the Eagle Cap Wilderness in Wallowa-Whitman National Forest; Northeast Oregon map 3, grid g4.

Campsites, facilities: There are six sites for tents or small, self-contained trailers or RVs. Picnic tables and fire grills are provided. Drinking water and vault toilets are available. All garbage must be packed out. Pets are permitted.

Reservations, fees: No reservations; no fee. Open June to late October.

Directions: From LaGrande drive southeast on Highway 203 for 14 miles to Union. Continue southeast on Highway 203 for 10 miles to Forest Road 7785. Turn east and drive four miles east on Forest Road 7785 to a fork. Bear left at the fork (still on 7785) and drive 3.5 miles northeast to the camp.

Contact: Wallowa-Whitman National Forest, LaGrande Ranger District, 3502 Hwy. 30, LaGrande, OR 97850; 541/963-7186; fax 541/962-8580.

36 Shady

6

This campground along the banks of the Lostine River at an elevation of 5,400 feet is close to trails that provide access to the Eagle Cap Wilderness, a beautiful and pristine area that's perfect for an extended backpacking trip. The camp has wooded as well as meadow areas. Mountain sheep can sometimes be spotted.

Location: On the Lostine River in Wallowa-Whitman National Forest; Northeast Oregon map 3, grid f5.

Campsites, facilities: There are 12 sites for tents, trailers, or RVs up to 16 feet long. Vault toilets are available, but there is no drinking water, and all garbage must be packed out. Picnic tables and fire grills are provided. Pets are permitted.

Reservations, fees: No reservations; no fee. Open mid-June to November.

Directions: From LaGrande turn north on Highway 82 and drive 52 miles to Lostine and Forest Road 8210. Turn south and drive 15 miles to the campground.

Contact: Wallowa-Whitman National Forest, Eagle Cap Ranger District Wallowa Mountains Visitor Center, 88401 Hwy. 82, Enterprise, OR 97828; 541/426-5546.

37 Two Pan

6

This campground lies at the end of a forest road on the banks of the Lostine River. Adjacent trails provide access to numerous lakes and streams in the Eagle Cap Wilderness. At 5,600 feet, this is a prime jump-off spot for a multiday wilderness adventure. Another campground option is Williamson, seven miles north on Forest Road 8210, or Shady.

Location: On the Lostine River in Wallowa-Whitman National Forest; Northeast Oregon map 3, grid g5.

Campsites, facilities: There are eight sites for tents or small, self-contained trailers or RVs. Vault toilets are available, but there is no drinking water, and all garbage must be packed out. Picnic tables and fire grills are provided. Pets are permitted.

Reservations, fees: No reservations; no fee. Open mid-June to November.

Directions: From LaGrande turn north on Highway 82 and drive 52 miles to Lostine and Forest Road 8210. Turn south and drive 17 miles to the campground.

Contact: Wallowa-Whitman National Forest, Eagle Cap Ranger District; Wallowa Mountains Visitor Center, 88401 Hwy. 82, Enterprise, OR 97828; 541/426-5546.

38 Hurricane Creek

5

This campground along Hurricane Creek at an elevation of 5,000 feet is on the edge of the Eagle Cap Wilderness and is a good place to begin a backcountry backpacking trip. There is no access for RVs, providing more of a wilderness environment. Obtaining maps of the area from the ranger district is essential.

Location: Near the Eagle Cap Wilderness in Wallowa-Whitman National Forest; Northeast Oregon map 3, grid f6.

Campsites, facilities: There are eight tent sites. Picnic tables and fire grills are provided. Firewood and vault toilets are available, but there is no drinking water, and all garbage must be packed out. Pets are permitted.

Reservations, fees: No reservations; no fee. Open mid-June to late October.

Directions: From LaGrande turn north on Highway 82 and drive 62 miles to Enterprise and Hurricane Creek Road. Turn south on Hurricane Creek Road and drive five miles to Hurricane Grange Hall and Forest Road 8205; bear right (off the paved road) and drive two miles to the campground.

Contact: Wallowa-Whitman National Forest, Eagle Cap Ranger District, Wallowa Mountains Visitor Center, 88401 Hwy. 82, Enterprise, OR 97828; 541/426-5546.

39 Mountain View Motel and Trailer Park

3

This park is centrally located for exploring the greater area within proximity of Wallowa Lake. There are views of the Seven Devils Mountains and of the Eagle Cap Wilderness. Nearby recreational facilities include a golf course, hiking trails, bike paths, and a riding stable. Fishing and jet boating are also nearby options. This park is under new ownership with considerable improvements made in late 2001.

Location: Near Wallowa Lake; Northeast Oregon map 3, grid f7.

Campsites, facilities: There are a few tent sites and 30 sites for trailers or RVs of any length; three are drive-through sites. Electricity, drinking water, sewer hookups, and picnic tables are provided at eight sites. Flush toilets and showers are available. Bottled gas, a store, a café, and a coin laundry are within two miles. Leashed pets are permitted.

Reservations, fees: Reservations accepted. Sites are $15–20 per night. Open year-round.

Directions: From LaGrande turn north on Highway 82 and drive 62 miles to Enterprise and the junction with Highway 3. Continue south on Highway 82 for four miles to the campground (1.5 miles north of Joseph).

Contact: Mountain View Motel and Trailer Park, 83450 Joseph Hwy., Joseph, OR 97846; tel./fax 541/432-2982.

40 Wallowa Lake State Park

8

Surrounded on three sides by 9,000-foot, snowcapped mountains and large, clear Wallowa Lake, this area is popular for fishing and boating recreation, including water-skiing and parasailing. You can also enjoy hiking, horseback riding, bumper boats, canoeing, miniature golf, or a tram ride up 4,000 feet to a mountaintop. A nearby artist community makes world-class bronze castings and tours are available. This is also the gateway to Hells Canyon, the deepest gorge in North America. Other highlights include a pretty one-mile nature trail and trailheads that provide access into the Eagle Cap Wilderness. A marina is nearby for boaters and anglers. Picnicking, swimming, and wildlife viewing are a few of the other activities available to visitors.

Location: On Wallowa Lake; Northeast Oregon map 3, grid f7.

Campsites, facilities: There are 89 tent sites and 121 full-hookup sites for trailers or RVs up to 90 feet long, some hiker/biker sites, three group tent areas, two yurts, and one deluxe cabin. Electricity, drinking water, sewer hookups, and picnic tables are provided. Garbage bins, flush toilets, sanitary disposal services, showers, and firewood are available. A store, a café, and ice are within one mile. Some facilities are wheelchair-accessible. Boat docks, launching facilities, and rentals are nearby. Leashed pets are permitted.

Reservations, fees: Reservations accepted ($6 reservation fee). Sites are $11–20 per night, hiker/biker sites are $4 per night, group areas are $60 per night, yurts are $29 per night, the deluxe cabin is $55–75 per night; an additional vehicle is $7 per night. Major credit cards accepted. Open year-round.

Directions: From LaGrande turn north on Highway 82 and drive 62 miles to Enterprise and the junction with Highway 3. Continue south on Highway 82 to Joseph. Continue for six miles to the south shore of the lake and the campground.

Contact: Wallowa Lake State Park, 72214 Marina Ln., Joseph, OR 97846; 541/432-4185, reservations 800/551-6949.

41 Lick Creek

🥾 🎣 🐕 🚐 ⛺ 7

This campground is set at an elevation of 5,400 feet in a parklike setting along the banks of Lick Creek in Hells Canyon National Recreation Area. It is secluded and pretty. Tall Douglas fir, white fir, tamarack, and lodgepole pine intersperse the campground, providing habitat for some of the birds and small mammals you might see.

Location: On Lick Creek in Wallowa-Whitman National Forest; Northeast Oregon map 3, grid g8.

Campsites, facilities: There are seven tent sites and five sites for trailers or RVs up to 30 feet long. Picnic tables and fire grills are provided. Vault toilets are available, but there is no drinking water, and garbage must be packed out. Pets are permitted.

Reservations, fees: No reservations. Sites are $5 per night. Senior discount available. Open mid-June to late November.

Directions: From LaGrande turn north on Highway 82 and drive 62 miles to Enterprise and the junction with Highway 3. Continue south on Highway 82 to Joseph and Highway 350. Turn east and drive 7.5 miles to Forest Road 39. Turn south and drive 15 miles to the campground.

Contact: Hells Canyon National Recreation Area, Wallowa Mountains Visitor Center, 88401 Hwy. 82, Enterprise, OR 97828; 541/426-5546.

42 Ollokot

🥾 🎣 🐕 🚐 ⛺ 5

This campground sits on the banks of the Imnaha River in Hells Canyon National Recreation Area at an elevation of 4,000 feet. It's named for Chief Joseph's brother, a member of the Nez Percé tribe. For those seeking a little more solitude, this could be the spot.

Location: On the Imnaha River in Wallowa-Whitman National Forest; Northeast Oregon map 3, grid c3.

Campsites, facilities: There are 12 sites for tents, trailers, or RVs up to 30 feet long. Picnic tables and fire grills are provided. Drinking water and vault toilets are available, but all garbage must be packed out. Pets are permitted.

Reservations, fees: No reservations. Sites are $5 per night. Senior discount available. Open June to late November.

Directions: From I-84 at LaGrande, turn north on Highway 82 and drive 62 miles to Enterprise. Continue six miles south to Joseph, and then drive eight miles east on Highway 350. Turn south on Forest Road 39 and drive 30 miles to the campground.

Contact: Hells Canyon National Recreation Area, Wallowa Mountains Visitor Center,

88401 Hwy. 82, Enterprise, OR 97828; 541/426-5546.

43 Buckhorn

8

Set at 5,200 feet elevation, adjacent to Buckhorn Springs, this small, primitive, and obscure camp gets little use. The elevation offers a spectacular view of the Imnaha River drainage from the nearby Buckhorn Lookout (not from campsites).

Location: Near Buckhorn Overlook in Wallowa-Whitman National Forest; Northeast Oregon map 4, grid c2.

Campsites, facilities: There are six sites for tents or small, self-contained trailers or RVs. Picnic tables and fire grills are provided. Vault toilets are available, but there is no drinking water and all garbage must be packed out. Pets are permitted.

Reservations, fees: No reservations; no fee. Open June to late November.

Directions: From LaGrande drive northeast on Highway 82 for 62 miles to Enterprise. Continue east for three miles on Highway 82 to County Road 772. Turn north and drive 32 miles to a junction at Thomason Meadows. Continue straight on Forest Road 46 for 10 miles to Forest Road 780. Turn right and drive one-quarter mile to the campground.

Contact: Hells Canyon National Recreation Area, Wallowa Mountains Visitor Center, 88401 Hwy. 82, Enterprise, OR 97828; 541/426-5546.

44 Saddle Creek

8

This campground is set at 6,800 feet in a wooded environment, on a ridge between two canyons, providing excellent views of the Seven Devils Mountains. Nearby trails provide access to Saddle Creek and Hells Canyon National Recreation Area. Note that a fire here has left its mark on the area.

Location: Near the Hells Canyon Wilderness in Wallowa-Whitman National Forest; Northeast Oregon map 4, grid d3.

Campsites, facilities: There are seven sites for tents. Picnic tables and fire grills are provided. Vault toilets are available, but there is no drinking water and all garbage must be packed out. Pets are permitted.

Note: RVs and trailers are not recommended on the access road.

Reservations, fees: No reservations; no fee. Open July to mid-November.

Directions: From LaGrande turn north on Highway 82 and drive 62 miles to Enterprise and the junction of Highway 3. At the junction bear south on Highway 82 and drive six miles to Joseph and Highway 350. Turn east on Highway 350 and drive 30 miles to the small town of Imnaha and Forest Road 4240. Drive straight up the hill on Forest Road 4240 and continue 19 miles to the campground.

Contact: Hells Canyon National Recreation Area, Wallowa Mountains Visitor Center, 88401 Hwy. 82, Enterprise, OR 97828; 541/426-5546.

45 Blackhorse

7

This campground along the banks of the Imnaha River in Hells Canyon National Recreation Area is in a secluded section of Wallowa-Whitman National Forest at an elevation of 4,000 feet.

Location: On the Imnaha River in Wallowa-Whitman National Forest; Northeast Oregon map 4, grid g1.

Campsites, facilities: There are 16 sites for tents, trailers, or RVs up to 30 feet long. Picnic tables and fire grills are provided. Drinking water and vault toilets are available, but all garbage must be packed out. Pets are permitted.

Reservations, fees: No reservations. Sites are $5 per night. Senior discount available. Open June to late November.

Directions: From I-84 at LaGrande, turn north on Highway 82 and drive 62 miles to Enterprise. Continue six miles south to Joseph and then drive eight miles east on Highway 350. Turn south on Forest Road 39 and drive 29 miles to the campground.

Contact: Hells Canyon National Recreation Area, Wallowa Mountains Visitor Center, 88401 Hwy. 82, Enterprise, OR 97828; 541/426-5546.

46 Lake Fork

🥾 🎣 🐕 🚐 🏕️ 6

This little campground (at 3,200 feet elevation) along the banks of Lake Fork Creek is tucked away off the main road and is an ideal jumping-off point for a backpacking trip. A trail from camp follows the creek west for about 10 miles to Fish Lake, then continues to several smaller lakes.

Location: On Lake Fork Creek in Wallowa-Whitman National Forest; Northeast Oregon map 4, grid g2.

Campsites, facilities: There are 10 sites for tents, trailers, or RVs up to 22 feet long. Picnic tables and fire grills are provided. Drinking water and vault toilets are available, but all garbage must be packed out. Pets are permitted.

Reservations, fees: No reservations accepted. Sites are $5 per night. Senior discount available. Open June to late November.

Directions: From Baker City drive east on Highway 86 for 82 miles to Forest Road 39. Turn north and drive eight miles to the campground entrance road on the left.

Contact: Hells Canyon National Recreation Area, Wallowa Mountains Visitor Center, 88401 Hwy. 82, Enterprise, OR 97828; 541/426-5546.

47 Hidden

🥾 🚲 🎣 🐕 🏕️ 6

River views and spacious sites can be found at this campground in a pretty spot along the banks of the Imnaha River in the Hells Canyon National Recreation Area. It's essential to obtain a map of Wallowa-Whitman National Forest that details back roads and hiking trails. If full, Coverdale Campground is an option just four miles northeast on Forest Road 3960.

Location: On the Imnaha River in Wallowa-Whitman National Forest; Northeast Oregon map 4, grid h1.

Campsites, facilities: There are 10 tent sites and three sites for tents or small, self-contained trailers or RVs. Picnic tables and fire grills are provided. Drinking water, firewood, and vault toilets are available, but all garbage must be packed out. Leashed pets are permitted.

Reservations, fees: No reservations. Sites are $5 per night. Senior discount available. Open June to late November.

Directions: From LaGrande drive east on Highway 82 for 62 miles to Enterprise. Continue six miles south to Joseph and Highway 350. Turn east and drive eight miles to Wallowa Mountain Loop Road (Forest Road 39). Turn south and drive 30 miles to Forest Road 3960. Turn right (southwest) and drive seven miles to the campground.

Contact: Hells Canyon National Recreation Area, Wallowa Mountains Visitor Center, 88401 Hwy. 82, Enterprise, OR 97828; 541/426-5546.

48 Evergreen

This campground can be found along the banks of the Imnaha River in Hells Canyon National Recreation Area. It's one of seven camps in the vicinity. The camp is popular with hunters in the fall.

Location: On the Imnaha River in Wallowa-Whitman National Forest; Northeast Oregon map 4, grid h1.

Campsites, facilities: This is a group campsite for tents, trailers, or RVs up to 31 feet long. Vault toilets are available, but there is no drinking water, and all garbage must be packed out. Picnic tables and fire grills are provided. Pets are permitted.

Reservations, fees: No reservations; no fee. Open June to late November.

Directions: From LaGrande turn north on Highway 82 and drive 62 miles to Enterprise and the junction with Highway 3. Continue on Highway 82 for six miles to Joseph and Highway 350. Turn east on Highway 350 and drive eight miles to Forest Road 39. Turn south and drive about 30 miles to Forest Road 3960. Turn right and drive seven miles to the campground.

Contact: Hells Canyon National Recreation Area, Wallowa Mountains Visitor Center, 88401 Hwy. 82, Enterprise, OR 97828; 541/426-5546.

49 Indian Crossing

This campground is set at an elevation of 4,500 feet and is more developed than nearby Evergreen and Hidden Campgrounds. A trailhead for the Eagle Cap Wilderness is near this camp. Obtain a U.S. Forest Service map for side-trip possibilities.

Location: On the Imnaha River in Wallowa-Whitman National Forest; Northeast Oregon map 4, grid h1.

Campsites, facilities: There are 14 sites for tents, trailers, or RVs up to 30 feet long. Drinking water, picnic tables, and fire grills are provided, but all garbage must be packed out. Vault toilets and horse facilities are available. Pets are permitted.

Reservations, fees: No reservations. Sites are $5 per night. Senior discount available. Open June to late November.

Directions: From LaGrande turn north on Highway 82 and drive 62 miles to Enterprise and the junction with Highway 3. Continue on Highway 82 for six miles to Joseph and Highway 350. Turn east on Highway 350 and drive eight miles to Forest Road 39. Turn south and drive about 30 miles to Forest Road 3960. Turn right and drive 10 miles to the campground at the end of the road.

Contact: Hells Canyon National Recreation Area, Wallowa Mountains Visitor Center, 88401 Hwy. 82, Enterprise, OR 97828; 541/426-5546.

50 Whistler

This is a trailhead camp for the Wildcat Trail heading into the Mill Creek Wilderness. The area is extremely popular with rock hounds, who search for thunder eggs, jasper, and agates (digging is forbidden in wilderness areas, however). Though primitive, this is a pretty camp in a conifer forest that guarantees quiet and privacy.

Location: In Ochoco National Forest; Northeast Oregon map 5, grid d5.

Campsites, facilities: There is a large area for dispersed tent camping. A picnic table and a vault toilet are provided. There is no drinking water, and garbage must be packed out. Horses are welcome. Leashed pets are permitted.

Reservations, fees: No reservations; no fee. Open late May to late October.

Directions: From Prineville drive east on U.S. 26 for about 30 miles to Forest Road 27 (just east of Bandit Spring State Rest Area, near Ochoco Pass). Turn left on Forest Road 27 and drive nine miles to the campground entrance on the left.

Contact: Ochoco National Forest, Prineville Ranger District, P.O. Box 490, Prineville, OR 97754; 541/416-6500.

51 Wildcat

🥾 🐕 🚐 ⛺   4

This quiet, cool campground is set at an elevation of 3,799 feet in conifer forest and in a canyon. Situated along the East Fork of Mill Creek, the camp is near the Twin Pillars Trailhead, which provides access into the Mill Creek Wilderness. Stein's Pillar and Twin Pillars, popular rock-climbing spots, are nearby. Ochoco Lake and Ochoco Lake State Park to the south provide side-trip possibilities.

Location: On the East Fork of Mill Creek in Ochoco National Forest; Northeast Oregon map 5, grid e3.

Campsites, facilities: There are 17 sites for tents, trailers, or RVs up to 30 feet long. Picnic tables and fire grills are provided. Drinking water and vault toilets are available, but garbage must be packed out. Leashed pets are permitted.

Reservations, fees: No reservations. Sites are $8 per night, plus $3 for each additional vehicle. Senior discount available. Open mid-April to late October.

Directions: From Prineville drive east on U.S. 26 for nine miles to Mill Creek Road (Forest Road 33). Turn left on Mill Creek Road and drive about 10 miles to the campground

Contact: Ochoco National Forest, Prineville Ranger District, P.O. Box 490, Prineville, OR 97754; 541/416-6500.

52 Ochoco Divide

🥾 🚴 🐕 ♿ 🚐 ⛺   5

This camp is set at an elevation of 4,700 feet amid an old-growth stand of ponderosa pine just off scenic U.S. 26. An unused forest road on the far side of the campground provides an easy stretch walk after a long day of driving. Most visitors arrive late in the day and leave early in the morning, so the area is normally quiet during the day. Marks Creek is nearby and the Bandit Springs Rest Stop one mile west is the jumping-off point for a network of trails.

Location: In Ochoco National Forest; Northeast Oregon map 5, grid e5.

Campsites, facilities: There are 28 sites for tents, trailers, or RVs up to 30 feet long, with a separate area with walk-in and bike-in sites. Picnic tables and fire pits are provided. Drinking water, garbage bins, and vault toilets are available. Some facilities are wheelchair-accessible. Leashed pets are permitted.

Reservations, fees: No reservations. Sites are $8 per night, $4 per night for an additional vehicle. Senior discount available. Open late May to mid-November, weather permitting.

Directions: From Prineville drive east on U.S. 26 for 30 miles to the campground at the summit of Ochoco Pass.

Contact: Ochoco National Forest, Big Summit Ranger District, 348855 Ochoco Ranger District, Prineville, OR 97754-9612; 541/416-6645.

53 Ochoco Forest Camp

🥾 🚴 🎣 🚗
🐕 ♿ 🚐 ⛺   4

Campsites here are set at an elevation of 4,000 feet, along Ochoco Creek in a lush setting of ponderosa pine and aspen. Fishing for rainbow trout is fair. A large, group picnic area with a beautiful log shelter is available for reservation. It's a perfect setting for weddings, family reunions, and other group events. The nearby Lookout Mountain Trail provides access to the Lookout Mountain Recreation Area of 15,000 acres without roads. But hey, the truth is: don't expect privacy and solitude at this campground.

Location: In Ochoco National Forest; Northeast Oregon map 5, grid e5.

Campsites, facilities: There are six sites for tents, trailers, or RVs up to 24 feet long. Picnic tables and fire rings are provided. Drinking water, garbage bins, and vault toilets are available. Some facilities are wheelchair-accessible. Boat-launching facilities are nearby (only electric motors are allowed). Leashed pets are permitted.

Reservations, fees: No reservations. Sites are $8 per night, $4 per night for an additional vehicle. Senior discount available. Open mid-May through November, weather permitting.

Directions: From Prineville drive east on U.S. 26 for 16.5 miles to County Road 23. Turn right on County Road 23 and drive nine miles (County Road 23 becomes Forest Road 42) to the campground, across from the Ochoco Ranger Station.

Contact: Ochoco National Forest, Big Summit Ranger District, 348855 Ochoco Ranger District, Prineville, OR 97754-9612; 541/416-6645.

Mountain. The lake is stocked with rainbow trout and the fishing can range from middle-of-the-road fair right up to downright excellent.

Location: On Walton Lake in Ochoco National Forest; Northeast Oregon map 5, grid e5.

Campsites, facilities: There are 30 sites for tents, trailers, or RVs up to 31 feet long, and one group site. Picnic tables, garbage bins, and fire grills are provided. Drinking water and vault toilets are available. Some facilities are wheelchair-accessible. Boat-launching facilities are nearby (only electric motors are allowed). Leashed pets are permitted.

Reservations, fees: Reservations required for the group site only ($8.65 reservation fee). Sites are $10 per night, $27 per night for the group site, $5 per night for an additional vehicle. Senior discount available. Open June to late September.

Directions: From Prineville drive east on U.S. 26 for 16.5 miles to County Road 23. Turn right (northeast) and drive nine miles (County Road 23 becomes Forest Road 42) to the Ochoco Ranger Station and Forest Road 22. Drive north on Forest Road 22 for seven miles to the campground.

Contact: Ochoco National Forest, Big Summit Ranger District, 348855 Ochoco Ranger District, Prineville, OR 97754-9612; 541/416-6645, reservations 877/444-6777; website (for reservations): www.reserveusa.com.

54 Walton Lake

7

This campground is along the shore of small Walton Lake, among old-growth ponderosa pine and mountain meadows, where fishing and swimming are popular; only non-motorized boats or those with electric motors are allowed. Hikers can explore a nearby trail that leads south to Round

55 Crook County RV Park

6

This campground is in a landscaped and grassy area near the Crooked River, where fly-fishing is popular. The camp is right next to the Crook County Fairgrounds. In season, it offers horse races, rodeos, and expositions.

Location: Near the Crooked River; Northeast Oregon map 5, grid f2.

Campsites, facilities: There are 81 sites for tents, trailers, or RVs up to 70 feet long, all with full hookups. There are also two cabins. Electricity, drinking water, and picnic tables are provided. Flush toilets, sanitary services, cable TV, vending machines, and showers are available. A minimart, restaurant, laundry facilities, ice, and propane are available within one mile. Some facilities are wheelchair-accessible. Leashed pets are permitted.

Reservations, fees: Reservations accepted by phone or fax. Sites are $9–22 per night; weekly and monthly rates are available. Cabins are $25 per night. Open year-round.

Directions: From Redmond drive east on Highway 126 for 18 miles to Prineville (Highway 126 becomes 3rd Street). Turn east on 3rd Street and drive to Main Street. Turn right on Main Street and drive about one-half mile south to the campground on the left, next to the fairgrounds.

Contact: Crook County RV Park, 1040 S. Main St., Prineville, OR 97754; 541/447-2599, reservations 800/609-2599; fax 541/416-9022.

56 Ochoco Lake County Park

6

This is one of the nicer camps along U.S. 26 in eastern Oregon. The state park is on the shore adjacent to Ochoco Lake, where boating and fishing are popular pastimes. Some quality hiking trails can be found in the area.

Location: On Ochoco Lake; Northeast Oregon map 5, grid f3.

Campsites, facilities: There are 22 primitive sites for tents, trailers, or self-contained RVs up to 30 feet long, and a special area for hikers and bicyclists. Picnic tables, garbage bins, and fire grills are provided. Drinking

water, firewood, hot showers, and flush toilets are available. Boat-launching facilities are nearby. Leashed pets are permitted.

Reservations, fees: No reservations. Sites are $14 per night, and $4 for hikers/bikers. Open April through October, weather permitting.

Directions: From Prineville drive east on U.S. 26 for seven miles to the park entrance on the right.

Contact: Crook County Parks and Recreation, 398 N.E. Fairview St., Prineville, OR 97754; 541/447-1209; fax 541/447-9894.

57 Crystal Corral RV Park

5

This RV park isn't far from Ochoco Lake State Park, where boating and fishing are among the activities. There's a golf course within two miles and there are hiking trails within five miles.

Location: Near Ochoco Lake State Park; Northeast Oregon map 5, grid f3.

Campsites, facilities: There are 20 tent sites and 22 sites for trailers or RVs of any length and another two sites that can accommodate trailers or RVs up to 40 feet. Electricity, drinking water, sewer hookups, flush toilets, bottled gas, showers, a store, a café, a laundry room, and ice are available. Boat docks, launching facilities are nearby. Leashed pets (one per site) and motorbikes are permitted.

Reservations, fees: Reservations accepted. Sites are $12–20 per night. Open year-round.

Directions: From Prineville drive east on U.S. 26 for eight miles to the park on the left.

Contact: Crystal Corral RV Park, 11777 N.E. Ochoco Hwy., Prineville, OR 97754; 541/447-5932.

58 Deep Creek

 5

This small camp is on the edge of high desert and gets little use, but it's in a nice spot—the confluence of Deep Creek and the North Fork of the Crooked River. Highlights include pretty, shady sites and river access. Fishing is possible here.

Location: On the North Fork of the Crooked River in Ochoco National Forest; Northeast Oregon map 5, grid f8.

Campsites, facilities: There are six sites for tents, trailers, or RVs up to 22 feet long. Picnic tables and fire grills are provided. Drinking water and vault toilets are available. Garbage must be packed out. Leashed pets are permitted.

Reservations, fees: No reservations. Sites are $8 per night, $3 per additional vehicle. Senior discount available. Open June to mid-October.

Directions: From Prineville drive east on U.S. 26 for 16.5 miles to County Route 23. Turn right (northeast) and drive 8.5 miles (it becomes Forest Road 42). Continue east on Forest Road 42 for 23.5 miles to the campground.

Contact: Ochoco National Forest, Big Summit Ranger District, 348855 Ochoco Ranger District, Prineville, OR 97754-9612; 541/416-6645.

59 Chimney Rock

6

This well-spaced campground is a favorite for picnicking and wildlife viewing. The Chimney Rock Trailhead, just across the highway, is the jump-off point for the 1.7-mile, moderately difficult hike to Chimney Rock. There are numerous scenic overlooks along the trail, and wildlife sightings are common. The

elevation here is 3,000 feet. Chimney Rock Campground is one of eight BLM camps along a six-mile stretch of Highway 27.

Location: On the Crooked River; Northeast Oregon map 5, grid g2.

Campsites, facilities: There are 20 sites for tents, trailers, or RVs of any length. Drinking water and picnic tables are provided. Vault toilets and garbage bins are available. Wheelchair-accessible toilets, tables, and a fishing dock are also available Leashed pets are permitted.

Reservations, fees: No reservations. Sites are $8 per night, $2 per night for an additional vehicle. Senior discount available. Open year-round.

Directions: In Prineville drive south on Highway 27 for 16.4 miles to the campground.

Contact: Bureau of Land Management, Prineville District, P.O. Box 550, Prineville, OR 97754; 541/416-6700; fax 541/416-6798; website: www.or.blm.gov.

60 Prineville Reservoir State Park

7

This state park is set along the shore of Prineville Reservoir, formed by damming the Crooked River. Swimming, boating, fishing, and water-skiing are among the activities here. The nearby boat docks and ramp are a bonus. The reservoir supports rainbow and cutthroat trout, small and largemouth bass, catfish, and crappie. You can even ice fish in the winter. This is one of two campgrounds on the lake; the other is Prineville Reservoir Resort (RVs only).

Location: On Prineville Reservoir; Northeast Oregon map 5, grid g3.

Campsites, facilities: There are 25 tent sites and 75 sites with partial hookups for trailers or RVs up to 40 feet long, two rustic cabins, and three deluxe cabins. Electricity, drinking water, sewer hookups, garbage bins, and picnic tables are provided. Flush toilets, showers, and firewood are available. Boat docks and launching facilities are nearby. Leashed pets are permitted.

Reservations, fees: Reservations accepted. Sites are $10–20 per night, cabins $35–55 per night. Major credit cards accepted. Open year-round.

Directions: From Prineville drive east on U.S. 26 for one mile to Combs Flat Road. Turn right (south) and drive one mile to Juniper Canyon Road. Turn right (south) and drive 18 miles to the campground.

Contact: Prineville Reservoir State Park, 19020 S.E. Parkland Dr., Prineville, OR 97754; 541/447-4363 or 800/452-5687.

61 Prineville Reservoir Resort

🧗 🚲 🏊

🎣 🚤 🐕 🚐   6

This resort is on the shore of Prineville Reservoir in the high desert, a good spot for water sports and fishing. The mostly shaded sites are a combination of dirt and gravel, and there is easy access to the reservoir. There are some colorful rock formations to check out.

Location: On Prineville Reservoir; Northeast Oregon map 5, grid g3.

Campsites, facilities: There are 70 sites for trailers or RVs of any length; four are drive-through sites. Electricity, drinking water, fire pits, and picnic tables are provided. Flush toilets, bottled gas, sanitary disposal services, showers, firewood, a store, a café, and ice are available. A full-service marina, boat ramp, and boat rentals, including personal watercraft, are on-site. Leashed pets are permitted.

Reservations, fees: Reservations accepted. Sites are $14–20 per night. Open mid-March to mid-October, weather permitting.

Directions: From Prineville drive east on U.S. 26 for one mile to Combs Flat Road. Turn right (south) and drive one mile to Juniper Canyon Road. Turn right (south) and drive 18 miles to the campground.

Contact: Prineville Reservoir Resort, 19600 S.E. Juniper Canyon Rd., Prineville, OR 97754; 541/447-7468; fax 541/447-6002.

62 Antelope Flat Reservoir

🎣 🚤 🐕 🚐 🏕   6

This pretty spot is set along the west shore of Antelope Flat Reservoir. The campground sits amid ponderosa pine and juniper on the edge of the high desert at an elevation of 4,600 feet. It has wide sites and easy access to the lake. Trout fishing can be good in the spring, and boating with motors is permitted. This is also a good lake for canoes.

Location: On Antelope Flat Reservoir in Ochoco National Forest; Northeast Oregon map 5, grid h5.

Campsites, facilities: There are 25 sites for tents, trailers, or RVs up to 30 feet long. Picnic tables and fire grills are provided. Drinking water and vault toilets are available, but all garbage must be packed out. Boat-launching facilities are nearby. Leashed pets are permitted.

Reservations, fees: No reservations. Sites are $8 per night, plus $3 for each additional vehicle. Senior discount available. Open early May to late October.

Directions: From Prineville drive southeast on Combs Flat Road (Paulina Highway) for 30 miles to Forest Road 17 (Antelope Reservoir Junction). Turn right on Forest Road 17 and drive about 10 miles to Forest Road 1700-600. Drive a quarter mile on Forest Road 1700-600 to the campground.

Contact: Ochoco National Forest, Prineville Ranger District, P.O. Box 490, Prineville, OR 97754; 541/416-6500.

63 Wiley Flat

🏃 🐕 🚐 ⛺ 3

This campground is set along Wiley Creek in a nice, hidden spot with minimal crowds and is popular with hunters. A map of Ochoco National Forest details nearby access roads. A good gut-thumping hike is the trip to Tower Point Lookout. It's one mile north of the camp—and a 1,000-foot climb straight up.

Location: On Wiley Creek in Ochoco National Forest; Northeast Oregon map 5, grid h6.

Campsites, facilities: There are five sites for tents, trailers, or RVs up to 30 feet long. Picnic tables and fire grills are provided. Vault toilets are available, but there is no drinking water, and all garbage must be packed out. Leashed pets are permitted.

Reservations, fees: No reservations; no fee. Open mid-June to late October.

Directions: From Prineville drive southeast on the Paulina Highway (Combs Flat Road) for 34 miles to Forest Road 16. Turn right (southeast) and drive 10 miles to Forest Road 1600-400. Turn right (west) and drive one mile to the camp.

Contact: Ochoco National Forest, Prineville Ranger District, P.O. Box 490, Prineville, OR 97754; 541/416-6500.

64 Bull Prairie

🏃 ⛵ 🦢 🚣 🐕 ♿ 🚐 ⛺ 8

This campground is set along the shore of Bull Prairie Lake, a 24-acre lake at 4,000 feet elevation. Boating (no motors permitted), swimming, fishing, and hunting are some of the options here. A hiking trail circles the lake. This spot attracts little attention from out-of-towners, yet it offers plenty of recreation opportunities, making it an ideal vacation destination for many.

Location: On Bull Prairie Lake in Umatilla National Forest; Northeast Oregon map 6, grid a3.

Campsites, facilities: There are 28 sites for tents, trailers, or RVs up to 31 feet long. Picnic tables and fire grills are provided. Drinking water, sanitary disposal services, garbage bins (summer only), firewood, and vault toilets are available. Boat docks, launching facilities, and a wheelchair-accessible boat ramp are on-site. Pets are permitted.

Reservations, fees: No reservations accepted. Sites are $12 per night, $5 per night for an additional vehicle. Senior discount available. Open May to October.

Directions: From Heppner, drive south on Highway 207 for roughly 35 miles to the national forest boundary and continue four miles to Forest Road 2039 (paved). Turn left and drive three miles northeast to the campground on the right.

Contact: Umatilla National Forest, Heppner Ranger District, P.O. Box 7, Heppner, OR 97836; 541/676-9187; fax 541/676-2105.

65 Fairview

🚣 〰️ 🐕 🚐 5

This rugged and primitive campground adjacent to Fairview Springs near Mahogany Butte is a small campsite known by very few people. In a remote area at 4,300 feet, it's primarily used as a base camp by hunters. Very easy to miss—and not even marked on maps for the Umatilla National Forest. Bull Prairie Lake is only four miles away.

Location: Near Bull Prairie Lake in Umatilla National Forest; Northeast Oregon map 6, grid a3.

Campsites, facilities: There are five sites for trailers or RVs up to 16 feet long. Picnic tables and fire grills are provided. Firewood and vault toilets are available. There is no drinking water and all garbage must be packed out. Boat docks and launching facilities are nearby at Bull Prairie Lake. Leashed pets are permitted.

Reservations, fees: No reservations; no fee. Open May to late October.

Directions: From Heppner, drive south on Highway 207 for roughly 35 miles to the national forest boundary. Continue four miles to Forest Road 2039 (the turnoff for Bull Prairie Lake). Continue on Highway 207 for one mile to Forest Road 400 (if you pass through the immediate series of hairpin turns, you have gone too far). Turn west and drive 500 yards to the campground.

Contact: Umatilla National Forest, Heppner Ranger District, P.O. Box 7, Heppner, OR 97836; 541/676-9187; fax 541/676-2105.

66 Wolf Creek

🥾 🎣 🏠 🚐 ⛺   5

This campground is set along the banks of Wolf Creek, a nice trout stream that runs through Ochoco National Forest. It's a quality spot. Some excellent hiking trails can be found to the northeast in the Black Canyon Wilderness.

Location: On Wolf Creek in Ochoco National Forest; Northeast Oregon map 6, grid g2.

Campsites, facilities: There are 11 sites for tents, trailers, or RVs up to 22 feet long. Picnic tables and fire grills are provided, but there is no drinking water, and all garbage must be packed out. Vault toilets are available. Leashed pets are permitted.

Reservations, fees: No reservations accepted. Sites are $6 per night, with a 14-day stay limit, and $3 per night for an additional vehicle. Senior discount available. Open May to early November.

Directions: From Prineville drive southeast on Combs Flat Road (Paulina Highway) for 55

miles to Paulina. Continue east for 3.5 miles to County Road 112. Turn left (north) and drive 6.5 miles to Forest Road 42. Turn north and drive 1.5 miles to the campground.

Contact: Ochoco National Forest, Paulina Ranger District, 71500 Beaver Creek Rd., Paulina, OR 97751; 541/473-3713; fax 541/416-6679.

67 Sugar Creek

🥾 🏊 🏠 ♿ 🚐 ⛺   6

This campground is on the banks of Sugar Creek, small, quiet, and remote. It is set at an elevation of 4,000 feet. A three-quarter-mile trail loops along Sugar Creek. There is also a covered group shelter in the day-use area and a wheelchair-accessible trail. Because of the presence of bald eagles, there may be seasonal closures on land access in the area. Be sure to check posted notices.

Location: On Sugar Creek in Ochoco National Forest; Northeast Oregon map 6, grid f2.

Campsites, facilities: There are 17 sites for tents, trailers, or RVs up to 21 feet long. Picnic tables, garbage bins, and fire grills are provided. Drinking water, a picnic shelter, and vault toilets are available. Some facilities are wheelchair-accessible. Leashed pets are permitted.

Reservations, fees: No reservations accepted. Sites are $8 per night, with a 14-day stay limit, and $3 per night for an additional vehicle. Senior discount available. Open June to early November.

Directions: From Prineville drive southeast on Combs Flat Road (Paulina Highway) for 55 miles to Paulina. Continue east and drive 3.5 miles to a fork with County Road 112. Bear left at the fork onto County Road 112 and drive 7.5 miles to Forest Road 58. Continue on Forest Road 58 for 2.25 miles to the campground on the right.

Contact: Ochoco National Forest, Paulina Ranger District, 71500 Beaver Creek Rd., Paulina, OR 97751; 541/473-3713; fax 541/416-6679.

68 Frazier

4

This small, remote, and little-used camp in a meadow setting is at an elevation of 4,300 feet. Some dirt roads adjacent to the camp are good for mountain biking in summer and cross-country skiing and snowmobiling in winter. The camp is popular for reunions during the holidays. This campground is set in an open, grassy area sprinkled with a few large trees.

Location: On Frazier Creek in Ochoco National Forest; Northeast Oregon map 6, grid f3.

Campsites, facilities: There are six sites for tents, trailers, or RVs up to 21 feet long. Picnic tables and fire grills are provided. Vault toilets are available. There is no drinking water and all garbage must be packed out. Leashed pets are permitted.

Reservations, fees: No reservations accepted. There is no fee. The stay limit is 14 days. Open June to early November.

Directions: From Prineville drive southeast on Combs Flat Road (Paulina Highway) for 55 miles to Paulina. Continue east and drive 3.5 miles to a fork with County Road 112. Bear left at the fork onto County Road 112 and drive 2.5 miles to County Road 135. Turn right (east) and drive 10 miles to Forest Road 58. Turn right and drive six miles to Forest Road 58-500. Turn left and drive two miles to the campground.

Contact: Ochoco National Forest, Paulina Ranger District, 71500 Beaver Creek Rd., Paulina, OR 97751; 541/473-3713; fax 541/416-6679.

69 Clyde Holliday State Recreation Site

7

Think of this campground as an oasis. Its tall, willowy cottonwood trees provide shade and serenity, giving you that private, secluded feeling. It borders the John Day River, and you're as likely to have wildlife neighbors as human ones; Rocky Mountain elk and mule deer are frequent visitors. You might also see steelhead rushing upriver to spawn.

Location: Near the John Day River; Northeast Oregon map 6, grid e8.

Campsites, facilities: There are 31 sites for trailers or RVs up to 60 feet long, a hiker/biker tent area, and two tepees. Electricity, picnic tables, and fire grills are provided. Drinking water, firewood, sanitary disposal services, showers, and flush toilets are available. Leashed pets are permitted.

Reservations, fees: No reservations accepted. Sites are $16 per night, $4 per night for hiker/bikers, $28 per night for tepees, and $7 per night for an additional vehicle. The campground is open March through November, weather permitting.

Directions: From John Day drive west on U.S. 26 for six miles to the park on the left.

Contact: Clyde Holliday State Recreation Site, P.O. Box 10, Mt. Vernon, OR 97865; 541/932-4453 or 800/551-6949.

70 Starr

4

This good layover spot (5,100 feet elevation) for travelers on U.S. 395 happens to be adjacent to Starr Ski Bowl, which is popular in winter for skiing and sledding. The camp itself doesn't offer much in the way of recreation, but to the northeast is the Strawberry Mountain Wilderness, which has a number of trails, lakes, and streams.

Location: On Starr Ridge in Malheur National Forest; Northeast Oregon map 6, grid f8.

Campsites, facilities: There are eight sites for tents, trailers, or RVs up to 25 feet long; one site is wheelchair-accessible. Picnic tables and fire grills are provided. Wheelchair-accesible vault toilets are available. There is no drinking water, and all garbage must be packed out. Leashed pets are permitted.

Reservations, fees: No reservations. Sites are $4 per night, $2 per night for an additional vehicle. Senior discount available. Open early May to November.

Directions: From John Day drive south on U.S. 395 for 15 miles to the campground.

Contact: Malheur National Forest, Blue Mountain Ranger District, P.O. Box 909, John Day, OR 97845; 541/575-3000; fax 541/575-3001.

71 Welch Creek

🏃 🚴 🎣 🐕 🚐 ⛺ 5

This primitive camp is on the banks of Desolation Creek. Road noise may be a problem for some, and there's little privacy among sites. There's trail access to the Desolation Area, both for nonmotorized and motorized traffic. Hunting and fishing are popular here.

Location: On Desolation Creek in Umatilla National Forest; Northeast Oregon map 7, grid a2.

Campsites, facilities: There are six primitive sites for tents, small RVs, or trailers. Picnic tables and fire rings are provided. A vault toilet is available. No drinking water. All garbage must be packed out. Leashed pets are permitted.

Reservations, fees: No reservations; sites are $5–10 per night. Senior discount available. Open late May through November.

Directions: From Pendleton drive south on U.S. 395 for 62 miles to Forest Road 55 (one

mile north of Dale; it's easier to find if you know the marker, Texas Bar Road). Turn left and drive one mile to Forest Road 10. Turn right and drive 13 miles to the campground.

Contact: Umatilla National Forest, North Fork John Day Ranger District, P.O. Box 158, Ukiah, OR 97880; 541/427-3231; fax 541/276-5026.

72 North Fork John Day

🏃 🎣 🐕 🚐 ⛺ 6

This campground is in a conifer stand along the banks of the North Fork of the John Day River and is an ideal base camp for a wilderness backpacking trip. There's a great view of salmon spawning in the river in the fall. A horse-handling area is also available for wilderness users. Trails from camp lead into the North Fork John Day Wilderness. The camp is set at an elevation of 5,200 feet at the intersection of Elkhorn and Blue Mountain National Forest Scenic Byways. No motorbikes are permitted in the wilderness.

Location: On the North Fork of the John Day River in Umatilla National Forest; Northeast Oregon map 7, grid a4.

Campsites, facilities: There are 15 sites for tents, trailers, or RVs up to 22 feet long, and two additional tent-only sites. Picnic tables and fire rings are provided. Vault toilets are available. There is no drinking water. All garbage must be packed out. Leashed pets are permitted.

Reservations, fees: No reservations. Sites are $5 per night, with a 14-day stay limit, $10 per night for group sites. Senior discount available. Open June 1 through November. For trailhead use only, a Northwest Forest Pass ($30 annual fee) or $5 daily fee per parked vehicle is required.

Directions: From Pendleton drive south on U.S. 395 for 50 miles to Highway 244. Turn east on Highway 244 and drive one mile to

Ukiah and Forest Road 52. Turn south on Forest Road 52 and drive 36 miles to the campground.

Contact: Umatilla National Forest, North Fork John Day Ranger District, P.O. Box 158, Ukiah, OR 97880; 541/427-3231; fax 541/276-5026.

73 Anthony Lakes

10

This campground is set at 7,100 feet elevation, adjacent to Anthony Lake, where boating without motors is permitted. Sites are wooded with good screening between them. Alas, mosquitoes are often in particular abundance. Several smaller lakes within two miles by car or trail are ideal for trout fishing from a raft, float tube, or canoe. Sometimes mountain goats can be seen from the Elkhorn Crest Trail, which begins near here. Weekends and holidays are full.

Location: On Anthony Lake in Wallowa-Whitman National Forest; Northeast Oregon map 7, grid a6.

Campsites, facilities: There are 37 sites for tents, trailers, or RVs up to 22 feet long, and one group site. Drinking water, fire grills, garbage bins (summer only), and picnic tables are provided. Vault toilets are available. Some facilities are wheelchair-accessible. Boat-launching facilities are nearby. Leashed pets are permitted.

Reservations, fees: Reservations for group sites. Sites are $8 per night. Senior discount available. Open July to late September.

Directions: From Baker City on I-84, turn north on U.S. 30. Drive north for 10 miles to Haines and County Road 1146 (signed for Anthony Lakes Ski Resort). Turn left on County Road 1146 and drive 20 miles (the road becomes Forest Road 73) to the campground on the left.

Contact: Wallowa-Whitman National Forest, Baker Ranger District, 3165 10th St., Baker City, OR 97814; 541/523-1932; fax 541/523-1965. Make group-site reservations through the concessionaire, Recreation Resource Management, 541/894-2505.

74 Grande Ronde Lake

8

This campground sits amid Douglas and white fir, set at an elevation of 6,800 feet along the shore of Grande Ronde Lake, a small lake where the trout fishing can be good. Mountain goats are sometimes seen in the area. Several trails are to the south near Anthony Lake. A map of Wallowa-Whitman National Forest details the possibilities.

Location: On Grande Ronde Lake in Wallowa-Whitman National Forest; Northeast Oregon map 7, grid a6.

Campsites, facilities: There are eight sites for tents, trailers, or RVs up to 16 feet long. Picnic tables and fire grills are provided. Drinking water and vault toilets are available, but garbage must be packed out. Boat docks and launching facilities are nearby. Leashed pets are permitted.

Reservations, fees: No reservations accepted. Sites are $8 per night. Senior discount available. Open July to mid-September.

Directions: From Baker City on I-84, turn north on U.S. 30. Drive north for 10 miles to Haines and County Road 1146 (signed for Anthony Lakes Ski Resort). Turn left on County Road 1146 and drive 20 miles (the road becomes Forest Road 73) to the campground on the right.

Contact: Wallowa-Whitman National Forest, Baker Ranger District, 3160 10th St., Baker City, OR 97814; 541/523-4476; fax 541/523-1965; concessionaire, Recreation Resource Management, 541/894-2505.

75 Mud Lake

⛿⛰ 🎣 🐕 🚐 ⛺ 7

This campground is in fir forest on the shore of small Mud Lake, where the trout fishing can be fairly good. Mud Lake is shallow and more marshy than muddy. The campground is tiny and pleasant, set at an elevation of 7,100 feet, with lots of vegetation and relatively little use. Bring your mosquito repellent.

Location: On Mud Lake in Wallowa-Whitman National Forest; Northeast Oregon map 7, grid a6.

Campsites, facilities: There are three tent sites and five sites for trailers or RVs up to 16 feet long. Picnic tables and fire grills are provided. Drinking water and vault toilets are available, but all garbage must be packed out. Boat docks and launching facilities are nearby at Anthony Lake. Leashed pets are permitted.

Reservations, fees: No reservations accepted. Sites are $8 per night. Senior discount available. Open July to mid-September.

Directions: From Baker City on I-84, turn north on U.S. 30. Drive north for 10 miles to Haines and County Road 1146 (signed for Anthony Lakes Ski Resort). Turn left on County Road 1146 and drive 21 miles (the road becomes Forest Road 73) to the campground on the right.

Contact: Wallowa-Whitman National Forest, Baker Ranger District, 3165 10th St., Baker City, OR 97814; 541/523-1932; fax 541/523-1965; concessionaire, Recreation Resource Management, 541/894-2505.

76 Olive Lake

9

This campground is set at 6,100 feet along the shore of Olive Lake, between two sections of the North Fork John Day Wilderness.

Dammed to hold an increased volume of water, the glacial lake is a beautiful tint of blue. Motorized boats are allowed, but water-skiing is prohibited. Fishing is fair for kokanee salmon, cutthroat, rainbow, and brook trout. Sections of the old wooden pipeline for the historical Fremont Powerhouse can still be seen. Nearby trails provide access to the wilderness. Motorbikes and mountain bikes are not permitted there. The old mining town of Granite is 12 miles east of camp.

Location: On Olive Lake in Umatilla National Forest; Northeast Oregon map 7, grid b4.

Campsites, facilities: There are 28 sites for tents, trailers, or RVs up to 31 feet long (four can handle up to 45 feet). Vault toilets are available, but there is no drinking water and garbage must be packed out. Picnic tables and fire grills are provided. Boat docks, launching facilities, and two picnic areas are available. Leashed pets are permitted.

Reservations, fees: No reservations accepted. Sites are $5 per night, with a 14-day stay limit; $10 for a group camp. Senior discount available. Open June to mid-October, weather permitting.

Directions: From Pendleton drive south on U.S. 395 for 62 miles to Forest Road 55 (one mile north of Dale). Turn right and drive one-half mile to Forest Road 10. Turn right on Forest Road 10 and drive 26 miles to the campground on the right.

Contact: Umatilla National Forest, North Fork John Day Ranger District, P.O. Box 158, Ukiah, OR 97880; 541/427-3231; fax 541/276-5026.

77 McCully Forks

⛿⛰ 🎣 🐕 ⛺ 5

Here's an easy-access campground at 4,600 elevation along the banks of McCully Creek that's tiny, free, and primitive. This tiny camp, wedged in between highway and mountains, gets moderately heavy use and is often full on weekends, and highway noise can be audible. Sites are wooded with alder and cottonwood.

Location: On McCully Creek in Wallowa-Whitman National Forest; Northeast Oregon map 7, grid b6.

Campsites, facilities: There are six tent sites. Picnic tables and fire grills are provided. Vault toilets are available. There is no drinking water and all garbage must be packed out. Leashed pets are permitted.

Reservations, fees: No reservations; no fee. Open late May to late October.

Directions: From Baker City drive southwest on Highway 7 for 29 miles (bear west at Salisbury) to Sumpter. Continue three miles past Sumpter (the road becomes Forest Road 24) to the campground.

Contact: Wallowa-Whitman National Forest, Baker Ranger District, 3165 10th St., Baker City, OR 97814; 541/523-1932; fax 541/523-1965.

78 Union Creek

8

This campground along the north shore of Phillips Lake is easy to reach, yet missed by most travelers on I-84. It's the largest of three camps on the lake and the only one with drinking water. An old narrow-gauge railroad has been restored and runs up the valley from McEwen Depot (six miles from the campground) to Sumpter (10 miles from the camp). An old dredge can be seen in Sumpter.

Location: On Phillips Lake in Wallowa-Whitman National Forest; Northeast Oregon map 7, grid c8.

Campsites, facilities: There are 58 sites for tents, trailers, or RVs up to 32 feet long. Electricity, drinking water, sewer hookups, garbage bins (summer only), and picnic

tables are provided. Flush toilets, a sanitary disposal station, firewood, and ice are available. There is a small concession stand for packaged goods and fishing tackle. Some facilities are wheelchair-accessible. Boat docks and launching facilities are adjacent to the campground. Leashed pets are permitted.

Reservations, fees: Reservations for groups only. Sites are $10–16 per night, $5–8 per night for an additional vehicle. Senior discount available. Open from mid-April to mid-September.

Directions: From Baker City drive southwest on Highway 7 for 20 miles to the campground.

Contact: Wallowa-Whitman National Forest, Baker Ranger District, 3165 10th St., Baker City, OR 97814; 541/523-1932; fax 541/523-1965; concessionaire, Recreation Resource Management, 541/894-2505. Reservations for groups only; call 541/894-2505.

79 Southwest Shore

7

This campground is set at 4,120 feet elevation along the south shore of Phillips Lake, a four-mile-long reservoir created by the Mason Dam on the Powder River. It's one of two primitive camps on the lake. The boat ramp is usable only when water is high in the reservoir. An old narrow-gauge railroad runs out of McEwen Depot. See the description of Union Creek.

Location: On Phillips Lake in Wallowa-Whitman National Forest; Northeast Oregon map 7, grid c8.

Campsites, facilities: There are 18 sites for tents, trailers, or RVs up to 24 feet long. Fire grills and vault toilets are available. There is no drinking water, and all garbage must be packed out. A boat ramp is adjacent to the campground. Pets are permitted.

Reservations, fees: No reservations accepted. Site are $10 per night. Senior discount available. Open from May to mid-November.

Directions: From Baker City drive southwest on Highway 7 for 24 miles (just past Phillips Lake) to Hudspeth Lane (County Road 667). Turn south on Hudspeth Lane and drive two miles to Forest Road 2220. Turn southeast and drive 2.5 miles to the campground.

Contact: Wallowa-Whitman National Forest, Baker Ranger District, 3165 10th St., Baker City, OR 97814; 541/523-1932; fax 541/523-1965; concessionaire, Recreation Resource Management, 541/894-2505.

80 Millers Lane

 7

This small campground is situated at an elevation of 4,120 feet along the south shore of Phillips Lake, a long, narrow reservoir that's the largest in the region. Millers Lane is one of two primitive camps on the lake. An old narrow-gauge railroad runs out of McEwen Depot. See the description of Union Creek.

Location: On Phillips Lake in Wallowa-Whitman National Forest; Northeast Oregon map 7, grid c8.

Campsites, facilities: There are seven sites for tents, trailers, or RVs up to 20 feet long. Picnic tables and fire grills are provided. Firewood and vault toilets are available. There is no drinking water, and all garbage must be packed out. A boat ramp is at Southwest Shore. Leashed pets are permitted.

Reservations, fees: No reservations. Sites are $10 per night. Senior discount available. Open from May to mid-November.

Directions: From Baker City, drive southwest on Highway 7 for 24 miles (just past Phillips Lake) to Hudspeth Lane (County Road 667). Turn south on Hudspeth Lane and drive two miles to Forest Road 2220. Turn

southeast and drive 3.5 miles to the campground.

Contact: Wallowa-Whitman National Forest, Baker Ranger District, 3165 10th St., Baker City, OR 97814; 541/523-1932; fax 541/523-1965; concessionaire, Recreation Resource Management, 541/894-2505.

81 Magone Lake

8

This campground is set along the shore of little Magone Lake at an elevation of 5,100 feet. A 1.8-mile trail rings the lake, and the section extending from the beach area to the campground (about a quarter mile) is barrier-free. A half-mile trail is routed to Magone Slide, an unusual geological formation. Swimming, fishing, sailing, and canoeing are some of the popular activities at this lake. Easy-access bike trails can be found within a quarter mile of the campground.

Location: On Magone Lake in Malheur National Forest; Northeast Oregon map 7, grid d1.

Campsites, facilities: There are three sites for tents and 18 sites for trailers or RVs up to 40 feet long; four are drive-through sites. There is a separate group camping site designed for 10 families and a picnic shelter that can accommodate 50 to 100 people. Some facilities are wheelchair-accessible, including two of the campsites. Picnic tables and fire grills are provided. Drinking water, composting toilets, a boat ramp, and a beach area are available. Boat docks and launching facilities are nearby. Leashed pets are permitted.

Reservations, fees: No reservations required, except for the group site and picnic shelter. Sites are $10 per night, $2.50 per night for an additional vehicle, group site $60 per night, picnic shelter $25 per day. Senior discount available. Open May through November, weather permitting.

Directions: From John Day drive east on U.S. 26 for eight miles to County Road 18. Turn north and drive 10 miles to Forest Road 3620. Turn west (left) on Forest Road 3620 and drive 1.5 miles to Forest Road 3618. Turn right (northwest) and drive 1.5 miles to the campground.

Contact: Malheur National Forest, Blue Mountain Ranger District, P.O. Box 909, John Day, OR 97845; 541/575-3000; fax 541/575-3001.

82 Middle Fork

Scattered along the banks of the Middle Fork of the John Day River at 4,100 feet elevation, this rustic spot is easy to reach off a paved road. Besides wildlife-watching and berry picking, the main activity at this camp is fishing, so bring along your fly rod, and pinch down your barbs for catch-and-release. The John Day is a state scenic waterway.

Location: On the Middle Fork of the John Day River in Malheur National Forest; Northeast Oregon map 7, grid c4.

Campsites, facilities: There are 10 sites for tents, trailers, or RVs up to 30 feet long. Picnic tables and fire grills are provided. Vault toilets are available. There is no drinking water, and all garbage must be packed out. Some facilities are wheelchair-accessible. Leashed pets are permitted.

Reservations, fees: No reservations. Sites are $5 per night, $2.50 per night for an additional vehicle. Senior discount available. Open May through November, weather permitting.

Directions: From John Day drive northeast on U.S. 26 for 28 miles to Highway 7. Turn left (north) and drive one mile to County Road

20. Turn left and drive five miles to the campground on the left.

Contact: Malheur National Forest, Blue Mountain Ranger District, P.O. Box 909, John Day, OR 97845; 541/575-3000; fax 541/575-3001.

83 Dixie

This campground is set at Dixie Summit (elevation 5,300 feet) near Bridge Creek, where you can toss in a fishing line. The camp is just off U.S. 26, close enough to provide easy access. It draws overnighters, but otherwise gets light use. The Sumpter Valley Railroad interpretive site is one mile west on U.S. 26.

Location: Near Dixie Summit in Malheur National Forest; Northeast Oregon map 7, grid d4.

Campsites, facilities: There are 11 sites for tents, trailers, or RVs up to 30 feet long. Picnic tables, vault toilets, and fire grills are provided. Drinking water is available, but all garbage must be packed out. A store, a café, gas, and ice are available within six miles. Some facilities are wheelchair-accessible. Leashed pets are permitted.

Reservations, fees: No reservations. Sites are $5 per night, $2.50 per night for an additional vehicle. Senior discount available. Open May through November, weather permitting.

Directions: From John Day drive northeast on U.S. 26 for 24 miles to Forest Road 365. Turn left and drive one-quarter mile to the campground.

Contact: Malheur National Forest, Blue Mountain Ranger District, P.O. Box 909, John Day, OR 97845; 541/575-3000; fax 541/575-3001.

84 Depot Park

🚶 🚴 🎣
🐕 ♿ 🚐 ⛺ 6

This urban park on grassy flatlands has access to the John Day River, a good trout fishing spot. The camp is a more developed alternative to the many U.S. Forest Service campgrounds in the area. A historic rail depot is in the camp, with a related museum. Nearby attractions include the Strawberry Mountain Wilderness (prime hiking trails) and Clyde Holliday State Recreation Site.

Location: On the John Day River; Northeast Oregon map 7, grid e3.

Campsites, facilities: There are 20 sites for tents, trailers, or RVs up to 35 feet. Restrooms, showers, a sanitary dump, gazebo, picnic area, and a public phone are provided. Leashed pets are permitted.

Reservations, fees: No reservations accepted. Sites are $16 per night. Open May through November, weather permitting.

Directions: From John Day drive east on U.S. 26 for 13 miles to Prairie City and the junction of U.S. 26 and Main Street. Turn right (south) on Main Street and drive one-half mile to the park (well signed).

Contact: Prairie City Hall, P.O. Box 370, Prairie City, OR 97869; 541/820-3605.

85 Wetmore

🚶 🎣 🐕 ♿ 🚐 ⛺ 7

This campground set at an elevation of 4,320 feet near the Middle Fork of the Burnt River is a nice base camp for a fishing or hiking trip. The stream can provide good trout fishing. Trails are detailed on a map of Wallowa-Whitman National Forest. In addition, an excellent half-mile, wheelchair-accessible trail passes through old-growth forest. Watch for bald eagles.

Location: On the Middle Fork of the Burnt River in Wallowa-Whitman National Forest; Northeast Oregon map 7, grid d6.

Campsites, facilities: There are 16 sites for tents, trailers, or RVs up to 28 feet long. Picnic tables and fire grills are provided. Drinking water, firewood, and vault toilets are available, but all garbage must be packed out. Some facilities are wheelchair-accessible. Leashed pets are permitted.

Reservations, fees: No reservations. Sites are $8 per night. Senior discount available. Open late May to mid-September.

Directions: From John Day drive east on U.S. 26 for 29 miles to Austin Junction. Continue east on U.S. 26 for 10 miles to the campground.

Contact: Wallowa-Whitman National Forest, Unity Ranger District, P.O. Box 38, Unity, OR 97884; 541/446-3351; fax 541/523-1479.

86 Oregon

🚶 🐕 🚐 ⛺ 6

This campground at 4,880 feet elevation is just off U.S. 26 and is a staging site for ATV trails. The camp is surrounded by hillside, Douglas fir, white fir, and tamarack. Bald eagles nest in the area.

Location: Near Austin Junction in Wallowa-Whitman National Forest; Northeast Oregon map 7, grid d6.

Campsites, facilities: There are 11 sites for tents, trailers, or RVs up to 28 feet long. Picnic tables and fire grills are provided. Drinking water and vault toilets are available, but garbage must be packed out. Pets are permitted.

Reservations, fees: No reservations. Sites are $5 per night. Senior discount available. Open May to mid-September.

Directions: From John Day drive east on U.S. 26 for 29 miles to Austin Junction. Continue east for 20 miles to the campground.

Contact: Wallowa-Whitman National Forest, Unity Ranger District, P.O. Box 38, Unity, OR 97884; 541/446-3351; fax 541/523-1479.

87 Yellow Pine

7

Highlights of this camp include easy access and good recreation potential, including hiking trails. One half-mile-long, wheelchair-accessible trail connects to the Wetmore Campground. This is similar to Oregon Campground, but larger. Keep an eye out for bald eagles in this area.

Location: Near Middle Fork Burnt River; Northeast Oregon map 7, grid d6.

Campsites, facilities: There are 21 sites for tents, trailers, or RVs up to 28 feet long. Picnic tables and fire grills are provided. Drinking water, a sanitary disposal station, and vault toilets are available, but all garbage must be packed out. Pets are permitted.

Reservations, fees: No reservations. Sites are $8 per night. Senior discount available. Open late May to mid-September.

Directions: From John Day drive east on U.S. 26 for 29 miles to Austin Junction. Continue east for 21 miles to the campground.

Contact: Wallowa-Whitman National Forest, Unity Ranger District, P.O. Box 38, Unity, OR 97884; 541/446-3351; fax 541/523-1479.

88 Unity Lake State Recreation Site

7

This camp is set along the east shore of Unity Reservoir and is a popular spot when the weather is good. Campers can choose from hiking, swimming, boating, fishing, picnicking, or enjoying the scenic views. Set in the high desert, the grassy park is a contrast to the sagebrush and cheat grass of the bordering land.

Location: On Unity Reservoir; Northeast Oregon map 7, grid d7.

Campsites, facilities: There are 35 sites with water and electrical hookups for tents or RVs of any length, a separate area for hikers and bicyclists, and two tepees. Picnic tables, garbage bins, and fire grills are provided. Drinking water, flush toilets, showers, a sanitary disposal station, and firewood are available. Some facilities are wheelchair-accessible. Boat docks and launching facilities are nearby. Leashed pets are permitted.

Reservations, fees: No reservations accepted. Sites are $13–15 per night, $4 per night for hikers/bikers, $27 per night for tepees, and $7 per night for an additional vehicle. Open mid-April to late October.

Directions: From John Day drive east on U.S. 26 for 50 miles to Highway 245. Turn north (left) on Highway 245 and drive three miles to the park on the left.

Contact: Unity Lake State Recreation Site, P.O. Box 10, Mt. Vernon, OR 97820; 541/932-4453 or 800/551-6949.

89 Mammoth Springs

4

The South Fork of the Burnt River is a nice trout creek with, according to the local ranger, "good evening bites for anglers who know how to sneak-fish." The camp is private and scenic. Popular with hunters in the fall, the camp is set in brush and Douglas firs. By the way, the hot springs consist of a spot the size of a washtub, not large enough for human use. Maybe a Lemurian could fit in.

Location: On the South Fork of the Burnt River in Wallowa-Whitman National Forest; Northeast Oregon map 7, grid e6.

Campsites, facilities: There is a dispersed camping area for tents, trailers, or RVs up to 28 feet long. Picnic tables and fire grills are provided. Vault toilets are available. Leashed pets are permitted. Pack out all garbage.

Reservations, fees: No reservations accepted. There is no fee. Open May to mid-September.

Directions: From John Day, drive east on U.S. 26 for 49 miles to Unity and County Road 600. Turn right on County Road 600 and drive west for six miles (the road becomes Forest Road 6005/South Fork Road) and continue past the forest boundary for two miles to a Y with Forest Road 2640. Bear right (west) and drive one-half mile to the camp.

Contact: Wallowa-Whitman National Forest, Unity Ranger District, P.O. Box 38, Unity, OR 97884; 541/446-3351; fax 541/523-1479.

90 South Fork

🚶‍♂️ 🎣 🐕 🚐 ⛺ 5

This campground is set at an elevation of 4,400 feet along the banks of the South Fork of the Burnt River, a nice trout creek with good evening bites for anglers who know how to sneak-fish. It's a gem of a spot, with drinking water, privacy, and scenery—all for free.

Location: On the South Fork of the Burnt River in Wallowa-Whitman National Forest; Northeast Oregon map 7, grid e6.

Campsites, facilities: There are 14 sites for tents, trailers, or RVs up to 28 feet long. Picnic tables and fire grills are provided. Drinking water and vault toilets are available, but all garbage must be packed out. Pets are permitted.

Reservations, fees: No reservations accepted. There is no fee. Open late May to mid-September.

Directions: From John Day, drive east on U.S. 26 for 49 miles to Unity and County Road 600. Turn right on County Road 600 and drive west for six miles (the road becomes Forest Road 6005/South Fork Road) and continue past the forest boundary for one mile to the campground on the left.

Contact: Wallowa-Whitman National Forest, Unity Ranger District, P.O. Box 38, Unity, OR 97884; 541/446-3351; fax 541/523-1479.

91 Stevens Creek

🚶‍♂️ 🎣 🐕 🚐 ⛺ 5

This campground along the banks of the South Fork of the Burnt River is an alternative to the other small camps along the river. It is set at an elevation of 4,480 feet. The trout fishing is often good here. See the description of South Fork for more information.

Location: On the South Fork of the Burnt River in Wallowa-Whitman National Forest; Northeast Oregon map 7, grid e6.

Campsites, facilities: There is one group area for up to six tents, trailers, or RVs of any length. Picnic tables and fire grills are provided, but there is no drinking water, and all garbage must be packed out. Vault toilets are available. Pets are permitted.

Reservations, fees: No reservations accepted. There is no fee. Open late May to mid-September.

Directions: From John Day, drive east on U.S. 26 for 49 miles to Unity and County Road 600. Turn right on County Road 600 and drive west for six miles (the road becomes Forest Road 6005/South Fork Road) and continue past the forest boundary for two miles to the campground on the right.

Contact: Wallowa-Whitman National Forest, Unity Ranger District, P.O. Box 38, Unity, OR 97884; 541/446-3351; fax 541/523-1479.

92 Long Creek

🥾 🎣 🐕 🚐 ⛺ 4

This small, little-known campground set at 4,430 feet elevation boasts good trout fishing in Long Creek Reservoir. Several nearby campgrounds are similar in surroundings and facilities: Mammoth Springs, Eldorado, and Elk Creek.

Location: On Long Creek Reservoir in Wallowa-Whitman National Forest; Northeast Oregon map 7, grid f6.

Campsites, facilities: There is one group site for tents, trailers, or RVs up to 28 feet long. Picnic tables and fire grills are provided. A vault toilet is available, but there is no drinking water, and all garbage must be packed out. Leashed pets are permitted.

Reservations, fees: No reservations accepted. There is no fee. Open May to mid-September.

Directions: From John Day, drive east on U.S. 26 for 49 miles to Unity, then continue for one mile to Forest Road 1680 (West Camp Creek Road). Turn south (right) and drive seven miles to the access road on the left for Long Creek Reservoir and campground. Turn left and drive three miles to the campground.

Contact: Wallowa-Whitman National Forest, Unity Ranger District, P.O. Box 38, Unity, OR 97884; 541/446-3351; fax 541/523-1479.

93 Eldorado

🥾 🎣 🐕 5

Trout fishing in spring and early summer at East Camp Creek is a draw here. The campground is also convenient for fishing at Murray Reservoir. It is set at an elevation of 4,600 feet.

Location: On East Camp Creek in Wallowa-Whitman National Forest; Northeast Oregon map 7, grid f6.

Campsites, facilities: There are six sites for tents, trailers, or RVs up to 28 feet long. Picnic tables and fire grills are provided. Vault toilets are available, but there is no drinking water, and all garbage must be packed out. Leashed pets are permitted.

Reservations, fees: No reservations accepted. There is no fee. Open May to mid-September.

Directions: From John Day, drive east on U.S. 26 for 49 miles to Unity, then continue 10 miles to Forest Road 16 (well signed, on the right). Turn right (south) and drive three miles to the campground on the left.

Contact: Wallowa-Whitman National Forest, Unity Ranger District, P.O. Box 38, Unity, OR 97884; 541/446-3351; fax 541/523-1479.

94 Strawberry

🥾 🎣 🐕 ♿ ⛺ 7

This campground is set along the banks of Strawberry Creek at 5,700 feet in elevation. Nearby trails provide access to the Strawberry Mountain Wilderness, Strawberry Lake, and Strawberry Falls. It's a pretty area with hiking and hunting options. Fishing in Strawberry Creek is another possibility.

Location: On Strawberry Creek in Malheur National Forest; Northeast Oregon map 7, grid f5.

Campsites, facilities: There are 11 sites for tents. Picnic tables and fire grills are provided. Drinking water and wheelchair-accessible vault toilets are available. Leashed pets are permitted. Pack out all garbage.

Reservations, fees: No reservations. Sites are $6 per night, $3 per night for an additional vehicle. Senior discount available. Open June to mid-October.

Directions: From John Day drive east on U.S. 26 for 13 miles to Prairie City and

County Road 62. Turn right (southeast) and drive one-half mile to County Road 60. Turn right and drive south on County Road 60 for 8.5 miles (County Road 60 becomes Forest Road 6001). Continue 2.5 miles to the campground.

Contact: Malheur National Forest, Prairie City Ranger District, P.O. Box 337, Prairie City, OR 97869; 541/820-3311; fax 541/820-3838.

95 Little Crane

 5

Small, primitive, quiet, and private all describe this camp along the banks of Little Crane Creek at an elevation of 5,500 feet. The stream is good for trout fishing (only artificial bait and artificial lures are allowed). There are also some nice hiking trails in the area, the closest one at the North Fork of the Malheur River, about 10 miles away.

Location: On Little Crane Creek in Malheur National Forest; Northeast Oregon map 7, grid f4.

Campsites, facilities: There are four tent and trailer sites. Picnic tables and fire grills are provided. Vault toilets are available. There is no drinking water, and all garbage must be packed out. Leashed pets are permitted.

Reservations, fees: No reservations accepted. There is no fee. Open June to mid-November.

Directions: From John Day drive east on U.S. 26 for 13 miles to Prairie City and County Road 62. Turn right and drive 8.5 miles to Forest Road 13. Turn left and drive 16 miles to Forest Road 16. Turn right and drive 5.5 miles south to the campground.

Contact: Malheur National Forest, Prairie City Ranger District, P.O. Box 337, Prairie City, OR 97869; 541/820-3311; fax 541/820-3838.

96 Trout Farm

6

This campground (4,900 feet elevation) is on the Upper John Day River, which provides good trout fishing with easy access for people who don't wish to travel off paved roads. A picnic shelter is available for family picnics, and a small pond at the campground has a wheelchair-accessible trail.

Location: Near Prairie City in Malheur National Forest; Northeast Oregon map 7, grid f4.

Campsites, facilities: There are six sites for tents, trailers, or RVs up to 21 feet long. Picnic tables and fire grills are provided. Drinking water and wheelchair-accessible vault toilets are available, but all garbage must be packed out. Leashed pets are permitted.

Reservations, fees: No reservations. Sites are $5 per night. Senior discount available. Open June to mid-October.

Directions: From John Day drive east on U.S. 26 for 13 miles to Prairie City and County Road 62. Turn right and drive 15 miles to the campground entrance on the right.

Contact: Malheur National Forest, Prairie City Ranger District, P.O. Box 337, Prairie City, OR 97869; 541/820-3311; fax 541/820-3838.

97 Wickiup

5

This campground sits along the forks of Wickiup Creek and Canyon Creek at a historic site, with many original Civilian Conservation Corps structures still in place. There is limited fishing in the creek. To the north are many trails that are routed into the Strawberry Mountain Wilderness.

Location: On Wickiup Creek in Malheur National Forest; Northeast Oregon map 7, grid g2.

Campsites, facilities: There are eight sites for tents, trailers, or RVs up to 25 feet long. Picnic tables and fire grills are provided. A wheelchair-accessible vault toilet and horse corrals are available. No drinking water is available and all garbage must be packed out. Leashed pets are permitted.

Reservations, fees: No reservation; no fee. Open early May to November.

Directions: From John Day drive south on U.S. 395 for 10 miles to Forest Road 15. Turn southeast and drive eight miles to the campground.

Contact: Malheur National Forest, Blue Mountain Ranger District, P.O. Box 909, John Day, OR 97845; 541/575-3000; fax 541/575-3001.

98 Canyon Meadows

 5

This campground is on the shore of Canyon Meadows Reservoir, where nonmotorized boating, plus swimming, sailing, fishing, and hiking, are recreation options. However, this reservoir dries up by the Fourth of July because of a leak in the dam. Several hiking trails nearby lead north into the Strawberry Mountain Wilderness.

Location: On Canyon Meadows Reservoir in Malheur National Forest; Northeast Oregon map 7, grid g2.

Campsites, facilities: There are 14 sites for tents, trailers, or RVs up to 25 feet long. Picnic tables and fire grills are provided. Wheelchair-accessible vault toilets are available. No drinking water is available and all garbage must be packed out. Leashed pets are permitted.

Reservations, fees: No reservations accepted. There is no fee. Open mid-May to late October.

Directions: From John Day drive south on U.S. 395 for 10 miles to Forest Road 15. Turn left and drive nine miles southeast to Forest Road 1520. Turn left and drive five miles to the campground.

Contact: Malheur National Forest, Blue Mountain Ranger District, P.O. Box 909, John Day, OR 97845; 541/575-3000; fax 541/575-3001.

99 Parish Cabin

 6

This campground along the banks of Little Bear Creek at an elevation of 4,900 feet is in a pretty spot that's not heavily used. Limited fishing is available in the creek. The road is paved all the way to the campground. This campground is popular with groups of families and hunters in season.

Location: On Little Bear Creek in Malheur National Forest; Northeast Oregon map 7, grid g2.

Campsites, facilities: There are 16 sites for tents, trailers, or RVs up to 32 feet long. Picnic tables and fire grills are provided. Drinking water, wheelchair-accessible vault toilets, and horse facilities are available. Leashed pets are permitted. All garbage must be packed out.

Reservations, fees: No reservations. Sites are $6 per night. Senior discount available. Open mid-May to late November.

Directions: From John Day drive south on U.S. 395 for 10 miles to Forest Road 15. Turn left and drive 16 miles southeast to Forest Road 16. Turn right onto Forest Road 16 and drive a short distance to the campground on the right.

Contact: Malheur National Forest, Blue Mountain Ranger District, P.O. Box 909, John Day, OR 97845; 541/575-3000; fax 541/575-3001.

100 Big Creek

6

This campground is set at an elevation of 5,100 feet along the banks of Big Creek. Nearby forest roads provide access to the Strawberry Mountain Wilderness. Fishing and mountain biking are other recreation options. Fishing is restricted to the use of artificial lures with a single, barbless hook. In the appropriate seasons, elk, bear, coyote, and deer are hunted here.

Location: Near the Strawberry Mountain Wilderness in Malheur National Forest; Northeast Oregon map 7, grid g3.

Campsites, facilities: There are 15 sites for tents, trailers, or RVs up to 16 feet long. Picnic tables and fire grills are provided. Drinking water and wheelchair-accessible vault toilets are available. All garbage must be packed out. Leashed pets are permitted.

Reservations, fees: No reservations. Sites are $5 per night, $2.50 per night for an additional vehicle. Senior discount available. Open mid-May to mid-November.

Directions: From John Day drive east on U.S. 26 for 13 miles to Prairie City and County Road 62. Turn right and drive 24 miles to Forest Road 16. Turn right and drive six miles to Forest Road 815. Turn right and drive one-half mile to the campground on the right.

Contact: Malheur National Forest, Prairie City Ranger District, P.O. Box 337, Prairie City, OR 97869; 541/820-3311; fax 541/820-3838.

101 Elk Creek

   8

This tiny, pretty camp at the confluence of the North and South Forks of Elk Creek (elevation 5,000 feet) has lots of hunting and fishing opportunities. This camp gets light use, except during the hunting season. North Fork Malheur is an alternate camp in the area.

Location: On Elk Creek in Malheur National Forest; Northeast Oregon map 7, grid f6.

Campsites, facilities: There are five tent sites. Picnic tables and fire grills are provided. Vault toilets are available. There is no drinking water and all garbage must be packed out. Leashed pets are permitted.

Reservations, fees: No reservations accepted. There is no fee. Open mid-May to mid-November.

Directions: From John Day drive east on U.S. 26 for 13 miles to Prairie City and County Road 62. Turn right (southeast) on County Road 62 and drive 8.5 miles to Forest Road 13. Turn left and drive 16 miles to Forest Road 16. Turn right and drive 1.5 miles south to the campground.

Contact: Malheur National Forest, Prairie City Ranger District, P.O. Box 337, Prairie City, OR 97869; 541/820-3311; fax 541/820-3838.

102 North Fork Malheur

🚶 🚲 🎣 🐕 🚐 ⛺   7

This secluded campground is set at an elevation of 4,700 feet along the banks of the North Fork of the Malheur River, a designated Wild and Scenic River. Hiking trails and dirt roads provide additional access to the river and backcountry streams. It's essential to obtain a U.S. Forest Service map. Good fishing, hunting, and mountain biking opportunities abound in the area. Fishing is restricted to the use of artificial lures with a single, barbless hook.

Location: On the North Fork of the Malheur River in Malheur National Forest; Northeast Oregon map 7, grid g5.

Campsites, facilities: There are five sites for tents or small, self-contained trailers or RVs. Picnic tables and fire grills are provided. Vault toilets are available. There is no drinking water, and all garbage must be packed out. Leashed pets are permitted.

Reservations, fees: No reservations accepted. There is no fee. Open mid-May to mid-November.

Directions: From John Day drive east on U.S. 26 for 13 miles to Prairie City and County Road 62. Turn right and drive 8.5 miles to Forest Road 13. Turn left and drive 16 miles to Forest Road 16. Turn right and drive two miles south to a fork with Forest Road 1675. Take the left fork to Forest Road 1675 and drive two miles to the camp on the right.

Contact: Malheur National Forest, Prairie City Ranger District, P.O. Box 337, Prairie City, OR 97869; 541/820-3311; fax 541/820-3838.

103 Rock Springs Forest Camp

 5

This camp is for you if you want to camp in a big forest filled with the scent of ponderosa pines. It is also sprinkled with pretty aspens and several little springs. This primitive camp is right on Rock Springs with Cave Spring, Sunshine Spring, and House Creek Spring within a few miles. Do not count on the springs for drinking water, however, without a water filter. The elevation is 4,800 feet.

Location: At Rock Springs in Malheur National Forest; Northeast Oregon map 7, grid h2.

Campsites, facilities: There are eight sites for tents, trailers, or RVs up to 20 feet long. Picnic tables and fire grills are provided. Vault toilets are available. There is no drinking water. Garbage must be packed out. Leashed pets are permitted.

Reservations, fees: No reservations, no fee. Open late May to mid-October.

Directions: From Burns drive north on U.S. 395 for 30 miles to Van-Silvies Highway (County Road 73). Turn right on Van-Silvies Highway (which turns into Forest Road 17) and drive four miles to Forest Road 054. Turn right (south) and drive 0.75 miles to the camp on the left.

Contact: Malheur National Forest, Emigrant Creek Ranger District, HC 74, P.O. Box 12870, Hines, OR 97738; 541/573-4300; fax 541/573-4398; website: www.fs.fed.us/c6/malheur.

104 Eagle Forks

6

This campground at 3,000 feet elevation is at the confluence of Little Eagle Creek and Eagle Creek. A trail follows the creek northwest for several miles, making for a prime day hike, though the spot attracts few people. It's quite pretty as well and perfect for a weekend getaway or an extended layover.

Location: On Eagle Creek in Wallowa-Whitman National Forest; Northeast Oregon map 8, grid a6.

Campsites, facilities: There are seven tent sites and five sites for trailers or RVs up to 21 feet long. Picnic tables and fire grills are provided. Drinking water and vault toilets are available, but all garbage must be packed out. Pets are permitted.

Reservations, fees: No reservations; no fee. Open June to late October.

Directions: From Baker City drive east on Highway 86 for 36 miles to Richland. Turn north on Eagle Creek Road and drive to Newbridge; continue on Forest Road 7735 for seven miles to the campground entrance on the left.

Contact: Wallowa-Whitman National Forest, Pine Ranger District, General Delivery, Halfway, OR 97834; 541/742-7511; fax 541/742-6705.

105 West Eagle Meadow

7

This campground in a big, open meadow is set at 5,200 feet elevation about a five-minute walk from West Eagle Creek. The West Eagle Trailhead is at the campground, providing access to the Eagle Cap Wilderness and offering a good opportunity to observe wildlife. The adjacent meadow is filled with wildflowers in the summer. There are also new stock facilities with water available in an adjacent separate campground for those with horses.

Location: Near West Eagle Creek in Wallowa-Whitman National Forest; Northeast Oregon map 8, grid a6.

Campsites, facilities: There are 24 sites for tents. There is an adjacent campground for those with horses with six sites. Picnic tables, garbage service (summer only), and fire rings are provided. There is no drinking water. Vault toilets are available. Stock facilities include water, corrals, hitching rails, and a nearby loading ramp. Some facilities are wheelchair-accessible. Pets are permitted.

Reservations, fees: No reservations; no fee. Open mid-June to late October.

Directions: From Baker City drive north on I-84 for six miles to Highway 203. Turn east and drive 17 miles to the town of Medical Springs and Forest Road 67. Turn on Forest Road 67 and drive 15.5 miles (across Eagle Creek) to Forest Road 77. Turn left and drive 20 miles to the campground on the left.

Contact: Wallowa-Whitman National Forest, LaGrande Ranger District, 3502 Hwy. 30, LaGrande, OR 97850; 541/963-7186; fax 541/962-8580.

106 Two Color

6

This campground is set at 4,800 feet elevation along the banks of Eagle Creek, about a mile north of Tamarack. Another option for campers is nearby Boulder Park campground, three miles northeast on Forest Road 7755.

Location: On Eagle Creek in Wallowa-Whitman National Forest; Northeast Oregon map 8, grid a6.

Campsites, facilities: There are 14 sites for tents and six sites for trailers or RVs up to 22 feet long. Picnic tables and fire grills are provided. Drinking water and vault toilets are available, but garbage must be packed out. Pets are permitted.

Reservations, fees: No reservations; no fee. Open mid-June to late October.

Directions: From Baker City drive north on I-84 for six miles to Highway 203. Turn

east on Highway 203 and drive 17 miles to Medical Springs and Big Springs Road (Forest Road 67). Turn left on Forest Road 67 and drive 15.5 miles (staying on Forest Road 67 at all Y junctions) to Forest Road 77. Turn left and drive one-quarter mile to the camp.

Contact: Wallowa-Whitman National Forest, LaGrande Ranger District, 3502 Hwy. 30, LaGrande, OR 97850; 541/963-7186; fax 541/962-8580.

107 Tamarack

5

At 4,600 feet on the banks of Eagle Creek in a beautiful area with lush vegetation and abundant wildlife, this camp is a good spot for a fishing and hiking trip in a remote setting.

Location: On Eagle Creek in Wallowa-Whitman National Forest; Northeast Oregon map 8, grid a6.

Campsites, facilities: There are 12 tent sites and 12 sites for trailers or RVs up to 22 feet long. Picnic tables and fire grills are provided. Drinking water and vault toilets are available, but all garbage must be packed out. Pets are permitted.

Reservations, fees: No reservations; no fee. Open June to late October.

Directions: From Baker City drive north on I-84 for six miles to Highway 203. Turn east on Highway 203 and drive 17 miles to Medical Springs and Big Springs Road (Forest Road 67). Turn left on Forest Road 67 and drive 15.5 miles (staying on Forest Road 67 at all Y junctions) to Forest Road 77. Turn right and drive one-quarter mile to the camp.

Contact: Wallowa-Whitman National Forest, Pine Ranger District, 38470 Pinetown Ln., Halfway, OR 97834; 541/742-7511; fax 541/742-6705.

108 McBride

🚶🎣🐕🚐🏕️ 6

This campground is set along the banks of Brooks Ditch at an elevation of 4,800 feet. It is little used, primitive, and obscure. Though not particularly scenic, it will work as a quick, free layover spot.

Location: On Brooks Ditch in Wallowa-Whitman National Forest; Northeast Oregon map 8, grid a7.

Campsites, facilities: There are 11 tent sites and eight sites for trailers or RVs up to 16 feet long. Picnic tables and fire grills are provided. Drinking water and vault toilets are available, but all garbage must be packed out. Leashed pets are permitted.

Reservations, fees: No reservations; no fee. Open mid-May to late October.

Directions: From Baker City drive east on Highway 86 for 52 miles to Halfway. Turn northwest on Highway 413 and drive six miles to Forest Road 7710. Turn west and drive 2.5 miles to the campground.

Contact: Wallowa-Whitman National Forest, Pine Ranger District, 38470 Pinetown Ln., Halfway, OR 97834; 541/742-7511; fax 541/742-6705.

109 Twin Lakes

🚶🎣🐕🏕️ 6

This campground is nestled at 6,500 feet elevation between the little Twin Lakes, both of which offer excellent fishing. Nearby trails provide access to backcountry lakes and streams. See a U.S. Forest Service map for details. Another campground option is Fish Lake, about six miles south on Forest Road 66.

Location: Near Twin Lakes in Wallowa-Whitman National Forest; Northeast Oregon map 8, grid a8.

Campsites, facilities: There are six tent sites. Picnic tables and fire grills are provid-

ed. Firewood and vault toilets are available, but there is no drinking water, and all garbage must be packed out. Pets are permitted.

Reservations, fees: No reservations; no fee. Open July to mid-September.

Directions: From Baker City on I-84, turn east on Highway 86. Drive east on Highway 86 for 52 miles to Halfway and County Road 733. Turn north on County Road 733 and drive five miles north to Fish Lake Road (Forest Road 66). Turn north and drive 24 miles to the campground.

Contact: Hells Canyon National Recreation Area, Wallowa Mountains Visitor Center, 88401 Hwy. 82, Enterprise, OR 97828; 541/426-5546; or Pine Ranger District, Wallowa-Whitman National Forest, 38470 Pinetown Ln., Halfway, OR 97834; 541/742-7511.

110 Fish Lake

🚶🏊🎣
🚐🐕🚐🏕️ 6

This pretty, well-forested camp at an elevation of 6,600 feet, with comfortable sites along the shore of Fish Lake, makes a good base for a fishing trip. Side-trip options include hiking on nearby trails that lead to mountain streams.

Location: On Fish Lake in Wallowa-Whitman National Forest; Northeast Oregon map 8, grid a8.

Campsites, facilities: There are 10 tent sites and five sites for trailers or RVs up to 22 feet long. Picnic tables and fire grills are provided. Drinking water and vault toilets are available. Boat-launching facilities are nearby. Leashed pets are permitted. Garbage must be packed out.

Reservations, fees: No reservations. Sites are $5 per night. Senior discount available. Open mid-June to late October.

Directions: From Baker City, drive north on I-84 for four miles to Highway 86. Turn east on Highway 86 and drive 52 miles to Halfway and County Road 733. Turn north on County Road 733 and drive five miles to Forest Road 66. Continue north on Forest Road 66 for 18.5 miles to the campground on the left.

Contact: Wallowa-Whitman National Forest, Pine Ranger District, 38470 Pinetown Ln., Halfway, OR 97834; 541/742-7511; fax 541/742-6705.

111 Mountain View Trav-L Park

6

This shaded, grassy campground is "the gateway to camping on the Oregon Trail," complete with an Oregon Trail Interpretive Center for those with a historical bent. The park is clean and cool, with spacious sites and many recreation options nearby. After a day of hiking, you can rest your bones in the indoor hot tub.

Location: In Baker City; Northeast Oregon map 8, grid b2.

Campsites, facilities: There are 11 tent sites and 69 full-hookup sites for trailers or RVs of any length; most are pull-through sites. Electricity, drinking water, sewer hookups, cable TV hookups, and picnic tables are provided. Flush toilets, sanitary disposal services, showers, a laundry room, ice, a playground, a meeting room, a convenience store, and a swimming pool are available. Bottled gas and a café are within one mile. Leashed pets and motorbikes are permitted.

Reservations, fees: Reservations accepted. Sites are $15.05–20.19 per night. Senior discount available. Open year-round, with limited winter facilities.

Directions: In Baker City on U.S. 84, take Exit 304 to Campbell Street. Drive west on Campbell Street for 1.5 miles to 10th Street. Turn right and drive one mile north to Hughes Lane. Turn east and drive one block.

Contact: Mountain View Trav-L Park, 2845 Hughes Ln., Baker City, OR 97814; 541/523-4824, reservations 800/806-4824.

112 Spring Rec

5

This campground along the banks of the Snake River Reservoir is one of two camps in or near Huntington. A more developed alternative is Farewell Bend State Recreation Area, which offers showers and all the other luxuries a camper could want. Fishing is popular at this reservoir.

Location: On the Snake River; Northeast Oregon map 8, grid f7.

Campsites, facilities: There are 35 sites for tents, trailers, or RVs. Picnic tables, garbage service, and fire grills are provided. Drinking water (summer only), sanitary disposal services, and vault toilets are available. Boat-launching facilities and a fish-cleaning station are on-site. Leashed pets are permitted.

Reservations, fees: No reservations accepted. Sites are $5 per night per vehicle, with a 14-day stay limit. Senior discount available. Open from March through October and some off-season weekends.

Directions: From Ontario (near the Oregon/Idaho border), drive northwest on I-84 for 28 miles to Huntington and Snake River Road. Turn northeast on Snake River Road and drive five miles to the campground.

Contact: Bureau of Land Management, Baker City Office, 3165 10th St., Baker City, OR 97814; 541/523-1256; fax 541/523-1285; website: www.or.blm.gov.

113 Farewell Bend State Recreation Area

7

This campground offers a desert experience on the banks of the Snake River's Brownlee

Reservoir. Situated along the Oregon Trail, there are historic interpretive displays and an evening interpretive program at the amphitheater. Among the amenities are horseshoe pits, basketball hoops, and a sand volleyball court.

Location: On the Snake River; Northeast Oregon map 8, grid f7.

Campsites, facilities: There are 45 primitive tent sites and 91 sites with partial hookups for trailers or RVs up to 56 feet long. There are also four tepees, two cabins, two covered camper wagons, and two group tent areas. Drinking water, garbage bins, barbecues, and picnic tables are provided. Flush toilets, sanitary disposal services, showers, and firewood are available. Boat-launching facilities are nearby. Leashed pets are permitted.

Reservations, fees: Reservations accepted ($6 reservation fee). Sites are $12–18 per night, tepees or covered wagons are $27 a night, and cabins are $35 per night; there is a $7 per night fee for an additional vehicle. Major credit cards accepted. Open year-round, with limited winter facilities.

Directions: From Ontario (near the Oregon/Idaho border), drive northwest on I-84 for 21 miles to Exit 353 and the park entrance on the right side of the road.

Contact: Farewell Bend State Recreation Area, 23751 Old Hwy. 30, Huntington, OR 97907; 541/869-2365 or 800/551-6949, reservations 800/452-5687.

114 Brogan Trailer Park and Camp

5

This rural campground is on the inner edge of the West's Great Basin, a high-desert area that extends to Idaho. Nearby side trips include Willow Creek, which runs along U.S. 26, and Malheur Reservoir, northwest of Brogan.

Location: Near Willow Creek; Northeast Oregon map 8, grid g4.

Campsites, facilities: There are four tent sites and 24 drive-through sites for trailers or RVs of any length. Electricity, drinking water, sewer hookups, and picnic tables are provided. Flush toilets, showers, laundry facilities, and ice are available. Bottled gas, a store, and a café are within one mile. Leashed pets are permitted.

Reservations, fees: Reservations accepted. Sites are $6–10 per night. Senior discount available. Open from April through December.

Directions: From Ontario (near the Oregon/Idaho border), drive west on U.S. 20/26 for 12 miles to Vale and U.S. 26. Turn northwest on U.S. 26 and drive 24 miles to Brogan. Continue into town to the campground on the left (Brogan is a very small town that consists of a few stores and this park on U.S. 26).

Contact: Brogan Trailer Park and Camp, 3029 6th St., Brogan, OR 97903; 541/473-3062.

115 Bully Creek Park

7

The reservoir is in a kind of high desert area, with sagebrush and poplar trees for shade. People swim, boat, water-ski, and fish in it, mostly for warm-water fish such as crappie and large and smallmouth bass. You can bike on the gravel roads. It's beautiful if you like the desert, and the sunsets are worth the trip. It's primitive with deer, jackrabbits, squirrels, and many birds around. The elevation is 2,300 feet.

Location: On Bully Creek Reservoir; Northeast Oregon map 8, grid h5.

Campsites, facilities: There are 33 double sites for tents, trailers, or RVs up to 30 feet of any length. There are also three group sites. Electricity, picnic tables, and fire pits are provided. Drinking water, flush toilets, showers, ice, garbage bins, a dump station, and a boat ramp and dock are available. A restaurant, café, grocery, minimart, gasoline, bottled gas, charcoal, and coin-operated laundry are within 10 miles. Bring your own firewood. Leashed pets are permitted.

Reservations, fees: Reservations are recommended by phone or fax. Reservations require a $10 deposit. Sites are $10 per sleeping unit per night. Open April through mid-November, weather permitting.

Directions: From Ontario (near the Oregon/Idaho border), drive west on U.S. 20/26 for 12 miles to Vale and Graham Boulevard. Turn northwest on Graham Boulevard and drive five miles to Bully Creek Road. Turn west (left) and drive three miles to Bully Creek Park.

Contact: Bully Creek Park, 2475 Bully Creek Rd., Vale, OR 97918; 541/473-2969; fax 541/473-9462.

THE SOUTHERN CASCADES

The Southern Cascades

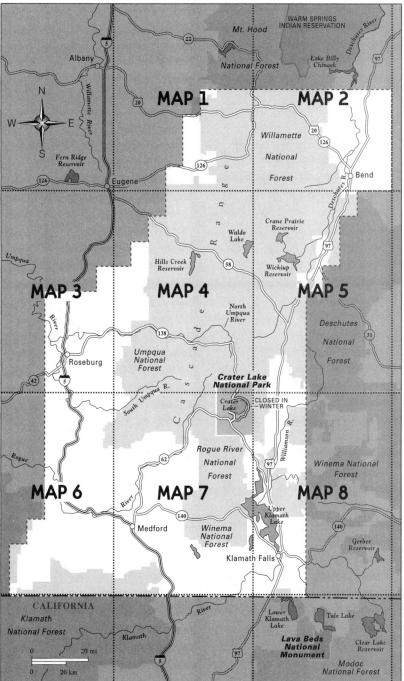

Map 1

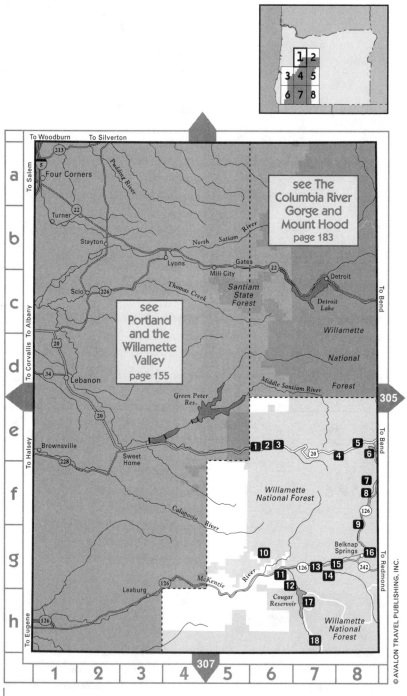

see The
Columbia River
Gorge and
Mount Hood
page 183

see
Portland
and the
Willamette
Valley
page 155

To Woodburn   To Silverton

To Salem

Four Corners

Turner

Stayton

Lyons

Mill City   Gates

Scio

Detroit

Detroit
Lake

Santiam State
Forest

Willamette

National

Forest

To Corvallis   To Albany

To Bend

Lebanon

Green Peter
Res.

Middle Santiam River

Brownsville

Sweet
Home

Willamette
National
Forest

To Bend

To Halsey

Calapooia   River

Belknap
Springs

To Redmond

Leaburg

McKenzie   River

Cougar
Reservoir

Willamette
National
Forest

To Eugene

Puddling River

North   Satiam   River

Thomas Creek

305

307

© AVALON TRAVEL PUBLISHING, INC.

Map 2

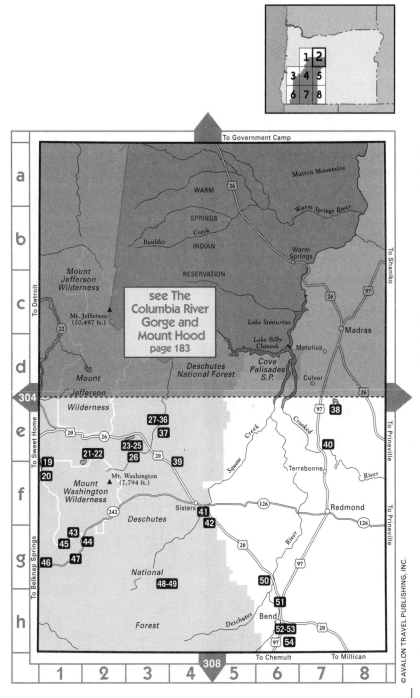

To Government Camp

a

Mutton Mountains

WARM

26

SPRINGS

Boulder

Creek

INDIAN

b

Warm Springs River

Warm
Springs

Mount
Jefferson
Wilderness

RESERVATION

To Detroit

c

Mt. Jefferson
(10,497 ft.)

22

see The
Columbia River
Gorge and
Mount Hood
page 183

Lake Simtustus

Lake Billy
Chinook

Metolius

26

97

To Shaniko

Madras

Deschutes
National Forest

Cove
Palisades
S.P.

d

Mount
Jefferson
Wilderness

Culver

26

304

e

To Sweet Home

20   26

21-22

23-25

26

27-36

37

20

39

Deschutes

97

Crooked

38

40

Squaw

Creek

Terrebonne

River

To Prineville

19

20

Mount
Washington
Wilderness

Mt. Washington
(7,794 ft.)

f

242

Sisters   41

42

126

Redmond

126

To Prineville

To Belknap Springs

g

43

45   44

47

National

48-49

20

River

97

50

51

52-53

54

h

Forest

Deschutes

Bend

20

97

To Chemult

To Millican

308

1   2   3   4   5   6   7   8

© AVALON TRAVEL PUBLISHING, INC.

Map 3

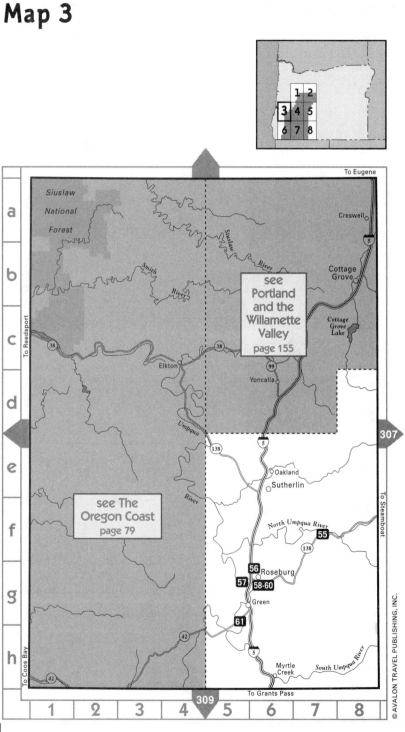

Map 4

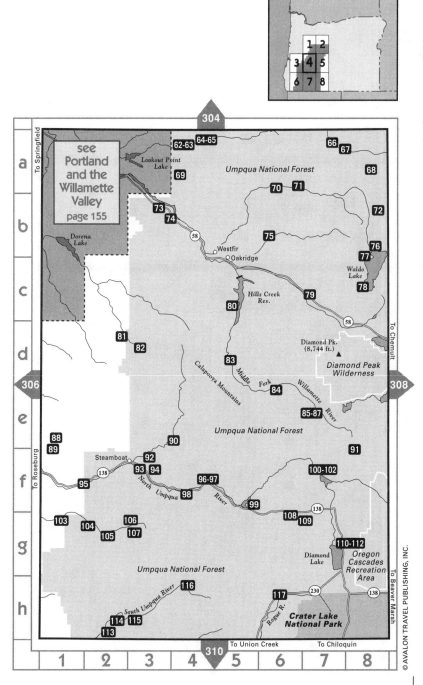

Map 5

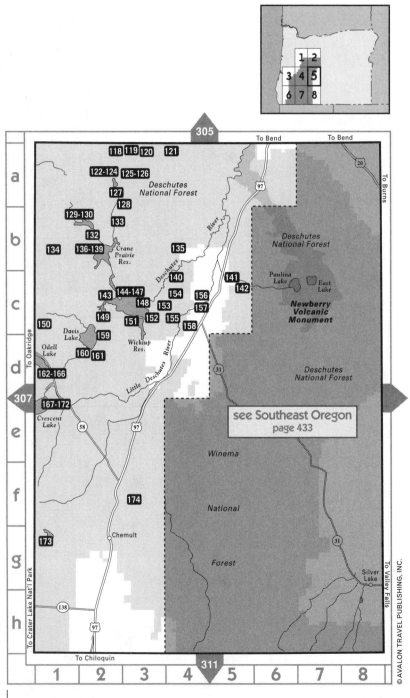

Map 6

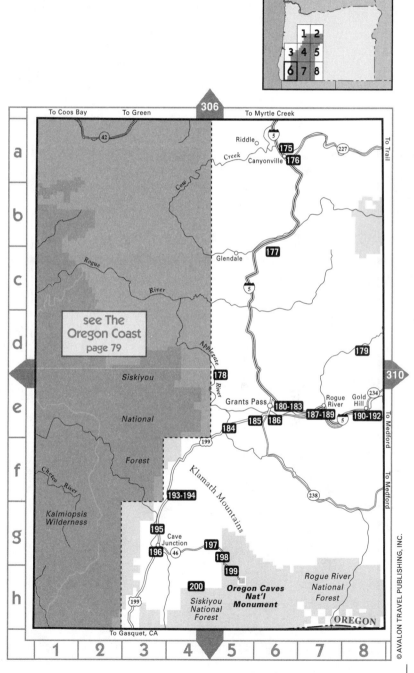

To Coos Bay · To Green · To Myrtle Creek

306

a

42
Riddle
175
Creek
Canyonville **176**
227
To Trail

b

Rogue
177

c

Glendale
River
5

see The
Oregon Coast
page 79

d

Applegate
Siskiyou
178
River
179

e

310

National
Grants Pass **180-183**
Rogue **Gold**
River **Hill** 234
185 **186** **187-189**
5
190-192
To Medford

Forest
199
184

f

Chetco River
Klamath Mountains
193-194
238
To Medford

g

Kalmiopsis
Wilderness
195
Cave
Junction
197
196 46
198
199

h

199
200
Siskiyou
National
Forest
Oregon Caves
Nat'l
Monument
Rogue River
National
Forest
OREGON

To Gasquet, CA

1 2 3 4 5 6 7 8

© AVALON TRAVEL PUBLISHING, INC.

Map 7

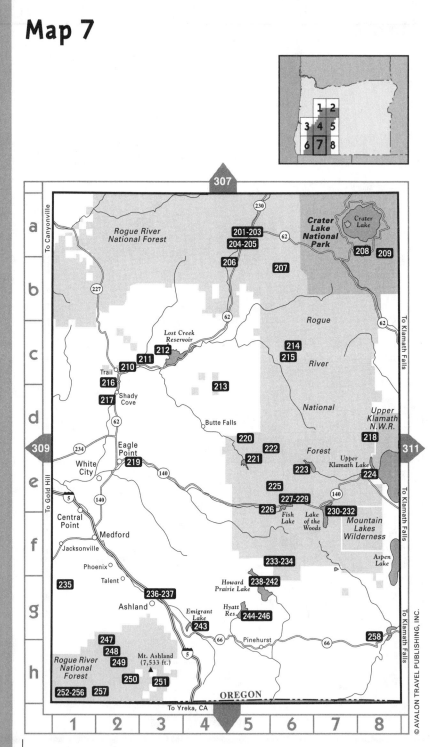

To Canyonville

a

Rogue River
National Forest

b

227

c

Lost Creek
Reservoir

212

210 211

Trail

216

217

Shady
Cove

62

234

d

Butte Falls

220

222
221

Eagle
Point

309

219

140

White
City

e

5

140

225

227-229

226

Fish
Lake

Central
Point

Medford

f

Jacksonville

Phoenix

235

Talent

236-237

g

Ashland

Emigrant
Lake

243

247

248

249

Rogue River
National Forest

h

250

251

Mt. Ashland
(7,533 ft.)

252-256 257

OREGON

To Yreka, CA

230

201-203
204-205

206

207

62

Crater
Lake
National
Park

Crater
Lake

208 209

Rogue

River

214
215

National

62

Forest

Upper
Klamath
N.W.R.

218

To Klamath Falls

223

Upper
Klamath Lake

224

230-232

Lake of
the Woods

Mountain
Lakes
Wilderness

Aspen
Lake

233-234

238-242

Howard
Prairie Lake

Hyatt
Res.

244-246

Pinehurst

66

66

258

To Klamath Falls

311

© AVALON TRAVEL PUBLISHING, INC.

1 2 3 4 5 6 7 8

To Gold Hill

Map 8

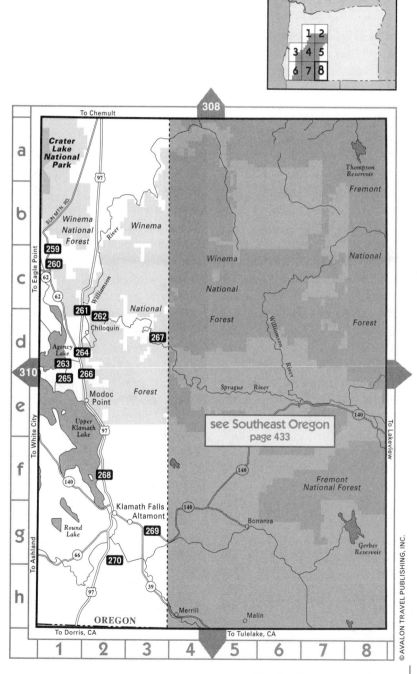

To Chemult

Crater Lake National Park

Winema National Forest

SUN MTN RD

259

260

To Eagle Point

62

62

261

262

Chiloquin

267

National

Agency Lake

264

263

266

265

Forest

Modoc Point

310

Sprague River

Williamson River

Winema

National

Forest

Williamson River

Winema National Forest

Thompson Reservoir

Fremont

National

Forest

To Lakeview

140

Upper Klamath Lake

97

To White City

268

140

Fremont National Forest

Klamath Falls

Altamont

269

140

Bonanza

Round Lake

To Ashland

66

270

Gerber Reservoir

97

39

Merrill

Malin

OREGON

see Southeast Oregon page 433

308

310

To Dorris, CA

To Tulelake, CA

1 2 3 4 5 6 7 8

a b c d e f g h

1 2
3 4 5
6 7 8

© AVALON TRAVEL PUBLISHING, INC.

The Southern Cascades

(CONTINUED ON NEXT PAGE)

◘ Trout Creek

8

This campground is set along the banks of the South Santiam River, about seven miles east of Cascadia. Fishing and swimming are some of the possibilities here. There is a historical shelter and remains of stonework from the era of the Civilian Conservation Corps. The Trout Creek Trail, just across the highway, is routed into the Menagerie Wilderness. The Long Ranch Elk Viewing Area is immediately west of the campground, and at the Trout Creek Trailhead you'll also find a short trail leading to an elk-viewing platform. Nearby is the Old Santiam Wagon Road.

Location: On the South Santiam River in Willamette National Forest; The Southern Cascades map 1, grid e6.

Campsites, facilities: There are 24 sites for tents, trailers, or RVs up to 22 feet long, including three sites for any length RV. Picnic tables, garbage bins, and fire grills are provided. Drinking water and vault toilets are available. Some facilities are wheelchair-accessible. Leashed pets are permitted.

Reservations, fees: No reservations. Sites are $10 per night, plus $5 for each additional vehicle. Senior discount available. Open May through October.

Directions: From Albany drive east on U.S. 20 for 45 miles (19 miles past Sweet Home) to the campground entrance on the right.

Contact: Willamette National Forest, Sweet Home Ranger District, 3225 U.S. Hwy. 20, Sweet Home, OR 97386; 541/367-5168; fax 541/367-5506.

◙ Yukwah

7

Yukwah campground is in a second-growth Douglas fir forest on the banks of the Santiam River. The camp is a quarter of a mile east of Trout Creek Campground and offers the same recreation possibilities. There is a half-mile-long, compacted-surface interpretive trail at the camp that's barrier-free.

Location: On the Santiam River in Willamette National Forest; The Southern Cascades map 1, grid e6.

Campsites, facilities: There are 19 sites for tents, trailers, or RVs of any length, including a deluxe group site for four or five families and three large RVs. Picnic tables, garbage bins, and fire grills are provided. Drinking water, vault toilets, a large picnic area, and a fishing platform are available. Some facilities are wheelchair-accessible, including a fishing platform. Leashed pets are permitted.

Reservations, fees: No reservations. Sites are $10 per night, plus $5 for each additional vehicle. The deluxe site is $16 per night. Senior discount available. Open May through October.

Directions: From Albany drive east on U.S. 20 for 45 miles (19 miles past Sweet Home) to the campground.

Contact: Willamette National Forest, Sweet Home Ranger District, 3225 U.S. Hwy. 20, Sweet Home, OR 97386; 541/367-5168; fax 541/367-5506.

◘ Fernview

This campground is set high above the confluence of Boulder Creek and the Santiam River just south of the Menagerie Wilderness. A stepped walkway leads down to the river. Just across U.S. 20 lies the Rooster Rock Trail, which leads to—where else?—Rooster Rock, the site of an old lookout tower. The Old Santiam Wagon Road runs through the back of the campground. The camp is better suited for tent and small RV camping; the sites are small.

Location: On the Santiam River in Willamette National Forest; The Southern Cascades map 1, grid e6.

Campsites, facilities: There are 11 sites for tents, trailers, or RVs up to 22 feet long. Picnic tables, garbage bins, and fire grills are provided. Drinking water and vault toilets are available. Some facilities are wheelchair-accessible. Leashed pets are permitted.

Reservations, fees: No reservations. Sites are $10 per night, plus $5 for each additional vehicle. Senior discount available. Open May through September.

Directions: From Albany drive east on U.S. 20 for 49 miles (23 miles past Sweet Home) to the campground entrance on the right.

Contact: Willamette National Forest, Sweet Home Ranger District, 3225 U.S. Hwy. 20, Sweet Home, OR 97386; 541/367-5168; fax 541/367-5506.

❹ House Rock

8

This campground is set at the confluence of Sheep Creek and the South Santiam River. Botany students come here from long distances to see firsthand many uncommon and spectacular specimens of varied plant life. The camp is in the midst of an old-growth forest and is surrounded by huge, majestic Douglas fir. Trout fishing can be good, particularly during summer evenings. History buffs should explore the short loop trail out of camp, which passes by House Rock, a historic shelter for Native Americans, and continues to the historic Old Santiam Wagon Road.

Location: On the Santiam River in Willamette National Forest; The Southern Cascades map 1, grid e8.

Campsites, facilities: There are 17 sites for tents, trailers, or RVs up to 22 feet long. Picnic tables, garbage bins, and fire grills are provided. Vault toilets and drinking water are available. Some facilities are wheelchair-accessible. Leashed pets are permitted.

Reservations, fees: No reservations. Sites are $10 per night, plus $5 for each additional vehicle. Open May through October.

Directions: From Albany drive east on U.S. 20 for 52.5 miles (26.5 miles past Sweet Home) to Squaw Creek Road (Forest Road 2044). Turn right and drive a short distance to the campground.

Contact: Willamette National Forest, Sweet Home Ranger District, 3225 U.S. Hwy. 20, Sweet Home, OR 97386; 541/367-5168; fax 541/367-5506.

❺ Lost Prairie

7

This campground is set along the banks of Hackleman Creek at 3,200 feet in an area of fir, spruce, and Douglas fir. Three excellent hiking trails can be found within five miles of the camp: Hackleman Old-Growth Grove, Cone Peak, and Iron Mountain. The latter two offer spectacular wildflower viewing in the late spring and early summer. This camp is an alternative to nearby Fish Lake.

Location: On Hackleman Creek in Willamette National Forest; The Southern Cascades map 1, grid e8.

Campsites, facilities: There are eight tent sites and two sites for trailers or RVs up to 22 feet long. Picnic tables, garbage bins, and fire grills are provided. Drinking water and vault toilets are available. Some facilities are wheelchair-accessible. Leashed pets are permitted.

Reservations, fees: No reservations. Sites are $8 per night, $4 per night for an additional vehicle. Senior discount available. Open mid-May through October, weather permitting.

Directions: From Albany drive east on U.S. 20 for 63 miles to the camp on the right.

Contact: Willamette National Forest, Sweet Home Ranger District, 3225 U.S. Hwy. 20, Sweet Home, OR 97386; 541/367-5168; fax 541/367-5506.

6 Fish Lake

7

This campground (3,200 feet elevation) is on the shore of Fish Lake, though the "lake" usually dries up by the middle of the summer. Interpretive information is set up at the guard station nearby. Across the road is a trail that follows the Old Santiam Wagon Road and the northern trailhead for the McKenzie River National Recreation Trail. The Clear Lake picnic area is two miles south off Highway 126.

Location: Near Clear Lake in Willamette National Forest; The Southern Cascades map 1, grid e8.

Campsites, facilities: There are eight sites for tents, trailers, or RVs up to 16 feet long. Picnic tables, garbage service, and fire grills are provided. Drinking water and vault toilets are available. Leashed pets are permitted.

Reservations, fees: No reservations. Sites are $6 per night, plus $3 for each additional vehicle. Senior discount available. Open late May to early September.

Directions: From Eugene drive east on Highway 126 for 47 miles to the town of McKenzie Bridge. Continue on Highway 126 for 23 miles to the campground entrance road on the left. Turn left and drive 100 yards to the campground.

Contact: Willamette National Forest, McKenzie Ranger District, 57600 McKenzie Hwy., McKenzie Bridge, OR 97413; 541/822-3381; fax 541/822-7254.

7 Lakes End Boat-In

9

This secluded boat-in campground is set along the shore of the headwaters of Smith Reservoir, a long narrow lake. You'll find no cars and no traffic. The trout fishing in this reservoir can be exceptional, and there's a 10 mph speed limit. The campground is split into two areas, providing camping opportunities on Smith Creek or on the reservoir.

Location: On Smith Reservoir in Willamette National Forest; The Southern Cascades map 1, grid f8.

Campsites, facilities: There are 17 boat-in tent sites. Picnic tables and fire grills are provided. Pit toilets are available, but there is no drinking water, and all garbage must be packed out. Boat docks are nearby. Leashed pets are permitted.

Reservations, fees: No reservations; no fee. Open late April to late September.

Directions: From Eugene drive east on Highway 126 for 47 miles to the town of McKenzie Bridge. Continue on Highway 126 for 13 miles to the signed turnoff for Lakes End at the north end of Trailbridge Reservoir. Turn left on Forest Road 1477 and drive a short distance; then bear left and continue (past Trailbridge Campground) for one-half mile to Forest Road 730 (Smith Reservoir Road). Continue three miles to the boat launch.

Contact: Willamette National Forest, McKenzie Ranger District, 57600 McKenzie Hwy., McKenzie Bridge, OR 97413; 541/822-3381; fax 541/822-7254.

8 Trailbridge

This campground is set along the shore of Trailbridge Reservoir, where boating, fishing, and hiking are recreation options. It's an exceptional spot for car campers. Highway 126 east of McKenzie Bridge is a designated scenic route, providing a pleasant trip to the camp. A good side trip is to take the beautiful 40-minute drive east to the little town of Sisters. From this camp there is access to the McKenzie River National Recreation Trail.

Location: On Trailbridge Reservoir in Willamette National Forest; The Southern Cascades map 1, grid f8.

Campsites, facilities: There are 28 sites for tents and 100-plus sites for trailers or RVs up to 45 feet long, with unlimited RV space at Trailbridge Flats. Picnic tables, garbage service, and fire grills are provided. Drinking water and vault and flush toilets are available. Boat ramps are nearby. Leashed pets are permitted.

Reservations, fees: No reservations. Sites are $6 per night, plus $3 for each additional vehicle. Senior discount available. Open late April to late September.

Directions: From Eugene drive east on Highway 126 for 47 miles to the town of McKenzie Bridge. Continue on Highway 126 for 13 miles to the signed turnoff for Trailbridge Reservoir. Turn left on Forest Road 1477 and drive a short distance; then bear left and continue one-quarter mile to the campground.

Contact: Willamette National Forest, McKenzie Ranger District, 57600 McKenzie Hwy., McKenzie Bridge, OR 97413; 541/822-3381; fax 541/822-7254.

9 Olallie

This campground (2,000 feet elevation) along the banks of the McKenzie River offers opportunities for boating, fishing, and hiking. Other bonuses include easy access from Highway 126. Fishing for rainbow trout usually is good. The campground is two miles southwest of Trailbridge Reservoir off Highway 126.

Location: On the McKenzie River in Willamette National Forest; The Southern Cascades map 1, grid g8.

Campsites, facilities: There are 17 sites for tents, trailers, or RVs up to 30 feet long. Picnic tables, garbage service, and fire grills are provided. Vault toilets and drinking water are available. A boat launch is nearby (non-motorized boats only). Leashed pets are permitted.

Reservations, fees: Reservations accepted ($8.65 reservation fee). Sites are $10 per night, plus $5 for each additional vehicle. Open mid-April through September, weather permitting.

Directions: From Eugene drive east on Highway 126 for 47 miles to the town of McKenzie Bridge. Continue on Highway 126 for 11 miles to the campground on the left.

Contact: Willamette National Forest, McKenzie Ranger District, 57600 McKenzie Hwy., McKenzie Bridge, OR 97413; 541/822-3381, reservations 877/444-6777; fax 541/822-7254; website (for reservations): www.reserveusa.com.

10 Mona

This forested campground is along the shore of Blue River Reservoir, close to where the Blue River joins it. A boat ramp is across the river from the campground. After launching a boat, campers can ground it near the campsite. This camp is extremely popular when the reservoir is full. Lookout Campground (next to the boat launch at Blue River Reservoir) is another option if this camp is full.

Location: Near Blue River Reservoir in Willamette National Forest; The Southern Cascades map 1, grid g6.

Campsites, facilities: There are 23 sites for tents, trailers, or RVs up to 21 feet long. Picnic tables, garbage bins, and fire grills are provided. Drinking water and flush toilets are available. Some facilities are wheelchair-accessible. Leashed pets are permitted.

Reservations, fees: No reservations. Sites are $12–20 per night. Senior discount available. Open mid-April to late September.

Directions: From Eugene drive east on Highway 126 for 41 miles to Blue River. Continue east on Highway 126 for three miles to Forest Road 15. Turn north and drive three miles to the campground.

Contact: Willamette National Forest, Blue River Ranger District, P.O. Box 199, Blue River, OR 97413; 541/822-3317; fax 541/822-1255.

11 Patio RV Park

7

This RV park is near the banks of the South Fork of the McKenzie River, not far from Cougar Lake, which offers opportunities for fishing, swimming, and water-skiing. Nearby recreation options include a golf course, hiking trails, and bike paths.

Location: Near the South Fork of the McKenzie River; The Southern Cascades map 1, grid g6.

Campsites, facilities: There are 60 sites for trailers or RVs of any length in this adult-only RV park. Electricity, drinking water, sewer hookups, and picnic tables are provided. Flush toilets, ice, showers, firewood, a recreation hall, video rentals, full group kitchen facilities, cable TV, and a laundry room are available. A store and a café are within two miles. Leashed pets are permitted.

Reservations, fees: Reservations accepted. Sites are $22–24 per night. Open year-round, weather permitting.

Directions: From Eugene drive east on Highway 126 for 37 miles to the town of Blue River. Continue east on Highway 126 for six miles to McKenzie River Drive. Turn east and drive two miles to the park on the right.

Contact: Patio RV Park, 55636 McKenzie River Dr., Blue River, OR 97413; 541/822-3596; fax 541/822-8292.

12 Delta

8

This is a popular campground along the banks of the McKenzie River. It is set in a heavily forested spot, primarily with old-growth Douglas fir. The Delta Old Growth Nature Trail, a half-mile wheelchair-accessible interpretive trail, is adjacent to the campground. There is an amphitheater in the camp. Nearby are Blue River and Cougar Reservoirs (seven and five miles away, respectively), both of which offer trout fishing, water-skiing, and swimming.

Location: On the McKenzie River in Willamette National Forest; The Southern Cascades map 1, grid g6.

Campsites, facilities: There are 38 sites for tents, trailers, or RVs up to 21 feet long. Picnic tables, garbage bins, and fire grills are provided. Drinking water and vault toilets are available. Some facilities are wheelchair-accessible. Leashed pets are permitted.

Reservations, fees: No reservations. Sites are $12–20 per night. Senior discount available. Open mid-May to late September.

Directions: From Eugene drive east on Highway 126 for 37 miles to the town of Blue River. Continue east on Highway 126 for five miles to Forest Road 19 (Aufderheide Scenic Byway). Turn south (right) and drive one-quarter mile to Forest Road 400. Turn right and drive one mile to the campground.

Contact: Willamette National Forest, Blue River Ranger District, P.O. Box 199, Blue River, OR 97413; 541/822-3317; fax 541/822-1255.

⓭ McKenzie Bridge

8

This campground (1,400 feet elevation) is set along the banks of the McKenzie River, one mile from the town of McKenzie Bridge. There is good evening fly-fishing for trout during summer on this stretch of river.

Location: On the McKenzie River in Willamette National Forest; The Southern Cascades map 1, grid g7.

Campsites, facilities: There are 20 sites for tents, trailers, or RVs up to 35 feet long. Picnic tables, garbage service, and fire rings are provided. Vault toilets and drinking water are available. A grocery store, gasoline, restaurants, and a pay phone are available within one mile. Leashed pets are permitted. Only nonmotorized boats are permitted.

Reservations, fees: Reservations accepted ($8.65 reservation fee). Sites are $10 per night, plus $5 for each additional vehicle. Senior discount available. Open late April to early September.

Directions: From Eugene drive east on Highway 126 for 46 miles to the campground entrance on the right (one mile west of the town of McKenzie Bridge).

Contact: Willamette National Forest, McKenzie Ranger District, 57600 McKenzie Hwy., McKenzie Bridge, OR 97413; 541/822-3381, reservations 877/444-6777; fax 541/

822-7254; website (for reservations): www.reserveusa.com.

⓮ Horse Creek Group Camp

9

This campground (1,400 feet elevation) reserved for groups is on the banks of Horse Creek near the town of McKenzie Bridge. In spite of the name, no horse camping is permitted, and fishing is catch-and-release only.

Location: On Horse Creek in Willamette National Forest; The Southern Cascades map 1, grid g7.

Campsites, facilities: There are 21 sites for tents, trailers, or RVs up to 35 feet long. Picnic tables, garbage service, and fire grills are provided. Drinking water and vault toilets are available. Leashed pets are permitted.

Reservations, fees: Reservations accepted ($8.65 reservation fee). Group sites are $40–60 per night. Senior discount available. Open late April through October.

Directions: From Eugene drive east on Highway 126 for 47 miles to the town of McKenzie Bridge and Horse Creek Road. Turn right (south) on Horse Creek Road and drive three miles to the campground on the left.

Contact: Willamette National Forest, McKenzie Ranger District, 57600 McKenzie Hwy., McKenzie Bridge, OR 97413; 541/822-3381, reservations 877/444-6777; fax 541/822-7254; website (for reservations): www.reserveusa.com.

⓯ Paradise

9

This campground (1,600 feet elevation) along the banks of the McKenzie River may be right off the highway, but it's in a rustic, streamside setting with access to the

McKenzie River National Recreation Trail. Trout fishing can be good here.

Location: On the McKenzie River in Willamette National Forest; The Southern Cascades map 1, grid g7.

Campsites, facilities: There are 64 sites for tents, trailers, or RVs up to 40 feet long. Picnic tables, garbage service, and fire rings are provided. Flush, vault, and pit toilets, drinking water, a boat ramp, and firewood are available. Leashed pets are permitted.

Reservations, fees: Reservations accepted ($8.65 reservation fee). Sites are $12 per night, plus $6 for each additional vehicle, and double sites are $20 per night. Senior discount available. Open late April to mid-October.

Directions: From Eugene drive east on Highway 126 for 47 miles to the town of McKenzie Bridge. Continue east on Highway 126 for 3.5 miles to the campground on the left.

Contact: Willamette National Forest, McKenzie Ranger District, 57600 McKenzie Hwy., McKenzie Bridge, OR 97413; 541/822-3381, reservations 877/444-6777; fax 541/822-7254; website (for reservations): www.reserveusa.com.

16 Belknap Springs Lodge

 9

This beautiful park has been featured on at least one magazine cover. It's in a wooded, mountainous area on the McKenzie River. Trout fishing can be excellent here. If you're looking for hiking opportunities, check out the Three Sisters and Mt. Washington Wilderness Areas, both accessible by driving west of Sisters on Highway 242. These are exceptionally scenic and pristine expanses of forest and well worth exploring. The Pacific Crest Trail runs north and south through both wilderness areas.

Location: On the McKenzie River; The Southern Cascades map 1, grid h7.

Campsites, facilities: There are 15 sites for tents and 42 sites for trailers or RVs with electrical and water hookups, and some with sewer hookups. There is also a lodge with 19 rooms, and six cabins are also available. Drinking water, restrooms, showers, a sanitary dump, and a public phone are provided. Recreational facilities include a hot-spring fed swimming pool, a recreation field, and a recreation hall. Some facilities are wheelchair-accessible. Leashed pets are permitted at the campground and in three of the cabins. Pets are not permitted in the other cabins and lodge rooms.

Reservations, fees: Reservations are recommended. Sites are $19–22 per night, lodge rooms are $80–200 per night, and cabins are $55–200 per night. Open year-round.

Directions: From Eugene drive east on Highway 126 for 56 miles to Belknap Spring Road. Turn left and drive a half mile. The road dead-ends at the lodge.

Contact: Belknap Springs Lodge, P.O. Box 2001, 59296 Belknap Springs Rd., McKenzie Bridge, OR 97413; 541/822-3512; fax 541/822-3327.

17 Slide Creek

6

This campground sits on a hillside overlooking Cougar Reservoir, which covers about 1,300 acres, has a paved boat landing, and offers opportunities for fishing, swimming, and water-skiing. The pretty lakeside camp is quite popular, so plan to arrive early on weekends. If this camp is full, Cougar Crossing (off Road 19) and Sunnyside (off Road 500) are nearby options.

Location: On Cougar Reservoir in Willamette National Forest; The Southern Cascades map 1, grid g8.

Campsites, facilities: There are 16 sites for tents, trailers, or RVs. Picnic tables, garbage bins, and fire grills are provided. Drinking water and vault toilets are available. A boat ramp is available. Leashed pets are permitted.

Reservations, fees: No reservations. Sites are $12–20 per night. Senior discount available. Open mid-May to mid-September.

Directions: From Eugene drive east on Highway 126 for 41 miles to the town of Blue River. Continue east on Highway 126 for five miles to Aufderheide Scenic Byway. Turn south (right) and drive 11 miles (along the west shore of Cougar Reservoir, crossing the reservoir bridge) to Eastside Road (Forest Road 500). Turn left and drive 1.5 miles northeast to the campground set on the southeast shore of the lake.

Contact: Willamette National Forest, Blue River Ranger District, P.O. Box 199, Blue River, OR 97413; 541/822-3317; fax 541/822-1255.

18 French Pete

 8

This quiet, wooded campground is on the banks of the South Fork of the McKenzie River and French Pete Creek. Fishing is catch-and-release only. A trail across the road from the campground provides access to the Three Sisters Wilderness. French Pete is only two miles from Cougar Reservoir, and the camp attracts campers wanting to use Cougar Reservoir facilities. Two more primitive camps (Homestead and Frissell Crossing) are a few miles southeast on the same road.

Location: On the South Fork of the McKenzie River in Willamette National Forest; The Southern Cascades map 1, grid h7.

Campsites, facilities: There are 17 sites for tents, trailers, or RVs. Picnic tables, garbage

containers, and fire grills are provided. Drinking water and vault toilets are available. Some facilities are wheelchair-accessible. Leashed pets are permitted.

Reservations, fees: No reservations. Sites are $12–20 per night. Senior discount available. Open mid-May to mid-September.

Directions: From Eugene drive east on Highway 126 for 41 miles to the town of Blue River. Continue east on Highway 126 for five miles to Forest Road 19 (Aufderheide Scenic Byway). Turn south (right) and drive 12 miles to the campground.

Contact: Willamette National Forest, Blue River Ranger District, P.O. Box 199, Blue River, OR 97413; 541/822-3317; fax 541/822-1255.

19 Coldwater Cove

 10

This campground (3,000 feet elevation) is on the south shore of Clear Lake, a spring-fed lake formed by a natural lava dam and the source of the McKenzie River. No motors are permitted on the lake, making it ideal for anglers in rowboats or canoes. The northern section of the McKenzie River National Recreation Trail passes by the camp.

Location: On Clear Lake in Willamette National Forest; The Southern Cascades map 2, grid f1.

Campsites, facilities: There are 35 sites for tents, trailers, or RVs up to 30 feet long. Picnic tables, garbage service, and fire grills are provided. Drinking water and vault toilets are available. Some facilities are wheelchair-accessible. Boat docks, launching facilities, rowboats, a store, a café, and cabin rentals are available nearby at Clear Lake Resort. Leashed pets are permitted.

Reservations, fees: Reservations accepted ($8.65

reservation fee). Sites are $12 per night, plus $6 for each additional vehicle. Open late May to early October.

Directions: From Eugene drive east on Highway 126 for 47 miles to the town of McKenzie Bridge. Continue on Highway 126 for 14 miles to Forest Road 770. Turn right (east) and drive to the campground.

Contact: Willamette National Forest, McKenzie Ranger District, 57600 McKenzie Hwy., McKenzie Bridge, OR 97413; 541/822-3381, reservations 877/444-6777; fax 541/822-7254; website (for reservations): www.reserveusa.com.

20 Ice Cap

This campground (3,000 feet elevation) is set on a hill above Carmen Reservoir, which was created by a dam on the McKenzie River. The McKenzie River National Recreation Trail passes by the camp, and Koosah Falls and Sahalie Falls are nearby. Clear Lake, a popular local vacation destination, is two miles away.

Location: On Carmen Reservoir in Willamette National Forest; The Southern Cascades map 2, grid f1.

Campsites, facilities: There are 11 tent sites and 11 sites for tents, trailers, or RVs up to 16 feet long. Picnic tables, garbage service, and fire grills are provided. Drinking water and flush toilets, boat-launching facilities, and boat rentals are about two miles away at Clear Lake Resort. Only nonmotorized boats are allowed on Carmen Reservoir. Leashed pets are permitted.

Reservations, fees: No reservations. Sites are $10 per night, plus $5 for each additional vehicle. Senior discount available. Open mid-May to mid-September.

Directions: From Eugene drive east on Highway 126 for 47 miles to the town of

McKenzie Bridge. Continue on Highway 126 for 19 miles to the campground entrance road on the left. Turn left and drive 200 yards to the campground.

Contact: Willamette National Forest, McKenzie Ranger District, 57600 McKenzie Hwy., McKenzie Bridge, OR 97413; 541/822-3381, reservations 877/444-6777; fax 541/822-7254; website (for reservations): www.reserveusa.com.

21 Big Lake

This jewel of a spot on the north shore of Big Lake at 4,650 feet elevation offers a host of activities, including fishing, swimming, water-skiing, and hiking. Big Lake has heavy motorized boat use. One of the better hikes is the five-mile wilderness loop trail (Patjens Lakes Trail) that heads out from the south shore of the lake and cuts past a few small lakes before returning. There's a great view of Mt. Washington from the lake. The Pacific Crest Trail is only one-half mile away.

Location: On Big Lake in Willamette National Forest; The Southern Cascades map 2, grid e1.

Campsites, facilities: There are 49 sites for tents, trailers, or RVs up to 16 feet long. Picnic tables, garbage service, and fire grills are provided. Drinking water and vault and flush toilets are available. Boat ramps and launching facilities are nearby. Leashed pets are permitted.

Reservations, fees: Reservations accepted ($8.65 reservation fee). Sites are $12 per night, plus $6 for each additional vehicle. Senior discount available. Open mid-June to early October.

Directions: From Eugene drive east on Highway 126 for 47 miles to the town of McKenzie Bridge. Continue northeast on Highway 126 for 40 miles to Big Lake Road (Forest Road

2690). Turn right and drive three miles to the campground on the left.

Contact: Willamette National Forest, McKenzie Ranger District, 57600 McKenzie Hwy., McKenzie Bridge, OR 97413; 541/822-3381, reservations 877/444-6777; fax 541/822-7254; website (for reservations): www.reserveusa.com.

22 Big Lake West Walk-In

 9

This spot, at an elevation of 4,650 feet west of the Big Lake Campground, has many of the same attractions, but the walk-in sites offer some seclusion and quiet. The Mt. Washington Wilderness and Patjens Lake access trails can be reached from here. See the description of Big Lake Campground.

Location: On Big Lake in Willamette National Forest; The Southern Cascades map 2, grid e1.

Campsites, facilities: There are 11 walk-in sites (only 200 feet from the road). Fire pits, garbage service, and picnic tables are provided. Drinking water and vault toilets are available. Leashed pets permitted.

Reservations, fees: No reservations. Sites are $16 per night, plus $8 for each additional vehicle, and double sites are $30 per night. Open late May to early October.

Directions: From Eugene drive east on Highway 126 for 47 miles to the town of McKenzie Bridge. Continue northeast on Highway 126 for 40 miles to Big Lake Road (Forest Road 2690). Turn right and drive four miles to the campground entrance on the left.

Contact: Willamette National Forest, McKenzie Ranger District, 57600 McKenzie Hwy., McKenzie Bridge, OR 97413; 541/822-3381, reservations 877/444-6777; fax 541/822-7254; website (for reservations): www.reserveusa.com.

23 South Shore

6

This campground is at 3,500 feet on the south shore of Suttle Lake, where water-skiing is permitted. A hiking trail winds around the lake. Fishing and windsurfing are other popular activities. The camp often fills up on weekends and holidays; reserve early. Quite a few dead trees have recently been removed, so the campground is now more open and spacious.

Location: On Suttle Lake in Deschutes National Forest; The Southern Cascades map 2, grid e3.

Campsites, facilities: There are 38 sites for tents, trailers, or RVs up to 40 feet long. Picnic tables, garbage service, and fire grills are provided. Drinking water and vault toilets are available. A fish-cleaning station, boat docks, launching facilities, and rentals are nearby. Leashed pets are permitted.

Reservations, fees: Reservations accepted ($8.65 reservation fee). Sites are $12 per night, $6 per night for an additional vehicle. Senior discount available. Open mid-April to late September.

Directions: From Albany, drive east on U.S. 20 to the junction with Highway 126. Continue east on Highway 126 for 12 miles to Forest Road 2070 (Suttle Lake). Turn right and proceed a short distance to the campground.

Contact: Deschutes National Forest, Sisters Ranger District, P.O. Box 249, Sisters, OR 97759; 541/549-7700, reservations 877/444-6777; fax 541/549-7746; website (for reservations): www.reserveusa.com.

24 Link Creek

 6

This campground (elevation 3,450 feet) is set at the west end of Suttle Lake. It's popular with water-skiers; the high-speed boating area is on this end of the lake. See the description of South Shore for recreation details.

Location: On Suttle Lake in Deschutes National Forest; The Southern Cascades map 2, grid e3.

Campsites, facilities: There are 33 sites for tents, trailers, or RVs up to 40 feet long. Picnic tables, garbage service, and fire grills are provided. Drinking water and vault toilets are available. Boat docks, launching facilities, and rentals are nearby. Leashed pets are permitted.

Reservations, fees: Reservations accepted ($8.65 reservation fee). Sites are $12 per night, $6 per night for an additional vehicle. Senior discount available. Open mid-April to mid-October.

Directions: From Albany drive east on U.S. 20 for 74 miles to the junction of U.S. 20 and Highway 126. Continue east on Highway 126 for 12 miles to Forest Road 2070 (Suttle Lake). Turn right and drive a short distance to the campground.

Contact: Deschutes National Forest, Sisters Ranger District, P.O. Box 249, Sisters, OR 97759; 541/549-7700, reservations 877/444-6777; fax 541/549-7746; website (for reservations): www.reserveusa.com.

25 Blue Bay

 7

This campground is set along the south shore of Suttle Lake, the low-speed end of the lake. It's a quieter campground, with more tree cover than South Shore or Link Creek. See the description of South Shore for recreation details.

Location: On Suttle Lake in Deschutes National Forest; The Southern Cascades map 2, grid e3.

Campsites, facilities: There are 25 sites for tents, trailers, or RVs up to 30 feet long. Picnic tables, garbage service, and fire grills are provided. Drinking water and vault toilets are available. A fish-cleaning station, boat docks, launching facilities, and rentals are nearby. Leashed pets are permitted.

Reservations, fees: Reservations accepted ($8.65 reservation fee). Sites are $12 per night, $6 per night for an additional vehicle. Senior discount available. Open mid-April to mid-October.

Directions: From Albany drive east on U.S. 20 for 74 miles to the junction of U.S. 20 and Highway 126. Continue east on Highway 126 for 12 miles to Forest Road 2070 (Suttle Lake). Turn right and drive a short distance to the campground.

Contact: Deschutes National Forest, Sisters Ranger District, P.O. Box 249, Sisters, OR 97759; 541/549-7700, reservations 877/444-6777; fax 541/549-7746; website (for reservations): www.reserveusa.com.

26 Scout Lake

5

This campground with a mix of sunny and shady sites is about half a mile from Suttle Lake and is a good spot for swimming and hiking. The camp is available for groups of up to 100 campers; reservations are required.

Location: On Scout Lake in Deschutes National Forest; The Southern Cascades map 2, grid e3.

Campsites, facilities: There are 10 sites for tents, trailers, or RVs up to 40 feet long. Picnic tables, garbage service, and fire grills are provided. Vault toilets and drinking water are available. Also available are a picnic shelter, volleyball court, and horseshoe pits. Leashed pets are permitted in the campground only (not in the day-use area).

Reservations, fees: Reservations accepted ($8.65 reservation fee). Sites are $11–25 per night, $5 per night for an additional vehicle. Open mid-April to mid-September.

Directions: From Eugene drive east on Highway 126 for 74 miles to the junction of U.S. 20 and Highway 126. Continue east on Highway 126 for 12 miles to Forest Road 2070 (Suttle Lake). Turn right and drive to Forest Road 2066. Turn left and drive less than one mile to the campground.

Contact: Deschutes National Forest, Sisters Ranger District, P.O. Box 249, Sisters, OR 97759; 541/549-7700, reservations 877/444-6777; fax 541/549-7746; website (for reservations): www.reserveusa.com.

27 Camp Sherman

6

Camp Sherman is set at an elevation of 2,950 feet along the banks of the Metolius River, where you can fish for wild trout. This place is for expert fly anglers seeking a quality fishing experience. It's advisable to obtain a map of the Deschutes National Forest that details back roads, trails, and streams. This is one of five camps in the immediate area.

Location: On the Metolius River in Deschutes National Forest; The Southern Cascades map 2, grid e3.

Campsites, facilities: There are 15 sites for tents, trailers, or RVs up to 40 feet long. Picnic tables, garbage service, and fire grills are provided. Vault toilets, a picnic shelter, and drinking water are available. Leashed pets are permitted.

Reservations, fees: No reservations. Sites are $12 per night, $6 per night for an addi-

tional vehicle. Senior discount available. Open April to mid-October.

Directions: From Albany drive east on U.S. 20 for 87 miles (near Black Butte) to the sign for Camp Sherman and Forest Road 14. Turn left on Forest Road 14 and drive five miles to Camp Sherman, the store, and Forest Road 900. Turn left on Forest Road 900 and drive one-half mile to the campground on the left.

Contact: Deschutes National Forest, Sisters Ranger District, P.O. Box 249, Sisters, OR 97759; 541/549-7700; fax 541/549-7746.

28 Allingham

5

This campground along the banks of the Metolius River is one of five camps in the immediate area. See the description of Camp Sherman for area details.

Location: On the Metolius River in Deschutes National Forest; The Southern Cascades map 2, grid e3.

Campsites, facilities: There are 10 sites for tents, trailers, or RVs up to 40 feet long. Picnic tables, garbage service, and fire grills are provided. Vault toilets and drinking water are available. A sanitary disposal station is nearby. Leashed pets are permitted.

Reservations, fees: No reservations. Sites are $12 per night, $6 per night for an additional vehicle. Senior discount available. Open April through mid-October.

Directions: From Albany drive east on U.S. 20 for 87 miles (near Black Butte) to the sign for Camp Sherman and Forest Road 14. Turn left on Forest Road 14 and drive five miles to Camp Sherman, the store, and Forest Road 900. Turn left on Forest Road 900 and drive one mile to the campground on the left.

Contact: Deschutes National Forest, Sisters Ranger

District, P.O. Box 249, Sisters, OR 97759; 541/549-7700; fax 541/549-7746.

29 Black Butte Motel and RV Park

 6

This RV park offers a choice of graveled or grassy sites in a clean, scenic environment. See the description of Camp Sherman for more area information.

Location: Near the Metolius River; The Southern Cascades map 2, grid e3.

Campsites, facilities: There are 30 sites with full hookups and 11 sites with partial hookups for trailers or RVs of any length. Electricity, drinking water, sewer hookups, and picnic tables are provided. Flush toilets, showers, firewood, and a laundry room are available. Bottled gas, sanitary services, a store, a café, and ice are within one block. Leashed pets and motorbikes are permitted.

Reservations, fees: Reservations encouraged. Sites are $12–21 per night. Senior discount available. Open year-round.

Directions: From Albany drive east on U.S. 20 for 87 miles (near Black Butte) to the sign for Camp Sherman. Turn north on Forest Road 1419 and drive 4.5 miles to a stop sign and the camp access road. Turn right and drive one-half mile to the campground on the right.

Contact: Black Butte Motel and RV Park, 25635 S.W. Forest Rd. 1419, Camp Sherman, OR 97730; 877/595-6514; fax 541/595-5971; website: www.blackbutte-resort.com.

30 Pine Rest

 5

This campground is set at an elevation of 2,900 feet along the banks of the Metolius River. See the description of Camp Sherman for more information.

Location: On the Metolius River in Deschutes National Forest; The Southern Cascades map 2, grid e3.

Campsites, facilities: There are eight tent sites. Picnic tables, garbage service, and fire grills are provided. Vault toilets, a picnic shelter, and drinking water are available. Leashed pets are permitted.

Reservations, fees: No reservations. Sites are $12 per night, $6 per night for an additional vehicle. Senior discount available. Open April through mid-October.

Directions: From Albany drive east on U.S. 20 for 87 miles (near Black Butte) to the sign for Camp Sherman and Forest Road 14. Turn left on Forest Road 14 and drive five miles to Camp Sherman, the store, and Forest Road 900. Turn left on Forest Road 900 and drive two miles to the campground on the left.

Contact: Deschutes National Forest, Sisters Ranger District, P.O. Box 249, Sisters, OR 97759; 541/549-7700; fax 541/549-7746.

31 Gorge

 5

Here is another of the camps set along the banks of the Metolius River. This campground is more open with less vegetation than many of the others, and it is set at an elevation of 2,900 feet. See the description of Camp Sherman for more details.

Location: On the Metolius River in Deschutes National Forest; The Southern Cascades map 2, grid e3.

Campsites, facilities: There are 18 sites for tents, trailers, or RVs up to 22 feet long. A few of the sites can accommodate RVs up to 40 feet long. Picnic tables, garbage service, and fire grills are provided. Vault toilets and drinking water are available. Leashed pets are permitted.

Reservations, fees: No reservations. Sites are $10 per night, plus $5 for each additional vehicle. Senior discount available. Open April through mid-October.

Directions: From Albany drive east on U.S. 20 for 87 miles (near Black Butte) to the sign for Camp Sherman and Forest Road 14. Turn left on Forest Road 14 and drive five miles to Camp Sherman, the store, and Forest Road 900. Turn left on Forest Road 900 and drive 2.5 miles to the campground on the left.

Contact: Deschutes National Forest, Sisters Ranger District, P.O. Box 249, Sisters, OR 97759; 541/549-7700; fax 541/549-7746.

32 Smiling River

5

Here's another camp along the banks of the Metolius River. It's set at an elevation of 2,900 feet. See the description of Camp Sherman for more details.

Location: On the Metolius River in Deschutes National Forest; The Southern Cascades map 2, grid e3.

Campsites, facilities: There are 37 sites for tents, trailers, or RVs up to 30 feet long. A few sites can accommodate RVs up to 40 feet in length. Picnic tables, garbage service, and fire grills are provided. Vault toilets and drinking water are available. Leashed pets are permitted.

Reservations, fees: No reservations. Sites are $12 per night, $6 per night for an additional vehicle. Senior discount available. Open May through mid-October.

Directions: From Albany drive east on U.S. 20 for 87 miles (near Black Butte) to the sign for Camp Sherman and Forest Road 14. Turn left on Forest Road 14 and drive five miles to Camp Sherman, the store, and Forest Road 900. Turn left on Forest Road 900 and drive one mile to the campground on the left.

Contact: Deschutes National Forest, Sisters Ranger District, P.O. Box 249, Sisters, OR 97759; 541/549-7700; fax 541/549-7746.

33 Allen Springs

7

This shady campground is in a conifer forest along the banks of the Metolius River, where fishing and hiking can be good. For an interesting side trip, head to the Wizard Falls Fish Hatchery about a mile away.

Location: On the Metolius River in Deschutes National Forest; The Southern Cascades map 2, grid e3.

Campsites, facilities: There are three tent sites and 12 sites for tents, trailers, or RVs up to 22 feet long. Picnic tables, garbage service, and fire grills are provided. Vault toilets and drinking water are available. A store, a café, and ice are within five miles. Leashed pets are permitted.

Reservations, fees: No reservations. Sites are $12 per night, $6 per night for an additional vehicle. Senior discount available. Open April-mid October.

Directions: From Albany drive east on U.S. 20 for 87 miles (near Black Butte) to the sign for Camp Sherman and Forest Road 14. Turn left on Forest Road 14 and drive about nine miles to the campground on the left.

Contact: Deschutes National Forest, Sisters Ranger District, P.O. Box 249, Sisters, OR 97759; 541/549-7700; fax 541/549-7746.

34 Lower Bridge

6

This campground is set along the banks of the Metolius River. See the description of Camp Sherman for details about the area. This camp is similar to Pioneer Ford, but with less vegetation.

Location: On the Metolius River in Deschutes National Forest; The Southern Cascades map 2, grid e3.

Campsites, facilities: There are 12 sites for tents, trailers, or RVs up to 22 feet long. Picnic tables, garbage service, and fire grills are provided. Vault toilets and drinking water are available. Leashed pets are permitted.

Reservations, fees: No reservations. Sites are $12 per night, $6 per night for an additional vehicle. Senior discount available. Open April-mid-October.

Directions: From Albany drive east on U.S. 20 for 87 miles (near Black Butte) to the sign for Camp Sherman and Forest Road 14. Turn left on Forest Road 14 and drive 12 miles to the campground on the left.

Contact: Deschutes National Forest, Sisters Ranger District, P.O. Box 249, Sisters, OR 97759; 541/549-7700; fax 541/549-7746.

35 Pioneer Ford

7

This quiet and serene wooded campground with grassy sites is along the banks of the Metolius River. See the description of Camp Sherman for recreation options.

Location: On the Metolius River in Deschutes National Forest; The Southern Cascades map 2, grid e3.

Campsites, facilities: There are two tent sites and 18 sites for tents, trailers, or RVs up to 40 feet long. Drinking water, garbage service, and fire grills are provided. Vault toilets, a barrier-free picnic shelter, and firewood are available. Leashed pets are permitted.

Reservations, fees: No reservations. Sites are $12 per night, $6 per night for an additional vehicle. Senior discount available. Open April through September.

Directions: From Albany drive east on U.S. 20 for 87 miles (near Black Butte) to the sign

for Camp Sherman and Forest Road 14. Turn left on Forest Road 14 and drive 11 miles to the campground on the left.

Contact: Deschutes National Forest, Sisters Ranger District, P.O. Box 249, Sisters, OR 97759; 541/549-7700; fax 541/549-7746.

36 Cold Springs Resort and RV Park

7

This pretty, wooded RV park on the Metolius River with an acre of riverfront lawn is world-famous for its fly-fishing. Nearby recreation options include a golf course, swimming, boating, water-skiing, windsurfing, hiking and biking trails, a riding stable, and tennis courts. Winter activities vary from alpine and Nordic skiing to sledding, snowmobiling, and winter camping. There is a private bridge from the resort to Camp Sherman, and the towns of Sisters and Bend are nearby (15 miles and 35 miles, respectively).

Location: On the Metolius River; The Southern Cascades map 2, grid e3.

Campsites, facilities: There are 45 sites with full hookups for trailers or RVs of any length, plus five cabins on the river. Fire pits, picnic tables, and patios are provided. Restrooms, showers, laundry facilities, firewood, and a riverfront picnic facility are available. Bottled gas, a store with groceries, fishing and sport supplies, a café, a coin-operated laundry, a post office, and ice are within one-quarter mile. Leashed pets are permitted.

Reservations, fees: Reservations accepted. Sites are $18–20 per night; cabins are $98–123 per night, depending on the season and the number of people. Open year-round.

Directions: From Albany drive east on U.S. 20 for 87 miles (near Black Butte) to the sign for Camp Sherman. Turn north and drive about five miles to the stop sign. Turn right at the stop sign and drive about 300 feet to Cold Springs Resort Lane. Turn right and drive through the forest and the meadow, crossing Cold Springs Creek, to the resort.

Contact: Cold Springs Resort and RV Park, 25615 Cold Springs Resort Ln., Camp Sherman, OR 97730; 541/595-6271; fax 541/595-1400; website: www.coldpsrings-resort.com

37 Riverside Walk-In

7

This campground is set 100 yards back from the banks of the Metolius River, less than a mile from Metolius Springs at the base of Black Butte. Because it's a tent-only campground and just far enough off the highway to be missed by most other people, it's very quiet; you'll find plenty of solitude here. After parking along the road, you must walk to the campsites, carrying your gear in the process.

Location: On the Metolius River in Deschutes National Forest; The Southern Cascades map 2, grid e3.

Campsites, facilities: There are 16 tent sites. Picnic tables and fire grills are provided. Vault toilets, garbage service, and drinking water are available. Leashed pets are permitted.

Reservations, fees: No reservations. Sites are $10 per night, $5 per night for an additional vehicle. Senior discount available. Open mid-April through September.

Directions: From Albany drive east on U.S. 20 for 87 miles to the sign for Camp Sherman and Forest Road 14. Turn left and drive five miles to Forest Road 800. Turn left and drive a short distance to the campground.

Contact: Deschutes National Forest, Sisters Ranger District, P.O. Box 249, Sisters, OR 97759; 541/549-7700; fax 541/549-7746.

38 Haystack Reservoir

5

This campground can be found in the high desert along the shore of Haystack Reservoir, where water-skiing, swimming, and fishing are some of the recreation options. There's lots of sheltering between sites and a view of Mt. Jefferson. The camping and fishing crowds are rated as moderate numbers.

Location: On Haystack Reservoir in Crooked River National Grassland; The Southern Cascades map 2, grid e7.

Campsites, facilities: There are 23 sites for tents, trailers, or RVs up to 22 feet long. Picnic tables and fire grills are provided. Vault toilets and drinking water are available. A store, a café, and ice are within five miles. Boat docks, launching facilities, and rentals are nearby. Leashed pets are permitted.

Reservations, fees: No reservations. Sites are $8 per night, plus $3 for each additional vehicle. Open mid-May through September.

Directions: From Madras drive south on U.S. 97 for nine miles to County Road 100. Turn southeast and drive three miles to Forest Road 96. Turn north and drive one-half mile to the campground.

Note: This camp is set along Haystack Reservoir, a bright spot in a expansive desert landscape. The camps feature a moderate amount of privacy, as well as views of nearby Mt. Jefferson. Haystack Lake receives moderate numbers of people who boat, water-ski, swim or fish.

Contact: Crooked River National Grassland, 813 S.W. Hwy. 97, Madras, OR 97741; 541/416-6640; fax 541/416-6694; website: www.fs.fed.us/r6/ochoco.

39 KOA Sisters

7

This park is amid wooded mountains outside of Sisters at an elevation of 3,200 feet. Branchwater Lake offers swimming and good trout fishing. See the description of Belknap Springs Lodge for information about the surrounding area.

Location: On Branchwater Lake; The Southern Cascades map 2, grid f4.

Campsites, facilities: There are 64 sites for tents, trailers, or RVs. Drinking water, air-conditioning, electric heat, cable TV, restrooms, showers, a sanitary dump, security, a public phone, a laundry room, limited groceries, ice, snacks, RV supplies, LP gas, and a barbecue are available. Recreational facilities include a sports field, a playground, a game room, horseshoes, a spa, and a heated swimming pool. Some facilities are wheelchair-accessible. Leashed pets are permitted.

Reservations, fees: Reservations recommended. Sites are $20–29 per night. Open year-round.

Directions: From Eugene drive east on Highway 126 to its junction with U.S. 20. Turn east and drive 26 miles to Sisters. Continue southeast on U.S. 20 for three miles to the park on the right side of the highway.

Contact: KOA Sisters, 67667 Hwy. 20 W, Bend, OR 97701; 541/549-3021; fax 541/549-8144; website: www.koa.com.

40 Crooked River Ranch RV Park

6

Spectacular wildlife abounds in this area. This campground is a short distance from Smith Rock State Park, which contains unusual, colorful volcanic formations overlooking the Crooked River Canyon. Lake Billy Chinook to the north is a good spot for water-skiing and fishing for bass and panfish. The park has a basketball court and a softball field; nearby recreation options include fishing, golf, and tennis. One of Oregon's nicest golf courses is nearby.

Location: Near Smith Rock State Park; The Southern Cascades map 2, grid f7.

Campsites, facilities: There are 40 tent sites and 88 sites for trailers or RVs of any length; 15 are drive-through sites. Electricity, drinking water, and sewer hookups are provided. Flush toilets, sanitary services, cable TV, showers, a store, a café, laundry facilities, ice, a playground, and a swimming pool are available. Leashed pets are permitted.

Reservations, fees: Reservations accepted. Sites are $12–21 per night. Senior discount available. Open mid-March through late October.

Directions: From Redmond drive north on U.S. 97 for six miles to Lower Bridge Way. Turn west on Lower Bridge Way at Terrebonne and drive to 43rd Street. Turn right and drive seven miles (the road names changes to Chinook, then to Clubhouse Road) to Hays Lane. Turn right on Hays Lane and drive one-quarter mile to the park.

Contact: Crooked River Ranch RV Park, P.O. Box 1448, Crooked River Ranch, OR 97760; 800/841-0563 or 541/923-1441; fax 541/548-0278; website: www.crookedriverranch.com.

41 Indian Ford

4

This campground is on the banks of Indian Ford Creek at an elevation of 3,250 feet. There's a lot of traffic noise from U.S. 20. The camp is used primarily by overnighters on their way to the town of Sisters. The campground is sprinkled with aspen trees, and great bird-watching opportunities are available.

Location: On Indian Ford Creek in Deschutes National Forest; The Southern Cascades map 2, grid f4.

Campsites, facilities: There are 25 sites for tents, trailers, or RVs up to 40 feet long. Picnic tables, garbage service, and fire grills are provided. Vault toilets are available. There is no drinking water. Leashed pets are permitted.

Reservations, fees: No reservations. Sites are $8 per night, $4 per night for an additional vehicle. Senior discount available. Open May through mid-October.

Directions: From Albany, drive east on U.S. 20 to the junction with Highway 126. Continue east on Highway 126 and drive 21 miles to the campground on the left.

Contact: Deschutes National Forest, Sisters Ranger District, P.O. Box 249, Sisters, OR 97759; 541/549-7700; fax 541/549-7746.

42 Cold Springs

7

This wooded campground is set at 3,400 feet along the source of a small creek. It's just far enough off the main drag to be missed by many campers. Spring and early summer are the times for great bird-watching in the area's abundant aspen.

Location: In Deschutes National Forest; The Southern Cascades map 2, grid f4.

Campsites, facilities: There are 23 sites for tents, trailers, or RVs up to 40 feet long. Picnic tables, fire grills, and garbage service are provided. Vault toilets and drinking water are available. Leashed pets are permitted.

Reservations, fees: No reservations. Sites are $9 per night, plus $5 for each additional vehicle. Senior discount available. Open May through September.

Directions: From Albany, drive east on U.S. 20 to the junction with Highway 126. Continue east on Highway 126 and drive 26 miles to

Sisters and Highway 242. Turn right and drive 4.2 miles to the campground on the right.

Contact: Deschutes National Forest, Sisters Ranger District, P.O. Box 249, Sisters, OR 97759; 541/549-7700; fax 541/549-7746.

43 Scott Lake Walk-In

10

This campground offers hike-in sites (only about an eighth of a mile from the road) set around Scott Lake at an elevation of 4,680 feet. Only nonmotorized boats are allowed on the lake. Trails leading out from camp provide access to several small lakes in the Mt. Washington Wilderness. There are great views of the Three Sisters Mountains from this camp. Mosquitoes are heavy during the spring and early summer.

Location: On Scott Lake in Willamette National Forest; The Southern Cascades map 2, grid g1.

Campsites, facilities: There are 12 walk-in tent sites. Picnic tables are provided. Vault toilets are available, but there is no drinking water, and garbage must be packed out. Leashed pets are permitted.

Reservations, fees: No reservations; no fee. Open late June to early October.

Directions: From Eugene drive east on Highway 126 and drive 54 miles to the junction with Highway 242 (part of the Santiam Scenic Byway). Turn right (east) on Highway 242 and drive 14.5 miles to Forest Road 260. Turn left and drive to the campground.

Note: Highway 242 is spectacularly scenic, but it's also very narrow, winding, and steep; not recommended for trailers. The maximum vehicle length is 35 feet.

Contact: Willamette National Forest, McKenzie Ranger District, 57600 McKenzie Hwy., McKenzie Bridge, OR 97413; 541/822-3381; fax 541/822-7254.

44 Lava Camp Lake

🥾 🎣 🐕 🚐 ⛺ 4

This campground is set at 5,200 feet among subalpine fir in the McKenzie Pass, not far from the Pacific Crest Trail. Other trails provide other hiking possibilities. A map of Deschutes National Forest details back roads, trails, and streams. Fishing is allowed, but don't expect to catch anything. Perhaps that is why this campground gets such light use.

Location: Near the Pacific Crest Trail in Deschutes National Forest; The Southern Cascades map 2, grid g2.

Campsites, facilities: There are 10 sites for tents, trailers, or RVs up to 22 feet long. Picnic tables and fire grills are provided. Pit toilets are available. There is no drinking water, and all garbage must be packed out. Leashed pets are permitted.

Reservations, fees: No reservations; no fee. Open June through September, weather permitting.

Directions: From Eugene drive east on Highway 126 for 47 miles to the town of McKenzie Bridge. Continue east on Highway 126 for five miles to Highway 242. Turn right (east) and drive 14.6 miles on Highway 242 to the campground entrance.

Note: Highway 242 is spectacularly scenic, but also very narrow, winding, and steep. RVs and trailers are discouraged (a 35-foot length limit is in effect).

Contact: Deschutes National Forest, Sisters Ranger District, P.O. Box 249, Sisters, OR 97759; 541/549-7700; fax 541/549-7746.

45 Whispering Pine Horse Camp

🥾 🐕 🚐 ⛺ 5

This wooded campground (elevation 4,400 feet) near Trout Creek Swamp is pretty, isolated, and private. Be sure to bring your own water. It's set up as a horse camp with corrals. Although generally not crowded, the camp is gaining in popularity, and groups of horse users occasionally fill it up. Hikers, beware; you'll be sharing the trails with horses.

Location: Near the Trout Creek Swamp in Deschutes National Forest; The Southern Cascades map 2, grid g1.

Campsites, facilities: There are nine primitive sites for tents, trailers, or RVs. Picnic tables, garbage service, and fire grills are provided. Pit toilets are available. There is no drinking water. Leashed pets are permitted.

Reservations, fees: No reservations. Sites are $10 per night, $5 per night for an additional vehicle. Senior discount available. Open June to mid-October.

Directions: From Eugene drive east on Highway 126 for 47 miles to the town of McKenzie Bridge. Continue east on Highway 126 for five miles to Highway 242. Turn right (east) and drive six miles on Highway 242 to Forest Road 1018. Turn left and drive four miles to the campground entrance.

Note: Highway 242 is spectacularly scenic, but also very narrow, winding, and steep. RVs and trailers are discouraged (a 35-foot length limit is in effect).

Contact: Deschutes National Forest, Sisters Ranger District, P.O. Box 249, Sisters, OR 97759; 541/549-7700; fax 541/549-7746.

46 Limberlost

🎣 🐕 ⛺ 9

This secluded campground is set at 1,800 feet elevation along Lost Creek about two miles from where it empties into the McKenzie River. It's relatively unknown and gets light use; it's a good base camp for a trout-fishing trip.

Location: On Lost Creek in Willamette National Forest; The Southern Cascades map 2, grid g1.

Campsites, facilities: There are two sites for tents only and 10 sites for tents or small trailers up to 16 feet long. Picnic tables, garbage service, and fire grills are provided. Vault toilets are available, but there is no drinking water. Leashed pets are permitted.

Reservations, fees: No reservations. Sites are $8 per night, plus $4 for each additional vehicle. Senior discount available. Open mid-April to mid-September.

Directions: From Eugene drive east on Highway 126 for 47 miles to the town of McKenzie Bridge. Continue east on Highway 126 for five miles to Highway 242. Turn right (east) and drive 1.5 miles on Highway 242 to the camp.

Note: Highway 242 is spectacularly scenic, but also very narrow, winding, and steep. RVs and trailers are discouraged (a 35-foot length limit is in effect).

Contact: Willamette National Forest, McKenzie Ranger District, 57600 McKenzie Hwy., McKenzie Bridge, OR 97413; 541/822-3381; fax 541/822-7254.

47 Alder Springs

7

Good hiking possibilities are a highlight of this remote campground at an elevation of 3,600 feet. There's hiking access to the Linton Lake Trail, and fishing is available at Linton Lake, a three-mile hike. The Three Sisters Wilderness is just south of the highway.

Location: In Willamette National Forest; The Southern Cascades map 2, grid g1.

Campsites, facilities: There are six tent sites. No drinking water is available, and all garbage must be packed out. Picnic tables and fire grills are provided. Vault toilets are available. Leashed pets are permitted.

Reservations, fees: No reservations; no fee. Open late May to late September, weather permitting.

Directions: From Eugene drive east on Highway 126 for 47 miles to the town of McKenzie Bridge. Continue east on Highway 126 for five miles to Highway 242. Turn right (east) and drive 10 miles on Highway 242 to the campground on the left.

Note: Highway 242 is spectacularly scenic, but also very narrow, winding, and steep. RVs and trailers are discouraged (a 35-foot length limit is in effect).

Contact: Willamette National Forest, McKenzie Ranger District, 57600 McKenzie Hwy., McKenzie Bridge, OR 97413; 541/822-3381; fax 541/822-7254.

48 Driftwood

9

This wooded campground at an elevation of 6,600 feet is often blocked by snowdrifts until July Fourth. At this high elevation, the views of Tam McArthur Rim are spectacular. Although it's on the lakeshore hidden from outsiders, the area can get very crowded. The campground is full most weekends from July Fourth to Labor Day. Fishing, swimming, hiking, and nonmotorized boating are some of the recreation options.

Location: On Three Creeks Lake in Deschutes National Forest; The Southern Cascades map 2, grid g3.

Campsites, facilities: There are 17 tent sites and five sites for tents, trailers, or RVs up to 16 feet long. Picnic tables, garbage service, and fire grills are provided. Pit toilets are available. There is no drinking water. Boats with motors are not allowed. Leashed pets are permitted.

Reservations, fees: No reservations. Sites are $10 per night, plus $5 for each additional vehicle. Senior discount available. Open mid-June to mid-September, weather permitting.

Directions: From Eugene drive east on Highway 126 to its junction with U.S. 20. Turn east and drive 26 miles to Sisters and Forest Road 16. Turn right and drive 16.4 miles to the campground.

Contact: Deschutes National Forest, Sisters Ranger District, P.O. Box 249, Sisters, OR 97759; 541/549-7700; fax 541/549-7746.

49 Three Creeks Lake

8

This wooded campground is set along the south shore of Three Creeks Lake in a pretty spot at 6,600 feet elevation. Fishing, swimming, hiking, and nonmotorized boating are the highlights. Also see the description of Driftwood.

Location: On Three Creeks Lake in Deschutes National Forest; The Southern Cascades map 2, grid g3.

Campsites, facilities: There are 10 sites for tents, trailers, or RVs up to 25 feet long. Picnic tables, garbage service, and fire grills are provided. Vault toilets are available. There is no drinking water. Boats with motors are not allowed. Leashed pets are permitted.

Reservations, fees: No reservations. Sites are $10 per night, plus $5 for each additional vehicle. Open mid-June to mid-October, weather permitting.

Directions: From Eugene drive east on Highway 126 to its junction with Highway 20. Turn east and drive 26 miles to Sisters and Forest Road 16. Turn right and drive 17 miles to the campground.

Contact: Deschutes National Forest, Sisters Ranger District, P.O. Box 249, Sisters, OR 97759; 541/549-7700; fax 541/549-7746.

50 Tumalo State Park

7

Trout fishing can be good at this camp along the banks of the Deschutes River, just five miles from Bend. Mount Bachelor is just up the road with plenty of winter recreation. The swimming area is safe and ideal for schoolchildren, and rafting is also an option here. See the description of Bend Keystone RV Park for more recreation information.

Location: On the Deschutes River; The Southern Cascades map 2, grid g6.

Campsites, facilities: There are 61 sites for tents, 21 sites with full hookups for trailers or RVs up to 44 feet long, a special camping area for hikers and bicyclists, four yurts, a group area for tent camping, and two tepees. Electricity, drinking water, sewer hookups, fire grills, and picnic tables are provided. Flush toilets, showers, firewood, and a playground are available. A store, a café, and ice are within one mile. Leashed pets are permitted.

Reservations, fees: Reservations accepted ($6 reservation fee). Sites are $13–19 per night, $4 per night for hikers/bikers, $29 per night for yurts and tepees, $64 per night for the group area, and $7 per night for an additional vehicle. Major credit cards accepted. Open year-round.

Directions: From Bend drive north on U.S. 97 for two miles to U.S. 20 west. Turn northwest and drive five miles to Tumalo Junction. Turn left at Tumalo Junction onto Cook Avenue, and drive one mile to the campground.

Contact: High Desert Management Unit, 62976 O. B. Riley Rd., Bend, OR 97701; 800/551-6949 or 541/388-6055, reservations 800/452-5687.

51 Bend Kampground

Recreation options near this camp include a golf course, hiking trails, bike paths, and tennis courts. See the description of Bend Keystone RV Park for additional recreation information.

Location: Near Bend; The Southern Cascades map 2, grid h6.

Campsites, facilities: There are 40 tent sites and 74 sites for trailers or RVs of any length; 40 are drive-through sites. Drinking water and picnic tables are provided. Electricity, sewer hookups, flush toilets, showers, a laundry room, a store, a deli, ice, firewood, a playground, a swimming pool, a recreation room, bottled gas, and a sanitary disposal station are available. Leashed pets are permitted.

Reservations, fees: Reservations accepted. Sites are $18–24 per night. Open year-round.

Directions: In Bend drive north on U.S. 97 for two miles to the park entrance road.

Contact: Bend Kampground, 63615 N. U.S. Hwy. 97, Bend, OR 97701; 541/382-7738.

52 Scandia RV and Mobile Park

This park near the Deschutes River is close to a golf course, a stable, bike paths, and tennis courts. See the description of Bend Keystone RV Park for additional recreation information.

Location: Near the Deschutes River; The Southern Cascades map 2, grid h6.

Campsites, facilities: There are 60 sites for tents, trailers, or RVs of any length; seven are drive-through sites. Electricity, drinking water, picnic tables, cable TV, and sewer hookups are provided. Flush toilets, showers, and a laundry room are available. Bot-tled gas, sanitary services, a store, a café, and ice are within one mile. Leashed pets are permitted.

Reservations, fees: Reservations accepted. Sites are $20 per night. Senior discount available. Open year-round.

Directions: In Bend drive south on U.S. 97 for a half mile to the park entrance.

Contact: Scandia RV and Mobile Park, 61415 S. U.S. Hwy. 97, Bend, OR 97702; 541/382-6206; fax 541/382-4087.

53 Bend Keystone RV Park

This park is right off the highway in Bend, a popular spot to use as a home base. The 100-mile Deschutes Forest Highway Loop connects here. Several state parks are within an hour's drive, and several city-managed parks provide access to the Deschutes River. Good side trips include the Oregon High Desert Museum, just six miles south of Bend on U.S. 97. A few miles farther is the Lava River Cave and the Lava Butte Geological Area.

Location: Near the Deschutes River; The Southern Cascades map 2, grid h6.

Campsites, facilities: There are 29 sites for trailers or RVs of any length. Electricity, cable TV, drinking water, and sewer hookups are provided. Flush toilets, showers, and a laundry room are available. Bottled gas, sanitary services, a store, a café, and ice are within one mile. Cats are permitted.

Reservations, fees: No reservations. Sites are $18 per night. Open year-round.

Directions: In Bend drive south on U.S. 97 for a half mile to the park entrance road.

Contact: Bend Keystone RV Park. 305 N.E. Burnside, Bend, OR 97701; 541/382-2335.

54 Crown Villa RV Park

 6

This RV park offers large and landscaped grassy sites. Nearby recreation options include horseback riding and golf. See the description of Bend Keystone RV Park for additional recreation information.

Location: Near Bend; The Southern Cascades map 2, grid h6.

Campsites, facilities: There are 124 sites for trailers or RVs of any length; 106 have full hookups, and 24 have partial hookups. Electricity, drinking water, sewer hookups, picnic tables, flush toilets, showers, cable TV, a laundry room, bottled gas, ice, a sanitary disposal station, and a playground are available. A store and a café are within one mile. Leashed pets are permitted.

Reservations, fees: Reservations accepted. Sites are $19–38.50 per night. Open year-round.

Directions: From Bend drive south on U.S. 97 for two miles to Brosterhous Road. Turn east and drive to the park.

Contact: Crown Villa RV Park, 60801 Brosterhous Rd., Bend, OR 97702; 541/388-1131.

55 Whistler's Bend

7

This county park along the banks of the North Umpqua River is an idyllic spot because it's just a 20-minute drive from I-5, yet it gets little pressure from outsiders. Two boat ramps accommodate boaters, and fishing is a plus. A wildlife reserve provides habitat for deer.

Location: On the North Umpqua River; The Southern Cascades map 3, grid f7.

Campsites, facilities: There are 23 sites for tents, trailers, or RVs up to 35 feet long, and two yurts. Group camping is available. Picnic tables and fire grills are provided. Drinking water, flush toilets, showers, a playground, and launching facilities are available. Leashed pets are permitted.

Reservations, fees: Reservations accepted for group sites and yurts only ($10 fee). Sites are $10 per night, yurts are $28 per night; call for group camping fees. Senior discount available for Douglas County residents. Open year-round.

Directions: From Roseburg drive east on Highway 138 for 12 miles to Whistler's Bend Park Road (well signed). Turn left and drive two miles to the end of the road and the park entrance.

Contact: Whistler's Bend, 2828 Whistlers Park Rd., Roseburg, OR 97470; 541/673-4863, reservations (group sites and yurts) 541/440-4500; website: www.co.douglas.or.us/parks.

56 John P. Amacher County Park

6

This prime layover spot for I-5 RV cruisers is in a wooded county park along the banks of the North Umpqua River, just far enough off the beaten track to be missed by most out-of-towners. An 18-hole golf course and tennis courts are close by. Riding stables are within a 20-minute drive, and Winchester Dam is within one-quarter mile. The camp was renovated in 2001.

Location: On the Umpqua River; The Southern Cascades map 3, grid g6.

Campsites, facilities: There are 10 sites for tents and 20 sites with full or partial hookups for trailers or RVs up to 30 feet long; 11 are drive-through sites. Electricity, drinking water, sewer hookups, and picnic tables are provided. Flush toilets, showers, a gazebo, and a playground are available. Bottled gas, a store, a café, a coin laundry, and ice are within one mile. Boat-launching facilities are available. Some facilities are wheelchair-accessible. Leashed pets and motorbikes are permitted.

Reservations, fees: No reservations accepted. Sites are $11–14 per night. Senior discount available. Open year-round.

Directions: From Roseburg drive five miles north on I-5 to Exit 129. Take that exit and drive south on Old Highway 99 for one-quarter mile to the park on the right (just across Winchester Bridge).

Contact: John P. Amacher County Park, P.O. Box 800, Winchester, OR 97495; 541/440-4500; fax 541/440-6248.

57 Twin Rivers Vacation Park

6

This wooded campground near the Umpqua River is the only camp in Roseburg with tent and RV sites. There are large shaded pull-through sites and more than 100 kinds of trees on the property. Nearby recreation options include a golf course, a county park, and bike paths.

Location: Near the Umpqua River; The Southern Cascades map 3, grid g5.

Campsites, facilities: There are four tent sites and 72 sites for trailers or RVs of any length; 35 are drive-through with full hookups. Electricity, drinking water, cable TV, sewer hookups, and picnic tables are provided. Flush toilets, bottled gas, showers, firewood, a store, a laundry room, ice, and a playground are available. Boat-launching facilities are nearby. Leashed pets and motorbikes are permitted.

Reservations, fees: Reservations accepted. Sites are $15–28 per night. Open year-round.

Directions: In Roseburg on I-5, take Exit 125. Take that exit to Garden Valley Road and drive west for five miles (over the river) to Old Garden Valley Road. Turn left and drive

1.5 miles to River Forks Road. Turn left and drive to the entrance to the park.

Contact: Twin Rivers Vacation Park, 433 River Forks Road, Roseburg, OR 97470; 541/673-3811.

58 Douglas County Fairgrounds RV Park

8

This county park is very easily accessible off the highway, and it covers 74 acres. It is also near the Umpqua River, one of Oregon's prettiest rivers. There is often good fishing in season. A golf course, bike paths, and tennis courts are nearby. Horse stalls and a boat ramp are available at the nearby fairgrounds. The campground fills up the third weekend in March during the annual fiddlers' convention.

Location: On the South Umpqua River; The Southern Cascades map 3, grid g6.

Campsites, facilities: There are 50 sites for tents, trailers, or RVs of any length with partial hookups. Tent camping is limited to two nights. Electricity, drinking water, and picnic tables are provided. Flush toilets, sanitary services, showers, and a dump station are available. A store, a café, a coin-operated laundry, and ice are within one mile. Some facilities are wheelchair-accessible. Leashed pets are permitted.

Reservations, fees: No reservations accepted. Sites are $15 per night, with a 14-day stay limit, $1 per night for an additional tent. Open year-round, except one week in August during the county fair. Phone ahead to confirm current status.

Directions: From I-5 in Roseburg, take Exit 123 and drive south under the freeway to Frear Street. Turn right and enter the park.

Contact: Douglas County Fairgrounds & Speedway, 2110 S.W. Frear St., Roseburg, OR 97470; 541/957-7010; fax 541/440-6023.

59 Alameda Avenue Trailer Park

🐕 🚐   3

Alameda Avenue Trailer Park, one of four parks in Roseburg, is near the Umpqua River and within walking distance to grocery stores and restaurants. A golf course, bike paths, and tennis courts are among the recreation possibilities in the area.

Location: Near the Umpqua River; The Southern Cascades map 3, grid g6.

Campsites, facilities: There are 35 sites for trailers or RVs up to 30 feet long. Electricity, drinking water, and sewer hookups are provided. Flush toilets, sanitary services, showers, and a laundry room are available. Bottled gas, a store, a café, and ice are within one mile. Leashed pets are permitted.

Reservations, fees: Reservations accepted. Sites are $20 per night. Open year-round.

Directions: In Roseburg on I-5, take the Garden Valley exit. Drive east on Garden Valley Road to Business Route 99. Turn north and drive one-quarter mile north to Northeast Alameda Avenue. The park is on the left.

Contact: Alameda Avenue Trailer Park, 581 N.E. Alameda Ave. #36, Roseburg, OR 97470; 541/672-2348.

60 Mount Nebo Trailer Park

🚲 🐕 🚐   5

This is an option for RVers stopping in Roseburg. The park is near the Umpqua River and close to a golf course, bike paths, and tennis courts.

Location: Near the Umpqua River; The Southern Cascades map 3, grid g6.

Campsites, facilities: There are 31 sites for trailers or RVs up to 45 feet long; four are drive-through sites. Electricity, drinking water, and sewer hookups are provided. Flush toilets, sanitary services, showers, and a laundry room are available. Bottled gas, a store, and a café are within one mile. Leashed pets under 20 pounds are permitted.

Reservations, fees: Reservations accepted. Sites are $17 per night. Open year-round.

Directions: From Roseburg on I-5, take Exit 125 to Garden Valley Road. Drive east on Garden Valley Road for three-quarters mile to Stephens Street. Turn left and drive less than a mile to the park on the right.

Contact: Mount Nebo Trailer Park, 2071 N.E. Stephens St., Roseburg, OR 97470; 541/673-4108; fax 541/679-7980.

61 Wildlife Safari RV Park

🚶 🚲 🐕 🚐   6

This park is part of the Wildlife Safari Park in Winston (near Roseburg), which offers a walk-through petting zoo. Nearby recreation options include an 18-hole golf course, hiking trails, and marked bike trails.

Location: Near Roseburg; The Southern Cascades map 3, grid g5.

Campsites, facilities: There are 18 drive-through sites for self-contained trailers or RVs. Electricity and a café are available. There is no drinking water. A gift shop is within one-half mile. Leashed pets and motorbikes are permitted.

Reservations, fees: No reservations accepted. Sites are $8–10 per night. The campground is closed in the winter.

Directions: From Roseburg drive south on I-5 for five miles to Exit 119 and Highway 42. Take Highway 42 southwest for three miles to Looking Glass Road (just before reaching Winston). Turn right and drive one block to Safari Road. Turn right and enter the park.

Contact: Wildlife Safari RV Park, P.O. Box 1600, Winston, OR 97496; 541/679-6761; fax 541/679-9210; website: www.maserith.com/safari.

62 Dolly Varden

This pretty campground is adjacent to Fall Creek and is at the lower trailhead for the scenic, 13.7-mile Fall Creek National Recreation Trail, which follows the creek and varies between 960 and 1,385 feet in elevation. This campground gets moderate to heavy use. It is set on the inlet stream for Fall Creek Reservoir.

Location: On Fall Creek in Willamette National Forest; The Southern Cascades map 4, grid a4.

Campsites, facilities: There are three sites for tents and two sites for tents, trailers, or RVs up to 16 feet long. Picnic tables, garbage service, and fire grills are provided. Vault toilets are available. There is no drinking water. Leashed pets are permitted.

Reservations, fees: No reservations. Sites are $8 per night, $4 per night for an additional vehicle. Senior discount available. Open May to mid-September.

Directions: From south Eugene on I-5, take Exit 188 to Highway 58. Drive 11 miles south to Lowell and Pioneer Street (at the covered bridge). Turn left and drive less than a quarter mile to West Boundary Road. Turn left and drive one block to Lowell Jasper Road. Turn right and drive 1.5 miles to Unity and Place Road. Turn right and drive about one mile to a fork with North Shore Road. Bear left onto North Shore Road (Big Fall Creek Road) and drive about 10 miles (the road becomes Forest Road 18) to the campground on the left.

Contact: Willamette National Forest, Lowell Service Center, 60 Pioneer St., Lowell, OR 97452; 541/937-2129; fax 541/937-2032.

63 Big Pool

This campground along Fall Creek at about 1,000 feet elevation is quiet, secluded, and primitive. The scenic Fall Creek National Recreation Trail passes the camp on the other side of the creek. See the description of Dolly Varden for more details on the area.

Location: On Fall Creek in Willamette National Forest; The Southern Cascades map 4, grid a4.

Campsites, facilities: There are three tent sites and two sites for tents, trailers, or RVs up to 16 feet long. Picnic tables, garbage containers, and fire grills are provided. Vault toilets are available. There is no drinking water. Leashed pets are permitted.

Reservations, fees: No reservations. Sites are $10 per night, plus $5 for each additional vehicle. Senior discount available. Open May to mid-September.

Directions: From south Eugene on I-5, take Exit 188 to Highway 58. Drive 11 miles south to Lowell and Pioneer Street (at the covered bridge). Turn left and drive less than a quarter mile to West Boundary Road. Turn left and drive one block to Lowell Jasper Road. Turn right and drive 1.5 miles to Unity and Place Road. Turn right and drive about one mile to a fork with North Shore Road. Bear left onto North Shore Road (Big Fall Creek Road) and drive about 12 miles (the road becomes Forest Road 18) to the campground on the right.

Contact: Willamette National Forest, Lowell Service Center, 60 Pioneer St., Lowell, OR 97452; 541/937-2129; fax 541/937-2032.

64 Bedrock

🚶 🚴 🏊
🎣 🐕 🚐 ⛺ 6

This campground along the banks of Fall Creek is one of the access points for the scenic Fall Creek National Recreation Trail, which offers access to Jones Trail, a six-mile uphill climb. See the description of Dolly Varden for trail information. The campground is also adjacent to the Jones Trail, which heads north for about six miles before joining a forest road.

Location: On Fall Creek in Willamette National Forest; The Southern Cascades map 4, grid a4.

Campsites, facilities: There are 20 sites for tents, trailers, or RVs up to 22 feet long. Picnic tables, garbage service, and fire grills are provided. Vault toilets and drinking water are available. Leashed pets are permitted.

Reservations, fees: No reservations. Sites are $10 per night, plus $5 for each additional vehicle. Senior discount available. Open May to late October.

Directions: From south Eugene on I-5, take Exit 188 to Highway 58. Drive 11 miles south to Lowell and Pioneer Street (at the covered bridge). Turn left and drive less than a quarter mile to West Boundary Road. Turn left and drive one block to Lowell Jasper Road. Turn right and drive 1.5 miles to Unity and Place Road. Turn right and drive about one mile to a fork with North Shore Road. Bear left onto North Shore Road (Big Fall Creek Road) and drive about 14 miles (the road becomes Forest Road 18) to the campground on the left.

Contact: Willamette National Forest, Lowell Service Center, 60 Pioneer St., Lowell, OR 97452; 541/937-2129; fax 541/937-2032.

65 Puma Creek

🚶 🚴 🏊
🎣 🐕 🚐 ⛺ 6

This campground is set along the banks of Fall Creek, across from the Fall Creek National Recreation Trail. It's one of four camps in the immediate area. See the description of Dolly Varden for more information.

Location: On Fall Creek in Willamette National Forest; The Southern Cascades map 4, grid a4.

Campsites, facilities: There are 11 sites for tents, trailers, or RVs up to 16 feet long. Picnic tables, garbage containers, and fire grills are provided. Vault toilets and drinking water are available. Leashed pets are permitted.

Reservations, fees: No reservations. Sites are $10 per night, plus $5 for each additional vehicle. Senior discount available. Open May to early October.

Directions: From I-5 south of Eugene, take Exit 188 to Highway 58. Drive about 11 miles to Lowell. Turn left at Pioneer Street (at the covered bridge), drive 0.2 mile and turn left on West Boundary Road. Drive one block and turn right at Lowell Jasper Road. Drive 1.5 miles to Place Road and turn right. Drive about one mile to a fork and bear left onto North Shore Road (Big Fall Creek Road). Drive about 16 miles (the road becomes Forest Road 18) to the campground on the left.

Contact: Willamette National Forest, Lowell Service Center, 60 Pioneer St., Lowell, OR 97452; 541/937-2129; fax 541/937-2032.

66 Homestead

This quiet little campground is set among the trees along the banks of the South Fork of the McKenzie River. It's primitive, little known, and free. Frissell Crossing is nearby and has water available from a hand pump.

Location: On the South Fork of the McKenzie River in Willamette National Forest; The Southern Cascades map 4, grid a7.

Campsites, facilities: There are eight sites for tents, trailers, or RVs. Picnic tables and fire grills are provided. Vault toilets are available, but there is no drinking water. All garbage must be packed out. Leashed pets are permitted.

Reservations, fees: No reservations; no fee. Open year-round.

Directions: From Eugene drive east on Highway 126 for 41 miles to Blue River. Continue east on Highway 126 for five miles to Forest Road 19 (Aufderheide Scenic Byway). Turn south on Forest Road 19 and drive 17 miles to the camp.

Contact: Willamette National Forest, Blue River Ranger District, P.O. Box 199, Blue River, OR 97413; 541/822-3317; fax 541/822-1255.

67 Frissell Crossing

8

This campground (elevation 2,800 feet) is on the banks of the South Fork of the McKenzie River, adjacent to a trailhead that provides access to the backcountry of the Three Sisters Wilderness. This is the only camp in the immediate area that has drinking water. If you're looking for solitude, this should be heaven to you. Homestead provides a free, primitive alternative.

Location: Near the Three Sisters Wilderness in Willamette National Forest; The Southern Cascades map 4, grid a7.

Campsites, facilities: There are 12 sites for tents, trailers, or RVs. Picnic tables, garbage bins, and fire grills are provided. Drinking water and vault toilets are available. Leashed pets are permitted.

Reservations, fees: No reservations. Sites are $10 per night. Senior discount available. Open mid-May to mid-September.

Directions: From Eugene drive east on Highway 126 for 37 miles to Blue River. Continue east on Highway 126 for five miles to Forest Road 19 (Aufderheide Scenic Byway). Turn south and drive 23 miles to the camp.

Contact: Willamette National Forest, Blue River Ranger District, P.O. Box 199, Blue River, OR 97413; 541/822-3317; fax 541/822-1255.

68 Box Canyon Horse Camp

4

Only 80 miles from Eugene, this secluded campground with sparse tree cover offers trails into wilderness, including the Chucksney Mountain Trail, Crossing-Way Trail, and Grasshopper Trail. It's a good base camp for a backpacking trip.

Location: Near Chucksney Mountain in Willamette National Forest; The Southern Cascades map 4, grid a8.

Campsites, facilities: There are 11 sites for tents, trailers, or RVs that allow horse and rider to camp close together. Picnic tables, fire grills, stock water, and corrals are provided. A manure disposal site and vault toilets are available. There is no drinking water and all garbage must be packed out. Leashed pets are permitted.

Reservations, fees: No reservations; no fee. Open year-round, weather permitting.

Directions: From Eugene drive east on Highway 126 for 41 miles to Blue River. Continue east on Highway 126 for five miles to Forest Road 19 (Aufderheide Scenic Byway). Turn south and drive 30 miles to the camp.

Contact: Willamette National Forest, Blue River Ranger District, P.O. Box 199, Blue River, OR 97413; 541/822-3317; fax 541/822-1255.

69 Winberry

6

This campground is on Winberry Creek in a tree-shaded area. The closest hiking option is Station Butte Trail, just downstream from the campground on Forest Road 1802-150. Be cautious—there is poison oak at the top of the butte.

Location: On Winberry Creek in Willamette National Forest; The Southern Cascades map 4, grid a4.

Campsites, facilities: There are five sites for tents and two sites for trailers or RVs up to 16 feet long. Picnic tables, garbage service, and fire grills are provided. Drinking water, vault toilets, and A-frame shelters are available. Leashed pets are permitted.

Reservations, fees: No reservations. Sites are $6–8 per night, plus $3 for each additional vehicle. Senior discount available. Open late May to mid-September.

Directions: From south Eugene on I-5, take Exit 188 to Highway 58. Drive 11 miles south to Lowell and Pioneer Street (at the covered bridge). Turn left and drive less than a quarter mile to West Boundary Road. Turn left and drive one block to Lowell Jasper Road. Turn right and drive 1.5 miles to Unity and Place Road. Turn right and drive about one mile to a fork with Winberry Road. Bear right and drive six miles (the road becomes Forest Road 1802). Continue 3.5 miles to the campground.

Contact: Willamette National Forest, Lowell Service Center, 60 Pioneer St., Lowell, OR 97452; 541/937-2129; fax 541/937-2032.

70 Blair Lake Walk-In

6

If you're looking for a pristine alpine, lakeside setting, you'll find it here. The lake is small (only 35 acres) and shallow (20 feet), set at 4,800 feet. It supports a population of brook and rainbow trout and is stocked in the summer. The surrounding meadows and woods are well known for their wide range of wildflowers and huckleberries.

Location: On Blair Lake in Willamette National Forest; The Southern Cascades map 4, grid b6.

Campsites, facilities: There are seven walk-in tent sites. Picnic tables and garbage bins are provided. Drinking water, fire rings, and a pit toilet are available. Leashed pets are permitted.

Reservations, fees: No reservations. Sites are $6 per night, plus $3 for each additional vehicle. Senior discount available. Open June to mid-October, weather permitting.

Directions: From south Eugene on I-5, take Exit 188 to Highway 58. Drive 35 miles southeast on Highway 58 to Oakridge. Turn left at the signal to downtown and Salmon Creek Road. Turn east and drive nine miles (it becomes Forest Road 24) to Forest Road 1934. Turn left and drive eight miles to Forest Road 733. Turn right and continue for less than one mile to the campground.

Contact: Willamette National Forest, Middle Fork Ranger District, 46375 Hwy. 58, Westfir, OR 97492; 541/782-2283; fax 541/782-5306.

71 Kiahanie

5

This is one heck of a spot for fly-fishing (the only kind allowed). This remote campground is set at 2,200 feet elevation along the North Fork of the Willamette River, a designated Wild and Scenic River. If you want beauty and quiet among enormous Douglas fir trees, you came to the right place. An even more remote campground is farther north on Forest Road 19 at Box Canyon Horse Camp.

Location: On the West Fork of the Willamette River in Willamette National Forest; The Southern Cascades map 4, grid a7.

Campsites, facilities: There are 19 sites for tents, trailers, or RVs up to 24 feet long. Picnic tables, garbage bins, a recycling center, and fire rings are provided. Drinking water and vault toilets are available. Leashed pets are permitted.

Reservations, fees: No reservations. Sites are $8 per night, plus $4 for each additional vehicle. Open late May through September.

Directions: From south Eugene on I-5, take Exit 188 to Highway 58. Drive 31 miles southeast on Highway 58 to Westfir. Take the Westfir exit and drive two miles to Westfir and the junction with Aufderheide Scenic Byway (Forest Road 19). Bear left (northeast) and drive 19 miles to the campground.

Contact: Willamette National Forest, Middle Fork Ranger District, 46375 Hwy. 58, Westfir, OR 97492; 541/782-2283; fax 541/782-5306.

72 Skookum Creek

7

This is a popular starting point for backcountry fishing, hiking, or horse use. The Erma Bell Lakes Trail begins here and is a portal into the Three Sisters Wilderness. This trail is maintained to be accessible for wheelchair users, though it is challenging.

Location: Near the Three Sisters Wilderness in Willamette National Forest; The Southern Cascades map 4, grid b8.

Campsites, facilities: There are eight walk-in tent sites, two of which are wheelchair-accessible. Picnic tables and fire rings are provided. Drinking water, hitching rails, and pit toilets are available. All garbage must be packed out. Leashed pets are permitted.

Reservations, fees: No reservations. Sites are $6 per night, plus $3 for each additional

vehicle. Senior discount available. Open mid-May through September, weather permitting.

Directions: From Eugene drive east on Highway 126 for 37 miles to Blue River. Continue east for five miles to Forest Road 19 (Aufderheide Scenic Byway). Turn right and drive 35 miles south to Forest Road 1957. Turn left (south) and drive four miles to the campground.

Contact: Willamette National Forest, Middle Fork Ranger District, 46375 Hwy. 58, Westfir, OR 97492; 541/782-2283; fax 541/782-5306.

73 Black Canyon

7

This campground is along the banks of the Middle Fork of the Willamette River, not far above Lookout Point Reservoir, where fishing and boating are available. The camp is pretty and wooded, with comfortable sites. Within the camp is a one-mile-long nature trail with interpretive signs. Weekend programs are offered in the amphitheater in July and August. You will hear train noise from the other side of the river.

Location: On the Middle Fork of the Willamette River in Willamette National Forest; The Southern Cascades map 4, grid b3.

Campsites, facilities: There are 72 sites for tents, trailers, or RVs up to 22 feet long. Picnic tables, garbage service, and fire grills are provided. Drinking water, vault toilets, and firewood are available. Sanitary services, a café, and a coin laundry are within six miles. Some of the facilities are wheelchair-accessible. Launching facilities are nearby at the south end of Lookout Point Reservoir. Leashed pets are permitted.

Reservations, fees: No reservations. Sites are $12–20 per night, plus $6 for each additional vehicle. Open May to late October.

Directions: From south Eugene on I-5, take Exit 188 to Highway 58. Drive southeast on Highway 58 for 27 miles to the camp on the left (six miles west of Oakridge).

Contact: Willamette National Forest, Lowell Service Center, 60 Pioneer St., Lowell, OR 97452; 541/937-2129; fax 541/937-2032.

74 Shady Dell Group Camp

 5

The camp is rented only for groups. It is set near the Middle Fork of the Willamette River, across from Lookout Point Reservoir, a long, narrow lake adjacent to Highway 58. Noteworthy here is a stand of old-growth cedars.

Location: On the Middle Fork of the Willamette River in Willamette National Forest; The Southern Cascades map 4, grid b3.

Campsites, facilities: There are group sites only for tents, trailers, or RVs up to 15 feet long. Picnic tables, garbage service, and fire grills are provided. Drinking water and vault toilets are available. Sanitary services, a café, and a coin laundry are available within five miles. Some of the facilities are wheelchair-accessible. Leashed pets are permitted.

Reservations, fees: Reservations required. Group sites are $40 per night. Open May to late October.

Directions: From south Eugene on I-5, take Exit 188 to Highway 58. Drive southeast on Highway 58 for 32 miles (five miles west of Oakridge) to the camp on the right.

Contact: Willamette National Forest, Lowell Service Center, 60 Pioneer St., Lowell, OR 97452; 541/937-2129; fax 541/937-2032.

75 Salmon Creek Falls

8

This pretty campground is in a lush, old-growth forest, right along Salmon Creek. The rocky gorge area creates two small

beautiful waterfalls and several deep pools in the clear, blue-green waters. Springtime brings a full range of wildflowers and wild thimbleberries; hazelnuts abound in the summer. This area is a popular recreation spot.

Location: On Salmon Creek in Willamette National Forest; The Southern Cascades map 4, grid b6.

Campsites, facilities: There are 14 sites for tents, trailers, or RVs up to 24 feet long. Picnic tables, garbage bins, and fire grills are provided. Drinking water and vault toilets are available. A store, a café, a coin laundry, and ice are available within five miles. Leashed pets are permitted.

Reservations, fees: No reservations. Sites are $12 per night, plus $6 for each additional vehicle. Senior discount available. Open late April through September.

Directions: From south Eugene on I-5, take Exit 188 to Highway 58. Drive southeast on Highway 58 for 35 miles to Oakridge and the signal light for downtown. Turn left on Crestview Street and drive one-fourth mile to 1st Street. Turn right and drive six miles (the road becomes Forest Road 24, Salmon Creek Road) to the campground entrance on the right.

Contact: Willamette National Forest, Middle Fork Ranger District, 49098 Salmon Creek Rd., Westfir, OR 97492; 541/782-2283; fax 541/782-5306.

76 North Waldo

10

This camp, at an elevation of 5,400 feet, is the most popular of the Waldo Lake campgrounds. The drier environment supports fewer mosquitoes, but they can still be plentiful in season. The boat launch is deeper than the others on the lake, making it more accommodating for large sailboats. North Waldo is also a popular starting point for many wilderness trails and lakes, most notably the Rigdon, Wahanna, and Torrey Lakes. Waldo Lake has the special distinction of being one of the three purest lakes in the world. Of those three lakes, two are in Oregon (the other is Crater Lake), and the third is in Siberia. Amphitheater programs are presented here on weekends from late July to Labor Day.

Location: On Waldo Lake in Willamette National Forest; The Southern Cascades map 4, grid b8.

Campsites, facilities: There are 58 sites for tents, trailers, or RVs up to 30 feet long. Picnic tables, garbage bins, a recycle center, and fire rings are provided. Drinking water, vault and flush toilets, a swimming area, and an amphitheater are available. Boat-launching facilities are available. Leashed pets are permitted.

Reservations, fees: No reservations. Sites are $10–12 per night, plus $5 for each additional vehicle. Senior discount available. Northwest Forest Pass ($30 annual fee) or $5 daily fee per parked vehicle is required at nearby boat launch and trailheads. Open July through September, weather permitting.

Directions: From Eugene drive south on I-5 for four miles to Exit 188 and Highway 58. Turn southeast and drive about 60 miles southeast to Waldo Lake Road (Forest Road 5897). Turn left and drive north on Waldo Lake Road for 14 miles to Forest Road 5898. Turn left and drive about two miles to the campground at the northeast end of Waldo Lake.

Contact: Willamette National Forest, Middle Fork Ranger District, 46375 Hwy. 58, Westfir, OR 97492; 541/782-2283; fax 541/782-5306.

77 Islet

10

You'll find sandy beaches and an interpretive sign at this campground at the north end of Waldo Lake. The winds blow consistently every afternoon. A picnic table placed strategically on the rock jetty is a great spot to enjoy a sunset. There's a one-mile shoreline trail between Islet and North Waldo Campground. Bring your mosquito repellent from June to August; you'll need it. For more information, see North Waldo.

Location: On Waldo Lake in Willamette National Forest; The Southern Cascades map 4, grid c8.

Campsites, facilities: There are 55 sites for tents, trailers, or RVs up to 30 feet long. Picnic tables, garbage bins, a recycling center, and fire rings are provided. Drinking water and vault toilets are available. Boat-launching facilities are available. Leashed pets are permitted.

Reservations, fees: No reservations. Sites are $12 per night, plus $6 for each additional vehicle. Multiple sites for group use are $20 per night. Senior discount available. Northwest Forest Pass ($30 annual fee) or $5 daily fee per parked vehicle is required at nearby boat launch and trailheads. Open July through September, weather permitting.

Directions: From Eugene drive south on I-5 for four miles to Exit 188 and Highway 58. Turn southeast and drive about 60 miles southeast to Waldo Lake Road (Forest Road 5897). Turn left and drive north on Waldo Lake Road for 14 miles to Forest Road 5898. Turn left and continue 1.5 miles to the campground at the northeast end of Waldo Lake.

Contact: Willamette National Forest, Middle Fork Ranger

District, 46375 Hwy. 58, Westfir, OR 97492; 541/782-2283; fax 541/782-5306.

78 Shadow Bay

10

This campground is on a large bay at the south end of Waldo Lake. It is a considerably wetter environment than either North Waldo or Islet, supporting a more diverse and prolific ground cover as well as more mosquitoes. The use rate is considerably lighter than North Waldo. You have access to the Shore Line Trail and then the Waldo Lake Trail from here. The boating speed limit is 10 mph for all of Waldo Lake.

Location: On Waldo Lake in Willamette National Forest; The Southern Cascades map 4, grid c8.

Campsites, facilities: There are 92 sites for tents, trailers, or RVs up to 24 feet long. Picnic tables, garbage bins, a recycle center, and fire grills are provided. Drinking water and vault and flush toilets are available. Boat-launching facilities are nearby. Leashed pets are permitted.

Reservations, fees: No reservations. Sites are $12 per night, plus $6 for each additional vehicle. Senior discount available. Northwest Forest Pass ($30 annual fee) or $5 daily fee per parked vehicle is required at nearby boat launch and trailheads. Open July through September, weather permitting.

Directions: From Eugene drive south on I-5 for four miles to Exit 188 and Highway 58. Turn southeast and drive about 60 miles southeast to Waldo Lake Road (Forest Road 5897). Turn left on Waldo Lake Road and drive north for 6.5 miles to the Shadow Bay turnoff. Turn left and drive on Forest Road 5896 to the campground at the south end of Waldo Lake.

Contact: Willamette National Forest, Middle Fork Ranger District, 46375 Hwy. 58, Westfir, OR 97492; 541/782-2283; fax 541/782-5306.

79 Blue Pool

4

This campground is situated in an old-growth forest alongside Salt Creek at 1,900 feet elevation. There is a large picnic area along the creek with picnic tables, a large grassy area, and fire stoves built in the 1930s by the Civilian Conservation Corps. One-half mile east of the campground on Highway 58 is McCredie Hot Springs. This spot is undeveloped, without any facilities. Exercise caution when using the hot springs; they can be very hot.

Location: On Salt Creek in Willamette National Forest; The Southern Cascades map 4, grid c7.

Campsites, facilities: There are 24 sites for tents, trailers, or RVs up to 18 feet long. Picnic tables, garbage bins, a recycle center, and fire rings are provided. Drinking water and pit and flush toilets are available. Leashed pets are permitted.

Reservations, fees: No reservations. Sites are $12 per night, plus $6 per additional vehicle. Senior discount available. Open mid-May to mid-September.

Directions: From Eugene drive south on I-5 for four miles to Exit 188 and Highway 58. Turn southeast and drive 35 miles to Oakridge. Continue east on Highway 58 for 10 miles to the campground.

Contact: Willamette National Forest, Middle Fork Ranger District, 46375 Hwy. 58, Westfir, OR 97492; 541/782-2283; fax 541/782-5306.

80 Packard Creek

 6

Situated on a large flat beside Hills Creek Reservoir, this campground is extremely popular with families and fills up on weekends and holidays. The mix of vegetation in the campground includes an abundance of poison oak. The speed limit around the swimming area and boat ramp is 5 mph.

Location: On Hills Creek Reservoir in Willamette National Forest; The Southern Cascades map 4, grid c5.

Campsites, facilities: There are 33 sites for tents, trailers, or RVs up to 30 feet long. Picnic tables, garbage bins, and fire rings are provided. Drinking water, vault toilets, and firewood are available. Some facilities are wheelchair-accessible. Fishing and boat docks, boat-launching facilities, a roped swimming area, a picnic shelter, and an amphitheater are available. Some sites have their own docks. Leashed pets are permitted.

Reservations, fees: No reservations. Sites are $12–20 per night, plus $6 per additional vehicle. Senior discount available. Open mid-April to mid-September.

Directions: From Eugene drive south on I-5 for four miles to Exit 188 and Highway 58. Turn southeast and drive 35 miles to Oakridge. Continue east on Highway 58 for two miles to Kitson Springs Road. Turn right and drive one-half mile to Forest Road 21. Turn right and continue six miles to the campground.

Contact: Willamette National Forest, Middle Fork Ranger District, 46375 Hwy. 58, Westfir, OR 97492; 541/782-2283; fax 541/782-5306.

81 Sharps Creek

5

Like nearby Rujada this camp on the banks of Sharps Creek is just far enough off the beaten path to be missed by most campers. It's quiet, primitive, and remote, and fishing, swimming, and gold-panning are popular activities in the day-use area.

Location: On Sharps Creek; The Southern Cascades map 4, grid d2.

Campsites, facilities: There are 10 sites for tents, trailers, or RVs up to 30 feet long. Picnic tables and fire pits are provided. Drinking water, vault toilets, and firewood are available. A camp host is here in summer. Some facilities are wheelchair-accessible. Leashed pets are permitted.

Reservations, fees: No reservations. Sites are $5 per night, with a 14-day stay limit, plus $3 for each additional vehicle. Senior discount available. Open mid-May to mid-October, weather permitting.

Directions: From Eugene drive south on I-5 to Cottage Grove and Exit 174. Take that exit and drive east on Row River Road for 18 miles to Sharps Creek Road. Turn south and drive four miles to the campground.

Contact: Bureau of Land Management, Eugene District, P.O. Box 10226, Eugene, OR 97440-2226; 541/683-6600; fax 541/683-6981; website: www.edo.or.blm.gov.

82 Rujada

7

This campground is situated on a river terrace on the banks of Layng Creek, right at the national forest border. The Swordfern Trail follows Layng Creek through a beautiful forest within a lush fern grotto. There is a fair swimming hole near the campground. Those with patience and persistence can fish in the creek. By continuing east on Forest Road 17, you reach a trailhead that leads one-half mile to beautiful Spirit Falls, a spectacular 60-foot waterfall. A bit farther east is another easy trail to Moon Falls, even more awe-inspiring at 125 feet. Another campground option is Cedar Creek, about six miles southeast on Brice Creek Road (County Road 2470).

Location: On Layng Creek in Umpqua National Forest; The Southern Cascades map 4, grid d3.

Campsites, facilities: There are 11 sites for tents, trailers, or RVs up to 22 feet long. Picnic tables, garbage bins, and fire pits are provided. Flush toilets, drinking water, and a softball field are available. Some facilities are wheelchair-accessible. Leashed pets are permitted.

Reservations, fees: No reservations for camping; reservations accepted for large groups for day-use. Sites are $7 per night, $3 per night for an additional vehicle. Senior discount available. Open late May to late September.

Directions: From Eugene drive south on I-5 to Cottage Grove and Exit 174. Take that exit and drive east on Row River Road for 19 miles to Layng Creek Road (Forest Road 17). Turn left and drive two miles to the campground on the right.

Contact: Umpqua National Forest, Cottage Grove Ranger District, 78405 Cedar Park Rd., Cottage Grove, OR 97424; 541/776-5000; fax 541/767-5075.

83 Sand Prairie

Situated at 1,600 feet in a mixed stand of Douglas fir, western hemlock, cedar, dogwood, and hazelnut, this campground is within easy access to the Middle Fork of the Willamette River. There's an access road to the south (upstream) end of the Hills Creek Reservoir. The 27-mile Middle Fork Trail begins at the south end of the campground.

Fishing is good here, where you can expect to catch large-scale suckers, rainbows, and cutthroat trout in the Middle Fork.

Location: On the Willamette River in Willamette National Forest; The Southern Cascades map 4, grid d5.

Campsites, facilities: There are 20 sites for tents, trailers, or RVs up to 22 feet long. Picnic tables, garbage bins, and fire rings are provided. Vault and flush toilets, a group picnic area, and drinking water are available. Some of the facilities are wheelchair-accessible. A boat launch is nearby on Hills Creek Reservoir. Leashed pets are permitted.

Reservations, fees: No reservations. Sites are $12 per night, plus $6 per additional vehicle. Senior discount available. Open May through September.

Directions: From Eugene drive south on I-5 for four miles to Exit 188 and Highway 58. Turn southeast and drive 35 miles to Oakridge. Continue east on Highway 58 for two miles to Kitson Springs Road. Turn right and drive one-half mile to Forest Road 21. Turn right and continue 11 miles to the campground.

Contact: Willamette National Forest, Middle Fork Ranger District, 46375 Hwy. 58, Westfir, OR 97492; 541/782-2283; fax 541/782-5306.

84 Sacandaga

This campground sits along the Middle Fork of the Willamette River, where a segment of the historic Oregon Central Military Wagon Road is visible. The Willamette River is accessible by two trails from the campground, and the Middle Fork Trail is in close proximity. There is also a short trail leading to a viewpoint with a bench for a short break. This campground gets low use and the sites are well separated by vegetation. Count on solitude here. The elevation is 2,400 feet.

Location: On the Willamette River in Willamette National Forest; The Southern Cascades map 4, grid e6.

Campsites, facilities: There are 16 sites for tents, trailers, or RVs up to 24 feet long. Picnic tables and fire rings are provided. Drinking water, vault toilets, and firewood are available. Leashed pets are permitted.

Reservations, fees: No reservations. Sites are $6 per night, $3 per night for an additional vehicle. Senior discount available. Open mid-April to mid-November, weather permitting.

Directions: From Eugene drive south on I-5 for four miles to Exit 188 and Highway 58. Turn southeast and drive 35 miles to Oakridge. Continue east on Highway 58 for two miles to Kitson Springs Road. Turn right and drive one-half mile to Forest Road 21. Turn right and drive 24 miles to the campground.

Contact: Willamette National Forest, Middle Fork Ranger District, 46375 Hwy. 58, Westfir, OR 97492; 541/782-2283; fax 541/782-5306.

85 Campers Flat

5

This pretty but small campground is on a small flat adjacent to the Middle Fork of the Willamette River. The river drowns out the sound of traffic from the road right next to the campground. There is an interpretive sign about the Oregon Central Military Wagon Road in the campground. Fishing is good with easy access to the water's edge. Young's Rock Trailhead is across the road from the campground entrance and is very popular with mountain bikers.

Location: On the Willamette River in Willamette National Forest; The Southern Cascades map 4, grid e7.

Campsites, facilities: There are five sites for tents, trailers, or RVs up to 21 feet long. Picnic tables, garbage bins, and fire grills are provided. Drinking water, vault toilets,

and firewood are available. Leashed pets are permitted.

Reservations, fees: No reservations. Sites are $10 per night, plus $5 for each additional vehicle. Open mid-April through September.

Directions: From Eugene drive south on I-5 for five miles to Exit 188 and Highway 58. Turn east and drive 35 miles to the town of Oakridge. From Oakridge continue east on Highway 58 about two miles to Kitson Springs Road. Turn right and drive one-half mile to Forest Road 21. Turn right and drive 19 miles to the campground.

Contact: Willamette National Forest, Middle Fork Ranger District, 46375 Hwy. 58, Westfir, OR 97492; 541/782-2283; fax 541/782-5306.

86 Secret

5

This small campground, set on the Middle Fork of the Willamette River, gets regular use from local know-hows. The tree cover is scant, but there is adequate vegetation to buffer the campsites from the nearby road noise. Fishing the Middle Fork Willamette is generally fair.

Location: On the Willamette River in Willamette National Forest; The Southern Cascades map 4, grid e7.

Campsites, facilities: There are six sites for tents, trailers, or RVs up to 15 feet long. Picnic tables, garbage bins, and fire rings are provided. Vault toilets are available, but there is no drinking water. Leashed pets are permitted.

Reservations, fees: No reservations. Sites are $8 per night, plus $4 for each additional vehicle. Senior discount available. Open mid-April through September.

Directions: From Eugene drive south on I-5 for five miles to Exit 188 and Highway

58. Turn east and drive 35 miles to the town of Oakridge. From Oakridge continue east on Highway 58 about two miles to Kitson Springs Road. Turn right and drive one-half mile to Forest Road 21. Turn right and drive 19 miles to the campground.

Contact: Willamette National Forest, Middle Fork Ranger District, 46375 Hwy. 58, Westfir, OR 97492; 541/782-2283; fax 541/782-5306.

87 Indigo Springs

 5

This is a small, semi-open campground at 2,800 feet elevation in a stand of old-growth Douglas fir. Nearby is a 250-foot walk to the origin of this cold water spring. A remnant of the historic Oregon Central Military Wagon Road passes near the campground, with an interpretive sign explaining it.

Location: Near the Willamette River in Willamette National Forest; The Southern Cascades map 4, grid e7.

Campsites, facilities: There are three sites for tents, trailers, or RVs up to 16 feet long. Picnic tables and fire grills are provided. Vault toilets and firewood are available. There is no drinking water. Leashed pets are permitted.

Reservations, fees: No reservations; no fee. Open mid-April to mid-November, weather permitting.

Directions: From Eugene drive south on I-5 for five miles to Exit 188 and Highway 58. Turn east and drive 35 miles to the town of Oakridge. From Oakridge continue east on Highway 58 about two miles to Kitson Springs Road. Turn right and drive one-half mile to Forest Road 21. Turn right and drive 27 miles to the campground.

Contact: Willamette National Forest, Middle Fork Ranger District, 46375 Hwy. 58, Westfir, OR 97492; 541/782-2283; fax 541/782-5306.

88 Rock Creek

8

Since we started roaming around the state 20 years ago, we've noticed that this campground on the banks of Rock Creek in a relatively obscure spot has been considerably improved by the BLM. It's not well known, either, so you're likely to have privacy as a bonus. No fishing is allowed in Rock Creek.

Location: On Rock Creek; The Southern Cascades map 4, grid e1.

Campsites, facilities: There are 17 sites for tents, trailers, or RVs up to 40 feet long. Picnic tables and fire grills are provided. A camp host is on-site, and vault toilets, drinking water, a pavilion, and firewood are available. Leashed pets are permitted.

Reservations, fees: No reservations. Sites are $8 per night, with a 14-day stay limit, plus $3 for each additional vehicle. Senior discount available. Open mid-May to mid-October.

Directions: From Roseburg drive east on Highway 138 for 22 miles to Rock Creek Road. Turn right (north) and drive seven miles to the campground on the right.

Contact: Bureau of Land Management, Roseburg District, 777 N.W. Garden Valley Blvd., Roseburg, OR 97470; 541/440-4930; fax 541/440-4948; website: www.or.blm.gov/roseburg.

89 Millpond

8

Rock Creek flows past Millpond and empties into the North Umpqua River five miles downstream. Just below this confluence is the Rock Creek Fish Hatchery, which is open year-round to visitors, with free access. This campground along the banks of Rock Creek is the first camp you'll see along Rock Creek Road, which accounts for its relative popularity in this area. Like Rock Creek Campground, it's primitive and remote. No fishing is allowed in Rock Creek. Note that a new campground called White Pine was planned just down the road, with construction beginning in 2002.

Location: On Rock Creek; The Southern Cascades map 4, grid e1.

Campsites, facilities: There are 12 sites for tents, trailers, or RVs up to 40 feet long. Picnic tables, garbage service, and fire grills are provided. A camp host is on-site, and flush and vault toilets, drinking water, firewood, a ball field, a playground, and a pavilion (with 24 picnic tables, sinks, electricity, and fireplaces), are available. Some facilities are wheelchair-accessible. Leashed pets are permitted.

Reservations, fees: No reservations. Sites are $8 per night, with a 14-day stay limit, plus $3 for each additional vehicle. Senior discount available. Open mid-May to mid-October.

Directions: From Roseburg drive east on Highway 138 for 22 miles to Rock Creek Road. Turn right (north) and drive five miles to the campground on the right.

Contact: Bureau of Land Management, Roseburg District, 777 N.W. Garden Valley Blvd., Roseburg, OR 97470; 541/440-4930; fax 541/440-4948; website: www.or.blm.gov/roseburg.

90 Steamboat Falls

8

There is excellent scenery at this campground on the banks of Steamboat Creek, at beautiful Steamboat Falls, which features a fish ladder that provides passage for steelhead and salmon on their upstream migration. No fishing is permitted in Steamboat Creek. Other camping options nearby are Island and Canton Creek.

Location: On Steamboat Creek in Umpqua National Forest; The Southern Cascades map 4, grid e4.

Campsites, facilities: There are 10 sites for tents, trailers, or RVs up to 24 feet long. Picnic tables, garbage bins, vault toilets, and fire grills are provided. There is no drinking water. Leashed pets are permitted.

Reservations, fees: No reservations. Sites are $6 per night, $3 more per night for additional vehicles. Senior discount available. Open year-round, with no fee from November through late May.

Directions: From Roseburg on I-5, take Exit 120 to Highway 138. Drive east on Highway 138 to Steamboat and Forest Road 38. Turn left on Forest Road 38 (Steamboat Creek Road) and drive six miles to a fork with Forest Road 3810. Bear right and drive one mile to the campground.

Contact: Umpqua National Forest, North Umpqua Ranger District, 18782 North Umpqua Hwy., Glide, OR 97443; 541/496-3532; fax 541/496-3534.

91 Timpanogas

8

At 5,200 feet elevation, this campground is situated in a stand of silver, grand, and noble fir. Timpanogas Lake is the headwaters of the Middle Fork Willamette River. Only nonmotorized boating is permitted. Fishing in the lake if often very good for cutthroat and brook trout. The Timpanogas Basin offers 23 miles of hiking trails, with a bonus of excellent views of Diamond Peak, Sawtooth, and Cowhorn Mountains. Warning: time it wrong and the mosquitoes will eat you alive if you forget your insect repellent.

Location: On Timpanogas Lake in Willamette National Forest; The Southern Cascades map 4, grid e8.

Campsites, facilities: There are 10 sites for tents, trailers, or RVs up to 24 feet long.

Picnic tables, garbage bins, and fire rings are provided. Drinking water, vault toilets, and firewood are available. Boat docks are nearby, but no boats with motors are allowed. Leashed pets are permitted.

Reservations, fees: No reservations. Sites are $6 per night, plus $3 for each additional vehicle. Senior discount available. Open mid-June to mid-October, weather permitting.

Directions: From Eugene drive south on I-5 for five miles to Exit 188 and Highway 58. Turn east and drive 35 miles to the town of Oakridge. Continue east on Highway 58 for two miles to Kitson Springs Road. Turn right and drive one-half mile to Forest Road 21. Turn right and drive 32 miles to Forest Road 2154. Turn left and drive about 10 miles to the campground.

Contact: Willamette National Forest, Middle Fork Ranger District, 46375 Hwy. 58, Westfir, OR 97492; 541/782-2283; fax 541/782-5306.

92 Scaredman

6

This small campground along the banks of Canton Creek is virtually unknown to out-of-towners. Set in an old-growth forest, it offers a chance to swim in the creek and it's also private and secluded. Scaredman gets its name from an old legend that says some early settlers camped here, heard a pack of hungry wolves, and then ran off, scared to death. This is one of the few free camps left in the region. It was considerably improved in 2001 with larger sites, new vault toilets, and revegetation. Even though fishing is closed on Canton Creek and all Steamboat drainages, the North Umpqua River 3.5 miles downstream offers fly-fishing for steelhead or salmon.

Location: On Canton Creek; The Southern Cascades map 4, grid f3.

Campsites, facilities: There are nine sites for tents, trailers, or RVs up to 25 feet long.

Picnic tables, garbage service, and fire grills are provided. Vault toilets are available and there is a camp host. Some facilities are wheelchair-accessible. There is no drinking water. Leashed pets are permitted.

Reservations, fees: No reservations; no fee. The stay limit is 14 days. Open year-round.

Directions: From Roseburg drive east on Highway 138 for 40 miles to Steamboat Creek Road. Turn north (left) and drive one-half mile to Canton Creek Road. Turn left (north) and drive three miles to the campground.

Contact: Bureau of Land Management, Roseburg District, 777 N.W. Garden Valley Blvd., Roseburg, OR 97470; 541/440-4930; fax 541/440-4948.

93 Island

8

The North Umpqua is one of Oregon's most beautiful rivers. This scenic campground is set along the banks of the North Umpqua River at a spot popular for both rafting and steelhead fishing (fly-fishing only and with a 20-inch minimum size limit). A hiking trail that leads east and west along the river is accessible by driving a short distance west. See a U.S. Forest Service map for details.

Location: On the Umpqua River in Umpqua National Forest; The Southern Cascades map 4, grid f3.

Campsites, facilities: There are seven sites for tents, trailers, or RVs up to 24 feet long. Picnic tables, garbage bins, and fire grills are provided. Some facilities are wheelchair-accessible. There is no drinking water. Leashed pets are permitted.

Reservations, fees: No reservations. Sites are $7 per night, $3 per night for an additional vehicle. Senior discount available. Open year-round.

Directions: From Roseburg drive east on Highway 138 for 40 miles (just past Steamboat). The campground is along the highway.

Contact: Umpqua National Forest, North Umpqua Ranger District, 18782 North Umpqua Hwy., Glide, OR 97443; 541/496-3532; fax 541/496-3534.

94 Canton Creek

8

This campground (1,195 feet elevation) at the confluence of Canton and Steamboat Creeks less than a mile from the North Umpqua River gets little overnight use, but there are lots of day swimmers in July and August. No fishing is permitted on Steamboat or Canton Creeks because they are spawning areas for steelhead and salmon. Steamboat Falls is six miles north on Forest Road 38. See the description of Steamboat Falls for other area details.

Location: Near the North Umpqua River in Umpqua National Forest; The Southern Cascades map 4, grid f3.

Campsites, facilities: There are five sites for tents, trailers, or RVs up to 22 feet long. Picnic tables, garbage bins, and fire grills are provided. Drinking water, a covered picnic gazebo, and flush toilets are available. Leashed pets are permitted.

Reservations, fees: No reservations. Sites are $7 per night, $3 per night for an additional vehicle. Senior discount available. Open mid-May to mid-October.

Directions: From Roseburg drive east on Highway 138 for 39 miles to Steamboat and Forest Road 38 (Steamboat Creek Road). Turn left and drive a quarter mile to the campground.

Contact: Umpqua National Forest, North Umpqua Ranger District, 18782 North Umpqua Hwy., Glide, OR 97443; 541/496-3532; fax 541/496-3534.

95 Susan Creek

9

This popular and pretty campground is set along the banks of the North Umpqua Wild and Scenic River. The setting is pretty, with lots of trees and river access. Highlights include two barrier-free trails, one traveling one-half mile to the day-use area. From there a hike of about three-quarters of a mile leads to the 50-foot Susan Creek Falls. Another 0.4 mile up the trail are the Susan Creek Indian Mounds. The moss-covered rocks are believed to be a spiritual site visited by Native Americans in search of guardian spirit visions. There is also an excellent osprey interpetive site with a viewing platform along the river.

Location: On the North Umpqua River; The Southern Cascades map 4, grid f1.

Campsites, facilities: There are 31 sites for trailers or RVs up to 35 feet long. Picnic tables, garbage service, and fire grills are provided. Flush toilets, drinking water, showers, and firewood are available, and there is a camp host. Some facilities and trails are wheelchair-accessible. Leashed pets are permitted.

Reservations, fees: No reservations. Sites are $11 per night, with a 14-day stay limit, plus $3 for each additional vehicle. Senior discount available. Open early May to late October.

Directions: From Roseburg drive east on Highway 138 for 29.5 miles to the campground (turnoff well signed).

Contact: Bureau of Land Management, Roseburg District, N.W. 777 Garden Valley Blvd., Roseburg, OR 97470; 541/440-4930; fax 541/440-4948; website: www.or.blm.gov/roseburg.

96 Eagle Rock

🎣 🐕 ♿ 🚐 ⛺ 9

This camp is set next to the North Umpqua River and adjacent to the Boulder Creek Wilderness. It is named after Eagle Rock, which towers above the campground along with Rattlesnake Rock. There are outstanding views of these unusual rock formations. The camp gets moderate use, even heavy on weekends. It is set at 1,676 feet elevation near Boulder Flat, a major launch point for rafting. Fishing is restricted here to the use of artificial lures with a single barbless hook.

Location: On the North Umpqua River in Umpqua National Forest; The Southern Cascades map 4, grid f4.

Campsites, facilities: There are 23 sites for tents, trailers, or RVs up to 30 feet long. Picnic tables and fire grills are provided. Vault toilets and garbage bins are available. There is no drinking water. A store, propane, and ice are within five miles. Some facilities are wheelchair-accessible. Leashed pets are permitted.

Reservations, fees: No reservations. Sites are $8 per night, $3 per night for an additional vehicle. Senior discount available. Open mid-May to mid-September.

Directions: From Roseburg drive east on Highway 138 for 53 miles to the campground on the left.

Contact: Umpqua National Forest, North Umpqua Ranger District, 18782 North Umpqua Hwy., Glide, OR 97443; 541/496-3532; fax 541/496-3534.

97 Boulder Flat

🎣 🚤 🐕 🚐 ⛺ 8

This campground is set along the banks of the North Umpqua River at the confluence of Boulder Creek. There's good trout fishing here (fly-fishing only) and outstanding scenery.

The camp is set at a major launching point for white-water rafting. Across the river from the campground a trail follows Boulder Creek north for 10.5 miles through the Boulder Creek Wilderness, a climb in elevation from 2,000 to 5,400 feet. Access to the trail is at Soda Springs Dam, two miles east of the camp. It's a good thumper for backpackers. A little over a mile to the east are some huge, dramatic pillars of volcanic rock, colored with lichen.

Location: On the North Umpqua River in Umpqua National Forest; The Southern Cascades map 4, grid f4.

Campsites, facilities: There are 11 sites for tents, trailers, or RVs up to 24 feet long. Picnic tables, garbage bins, and fire grills are provided. Vault toilets are available. There is no drinking water. A store, propane, and ice are within five miles. A raft launch is on-site. Leashed pets are permitted.

Reservations, fees: No reservations. Sites are $7 per night, $3 per night for an additional vehicle. Senior discount available. Open year-round.

Directions: From Roseburg drive east on Highway 138 for 54 miles to the campground on the left.

Contact: Umpqua National Forest, North Umpqua Ranger District, 18782 North Umpqua Hwy., Glide, OR 97443; 541/496-3532; fax 541/496-3534.

98 Horseshoe Bend

🚶 🚴 🎣 🚤
🐕 ♿ 🚐 ⛺ 8

This campground is in the middle of a big bend in the North Umpqua River, set at an elevation of 1,300 feet. This is a major launching point for white-water rafting. Fly-fishing is popular here.

Location: On the Umpqua River in Umpqua National Forest; The Southern Cascades map 4, grid f4.

Campsites, facilities: There are 24 sites for tents, trailers, or RVs up to 35 feet long and one group site. Picnic tables, fire grills, garbage bins, drinking water, and flush toilets are provided. A coin-operated laundry, a store, gas, and propane are available one mile east. Some facilities are wheelchair-accessible. Raft launching facilities are nearby. Leashed pets are permitted.

Reservations, fees: Reservations accepted for the group site only. Individual sites are $11 per night, and the group site is $60 per night; $3 per night for an additional vehicle. Senior discount available. Open from mid-May to late September.

Directions: From Roseburg on I-5, take Exit 120. Drive east on Highway 138 for 47 miles to Forest Road 4750. Turn right and drive south a short distance to the campground.

Contact: Umpqua National Forest, North Umpqua Ranger District, 18782 North Umpqua Hwy., Glide, OR 97443; 541/496-3532; fax 541/496-3534.

99 Toketee Lake

7

This campground is just north of Toketee Lake, set at an elevation of 2,200 feet. The North Umpqua River Trail passes near camp and continues east along the river for many miles. Diehard hikers can also take it west, where it meanders for a while before heading north near the Boulder Creek Wilderness. Toketee Lake is an 80-acre reservoir offering a good population of brown and rainbow trout and many recreation options. A worthwhile point of interest is Toketee Falls, just west of the lake turnoff. Another is Umpqua Hot Springs, a few miles northeast of the camp. There's a wide variety of wildlife in the area. You might see otter, beaver, great blue heron, kingfishers, a variety of ducks and geese, and bald eagles in fall and winter.

Location: On Toketee Lake in Umpqua National Forest; The Southern Cascades map 4, grid f5.

Campsites, facilities: There are 32 sites for tents, trailers, or RVs up to 22 feet long, and one group site. Picnic tables, garbage bins, and fire grills are provided. Vault toilets are available, but there is no drinking water. Boat docks and launching facilities are nearby. Leashed pets are permitted.

Reservations, fees: Reservations required for the group site. Sites are $6 per night, $15 per night for the group site, $2 per night for an additional vehicle. Open year-round.

Directions: From Roseburg drive east on Highway 138 for 60 miles to Forest Road 34. Turn north and drive one mile to the campground on the right.

Contact: Umpqua National Forest, Diamond Lake Ranger District, 2020 Toketee Ranger Station Rd., Idleyld Park, OR 97447; 541/498-2531; fax 541/498-2515.

100 East Lemolo

8

This campground is on the southeastern shore of Lemolo Lake, where boating and fishing are some of the recreation possibilities. Boats with motors are allowed. The North Umpqua River and its adjacent trail are just beyond the north shore of the lake. If you hike for two miles northwest of the lake, you can reach spectacular Lemolo Falls. Large German brown trout, a wild, native fish, can be taken on troll and fly. Lemolo Lake also provides fishing for kokanee, brook trout, and a sprinkling of rainbow trout.

Location: On Lemolo Lake in Umpqua National Forest; The Southern Cascades map 4, grid f7.

Campsites, facilities: There are 15 sites for tents or small RVs up to 22 feet long. No drinking water is available. Picnic tables, garbage bins, and fire rings are provided. Vault toilets are available. Boat docks, launching facilities, and rentals are nearby. Leashed pets are permitted.

Reservations, fees: No reservations. Sites are $6 per night, $2 per night for an additional vehicle. Senior discount available. Open mid-May to late October.

Directions: From Roseburg drive east on Highway 138 for 74 miles to Forest Road 2610 (three miles east of Clearwater Falls). Turn north and drive three miles to Forest Road 2610-400. Turn right and drive two miles to Forest Road 2610-430. Turn left and drive a short distance to the campground at the end of the road.

Contact: Umpqua National Forest, Diamond Lake Ranger District, 2020 Toketee Ranger Station Rd., Idleyld Park, OR 97447; 541/498-2531; fax 541/498-2515.

101 Poole Creek

8

This campground on the western shore of Lemolo Lake isn't far from Lemolo Lake Resort, which is open for recreation year-round. The camp is just south of the mouth of Poole Creek in a lodgepole pine, mountain hemlock, and Shasta red fir forest. This is by far the most popular U.S. Forest Service camp at the lake, especially with water-skiers, who are allowed to ski in designated areas of the lake. See the description of East Lemolo for more information.

Location: On Lemolo Lake in Umpqua National Forest; The Southern Cascades map 4, grid f7.

Campsites, facilities: There are 59 sites for tents, trailers, or RVs up to 30 feet long, including group sites. Picnic tables and fire grills are provided. Drinking water and vault toilets are available. A grocery store, restaurant, lounge, boat docks, launching facilities, and rentals are nearby. Leashed pets are permitted.

Reservations, fees: Reservations required for group sites ($8.65 reservation fee). Sites are $9–12 per night, $3 per night for an additional vehicle. Senior discount available. Open late April to late October.

Directions: From Roseburg drive east on Highway 138 for 72 miles to Forest Road 2610 (Bird's Point Road). Turn north and drive four miles to the signed turnoff on the right for the campground entrance.

Contact: Umpqua National Forest, Diamond Lake Ranger District, 2020 Toketee Ranger Station Rd., Idleyld Park, OR 97447; 541/498-2531; fax 541/498-2515; website (for reservations): www.reserveusa.com. Reservations 877/444-6777

102 Inlet

5

This campground is on the eastern inlet of Lemolo Lake, hidden in the deep, green, and quiet forest, where the North Umpqua River rushes into Lemolo Reservoir. The lake exceeds 100 feet in depth in some spots. The camp is just across the road from the North Umpqua River Trail, which is routed east into the Oregon Cascades Recreation Area and the Mt. Thielsen Wilderness. See the description of East Lemolo for more recreation details.

Location: On Lemolo Lake in Umpqua National Forest; The Southern Cascades map 4, grid f7.

Campsites, facilities: There are 14 sites for tents, trailers, or RVs up to 22 feet long. Vault toilets are available, but there is no drinking water. Picnic tables, garbage bins, and fire grills are provided. Boat docks, launching facilities, rentals, a restaurant, lounge, groceries, and gas station are available nearby. Leashed pets are permitted.

Reservations, fees: No reservations accepted. Sites are $6 per night, $2 per night for an additional vehicle. Senior discount available. Open mid-May to late October.

Directions: From Roseburg drive east on Highway 138 for 74 miles to Forest Road 2610. Turn north and drive three miles to Forest Road 2610-400. Turn east and drive three miles to the campground.

Contact: Umpqua National Forest, Diamond Lake Ranger District, 2020 Toketee Ranger Station Rd., Idleyld Park, OR 97447; 541/498-2531; fax 541/498-2515.

103 Wolf Creek

6

This pretty camp is at the entrance to the national forest along the banks of the Little River near the Wolf Creek Civilian Conservation Center. It is set at an elevation of 1,100 feet, close to civilization with easy access. This camp has abundant wildflowers in the spring. If you want to get deeper into the interior of the Cascades, Hemlock Lake and Lake of the Woods are about 21 and 15 miles east, respectively.

Location: On the Little River in Umpqua National Forest; The Southern Cascades map 4, grid g1.

Campsites, facilities: There are eight sites for tents, trailers, or RVs up to 30 feet long and one group site. A covered pavilion for groups, 14 tables, and stone fireplaces are available. Picnic tables, fire grills, garbage bins, horseshoe pits, softball field, and volleyball court are provided. Flush toilets and drinking water are available. Some facilities are wheelchair-accessible. Leashed pets are permitted.

Reservations, fees: Reservations required for groups. Individual sites are $8 per night, the group site is $70 per night; $3 per night for an additional vehicle. Senior discount available. Open from mid-May through September.

Directions: From Roseburg on I-5, take Exit 120. Drive east on Highway 138 for 18 miles to Glide and County Road 17. Turn southeast and drive 12 miles southeast (the road becomes Little River Road) to the campground.

Contact: Umpqua National Forest, North Umpqua Ranger District, 18782 North Umpqua Hwy., Glide, OR 97443; 541/496-3532; fax 541/496-3534.

104 Coolwater

6

This campground along the banks of the Little River gets moderate use. It is set at 1,300 feet elevation and is in a pretty forest setting with some scenic hiking trails nearby. Overhang Trail is within one-half mile of the campground. Fishing and swimming are also options here. Scenic Grotto Falls can be reached by traveling north on Forest Road 2703 (across the road from the camp). Near the falls is Emile Grove, home of a thicket of old-growth Douglas firs and the huge "Bill Taft Tree," named after the former president.

Location: On the Little River in Umpqua National Forest; The Southern Cascades map 4, grid g2.

Campsites, facilities: There are seven sites for tents, trailers, or RVs up to 24 feet long. Picnic tables and fire grills are provided.

Vault toilets and drinking water are available. Leashed pets are permitted.

Reservations, fees: No reservations. Sites are $5 per night; $3 per night for an additional vehicle. Senior discount available. Open year-round.

Directions: From Roseburg on I-5, take Exit 120. Drive east on Highway 138 for 18 miles to Glide and County Road 17. Turn southeast and drive 15.5 miles southeast (the road becomes Little River Road) to the campground on the right.

Contact: Umpqua National Forest, North Umpqua Ranger District, 18782 North Umpqua Hwy., Glide, OR 97443; 541/496-3532; fax 541/496-3534.

105 White Creek

6

Hiking and fishing are two of the recreation options at this campground set at the confluence of White Creek and the Little River. There is a sandy beach on shallow Little River. See the description of Coolwater for other details about the area.

Location: On the Little River in Umpqua National Forest; The Southern Cascades map 4, grid g2.

Campsites, facilities: There are four sites for tents, trailers, or RVs up to 30 feet long. Picnic tables, fire grills, and garbage bins are provided. Vault toilets are available. There is no drinking water. Leashed pets are permitted.

Reservations, fees: No reservations. Sites are $5 per night (with no fee from November through May 20), $3 per night for an additional vehicle. Senior discount available. Open year-round.

Directions: From Roseburg on I-5, take Exit 120. Drive east on Highway 138 for 18 miles to Glide and County Road 17. Turn southeast and drive 17 miles southeast (the road becomes Little River Road) to Forest Road 2792 (Red Butte Road). Bear right and drive one-quarter mile to the campground on the left.

Contact: Umpqua National Forest, North Umpqua Ranger District, 18782 North Umpqua Hwy., Glide, OR 97443; 541/496-3532; fax 541/496-3534.

106 Lake in the Woods

7

The shore of little Lake in the Woods is the setting of this camp, which makes a nice home base for several good hikes. One of them leaves the camp and heads south for about three miles to the Hemlock Lake Campground. Two other nearby trails provide short, scenic hikes to either Hemlock Falls or Yakso Falls. The campground is set at 3,200 feet elevation. There is a man-made, four-acre lake, eight feet at its deepest point. Boats without motors are allowed.

Location: On Lake in the Woods in Umpqua National Forest; The Southern Cascades map 4, grid g3.

Campsites, facilities: There are 11 sites for tents, trailers, or RVs up to 35 feet long. Picnic tables, fire grills, and garbage bins are provided. Flush toilets are available. There is no drinking water. Leashed pets are permitted.

Reservations, fees: No reservations. Sites are $8 per night, $3 per night for an additional vehicle. Senior discount available. Open from June to late October.

Directions: From Roseburg on I-5, take Exit 120. Drive east on Highway 138 for 18 miles to Glide and County Road 17. Turn southeast and drive 16.5 miles southeast (the road becomes Little River Road) to Forest Road 27. Continue 11 miles to the campground. The last seven miles are gravel.

Contact: Umpqua National Forest, North Umpqua Ranger District, 18782 North Umpqua Hwy., Glide, OR 97443; 541/496-3532; fax 541/496-3534.

107 Hemlock Lake

8

This is a little-known jewel of a spot. For starters, it's set along the shore of Hemlock Lake at 4,400 feet elevation. There is a 28-acre, man-made reservoir that is 33 feet at its deepest point. An eight-mile loop trail called the Yellow Jacket Loop is just south of the campground. Another trail leaves camp and heads north for about three miles to the Lake of the Woods Campground. From there, it's just a short hike to either Hemlock Falls or Yakso Falls, both spectacularly scenic.

Location: On Hemlock Lake in Umpqua National Forest; The Southern Cascades map 4, grid g3.

Campsites, facilities: There are 13 sites for tents, trailers, or RVs up to 35 feet long. Picnic tables, fire grills, and garbage bins are provided. Vault toilets are available, but there is no drinking water. Boat docks and launching facilities are nearby. No motors are allowed on the lake. Leashed pets are permitted.

Reservations, fees: No reservations. Sites are $7 per night (with no fee from November through May 20), $3 per night for an additional vehicle. Senior discount available. Open year-round, weather permitting.

Directions: From Roseburg on I-5, take Exit 120. Drive east on Highway 138 for 18 miles to Glide and County Road 17. Turn southeast and drive 32 miles to the campground.

Contact: Umpqua National Forest, North Umpqua Ranger District, 18782 North Umpqua Hwy., Glide, OR 97443; 541/496-3532; fax 541/496-3534.

108 Whitehorse Falls

8

This campground is along the Clearwater River, one of the coldest streams in Umpqua National Forest. Even though the camp is adjacent to the highway, the setting is primitive. It is shaded by old-growth Douglas fir and is set at an elevation of 3,790 feet. Pretty Clearwater Falls, a few miles east, is a good side-trip option. Fishing and hiking are among the other recreation possibilities.

Location: On the Clearwater River in Umpqua National Forest; The Southern Cascades map 4, grid g6.

Campsites, facilities: There are five tent sites. Picnic tables, fire grills, and garbage bins are provided. Vault toilets are available, but there is no drinking water. Leashed pets are permitted.

Reservations, fees: Reservations accepted. Sites are $6 per night, $2 per night for an additional vehicle. Senior discount available. Open from June to late October.

Directions: From Roseburg on I-5, take Exit 120. Drive east on Highway 138 for 67 miles (before reaching the Lemolo Lake turnoff) to the campground.

Contact: Umpqua National Forest, Diamond Lake Ranger District, 2020 Toketee Ranger Station Rd., Idleyld Park, OR 97447; 541/498-2531; fax 541/498-2515.

109 Clearwater Falls

8

The main attraction at this campground along the banks of the Clearwater River is the cascading section of stream called Clearwater Falls. It is set at an elevation of 4,100 feet. See the description of Whitehorse Falls for area details. There is another camping area two miles away within Clearwater Falls with eight more sites that include picnic tables and fire rings.

Location: On the Clearwater River in Umpqua National Forest; The Southern Cascades map 4, grid g7.

Campsites, facilities: There are nine sites for tents or self-contained trailers or RVs up to 30 feet long. Picnic tables, fire grills, and garbage bins are provided. Vault toilets are available, but there is no drinking water. Leashed pets are permitted.

Reservations, fees: No reservations. Sites are $6 per night, $3 per night for an additional vehicle. Senior discount available. Open from mid-May to late October.

Directions: From Roseburg on I-5, take Exit 120 for Highway 138. Drive east on Highway 138 for 70 miles to a signed turn for Clearwater Falls. Turn right and drive one mile to the campground.

Contact: Umpqua National Forest, Diamond Lake Ranger District, 2020 Toketee Ranger Station Rd., Idleyld Park, OR 97447; 541/498-2531; fax 541/498-2515.

110 Broken Arrow

 6

This campground is set at 5,190 feet near the south shore of Diamond Lake, the largest natural lake in Umpqua National Forest. It is set back from the lake and surrounded by lodgepole pine with views of Mt. Bailey and Mt. Thielsen. Boating, fishing, swimming, hiking, and bicycling keep visitors busy here. Concerns over the size of the trout have initiated a trout-planting program of one- and two-pound rainbow trout. Diamond Lake is adjacent to the Mt. Thielsen Wilderness, Crater Lake National Park, and Mt. Bailey, all of which offer a variety of recreation opportunities year-round. Diamond Lake is quite popular with anglers because of its good trout trolling, particularly in early summer.

Location: On Diamond Lake in Umpqua National Forest; The Southern Cascades map 4, grid g7.

Campsites, facilities: There are 117 sites for tents, trailers, or RVs up to 35 feet long. Picnic tables, fire grills, and garbage bins are provided. Flush toilets, showers, a sanitary disposal station, and drinking water are available. Some facilities are wheelchair-accessible. Boat docks, launching facilities, and rentals are nearby. Leashed pets are permitted.

Reservations, fees: Reservations accepted for groups only ($8.65 reservation fee). Individual sites are $9–12 per night and $3 per night for an additional vehicle. Senior discount available. Open from late May to mid-September.

Directions: From Roseburg on I-5, take Exit 120. Drive east on Highway 138 for 80 miles to Diamond Lake Loop (Forest Road 4795). Turn right and drive a short distance to the junction with the loop road. Turn south and drive four miles (along the east shore) to the campground at the southern end of the lake.

Contact: Umpqua National Forest, Diamond Lake Ranger District, 2020 Toketee Ranger Station Rd., Idleyld Park, OR 97447; 541/498-2531; fax 541/498-2515. Reservations 877/444-6777.

111 Thielsen View

7

This campground sits along the west shore of Diamond Lake in the shadow of majestic Mt. Bailey. There is a beautiful view of Mt. Thielsen from here. See the description of Broken Arrow for information on recreation opportunities.

Location: On Diamond Lake in Umpqua National Forest; The Southern Cascades map 4, grid g7.

Campsites, facilities: There are 60 sites for tents, trailers, or RVs up to 30 feet long. Picnic tables, fire grills, and garbage bins are provided. Drinking water and vault toilets are available. Some facilities are wheelchair-accessible. Boat docks, launching facilities, and rentals are nearby. Leashed pets are permitted.

Reservations, fees: No reservations. Sites are $9–12 per night; $3 per night for an additional vehicle. Senior discount available. Open from late May to late September.

Directions: From Roseburg on I-5, take Exit 120. Drive east on Highway 138 for 80 miles to Diamond Lake Loop (Forest Road 4795). Turn right and drive a short distance to the junction with the loop road. Continue straight on the loop road and drive four miles to the campground on the left.

Contact: Umpqua National Forest, Diamond Lake Ranger District, 2020 Toketee Ranger Station Rd., Idleyld Park, OR 97447; 541/498-2531; fax 541/498-2515.

112 Diamond Lake

 9

This extremely popular camp along the east shore of Diamond Lake has all the luxuries: flush toilets, showers, and drinking water. There are campfire programs every Friday and Saturday night in the summer. See the description of Broken Arrow for recreation information.

Location: On Diamond Lake in Umpqua National Forest; The Southern Cascades map 4, grid g8.

Campsites, facilities: There are 238 sites for tents, trailers, or RVs up to 45 feet long. Picnic tables, garbage bins, and fire grills

are provided. Flush toilets, showers, drinking water, sanitary disposal station, firewood, and an amphitheater are available. Boat docks, launching facilities, rentals, and fish-cleaning station are nearby. Leashed pets are permitted.

Reservations, fees: Some sites can be reserved ($8.65 reservation fee). Sites are $10–20 per night; $5 per night for an additional vehicle. Senior discount available. Open from late April to late October.

Directions: From Roseburg on I-5, take Exit 120. Drive east on Highway 138 for 80 miles to Diamond Lake Loop (Forest Road 4795). Turn right and drive a short distance to the junction with a loop road. Turn south and drive two miles (along the east shore) to the campground on the right.

Contact: Umpqua National Forest, Diamond Lake Ranger District, 2020 Toketee Ranger Station Rd., Idleyld Park, OR 97447; 541/498-2531; fax 541/498-2515. Reservations 877/444-6777.

113 Boulder Creek

This campground is on the banks of the South Umpqua River near Boulder Creek. No fishing is allowed here. It is set at 1,400 feet elevation. See the description of Dumont Creek for information on the area.

Location: On the South Umpqua River in Umpqua National Forest; The Southern Cascades map 4, grid h2.

Campsites, facilities: There are 12 sites for tents, trailers, or RVs up to 25 feet long. Picnic tables, fire grills, and garbage bins are provided. Vault toilets are available, but there is no drinking water. Leashed pets are permitted.

Reservations, fees: No reservations; no fee. Open from late May to late October.

Directions: At Canyonville on I-5, take Exit 99 to County Road 1. Drive east on County Road 1 for 25 miles to Tiller and County Road 46. Turn left and drive six miles northeast (County Road 46 turns into South Umpqua Road/Forest Road 28). Continue northeast and drive seven miles to the camp.

Contact: Umpqua National Forest, Tiller Ranger District, 27812 Tiller Trail Hwy., Tiller, OR 97484; 541/825-3201; fax 541/825-3259.

114 Dumont Creek

🏊 🐕 🚐 ⛺ 4

This campground set at 1,300 feet elevation along the banks of the South Umpqua River just above the mouth of Dumont Creek is quiet, primitive, and remote. It gets moderate to heavy use. A short trail leads to a small beach on the river. No fishing is allowed at this camp, and there is no trailer turnaround here. Boulder Creek, just a few miles east, provides a camping option. A good side trip is nearby South Umpqua Falls, a beautiful, wide waterfall featuring a fish ladder and a platform so you can watch the fish struggle upstream.

Location: On the South Umpqua River in Umpqua National Forest; The Southern Cascades map 4, grid h2.

Campsites, facilities: There are five sites for tents, trailers, or RVs up to 16 feet long. Picnic tables, fire grills, and garbage bins are provided. Vault toilets are available, but there is no drinking water. Leashed pets are permitted.

Reservations, fees: No reservations; no fee. Open all year.

Directions: At Canyonville on I-5, take Exit 99 to County Road 1. Drive east on County Road 1 for 25 miles to Tiller and County Road 46. Turn left and drive six miles northeast (County Road 46 turns into South Umpqua

Road/Forest Road 28). Continue northeast and drive 5.5 miles to the camp.

Contact: Umpqua National Forest, Tiller Ranger District, 27812 Tiller Trail Hwy., Tiller, OR 97484; 541/825-3201; fax 541/825-3259.

115 Cover

🏃 🐕 🚐 ⛺ 4

If you want quiet, this camp set at 1,700 feet elevation along the banks of Jackson Creek is the right place, since hardly anyone knows about it. It gets light use during the summer. During the fall hunting season, however, it is known to fill. If you head east to Forest Road 68 and follow it south, you'll have access to a major trail into the Rogue-Umpqua Divide Wilderness. Be sure not to miss the world's largest sugar pine tree, a few miles west of camp. No fishing is allowed here.

Location: On Jackson Creek in Umpqua National Forest; The Southern Cascades map 4, grid h2.

Campsites, facilities: There are seven sites for tents, trailers, or RVs up to 22 feet long. Picnic tables, fire grills, and garbage bins are provided. Vault toilets are available, but there is no drinking water. Leashed pets are permitted.

Reservations, fees: No reservations; no fee. Open year-round.

Directions: At Canyonville on I-5, take Exit 99 to County Road 1. Drive east on County Road 1 for 25 miles to Tiller and County Road 46. Turn left and drive five miles to Forest Road 29 (Jackson Creek Road). Turn right and drive east for 12 miles to the campground on the right.

Contact: Umpqua National Forest, Tiller Ranger District, 27812 Tiller Trail Hwy., Tiller, OR 97484; 541/825-3201; fax 541/825-3259.

116 Camp Comfort

 6

This campground is set near the upper South Umpqua River, deep in the Umpqua National Forest, at an elevation of 2,000 feet. Campsites are shaded by large old-growth cedar. No fishing is permitted. A good side trip is visiting South Umpqua Falls (you will pass the access point while driving to this camp). Trailheads are nearby (see map of Umpqua National Forest) that provide access to Rogue-Umpqua Divide Wilderness. By the way, those familiar with this camp might remember a rain shelter. It's gone now, having burned down.

Location: On the South Umpqua River in Umpqua National Forest; The Southern Cascades map 4, grid h3.

Campsites, facilities: There are five sites for tents, trailers, or RVs up to 22 feet long. Picnic tables, fire grills, and garbage bins are provided. A wheelchair-accessible vault toilet is available. There is no drinking water. Leashed pets are permitted.

Reservations, fees: No reservations; no fee. Open year round.

Directions: At Canyonville on I-5, take Exit 99 to County Road 1. Drive east on County Road 1 for 25 miles to Tiller and County Road 46. Turn left and drive six miles northeast (County Road 46 turns into South Umpqua Road/Forest Road 28). Continue northeast and drive 18 miles to the camp on the right.

Contact: Umpqua National Forest, Tiller Ranger District, 27812 Tiller Trail Hwy., Tiller, OR 97484; 541/825-3201; fax 541/825-3259.

117 Hamaker

8

Set at 4,000 feet near the Upper Rogue River, this is a beautiful little spot high in a mountain meadow. Wildflowers and wild-

life abound in the spring and early summer. This is one of the least-used camps in the area, and it's a prime camp for Crater Lake visitors.

Location: Near the Upper Rogue River in Rogue River National Forest; The Southern Cascades map 4, grid h6.

Campsites, facilities: There are 10 sites for tents, trailers, or RVs up to 30 feet long. Picnic tables, fire grills, garbage service, and stoves are provided. Drinking water and vault toilets are available. Firewood is available for purchase. Leashed pets are permitted.

Reservations, fees: No reservations. Sites are $8 per night, plus $4 per extra vehicle a night. Senior discount available. Open late May to late October.

Directions: From Medford drive northeast on Highway 62 for 57 miles (just past Union Creek) to Highway 230. Turn left (north) and drive 11 miles to a junction with Forest Road 6530. Continue on Forest Road 6530 for a half mile to Forest Road 6530-900. Turn right and drive one-half mile to the campground on the right.

Contact: Rogue Recreation, 2990 N. Pacific Hwy., Medford, OR 97501; 541/770-5146; fax 541/770-1552; website: www.roguerec.com.

118 Quinn Meadow Horse Camp

8

This scenic campground is open only to horse camping and gets high use. The Elk-Devil's Trail or Wickiup Plains Trail offer access to the Three Sisters Wilderness. There's also a horse route via Katsuk Trail to Devil's Lake. It is set at an elevation of 5,100 feet.

Location: Near Quinn Creek in the Deschutes National Forest; The Southern Cascades map 5, grid a2.

Campsites, facilities: There are 24 sites for tents, trailers, or RVs up to 30 feet long. Picnic tables, fire rings, and horse corrals are provided. Drinking water, vault toilets, and garbage bins are available. Toilets are wheelchair-accessible. Leashed pets are permitted.

Reservations, fees: Reservations required ($8.65 reservation fee). Two-horse corral sites are $12 and four-horse sites are $16; plus $10 for each additional RV and $5 for each additional vehicle. Senior discount available. Open late June through September, weather permitting.

Directions: From Bend drive southwest on Cascades Lakes Highway (also called Century Drive Highway and County Road 46) for 31.2 miles to the campground entrance.

Contact: Deschutes National Forest, Bend-Fort Rock Ranger District, 1230 N.E. 3rd St., Bend, OR 97701; 541/383-4000, reservations 877/444-6777; fax 541/383-4700; website (for reservations): www.reserveusa.com.

119 Devil's Lake Walk-In

🏃 🎣 🐕 🚤 ⛺   8

This walk-in campground is set along the shore of a scenic alpine lake with aqua-jade water and fishing access. Devil's Lake, set at 5,500 feet, is a popular rafting and canoeing spot, and there are several trailheads that lead from the lake into the wilderness. The Elk-Devil's Trail or Wickiup Plains Trail offer access to the Three Sisters Wilderness. There's also a horse route via Katsuk Trail to Quinn Meadow Horse Camp.

Location: On Devil's Lake in Deschutes National Forest; The Southern Cascades map 5, grid a2.

Campsites, facilities: There are nine walk-in tent sites. Picnic tables and fire grills are provided. Vault toilets are available. There is no drinking water, and all garbage must be packed out. Leashed pets are permitted.

Reservations, fees: No reservations. Northwest Forest Pass ($30 annual fee) or $5 daily fee per parked vehicle is required. Open July through September, weather permitting.

Directions: From Bend drive southwest on Cascades Lakes Highway (Century Drive Highway, which becomes County Road 46) for 28.7 miles to the parking area. Walk 200 yards to the campground.

Contact: Deschutes National Forest, Bend-Fort Rock Ranger District, 1230 N.E. 3rd St., Bend, OR 97701; 541/383-4000; fax 541/383-4700.

120 Soda Creek

🏃 🎣 🚤 🐕 🚐 ⛺   5

This campground is on the road to Sparks Lake, nestled between two meadows in a pastoral setting at 5,450 feet elevation. Boating—particularly canoeing—is ideal at Sparks Lake, about a two-mile drive away. Also at Sparks Lake is a trail that loops the lake; about one-half mile of it is paved and barrier-free. Only fly-fishing is permitted.

Location: Near Sparks Lake in Deschutes National Forest; The Southern Cascades map 5, grid a2.

Campsites, facilities: There are 10 sites for tents, trailers, or RVs up to 22 feet long. Picnic tables and fire grills are provided. Vault toilets are available. There is no drinking water and all garbage must be packed out. Leashed pets are permitted.

Reservations, fees: No reservations. Northwest Forest Pass ($30 annual fee) or $5 daily fee per parked vehicle is required. Senior discount available. Open July through October, weather permitting.

Directions: From Bend drive southwest on Cascades Lakes Highway (also called Century Drive Highway and County Road 46) for 26.2 miles to Forest Road 400 (at sign for

Sparks Lake). Turn east (left) and drive 100 yards to the campground.

Contact: Deschutes National Forest, Bend-Fort Rock Ranger District, 1230 N.E. 3rd St., Bend, OR 97701; 541/383-4000; fax 541/383-4700.

121 Todd Lake Hike-In

 8

This is a trailhead camp, with a trail access point here for hikers and horses for the Three Sisters Wilderness. This is one of numerous camps in the area that offer a pristine mountain experience yet can be reached by car. Small Todd Lake Campground is one-half mile from the shore of an alpine lake at 6,150 feet. It's popular for canoeing and offers great views. No bikes or horses are allowed on the trail around the lake.

Location: Near Todd Lake in Deschutes National Forest; The Southern Cascades map 5, grid a2.

Campsites, facilities: There are 11 hike-in tent sites. Picnic tables and fire grills are provided. Vault toilets are available. There is no drinking water, and all garbage must be packed out. Leashed pets are permitted.

Reservations, fees: No reservations. Northwest Forest Pass ($30 annual fee) or $5 daily fee per parked vehicle is required. Open July to October, weather permitting.

Directions: From Bend drive southwest on Cascades Lakes Highway (also called Century Drive Highway and County Road 46) for 24 miles to Forest Road 370. Turn north (right) and drive one-half mile to the parking area. Hike one-half mile to the campground.

Contact: Deschutes National Forest, Bend-Fort Rock Ranger District, 1230 N.E. 3rd St., Bend, OR 97701; 541/383-4000; fax 541/383-4700.

122 Point

 8

This campground is along the shore of Elk Lake at an elevation of 4,900 feet. Fishing for kokanee salmon, rainbow trout and brown trout, and hiking can be good. Swimming and water sports are popular during warm weather.

Location: On Elk Lake in Deschutes National Forest; The Southern Cascades map 5, grid a2.

Campsites, facilities: There are 10 sites for tents, trailers, or RVs up to 22 feet long. Picnic tables, garbage service, and fire grills are provided. Vault toilets and drinking water are available. Boat docks and launching facilities are on-site. Boat rentals, a store, a restaurant, gas, and propane are at Elk Lake Resort, one mile away. Leashed pets are permitted.

Reservations, fees: No reservations. Sites are $10 per night, plus $5 per additional vehicle, $10 for additional RV. Senior discount available. Open late May to late September, weather permitting.

Directions: From Bend drive southwest on Cascades Lakes Highway (Century Drive Highway, which becomes County Road 46) for 34 miles to the campground on the left.

Contact: Deschutes National Forest, Bend-Fort Rock Ranger District, 1230 N.E. 3rd St., Bend, OR 97701; 541/383-4000; fax 541/383-4700.

123 Elk Lake

 8

This campground is on the shore of Elk Lake at 4,900 feet. It is adjacent to Elk Lake Resort, which has boat rentals, a store, a restaurant, gas, and propane. Elk Lake is popular for windsurfing and sailing. See the description of Point for recreation options.

Location: On Elk Lake in Deschutes National Forest; The Southern Cascades map 5, grid a2.

Campsites, facilities: There are 23 sites for tents, trailers, or RVs up to 22 feet long. Picnic tables, garbage service, and fire grills are provided. Vault toilets and drinking water are available. Boat-launching facilities are on-site. Boat rentals can be obtained nearby. Leashed pets are permitted.

Reservations, fees: No reservations. Sites are $10 per night, plus $5 per additional vehicle. Senior discount available. Open June through September, weather permitting.

Directions: From Bend drive southwest on Cascades Lakes Highway (Century Drive Highway, which becomes County Road 46) and drive 33.1 miles to the campground at the north end of Elk Lake.

Contact: Deschutes National Forest, Bend-Fort Rock Ranger District, 1230 N.E. 3rd St., Bend, OR 97701; 541/383-4000; fax 541/383-4700.

124 Little Fawn

 5

Choose between sites on the water's edge or nestled nearby in the forest at this campground along the eastern shore of Elk Lake at 4,900 feet elevation. Afternoon winds are common here, making this a popular spot for sailing and windsurfing. A play area for children can be found at one of the lake's inlets. See the description of Point for recreation options. Little Fawn Group Camp is just beyond Little Fawn campground.

Location: On Elk Lake in Deschutes National Forest; The Southern Cascades map 5, grid a2.

Campsites, facilities: There are 20 sites for tents, trailers, or RVs up to 22 feet long, and one group site that can accommodate up to

60 campers. Picnic tables, garbage service, drinking water, and fire grills are provided. Vault toilets are available. Boat-launching facilities and rentals are on-site. Leashed pets are permitted.

Reservations, fees: Reservations required for the group sites. Sites are $8 per night; the group site is $70 per night; there is a fee of $5 per night for an additional vehicle. Open June through September, weather permitting.

Directions: From Bend drive southwest on Cascades Lakes Highway (Century Drive Highway, which becomes County Road 46) and drive 35.5 miles to Forest Road 4625. Turn east (left) and drive 1.7 miles to the campground.

Contact: Deschutes National Forest, Bend-Fort Rock Ranger District, 1230 N.E. 3rd St., Bend, OR 97701; 541/383-4000; fax 541/383-4700.

125 Mallard Marsh

8

This quiet campground is on the shore of Hosmer Lake, elevation 5,000 feet. The lake is stocked with brown trout and Atlantic salmon and reserved for catch-and-release fly-fishing only. The lake is ideal for canoeing. You'll get a pristine, quality fishing experience. Nonmotorized boats only.

Location: On Hosmer Lake in Deschutes National Forest; The Southern Cascades map 5, grid a2.

Campsites, facilities: There are 15 sites for tents, trailers, or RVs up to 22 feet long. Picnic tables, garbage service, and vault toilets are provided. No drinking water is available. Boat-launching facilities are nearby. Leashed pets are permitted.

Reservations, fees: No reservations. Sites are $5 per night per vehicle. Open late May to late September.

Directions: From Bend drive southwest on Cascades Lakes Highway (Century Drive Highway, which becomes County Road 46)

and drive 35.5 miles to Forest Road 4625. Turn left (southeast) and drive 1.3 miles to the camp.

Contact: Deschutes National Forest, Bend-Fort Rock Ranger District, 1230 N.E. 3rd St., Bend, OR 97701; 541/383-4000; fax 541/383-4700.

126 South

 8

This campground is along the shore of Hosmer Lake, adjacent to Mallard Marsh. See the description of Mallard Marsh for recreation details.

Location: On Hosmer Lake in Deschutes National Forest; The Southern Cascades map 5, grid a3.

Campsites, facilities: There are 23 sites for tents, trailers, or RVs up to 22 feet long. Picnic tables, garbage service, and fire grills are provided. Vault toilets and boat launch facilities are available. No drinking water is provided. Leashed pets are permitted.

Reservations, fees: No reservations. Sites are $5 per night per vehicle. Senior discount available. Open late May to late September, weather permitting.

Directions: From Bend drive southwest on Cascades Lakes Highway (Century Drive Highway, which becomes County Road 46) and drive 35.5 miles to Forest Road 4625. Turn left (east) and drive 1.2 miles to the campground on the right.

Contact: Deschutes National Forest, Bend-Fort Rock Ranger District, 1230 N.E. 3rd St., Bend, OR 97701; 541/383-4000; fax 541/383-4700.

127 Lava Lake

10

This is a well-designed campground on the shore of pretty Lava Lake, set at 4,750 feet elevation. Mount Bachelor and the Three Sisters are in the background, making a classic picture. Boating and fishing are popular here. A bonus is nearby Lava Lake Resort, which has showers, laundry facilities, a sanitary disposal station, a store, gasoline, and propane.

Location: On Lava Lake in Deschutes National Forest; The Southern Cascades map 5, grid a2.

Campsites, facilities: There are 43 sites for tents, trailers, or RVs up to 28 feet long. Picnic tables, garbage service, and fire grills are provided. Vault toilets, drinking water, and a fish-cleaning station are available. Some facilities are wheelchair-accessible. Boat docks and launching facilities are on-site. Boat rentals are nearby. Leashed pets are permitted.

Reservations, fees: No reservations. Sites are $10 per night, plus $5 per additional vehicle. Senior discount available. Open mid-April through October, weather permitting.

Directions: From Bend drive southwest on Cascades Lakes Highway (Century Drive Highway, which becomes County Road 46) and drive 38.4 miles to Forest Road 4600-500. Turn east (left) and drive one mile to the campground.

Contact: Deschutes National Forest, Bend-Fort Rock Ranger District, 1230 N.E. 3rd St., Bend, OR 97701; 541/383-4000; fax 541/383-4700.

128 Little Lava Lake

8

Boating, fishing, swimming, and hiking are some of the recreation options. This lake feeds into the Deschutes River. Some sites are lakeside and some are along the river. The elevation is 4,750 feet.

Location: On Little Lava Lake in Deschutes National Forest; The Southern Cascades map 5, grid b3.

Campsites, facilities: There are 12 sites for tents, trailers, or RVs up to 22 feet long. Picnic tables, garbage service, and fire grills are provided. Vault toilets and drinking water are available. Boat launch, docks, and rentals are nearby. Launching facilities are on-site. Leashed pets are permitted.

Reservations, fees: No reservations. Sites are $5 per night per vehicle. Senior discount available. Open May to late September, weather permitting.

Directions: From Bend drive southwest on Cascades Lakes Highway (Century Drive Highway, which becomes County Road 46) and drive 38.4 miles to Forest Road 4600-500. Turn east (left) and drive 0.7 mile to Forest Road 4600-520. Continue east for 0.4 mile to the campground.

Contact: Deschutes National Forest, Bend-Fort Rock Ranger District, 1230 N.E. 3rd St., Bend, OR 97701; 541/383-4000; fax 541/383-4700.

129 West Cultus Hike-In/ Boat-In

🥾 🏊 🎣 🛶 🐕 ⛺ 5

This campground set at 4,700 feet along the west shore of Cultus Lake is accessible by boat or trail only. It's about three miles by trail from the parking area to the campground. This is a good spot for water-skiing, fishing, and swimming. Trails branch out from the campground and provide access to numerous small backcountry lakes. Drinking water and boat-launching facilities are available at Cultus Lake.

Location: On Cultus Lake in Deschutes National Forest; The Southern Cascades map 5, grid b1.

Campsites, facilities: There are 12 boat-in or hike-in tent sites. Picnic tables and fire grills are provided. Vault toilets are available. There is no drinking water and all garbage must be packed out. Boat docks are available on-site; boat rentals are at Cultus Lake Resort. Leashed pets are permitted.

Reservations, fees: No reservations. Northwest Forest Pass ($30 annual fee) or $5 daily fee per parked vehicle is required. Open June to late September, weather permitting.

Directions: From Bend drive southwest on Cascades Lakes Highway (Century Drive Highway, which becomes County Road 46) and drive 46 miles to Forest Road 4635. Turn west (right) and drive two miles to the parking area. Boat in or hike in about three miles to the west end of the lake.

Contact: Deschutes National Forest, Bend-Fort Rock Ranger District, 1230 N.E. 3rd St., Bend, OR 97701; 541/383-4000; fax 541/383-4700.

130 Cultus Lake

🥾 🏊 🎣 🚗 🐕 🚐 ⛺ 7

This camp along the east shore of Cultus Lake is set at 4,700 feet elevation. It is a popular spot for windsurfing, water-skiing, swimming, fishing, and hiking. It fills up early on weekends and holidays.

Location: On Cultus Lake in Deschutes National Forest; The Southern Cascades map 5, grid b2.

Campsites, facilities: There are 54 sites for tents, trailers, or RVs up to 30 feet long. Picnic tables, garbage service, and fire grills are provided. Drinking water and vault toilets are available. Boat docks and launching facilities are on-site. Boat rentals are nearby. A restaurant, gasoline, and cabins are available at Cultus Lake Resort nearby. Leashed pets are permitted.

Reservations, fees: No reservations. Sites are $10 per night, plus $5 per additional vehicle. Senior discount available. Open June to October.

Directions: From Bend drive southwest on Cascades Lakes Highway (Century Drive Highway, which becomes County Road 46) and drive 46 miles to Forest Road 4635. Turn west (right) and drive two miles to the campground.

Contact: Deschutes National Forest, Bend-Fort Rock Ranger District, 1230 N.E. 3rd St., Bend, OR 97701; 541/383-4000; fax 541/383-4700.

131 Cultus Corral Horse Camp
3

This campground is set at 4,450 feet elevation, about one mile from Cultus Lake, in a stand of lodgepole pine. Many trees have been removed because of disease. The camp is near many trails that provide access to backcountry lakes. This is a good overflow campground for Quinn Meadow Horse Camp.

Location: Near Cultus Lake in Deschutes National Forest; The Southern Cascades map 5, grid b1.

Campsites, facilities: There are 11 sites for tents, trailers, or RVs of any length. Picnic tables, garbage service, fire grills, and four-horse corrals are provided. Drinking water and vault toilets are available. Leashed pets are permitted.

Reservations, fees: No reservations. Sites are $5 per night per vehicle. Senior discount available. Open June to October.

Directions: From Bend drive southwest on Cascades Lakes Highway (Century Drive Highway, which becomes County Road 46) and drive 44.7 miles to Forest Road 4630. Turn west (right) and drive 0.4 miles to the campground entrance.

Contact: Deschutes National Forest, Bend-Fort Rock Ranger District, 1230 N.E. 3rd St., Bend, OR 97701; 541/383-4000; fax 541/383-4700.

132 Little Cultus Lake
7

This campground is set near the shore of Little Cultus Lake at an elevation of 4,800 feet. It's a popular spot for swimming, fishing, boating (10 mph speed limit), and hiking. Nearby trails offer access to numerous backcountry lakes, and the Pacific Crest Trail passes about six miles west of the camp.

Location: On Little Cultus Lake in Deschutes National Forest; The Southern Cascades map 5, grid b2.

Campsites, facilities: There are 20 sites for tents, trailers, or RVs up to 22 feet long. Picnic tables, garbage service, and fire grills are provided. Drinking water, vault toilets, and a boat launch are available. Leashed pets are permitted.

Reservations, fees: No reservations. Sites are $5 per night. Senior discount available. Open late May to late September, weather permitting.

Directions: From Bend drive southwest on Cascades Lakes Highway (Century Drive Highway, which becomes County Road 46) and drive 46 miles to Forest Road 4635. Turn west (right) and drive two miles to Forest Road 4630. Turn south (left) and drive 1.7 miles to Forest Road 4636. Turn west (right) and drive one mile to the campground.

Contact: Deschutes National Forest, Bend-Fort Rock Ranger District, 1230 N.E. 3rd St., Bend, OR 97701; 541/383-4000; fax 541/383-4700.

133 Deschutes Bridge
5

This wooded campground is on the banks of the Deschutes River in a beautiful green spot. It's set at 4,650 feet elevation. Fishing prospects are often difficult and are restricted to artificial lures with a single barbless hook.

Location: On the Upper Deschutes River in the Deschutes National Forest; The Southern Cascades map 5, grid b3.

Campsites, facilities: There are 12 sites for tents, trailers, or RVs up to 22 feet long. Picnic tables, garbage service, and fire grills are provided. Drinking water and vault toilets are available. Leashed pets are permitted.

Reservations, fees: No reservations. Sites are $5 per night per vehicle. The entire camp is $50 per night, with a two-night minimum on weekends and a three-night minimum on holidays. Senior discount available. Open June to October.

Directions: From Bend drive southwest on Cascades Lakes Highway (Century Drive Highway, which becomes County Road 46) and drive 41.1 miles to the campground on the left (just past the Deschutes River Bridge).

Contact: Deschutes National Forest, Bend-Fort Rock Ranger District, 1230 N.E. 3rd St., Bend, OR 97701; 541/383-4000; fax 541/383-4700.

134 Irish and Taylor

7

Little known and beautiful, this remote campground is set between two small lakes at 5,550 feet elevation about a mile from the Pacific Crest Trail. Other nearby trails provide access into the Three Sisters Wilderness. A four-wheel-drive with high clearance is recommended for access.

Location: Near Irish and Taylor Lakes in Deschutes National Forest; The Southern Cascades map 5, grid b1.

Campsites, facilities: There are six tent sites. Picnic tables and fire grills are provided. Vault toilets are available. There is no drinking water. Leashed pets are permitted.

Reservations, fees: No reservations. Northwest Forest Pass ($30 annual fee) or $5 daily fee per parked vehicle is required. Open mid-June to mid-September.

Directions: From Bend drive southwest on Cascades Lakes Highway (Century Drive Highway, which becomes County Road 46) and drive 46 miles to Forest Road 4635. Turn west (right) on Forest Road 4635 and drive a short distance to Forest Road 4630. Turn south and drive 1.7 miles to Forest Road 4636. Turn west and drive 6.4 miles to the campground. A high-clearance vehicle is needed for the last four miles.

Contact: Deschutes National Forest, Bend-Fort Rock Ranger District, 1230 N.E. 3rd St., Bend, OR 97701; 541/383-4000; fax 541/383-4700.

135 Fall River

5

This campground is on the Fall River, where fishing is restricted to fly-fishing only. Check the regulations for other restrictions. Fall River is beautiful, crystal clear, and cold. Fall River Trail meanders along the river for 3.5 miles and is open for bicycling. The elevation is 4,300 feet.

Location: On the Fall River in Deschutes National Forest; The Southern Cascades map 5, grid b4.

Campsites, facilities: There are 10 sites for tents, trailers, or RVs up to 22 feet long. Picnic tables, garbage service, and fire grills are provided. Vault toilets are available. There is no drinking water. Leashed pets are permitted.

Reservations, fees: No reservations. Sites are $5 per night per vehicle. Senior discount available. Open mid-April through October, weather permitting.

Directions: From Bend drive south on U.S. 97 for 17.3 miles to Forest Road 42. Turn southwest (right) and drive 12.2 miles to the campground.

Contact: Deschutes National Forest, Bend-Fort Rock Ranger District, 1230 N.E. 3rd St., Bend, OR 97701; 541/383-4000; fax 541/383-4700.

136 Cow Meadow

 6

This campground is set near the north end of Crane Prairie Reservoir and near the Deschutes River. It's a pretty spot and the price is right. This is a great spot for fly-fishing and bird-watching. The elevation is 4,450 feet.

Location: On Crane Prairie Reservoir in Deschutes National Forest; The Southern Cascades map 5, grid b2.

Campsites, facilities: There are 21 sites for tents, trailers, or RVs up to 22 feet long. Picnic tables, garbage service, and fire grills are provided. Vault toilets are available. There is no drinking water. A boat launch for small boats is available nearby. Leashed pets are permitted.

Reservations, fees: No reservations. Sites are $5 per night per vehicle. Open May to mid-October.

Directions: From Bend drive southwest on Cascades Lakes Highway (Century Drive Highway, which becomes County Road 46) for 44.7 miles to Forest Road 40. Turn east (left) on Forest Road 40 and drive 0.4 miles to Forest Road 4000-970. Turn south (right) and drive two miles to the campground on the right.

Contact: Deschutes National Forest, Bend-Fort Rock Ranger District, 1230 N.E. 3rd St., Bend, OR 97701; 541/383-4000; fax 541/383-4700.

137 Crane Prairie

6

This campground along the north shore of Crane Prairie Reservoir is a good spot for fishing and boating. This reservoir is world-renowned for rainbow trout fishing and is also popular for bass fishing.

Location: On Crane Prairie Reservoir in Deschutes National Forest; The Southern Cascades map 5, grid b2.

Campsites, facilities: There are six sites for tents and 140 sites for trailers or RVs. Picnic tables, garbage service, and fire grills are provided. Drinking water and vault toilets are available. Some facilities are wheelchair-accessible. Boat docks, launching facilities, and a fish-cleaning station are available on-site. Boat rentals, showers, gas, and laundry facilities are nearby. Leashed pets are permitted.

Reservations, fees: No reservations. Sites are $10–12 per night, plus $5 per additional vehicle. Senior discount available. Open April 20 through October, weather permitting.

Directions: From Bend drive south on U.S. 97 for 26.8 miles to Wickiup Junction and County Road 43. Turn west (right) on County Road 43 and drive 11 miles to Forest Road 42. Continue west on Forest Road 42 for 5.4 miles to Forest Road 4270. Turn north (right) and drive 4.2 miles to the campground on the left.

Contact: Deschutes National Forest, Bend-Fort Rock Ranger District, 1230 N.E. 3rd St., Bend, OR 97701; 541/383-4000; fax 541/383-4700.

138 Quinn River

5

This campground is set along the western shore of Crane Prairie Reservoir, a popular spot for anglers and a great spot for bird-watching. A separate, large parking lot is available for boats and trailers. Boat speed is limited to 10 mph here. The elevation is 4,450 feet.

Location: On Crane Prairie Reservoir in Deschutes

National Forest; The Southern Cascades map 5, grid b2.

Campsites, facilities: There are 41 sites for tents, trailers, or RVs up to 30 feet long. Picnic tables, garbage service, and fire grills are provided. Drinking water and vault toilets are available. Some facilities are wheelchair-accessible. Boat launch facilities are available. Leashed pets are permitted.

Reservations, fees: No reservations. Sites are $10 per night, plus $5 per additional vehicle. Senior discount available. Open late April to mid-October.

Directions: From Bend drive southwest on Cascade Lakes Highway (Century Drive Highway, which becomes County Road 46) and drive 48 miles to the campground.

Contact: Deschutes National Forest, Bend-Fort Rock Ranger District, 1230 N.E. 3rd St., Bend, OR 97701; 541/383-4000; fax 541/383-4700.

139 Rock Creek

5

This campground is set along the west shore of Crane Prairie Reservoir. See the description of Quinn River. The elevation is 4,450 feet.

Location: On Crane Prairie Reservoir in Deschutes National Forest; The Southern Cascades map 5, grid b2.

Campsites, facilities: There are 31 sites for tents, trailers, or RVs up to 22 feet long. Picnic tables, garbage service, and fire grills are provided. Drinking water, a fish-cleaning station, and vault toilets are available. Some facilities are wheelchair-accessible. Boat docks and launching facilities are on-site. Leashed pets are permitted.

Reservations, fees: No reservations. Sites are $10 per night, plus $5 per additional vehicle. Senior discount available. Open mid-April through October, weather permitting.

Directions: From Bend drive southwest on Cascade Lakes Highway (Century Drive Highway, which becomes County Road 46) and drive 48.8 miles to the campground.

Contact: Deschutes National Forest, Bend-Fort Rock Ranger District, 1230 N.E. 3rd St., Bend, OR 97701; 541/383-4000; fax 541/383-4700.

140 Big River

4

This is a good spot between the banks of the Deschutes River and the road. Rafting, fishing, and motorized boating are permitted. Access is easy. This is a popular overnight spot.

Location: On the Deschutes River in Deschutes National Forest; The Southern Cascades map 5, grid c4.

Campsites, facilities: There are two tent sites and nine sites for tents, trailers, or RVs up to 22 feet long. There is also one group site that can accommodate up to 60 people. Picnic tables, garbage service, and fire grills are provided. Vault toilets are available. There is no drinking water. Some facilities are wheelchair-accessible. Boat-launching facilities are on-site. Leashed pets are permitted.

Reservations, fees: No reservations. Individual sites are $5 per night per vehicle. Senior discount available. Open April through September.

Directions: From Bend drive south on U.S. 97 for 17.3 miles to Forest Road 42. Turn west (right) and drive 7.9 miles to the campground.

Contact: Deschutes National Forest, Bend-Fort Rock Ranger District, 1230 N.E. 3rd St., Bend, OR 97701; 541/383-4000; fax 541/383-4700.

141 Prairie

4

Here's another good overnight campground that is quiet and private. This camp along the banks of Paulina Creek is about one-half mile from the trailhead for the Peter Skene Ogden National Recreation Trail. The elevation is 4,300 feet.

Location: On Paulina Creek in Deschutes National Forest; The Southern Cascades map 5, grid c5.

Campsites, facilities: There are 16 sites for tents, trailers, or RVs up to 30 feet long. Picnic tables, garbage service, and fire grills are provided. Drinking water, firewood, and vault toilets are available. Leashed pets are permitted.

Reservations, fees: No reservations. Sites are $10 per night, $5 per additional vehicle. Senior discount available. Open mid-May through October, weather permitting.

Directions: From Bend drive south on U.S. 97 for 23.5 miles to County Road 21 (Paulina/East Lake Road). Turn east (left) and drive 3.1 miles to the campground.

Contact: Deschutes National Forest, Bend-Fort Rock Ranger District, 1230 N.E. 3rd St., Bend, OR 97701; 541/383-4000; fax 541/383-4700.

142 McKay Crossing

6

This pleasant little campground is set along the banks of Paulina Creek. This is an outstanding site for bird-watching. The elevation is 4,300 feet. The nearby Peter Skene Ogden National Recreation Trail travels east for six miles to Paulina Lake (also reachable by car). This is the gateway to Newberry National Volcanic Monument, about 10 miles east on County Road 21.

Location: On Paulina Creek in Deschutes National Forest; The Southern Cascades map 5, grid c5.

Campsites, facilities: There are 16 sites for tents, trailers, or RVs up to 22 feet long. Picnic tables, garbage service, and fire grills are provided. Vault toilets are available.

There is no drinking water. Leashed pets are permitted.

Reservations, fees: No reservations. Sites are $10 per night per vehicle, $5 extra vehicle per night. Senior discount available. Open June to late October.

Directions: From Bend drive south on U.S. 97 for 23.5 miles to County Road 21 (Paulina/East Lake Road). Turn east (left) and drive 3.2 miles to Forest Road 2120. Continue east for 2.7 miles to the campground.

Contact: Deschutes National Forest, Bend-Fort Rock Ranger District, 1230 N.E. 3rd St., Bend, OR 97701; 541/383-4000; fax 541/383-4700.

143 Sheep Bridge

3

This campground is set along the north Deschutes River Channel of Wickiup Reservoir in an open, treeless area that has minimal privacy and is dusty in summer. Dispersed sites here are popular with group campers. The elevation is 4,350 feet.

Location: Near Wickiup Reservoir in Deschutes National Forest; The Southern Cascades map 5, grid c2.

Campsites, facilities: There are 18 sites for tents, trailers, or RVs of any length. Picnic tables, garbage service, and fire grills are provided. Drinking water, vault toilets, boat-launching facilities, and a picnic area are available. Leashed pets are permitted.

Reservations, fees: No reservations. Sites are $5 per night per vehicle. Senior discount available. Open April through October, weather permitting.

Directions: From Bend drive south on U.S. 97 for 26.8 miles to Wickiup Junction. Turn west (right) on County Road 43 and drive 11 miles to Forest Road 42. Continue 4.6 miles west on Forest Road 42 to Forest Road 4260. Turn south (left)

and drive three-quarters of a mile to the campground on the right.

Contact: Deschutes National Forest, Bend-Fort Rock Ranger District, 1230 N.E. 3rd St., Bend, OR 97701; 541/383-4000; fax 541/383-4700.

144 North Twin Lake

 6

This campground on the shore of North Twin Lake is a popular weekend spot for families. It's small and fairly primitive, but it has lake access and a pretty setting. Only nonmotorized boats are permitted. The elevation is 4,350 feet.

Location: On North Twin Lake in Deschutes National Forest; The Southern Cascades map 5, grid c3.

Campsites, facilities: There are 19 sites for tents, trailers, or RVs up to 22 feet long. Picnic tables and fire grills are provided. Vault toilets are available. There is no drinking water. Boat-launching facilities are on-site. Leashed pets are permitted.

Reservations, fees: No reservations. Sites are $5 per night per vehicle. Senior discount available. Open June to late September, weather permitting.

Directions: From Bend drive southwest on Cascade Lakes Highway (Century Drive Highway, which becomes County Road 46) for 52 miles and drive past Crane Prairie Reservoir to Forest Road 42. Turn east and drive four miles to Forest Road 4260. Turn right (south) and drive a quarter mile to the campground.

Contact: Deschutes National Forest, Bend-Fort Rock Ranger District, 1230 N.E. 3rd St., Bend, OR 97701; 541/383-4000; fax 541/383-4700.

145 Twin Lakes Resort

8

This resort is a popular family vacation destination, with a full-service marina and all the amenities, including beach areas. Recreational activities vary from hiking to fishing, swimming, and boating on Wickiup Reservoir. Nearby South Twin Lake is popular with paddleboaters and kayakers. It's stocked with rainbow trout. See the description of West South Twin and South Twin Lake.

Location: On Twin Lakes; The Southern Cascades map 5, grid c3.

Campsites, facilities: There are 22 full-hookup sites for trailers and RVs of any length. There are also 14 cabins. Restrooms, showers, a sanitary dump, a public telephone, a laundry room, a store, a full-service restaurant, ice, snacks, some RV supplies, LP gas, gasoline, and a barbecue are available. A boat ramp, rentals, and a dock are provided; no motors are permitted on South Twin Lake. Leashed pets are permitted.

Reservations, fees: Reservations are recommended. Sites are $26 per night, and cabins are $55–135 per night. Open late April to mid-October.

Directions: From Bend drive south on U.S. 97 for 26.8 miles to Wickiup Junction. Turn west (right) on County Road 43 and drive 11 miles to Forest Road 42. Continue 4.6 miles west on Forest Road 42 to Forest Road 4260. Turn south (left) and drive two miles to the resort.

Contact: Twin Lakes Resort, P.O. Box 3550, Sun River, OR 97707; 541/593-6526; fax 541/410-4688.

146 South Twin Lake

6

This campground is on the shore of South Twin Lake, a popular spot for swimming, fishing, and boating (nonmotorized only). See the description of West South Twin. The elevation is 4,350 feet.

Location: On South Twin Lake in Deschutes National Forest; The Southern Cascades map 5, grid c3.

Campsites, facilities: There are 24 sites for tents, trailers, or RVs up to 22 feet long. Picnic tables, garbage service, and fire grills are provided. Drinking water and vault and flush toilets are available. Some facilities are wheelchair-accessible. Boat-launching facilities (small boats only), boat rentals, showers, and laundry facilities are nearby. Leashed pets are permitted.

Reservations, fees: No reservations. Sites are $12 per night, plus $5 per additional vehicle. Senior discount available. Open mid-April through October, weather permitting.

Directions: From Bend drive south on U.S. 97 for 26.8 miles to Wickiup Junction. Turn west (right) on County Road 43 and drive 11 miles to Forest Road 42. Continue west on Forest Road 42 for 4.6 miles to Forest Road 4260. Turn left (south) and drive two miles to the campground on the left.

Contact: Deschutes National Forest, Bend-Fort Rock Ranger District, 1230 N.E. 3rd St., Bend, OR 97701; 541/383-4000; fax 541/383-4700.

147 West South Twin

4

This camp is set on South Twin Lake adjacent to Wickiup Reservoir, and it is a major access point to the Wickiup Reservoir. It's a popular angling spot with very good kokanee salmon fishing. Twin Lakes Resort is adjacent to West South Twin. The elevation is 4,350 feet.

Location: On South Twin Lake in Deschutes National Forest; The Southern Cascades map 5, grid c3.

Campsites, facilities: There are 24 sites for trailers or RVs up to 22 feet long. Picnic tables, garbage service, and fire grills are provided. Drinking water and flush toilets are available. Boat-launching facilities are on-site, and boat rentals, a restaurant, showers, coin-operated laundry, gas, propane, cabins, and a store are nearby. Leashed pets are permitted.

Reservations, fees: No reservations. Sites are $10 per night, plus $5 per additional vehicle. Senior discount available. Open mid-May to mid-October, weather permitting.

Directions: From Bend drive southwest on Cascade Lakes Highway (Century Drive Highway, which becomes County Road 46) for 52 miles (past Crane Prairie Reservoir) to Forest Road 42. Turn east and drive four miles to Forest Road 4260. Turn right (south) and drive a quarter mile to the campground.

Contact: Deschutes National Forest, Bend-Fort Rock Ranger District, 1230 N.E. 3rd St., Bend, OR 97701; 541/383-4000; fax 541/383-4700.

148 Gull Point

5

This campground is in an open ponderosa stand on the north shore of Wickiup Reservoir. You'll find good fishing for kokanee salmon here. It's about two miles from West South Twin Campground. This is the most popular campground on Wickiup Reservoir.

Location: On Wickiup Reservoir in Deschutes National Forest; The Southern Cascades map 5, grid c3.

Campsites, facilities: There are 79 sites for tents, trailers, or RVs up to 30 feet long. There are also two sites available for groups of up to 25 people. Picnic tables, garbage service, and fire grills are provided. Drinking water, a sanitary dump station, and flush and vault toilets are available. Some facilities are wheelchair-accessible. Boat-launching facilities and fish-cleaning stations are onsite. Leashed pets are permitted.

Reservations, fees: Reservations accepted for group sites only. Individual sites are $10–12 per night, and group sites are $40 per night, plus $5 per additional vehicle. Senior discount available. Open mid-April through October, weather permitting.

Directions: From Bend drive south on U.S. 97 for about 26.8 miles to County Road 43 (three miles north of LaPine). Turn west on County Road 43 and drive 11 miles to Forest Road 42. Turn west on Forest Road 42 and drive 4.6 miles to Forest Road 4260. Turn south (left) and drive three miles to the campground on the right.

Contact: Deschutes National Forest, Bend-Fort Rock Ranger District, 1230 N.E. 3rd St., Bend, OR 97701; 541/383-4000; fax 541/383-4700.

149 North Davis Creek

4

This remote, secluded campground is set along a western channel that feeds into Wickiup Reservoir and receives little use. It can be used as an overflow camp if campsites are filled at Wickiup. In late summer, the reservoir level tends to drop. Fishing for brown and rainbow trout as well as kokanee salmon is good here. The elevation is 4,350 feet.

Location: On North Davis Creek in Deschutes National Forest; The Southern Cascades map 5, grid c2.

Campsites, facilities: There are 15 sites for tents, trailers, or RVs up to 22 feet long. Picnic tables, garbage service, and fire grills are provided. Drinking water and vault toilets are available. Boat-launching facilities are on-site. Leashed pets are permitted.

Reservations, fees: No reservations. Sites are $8 per night, $5 for each addtional vehicle. Senior discount available. Open May to late October.

Directions: From Bend drive southwest on Cascade Lake Highway (Highway 46/Forest Road 46) for 56.2 miles to the campground on the left.

Contact: Deschutes National Forest, Bend-Fort Rock Ranger District, 1230 N.E. 3rd St., Bend, OR 97701; 541/383-4000; fax 541/383-4700.

150 Gold Lake

8

This campground wins the popularity contest for high use. Although motors are not allowed on this small lake (100 acres, 25 feet deep), rafts and rowboats provide excellent fishing access. A primitive log shelter built in the early 1940s provides a dry picnic area. In the spring and summer, this area abounds with wildflowers and huckleberries. The Gold Lake Bog is another special attraction where one can often see deer, elk, and smaller wildlife.

Location: On Gold Lake in Willamette National Forest; The Southern Cascades map 5, grid c1.

Campsites, facilities: There are 25 sites for tents, trailers, or RVs up to 22 feet long. Picnic tables, garbage bins, and fire grills are provided. Drinking water and vault toilets are available. Boat docks and launching facilities are nearby. Leashed pets are permitted.

Reservations, fees: No reservations. Sites are $10 per night, plus $5 for each additional vehicle. Senior discount available. Open June through September, weather permitting.

Directions: From Eugene drive south on I-5 for five miles to Exit 188 and Highway 58. Turn east and drive 35 miles to the town of Oakridge. From Oakridge, continue east on

Highway 58 for 28 miles to Gold Lake Road (Forest Road 500). Turn left (north) and drive two miles to the campground on the right.

Contact: Willamette National Forest, Middle Fork Ranger District, 46375 Hwy. 58, Westfir, OR 97492; 541/782-2283; fax 541/782-5306.

151 Reservoir

 4

This campground is set along the south shore of Wickiup Reservoir, where the kokanee salmon fishing is good. The camp is best in early summer, before the lake level drops. This campground gets little use, so you won't find crowds here. The elevation is 4,350 feet.

Location: On Wickiup Reservoir in Deschutes National Forest; The Southern Cascades map 5, grid c3.

Campsites, facilities: There are 28 sites for tents, trailers, or RVs up to 22 feet long. Picnic tables, garbage service, and fire grills are provided. Boat-launching facilities and vault toilets are available, but there is no drinking water. Leashed pets are permitted.

Reservations, fees: No reservations. Sites are $5 per night per vehicle. Senior discount available. Open May to late October, weather permitting.

Directions: From Bend drive southwest on Cascade Lakes Highway (Century Drive Highway, which becomes County Road 46) and drive 57.8 miles to Forest Road 44. Turn left (east) and drive 1.7 miles to the campground.

Contact: Deschutes National Forest, Bend-Fort Rock Ranger District, 1230 N.E. 3rd St., Bend, OR 97701; 541/383-4000; fax 541/383-4700.

152 Wickiup Butte

4

This campground is set along the southeast shore of Wickiup Reservoir at 4,350 feet, where kokanee salmon fishing is good during the early summer. Wickiup Butte is more remote than the other campgrounds on Wickiup Reservoir.

Location: On Wickiup Reservoir in Deschutes National Forest; The Southern Cascades map 5, grid c3.

Campsites, facilities: There are eight sites for tents, trailers, or RVs up to 22 feet long. Picnic tables, garbage service, and fire grills are provided. Vault toilets are available. There is no drinking water. Boat-launching facilities are nearby. Leashed pets are permitted.

Reservations, fees: No reservations. Sites are $5 per night per vehicle. Senior discount available. Open May to late October, weather permitting.

Directions: From Bend drive south on U.S. 97 for 26.8 miles to Wickiup Junction. Turn west (right) on County Road 43 and drive 10.4 miles to Forest Road 4380. Turn south (left) and drive 3.6 miles to Forest Road 4260. Turn east (left) and drive three miles to the campground.

Contact: Deschutes National Forest, Bend-Fort Rock Ranger District, 1230 N.E. 3rd St., Bend, OR 97701; 541/383-4000; fax 541/383-4700.

153 Bull Bend

5

This campground is on the inside of a major bend in the Deschutes River at 4,300 feet. A mini-float trip can be made by starting at the upstream end of camp, floating around the bend, and then taking out at the downstream end of camp. This is a low-use getaway spot.

Location: On the Deschutes River in Deschutes National Forest; The Southern Cascades map 5, grid c3.

Campsites, facilities: There are 12 sites for tents, trailers, or RVs. Picnic tables, garbage service, fire grills, vault toilets, and boat-launching facilities are available. There is no drinking water. Leashed pets are permitted.

Reservations, fees: No reservations. Sites are $5 per night per vehicle. Senior discount available. Open April through September, weather permitting.

Directions: From Bend drive south on U.S. 97 for 26.8 miles to Wickiup Junction. Turn west (right) on County Road 43 and drive eight miles to Forest Road 4370. Turn south (left) and drive 1.5 miles to the campground.

Contact: Deschutes National Forest, Bend-Fort Rock Ranger District, 1230 N.E. 3rd St., Bend, OR 97701; 541/383-4000; fax 541/383-4700.

154 Pringle Falls
4

This campground is set along the Deschutes River and is less than a mile from Pringle Falls. The camp gets light use and is pretty and serene.

Location: On the Deschutes River in Deschutes National Forest; The Southern Cascades map 5, grid c4.

Campsites, facilities: There are six sites for tents, trailers, or RVs up to 22 feet long. Picnic tables, garbage service, and fire grills are provided. Vault toilets are available. There is no drinking water. Leashed pets are permitted.

Reservations, fees: No reservations. Sites are $5 per night per vehicle. Senior discount available. Open April through September, weather permitting.

Directions: From Bend drive south on U.S. 97 for 26.8 miles to Wickiup Junction. Turn west (right) on County Road 43 and drive 7.4 miles to Forest Road 4330-500. Turn right (north) and drive one mile to the campground.

Contact: Deschutes National Forest, Bend-Fort Rock Ranger District, 1230 N.E. 3rd St., Bend, OR 97701; 541/383-4000; fax 541/383-4700.

155 LaPine State Park
7

Here is a clean, quiet campground next to a twisting, cold river brimming with trout and a nearby legendary fly-fishing spot and giant tree. Be sure to visit Oregon's "Big Tree," the largest ponderosa pine in the state. The camp is set in a subalpine pine forest, and you just might see an eagle or red-tailed hawk grabbing breakfast right in front of you. Many high mountain lakes are in proximity, as is snow-skiing in the winter.

Location: On the Deschutes River; The Southern Cascades map 5, grid c4.

Campsites, facilities: There are 141 sites, including 92 with full hookups and 49 with partial hookups for tents, trailers or RVs up to 85 feet long. There are also five cabins and three yurts. Picnic tables and fire grills are provided. Drinking water, restrooms with flush toilets and showers, garbage bins, a dump station, and firewood are available. Leashed pets are permitted.

Reservations, fees: Reservations accepted ($6 reservation fee). Sites are $13–15 per night, with a charge of $7 per additional vehicle. Yurts are $27 per night, and cabins are $35 per night. Major credit cards accepted. Open year-round.

Directions: From Bend turn south on U.S. 97 and drive 23 miles to State Recreation Road. Turn right and drive four miles to the park.

Contact: LaPine State Park, Oregon State Parks, 15800 State Recreation Rd., LaPine, OR 97739; 800/551-6949 or 541/536-2071, reservations 800/452-5687.

156 Highlander Motel and Trailer Park
5

This campground is near the Little Deschutes River. A golf course and tennis courts are close by.

Location: Near the Little Deschutes River; The Southern Cascades map 5, grid c4.

Campsites, facilities: There are 30 sites for trailers or RVs up to 35 feet long; 16 are drive-through sites. Electricity, drinking water, and sewer hookups are provided. Flush toilets, bottled gas, sanitary services, showers, a store, a café, and ice are available. A coin laundry is within one mile. Leashed pets are permitted.

Reservations, fees: Reservations accepted. Sites are $15 per night. Open year-round.

Directions: From I-5 south of Eugene, take Exit 188 and turn east on Highway 58. Drive 86 miles east to U.S. 97. Turn north on U.S. 97 and drive 26 miles to LaPine. The campground is at the north edge of town on the left.

Contact: Highlander Motel and Trailer Park, P.O. Box 322, LaPine, OR 97739; 541/536-2131; fax 541/536-5246.

157 Riverview Trailer Park

8

This grassy campground is set along the bank of the Little Deschutes River, which offers excellent trout fishing. It's missed by a lot of highway travelers; they just plain don't know about it.

Location: On the Little Deschutes River; The Southern Cascades map 5, grid c4.

Campsites, facilities: There are 15 tent sites and 20 sites for trailers or RVs of any length. Electricity, cable TV, well water, sewer hookups, and picnic tables are provided. Flush toilets, showers, a recreation hall, and a laundry room are available. Small leashed pets are permitted.

Reservations, fees: Reservations accepted. Sites are $13–20 per night. Open year-round.

Directions: From Eugene drive south on I-5 for five miles to Exit 188 and Highway 58. Turn

east and drive 86 miles to U.S. 97. Turn north on U.S. 97 and drive 26 miles to LaPine. Continue 2.5 miles northeast on U.S. 97 to Wickiup Junction and County Road 43 (Burgess Road). Turn left and drive one mile to Huntington Road. Turn right and drive one mile to the park on the left.

Contact: Riverview Trailer Park, 52731 Huntington Rd., LaPine, OR 97739; 541/536-2382.

158 Hidden Pines RV Park

7

So you think you've come far enough, eh? If you want a spot in a privately run RV park two miles from the bank of the Little Deschutes River, you've found it. Within a 30-minute drive are two reservoirs, four lakes, and a golf course. The nearby town of LaPine is the gateway to the Newberry National Volcanic Monument.

Location: Near the Little Deschutes River; The Southern Cascades map 5, grid c4.

Campsites, facilities: There are six tent sites and 25 sites for RVs up to 40 feet; 16 are pull-through sites. Electricity, drinking water, cable TV, sewer hookups (19 sites only), and picnic tables are provided. Flush toilets, sanitary services, showers, a laundry room, RV supplies, LP gas, a community fire ring with firewood, and ice are available. The full-service community of LaPine is about five miles away. Leashed pets allowed with restrictions; call first.

Reservations, fees: Reservations accepted. Sites are $16.50–21.50 per night. Open from mid-April to mid-October.

Directions: From Bend drive south on U.S. 97 for 24 miles to Wickiup Junction and milepost 165 and County Road 43/Burgess Road (lighted). Turn west (right) on County Road 43 (Burgess Road) and drive 2.4 miles to

Pine Forest Road. Turn left and drive 0.7 mile to Wright Avenue. Turn left and drive one block to the campground.

Contact: Hidden Pines RV Park, 52158 Elderberry Ln., LaPine, OR 97739; 541/536-2265.

159 Lava Flow

🎣 🚤 🏠 🚐 ⛺ 8

This campground is set in old-growth forest, along the northeast shore of Davis Lake, a very shallow lake formed by lava flow. The water level fluctuates here, and this campground can sometimes be closed in summer. There's good duck hunting during the fall. Fishing can be decent, but only fly fishing is allowed. Boat speed is limited to 10 mph.

Location: On Davis Lake in Deschutes National Forest; The Southern Cascades map 5, grid c2.

Campsites, facilities: There is a dispersed camping area for 12 tents, trailers, or RVs up to 22 feet long. Picnic tables and fire grills are provided. Vault toilets and firewood (to be gathered from the surrounding area) are available. There is no drinking water, and all garbage must be packed out. A boat launch is nearby. Leashed pets are permitted.

Reservations, fees: No reservations; no fee. Open September through December, weather permitting.

Directions: From Eugene drive south on I-5 for five miles to Exit 188 and Highway 58. Turn east on Highway 58 and drive 86 miles to County Road 61. Turn left and drive three miles to Forest Road 46. Turn left and drive 7.7 miles to Forest Road 850. Turn left and drive 1.8 miles to the campground.

Contact: Deschutes National Forest, Crescent Ranger District, P.O. Box 208, Crescent, OR 97733; 541/433-3200; fax 541/433-3224.

160 West Davis Lake

🚶 🚴 🏊
🚗 🐕 🚐 ⛺ 9

Spacious sites and easy access to the water are highlights of this campground on the south shore of Davis Lake. Only fly-fishing is permitted, and the boat speed limit is 10 mph. See notes for East Davis Lake.

Location: On Davis Lake in Deschutes National Forest; The Southern Cascades map 5, grid d2.

Campsites, facilities: There are 21 sites for tents, trailers, or RVs up to 22 feet long. Picnic tables, garbage service, and fire grills are provided. Drinking water, vault toilets, and firewood (to be gathered from the surrounding area) are available. A boat launch is on-site. Leashed pets are permitted.

Reservations, fees: No reservations. Sites are $8 per night, plus $4 for each additional vehicle. Senior discount available. Open May to late October, weather permitting.

Directions: From Eugene drive south on I-5 for five miles to Exit 188 and Highway 58. Turn east and drive 73 miles to County Road 61. Turn left (east) and drive three miles to Forest Road 46. Turn left and drive three miles north to Forest Road 4660. Turn left and drive three miles to Forest Road 4669. Turn right and drive 1.5 miles to the campground.

Contact: Deschutes National Forest, Crescent Ranger District, P.O. Box 208, Crescent, OR 97733; 541/433-3200; fax 541/433-3224.

161 East Davis Lake

🚶 🚴 🎣
🚗 🐕 🚐 ⛺ 9

This campground is nestled in the lodgepole pines along the south shore of Davis Lake. Recreation options include fly-fishing, boating (speed limit is 10 mph), and hiking. Leeches prevent swimming here.

Bald eagles and sandhill cranes are frequently seen.

Location: On Davis Lake in Deschutes National Forest; The Southern Cascades map 5, grid d2.

Campsites, facilities: There are 33 sites for tents, trailers, or RVs up to 22 feet long. Picnic tables, garbage service, fire grills, drinking water, and vault toilets are provided. Firewood may be gathered from the surrounding area. Primitive boat-launching facilities are available on-site. Leashed pets are permitted.

Reservations, fees: No reservations. Sites are $8 per night, plus $4 for each additional vehicle. Senior discount available. Open May to late October, weather permitting.

Directions: From Eugene drive south on I-5 for five miles to Exit 188 and Highway 58. Turn east and drive 73 miles to County Road 61. Turn left (east) and drive three miles to Forest Road 46. Turn left and drive 7.7 miles to Forest Road 850. Turn left and drive one-quarter mile to Forest Road 855. Turn left and drive two miles to the campground.

Contact: Deschutes National Forest, Crescent Ranger District, P.O. Box 208, Crescent, OR 97733; 541/433-3200; fax 541/433-3224.

162 Trapper Creek

The west end of Odell Lake is the setting for this camp. Boat docks and rentals are nearby at the Shelter Cove Resort. The lake is one of the prime fisheries in Oregon for kokanee salmon and mackinaw (lake trout). There are also some huge brown trout in this lake.

Location: On Odell Lake in Deschutes National Forest; The Southern Cascades map 5, grid d1.

Campsites, facilities: There are 32 sites for tents, trailers, or RVs up to 22 feet long. Picnic

tables, garbage service, and fire grills are provided. Drinking water, vault toilets, and a boat launch are available. Firewood may be gathered from the surrounding area. A store, a coin laundry, and ice are within one mile. Leashed pets are permitted.

Reservations, fees: No reservations. Sites are $10–12 per night, $5 per night for an additional vehicle. Senior discount available. Open June through September, weather permitting.

Directions: From Eugene drive south on I-5 for five miles to Exit 188 and Highway 58. Turn east and drive 61 miles to the turnoff for Odell Lake and Forest Road 5810. Turn right on Forest Road 5810 and drive 1.9 miles to the campground on the left.

Contact: Deschutes National Forest, Crescent Ranger District, P.O. Box 208, Crescent, OR 97733; 541/433-3200; fax 541/433-3224.

163 Shelter Cove Resort

This private resort along the north shore of Odell Lake is at the base of the Diamond Peak Wilderness and offers opportunities for hiking, fishing, and swimming. The cabins are right on the lakefront. A general store and tackle shop are available.

Location: On Odell Lake; The Southern Cascades map 5, grid d1.

Campsites, facilities: There are 18 tent sites and 54 drive-through sites for trailers or RVs up to 40 feet long, and 12 cabins. Electricity and picnic tables are provided. Drinking water, flush toilets, showers, a store, laundry facilities, and ice are available. Boat docks, launching facilities, and boat rentals are on-site. Leashed pets are permitted.

Reservations, fees: Reservations are recommended. Sites are $12–19 per night, and cabins are $65–225 per night. Open year-round.

Directions: From Eugene drive south on I-5 for five miles to Exit 188 and Highway 58. Turn east and drive 61 miles to the turnoff for Odell Lake and West Odell Lake Road. Take that road and drive south for 1.8 miles to the camp.

Contact: Shelter Cove Resort, West Odell Lake Road, Highway 58 P.O. Box 52, Crescent Lake, OR 97425; (541) 433-2548; reservations 1-800-647-2729; website: www.sheltercoveresort.com.

164 Odell Creek

9

You can fish, swim, and hike at this campground (4,800 feet elevation) along the east shore of Odell Lake. A trail from the nearby Crater Buttes trailhead heads southwest into the Diamond Peak Wilderness and provides access to several small lakes in the backcountry. Another trail follows the north shore of the lake. Boat docks, launching facilities, and rentals are nearby at the Odell Lake Lodge and Resort, adjacent to the campground. Windy afternoons are common here.

Location: On Odell Lake in Deschutes National Forest; The Southern Cascades map 5, grid d1.

Campsites, facilities: There are 21 sites for tents, trailers, or RVs up to 22 feet long. Picnic tables, garbage service, and fire grills are provided. Drinking water and vault toilets are available. Firewood may be gathered from the surrounding area. Leashed pets are permitted.

Reservations, fees: No reservations. Sites are $10 per night, plus $5 for each additional vehicle. Senior discount available. Open mid-May to late September, weather permitting.

Directions: From Eugene drive south on I-5 for five miles to Exit 188 and Highway 58. Turn east and drive 68 miles to Odell Lake and Forest Road 680 (at the east end of the lake). Turn right on Forest Road 680 and drive 400 yards to the campground on the right.

Contact: Deschutes National Forest, Crescent Ranger District, P.O. Box 208, Crescent, OR 97733; 541/433-3200; fax 541/433-3224.

165 Sunset Cove

8

This campground is on the northeast shore of Odell Lake. Boat docks and rentals are available nearby at Odell Lake Lodge and Resort. Campsites are surrounded by large Douglas fir and some white pine. The camp backs up to the highway; expect to hear the noise.

Location: On Odell Lake in Deschutes National Forest; map The Southern Cascades map 5, grid d1.

Campsites, facilities: There are 20 sites for tents, trailers, or RVs up to 22 feet long. Picnic tables and fire grills are provided. Drinking water, vault toilets, a barrier-free boat launch and day-use area, and fish-cleaning facilities are available. Firewood may be gathered from the surrounding area. Leashed pets are permitted.

Reservations, fees: No reservations. Sites are $10 per night, plus $5 for each additional vehicle. Senior discount available. Open mid-May to mid-October, weather permitting.

Directions: From Eugene drive south on I-5 for five miles to Exit 188 and Highway 58. Turn east and drive 67 miles to the campground on the right.

Contact: Deschutes National Forest, Crescent Ranger District, P.O. Box 208, Crescent, OR 97733; 541/433-3200; fax 541/433-3224.

166 Princess Creek

🚶 🏊 🎣
🚤 🐕 🚐 ⛺ 9

This wooded campground is on the northeast shore of Odell Lake, but it backs up to the highway; expect traffic noise. See the description of Odell Creek for recreation details. Boat docks and rentals are available nearby at the Shelter Cove Resort.

Location: On Odell Lake in Deschutes National Forest; The Southern Cascades map 5, grid d1.

Campsites, facilities: There are 46 sites for tents, trailers, or RVs up to 22 feet long. Picnic tables and fire grills are provided. Drinking water, vault toilets, and boat-launching facilities are available. Firewood may be gathered from the surrounding area. Showers, a store, coin-operated laundry facilities, and ice are within five miles. Leashed pets are permitted.

Reservations, fees: No reservations. Sites are $10–12 per night, plus $5 for each additional vehicle. Senior discount available. Open mid-May through September, weather permitting.

Directions: From Eugene drive south on I-5 for five miles to Exit 188 and Highway 58. Turn east and drive 64 miles to the campground on the right.

Contact: Deschutes National Forest, Crescent Ranger District, P.O. Box 208, Crescent, OR 97733; 541/433-3200; fax 541/433-3224.

167 Simax Group Camp

🚶 🏊 🎣 🚤
🐕 ♿ 🚐 ⛺ 8

This camp is set at an elevation of 4,850 feet on Crescent Lake with trails to day-use beaches. Fishing is variable year to year and is usually better earlier in the season. A boat launch is available at Crescent Lake, about two miles away. See neighboring Crescent Lake for more details.

Location: On Crescent Lake in Deschutes National Forest; The Southern Cascades map 5, grid e1.

Campsites, facilities: There are three group campsites for 30 to 40 campers each. Drinking water, tent pads, flush toilets, showers, picnic tables, garbage service, fireplaces, and a group shelter (with an electrical outlet) that accommodates 50 campers are available. Tents must be placed on tent pads. Facilities are wheelchair-accessible. Leashed pets are permitted.

Reservations, fees: Reservations required ($8.65 reservation fee). Rates are $65 per night for Site A (the most accessible) and $85 per night for Sites B and C. Site B is the most difficult to reach and only tents are advised; Site C is best for RVs. The group shelter fee is $25 per day. The campground is generally open from Memorial Day through Labor Day, weather permitting.

Directions: From Eugene drive south on I-5 for five miles to Exit 188 and Highway 58. Turn east and drive 70 miles to Crescent Lake Highway (Forest Road 50). Turn right and drive two miles to Forest Road 6005. Turn left and drive one mile to the campground on the right.

Contact: Deschutes National Forest, Crescent Ranger District, P.O. Box 208, Crescent, OR 97733; 541/433-3200; reservations 877/444-6777; fax 541/433-3224; website (for reservations): www.reserveusa.com.

168 Crescent Lake

🚶 🏊 🎣
🚤 🐕 🚐 ⛺ 8

This campground is set along the north shore of Crescent Lake, and it is often windy here in the afternoon. Boat docks, launching facilities, and rentals are also nearby at Crescent Lake Resort, adjacent to the campground. A trail from camp heads into the Diamond Peak Wilderness and also branches north to Odell Lake.

Location: On Crescent Lake in Deschutes National Forest; The Southern Cascades map 5, grid e1.

Campsites, facilities: There are 47 sites for tents, trailers, or RVs up to 35 feet long. Picnic tables, garbage service, and fire grills are provided. Drinking water, vault toilets, and boat-launching facilities are available. Firewood may be gathered from the surrounding area. Leashed pets are permitted.

Reservations, fees: No reservations. Sites are $10–12 per night, plus $5 for each additional vehicle. Senior discount available. Open mid-May to late October, weather permitting.

Directions: From Eugene drive south on I-5 for five miles to Exit 188 and Highway 58. Turn east and drive 70 miles to Crescent Lake Highway (Forest Road 60). Turn right (west) and drive 2.2 miles southwest. Bear right to remain on Forest Road 60, and drive another one-quarter mile to the campground on the left.

Contact: Deschutes National Forest, Crescent Ranger District, P.O. Box 208, Crescent, OR 97733; 541/433-3200; fax 541/433-3224.

169 Spring

8

This campground is on the southern shore of Crescent Lake at an elevation of 4,850 feet. In a lodgepole pine forest, sites are open and some are on the lake with Diamond Peak views. See Contorta Point for more information.

Location: On Crescent Lake in Deschutes National Forest; The Southern Cascades map 5, grid e1.

Campsites, facilities: There are 68 sites for tents, trailers, or RVs up to 22 feet long. Picnic tables, garbage service, and fire grills are provided. Drinking water, vault toilets, boat-launching facilities, and firewood (to be gathered from the surrounding area) are available. Leashed pets are permitted.

Reservations, fees: No reservations. Sites are $10–12 per night, plus $5 for each additional vehicle. Senior discount available. Open June through September, weather permitting.

Directions: From Eugene drive south on I-5 for five miles to Exit 188 and Highway 58. Turn east and drive 70 miles to Crescent Lake Highway (Forest Road 60). Turn right and drive eight miles west to the campground entrance road on the left. Turn left and drive one mile to the campground.

Contact: Deschutes National Forest, Crescent Ranger District, P.O. Box 208, Crescent, OR 97733; 541/433-3200; fax 541/433-3224.

170 Contorta Point

8

This campground at 4,850 feet elevation is on the southern shore of Crescent Lake, where swimming, boating, and water-skiing are among the summer pastimes. A number of trails from the nearby Windy-Oldenburg Trailhead provide access to lakes in the Oregon Cascades Recreation Area. Motorized vehicles are restricted to open roads only.

Location: On Crescent Lake in Deschutes National Forest; The Southern Cascades map 5, grid e1.

Campsites, facilities: There are about 15 sites in an area for dispersed camping for tents, trailers, or RVs up to 22 feet long. There is no drinking water, and all garbage must be packed out. Picnic tables and vault toilets are provided. Boat docks and launching facilities are three miles away at Spring Campground. Leashed pets are permitted.

Reservations, fees: No reservations. There is no fee. Open May to late October, weather permitting.

Directions: From Eugene drive south on I-5 for five miles to Exit 188 and Highway 58. Turn east and drive 70 miles to Crescent Lake Highway (Forest Road 60). Turn right and drive 9.9 miles to Forest Road 280. Turn left and drive one mile to the campground.

Contact: Deschutes National Forest, Crescent Ranger District, P.O. Box 208, Crescent, OR 97733; 541/433-3200; fax 541/433-3224.

171 Whitefish Horse Camp

5

This just might be the best horse camp in the state. Horse camping only is allowed here, and manure removal is required. High lines are not allowed; horses must be kept in stalls. On Whitefish Creek at the west end of Crescent Lake, this campground is set in lodgepole pine with shaded sites. It's across the road from the lake in a flat area with no lake view from the campground. Moderately to heavily used, at 4,850 feet elevation, it has access to about 100 miles of trail, including Diamond Peak Wilderness, the Oregon Cascades Recreation Area, many high mountain lakes, and the Metolius-Windigo National Recreation Trail.

Location: On Whitefish Creek in Deschutes National Forest; The Southern Cascades map 5, grid e1.

Campsites, facilities: There are 17 sites for tents, trailers, or RVs up to 40 feet long. Picnic tables, horse corrals, and fire rings are provided. Drinking water and garbage bins are available in the summer only. Vault toilets are available. Firewood may be gathered from the surrounding area. Leashed pets are permitted.

Reservations, fees: Reservations accepted ($8.65 reservation fee). Sites are $10 per night for two stalls, and $12 per night for four stalls, plus $5 for each additional vehicle. Open May through November, weather permitting.

Directions: From Eugene drive south on I-5 for five miles to Exit 188 and Highway 58. Turn east and drive 70 miles to Crescent Lake Highway (Forest Road 60). Turn right (west) and drive 2.2 miles southwest. Stay to the right to remain on Forest Road 60, and drive six miles to the campground on the right.

Contact: Deschutes National Forest, Crescent Ranger District, P.O. Box 208, Crescent, OR 97733; 541/433-3200, reservations 877/444-6777; fax 541/433-3224; website (for reservations): www.reserveusa.com.

172 Crescent Creek

7

This is one of the Cascade's classic hidden campgrounds, set along the banks of Crescent Creek at 4,500 feet. The buzzwords here are pretty, developed, and private. Hunters are the primary users of this campground, mainly in the fall. Otherwise, it gets light use. There's some highway noise here, and even if you can't hear it, traffic is visible from some sites.

Location: On Crescent Creek in Deschutes National Forest; The Southern Cascades map 5, grid e1.

Campsites, facilities: There are 10 sites for tents, trailers, or RVs up to 22 feet long. Picnic tables, garbage service, and fire grills are provided. Drinking water and vault toilets are available. Firewood may be gathered from the surrounding area. Leashed pets are permitted.

Reservations, fees: No reservations. Sites are $8 per night, plus $4 for each additional vehicle. Senior discount available. Open May to late October, weather permitting.

Directions: From Eugene drive south on I-5 for five miles to Exit 188 and Highway 58. Turn east and drive 73 miles to County Road 61. Turn left (east) and drive three miles to the campground on the right.

Contact: Deschutes National Forest, Crescent Ranger District, P.O. Box 208, Crescent, OR 97733; 541/433-3200; fax 541/433-3224.

173 Digit Point

7

This campground is set in lodgepole forest at 5,600 feet on the shore of Miller Lake, a popular spot for boating, fishing, and swimming. Nearby trails provide access to the Mt. Thielsen Wilderness and the Pacific Crest Trail.

Location: On Miller Lake in Winema National Forest; The Southern Cascades map 5, grid g1.

Campsites, facilities: There are 64 sites for tents, trailers, or RVs up to 30 feet long. Picnic tables, garbage bins, and fire grills are provided. Drinking water, a sanitary disposal station, and flush toilets are available. Boat docks and launching facilities are nearby. Leashed pets are permitted.

Reservations, fees: No reservations. Sites are $8 per night, $4 per night for an additional vehicle. Senior discount available. Open from Memorial Day to mid-October.

Directions: From Eugene drive southeast on Highway 58 for 86 miles to U.S. 97. Turn south and drive seven miles to Forest Road 9772 (one mile north of Chemult). Turn right and drive 12 miles west to the campground.

Contact: Winema National Forest, Chemult Ranger District, P.O. Box 150, Chemult, OR 97731; 541/365-7001; fax 541/365-7019.

174 Corral Spring

4

This flat campground with no water source is next to Corral Spring at 4,900 feet elevation. The main attraction is solitude; it's primitive, remote, and quiet. It is set in an area with stands of lodgepole pine, interspersed by several small meadows.

Location: In Winema National Forest; The Southern Cascades map 5, grid f3.

Campsites, facilities: There are six sites for tents, trailers, or RVs up to 34 feet long. Picnic tables, garbage bins, and fire grills are provided. Vault toilets are available, but there is no drinking water. A store, a café, a coin-operated laundry, and ice are within five miles. Leashed pets are permitted.

Reservations, fees: No reservations; no fee. Open mid-May to late October.

Directions: From Eugene drive southeast on Highway 58 for 86 miles to U.S. 97. Turn south and drive 6.5 miles to Forest Road 9774 (2.5 miles north of Chemult). Turn right and drive two miles west to the campground.

Contact: Winema National Forest, Chemult Ranger District, P.O. Box 150, Chemult, OR 97731; 541/365-7001; fax 541/365-7019.

175 Surprise Valley RV Park

7

This RV park is near the South Umpqua River about two miles from a gambling casino. If you desire a more remote setting, the following sites are the answer: Dumont Creek, Boulder Creek, and Camp Comfort. This is a nice park with new restrooms, gravel on the roads, and grass at all sites.

Location: On the South Umpqua River; The Southern Cascades map 6, grid a6.

Campsites, facilities: There are 15 tent sites and four drive-through sites for trailers or RVs of any length. Electricity, drinking water, sewer hookups, and picnic tables are provided. Flush toilets, showers, and a laundry room are available. Leashed pets are permitted.

Reservations, fees: No reservations accepted. Sites are $15 per night. Open year-round.

Directions: In Canyonville drive north on I-5 for three miles to Exit 102. Take that exit and drive east on Gazley Road for one mile to the campground.

Contact: Surprise Valley RV Park, P.O. Box 909, Canyonville, OR 97417; 541/839-6634.

176 Charles V. Stanton Park

7

This campground set along the banks of the South Umpqua River is an all-season spot with a nice beach for swimming in the summer, good steelhead fishing in the winter, and wild grape picking in the fall.

Location: On the South Umpqua River; The Southern Cascades map 6, grid a6.

Campsites, facilities: There are 20 tent sites and 20 sites for trailers or RVs up to 30 feet long. Electricity, sewer hookups, and picnic tables are provided. Drinking water, flush toilets, showers, a dump station, a pavilion, and a playground are available. Bottled gas, a store, a café, a coin laundry, and ice are within one mile. Leashed pets and motorbikes are permitted.

Reservations, fees: Reservations accepted for pavilion only. Sites are $11–14 per night. Senior discount available for county residents. Open year-round.

Directions: Depending on your heading on I-5, there are two routes to reach this campground. In Canyonville northbound on I-5, take Exit 99 and drive one mile north on the frontage road to the campground on the right.

Otherwise: in Canyonville southbound on I-5, take Exit 101 and drive one mile south on the frontage road to the campground on the left.

Contact: Charles V. Stanton Park, 1540 Stanton Park Rd., Canyonville, OR 97417; 541/839-4483, reservations (for pavilion) 541/440-4500.

177 Meadow Wood RV Resort and Camp

6

This is a good option for RVers looking for a camping spot along I-5. There are 80 wooded acres. All the amenities are available. Nearby attractions include a ghost town, gold panning, and Wolf Creek Tavern.

Location: In Glendale; The Southern Cascades map 6, grid c6.

Campsites, facilities: There are 25 tent sites and 34 drive-through sites for trailers or RVs of any length; 23 sites have full hookups. Electricity, drinking water, and picnic tables are provided. Flush toilets, bottled gas, sanitary disposal services, showers, firewood, a store, a laundry room, ice, a playground, and a heated swimming pool are available. Leashed pets are permitted.

Reservations, fees: Reservations accepted. Sites are $12–20 per night. Senior discount available. Open year-round.

Directions: Depending on your heading on I-5, there are two routes to reach this campground. From Roseburg drive south on I-5 to Exit 86 (near Glendale). Take that exit and drive south on the frontage road for three miles to Barton Road. Turn east and drive a quarter mile to Autumn Lane. Turn south on Autumn Lane and drive three-quarters of a mile to the park. From Grants Pass drive north on I-5 to Exit 83 (near Glendale) and drive east for a quarter mile to Autumn Lane. Turn south on

Autumn Lane and drive three-quarters of a mile to the camp.

Contact: Meadow Wood RV Resort and Camp, 869 Autumn Ln., Glendale, OR 97442; 800/606-1279 or 541/832-3114; fax 541/832-2454.

178 Indian Mary Park

 9

This park is the crown jewel of the Josephine County parks. Set right on the Rogue River at an elevation of 900–1,000 feet, the park sports hiking trails, a picnic shelter for 150 people, swimming (unsupervised), fishing, disc golf (Frisbee golf), and a historic mining town nearby. Rogue River is famous for its rafting, which can be done commercially or on your own.

Location: On the Rogue River; The Southern Cascades map 6, grid d5.

Campsites, facilities: There are 34 sites for tents and 68 sites for trailers or RVs of up to 40 feet; 44 are full hookup, and 14 are partial. There is also a group site of six sites together, and two yurts. Picnic tables and fire pits are provided. Drinking water, restrooms with flush toilets and coin-operated showers, a barrier-free campsite and restroom, garbage bins, dump station, boat ramp, playground, ice, and firewood are available. A store and café are seven miles away, and a laundry is 16 miles away. Leashed pets are permitted.

Reservations, fees: Reservations recommended. Family sites are $15–20 per night, $5 for a third vehicle, $28 for a yurt per night with a $28 refundable cleaning deposit. Call for group rates. Open year-round.

Directions: From Grants Pass drive north on I-5 for 3.5 miles to Exit 61 (Merlin-Galice Road). Take that exit and drive northwest for 10 miles to Indian Mary Park on the right.

Contact: Josephine County Parks, 125 Ringuette St., Grants Pass, OR 97527; 541/474-5285; fax 541/474-5288; website: www.co.josephine.or.us/planning/parks, (reservations) www.jocopark@magick.net.

179 Elderberry Flat

7

Virtually unknown, this campground on the banks of Evans Creek is only about a 30-minute drive from I-5. It's small and primitive, and swimming holes are along the creek. ATV/motorcycle trails originate from this area. No fishing is allowed in the creek.

Location: On West Fork Evans Creek; The Southern Cascades map 6, grid d8.

Campsites, facilities: There are nine primitive tent sites. Picnic tables and fire grills are provided. Vault toilets and garbage service are available, but there is no drinking water. Some facilities are wheelchair-accessible. Leashed pets are permitted.

Reservations, fees: No reservations; no fee. There is a 14-day stay limit. Open mid-April to mid-November.

Directions: From Grants Pass drive south on I-5 for 10 miles to the Rogue River exit. Take that exit and turn right on Depot Street and drive to Pine Street. Turn left and drive 18 miles (it becomes East Evans Creek Road) to West Fork Evans Creek Road. Turn left and drive nine miles to the campground.

Contact: Bureau of Land Management, Medford District, 3040 Biddle Rd., Medford, OR 97504; 541/618-2200; fax 541/618-2400; website: www.or.blm.gov/medford.

180 Bend O' the River RV Park

7

This campground is set along the banks of the Rogue River. It's a pretty spot far enough out of Grants Pass to have a unique feel.

Location: On the Rogue River; The Southern Cascades map 6, grid e6.

Campsites, facilities: There are no tent sites and 25 sites for trailers or RVs of any length. Electricity, drinking water, sewer hookups, and picnic tables are provided. Flush toilets, sanitary disposal services, showers, firewood, a store, a laundry room, and ice are available. Leashed pets are permitted.

Reservations, fees: Reservations accepted. Sites are $16 per night. Open year-round.

Directions: In Grants Pass on I-5, take Exit 58 to 6th Street. Drive south on 6th Street to G Street. Turn west and drive 7.5 miles (the road becomes Upper River Road, then Lower River Road) to the park.

Contact: Bend O' the River RV Park, 7501 Lower River Rd., Grants Pass, OR 97526; 541/479-2547.

181 White Horse

9

This pleasant county park on the banks of the Rogue River is one of several parks in the Grants Pass area that provide opportunities for trout fishing, hiking, and boating. Wildlife Images, a wildlife rehabilitation center, is nearby. Possible side trips include Oregon Caves, Kerby Museum, and Crater Lake National Monument (two hours away).

Location: On the Rogue River; The Southern Cascades map 6, grid e6.

Campsites, facilities: There are 42 sites for tents, trailers, or RVs including eight with full hookups, one group site for 12 to 18 people, and one yurt. Drinking water and picnic tables are provided. Restrooms, coin-operated showers, a public phone, fire grills, horseshoes, a reservable picnic shelter, and a playground are available. Leashed pets are permitted.

Reservations, fees: Reservations accepted. Sites are $14 per night, plus $5 for a third vehicle; $28 for a yurt per night with a $28 re-

fundable cleaning deposit. Major credit cards accepted. Open year-round, but only to self-contained RVs in the winter.

Directions: In Grants Pass on I-5, take Exit 58 to 6th Street. Drive south on 6th Street to G Street. Turn west and drive seven miles (the road becomes Upper River Road, then Lower River Road). The park is on the left at 7600 Lower River Road.

Contact: Josephine County Parks, 125 Ringuette St., Grants Pass, OR 97527; 541/474-5285; fax 541/474-5288; website: www.co.josephine.or.us/planning/parks.

182 Grants Pass Overniters

7

This wooded park is set in a rural area just outside Grants Pass and is mostly shaded. Several other campgrounds are in the area.

Location: Near Grants Pass; The Southern Cascades map 6, grid e6.

Campsites, facilities: There are eight tent sites and 26 drive-through sites for trailers or RVs of any length. Electricity, drinking water, sewer hookups, and picnic tables are provided. Flush toilets, showers, a laundry room, and a swimming pool are available. A store is within one mile. Leashed pets are permitted.

Reservations, fees: Reservations accepted. Sites are $12–18 per night. Open year-round.

Directions: From Grants Pass drive north on I-5 for three miles to Exit 61 (and bear right) to a stop sign and Highland Avenue. Turn left and drive a very short distance to the campground on the right.

Contact: Grants Pass Overniters, 5941 Highland Ave., Grants Pass, OR 97526; 541/479-7289.

183 River Park RV Resort

🚶 🚴 🏊
🎣 🐕 🚐 ⛺ 6

This park has a quiet, serene riverfront setting, yet it is close to all the conveniences of a small city. Highlights here include 700 feet of Rogue River frontage for trout fishing and swimming. It's one of several parks in the immediate area.

Location: On the Rogue River; The Southern Cascades map 6, grid e6.

Campsites, facilities: There are three tent sites and 47 sites for trailers or RVs. Cable TV, restrooms, showers, a sanitary dump, a public phone, laundry facilities, and ice are available. Leashed pets are permitted.

Reservations, fees: Reservations recommended. Sites are $22.50 per night. Open year-round.

Directions: In Grants Pass on I-5, take Exit 55 west fo Highway 199. Drive west two miles to Parkdale. Turn left on Parkdale and drive one block to Highway 99. Turn left on Highway 99 and drive two miles to the park on the left.

Contact: River Park RV Resort, 2956 Rogue River Hwy., Grants Pass, OR 97527; 800/677-8857 or 541/479-0046; fax 541/471-1448; website: www.riverparkrvresort.com.

184 Grants Pass/Redwood KOA

🚶 🚴 🐕 🚶 🚐 ⛺ 8

This KOA campground along a stream in the hills outside of Grants Pass is popular with bird-watchers. It's a perfect layover spot for travelers who want to get away from the highway for a while. For an interesting side trip, drive south down scenic U.S. 199 to Cave Junction or Illinois River State Park.

Location: Near Grants Pass; The Southern Cascades map 6, grid e5.

Campsites, facilities: There are 40 sites for tents, trailers, or RVs. Restrooms, showers, drinking water, a sanitary dump, security, a public phone, a laundry room, limited groceries, ice, RV supplies, LP gas, and a barbecue are available. There are also a recreation hall, a playground, and a recreation field. Leashed pets are permitted.

Reservations, fees: Reservations recommended. Sites are $19–24 per night. Open year-round.

Directions: In Grants Pass on I-5, take the U.S. 199 exit. Turn southwest on U.S. 199 and drive for 14.5 miles to the campground on the right (at milepost 14.5).

Contact: Grants Pass/ Redwood KOA, 13370 Redwood Hwy., Wilderville, OR 97543; 541/476-6508; website: www.koa.com.

185 Schroeder

🏊 🎣 🚤 🐕
🚶 ♿ 🚐 ⛺ 9

Trout fishing, swimming, and boating are among the possibilities at this camp along the Rogue River. Just a short jog off the highway, it makes an excellent layover for I-5 travelers. It's not a highly publicized camp, so many tourists pass by it in favor of the more commercial camps in the area. The park is set close to Hellgate Excursions, which provides jetboat trips on the Rogue River. Tennis courts are close by, and horse rentals are available within a 10-minute drive.

Location: On the Rogue River; The Southern Cascades map 6, grid e5.

Campsites, facilities: There are 22 tent sites and 28 sites for trailers and RVs; three are partial hookups. Restrooms, coin-operated showers, and a public phone are available. Recreational facilities include horseshoes, a recreation field, a barbecue, a playground, and a boat ramp. Some facilities are wheelchair-accessible. Leashed pets are permitted.

Reservations, fees: Reservations accepted. Sites are $12–18 per night. Major credit cards accepted. Open year-round.

Directions: In Grants Pass on I-5, take Exit 58 to U.S. 199. Drive west on U.S. 199 for four miles to the campground.

Contact: Josephine County Parks, 125 Ringuette St., Grants Pass, OR 97527; 541/474-5285; fax 541/474-5288; website: www.co.josephine.or.us/planning/parks.

186 Rogue Valley Overniters

5

This park is just off the freeway in Grants Pass, the jumping-off point for trips down the Rogue River. The summer heat in this part of Oregon can surprise visitors in late June and early July. This is a nice comfortable park with shade trees.

Location: Near the Rogue River; The Southern Cascades map 6, grid e6.

Campsites, facilities: There are 110 sites for tents, trailers, and RVs; 26 are drive-through sites. Electricity, drinking water, cable TV, and sewer hookups are provided. Flush toilets, sanitary disposal services, showers, and a laundry room are available. Bottled gas, a store, a café, and ice are available within one mile. Leashed pets are permitted.

Reservations, fees: Reservations accepted. Sites are $20–22 per night. Senior discount available. Open year-round.

Directions: In Grants Pass on I-5, take Exit 58 to 6th Street. Drive south on 6th Street for a quarter mile to the park on the right.

Contact: Rogue Valley Overniters, 1806 N.W. 6th St., Grants Pass, OR 97526; 541/479-2208.

187 Circle W Campground

6

This campground along the Rogue River is close to chartered boat trips down the Rogue and a golf course. Fishing and swimming access are available from the campground.

Location: On the Rogue River; The Southern Cascades map 6, grid e7.

Campsites, facilities: There are 25 sites for trailers or RVs of any length; four are drive-through sites. Electricity, drinking water, sewer hookups, and picnic tables are provided. Flush toilets, sanitary disposal services, showers, a laundry room, and ice are available. A boat dock is nearby. Leashed pets are permitted.

Reservations, fees: Reservations accepted. Sites are $18 per night. Senior discount available. Open year-round.

Directions: From Grants Pass drive south on I-5 for 10 miles to Exit 48 at Rogue River. Take that exit west (over the bridge) to Highway 99. Turn right and drive west one mile to the camp.

Contact: Circle W Campground, 8110 Rogue River Hwy., Grants Pass, OR 97527; 541/582-1686.

188 Have a Nice Day Campground

6

This campground with grassy, shaded sites is set along the Rogue River, where fishing, swimming, and boating are options. This camp has nice river views.

Location: On the Rogue River; The Southern Cascades map 6, grid e7.

Campsites, facilities: There are 22 sites for tents, trailers, or RVs and 18 for trailers or

RVs only, including some sites that are drive-through and some with sewer hook-ups. Electricity, drinking water, and picnic tables are provided. Flush toilets, sanitary disposal services, showers, a laundry room, and a playground are available. A store and a café are within two miles. Boat docks and launching facilities are nearby. Leashed pets and motorbikes are permitted.

Reservations, fees: Reservations accepted. Sites are $17 per night. Open year-round, weather permitting, with limited winter facilities.

Directions: From Grants Pass drive south on I-5 for seven miles to Exit 48 at Rogue River. Take that exit and drive west over the bridge to Highway 99. Turn right (downriver) and drive west for 2.5 miles to the campground (on both sides of the road).

Contact: Have a Nice Day Campground, 7275 Rogue River Hwy., Grants Pass, OR 97527; 541/582-1421.

189 Riverfront Trailer Park

🥾 🏊 🎣 🚗 🐕 🚐   6

This spot is convenient to good fishing, swimming, and boating on the Rogue River. Many of these large sites face the river. This park features a round driveway, so there is no backing up.

Location: On the Rogue River; The Southern Cascades map 6, grid e7.

Campsites, facilities: There are 22 sites for trailers or RVs of any length; 19 have full and three have partial hookups. Electricity, drinking water, sewer and cable TV hookups, and picnic tables are provided. Flush toilets, sanitary disposal services, showers, a laundry room, and ice are available. Bottled gas, a store, and a café are within two miles. Fishing docks, boat docks, and launching facilities are nearby. Small leashed pets are permitted.

Reservations, fees: Reservations accepted. Sites are $20 per night. Open year-round.

Directions: From Grants Pass, drive south on I-5 for seven miles to Exit 48 and Highway 99. Take that exit and bear west on Highway 99 and drive two miles to the park on the right.

Contact: Riverfront Trailer Park, 7060 Rogue River Hwy., Grants Pass, OR 97527; 541/582-0985.

190 Lazy Acres RV

🥾 🏊 🎣
🚗 🐕 🚣 🚐   6

This wooded campground on the Rogue River may be a bit less scenic than KOA Gold n' Rogue, but there are evergreen, maple, and birch trees that still make this a beautiful spot. It also offers the same recreation options.

Location: On the Rogue River; The Southern Cascades map 6, grid e8.

Campsites, facilities: There are 68 sites with full hookups for trailers or RVs of any length. Electricity, drinking water, sewer hookups, and picnic tables are provided. Flush toilets, bottled gas, cable TV, a dump station, a playground, and a laundry room are available. Boat docks are nearby. Leashed pets are permitted.

Reservations, fees: Reservations accepted. Sites are $20 per night. Open year-round.

Directions: From Medford drive north on I-5 for 18 miles to the South Gold Hill exit. Take that exit and drive one-quarter mile north to 2nd Avenue. Turn west and drive 1.2 miles to the campground on the left.

Contact: Lazy Acres RV, 1550 2nd Ave., Gold Hill, OR 97525; 541/855-7000.

191 Valley of the Rogue State Park

7

With easy highway access, this popular spot along the banks of the Rogue River is often filled to near capacity during the summer. Recreation options include fishing and boating. This is a good base camp for taking in the Rogue Valley and surrounding attractions: Crater Lake National Park, Oregon Caves National Monument, historic Jacksonville, Ashland's Shakespeare Festival, or the Britt Music Festival.

Location: On the Rogue River; The Southern Cascades map 6, grid e8.

Campsites, facilities: There are 21 sites for tents or self-contained RVs and 146 sites with full or partial hookups for trailers or RVs up to 75 feet long. Three group tent areas and six yurts are available. Picnic tables and fire grills are provided. Flush toilets, drinking water, garbage bins, sanitary disposal station, showers, firewood, two laundry rooms, a meeting hall, and playgrounds are available. A restaurant is nearby. Some facilities are wheelchair-accessible. Boat-launching facilities are nearby. Leashed pets are permitted.

Reservations, fees: Reservations accepted ($6 reservation fee). Sites are $15–18 per night. Group areas are $60 per area, yurts are $27 per night, and additional vehicles are $7 per night. Open year-round. Major credit cards accepted.

Directions: From Grants Pass drive south on I-5 for 12 miles to Exit 45B. Take that exit and turn right and drive one mile to the park on the right.

Contact: Valley of the Rogue State Park, 3792 N. River Rd., Gold Hill, OR 97525; 541/582-1118, reservations 800/452-5687.

192 KOA Gold n' Rogue

6

This campground is set a half mile from the Rogue River, with a golf course, bike paths, and the Oregon Vortex in the vicinity. It's one of the many camps between Gold Hill and Grants Pass.

Location: On the Rogue River; The Southern Cascades map 6, grid e8.

Campsites, facilities: There are 12 tent sites and 53 sites for trailers or RVs of any length; 27 are drive-through sites. Electricity, drinking water, sewer hookups, and picnic tables are provided. Flush toilets, bottled gas, sanitary disposal services, showers, firewood, a store, a laundry room, ice, a playground, and a swimming pool are available. A café is within one mile, and boat-launching facilities are within five miles. Leashed pets and motorbikes are permitted.

Reservations, fees: Reservations accepted. Sites are $19–24 per night. Major credit cards accepted. Open year-round.

Directions: From Medford drive north on I-5 for 10 miles to South Gold Hill and Exit 40. Take that exit and turn right and drive a quarter mile to Blackwell Road. Turn right (on a paved road) and drive a quarter mile to the park.

Contact: KOA Gold n' Rogue, P.O. Box 320, Gold Hill, OR 97525; 541/855-7710; website: www.koa.com.

193 Lake Selmac

9

Nestled in a wooded, mountainous area, this 300-acre park offers swimming, hiking, boating, sailing, and good trout fishing on beautiful Lake Selmac. There are seasonal hosts and an assistant park ranger on-site.

Location: On Lake Selmac; The Southern Cascades map 6, grid f4.

Campsites, facilities: There are 81 sites for tents, trailers, or RVs up to 32 feet long, and two yurts. Drinking water and picnic tables are provided. Facilities include restrooms, coin-operated showers, a sanitary dump, a public phone, snacks, a barbecue, horseshoes, a playground, a recreation field, and two boat ramps and dock. Facilities are wheelchair-accessible. Leashed pets are permitted.

Reservations, fees: Reservations recommended. Sites are $15–20 per night, plus $5 for a third vehicle; $28 per night for a yurt plus a $28 refundable deposit. Major credit cards accepted. Open year-round, with limited winter service.

Directions: In Grants Pass on I-5, take the U.S. 199 exit. Turn southwest on U.S. 199 and drive for 23 miles to Selma and the Lake Selmac exit (Lakeshore Drive). Turn left (east) and drive two miles to the lake and the campground entrance.

Contact: Josephine County Parks, 125 Ringuette St., Grants Pass, OR 97527; 541/474-5285; fax 541/474-5288; website: www.co.josephine.or.us/planning/parks.

194 Lake Selmac Resort

🚶 🚴 🏊 🎣
🚗 🐕 🛶 🚐   7

This resort is along the shore of Lake Selmac. About 30 miles away is Oregon Caves National Monument. Fishing is great for largemouth bass (the state record has been set here three times). Trout, crappie, bluegill, and catfish are also catchable here. There is a 5 mph speed limit on the lake. A trail circles the lake, and hikers, bikers, and horses are welcome. A golf course is about six

miles away. The campground was renovated in 2001.

Location: On Lake Selmac; The Southern Cascades map 6, grid f4.

Campsites, facilities: There are 29 sites for trailers or RVs of any length. Electricity, drinking water, fire rings, and picnic tables are provided. Flush toilets, showers, firewood, a store, a café, a laundry room, ice, and a playground are available. Boat docks and launching facilities are nearby, and rentals are on-site. Horseback riding trails are available in the summer. Leashed pets and motorbikes are permitted. Corrals are available for horse campers.

Reservations, fees: Reservations accepted. Sites are $18 per night. Open year-round, with limited winter facilities.

Directions: In Grants Pass on I-5, take the U.S. 199 exit. Turn southwest on U.S. 199 and drive for 23 miles to Selma and the Lake Selmac exit (Lakeshore Drive). Turn left (east) and drive 2.5 miles to the lake and the resort on the left.

Contact: Lake Selmac, 2700 Lakeshore Dr., Selma, OR 97538; 541/597-2277; website: www.lakeselmacresort.com.

195 Kerby Trailer Park

🚶 🚴 🏊
🛶 🚐 🐕 🚐   5

This small park is near the Illinois River, a good stream during the summer for swimming. Lake Selmac provides a nearby side trip. Other recreation options include an 18-hole golf course, hiking trails, and tennis courts.

Location: Near the Illinois River; The Southern Cascades map 6, grid g3.

Campsites, facilities: There are five sites for trailers and RVs with full hookups. Electricity, drinking water, and sewer hookups are provided. A laundry room is available. A store and ice are within 1.5 miles. One pet per site and motorbikes are permitted.

Reservations, fees: Reservations accepted. Sites are $15 per night. Open year-round.

Directions: In Grants Pass drive south on U.S. 199 for 26 miles to Kerby. Continue south on U.S. 199 for a quarter mile to the campground on the right.

Contact: Kerby Trailer Park, P.O. Box 3256, Kerby, OR 97531; 541/592-2897.

196 Town and Country RV Park

 7

This park on the Illinois River provides good opportunities for swimming and boating (no motors are permitted). Nearby side trips include Oregon Caves National Monument (21 miles) and Grants Pass (31 miles). Crescent City is 50 miles away.

Location: On the Illinois River; The Southern Cascades map 6, grid g3.

Campsites, facilities: There are 51 sites for tents, trailers, or RVs. Cable TV, showers, restrooms, a sanitary dump, a public phone, a laundry room, and ice are available. Horseshoe pits, a clubhouse, and a playground are also provided. Leashed pets are permitted.

Reservations, fees: Reservations recommended. Sites are $16.50 for two people per night, $2 per additional person per night. Open year-round.

Directions: In Grants Pass on I-5, take Exit 55 for U.S. 199. Bear southwest on U.S. 199 for 30 miles to Cave Junction and the campground.

Contact: Town and Country RV Park, 28288 Redwood Hwy., Cave Junction, OR 97523; tel./fax 541/592-2656.

197 Country Hills Resort

7

Lots of sites at this wooded camp border Sucker Creek, a popular spot for swimming.

Lake Selmac and Oregon Caves National Monument provide nearby side-trip options.

Location: Near Oregon Caves National Monument; The Southern Cascades map 6, grid g5.

Campsites, facilities: There are 12 tent sites and 20 sites for trailers or RVs of any length; two are drive-through sites. There are also six cabins. Picnic tables are provided. Flush toilets, showers, drinking water, electricity, firewood, a small store, a laundry room, motel, ice cream parlor, and ice are available. Leashed pets are permitted.

Reservations, fees: Reservations accepted. Tent sites are $13 per night, RV sites are $17 per night, cabins are $45–63 per night. Open year-round.

Directions: In Grants Pass on I-5, take Exit 55 for U.S. 199. Bear southwest on U.S. 199 for 30 miles to Cave Junction and Highway 46. Turn east on Highway 46 and drive eight miles to the campground on the right.

Contact: Country Hills Resort, 7901 Caves Hwy., Cave Junction, OR 97523; 541/592-3406; fax 541/592-3406.

198 Grayback

7

This wooded campground at an elevation of 2,000 feet along the banks of Sucker Creek has sites with ample shade and is a good choice if you're planning to visit Oregon Caves National Monument, which is about 10 miles away. The camp is in a grove of old-growth firs and is a prime place for bird-watching. A half-mile barrier-free trail cuts through the camp.

Location: Near Oregon Caves National Monument in Siskiyou National Forest; The Southern Cascades map 6, grid g5.

Campsites, facilities: There are 37 sites for tents, trailers, or RVs up to 22 feet long; one site has a full hookup. Picnic tables, garbage bins, and fire grills are provided. Flush toilets and drinking water are available. Some facilities are wheelchair-accessible. Leashed pets are permitted.

Reservations, fees: Some sites can be reserved ($8.65 reservation fee). Sites are $15 per night. Senior discount available. Open May through October.

Directions: In Grants Pass on I-5, take Exit 55 for U.S. 199. Bear southwest on U.S. 199 for 30 miles to Cave Junction and Highway 46. Turn east on Highway 46 and drive 12 miles to the campground.

Contact: Siskiyou National Forest, Illinois Valley Ranger District, P.O. Box 389, Cave Junction, OR 97523; 541/592-4000, reservations 541/592-3311; fax 541/592-4010.

199 Cave Creek

7

No campground is closer to Oregon Caves National Monument than this U.S. Forest Service camp, a mere four miles away. There is even a two-mile trail out of camp that leads directly to the caves. The camp, at an elevation of 2,500 feet, lies in a grove of old-growth timber along the banks of Cave Creek, a small stream with some trout fishing opportunities (catch-and-release only). The sites are shaded, and an abundance of wildlife can be spotted in the area. Hiking opportunities abound.

Location: Near Oregon Caves National Monument in Siskiyou National Forest; The Southern Cascades map 6, grid h5.

Campsites, facilities: There are 18 tent sites. Drinking water, garbage bins, vault toilets, and picnic tables are provided. Showers are within eight miles. Leashed pets are permitted.

Reservations, fees: No reservations. Sites are $12 per night. Senior discount available. Open mid-May to mid-September.

Directions: In Grants Pass on I-5, take Exit 55 for U.S. 199. Bear southwest on U.S. 199 for 30 miles to Cave Junction and Highway 46. Turn east on Highway 46 and drive 16 miles to Forest Road 4032. Turn right and drive south for one mile to the campground.

Contact: Siskiyou National Forest, Illinois Valley Ranger District, P.O. Box 389, Cave Junction, OR 97523; 541/592-4000; fax 541/592-4010.

200 Bolan Lake

9

Very few out-of-towners know about this camp set at an elevation of 5,500 feet, with pretty, shaded sites along the shore of 15-acre Bolan Lake. The lake is stocked with trout. Only nonmotorized boats are allowed. A trail from the lake leads up to a fire lookout and ties into miles of other trails, including the Bolan Lake Trail. This spot is truly a bird-watcher's paradise, with a variety of species to view. The fishing can be good here.

Location: On Bolan Lake in Siskiyou National Forest; The Southern Cascades map 6, grid h5.

Campsites, facilities: There are 12 sites for tents, trailers, or RVs up to 16 feet long. Picnic tables and fire grills are provided. Vault toilets and firewood are available, but there is no drinking water, and all garbage must be packed out. Leashed pets are permitted.

Reservations, fees: No reservations. Site are $5 per night. Senior discount available. Open July through October.

Directions: In Grants Pass drive south on U.S. 199 for 30 miles to Cave Junction and Rockydale Road (County Road 5560). Turn southeast on Rockydale Road and drive eight miles to County Road 5828 (also called Waldo Road and Happy Camp Road). Turn southeast and drive 14 miles to Forest Road 4812. Turn east and drive four miles to Forest Road

4812-040. Turn south and drive two miles to the campground. This access road is very narrow and rough. Large trailers or RVs are strongly discouraged.

Contact: Siskiyou National Forest, Illinois Valley Ranger District, P.O. Box 389, Cave Junction, OR 97523; 541/592-4000; fax 541/592-4010.

201 Farewell Bend

7

This extremely popular campground is set at an elevation of 3,400 feet along the banks of the Upper Rogue River near the Rogue River Gorge. A quarter-mile barrier-free trail leads from camp to the Rogue Gorge Viewpoint and is definitely worth the trip. The Upper Rogue River Trail passes near camp. It attracts a lot of the campers who also visit Crater Lake. See description of Union Creek.

Location: On the Upper Rogue River in Rogue River National Forest; The Southern Cascades map 7, grid a5.

Campsites, facilities: There are 61 sites for tents, trailers, or RVs up to 40 feet long. Picnic tables, fire grills, and fire rings are provided. Drinking water, firewood for purchase, and flush toilets are available. Some facilities are wheelchair-accessible. Leashed pets are permitted.

Reservations, fees: No reservations. Sites are $12 per night, plus $5 per extra vehicle a night. Senior discount available. Open late May to late October.

Directions: From Medford drive northeast on Highway 62 for 59 miles (near Union Creek) to the campground on the left.

Contact: Rogue Recreation, 2990 N. Pacific Hwy., Medford, OR 97501; 541/770-5146; fax 541/770-1552; website: www.roguerec.com.

202 Union Creek

8

One of the most popular camps in the district, this spot is more developed than the nearby camps of Mill Creek, River Bridge, and Natural Bridge. It's set along the banks of Union Creek at 3,200 feet elevation, where it joins the Upper Rogue River. The Upper Rogue River Trail passes near camp. Interpretive programs are offered in the summer, and a convenience store and a restaurant are within walking distance. A private riding stable is less than one mile away.

Location: Near the Upper Rogue River in Rogue River National Forest; The Southern Cascades map 7, grid a5.

Campsites, facilities: There are 78 sites for tents, trailers, or RVs up to 30 feet long. Picnic tables, garbage service, and fire grills are provided. Drinking water and vault toilets are available. Firewood is available for purchase. A store and a restaurant are within walking distance. At least one toilet and one site are wheelchair-accessible. Leashed pets are permitted.

Reservations, fees: No reservations accepted. Sites are $10 per night, plus $4 per second vehicle a night. Senior discount available. Open mid-May to mid-October.

Directions: From Medford drive northeast on Highway 62 for 56 miles (near Union Creek) to the campground on the left.

Contact: Rogue Recreation, 2990 N. Pacific Hwy., Medford, OR 97501; 541/770-5146; fax 541/770-1552; website: www.roguerec.com.

203 Natural Bridge

8

Expect lots of company in midsummer at this popular camp, which is at an elevation of 3,200 feet, where the Upper Rogue River runs underground. The Upper Rogue River Trail passes by the camp and follows the river for many miles to the Pacific Crest Trail in Crater Lake National Park. There is an interpretive area and a spectacular geological viewpoint adjacent to the camp. A quarter-mile, barrier-free trail is also available.

Location: On the Upper Rogue River Trail in Rogue River National Forest; The Southern Cascades map 7, grid a5.

Campsites, facilities: There are 17 sites for tents, trailers, or RVs up to 30 feet long. Picnic tables, garbage service, and fire grills are provided. Vault toilets are available, but there is no drinking water. One toilet and one site are wheelchair-accessible. Leashed pets are permitted.

Reservations, fees: No reservations. Sites are $3 per night, $2.50 per night for an additional vehicle. Senior discount available. Open early May to early November.

Directions: From Medford drive northeast on Highway 62 for 54 miles (near Union Creek) to Forest Road 300. Turn left and drive one mile west to the campground on the right.

Contact: Rogue River National Forest, Prospect Ranger District, 47201 Hwy. 62, Prospect, OR 97536; 541/560-3400; fax 541/560-3444.

204 Abbott Creek

🏊 🎣 🐕 🚐 ⛺   8

Set at an elevation of 3,100 feet, at the confluence of Abbott and Woodruff Creeks about two miles from the Upper Rogue River, this is a better camp for visitors with children than some of the others along the Rogue River. Abbott Creek is small and tame compared to the roaring Rogue. The kids probably still won't be tempted to dip their toes, however, because the water usually runs at a body-numbing 42 degrees, even in the summer.

Location: On Abbott and Woodruff Creeks in Rogue River National Forest; The Southern Cascades map 7, grid a5.

Campsites, facilities: There are 25 sites for tents, trailers, or RVs up to 20 feet long. Picnic tables, garbage service, and fire grills are provided. Drinking water and vault toilets are available. Firewood is available for purchase. Leashed pets are permitted.

Reservations, fees: No reservations. Sites are $8 per night, plus $4 per extra vehicle a night. Senior discount available. Open late May to late October.

Directions: From Medford drive northeast on Highway 62 for 47 miles (near Union Creek) to Forest Road 68. Turn left and drive 3.5 miles west to the campground on the left.

Contact: Rogue Recreation, 2990 N. Pacific Hwy., Medford, OR 97501; 541/770-5146; fax 541/770-1552; website: www.roguerec.com.

205 Mill Creek

🎣 🐕 ⛺   7

This campground along the banks of Mill Creek at an elevation of 2,800 feet, about two miles from the Upper Rogue River, has beautiful, private sites and is heavily vegetated. It's one in a series of remote, primitive camps near Highway 62 missed by out-of-towners and is an excellent choice for tenters.

Location: Near the Upper Rogue River in Rogue River National Forest; The Southern Cascades map 7, grid a5.

Campsites, facilities: There are eight sites for tents. Picnic tables, garbage service, and fire grills are provided. Vault toilets are available. There is no drinking water. Leashed pets are permitted.

Reservations, fees: No reservations. Sites are $5 per night, $2.50 per night for an additional vehicle. Senior discount available. Open April to November.

Directions: From Medford drive north on Highway 62 for 47 miles (near Union Creek) to Forest Road 30. Turn right (southeast) and drive one mile to the campground on the right.

Contact: Rogue River National Forest, Prospect Ranger District, 47201 Hwy. 62, Prospect, OR 97536; 541/560-3400; fax 541/560-3444.

206 River Bridge

7

This campground situated at 2,900 feet elevation along the banks of the Upper Rogue River is particularly scenic, with secluded sites and river views. This is a calmer part of the Wild and Scenic Upper Rogue, though swimming and rafting are not recommended. The Upper Rogue River Trail passes by the camp and follows the river for many miles to the Pacific Crest Trail in Crater Lake National Park.

Location: On the Upper Rogue River in Rogue River National Forest; The Southern Cascades map 7, grid b5.

Campsites, facilities: There are six sites for tents. Picnic tables, garbage service, and fireplaces are provided. Vault toilets are available. There is no drinking water. Leashed pets are permitted.

Reservations, fees: No reservations. Sites are $5 per night, $2.50 per night for an additional vehicle. Senior discount available. Open April to November, weather permitting.

Directions: From Medford drive northeast on Highway 62 (Crater Lake Highway) for 42 miles (before reaching Union Creek) to Forest Road 6210. Turn left and drive one mile north to the campground on the left.

Contact: Rogue River National Forest, Prospect Ranger District, 47201 Hwy. 62, Prospect, OR 97536; 541/770-5146; fax 541/560-3444.

207 Huckleberry Mountain

6

Here's a hideaway for Crater Lake visitors. The camp is at the site of an old 1930s Civilian Conservation Corps camp, and an ATV trail runs through and next to the campground. Set at an elevation of 5,400 feet, this camp, about 15 miles from the entrance to Crater Lake National Park, really does get overlooked by highway travelers, so you have a good shot at privacy.

Location: Near Crater Lake National Park in Rogue River National Forest; The Southern Cascades map 7, grid b6.

Campsites, facilities: There are 25 primitive sites for tents, trailers, or RVs up to 26 feet long. Picnic tables and fireplaces are provided. Drinking water and vault toilets are available, but all garbage must be packed out. Leashed pets are permitted.

Reservations, fees: No reservations; no fee. Open June to late October.

Directions: From Medford drive north on Highway 62 for 52 miles (near Union Creek) to Forest Road 60. Turn south and drive 12 miles to the campground on the right.

Note: The access road is quite rough; trailers are not recommended.

Contact: Rogue River National Forest, Prospect Ranger District, 47201 Hwy. 62, Prospect, OR 97536; 541/560-3400; fax 541/560-3444.

208 Mazama

6

This is one of two campgrounds at Crater Lake; the other is Lost Creek. This one is set at 6,000 feet and is known for cold nights, even in late June and early September; I once got caught in a snowstorm here at the opening in mid-June. A nearby store is a great convenience. The Pacific Crest Trail passes near the camp, but the only trail access down to Crater Lake is at Cleetwood Cove. Note that winter access to the park is from the west only on Highway 62 to Rim Village.

Location: Near the Pacific Crest Trail in Crater Lake National Park; The Southern Cascades map 7, grid a8.

Campsites, facilities: There are 213 sites for tents, trailers, or RVs up to 32 feet long. Picnic tables, fire grills, and garbage bins are provided. Drinking water, flush toilets, sanitary disposal services, coin-operated showers, a laundry room, gas pumps, a mini-mart, firewood, and ice are available. Some facilities are wheelchair-accessible. Leashed pets and motorbikes are permitted on paved roads only.

Reservations, fees: No reservations. Sites are $15–19 for two campers and $3.50 per night for each additional person. Senior discount available. Open from late June to early October.

Directions: From I-5 at Medford, turn east on Highway 62 and drive 72 miles into Crater Lake National Park and to Annie Springs junction. Turn left and drive to the national park entrance kiosk. Just beyond the kiosk, turn right to the campground and Mazama store entrance.

Contact: Mazama Campground, P.O. Box 2704, White City, OR 97503; 541/830-8700; fax 541/830-8514; website: www.crater-lake.com.

209 Lost Creek

🥾 🚴 🎣 🐕 ⛺   6

In good weather this is a prime spot in Crater Lake National Park; you avoid most of the crowd driving the Rim Drive. This campground is set near little Lost Creek and the Pinnacles, a series of spires. The only trail

access down to Crater Lake is at Cleetwood Cove. This campground is set in a lodgepole pine forest and is more private than Mazama Campground. There are paved roads in the campground and there is a possibility (hint, hint) that a black bear could visit your campsite. Follow all bear precautions described in the Camping Tips section of this book.

Location: Near the Crater Lake Pinnacles in Crater Lake National Park; The Southern Cascades map 7, grid b8.

Campsites, facilities: There are 16 sites for tents. Picnic tables and fire grills are provided. Drinking water, flush toilets, and garbage bins are available. Leashed pets and motorbikes are permitted on paved roads only.

Reservations, fees: Reservations are not accepted. Sites are $10 for two campers and $3 per night for each additional camper. Senior discount available. Open from mid-July to mid-September, weather permitting.

Directions: From I-5 at Medford, turn east on Highway 62 and drive 72 miles into Crater Lake National Park and to Annie Springs junction. Turn left and drive to the junction with Rim Drive. Turn right and drive east on Rim Drive to Pinnacles Road Junction. Turn right on Pinnacles Road and drive five miles to the campground.

Contact: Crater Lake National Park, P.O. Box 7, Crater Lake, OR 97604; 541/594-2211; fax 541/594-2299.

210 Bear Mountain RV Park

🏊 🎣 🛶
🐕 🧗 🚐 ⛺   7

This campground is in an open, grassy area on the Rogue River about six miles from Lost Creek Lake, where boat ramps and picnic areas are available for day use. The campsites are spacious and shaded.

Location: On the Rogue River; The Southern Cascades map 7, grid c2.

Campsites, facilities: There are some tent sites and 37 drive-through sites for trailers or RVs of any length; 30 have full hookups and seven have partial hookups. Electricity, drinking water, sewer hookups, and picnic tables are provided. Flush toilets, bottled gas, sanitary disposal services, showers, a laundry room, ice, and a playground are available. A store and a café are within one mile. Boat docks and launching facilities are nearby. Leashed pets and motorbikes are permitted.

Reservations, fees: Reservations accepted. Sites are $14–18 per night. Senior discount available. Open year-round.

Directions: From Medford drive northeast on Highway 62 to the junction with Highway 227. Continue east on Highway 62 for 2.5 more miles to the campground.

Contact: Bear Mountain RV Park, 27301 Hwy. 62, Trail, OR 97541; 541/878-2400.

211 Rogue Elk Campground

8

Set right on the Rogue River at an elevation of 1,476 feet, the park has hiking trails, creek swimming (unsupervised), fishing, rafting, a Douglas fir forest, and wildlife. The forest is very beautiful here. Lost Creek Lake on Highway 62 is in the vicinity.

Location: On the Rogue River east of the city of Trail; The Southern Cascades map 7, grid c3.

Campsites, facilities: There are 37 sites for tents, trailers, or RVs of up to 25 feet; 15 are partial hookups. Picnic tables and fire pits are provided. Drinking water, restrooms with flush toilets and coin-operated showers, a barrier-free campsite and restroom, garbage bins, dump station, soft drink machine, boat ramp, and playground are available. A café,

minimart, ice, laundry facilities, and firewood are available within three miles. Leashed pets are permitted.

Reservations, fees: No reservations. Family sites are $16–18 per night, $6 for a third vehicle. There is a pet fee of $1. Open mid-April through mid-October.

Directions: From Medford, take Exit 30 for the Crater Lake Highway (Highway 62) and drive northeast on Highway 62 for 29 miles to the park entrance (well signed).

Contact: Jackson County Parks, 400 Antelope Rd., White City, OR 97503; 541/774-8183; fax 541/774-6320.

212 Joseph H. Stewart State Park

7

This state park is on the shore of Lost Creek Reservoir, a lake with a marina, a beach, and boat rentals. The park is home to eight miles of hiking and biking trails. The park is about 40 miles from Crater Lake National Park and makes an excellent jumping-off point for an exploration of southern Oregon.

Location: On Lost Creek Reservoir; The Southern Cascades map 7, grid c3.

Campsites, facilities: There are 151 sites with partial hookups (water and electricity) for tents, trailers or RVs, including some sites for RVs up to 80 feet long, and 50 sites for tents or self-contained trailers or RVs, two group tent areas. Picnic tables and fire grills are provided. Flush toilets, garbage bins, drinking water, sanitary disposal services, showers, firewood, and a playground are available. Boat rentals and launching facilities are nearby. Leashed pets are permitted.

Reservations, fees: No reservations. Sites are $14–15 per night, $7 per night for an additional vehicle. Group camping is $60 per area. Open from mid-April to late October.

Directions: From Medford drive northeast on Highway 62 for 34 miles to the Lost Creek Reservoir and the campground on the left.

Contact: Joseph H. Stewart State Park, 35251 Hwy. 62, Trail, OR 97524; 800/551-6949 or 541/560-3334.

213 Whiskey Springs

9

This campground at Whiskey Springs, near Fourbit Ford Campground, is one of the larger, more developed backwoods U.S. Forest Service camps in the area. A one-mile, wheelchair-accessible nature trail is nearby. You can see beaver dams and woodpeckers here. The camp is set at 3,200 feet elevation.

Location: Near Burre Falls in Rogue River National Forest; The Southern Cascades map 7, grid c5.

Campsites, facilities: There are 34 sites for tents, trailers, or RVs up to 30 feet long. Picnic tables, garbage service, and fire grills are provided. Drinking water and vault toilets are available. Firewood is available for purchase. Boat docks, launching facilities, and rentals are within 1.5 miles. Some facilities are wheelchair-accessible. Leashed pets are permitted.

Reservations, fees: No reservations. Sites are $8 per night, plus $4 per extra vehicle a night. Senior discount available. Open late May through September.

Directions: From Medford drive northeast on Highway 62 for 16 miles to the Butte Falls Highway. Turn right and drive east for 16 miles to the town of Butte Falls. Continue southeast on Butte Falls Highway for nine miles to Forest Road 3065. Turn left on Forest Road

3065 and drive 300 yards to the campground on the left.

Contact: Rogue Recreation, 2990 N. Pacific Hwy., Medford, OR 97501; 541/770-5146; fax 541/770-1552; website: www.roguerec.com.

214 Imnaha

7

This campground along Imnaha Creek at an elevation of 3,800 feet is a good base camp for a wilderness trip. Trailheads at the ends of the nearby forest roads lead east into the Sky Lakes Wilderness and there are two, shorter interpretive trails.

Location: Near the Sky Lakes Wilderness in Rogue River National Forest; The Southern Cascades map 7, grid c6.

Campsites, facilities: There are four sites for tents. Picnic tables, garbage service, and fire grills are provided. Drinking water and vault toilets are available. A furnished cabin is also available. Leashed pets are permitted.

Reservations, fees: No reservations. Sites are $5 per night, $2.50 per night for an additional vehicle. Reservations required for the cabin, $50 per night. Senior discount available. Open mid-June to mid-November.

Directions: From Medford drive northeast on Highway 62 for about 35 miles to Prospect and Mill Creek Drive. Turn right and drive one mile to County Road 992/Butte Falls Prospect Highway. Turn right and drive 2.5 miles to Forest Road 37. Turn left and drive 10 miles east to the campground.

Contact: Rogue River National Forest, Butte Falls Ranger District, 800 Laurel St., Butte Falls, OR 97522; 541/865-2700; fax 541/865-2795.

215 South Fork

7

This campground is set at an elevation of 4,000 feet along the South Rogue River. To the east, trails at the ends of the nearby forest roads provide access to the Sky Lakes Wilderness. The Southfork Trail is across the road from the campground and has a good biking trail in one direction and a hiking trail in the other. A map of Rogue River National Forest details all back roads, trails, and waters.

Location: On the South Rogue River in Rogue River National Forest; The Southern Cascades map 7, grid c6.

Campsites, facilities: There are two sites for tents, four sites for tents, trailers, or RVs up to 15 feet long. Picnic tables, drinking water, garbage service, and fire grills are provided. Vault toilets are available. Leashed pets are permitted.

Reservations, fees: No reservations. Sites are $3 per night, $1.50 per night for an additional vehicle. Senior discount available. Open mid-June to mid-November.

Directions: From Medford drive northeast on Highway 62 for 16 miles to Butte Falls Highway. Turn right and drive 16 miles east to the town of Butte Falls. Continue one mile past Butte Falls to County Road 992 (Butte Falls Prospect Highway) and drive nine miles to Forest Road 34. Turn right and drive 8.5 miles to the campground on the right.

Contact: Rogue River National Forest, Butte Falls Ranger District, P.O. Box 227, Butte Falls, OR 97522; 541/865-2700; fax 541/865-2795.

216 Fly-Casters RV Park

6

This spot along the banks of the Rogue River is a good base camp for RVers who want to fish or hike. The county park in

Shady Cove offers picnic facilities and a boat ramp. Lost Creek Lake is about a 15-minute drive northeast.

Location: On the Rogue River; The Southern Cascades map 7, grid d2.

Campsites, facilities: There are 47 sites for trailers or RVs of any length; two are drive-through sites. Electricity, drinking water, sewer hookups, and picnic tables are provided. Flush toilets, bottled gas, showers, cable, a clubhouse, and a laundry room are available. A store, a café, and ice are within one mile. Boat-launching facilities are nearby. Leashed pets are permitted.

Reservations, fees: Reservations accepted. Sites are $16–30 per night. Open year-round.

Directions: From Medford drive northeast on Highway 62 for 23 miles to the campground on the right (it is 2.7 miles south of the junction of Highways 62 and 227).

Contact: Fly-Casters RV Park, P.O. Box 699, Shady Cove, OR 97539; 541/878-2749; fax 541/878-2742.

217 Shady Trails RV Park and Camp

7

This grassy park is set along the banks of the Rogue River in a wooded, mountainous area with many shaded sites. Recreation options include fishing on the Rogue River or exploring Casey State Park.

Location: On the Rogue River; The Southern Cascades map 7, grid d2.

Campsites, facilities: There are 10 tent sites and 49 sites for trailers or RVs of any length. Electricity, drinking water, sewer hookups, and picnic tables are provided. Flush toilets, cable TV, bottled gas, sanitary disposal services, showers, a store, ice, and a playground are available. A café is within one mile. Boat-launching facilities are nearby. Pets and motorbikes are permitted.

Reservations, fees: Reservations accepted. Sites are $22–26 per night, $2 per night for each additional person. Open year-round.
Directions: From I-5 at Medford, drive northeast on Highway 62 for 23 miles to the campground.
Contact: Shady Trails RV Park and Camp, 1 Meadow Ln., Shady Cove, OR 97539; 541/878-2206.

218 Odessa

4

This campground is set at an elevation of 4,100 feet along Odessa Creek, near the shore of Upper Klamath Lake. The lake is the main attraction, with fishing the main activity. Campsites are in among scattered mixed conifers and native brush. Boating is popular. The lake can provide excellent fishing for rainbow trout on both flies and Rapalas.

Location: Near Klamath Lake in Winema National Forest; The Southern Cascades map 7, grid d8.
Campsites, facilities: There are five tent sites. Picnic tables, garbage bins, and fire grills are provided. Vault toilets are available, but there is no drinking water. Leashed pets are permitted.
Reservations, fees: No reservations; no fee. Open year-round, weather permitting.
Directions: From Klamath Falls drive north on Highway 140 about 18 miles to Forest Road 3639. Turn northeast and drive one miles to the campground.
Contact: Winema National Forest, Klamath Ranger District, 1936 California Ave., Klamath Falls, OR 97601; 541/885-3400; fax 541/885-3452.

219 Medford Oaks Campark

6

This park is in a quiet, rural setting among the trees. Just a short hop off I-5, it's an excellent choice for travelers heading south to California. The campground is along the shore of a pond that provides good fishing.

Location: Near Eagle Point; The Southern Cascades map 7, grid e2.
Campsites, facilities: There are 60 sites for tents, trailers, or RVs of any length. Cabins are also available. Restrooms, showers, a sanitary dump, a public phone, a laundry room, limited groceries, ice, RV supplies, and LP gas are available. Recreational facilities include a seasonal, heated swimming pool, movies, horseshoe pits, table tennis, a recreation field for baseball and volleyball, and a playground. Call for pet policy.
Reservations, fees: Reservations are recommended. Sites are $14–50 per night. Group rates are available. Call for cabin information. Open year-round.
Directions: From Medford drive northeast on Highway 62 for five miles to Exit 30 and Highway 140. Turn east on Highway 140 and drive 6.8 miles to the campground on the left.
Contact: Medford Oaks Campark, 7049 Hwy. 140, Eagle Point, OR 97524; 541/826-5103; fax 541/826-5984; website: www.gocamping america.com/medfordoaks.

220 Fourbit Ford

6

This campground set at an elevation of 3,200 feet along Fourbit Creek is one in a series of hidden spots tucked away near County Road 821.

Location: On Fourbit Creek in Rogue River National Forest; The Southern Cascades map 7, grid d5.

Campsites, facilities: There are seven sites for tents. Picnic tables, garbage service, and fire grills are provided. Drinking water and vault toilets are available. A store, a café, and ice are within five miles. Boat docks, launching facilities, and rentals are nearby. Leashed pets are permitted.

Reservations, fees: No reservations. Sites are $8 per night, plus $4 per extra vehicle per night. Open late May to late September.

Directions: From Medford drive northeast on Highway 62 for 16 miles to Butte Falls Highway. Turn right and drive 16 miles east to the town of Butte Falls and County Road 821. Turn left and drive nine miles southeast to Forest Road 3065. Turn left and drive one mile to the campground on the left.

Contact: Rogue Recreation, 2990 N. Pacific Hwy., Medford, OR 97501; 541/770-5146; fax 541/770-1552; website: www.roguerec.com.

221 Willow Lake Resort

This campground is on the shore of Willow Lake. There is a hiking trail that starts near camp.

Location: On Willow Lake; The Southern Cascades map 7, grid e5.

Campsites, facilities: There are 29 tent sites, 20 drive-through sites with full hookups for trailers or RVs, and 17 sites with electricity and water for trailers or RVs. There are also four cabins for up to six people each. Picnic tables and fire rings are provided. Flush toilets, sanitary disposal services, coin-operated showers, and firewood are available. Leashed pets are permitted.

Reservations, fees: Reservations accepted for groups and cabins only. Sites are $12–18 per night. Major credit cards accepted with reservations only. Open year-round.

Directions: From Medford drive northeast on Highway 62 for 15 miles to Butte Falls Highway. Turn east and drive 25 miles to Willow Lake Road. Turn south and drive two miles to the campground.

Contact: Jackson County Parks, 400 Antelope Rd., White City, OR 97503; 541/774-8183; fax 541/774-6320.

222 Parker Meadows

7

Fantastic views of nearby Mt. McLoughlin are among the highlights of this rustic camp set at 5,000 feet elevation in a beautiful meadow. Trailheads at the ends of the forest roads lead into the Sky Lakes Wilderness. This is a nice spot, complete with water and lots of privacy between sites. Except during hunting season in the fall, Parker Meadows does not get much use.

Location: On Parker Meadow in Rogue River National Forest; The Southern Cascades map 7, grid e6.

Campsites, facilities: There are three sites for tents, five sites for tents, trailers, or RVs up to 15 feet long. Picnic tables, garbage service, and fire grills are provided. Drinking water and vault toilets are available. Leashed pets are permitted.

Reservations, fees: No reservations. Sites are $3 per night, $1.50 per night for an additional vehicle. Senior discount available. Open mid-June to late October.

Directions: From Medford drive northeast on Highway 62 for 16 miles to Butte Falls Highway. Turn right and drive 16 miles east to the town of Butte Falls and County Road 821. Turn left and drive 10 miles southeast to Forest Road 37. Turn left and drive 11 miles to the campground on the left.

Contact: Rogue River National Forest, Butte Falls Ranger District, 800 Laurel

St., Butte Falls, OR 97522; 541/865-2700; fax 541/865-2795.

223 Fourmile Lake

8

This beautiful spot is the only camp on the shore of Fourmile Lake. Several nearby trails provide access to the Sky Lakes Wilderness. The Pacific Crest Trail passes about two miles from camp. This campground is near the foot of Mt. McLoughlin (9,495 feet). More primitive and with lots of solitude, it attracts a calm and quiet crowd. Afternoon winds can be a problem, and in the evening, if the wind isn't blowing, the mosquitoes often arrive. There is no view of Mt. McLoughlin from the campground, but there is a good view from the lake.

Location: At Fourmile Lake in Winema National Forest; The Southern Cascades map 7, grid e6.

Campsites, facilities: There are 25 sites for tents, trailers, or RVs up to 22 feet long. Picnic tables, garbage bins, and fire grills are provided. Drinking water and vault toilets are available. Leashed pets are permitted.

Reservations, fees: No reservations. Sites are $9 per night, $4 per night for an additional vehicle. Senior discount available. Open from June to late September.

Directions: From Medford drive northeast on Highway 62 for five miles to Exit 30 and Highway 140. Turn east on Highway 140 and drive approximately 40 miles to Forest Road 3661. Turn north and drive six miles to the campground.

Contact: Winema National Forest, Klamath Ranger District, 1936 California Ave., Klamath Falls, OR 97601; 541/885-3400; fax 541/885-3452.

224 Rocky Point Resort

7

Rocky Point Resort is at the Upper Klamath Wildlife Refuge with 10 miles of canoe trails, with opportunities for fishing, boating, and canoeing.

Location: On Upper Klamath Lake; The Southern Cascades map 7, grid e8.

Campsites, facilities: There are 28 sites, some drive-through sites, with partial or full hookups for RVs, and four tent sites. Picnic tables are provided. Restrooms, drinking water, flush toilets, showers, firewood, a store, a laundry room, ice and marina with boat gas, boat and canoe rentals are available. There is a free boat launch and game area. A restaurant and lounge overlook the lake. Leashed pets are permitted.

Reservations, fees: Reservations accepted. Sites are $14–21 per night. Open April through November.

Directions: From Klamath Falls drive northeast on Highway 140 for about 25 miles to Rocky Point Road. Turn north and drive three miles to the campground.

Contact: Rocky Point Resort, 28121 Rocky Point Rd., Klamath Falls, OR 97601; 541/356-2287; fax 541/356-2222; website: www.rockypointoregon.com.

225 Willow Prairie

7

Next to this camp is a beaver swamp and several large ponds that attract sandhill cranes, ducks, geese, elk, and deer. This spot near the origin of the west branch of Willow Creek has riding trails nearby and is primarily used as a horse camp. A map of Rogue River National Forest details the back roads and can help you get here. Fish Lake is four miles south.

Location: Near Fish Lake in Rogue River National Forest; The Southern Cascades map 7, grid e6.

Campsites, facilities: There are 10 sites for tents, trailers, or RVs up to 15 feet long, and one primitive cabin with cots. Picnic tables and fire grills are provided. Drinking water, vault toilets, garbage service, two stock water troughs, and horse corrals are available. A store, a café, and ice are within five miles. Boat docks, launching facilities, and rentals are nearby. A camp host is on-site. Leashed pets are permitted.

Reservations, fees: Reservations required during the summer. Sites are $6 per night, $3 per night for an additional vehicle. The cabin is $15 per night. Senior discount available. Open late May to late October.

Directions: From Medford drive northeast on Highway 62 for five miles to Exit 30 and Highway 140. Turn east on Highway 140 and drive 31.5 miles to Forest Road 37. Turn left and drive north 1.5 miles to Forest Road 3738. Turn left and drive one mile west to Forest Road 3735. Turn left and drive 100 yards to the campground.

Contact: Rogue River National Forest, Butte Falls Ranger District, 800 Laurel St., Butte Falls, OR 97522; 541/865-2700; fax 541/865-2795.

226 North Fork

7

Here is a small, pretty campground with easy access from the highway and proximity to Fish Lake. It is situated on the North Fork of Little Butte Creek at an elevation of 4,500 feet. It's fairly popular, so reserve your spot early. Excellent fly-fishing can be found along the Fish Lake Trail, which leads directly out of camp.

Location: Near Fish Lake in Rogue River National Forest; The Southern Cascades map 7, grid e6.

Campsites, facilities: There are six tent sites and three sites for trailers or RVs up to 24 feet long. Picnic tables and fire grills are provided. All garbage must be packed out. Vault toilets and drinking water are available. Boat docks, launching facilities, and rentals are nearby. Some facilities are wheelchair-accessible, including a barrier-free vault toilet. Leashed pets are permitted.

Reservations, fees: No reservations. There is no fee, but donations are accepted. Open from early May to mid-November.

Directions: From Medford drive northeast on Highway 62 for five miles to Exit 30 and Highway 140. Turn east on Highway 140 and drive 31.5 miles to Forest Road 37. Turn south and drive a half mile to the campground.

Contact: Rogue River National Forest, Ashland Ranger District, 645 Washington St., Ashland, OR 97520; 541/482-3333; fax 541/858-2402.

227 Fish Lake

8

Bikes can be rented by the hour or by the day, a nice bonus. Same with boats. Add it up: boating, fishing, hiking, and bicycling are among the recreation options at this campground on the north shore of Fish Lake. Easy one-mile access to the Pacific Crest Trail is also available. If this campground is full, Doe Point and Fish Lake Resort are nearby.

Location: On Fish Lake in Rogue River National Forest; The Southern Cascades map 7, grid e6.

Campsites, facilities: There are 19 sites for tents, trailers, or RVs up to 32 feet long, and two walk-in sites for tents. There is one wheelchair-accessible site. Picnic tables, fire grills, and garbage bins are provided. Drinking water, showers, flush toilets, sanitary disposal station, a wheelchair-accessible picnic shelter, a store, a café, and ice are available. Firewood is available for purchase. Boat docks, launching facilities, and rentals are nearby. Leashed pets are permitted.

Reservations, fees: Group reservations only. Sites are $12 per night, plus $5 per extra vehicle a night. Boat ramp parking is $2. Senior discount available. Open from mid-May to mid-October, weather permitting.

Directions: From Medford drive northeast on Highway 62 for five miles to Exit 30 and Highway 140. Turn east on Highway 140 and drive 30 miles to the campground on the right.

Contact: Rogue River National Forest, Ashland Ranger District, 645 Washington St., Ashland, OR 97520; 541/482-3333, reservations (groups only) 800/416-6992; fax 541/858-2402.

228 Doe Point

8

This campground (at 4,600 feet elevation) is along the north shore of Fish Lake, nearly adjacent to Fish Lake Campground. Doe Point is slightly preferable because it's densely vegetated, offering shaded, quiet, well-screened sites. Privacy, rare at many campgrounds, can be found here. Recreation options include boating, fishing, hiking, and biking, plus an easy one-mile access trail to the Pacific Crest Trail.

Location: On Fish Lake in Rogue River National Forest; The Southern Cascades map 7, grid e6.

Campsites, facilities: There are five walk-in tent sites and 25 sites for tents, trailers, or RVs up to 32 feet long. Picnic tables and fire grills are provided. Drinking water, garbage service, flush toilets, a store, a café, and ice are available. Firewood is available for purchase. Boat docks, launching facilities, boat rentals, showers, and a sanitary

disposal station are nearby. Leashed pets are permitted.

Reservations, fees: No reservations. Sites are $12 per night, plus $5 per extra vehicle a night. Senior discount available. Open mid-May to late September.

Directions: From Medford drive northeast on Highway 62 for five miles to Exit 30 and Highway 140. Turn east on Highway 140 and drive 30 miles to the campground on the right.

Contact: Rogue River National Forest, Ashland Ranger District, 645 Washington St., Ashland, OR 97520; 541/482-3333; fax 541/858-2402.

229 Fish Lake Resort

7

This resort along Fish Lake is privately operated under permit by the U.S. Forest Service and offers a resort-type feel, catering primarily to families. Hiking, bicycling, fishing, and boating are some of the activities here. This is the largest and most developed of the three camps at Fish Lake. Cozy cabins are available for rental. Boat speed on the lake is limited to 10 mph.

Location: On Fish Lake; The Southern Cascades map 7, grid e6.

Campsites, facilities: There are six tent sites and 45 sites for trailers or RVs up to 30 feet long, plus 11 cabins. Electricity, drinking water, sewer hookups, garbage bins, and picnic tables are provided. Flush toilets, bottled gas, sanitary disposal services, showers, a recreation hall, a store, a café, a laundry room, ice, boat docks, boat rentals, and launching facilities are available. Leashed pets and motorbikes are permitted.

Reservations, fees: Reservations accepted. Sites are $16–22 per night; cabins are $50–170 per night. Open May through October, weather permitting.

Directions: From Medford drive northeast on Highway 62 for five miles to Exit 30 and Highway 140. Turn east on Highway 140 and drive 30 miles to Fish Lake Road. Turn right (south) and drive half a mile to the campground on the left.

Contact: Fish Lake Resort, P.O. Box 990, Gayle Point, OR 97524; 541/949-8500.

230 Lake of the Woods Resort

9

On beautiful Lake of the Woods, this resort offers fishing (four kinds of trout, catfish, and bass) and boating in a secluded forest setting. It's on one of the most beautiful lakes in the Cascade mountains, surrounded by tall pine trees. It's a family-oriented campground with all the amenities. In the winter, snowmobiling and cross-country skiing are popular (you can rent equipment at the resort). Attractions in the area include the Mountain Lakes Wilderness and the Pacific Crest Trail.

Location: On Lake of the Woods; The Southern Cascades map 7, grid f7.

Campsites, facilities: There are 27 sites for tents, trailers, or RVs up to 35 feet long, plus eight cabins that can accommodate from one to six people. Restrooms, showers, a sanitary dump, a public phone, a laundry room, ice, snacks, a restaurant, a lounge, and LP gas bottles are available. There are also a boat ramp, dock, marina, boat and mountain bike rentals, and a barbecue. Leashed pets are permitted.

Reservations, fees: Reservations recommended. Sites are $14–20 per night, and cabins are $45–249 per night. Open year-round, weather permitting.

Directions: In Medford on I-5, take Exit 14 to Highway 66. Drive east for less than a mile to Dead Indian Memorial Road. Turn left (east)

and drive 40 miles to Lake of the Woods Road. Turn north and drive less than one-half mile to the resort.

Contact: Lake of the Woods Resort, 950 Harriman Route, Klamath Falls, OR 97601; 541/949-8300; website: www.lakeowoods.com.

231 Aspen Point

8

This campground (at 5,000 feet elevation) is near the north shore of Lake of the Woods, adjacent to Lake of the Woods Resort. It's heavily timbered with old growth fir and has a great view of Mt. McLoughlin (9,495 feet). A hiking trail just north of camp leads north for several miles, wandering around Fourmile Lake and extending into the Sky Lakes Wilderness. Other trails nearby head into the Mountain Lakes Wilderness. Fishing, swimming, boating, and water-skiing are among the activities here.

Location: On Lake of the Woods in Winema National Forest; The Southern Cascades map 7, grid f7.

Campsites, facilities: There are 60 sites for tents, trailers, or RVs up to 55 feet long. Picnic tables, garbage bins, and fire grills are provided. Drinking water, a sanitary disposal station, and flush toilets are available. Boat docks, launching facilities, and rentals are nearby. Leashed pets are permitted.

Reservations, fees: Reservations accepted ($8.65 reservation fee). Sites are $12 per night, $6 per night for an additional vehicle. Senior discount available. Open from late May to late September.

Directions: In Medford on I-5, take Exit 14 to Highway 66. Drive east for less than a mile to Dead Indian Memorial Road. Turn left (east) and drive 40 miles to Lake of the Woods. Continue along the east shore to the campground turnoff on the left.

Contact: Winema National Forest, Klamath Ranger District, 1936 California Ave., Klamath Falls, OR 97601; 541/885-3400, reservations 877/444-6777; fax 541/885-3452; website (for reservations): www.reserveusa.com.

232 Sunset

 8

This campground at 5,000 feet elevation near the eastern shore of Lake of the Woods is fully developed and offers a myriad of recreation options. It's popular for both fishing and boating.

Location: Near Lake of the Woods in Winema National Forest; The Southern Cascades map 7, grid f7.

Campsites, facilities: There are 67 sites for tents, trailers, or RVs up to 55 feet long. Picnic tables, garbage bins, and fire grills are provided. Drinking water and flush toilets are available. Some facilities are wheelchair-accessible. Boat docks, launching facilities, and rentals are nearby. Leashed pets are permitted.

Reservations, fees: Reservations accepted ($8.65 reservation fee). Sites are $12 per night, $6 per night for an additional vehicle. Senior discount available. Open from June to mid-September.

Directions: In Medford on I-5, take Exit 14 to Highway 66. Drive east for less than a mile to Dead Indian Memorial Road. Turn left (east) and drive 40 miles to Lake of the Woods. Continue along the east shore to Forest Road 3738. Turn west and drive one-half mile to the camp.

Contact: Winema National Forest, Klamath Ranger District, 1936 California Ave., Klamath Falls, OR 97601; 541/885-3400, reservations 877/444-6777; fax 541/885-3452; website (for reservations): www.reserveusa.com.

233 Daley Creek

6

This campground (at 4,500 feet elevation) along the banks of Daley Creek among old-growth Douglas and white fir is a primitive and free alternative to some of the more developed spots in the area. The camp is near the confluence of Beaver Dam and Daley Creeks. The Beaver Dam Trail heads right out of camp, leading along the creek. Fishing can be decent downstream from here.

Location: On Daley Creek in Rogue River National Forest; The Southern Cascades map 7, grid f6.

Campsites, facilities: There are three tent sites and three sites for trailers or RVs up to 18 feet long. Picnic tables, garbage bins, and fire grills are provided, but there is no drinking water. Some facilities are wheelchair-accessible, including two campsites and a barrier-free vault toilet. Leashed pets are permitted.

Reservations, fees: No reservations. There is no fee, but donations are accepted. Open early May to mid-November.

Directions: In Ashland on I-5, take Exit 14 to Highway 66. Drive east for less than a mile to Dead Indian Memorial Road. Turn left (east) and drive 22 miles to Forest Road 37. Turn north and drive 1.5 miles to the campground.

Contact: Rogue River National Forest, Ashland Ranger District, 645 Washington St., Ashland, OR 97520; 541/482-3333; fax 541/858-2402.

234 Beaver Dam

5

This campground sits at an elevation of 4,500 feet along Beaver Dam Creek. Look for beaver dams. There's not much screening between sites, but it's a pretty, rustic, and quiet spot, with unusual vegetation along the creek for botany fans. The trailhead for the

Beaver Dam Trail is also here. The camp is adjacent to Daley Creek Campground.

Location: On Beaver Dam Creek in Rogue River National Forest; The Southern Cascades map 7, grid f6.

Campsites, facilities: There are two primitive tent sites and two sites for trailers or RVs up to 16 feet long. Picnic tables, garbage bins, and fire grills are provided. Vault toilets are available, but there is no drinking water. Leashed pets are permitted.

Reservations, fees: No reservations. There is no fee, but donations are accepted. Open early May to early November.

Directions: In Medford on I-5, take Exit 14 to Highway 66. Drive east for less than a mile to Dead Indian Memorial Road. Turn left (east) and drive 22 miles to Forest Road 37. Turn left (north) and drive 1.5 miles to the campground.

Contact: Rogue River National Forest, Ashland Ranger District, 645 Washington St., Ashland, OR 97520; 541/482-3333; fax 541/858-2402.

235 Cantrall-Buckley Park

8

This county park outside of Medford offers pleasant, shady sites in a wooded setting. The Applegate River, which has good trout fishing, runs nearby.

Location: On the Applegate River; The Southern Cascades map 7, grid g1.

Campsites, facilities: There are 25 sites for tents, trailers, and RVs up to 25 feet long. Picnic tables and fire pits are provided. Drinking water, restrooms, coin-operated showers, and a public phone are available. Recreational facilities include horseshoes, a playground, and a recreation field. Leashed pets are permitted.

Reservations, fees: Group site reservations accepted. Sites are $10 per night. Major

credit cards accepted with reservations only. Open year-round.

Directions: In Medford on I-5, take the Jacksonville exit to the Jacksonville Highway. Drive west on the Jacksonville Highway (Highway 238) for seven miles to Jacksonville. Bear left on Highway 238 and drive to Hamilton Road. Turn south on Hamilton Road and drive to Cantrall Road. Turn right on Cantrall and drive to the campground.

Contact: Jackson County Parks, 400 Antelope Rd., White City, OR 97503; 541/774-8183; fax 541/826-8360; website: www.co.jackson.or.us.

236 Jackson Hot Springs

5

This wooded campground has mineral hot springs that empty into a swimming pool, not a hot pool (76 degrees). Hot mineral baths are available in private rooms. This is an old Indian birthing ground. Nearby recreation options include a golf course, hiking trails, bike path, and tennis courts. Boating, fishing, and water-skiing are within 10 miles.

Location: Near Ashland; The Southern Cascades map 7, grid g3.

Campsites, facilities: There are 30 tent sites and 20 drive-through sites for trailers or RVs of any length. Electricity, drinking water, sewer hookups, and picnic tables are provided. Flush toilets, showers, a laundry room, ice, and a swimming pool are available. Bottled gas is within one mile. Pets are permitted with deposit.

Reserations, fees: No reservations. Sites are $16–20 per night. Open year-round.

Directons: From Ashland drive north on I-5 to Exit 19. Take that exit and drive west for one-quarter mile to the stoplight at Highway 99. Turn right and drive 500 feet to the campground.

Contact: Jackson Hot Springs, 2253 Hwy. 99 N, Ashland, OR 97520; 541/482-3776.

237 Glenyan Campground of Ashland

🏕️ 🚲 🏊 🎣
🐕 🎠 🚐 🏕️   7

This campground within seven miles of Ashland offers shady sites near Emigrant Lake. Recreation options in the area include a golf course, hiking trails, bike path, and tennis courts. It's an easy jump from I-5 at Ashland.
Location: Near Emigrant Lake; The Southern Cascades map 7, grid g3.

Campsites, facilities: There are 68 sites for tents, trailers, or RVs of any length; 12 have full and 38 have partial hookups. Electricity, drinking water, sewer hookups, and picnic tables are provided. Flush toilets, bottled gas, sanitary disposal services, showers, firewood, a recreation hall, a store, a laundry room, ice, a playground, and a swimming pool are available. Leashed pets are permitted.

Reservations, fees: Reservations accepted. Sites are $18.50–23 per night. Senior discount available. Open year-round.

Directions: From Ashland drive east on Highway 66 for 3.5 miles to the campground on the right.

Contact: Glenyan Campground of Ashland, 5310 Hwy. 66, Ashland, OR 97520; 541/488-1785; website: www.glenyancampground.com.

238 Howard Prairie Lake Resort

🏕️ 🚲 🎣 🏊
🚐 🐕 🚐 🏕️   7

This wooded campground is along the shore of Howard Prairie Lake, where hiking, swimming, fishing, and boating are among the recreation options. This is one of the largest campgrounds in more than 100 miles.

Location: On Howard Prairie Lake; The Southern Cascades map 7, grid g5.

Campsites, facilities: There are 300 sites for tents, trailers, or RVs of any length. Electricity, drinking water, sewer hookups, 24-hour security, and picnic tables are provided. Flush toilets, bottled gas, sanitary disposal services, showers, firewood, a store, a café, a laundry room, boat docks, boat rentals, moorage, and launching facilities are available. Leashed pets are permitted.

Reservations, fees: No reservations. Sites are $17–21 per night. Open from mid-April through October.

Directions: In Ashland on I-5, take Exit 14 to Highway 66. Drive east for less than a mile to Dead Indian Memorial Road. Turn left (east) and drive 17 miles to Howard Prairie Road. Turn right (south) and drive two miles to the reservoir.

Contact: Howard Prairie Lake Resort, 3249 Hyatt Prairie Rd., Ashland, OR 97520; 541/482-1979; fax 541/488-7485; website: www.howard prairieresort.com.

239 Lily Glen Campground

🏕️ 🚲 🏊 🎣
🚐 🐕 ♿ 🚐 🏕️   6

Set along the shore of Howard Prairie Lake, this horse camp is a secluded, primitive getaway. Trout fishing is available. Tubb Springs Wayside State Park and the nearby Rogue River National Forest are possible side trips. There is also nearby access to the Pacific Crest Trail.

Location: Near Howard Prairie Lake; The Southern Cascades map 7, grid g5.

Campsites, facilities: There are 26 sites for tents, trailers, or RVs, with no hookups. Picnic tables, drinking water, vault toilets, individual corrals, and a large barn are available. Some facilities are wheelchair-accessible. Leashed pets are permitted.

Reservations, fees: Reservations for groups are accepted. Sites are $12 per night. Major credit cards accepted for reservations. Open year-round, with limited winter services.

Directions: In Ashland on I-5, take Exit 14 to Highway 66. Drive east for less than a mile to Dead Indian Memorial Road. Turn left (east) and drive 21 miles to the campground.

Contact: Jackson County Parks, 400 Antelope Rd., White City, OR 97503; 541/774-8183; fax 541/774-6320.

240 Grizzly

Grizzly is one of a series of three county campgrounds at Howard Prairie Lake. This one features well-spaced campsites amid a forest and lake setting. The lake level is known to fluctuate, and in low-water years, this camp is subject to being shut down. It gets moderate use. The elevation is 4,550 feet.

Location: Near Howard Prairie Lake; The Southern Cascades map 7, grid g5.

Campsites, facilities: There are 21 sites for tents, trailers, or RVs, with no hookups. Picnic tables and fire rings are provided. Drinking water, vault toilets, and garbage bins are available. Some facilities are wheelchair-accessible. A boat ramp is nearby. A store, café, laundry facilities, and boat rentals are available within two miles. Leashed pets are permitted.

Reservations, fees: No reservations. Sites are $12 per night for the first two vehicles, $1 per pet per night. Senior discount available. Open mid-April through October.

Directions: In Ashland on I-5, take Exit 14 to Highway 66. Drive east for less than a mile to Dead Indian Memorial Road. Turn left (east) and drive 17 miles to Howard Prairie Road. Turn right (south) and drive eight

miles to Howard Prairie Dam Road. Turn left (east) and drive one-quarter mile to the campground.

Contact: Jackson County Parks, 400 Antelope Rd., White City, OR 97503; 541/774-8183; fax 541/774-6320.

241 Willow Point

This is the most popular of the three county campgrounds on Howard Prairie Lake. It is similar to Grizzly, with flat tent sites in an area well covered by trees.

Location: Near Howard Prairie Lake; The Southern Cascades map 7, grid g5.

Campsites, facilities: There are 40 sites for tents, trailers, or RVs, with no hookups. Picnic tables and fire rings are provided. Drinking water, vault toilets, and garbage bins are available. Some facilities are wheelchair-accessible. A boat ramp is nearby. A store, café, laundry facilities, and boat rentals are availabile within four miles. Leashed pets are permitted.

Reservations, fees: Reservations for groups are accepted. Sites are $12 per night for first two vehicles, $1 per pet per night. Senior discount available. Open mid-April through October.

Directions: In Ashland on I-5, take Exit 14 to Highway 66. Drive east for less than a mile to Dead Indian Memorial Road. Turn left (east) and drive 17 miles to Howard Prairie Road. Turn right (south) and drive three miles to the reservoir.

Contact: Jackson County Parks, 400 Antelope Rd., White City, OR 97503; 541/774-8183; fax 541/774-6320.

242 Klum Landing

7

This is one of three county campgrounds on Howard Prairie Lake. The others are Grizzly and Lookout Point. A bonus at this one is that coin-operated showers are available.

Location: Near Howard Prairie Lake; The Southern Cascades map 7, grid g5.

Campsites, facilities: There are 30 sites for tents, trailers, or RVs, with no hookups. Picnic tables and fire rings are provided. Drinking water, garbage bins, and restrooms with flush toilets and showers are available. Some facilities are wheelchair-accessible. A boat ramp is nearby. A store, café, laundry facilities, and boat rentals are availabile at Howard Prairie Lake Resort. Leashed pets are permitted.

Reservations, fees: Reservations for groups are accepted. Sites are $12 per night for first two vehicles, $1 per pet per night. Senior discount available. Open mid-April through October.

Directions: In Ashland on I-5, take Exit 14 to Highway 66. Drive east for less than a mile to Dead Indian Memorial Road. Turn left (east) and drive 17 miles to Howard Prairie Road. Turn right (south) and drive eight miles to Howard Prairie Dam Road. Turn left (east) and drive one mile to the campground.

Contact: Jackson County Parks, 400 Antelope Rd., White City, OR 97503; 541/774-8183; fax 541/774-6320.

243 Emigrant Campground

8

This camp is nestled among the trees above Emigrant Lake. Emigrant Lake is a well-known recreational area, and activities at this park include swimming, hiking, boating,

water-skiing, and fishing. There are also two super water slides. The park has its own swimming cove (unsupervised). Side-trip possibilities include exploring nearby Mt. Ashland, where a ski area operates in the winter, and visiting the world-renowned Shakespeare Festival in Ashland, as well as historic Jacksonville and the Britt Music Festival.

Location: On Emigrant Lake; The Southern Cascades map 7, grid g4.

Campsites, facilities: There are 42 sites for tents, trailers, and self-contained RVs, 32 with full hookups, plus an overflow area. Two group camp areas and the picnic and barbecue areas can be reserved. Restrooms, coin-operated showers, a sanitary dump, a public phone, snacks in summer, and a barbecue are available. Recreational facilities include horseshoe pits, volleyball, and a recreation field. Two boat ramps are provided. Some facilities are wheelchair-accessible. Laundry and food facilities are within six miles. Pets are permitted in designated areas only.

Reservations, fees: Reservations accepted for the group camps, picnic areas, and RV sites. Sites are $14 per night, $20 for RV sites, $1 per pet per night. Children 15 and under are free. Open from mid-March to mid-October.

Directions: From Ashland drive east on Highway 66 for five miles to the campground.

Contact: Jackson County Parks, 400 Antelope Rd., White City, OR 97503; 541/774-8183; fax 541/774-6320.

244 Hyatt Lake

8

This campground is on the south end of Hyatt Reservoir, which has six miles of shoreline. Fishing is good for brook and rainbow trout and smallmouth bass. Another campground option is Wildcat, about two miles north, with 12 semi-primitive sites. Boat speed limit here is 10 mph.

Location: On Hyatt Lake; The Southern Cascades map 7, grid g5.

Campsites, facilities: There are 47 sites for tents, trailers, or RVs up to 40 feet in length, one horse campsite, one group site, and a few walk-in tent sites. Picnic tables and fire grills are provided. Drinking water, flush toilets, showers, garbage service, a sanitary disposal station, group kitchen, a fish-cleaning station, a day-use area, athletic fields, a playground, horseshoe pits, and two boat ramps are available. Some sites and facilities are wheelchair-accessible. Leashed pets are permitted.

Reservations, fees: No reservations. Sites are $12–15 per night, with a 14-day stay limit. Campsites with horse facilities are $10 per night, group kitchen is $45. Sites at nearby primitive Wildcat Campground are $7 per night. Senior discount available. Open late April through October, weather permitting.

Directions: From Ashland drive east on Highway 66 for 17 miles to East Hyatt Lake Road. Turn north and drive three miles to the campground entrance on the left.

Contact: Bureau of Land Management, Medford District, 3040 Biddle Rd., Medford, OR 97504; 541/618-2200; fax 541/618-2400; website: www.or.blm.gov/medford.

245 Hyatt Lake Resort

🥾 🏊 🎣 🚤 🐴 🚐   7

This campground is set along the shore of Hyatt Lake, just west of the dam, where hiking and fishing are some of the recreation options. This is a scaled-down alternative to the resort at adjacent Howard Prairie Lake. The Pacific Crest Trail is just half a mile away.

Location: On Hyatt Lake; The Southern Cascades map 7, grid g5.

Campsites, facilities: There are 13 no-hookup and 22 full-hookup sites for trailers or RVs of any length, including four drive-through sites. There are also four cabins with no kitchen facilities; each sleeps four. Electricity (10 sites have 50-amp), drinking water, sewer hookups, and picnic tables are provided. Flush toilets, sanitary disposal services, showers, a store, a laundry room, ice, and boat rentals are available. Boat docks and launching facilities are on the resort property. Leashed pets and motorbikes are permitted.

Reservations, fees: Reservations accepted. Sites are $15–20 per night; call for cabin fees (monthly rates are available). Open from April through October.

Directions: From Ashland drive east on Highway 66 for 17 miles to East Hyatt Lake Road. Turn north and drive three miles to Hyatt Prairie Road. Turn left and drive one mile to the resort.

Contact: Hyatt Lake Resort, 7979 Hyatt Prairie Rd., Ashland, OR 97520; 541/482-3331; website: www.hyattlake.resort.com.

246 Camper's Cove

🥾 🚲 🏊 🎣 🚤 🐕 🚐   7

This campground is set about 400 feet from the shore of Hyatt Lake, with the Pacific Crest Trail passing about a mile away. It is in a cove east of the dam.

Location: On Hyatt Lake; The Southern Cascades map 7, grid g5.

Campsites, facilities: There are 23 sites for trailers or RVs up to 30 feet long; seven are drive-through sites. Picnic tables are provided. Electricity, drinking water, sewer hookups, flush toilets, showers, firewood, a store, a café, bar, lounge, and ice are available. Boat docks are nearby. Leashed pets are permitted.

Reservations, fees: Reservations accepted. Sites are $15 per night. Open year-round.
Directions: From Ashland drive east on Highway 66 for 17 miles to East Hyatt Lake Road. Turn north and drive three miles to Hyatt Prairie Road. Turn right and drive 2.5 miles (over the dam) to the resort.
Contact: Camper's Cove, 7900 Hyatt Prairie Rd., Ashland, OR 97520; 541/482-1201.

247 Flumet Flat

 7

This campground is set at an elevation of 1,700 feet along the banks of the Applegate River about six miles north of Applegate Reservoir. The Gin-Lin National Recreation Trail, named for the Chinese miner who struck it rich in local gold mines, is nearby. The camp has a large parklike lawn area with a lot of willow and cottonwood trees. Four of the sites require a short walk in and are secluded.
Location: On the Applegate River in Rogue River National Forest; The Southern Cascades map 7, grid h2.
Campsites, facilities: There are 23 sites for tents, trailers, or RVs up to 40 feet long, and four walk-in tent sites. Picnic tables, garbage bins (summer only), and fire grills are provided. Drinking water (summer only) and flush toilets are available. Showers, a store, a café, a laundry room, and ice are available nearby at McKee Bridge. Leashed pets are permitted.
Reservations, fees: Reservations available for groups only. Sites are $8 per night, plus $4 for each additional vehicle. Senior discount available. Open year-round.
Directions: In Medford on I-5, take the Jacksonville exit to the Jacksonville Highway. Drive west on the Jacksonville Highway (Highway 238) for seven miles to Jacksonville. Bear left

on Highway 238 and drive eight miles to the town of Ruch and Upper Applegate Road (County Road 10). Turn left and drive nine miles to Forest Road 1095. Continue one mile to the campground.
Contact: Rogue River National Forest, Applegate Ranger District, 6941 Upper Applegate Rd., Jacksonville, OR 97530; 541/899-1812; fax 541/858-2401.

248 Jackson

This camp at 1,700 feet elevation is nestled in an old mining area. It's between the Applegate River and the road, in a canopy of ponderosa pine, with a swimming hole and good trout fishing. Mine tailings can be seen from the camp. Trailers are not advised.
Location: On the Applegate River in Rogue River National Forest; The Southern Cascades map 7, grid h2.
Campsites, facilities: There are 10 sites for tents. Drinking water (summer only), garbage service (summer only), and flush toilets are available. Leashed pets are permitted. Some facilities are wheelchair-accessible.
Reservations, fees: No reservations accepted. Sites are $8 per night, plus $8 for each additional vehicle. Senior discount available. Open year-round, with limited winter services.
Directions: In Medford on I-5, take the Jacksonville exit to the Jacksonville Highway. Drive west on the Jacksonville Highway (Highway 238) for seven miles to Jacksonville. Bear left on Highway 238 and drive eight miles to the town of Ruch and Upper Applegate Road (County Road 10). Turn left and drive 10 miles to the campground on the right (this camp is directly across from Flumet Flat Campground).
Contact: Rogue River National Forest, Applegate Ranger District, 6941 Upper Applegate

Rd., Jacksonville, OR 97530; 541/899-1812; fax 541/858-2401.

249 Beaver Sulphur

7

Tiny and hidden, this camp is set at an elevation of 2,100 feet and situated in an area with mixed tree cover, including maple, live oak, and tall Douglas fir. Along the banks of Beaver Creek, the camp is about nine miles from Applegate Reservoir, has pretty, shaded sites, and offers easy access to the creek. Fishing is a possibility. Some recreational mining is done here; a permit can be obtained at the ranger station.

Location: On Beaver Creek in Rogue River National Forest; The Southern Cascades map 7, grid h2.

Campsites, facilities: There are 10 sites for tents. Picnic tables and fire grills are provided. One site is barrier-free, but there are no wheelchair-accessible toilets. Vault toilets, garbage bins (summer only), and drinking water are available. Leashed pets are permitted.

Reservations, fees: No reservations accepted. Sites are $4 per night, plus $2 per extra vehicle. Open May through November.

Directions: In Medford on I-5, take the Jacksonville exit to the Jacksonville Highway. Drive west on the Jacksonville Highway (Highway 238) for seven miles to Jacksonville. Bear left on Highway 238 and drive eight miles to the town of Ruch and Upper Applegate Road (County Road 10). Turn south (left) and drive 9.5 miles to Forest Road 20. Continue three miles to the campground.

Contact: Rogue River National Forest, Applegate Ranger District, 6941 Upper Applegate Rd., Jacksonville, OR 97530; 541/899-1812; fax 541/858-2401.

250 Wrangle

10

This campground is set at the headwaters of Glade Creek in the Siskiyou Mountains at an elevation of 6,400 feet. The Pacific Crest Trail passes near camp. Dutchman Peak Lookout, built in the late 1920s and featured in the National Historic Register, is within five miles. This is a lovely campground, in a beautiful, high country setting, with huge Shasta red firs and views of the Siskiyou Mountains. Wrangle is along the Scenic Siskiyou Loop driving tour.

Location: Near the Pacific Crest Trail in Rogue River National Forest; The Southern Cascades map 7, grid h2.

Campsites, facilities: There are five sites for tents. Picnic tables and fire grills are provided. The availability of drinking water is intermittent. All garbage must be packed out. Vault toilets and a community kitchen are available. Leashed pets are permitted.

Reservations, fees: No reservations; no fee. Open early June to late October, weather permitting.

Directions: In Ashland on I-5, take the Jacksonville exit. Drive east on the Jacksonville Highway to Jacksonville and Highway 238. Bear left on Highway 238 and drive eight miles to the town of Ruch and County Road 10 (Upper Applegate Road). Turn left and drive 9.5 miles to Forest Road 20. Turn left and drive 21 miles to Forest Road 2030. Continue one mile on Forest Road 2030 to the campground.

Contact: Rogue River National Forest, Applegate District, 6941 Upper Applegate Rd., Jacksonville, OR 97530; 541/899-1812; fax 541/858-2401.

251 Mount Ashland

 8

Set at 6,600 feet along the Pacific Crest Trail, this beautiful site is heavily wooded and has abundant wildlife. On clear days there are great lookouts nearby from Siskiyou Peak, particularly to the south, where California's 14,162-foot Mt. Shasta is an awesome sight. Mount Ashland Ski Resort is one mile west of the campground.

Location: On the Pacific Crest Trail in Klamath National Forest; The Southern Cascades map 7, grid h3.

Campsites, facilities: There are nine sites for tents, trailers, or RVs up to 15 feet long, with extremely limited space for RVs. Picnic tables and fire grills are provided. Vault toilets are available. There is no drinking water. All garbage must be packed out. Leashed pets are permitted.

Reservations, fees: No reservations; no fee. Open from May to late October, weather permitting.

Directions: From Ashland drive south on I-5 for 12 miles to Mount Ashland Ski Park Road (County Road 993). Turn west and drive 10 miles (the road becomes Forest Road 20) to the campground.

Contact: Klamath National Forest, Scott River Ranger District, 11263 N. Hwy. 3, Fort Jones, CA 96032; 530/468-5351; fax 530/468-1290.

252 Hart-tish Recreation Area Walk-In

7

This concessionaire-managed campground on Applegate Lake has a great view of the lake and shaded sites. Bald eagles and osprey nest in the area, and it's a treat to watch them fish. A nearby boat launch and boat rentals are available. The walk-in sites are only 200 yards from the parking area.

Location: On Applegate Reservoir, Rogue River National Forest; The Southern Cascades map 7, grid h1.

Campsites, facilities: There are five walk-in tent sites and eight RV parking lot sites. Picnic tables and fire pits are provided. Drinking water, flush toilets, garbage bins, firewood, a minimart, and wheelchair facilities (restroom, one site, and a barrier-free loading ramp) are available. Leashed pets are permitted.

Reservations, fees: No reservations accepted, except for groups. Sites are $10 per night. There is an additional charge of $5 per each additional vehicle. Open Memorial Day through September.

Directions: In Medford on I-5, take the Jacksonville exit to the Jacksonville Highway. Drive west on the Jacksonville Highway (Highway 238) for seven miles to Jacksonville. Bear left on Highway 238 and drive eight miles to the town of Ruch and Upper Applegate Road (County Road 10). Turn south (left) and drive 15.5 miles to the campground.

Contact: Rogue River National Forest, Applegate Ranger District, 6941 Upper Applegate Rd., Jacksonville, OR 97530; 541/899-1812; fax 541/858-2401.

253 Watkins

6

On the southwest shore of Applegate Reservoir at an elevation of 2,000 feet, this campground, like Carberry Walk-In and French Gulch, is small and quite primitive, but it's pretty and offers all the same recreation options. Few campers know about this spot, so it usually doesn't fill up quickly. There are good views of the lake and the surrounding Siskiyou Mountains.

Location: On Applegate Reservoir in Rogue River National Forest; The Southern Cascades map 7, grid h1.

Campsites, facilities: There are 14 walk-in sites for tents. Picnic tables, drinking water, garbage bins, and fire grills are provided. Vault toilets and firewood are available. Boat docks and launching facilities are within two miles. Some facilities are wheelchair-accessible. Leashed pets are permitted.

Reservations, fees: No reservations accepted. Sites are $8 per night, plus $4 for each additional vehicle. Senior discount available. Open May through September.

Directions: In Medford on I-5, take the Jacksonville exit to the Jacksonville Highway. Drive west on the Jacksonville Highway (Highway 238) for seven miles to Jacksonville. Bear left on Highway 238 and drive eight miles to the town of Ruch and Upper Applegate Road (County Road 10). Turn south (left) and drive 17 miles to the campground.

Contact: Rogue River National Forest, Applegate Ranger District, 6941 Upper Applegate Rd., Jacksonville, OR 97530; 541/899-1812; fax 541/858-2401.

254 Latgawa Cove Boat-In

The elevation of this lake is 2,000 feet. Latgawa Cove has semi-primitive lakeshore campsites with tree cover providing shade. A mountain bike trail runs through the campground. The water level fluctuates, sometimes preventing boat access. Several boat launches can be used to reach this campground and the other boat-in campgrounds on Applegate Lake: Harr Point and Typsu Tyee, both with similar amenities as Latgawa and within three miles of each other by boat.

Location: On Applegate Reservoir, Rogue River National Forest; The Southern Cascades map 7, grid h1.

Campsites, facilities: There are five boat-in sites. No drinking water is available, but picnic tables and fire rings are provided. Pit toilets are available. Pack out all garbage. Leashed pets are permitted.

Reservations, fees: No reservations accepted. No fee. Open year-round.

Directions: In Medford on I-5, take the Jacksonville exit to the Jacksonville Highway. Drive west on Jacksonville Highway (Highway 238) for seven miles to Jacksonville. Bear left on Highway 238 and drive eight miles to the town of Ruch and Upper Applegate Road (County Road 10). Turn left and drive 15 miles to Forest Road 1075. Turn right and drive 1.5 miles to the parking area for French Gulch Campground and the boat ramp. Boat-in to Latgawa Cove Campground.

Contact: Rogue River National Forest, Applegate Ranger District, 6941 Upper Applegate Rd., Jacksonville, OR 97530; 541/899-1812; fax 541/858-2401.

255 Carberry Walk-In

5

You'll find recreational opportunities aplenty at this campground on Cougar Creek near the southwest shore of Applegate Reservoir, including fishing, boating, hiking, mountain biking, and swimming. Dense forest covers the campsites providing much-needed shade. This camp is similar to French Gulch and Watkins Walk-in.

Location: Near Applegate Reservoir in Rogue River National Forest; The Southern Cascades map 7, grid h1.

Campsites, facilities: There are 10 walk-in sites for tents. Space is available in the parking lot for trailers or RVs. Picnic tables and fire grills are provided. Vault toilets and drinking water are available. Boat docks and launching facilities are within two miles. Leashed pets are permitted. Some facilities are wheelchair-accessible.

Reservations, fees: No reservations accepted. Sites are $8 per night, plus $4 for each additional vehicle. Senior discount available. Open year-round, weather permitting, with limited services and no fee in winter.

Directions: In Medford on I-5, take the Jacksonville exit to the Jacksonville Highway. Drive west on the Jacksonville Highway (Highway 238) for seven miles to Jacksonville. Bear left on Highway 238 and drive eight miles to the town of Ruch and Upper Applegate Road (County Road 10). Turn south (left) and drive 18 miles to the campground parking area. A short walk is required.

Contact: Rogue River National Forest, Applegate Ranger District, 6941 Upper Applegate Rd., Jacksonville, OR 97530; 541/899-1812; fax 541/858-2401.

256 French Gulch Walk-In

🏃 🚴 🛶
🎣 🚤 🐕 ⛺ 5

This campground along the shore of Applegate Reservoir at an elevation of 2,000 feet is a popular summer fishing spot for anglers. It's also a good boat-in campground when the lake level allows. A seasonal launch ramp is not far from the camp. A 10 mph speed limit is in effect for boats. Mountain biking is available around the lake. See the description of Watkins and Carberry Walk-in.

Location: On Applegate Reservoir in Rogue River National Forest; The Southern Cascades map 7, grid h1.

Campsites, facilities: There are nine walk-in sites for tents. Picnic tables and fire grills are provided. Drinking water and vault toi-

lets are available. Boat-launching facilities are within one-half mile. Leashed pets are permitted.

Reservations, fees: No reservations accepted. Sites are $8 per night, plus $4 for each additional vehicle. Senior discount available. Open May through October.

Directions: In Medford on I-5, take the Jacksonville exit to the Jacksonville Highway. Drive west on the Jacksonville Highway (Highway 238) for seven miles to Jacksonville. Bear left on Highway 238 and drive eight miles to the town of Ruch and Upper Applegate Road (County Road 10). Turn left and drive 15 miles to Forest Road 1075. Turn left and drive 1.5 miles to the parking area. A short walk is required.

Contact: Rogue River National Forest, Applegate Ranger District, 6941 Upper Applegate Rd., Jacksonville, OR 97530; 541/899-1812; fax 541/858-2401.

257 Squaw Lake Hike-In

🏃 🚴 🏊 🎣
🚤 🐕 ♿ ⛺ 10

"Paradise Found" should be the name here. Numerous trails crisscross the area around this camp (3,000 feet elevation) on the shore of spectacular Squaw Lake. The setting is more intimate than the larger Applegate Reservoir to the west. This spot has a mix of developed and primitive sites and is also more popular. It's the only campground in the district that requires reservations. This area attracts the canoe/kayak crowd. Be sure to call ahead for a space. Campers with disabilities are welcome, but arrangements should be made in advance with the local U.S. Forest Service office.

Location: On Squaw Lake in Rogue River National Forest; The Southern Cascades map 7, grid h1.

Campsites, facilities: There are 17 walk-in sites for tents and two family group sites that can accommodate up to 10 people each. Picnic tables, garbage bins (summer only), and fire grills are provided. Vault toilets are available. Drinking water is available at one end of the camp during the summer only. Two sites are barrier-free. Leashed pets are permitted.

Reservations, fees: Reservations required during summer. Sites are $10 per night, group sites are $20 per night. Senior discount available. Open year-round, with limited winter services.

Directions: In Medford on I-5, take the Jacksonville exit to the Jacksonville Highway. Drive west on the Jacksonville Highway (Highway 238) for seven miles to Jacksonville. Bear left on Highway 238 and drive eight miles to the town of Ruch and Upper Applegate Road (County Road 10). Turn south (left) and drive 15 miles to Forest Road 1075. Continue eight miles to Squaw Lake and trailhead. Hike one mile to the campsites.

Contact: Rogue River National Forest, Applegate Ranger District, 6941 Upper Applegate Rd., Jacksonville, OR 97530; 541/899-1812; fax 541/858-2401.

258 Topsy

 7

This campground is on Boyle Reservoir near the Upper Klamath River, a good spot for trout fishing and a top river for rafters (experts only, or nonexperts with professional licensed guides). There are Class IV and V rapids about four miles southwest at Caldera, Satan's Gate, and Hells Corner. I flipped at Caldera and ended up swimming for it, finally getting out at an eddy. Luckily, I was wearing a dry suit and the best lifejacket available, perfect fitting, which saved my butt. The area is good for mountain biking, too.

Location: On the Upper Klamath River; The Southern Cascades map 7, grid h8.

Campsites, facilities: There are 13 sites for trailers or RVs up to 40 feet long. Picnic tables and fire grills are provided. Drinking water, vault toilets, garbage service, and a sanitary disposal station are available. Facilities are wheelchair-accessible. Boat-launching facilities are nearby. A camp host is on-site. Leashed pets are permitted.

Reservations, fees: No reservations. Sites are $7 per night, $4 per night for an additional vehicle, with a 14-day stay limit. Senior discount available. Open mid-May through mid-September.

Directions: From Klamath Falls drive west on Highway 66 for 20 miles to Topsy Road. Turn south on Topsy Road and drive 1.5 miles to the campground on the right.

Contact: Bureau of Land Management, Klamath Falls Resource Area, 2795 Anderson Ave., Building 25, Klamath Falls, OR 97603; 541/883-6916; fax 541/884-2097; website: www.or.blm.gov/lakeview.

259 Jackson F. Kimball State Park

7

This primitive state campground at the headwaters of the Wood River is another nice spot just far enough off the main drag to remain a secret. Wood River offers fine fishing that's accessible from the park by canoe. A walking trail leads from the campground to a clear spring bubbling from a rocky hillside.

Location: On the Wood River; The Southern Cascades map 8, grid c1.

Campsites, facilities: There are 10 primitive sites for tents, trailers, or self-contained RVs up to 45 feet long. Picnic tables, fire grills, and garbage bins are provided. Vault toilets are available. There is no drinking water. Leashed pets are permitted.

Reservations, fees: No reservations. Sites are $7.42 per night, $7 per night for an additional vehicle. Open from mid-April to late October.

Directions: From Klamath Falls drive north on U.S. 97 for 21 miles to Highway 62. Turn northwest on Highway 62 and drive 10 miles to Highway 232 (near Fort Klamath). Turn north and drive three miles to the campground.

Contact: Jackson F. Kimball State Park, 46000 Hwy. 97 N, Chiloquin, OR 97624; 800/551-6949 or 541/783-2471. This park is managed by Collier Memorial State Park.

260 Crater Lake Resort

6

This campground set among huge pine trees is on the banks of the beautiful, crystal-clear Fort Creek, just outside Fort Klamath, the site of numerous military campaigns against the Modoc Indians in the late 1800s.

Location: On the Wood River; The Southern Cascades map 8, grid c1.

Campsites, facilities: There are some tent sites and 23 sites for trailers or RVs of any length; 11 have full hookups and 12 have partial hookups. Electricity, drinking water, sewer hookups, and picnic tables are provided. Flush toilets, showers, a recreation hall, and a laundry room are available. Bottled gas, a store, a café, and ice are within one mile. Leashed pets and motorbikes are permitted.

Reservations, fees: Reservations accepted. Sites are $16–22 per night. Open from mid-April to mid-October.

Directions: From Klamath Falls drive north on U.S. 97 for 21 miles to Highway 62. Bear

left on Highway 62 and drive 12.5 miles north to the campground (just before reaching Fort Klamath).

Contact: Crater Lake Resort, P.O. Box 457, Fort Klamath, OR 97626; 541/381-2349; website: www.craterlakeresort.com.

261 Collier Memorial State Park

7

This campground is set at the confluence of Spring Creek and the Williamson River, both of which are superior trout streams. A nature trail is also available. The park features a pioneer village and one of the state's finer logging museums. Movies about old-time logging and other activities are shown on weekend nights during the summer.

Location: On the Williamson River; The Southern Cascades map 8, grid c2.

Campsites, facilities: There are 18 sites for tents or self-contained RVs and 50 sites with full hookups for trailers or RVs up to 60 feet long. Picnic tables, fire grills, garbage bins, and drinking water are provided. Flush toilets, sanitary disposal services, showers, firewood, a laundry room, a playground, and a day-use hitching area are available. Some facilities are wheelchair-accessible. Leashed pets are permitted.

Reservations, fees: No reservations. Sites are $15–18 per night, $7 per night for an additional vehicle. Open from April to late October, weather permitting.

Directions: From Klamath Falls drive north on U.S. 97 for 28 miles to the park on the left (well signed).

Contact: Collier Memorial State Park, 46000 Hwy. 97 N, Chiloquin, OR 97624; 800/551-6949 or 541/783-2471.

262 Williamson River

🎣 🐕 ♿ 🚐 ⛺ 6

Another great little spot is discovered, this one at 4,200 feet elevation, with excellent trout fishing along the banks of the Williamson River. It's a world-famous fly-fishing river, but the camp does not get high use. Mosquitoes are numerous in spring and early summer, and that can drive people away. A map of Winema National Forest details the back roads and trails. Collier Memorial State Park provides a nearby side-trip option.

Location: Near Collier Memorial State Park in Winema National Forest; The Southern Cascades map 8, grid d2.

Campsites, facilities: There are three tent sites and seven sites for trailers or RVs up to 30 feet long. Picnic tables, garbage bins, and fire grills are provided. Drinking water and vault toilets are available. Some facilities are wheelchair-accessible. A restaurant is within five miles. Leashed pets are permitted.

Reservations, fees: No reservations. Sites are $6 per night, plus $2 for each additional vehicle. Senior discount available. Open from May 15 to November 25, weather permitting.

Directions: From Klamath Falls drive north on U.S. 97 for 30 miles to Chiloquin. Continue north on U.S. 97 for 5.5 miles to Forest Road 9730 on the right. Turn northeast and drive one mile to the campground.

Contact: Winema National Forest, Klamath Ranger District, 1936 California Ave., Klamath Falls, OR 97601; 541/885-3400; fax 541/885-3452.

263 Agency Lake Resort

 5

This campground is on Agency Lake in an open, grassy area with some shaded sites. It has more than 700 feet of lakefront property,

with world-class trout fishing. Look across the lake and watch the sun set on the Cascades. See the description of Rocky Point Resort for more information.

Location: On Agency Lake; The Southern Cascades map 8, grid d1.

Campsites, facilities: There are 15 tent sites and 25 sites for trailers or RVs of any length, plus four cabins. Electricity, drinking water, sewer hookups, and picnic tables are provided. Flush toilets, showers, a general store, ice, boat docks, launching facilities, and marine gas are available. Leashed pets and motorbikes are permitted.

Reservations, fees: Reservations accepted. Sites are $8–16 per night, and cabins start at $45 per night. Open year-round.

Directions: From Klamath Falls drive north on U.S. 97 for 17 miles to Modoc Point Road. Turn left (north) and drive about 10 miles to the campground on the left.

Contact: Agency Lake Resort, 37000 Modoc Point Rd., Chiloquin, OR 97624; 541/783-2489.

264 Walt's Cozy Camp

🚶 🚲 🎣 🐕 🚐 ⛺ 7

This heavily treed campground, across the highway from the Williamson River near Collier Memorial State Park, is one of three camps in the immediate area. For a more remote setting, Potter's Trailer Park (in this chapter) and Head of the River (in the Southeast Oregon chapter) are to the east. The Williamson River has excellent trout fishing. And by the way, the "Walt" who started this place is still here, providing friendly advice as he has for years.

Location: On the Williamson River; The Southern Cascades map 8, grid d1.

Campsites, facilities: There are 20 tent sites and 34 sites for trailers or RVs of any length; six are drive-through sites. Electricity, drinking water, sewer hookups, and picnic tables are provided. Flush toilets, showers, firewood, a laundry room, and ice are available. A café is available within one-quarter mile and a store is available in Chiloquin. Leashed pets and motorbikes are permitted.

Reservations, fees: Reservations accepted. Sites are $12 per night. Open from April to mid-October, weather permitting.

Directions: From Klamath Falls drive north on U.S. 97 for 24 miles to Chiloquin Junction. Continue north for one-quarter mile to the campground (adjacent to the Chiloquin Ranger Station) on the left.

Contact: Walt's Cozy Camp, P.O. Box 243, Chiloquin, OR 97624; 541/783-2537.

265 Williamson River Resort

This little RV park is along the banks of the Williamson River. The Williamson is one of Oregon's famous fishing streams, attracting anglers from many miles away. It can be fished by drift boat or by motorboat, and it is one of Oregon's preeminent fly-fishing destinations for large rainbow trout.

Location: On the Williamson River; The Southern Cascades map 8, grid e1.

Campsites, facilities: There are eight sites for trailers or RVs of any length. Electricity, drinking water, and picnic tables are provided. A dump station, a store, and ice are available. Boat docks, launching facilities, and rentals are on-site. Leashed pets are permitted.

Reservations, fees: Reservations accepted. Sites are $14 per night; open April to November, weather permitting.

Directions: From Klamath Falls drive north on U.S. 97 for 17 miles to Modoc Point Road (the first turnoff north of Klamath Lake). Turn left on Modoc Point Road and drive 3.5 miles to the park.

Contact: Williamson River Resort, 31900 Modoc Point Rd., Chiloquin, OR 97624; 541/783-2071.

266 Waterwheel Camp and RV Park

This rural campground right on the Williamson River is close to hiking trails. Fishing can be excellent here, with a boat ramp and fishing tackle right at the camp.

Location: On the Williamson River; The Southern Cascades map 8, grid d2.

Campsites, facilities: There are six tent sites and 28 sites for trailers or RVs of any length; 22 are drive-through sites. Electricity, drinking water, sewer hookups, and picnic tables are provided. Flush toilets, bottled gas, sanitary disposal services, showers, firewood, a store, a laundry room, ice, and a playground are available. A café is within one mile. Boat docks and launching facilities are nearby. Leashed pets and motorbikes are permitted.

Reservations, fees: Reservations accepted. Sites are $16–22 per night. Open year-round, weather permitting.

Directions: From Klamath Falls drive north on U.S. 97 for 20 miles to the campground (a quarter mile south of the junction of U.S. 97 and Highway 62).

Contact: Waterwheel Camp and RV Park, 200 Williamson River Dr., Chiloquin, OR 97624; 541/783-2738.

267 Potter's Trailer Park

This park on a bluff overlooking the river is in woods and bordered by the Sprague River and the Winema National Forest. For the most part the area east of Klamath Lake doesn't get much attention. But if you want to check out a relatively close spot that's out in remote country, try Head of the River (in the Southeast Oregon chapter).

Location: On the Sprague River; The Southern Cascades map 8, grid d3.

Campsites, facilities: There are 17 tent sites and 23 full-hookup sites for trailers or RVs of any length. Electricity, drinking water, sewer hookups, and picnic tables are provided. Flush toilets, showers, firewood, convenience store, café, tavern, laundry room, telephone, and ice are available. Pets and motorbikes are permitted.

Reservations, fees: Reservations accepted. Sites are $15 per night. Open year-round, with limited winter facilities.

Directions: From Klamath Falls drive north on U.S. 97 for 27 miles to Chiloquin and Sprague River Highway. Turn east on Sprague River Highway and drive 12 miles to the resort.

Contact: Potter's Trailer Park, 11700 Sprague River Rd., Chiloquin, OR 97624; 541/783-2253.

268 Oregon 8 Motel and RV Park

 6

This campground, surrounded by mountains, big rocks, and trees, is near Hanks Marsh on the southeast shore of Upper Klamath Lake, within 50 miles of Crater Lake. Nearby recreation options include a golf course, bike paths, and a marina.

Location: On Upper Klamath Lake; The Southern Cascades map 8, grid f2.

Campsites, facilities: There are 10 tent sites and 29 drive-through sites for trailers or RVs of any length. Electricity, drinking water, cable TV, sewer hookups, and picnic tables are provided. Flush toilets, showers, a recreation hall, a laundry room, ice, and a swimming pool are available. Bottled gas, a store, and a café are within one mile. Leashed pets and motorbikes are permitted.

Reservations, fees: Reservations accepted. Sites are $19–25 per night. Open year-round, with limited winter facilities.

Directions: From Klamath Falls drive north on U.S. 97 for 3.5 miles to the campground on the right.

Contact: Oregon 8 Motel and RV Park, 5225 Hwy. 97 N, Klamath Falls, OR 97601; 541/883-3431.

269 Wiseman's Mobile Court and RV

5

This is a suburban RV park with the barest essentials, including trees and lawn. It's a decent layover spot if you need a quick place to stay. You can find golf within two miles.

Location: Near Upper Klamath Lake; The Southern Cascades map 8, grid g3.

Campsites, facilities: There are 17 sites for trailers or RVs of any length. Electricity, drinking water, and sewer hookups are provided. Flush toilets, sanitary disposal services, showers, and laundry facilities are available. Bottled gas is within one block. Leashed pets are permitted.

Reservations, fees: Reservations accepted. Sites are $18 per night. Open year-round.

Directions: From Klamath Falls drive east on Highway 140 for 4.5 miles to the park.

Contact: Wiseman's Mobile Court and RV, 6800 S. 6th St., Klamath Falls, OR 97603; 541/884-4327.

270 Tingley Lake Estates

🚶 🚴 🏊 🎣
🚐 🐕 🛶 🚍 ⛺ **7**

This privately operated RV park provides a layover for travelers crossing the Oregon border on U.S. 97. You can see Mt. Shasta in California from this park right on the lake. All sites have a view of the lake. Tingley Lake has opportunities for bass fishing, boating, and swimming.

Location: On Tingley Lake; The Southern Cascades map 8, grid h2.

Campsites, facilities: There are six tent sites and 10 sites for trailers or RVs of any length; three have full and seven have partial hookups. Electricity, drinking water, sewer hookups, and picnic tables are provided. Telephone and cable TV hookups, flush toilets, showers, boat docks, and a playground are available. A store, a café, and ice are within two miles. Leashed pets are permitted.

Reservations, fees: Reservations accepted. Sites are $15–17 per night. Open year-round, weather permitting, with limited winter services.

Directions: From Klamath Falls drive southwest on U.S. 97 for seven miles to Old Midland Road. Turn east and drive two miles to Tingley Lane. Turn right (south) and drive a half mile to the park.

Contact: Tingley Lake Estates, 11800 Tingley Ln., Klamath Falls, OR 97603, tel./fax 541/882-8386.

SOUTHEAST OREGON

Southeast Oregon

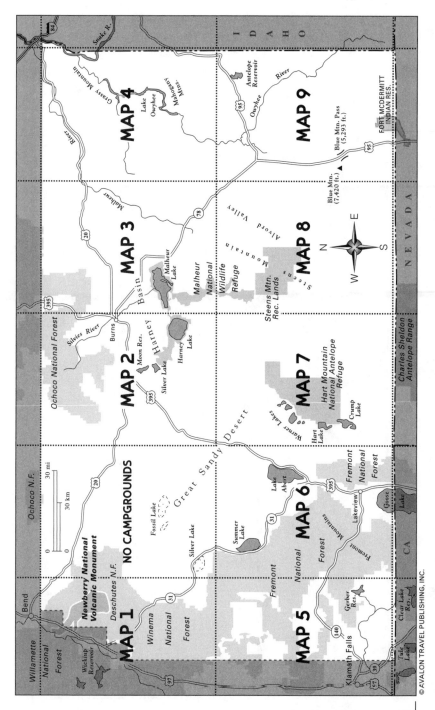

MAP 1

MAP 2

MAP 3

MAP 4

MAP 5

MAP 6

MAP 7

MAP 8

MAP 9

NO CAMPGROUNDS

Newberry National Volcanic Monument

Deschutes N.F.

Winema National Forest

Ochoco N.F.

Ochoco National Forest

Great Sandy Desert

Harney Basin

Fremont National Forest

Fremont National Forest

Fremont Mountains

Hart Mountain National Antelope Refuge

Malheur National Wildlife Refuge

Steens Mtn. Rec. Lands

Steens Mountain

Alvord Valley

Charles Sheldon Antelope Range

Willamette National Forest

Bend

Wickiup Reservoir

Klamath Falls

Tule Lake

Clear Lake Res.

Goose Lake

Garber Res.

Lakeview

Lake Abert

Summer Lake

Silver Lake

Fossil Lake

Silver Lake

Moon Res.

Harney Lake

Burns

Silvies River

Malheur Lake

Malheur River

Warner Lakes

Hart Lake

Crump Lake

Grassy Mountain

Snake R.

Lake Owyhee

Mahogany Mtns.

Owyhee River

Antelope Reservoir

Owyhee River

Blue Mtn. (7,420 ft.)

Blue Mtn. Pass (5,293 ft.)

FORT MCDERMITT INDIAN RES.

I D A H O

N E V A D A

CA

N E W
S

30 mi
30 km
0

© AVALON TRAVEL PUBLISHING, INC.

Southeast Oregon 433

Map 1

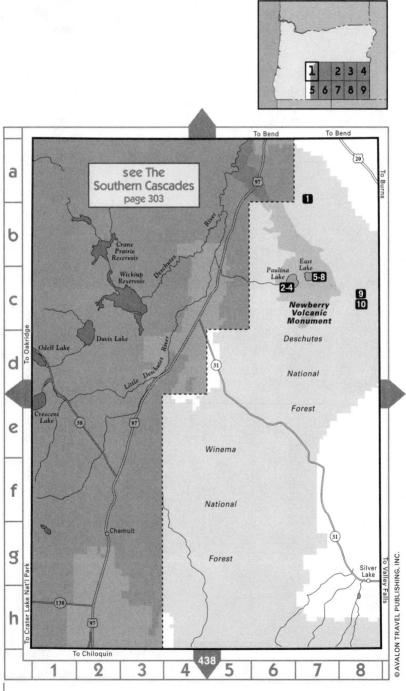

Map 2

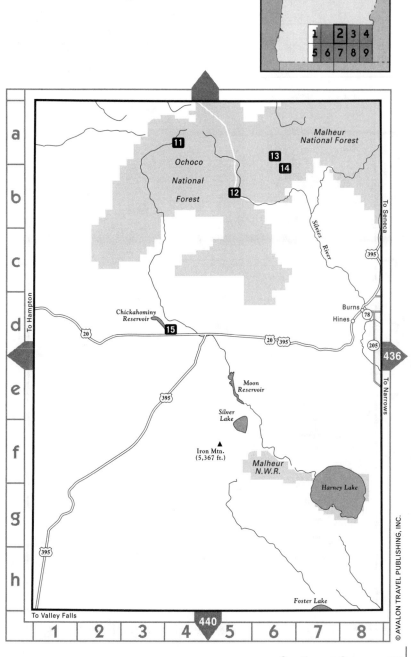

© AVALON TRAVEL PUBLISHING, INC.

Map 3

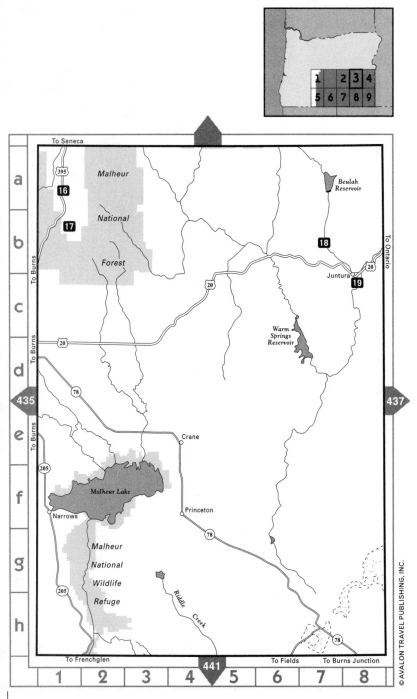

Map 4

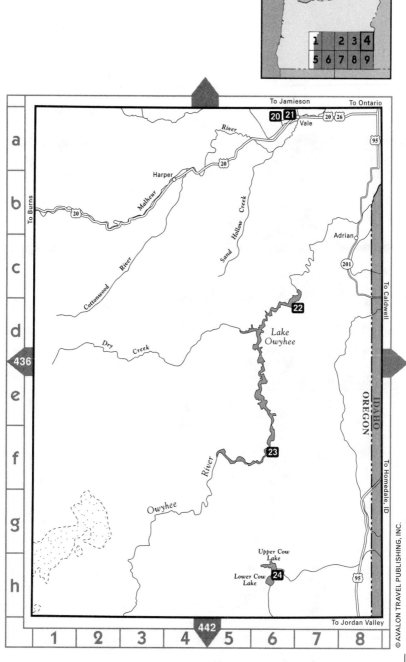

To Jamieson   To Ontario

20 21 — Vale   20 26

95

a

Harper

20

To Burns

b

20   Malheur   River   Sand Hollow Creek

Adrian

201   To Caldwell

c

Cottonwood   River

22

d

Dry   Creek   Lake Owyhee

436

e

IDAHO
OREGON

f

River   23

To Homedale, ID

g

Owyhee

Upper Cow Lake

h

Lower Cow Lake   24   95

To Jordan Valley

442

1   2   3   4   5   6   7   8

© AVALON TRAVEL PUBLISHING, INC.

Map 5

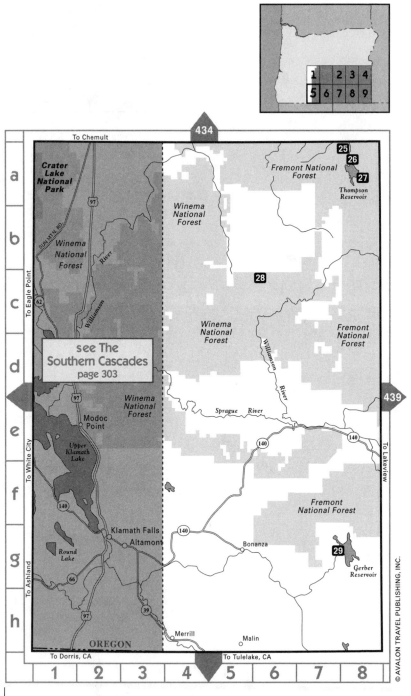

© AVALON TRAVEL PUBLISHING, INC.

Map 6

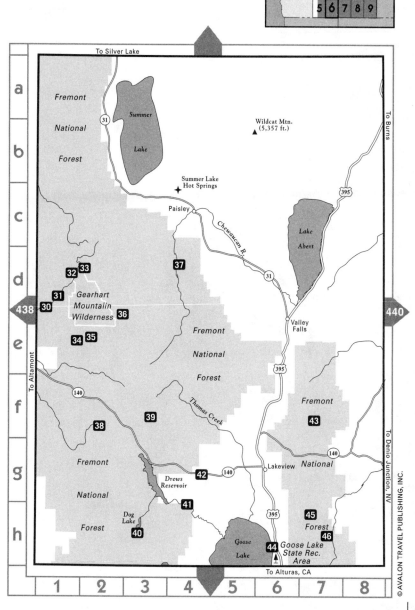

To Silver Lake

a
Fremont
Summer

National
Lake

b
Forest

Wildcat Mtn.
(5,357 ft.)

▲

31

To Burns

Summer Lake
Hot Springs

✦

Paisley

Chewaucan R.

c

395

Lake
Abert

32 33
37

d
31

30

Gearhart
Mountaiin
Wilderness
36

31

438
440

34 35
e
Fremont

National

Forest

Valley
Falls

140
395

f
39
Fremont

To Altamont

Thomas Creek

43

38

140

g
Fremont
Drews
Reservoir

42
140

Lakeview

National

140

To Denio Junction, NV

National

41

Dog
Lake

395

45

h
Forest
40

Goose
Lake

44

Forest
46

Goose Lake
State Rec.
Area

To Alturas, CA

1   2   3   4   5   6   7   8

© AVALON TRAVEL PUBLISHING, INC.

Map 7

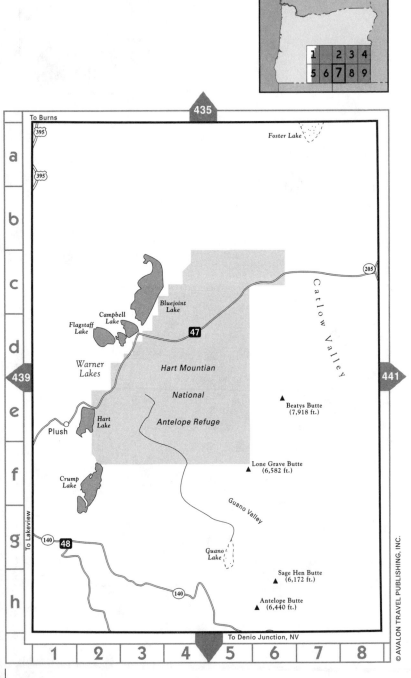

To Burns

395

395

Foster Lake

a

b

c

Bluejoint
Lake

Campbell
Lake

Flagstaff
Lake

47

Catlow Valley

205

d

Warner
Lakes

Hart Mountain

439

National

441

e

Plush

Hart
Lake

Antelope Refuge

Beatys Butte
(7,918 ft.)

f

Crump
Lake

Lone Grave Butte
(6,582 ft.)

Guano Valley

g

To Lakeview

140 48

Guano
Lake

Sage Hen Butte
(6,172 ft.)

h

140

Antelope Butte
(6,440 ft.)

To Denio Junction, NV

1 2 3 4 5 6 7 8

© AVALON TRAVEL PUBLISHING, INC.

Map 8

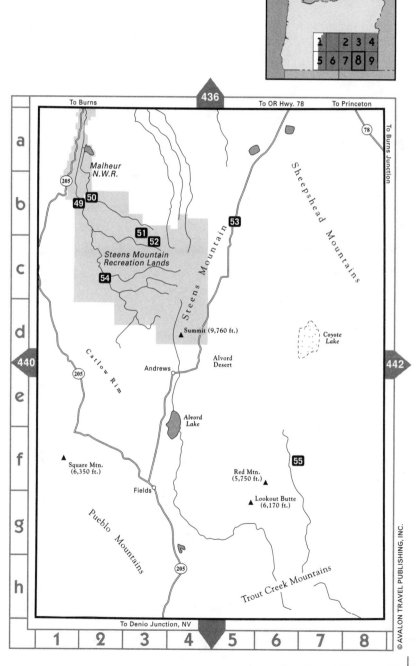

To Burns
To OR Hwy. 78
To Princeton

436

78

To Burns Junction

a

Malheur
N.W.R.

205

b

49 50

53

Sheepshead Mountains

51 52

Steens Mountain
Recreation Lands

c

54

Steens Mountain

d

Summit (9,760 ft.)

Coyote
Lake

Alvord
Desert

440

Andrews

442

205

Catlow Rim

e

Alvord
Lake

f

Square Mtn.
(6,350 ft.)

Red Mtn.
(5,750 ft.)

55

Fields

Lookout Butte
(6,170 ft.)

g

Pueblo Mountains

205

Trout Creek Mountains

h

To Denio Junction, NV

1   2   3   4   5   6   7   8

© AVALON TRAVEL PUBLISHING, INC.

Map 9

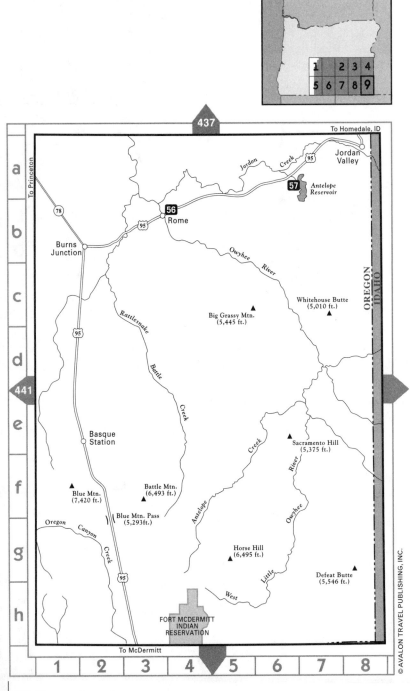

To Princeton

437

To Homedale, ID

Jordon Creek

95

Jordan Valley

57 Antelope Reservoir

78

56 Rome

95

Burns Junction

Ouyhee River

OREGON
IDAHO

Rattlesnake

Big Grassy Mtn.
(5,445 ft.)

Whitehouse Butte
(5,010 ft.)

95

Battle

Creek

Basque Station

Creek

Sacramento Hill
(5,375 ft.)

Blue Mtn.
(7,420 ft.)

Battle Mtn.
(6,493 ft.)

Owyhee River

Blue Mtn. Pass
(5,293 ft.)

Oregon

Canyon

Creek

Antelope

Horse Hill
(6,495 ft.)

Little

Defeat Butte
(5,546 ft.)

95

FORT MCDERMITT
INDIAN
RESERVATION

West

To McDermitt

© AVALON TRAVEL PUBLISHING, INC.

Southeast Oregon

■ Swamp Wells Horse Camp

🏃 🐴 🚐 ⛺   3

If you look at the map, this campground may appear to be quite remote, but it's actually in an area that is less than 30 minutes from Bend. It is set at an elevation of 5,450 feet. This is a good place for horseback riding, and trails heading south reenter the forested areas. The system of lava tubes nearby at the Arnold Ice Caves is fun to explore; bring flashlight, bicycle helmet, and knee pads. A U.S. Forest Service map details trail options. You don't need a horse to enjoy this spot.

Location: Near the Arnold Ice Caves in Deschutes National Forest; Southeast Oregon map 1, grid a7.

Campsites, facilities: There are six primitive sites for tents, trailers, or RVs up to 22 feet long. Picnic tables and fire grills are provided. There are vault toilets, but no drinking water, and all garbage must be packed out. Leashed pets are permitted.

Reservations, fees: No reservations; no fee. Open April to late November.

Directions: From Bend drive south on U.S. 97 for four miles to Forest Road 18. Turn southeast and drive 5.4 miles to Forest Road 1810. Turn south (right) and drive 5.8 miles to Forest Road 1816. Turn east (left) and drive three miles to the campground.

Contact: Deschutes National Forest, Bend-Fort Rock Ranger District, 1230 N.E. 3rd St., Bend, OR 97701; 541/388-5664; fax 541/383-4700.

■ Paulina Lake

This campground is set along the south shore of Paulina Lake at 6,350 feet and within the Newberry National Volcanic Monument. The lake itself sits in a volcanic crater. Nearby trails provide access to the remains of volcanic activity, including craters and obsidian flows. The state's record brown trout was caught here by my longtime friend Guy Carl, right after I'd written a story about his unique method of using giant Rapala and Rebel bass lures for giant browns. The boat speed limit is 10 mph. The camp is adjacent to Paulina Lake Resort. The recreation options here include boating, sailing, fishing, and hiking. Note that food-raiding bears are common at all the campgrounds in the Newberry Caldera area, and that all food must be kept out of reach. Do not store food in vehicles.

Location: On Paulina Lake in Deschutes National Forest; Southeast Oregon map 1, grid c6.

Campsites, facilities: There are 69 sites for trailers or RVs up to 30 feet long. Picnic tables, garbage service, and fire grills are provided. Flush and vault toilets, showers, and a coin-operated laundry are within five miles. Drinking water is available. Some facilities are wheelchair-accessible. Boat docks, launching facilities, boat rentals, a small store, restaurant, cabins, gas, and propane are within five miles. The Newberry RV dump station is nearby ($5). Leashed pets are permitted.

Reservations, fees: No reservations. Sites are $10–12 per night, $5 for each additional vehicle. Senior discount available. Open late May to late October.

Directions: From Bend drive south on U.S. 97 for 23.5 miles to County Road 21 (Paulina/East Lake Road). Turn east (left) and drive 12.9 miles to the campground.

Contact: Deschutes National Forest, Bend-Fort Rock Ranger District, 1230 N.E. 3rd St., Bend, OR 97701; 541/388-5664; fax 541/383-4700.

■ Chief Paulina Horse Camp

🏃 🚲 🐴 🚐 ⛺   4

This campground is set at an elevation of 6,400 feet, about one-quarter mile from the south shore of Paulina Lake. Horse trails and a vista point are close by. See the description of Paulina Lake for additional recreation information.

Location: On Paulina Lake in Deschutes National Forest; Southeast Oregon map 1, grid c6.

Campsites, facilities: There are 14 sites for tents, trailers, or RVs up to 30 feet long. Picnic tables, garbage service, and fire grills are provided. Vault toilets are available, but there is no drinking water. Boat docks and rentals are nearby. Leashed pets are permitted.

Reservations, fees: No reservations. Sites are $12 per night, $5 per additional vehicle. The entire camp can be reserved for $45 a night. Senior discount available. Open late May to late October, weather permitting.

Directions: From Bend drive south on U.S. 97 for 23.5 miles to County Road 21 (Paulina/East Lake Road). Turn east (left) and drive 14 miles to the campground.

Contact: Deschutes National Forest, Bend-Fort Rock Ranger District, 1230 N.E. 3rd St., Bend, OR 97701; 541/388-5664; fax 541/383-4700.

❹ Little Crater

🏃🚴🏊🎣
🚐🐕♿🚙⛺ 8

This campground is set at 6,350 feet near the east shore of Paulina Lake in Newberry National Volcanic Monument, a caldera. This camp is very popular. See the description of Paulina Lake for more information.

Location: Near Paulina Lake in Deschutes National Forest; Southeast Oregon map 1, grid c7.

Campsites, facilities: There are 50 sites for tents, trailers, or RVs up to 30 feet long. Picnic tables, garbage service, and fire grills are provided. Drinking water and vault toilets are available. Boat docks and launching facilities are on-site, and boat rentals are nearby.

Some facilities are wheelchair-accessible. Leashed pets are permitted.

Reservations, fees: No reservations. Sites are $14 per night, plus $5 per additional vehicle. Senior discount available. Parking at the trailhead at the campground requires a Northwest Forest Pass ($30 annual fee) or a $5 daily fee per parked vehicle. Open late May to late October.

Directions: From Bend drive south on U.S. 97 for 23.5 miles to County Road 21 (Paulina/East Lake Road). Turn east (left) and drive 14.5 miles to Forest Road 2110. Turn north (left) and drive one-half mile to the campground.

Contact: Deschutes National Forest, Bend-Fort Rock Ranger District, 1230 N.E. 3rd St., Bend, OR 97701; 541/388-5664; fax 541/383-4700.

❺ Cinder Hill

🏃🚴🏊🎣
🚐🐕♿🚙⛺ 7

The campground is situated along the northeast shore of East Lake at an elevation of 6,400 feet. Within the Newberry National Volcanic Monument, this is a good base camp for area activities. Boating, fishing, and hiking are among the recreation options here. Boat speed is limited to 10 mph.

Location: On East Lake in Deschutes National Forest; Southeast Oregon map 1, grid c7.

Campsites, facilities: There are 110 sites for tents, trailers, or RVs up to 30 feet long. Picnic tables, garbage service, and fire grills are provided. Drinking water and flush and vault toilets are available. Boat docks and launching facilities are on-site, and boat rentals, a store, restaurant, showers, coin-operated laundry, and cabins are nearby at East Lake Resort. Some facilities are wheelchair-accessible. Leashed pets are permitted.

Reservations, fees: No reservations. Sites are $10–12 per night, plus $5 per additional vehicle. Parking at the trailhead at the campground requires a Northwest Forest Pass ($30 annual fee) or a $5 daily fee per parked vehicle. Senior discount available. Open late May to late October.

Directions: From Bend drive south on U.S. 97 for 23.5 miles to County Road 21 (Paulina/East Lake Road). Turn east (left) and drive 17.6 miles to Forest Road 2110-700. Turn north (left) and drive one-half mile to the campground.

Contact: Deschutes National Forest, Bend-Fort Rock Ranger District, 1230 N.E. 3rd St., Bend, OR 97701; 541/388-5664; fax 541/383-4700.

6 East Lake

 8

This campground is set along the south shore of East Lake at an elevation of 6,400 feet. Boating and fishing are popular here, and hiking trails provide access to signs of former volcanic activity in the area. East Lake Campground is similar to Cinder Hill, but smaller. Boat speed is limited to 10 mph.

Location: On East Lake in Deschutes National Forest; Southeast Oregon map 1, grid c7.

Campsites, facilities: There are 29 sites for tents, trailers, or RVs up to 30 feet long. Picnic tables, garbage service, and fire grills are provided. Drinking water and flush and vault toilets are available. Some facilities are wheelchair-accessible. Boat docks, launching facilities, and rentals are nearby. Leashed pets are permitted.

Reservations, fees: No reservations. Sites are $10–12 per night, plus $5 per additional vehicle. Senior discount available. Open late May to late October.

Directions: From Bend drive south on U.S. 97 for 23.5 miles to County Road 21 (Paulina/East

Lake Road). Turn east (left) and drive 16.6 miles to the campground.

Contact: Deschutes National Forest, Bend-Fort Rock Ranger District, 1230 N.E. 3rd St., Bend, OR 97701; 541/388-5664; fax 541/383-4700.

7 Hot Springs

 5

Don't be fooled by the name. There are no hot springs at this campsite. It lies across the road from East Lake at 6,400 feet elevation. It's a good tent camping spot if you want to be near East Lake but farther away from RVs. See the description of East Lake for additional recreation information.

Location: Near East Lake in Deschutes National Forest; Southeast Oregon map 1, grid c7.

Campsites, facilities: There are 52 sites for tents, trailers, or RVs up to 30 feet long. Picnic tables, garbage service, and fire grills are provided. Drinking water and vault toilets are available. Boat docks, launching facilities, and rentals are nearby. Leashed pets are permitted.

Reservations, fees: No reservations. Sites are $7 per night, plus $5 per additional vehicle. Senior discount available. Open late May to late October.

Directions: From Bend drive south on U.S. 97 for 23.5 miles to County Road 21 (Paulina/East Lake Road). Turn east (left) and drive 17.2 miles to the campground.

Contact: Deschutes National Forest, Bend-Fort Rock Ranger District, 1230 N.E. 3rd St., Bend, OR 97701; 541/388-5664; fax 541/383-4700.

8 East Lake Resort and RV Park

 7

This resort is in a wooded, mountainous setting with shaded sites on the east shore of

East Lake. Opportunities for fishing, boating, and swimming abound.

Location: On East Lake; Southeast Oregon map 1, grid c7.

Campsites, facilities: There are 38 sites for tents, trailers, or RVs up to 36 feet in length. Electricity, drinking water, and picnic tables are provided. Flush toilets, bottled gas, showers, barbecues, cabins, firewood, a store, a café, a laundry room, ice, boat-launching facilities, boat rentals, and a playground are available. A dump station is on-site. Leashed pets are permitted.

Reservations, fees: Reservations accepted. Sites are $15 per night. Open mid-May to mid-October, weather permitting.

Directions: From Bend drive south on U.S. 97 for 23.5 miles to County Road 21 (Paulina/East Lake Road). Turn east (left) and drive 22 miles to the campground at the end of the road.

Contact: East Lake Resort and RV Park, P.O. Box 95, La Pine, OR 97739; 541/536-2230; website: www.eastlakeresort.com.

9 China Hat

 3

This remote campground is set at 5,100 feet in a rugged, primitive area. There is direct trail access here to the East Fort Rock OHV Trail System. Hunters use it as a base camp in the fall, but it is a summer base camp for off-road motorcyclists.

Location: In Deschutes National Forest; Southeast Oregon map 1, grid c8.

Campsites, facilities: There are 14 sites for tents, trailers, or RVs up to 30 feet long. Picnic tables and fire grills are provided. Vault toilets are available. There is no drinking water, and all garbage must be packed out. Leashed pets are permitted.

Reservations, fees: No reservations; no fee. Open May to late October, weather permitting.

Directions: From Bend drive south on U.S. 97 for 29.6 miles to Forest Road 22. Turn east (left) and drive 26.4 miles to Forest Road 18. Turn north (left) and drive 5.9 miles to the campground on the left.

Contact: Deschutes National Forest, Bend-Fort Rock Ranger District, 1230 N.E. 3rd St., Bend, OR 97701; 541/388-5664; fax 541/383-4700.

10 Cabin Lake

![] 3

This remote campground set at 4,500 feet is adjacent to a bird blind that's more than 80 years old—it's a great place to watch birds. The spot is primitive and secluded with sparse tree cover and it receives little use even in the busy summer months.

Location: In Deschutes National Forest; Southeast Oregon map 1, grid c8.

Campsites, facilities: There are 14 sites for tents, trailers, or RVs up to 30 feet long. Picnic tables and fire grills are provided. Vault toilets and drinking water are available. All garbage must be packed out. Leashed pets are permitted.

Reservations, fees: No reservations; no fee. Open mid-May to late October.

Directions: From Bend drive south on U.S. 97 for 29.6 miles to Forest Road 22. Turn east (left) and drive 26.4 miles to Forest Road 18. Turn north (left) and drive six miles to the campground on the left.

Contact: Deschutes National Forest, Bend-Fort Rock Ranger District, 1230 N.E. 3rd St., Bend, OR 97701; 541/388-5664; fax 541/383-4700.

11 Delintment Lake

![] 7

This very pretty, forested camp is set along the shore of Delintment Lake.
It was originally a beaver pond, which was gradually

developed into a lake covering 57 acres. It is now pretty and blue and is stocked with trout, providing good bank and boat fishing. Here's an insider's note: rainbow trout here average 12–18 inches.

Location: On Delintment Lake in Malheur National Forest; Southeast Oregon map 2, grid a3.

Campsites, facilities: There are 29 sites for tents, trailers, or RVs up to 30 feet long. Picnic tables and fire grills are provided. Drinking water, a group picnic area on the lake with tables and grills, and vault toilets are available. All garbage must be packed out. Wheelchair-accessible facilities include five sites and three toilets. Launching facilities are in the campground. Leashed pets are permitted.

Reservations, fees: No reservations accepted. Sites are $7–10 per night, $3 per night for an additional vehicle. Senior discount available. Open May through October.

Directions: From Burns drive southwest on U.S. 20 for three miles to County Road 127. Turn right (northwest) and drive about 18 miles to Forest Road 41. Turn left on Forest Road 41 and drive about 35 miles (staying on Forest Road 41 at all junctions, paved all the way) to the campground at the lake.

Contact: Malheur National Forest, Emigrant Creek Ranger District, HC 74, P.O. Box 12870, Hines, OR 97738; 541/573-4300; fax 541/573-4398.

try dirt roads are good for mountain biking. See a U.S. Forest Service map for details.

Location: Near Emigrant Creek in Malheur National Forest; Southeast Oregon map 2, grid b5.

Campsites, facilities: There are six sites for tents, trailers, or RVs up to 30 feet long. Picnic tables and fire grills are provided, but there is no drinking water, and all garbage must be packed out. Vault toilets are available. Some facilities are wheelchair-accessible. Leashed pets are permitted. Drinking water is available nearby at Falls.

Reservations, fees: No reservations accepted. Sites are $7 per night, $3.50 per night for an additional vehicle. Senior discount available. Open May through October. From Burns, drive southwest on U.S. 20 for three miles to County Road 127. Turn right (northwest) and drive 25 miles (passing Forest Road 41 on the left) to Forest Road 43 and the junction for Allison Guard Station, Delintment Lake, and Paulina. Turn left on Forest Road 43 and drive 9.75 miles to Forest Road 4340. Turn left and drive on Forest Road 4340-050 to the campground.

Contact: Malheur National Forest, Emigrant Creek Ranger District, HC 74, P.O. Box 12870, Hines, OR 97738; 541/573-4300; fax 541/573-4398; website: www.fs.fed.us/c6/malheur.

12 Emigrant

4

You'll get peace and quiet here because this spot is usually uncrowded. One of two camps in the immediate area, it is set at an elevation of 5,200 feet in Malheur National Forest, in a meadow near Emigrant Creek. There's good fly-fishing here in the spring and early summer. Falls is busier but has drinking water and is two miles away. Several nearby backcoun-

13 Yellowjacket

8

This campground (elevation 4,800 feet) in the ponderosa pines is set along the shore of Yellowjacket Lake, where fishing for rainbow trout can be very good in the summer. Boats without motors are encouraged. The camp is quiet and uncrowded.

Location: On Yellowjacket Lake in Malheur National Forest; Southeast Oregon map 2, grid a6.

Campsites, facilities: There are 20 sites for tents, trailers, or RVs up to 22 feet long. Picnic tables, drinking water, and pit or vault toilets are available, but all garbage must be packed out. A boat launch is nearby. Leashed pets are permitted.

Reservations, fees: No reservations. Sites are $7–9 per night, $3 per night for an additional vehicle. Senior discount available. Open late May through October, weather permitting.

Directions: From Burns, drive southwest on U.S. 20 for three miles to County Road 127. Turn right (northwest) and drive 32 miles to Forest Road 37. Turn right and drive three miles to Forest Road 3745. Turn right and drive one mile to the campground on the right.

Contact: Malheur National Forest, Emigrant Creek Ranger District, HC 74, P.O. Box 12870, Hines, OR 97738; 541/573-4300; fax 541/573-4398.

14 Falls

 5

Falls Camp is set in a beautiful meadow next to Emigrant Creek. This campground is a great place to see wildflowers in the early summer. It is also surrounded by ponderosa pine forests. There is a short trail to a small waterfall on the creek, from which the camp gets its name. Flyfishing and mountain biking are good here, as at nearby Emigrant, set two miles down the road. The elevation is 5,200 feet.

Location: Near Emigrant Creek in Malheur National Forest; Southeast Oregon map 2, grid b6.

Campsites, facilities: There are seven sites for tents, trailers, or RVs up to 30 feet long. Picnic tables and fire grills are provided.

Drinking water and vault toilets are available. Garbage must be packed out. Some facilities are wheelchair-accessible. Leashed pets are permitted.

Reservations, fees: No reservations accepted. Sites are $7 per night, $3.50 per night for an additional vehicle. Senior discount available. Open May through October.

Directions: From Burns, drive southwest on U.S. 20 for three miles to County Road 127. Turn right (northwest) and drive 25 miles (passing Forest Road 41 on the left) to Forest Road 43 and the junction for Allison Guard Station, Delintment Lake, and Paulina. Turn left on Forest Road 43 and drive eight miles to the campground on the left.

Contact: Malheur National Forest, Emigrant Creek Ranger District, HC 74, P.O. Box 12870, Hines, OR 97738; 541/573-4300; fax 541/573-4398; website: www.fs.fed.us/c6/malheur.

15 Chickahominy Reservoir

4

This is a good spot for group camping, but it's in the high desert with no shade. Weather conditions can be extreme, so come prepared. The camp is used primarily as an overnight stop for travelers driving through the area. Boats with motors are allowed on the reservoir. There is a new access road on the northwest side of the reservoir for day use. The nearest services are eight miles east (via U.S. 20) in Riley.

Location: On Chickahominy Reservoir; Southeast Oregon map 2, grid d4.

Campsites, facilities: There are 28 sites for tents, trailers, or RVs up to 35 feet long. Picnic tables, garbage bins, and fire grills are provided. Drinking water and vault toilets are available. A fish-cleaning station is available nearby. Some facilities are wheelchair-accessible. Leashed pets are permitted.

Reservations, fees: No reservations. Sites are $6 per night per vehicle, with a stay limit of 14 days. Open April through October, weather permitting.

Directions: From Burns drive west on U.S. 20 for 30 miles to the campground on the right.

Contact: Bureau of Land Management, Burns District, HC 74-12533, U.S. Highway 20 West, Hines, OR 97738; 541/573-4400; fax 541/573-4411; website: www.or.blm.gov/burns.

16 Joaquin Miller Horse Camp

5

Campsites are spread out and there's a fair amount of privacy here among mature ponderosa pine and adjacent to a meadow. Expect some highway noise. Lots of old logging roads are available for walking, biking, and horseback riding. The camp gets low use, but even though it caters to horse campers, all are welcome. Campers with horses are strongly advised to arrive early before weekends to claim the campsites set nearest to the corrals.

Location: In Malheur National Forest; Southeast Oregon map 3, grid a1.

Campsites, facilities: There are 18 sites for tents, trailers, or RVs up to 28 feet long. Picnic tables and fire rings are provided. Drinking water and vault toilets are available. All garbage must be packed out. Stock facilities include four corrals and hitching rails. Leashed pets are permitted.

Reservations, fees: No reservations; no fee. Open mid-May through November, weather permitting.

Directions: From Burns drive north on U.S. 395 for 19 miles to the campground on the left (this turnoff is easy to miss; watch for a very small green sign on the right that says, Joaquin Miller Horse Camp).

Contact: Malheur National Forest, Emigrant Creek Ranger District, HC 74, P.O. 12870, Hines, OR 97738; 541/573-4300; fax 541/573-4398.

17 Idlewild

8

This campground is set at an elevation of 5,300 feet in Devine Canyon, a designated sno-park in the winter that's popular with locals for snowmobiling and cross-country skiing. Several hiking and biking trailheads start here, including the Divine Summit Interpretive Loop Trail and the Idlewild Loop Trail. It's also a popular spot for visitors traveling up U.S. 395 and in need of a stopover, since it provides easy access and a pretty setting. Bird-watching for white-headed woodpeckers and goshawks is popular. Expect to hear some highway noise. But the ponderosa pine forest and area trails are so beautiful that it can feel divine, even if Devine Canyon and neighboring Devine Ridge are spelled after the guy who named the place in the good old days where nobody worried about spelling.

Location: In Devine Canyon in Malheur National Forest; Southeast Oregon map 3, grid b1.

Campsites, facilities: There are 26 sites for tents and five sites for trailers or RVs up to 30 feet long. Picnic tables, fire grills, and picnic areas are provided. Drinking water, a group shelter, and vault toilets are available. All garbage must be packed out. Some facilities are wheelchair-accessible. Leashed pets are permitted.

Reservations, fees: No reservations. Sites are $7 per night, $3.50 per night for an additional vehicle. Senior discount available. Open late May to mid-October.

Directions: From Burns drive north on U.S. 395 for 17 miles to the campground on the right.

Contact: Malheur National Forest, Emigrant Creek Ranger District, HC 74, P.O. 12870, Hines, OR 97738; 541/573-4300; fax 541/573-4398.

18 Chukar Park

7

This campground is set along the banks of the North Fork of the Malheur River. The area in general provides habitat for chukar, an upland game bird species. Hunting can be good in season during the fall, but requires much hiking in rugged terrain. Trout fishing is also a popular here. BLM asks that visitors please respect the surrounding private property.

Location: Near the North Fork of the Malheur River; Southeast Oregon map 3, grid b7.

Campsites, facilities: There are 18 sites for tents, trailers, or RVs up to 28 feet long. Picnic tables, fire grills, and garbage services are provided. Drinking water (May through October only) and vault toilets are available. Leashed pets are permitted.

Reservations, fees: No reservations. Sites are $5 per night per vehicle, with a 14-day stay limit. Senior discount available. Open year-round, with limited winter facilities.

Directions: From Burns drive north on U.S. 395 for three miles to U.S. 20. Turn east and drive 55 miles to Juntura and Beulah Reservoir Road. Turn northwest and drive six miles to the campground.

Contact: Bureau of Land Management, Vale District, 100 Oregon St., Vale, OR 97918-9630; 541/473-3144; fax 541/473-6213; website: www.or.blm.gov/vale.

19 Oasis RV Park

6

One of the only camps in the area, this well-maintained RV park is close to Chukar Park. See the description of Chukar Park for more details.

Location: In Juntura; Southeast Oregon map 3, grid c8.

Campsites, facilities: There are 22 sites for trailers or RVs of any length; eight are drive-through. Electricity, drinking water, and sewer hookups are provided. Flush toilets, showers, a café, and ice are available. Leashed pets are permitted.

Reservations, fees: No reservations accepted. Sites are $16 per night. Open year-round.

Directions: From Burns, drive north on U.S. 395 for three miles to U.S. 20. Turn east and drive 55 miles to Juntura. The park is in Juntura (a very small town) along U.S. 20.

Contact: Oasis RV Park, P.O. Box 277, Juntura, OR 97911; 541/277-3605; fax 541/277-3312.

20 Prospector Travel Trailer Park

5

This is one of two camps (Westerner Trailer Park is the other) for travelers in the Vale area. This one is more comfortable for tents, with a specifically designated wooded and grassy area. It claims to be a fishing and hunting paradise, and it even has a game bird cleaning room. It is set on the historical Oregon Trail.

Location: In Vale; Southeast Oregon map 4, grid a6.

Campsites, facilities: There are 10 tent sites and 28 drive-through sites for trailers or RVs of any length, plus a separate area for tents. Picnic tables are provided. Flush toilets, bottled gas, sanitary disposal services, showers, a laundry room, and ice are available. A store and a café are within one mile. Leashed pets and motorbikes are permitted.

Reservations, fees: Reservations accepted. Sites are $8 per person and $18–20 per RV a night. Senior discount available. Major credit cards accepted. Open year-round.

Directions: From Ontario (near the Oregon/Idaho border) drive west on U.S. 20/26 for 12 miles to Vale and U.S. 26. Turn north on U.S. 26 and drive one-half mile to Hope Street. Turn east and drive one block east to park on the left.

Contact: Prospector Travel Trailer Park, 511 N. 11th St. E, Vale, OR 97918; 541/473-3879; fax 541/473-2338.

21 Westerner Trailer Park

 5

This campground on the banks of Willow Creek is a good layover spot for travelers heading to or from Idaho on U.S. 20/26. See the description of Prospector Travel Trailer Park for more information.

Location: On Willow Creek; Southeast Oregon map 4, grid a6.

Campsites, facilities: There are 10 sites for tents, trailers, or RVs of any length. Electricity, drinking water, cable TV, sewer hookups, and picnic tables are provided. Flush toilets, showers, a laundry room, and ice are available. Bottled gas, a store, a café, and a swimming pool are within two blocks. Leashed pets and motorbikes are permitted.

Reservations, fees: Reservations accepted. Sites are $10 per night. Open year-round.

Directions: From Ontario (near the Oregon/Idaho border) drive west on U.S. 20/26 for 12 miles to Vale and to the junction of U.S. 26. The campground is on the left at the junction of U.S. 20 and U.S. 26.

Contact: Westerner Trailer Park, 317 A St. E, Vale, OR 97918; 541/473-3947.

22 Lake Owyhee State Park

7

This state park is set along the shore of 53-mile long Owyhee Lake, a good lake for water-

skiing in the day and fishing for warm-water species in the morning and evening. Owyhee is famous for its superb bass fishing. The place even has floating restrooms. Other highlights include views of unusual geological formations and huge rock pinnacles from the park. Bighorn sheep, pronghorn antelope, golden eagles, coyotes, mule deer, wild horses, and mountain lions live around here.

Location: On Owyhee Lake; Southeast Oregon map 4, grid d7.

Campsites, facilities: There are seven sites for tents or self-contained RVs, and 33 sites with water and electrical hookups for trailers or RVs up to 55 feet long. There are also two tepees. Drinking water, garbage bins, picnic tables, and fire grills are provided. Flush toilets, a sanitary disposal station, and showers are available. Boat docks and launching facilities are available nearby. Leashed pets are permitted.

Reservations, fees: Reservations accepted for tepees ($6 reservation fee). Sites are $12–19 per night, tepees are $27 per night; $7 per night for an additional vehicle. Open from mid-April through October.

Directions: From Ontario (near the Oregon/Idaho border), drive south on U.S. 20/U.S. 26 for six miles to the Nyssa exit. Turn south and drive eight miles to Nyssa and Highway 201. Turn southeast on Highway 201 and drive eight miles to Owyhee. Turn east and drive about 20 miles to road's end and the entrance to the park.

Contact: Lake Owyhee State Park, 3012 Island Ave., LaGrande, OR 97850; 800/551-6949 or 541/339-2331, reservations (for tepees) 800/452-5687.

23 Leslie Gulch-Slocum Creek

 6

This campground is on the eastern shore of Owyhee Lake, not far from the Oregon/Idaho border. Warm-water fishing, water-skiing, and hiking are among the recreation options in this high desert area. Lake Owyhee State Park provides the other nearby recreation destination.

Location: On Owyhee Lake; Southeast Oregon map 4, grid f6.

Campsites, facilities: There are 10 undeveloped sites for tents, trailers, or RVs up to 20 feet long. Picnic tables and garbage service are provided. Vault toilets are available. There is no drinking water. Boat-launching facilities are available on-site. Leashed pets are permitted.

Reservations, fees: No reservations accepted. There is no fee. The campground is open from mid-March to mid-November.

Directions: From U.S. 95 where it crosses the Idaho/Oregon border, drive north for five miles to McBride Creek Road. Turn west and drive 10 miles to Leslie Gulch Road. Turn left (west) and drive 15 miles to the campground.

Contact: Bureau of Land Management, Vale District, 100 Oregon St., Vale, OR 97918-9630; 541/473-3144; fax 541/473-6213.

24 Cow Lakes

 6

This little-used campground is adjacent to an old lava flow. The lake is shallow and murky, which makes fishing popular here. The campsites are open and treeless, and the road is rutted and rough in places.

Location: Near Cow Lakes; Southeast Oregon map 4, grid h6.

Campsites, facilities: There are 10 sites for tents, small trailers, or RVs. Picnic tables and fire rings are provided. Vault toilets and a boat ramp are available. No drinking water is available, and all garbage must be packed out. Leashed pets are permitted.

Reservations, fees: No reservations. No fee. Open year-round, weather permitting.

Directions: From Burns Junction, drive east on U.S. 95 for 30 miles to Danner Loop Road. Turn left (north) and drive 14 miles (past Danner) to Cow Lakes and the campground.

Contact: Bureau of Land Management, Vale District, 100 Oregon St., Vale, OR 97918-9630; 541/473-3144; fax 541/473-6213.

25 Silver Creek Marsh

4

A trailhead and terminus for segments of the National Recreational Trail are at this small, quiet, and primitive camp that gets little attention. It's a short walk to the creek, a popular fishing spot. It is also set close to the wildlife area boundary.

Location: Near Silver Creek in Fremont National Forest; Southeast Oregon map 5, grid a8.

Campsites, facilities: There are 17 tent sites. Picnic tables and fire grills are provided. Drinking water, vault toilets, and hitching rails and corrals for horses are available. Firewood is available nearby. All garbage must be packed out. Leashed pets are permitted.

Reservations, fees: No reservations; no fee. Open May to mid-November.

Directions: From Bend drive south on U.S. 97 for 32 miles to Highway 31. Turn southeast on Highway 31 and drive 48 miles to County Road 4-11 (one mile west of the town of Silver Lake). Turn right and drive six miles (the road becomes Forest Road 27) and continue south for five miles to the campground entrance road on the left.

Contact: Fremont National Forest, Silver Lake Ranger District, P.O. Box 129, Silver Lake, OR 97638; 541/576-2107; fax 541/576-7587.

26 Thompson Reservoir

🚶🏊🎣
🚐🐕🚙🏕️ 3

On the north shore of Thompson Reservoir among black bark ponderosa pine the height of telephone poles, this camp is simple and pretty, with shaded sites close to the water. This is a popular fishing and boating area. See description of East Bay. Water in the reservoir fluctuates and sometimes dries up altogether in late summer.

Location: On Thompson Reservoir in Fremont National Forest; Southeast Oregon map 5, grid a8.

Campsites, facilities: There are 19 sites for tents, trailers, or RVs up to 22 feet long, plus a separate group camping area. Picnic tables and fire grills are provided. Drinking water and vault toilets are available, but all garbage must be packed out. Boat-launching facilities are nearby. Leashed pets are permitted.

Reservations, fees: No reservations; no fee. Open May to mid-November.

Directions: From Bend drive south on U.S. 97 for 32 miles to Highway 31. Turn southeast on Highway 31 and drive 48 miles to County Road 4-11 (one mile west of the town of Silver Lake). Turn right and drive six miles (the road becomes Forest Road 27) and continue south for nine miles to the campground entrance road. Turn left and drive one mile to the camp.

Contact: Fremont National Forest, Silver Lake Ranger District, P.O. Box 129, Silver Lake, OR 97638; 541/576-2107; fax 541/576-7587.

27 East Bay

🚶🏊🎣🚤
🐕♿🚙🏕️ 3

This campground on the east shore of Thompson Reservoir has paved roads, but it's still a long way from home, so be sure to bring all of your supplies with you. A day-use area is ad-jacent to the camp. Silver Creek Marsh Campground is an even more primitive setting along a stream.

Location: On Thompson Reservoir in Fremont National Forest; Southeast Oregon map 5, grid a8.

Campsites, facilities: There are 17 sites for tents, trailers, or RVs. Picnic tables, garbage bins, and fire grills are provided. Drinking water, vault toilets, and a fishing pier are available. The facilities are wheelchair-accessible. Boat-launching facilities are nearby. Leashed pets are permitted.

Reservations, fees: No reservations accepted. Sites are $8 per night, $5 per extra vehicle. Senior discount available. Open May to mid-November.

Directions: From Bend drive south on U.S. 97 for 32 miles to Highway 31. Turn southeast on Highway 31 and drive 49 miles to Silver Lake. Continue east a short distance on Highway 31 to Forest Road 28. Turn right on Forest Road 28 and drive 13 miles to Forest Road 014. Turn right on Forest Road 014 and drive two miles to the campground.

Contact: Fremont National Forest, Silver Lake Ranger District, P.O. Box 129, Silver Lake, OR 97638; 541/576-2107; fax 541/576-7587.

28 Head of the River

🐕🎣🚙🏕️ 8

Almost nobody knows about this small, extremely remote spot on the edge of meadow in the lodgepole and ponderosa pine, though hunters use it in the fall. The only camp for miles around, it's set at 4,500 feet elevation along the Williamson River headwaters, where you can actually see the beginning of the river bubbling up from underground springs.

Location: On the Williamson River in Winema National Forest; Southeast Oregon map 5, grid c6.

Campsites, facilities: There are five sites for tents, trailers, or RVs up to 30 feet long. Picnic tables, garbage bins, and fire pits are provided. Vault toilets are available. There is no drinking water. Leashed pets are permitted.

Reservations, fees: No reservations; no fee. Open from Memorial Day through late November.

Directions: From Klamath Falls drive north on U.S. 97 for 30 miles to Chiloquin and Sprague River Highway. Turn east on Sprague River Highway and drive five miles to Williamson River Road. Turn northeast and drive 20 miles to Forest Road 4648. Turn north on Forest Road 4648 and drive one-half mile to the campground.

Contact: Winema National Forest, Klamath Ranger District, 1936 California Ave., Klamath Falls, OR 97601; 541/885-3400; fax 541/885-3452.

29 Gerber Reservoir

 6

This camp can be found at an elevation of 4,800 feet alongside the west shore of Gerber Reservoir (10 mph boat speed limit). Gerber is off the beaten path and is used mainly by locals. Recreation options include swimming, fishing, boating, and hiking.

Location: On Gerber Reservoir; Southeast Oregon map 5, grid g7.

Campsites, facilities: There are 50 sites for tents, trailers, or RVs up to 30 feet long. Picnic tables and fire grills are provided. Drinking water, firewood, a sanitary dump station, wheelchair-accessible vault toilets, a boat ramp, a boat dock, launching facilities, and a fish-cleaning station are available. Leashed pets are permitted.

Reservations, fees: No reservations accepted. Sites are $7 per night, $4 per night for an additional vehicle. Senior discount available. Open year-round, with drinking water and services available May to mid-September.

Directions: From Klamath Falls drive east on Highway 140 for 16 miles to Dairy and Highway 70. Turn south on Highway 70 and drive seven miles to Bonanza and East Langell Valley Road. Turn east on East Langell Valley Road and drive for 11 miles to Gerber Road. Turn left on Gerber Road and drive eight miles to the campground on the right.

Contact: Bureau of Land Management, Klamath Falls Resource Area, 2795 Anderson Ave., Building 25, Klamath Falls, OR 97603; 541/883-6916; fax 541/884-2097; website: www.or.blm.gov/lakeview.

30 Lee Thomas

 6

The campsite is set near the trailhead that provides access to the Dead Horse Rim Trail. Nestled along the North Fork of the Sprague River in the interior of Fremont National Forest, this small, cozy camp is a genuine hideaway, with all the necessities provided. It is set at an elevation of 6,306 feet. Like Sandhill Crossing Campground, two miles downstream, this camp is popular with fishermen and hunters in the fall. Lee Thomas is two miles upstream from Sandhill Crossing and is set in a meadow.

Location: Near the North Fork of the Sprague River in Fremont National Forest; Southeast Oregon map 6, grid d1.

Campsites, facilities: There are eight sites for tents, trailers, or RVs up to 16 feet long. Picnic tables and fire grills are provided. Drinking water and vault toilets are available. All garbage must be packed out. Leashed pets are permitted.

Reservations, fees: No reservations; no fee. Open June to late October.

Directions: From Lakeview drive north on U.S. 395 for 23 miles to Highway 31. Turn northwest and drive 22 miles to Paisley. Continue on Highway 31 for one-half mile to Mill Street. Turn west on Mill Street and drive 20 miles (the road becomes Forest Road 33) and continue to the T intersection with Forest Road 28. Turn right and drive 11 miles to Forest Road 3411. Turn left and drive five miles to the campground.

Contact: Fremont National Forest, Paisley Ranger District, P.O. Box 67, Paisley, OR 97636; 541/943-3114; fax 541/943-4479.

31 Sandhill Crossing

6

If you're looking for a combination of beauty and solitude, you've found it. This camp is set at 6,306 feet elevation on the banks of the designated Wild and Scenic North Fork Sprague River, where fishing is superior. This is a low-use camp, but it is popular with anglers and hunters in the fall. It is also set near a trailhead for the Gearheart Wilderness.

Location: On the North Fork of the Sprague River in Fremont National Forest; Southeast Oregon map 6, grid d1.

Campsites, facilities: There are five sites for tents, trailers, or RVs; some are drive-through sites. Picnic tables, fire grills, vault toilets, and drinking water are provided. All garbage must be packed out. Leashed pets are permitted.

Reservations, fees: No reservations; no fee. Open June through October.

Directions: From Lakeview drive north on U.S. 395 for 23 miles to Highway 31. Turn northwest and drive 22 miles to Paisley. Continue on Highway 31 for one-half mile to Mill Street. Turn west on Mill Street and drive 20 miles (the road becomes Forest Road 33) and continue to the T intersection with Forest Road 28. Turn right and drive 11 miles to Forest Road 3411. Turn left and drive eight miles to the campground.

Contact: Fremont National Forest, Paisley Ranger District, P.O. Box 67, Paisley, OR 97636; 541/943-3114; fax 541/943-4479.

32 Dead Horse Lake

9

The shore of Dead Horse Lake is home to this camp (at 7,372 feet elevation). It is generally full on most weekends and holidays. A hiking trail winds around the perimeter of the lake, hooking up with other trails along the way. One original Civilian Conservation Corps canoe is left in the lake, a relic of the 1930s. Good side trips are nearby in Fremont National Forest. See description of Campbell Lake.

Location: On Dead Horse Lake in Fremont National Forest; Southeast Oregon map 6, grid d1.

Campsites, facilities: There are nine sites for tents or self-contained trailers, or RVs up to 16 feet long, and a separate area with seven sites for group camping. Picnic tables and fire grills are provided. Drinking water and vault toilets are available, but all garbage must be packed out. A boat launch is nearby. Boats with electric motors are permitted, but gas motors are prohibited. All garbage must be packed out. Leashed pets are permitted.

Reservations, fees: No reservations; no fee. Open July through October.

Directions: From Lakeview drive north on U.S. 395 for 23 miles to Highway 31. Turn northwest and drive 22 miles to Paisley. Continue on Highway 31 for one-half mile to Mill Street. Turn west on Mill Street and drive 20 miles (the road becomes Forest Road 033) and continue to the T intersection with Forest Road 28. Turn right and drive 11 miles (watch for the turn to Campbell-Dead Horse Lakes) to Forest Road 033. Turn left and drive three miles (gravel road) to the campground.

Contact: Fremont National Forest, Paisley Ranger District, P.O. Box 67, Paisley, OR 97636; 541/943-3114; fax 541/943-4479.

33 Campbell Lake

9

This campground on the pebbled shore of Campbell Lake is near Dead Horse Lake Campground. These high-elevation, crystal-clear lakes were formed during the glacier period. Evidence of the past glacial nature of this area can be found on the nearby Lakes Trail system. Both camps are very busy and are full most weekends in July and August. No boats with gas motors are permitted on Campbell Lake. Good side trips are available in Fremont National Forest. A U.S. Forest Service map details the back roads.

Location: On Campbell Lake in Fremont National Forest; Southeast Oregon map 6, grid d2.

Campsites, facilities: There are 21 sites for tents, trailers, or RVs up to 16 feet long. Picnic tables and fire grills are provided. Drinking water and vault toilets are available. A boat launch is adjacent to the camp. Boats with electric motors are permitted, but gas motors are prohibited. All garbage must be packed out. Leashed pets are permitted.

Reservations, fees: No reservations; no fee. Open July to late October.

Directions: From Lakeview drive north on U.S. 395 for 23 miles to Highway 31. Turn northwest and drive 22 miles to Paisley. Continue on Highway 31 for one-half mile to Mill Street. Turn west on Mill Street and drive 20 miles (the road becomes Forest Road 33) and continue to the T intersection with Forest Road 28. Turn right and drive eight miles to

Forest Road 033. Turn left and drive two miles to the campground.

Contact: Fremont National Forest, Paisley Ranger District, P.O. Box 67, Paisley, OR 97636; 541/943-3114; fax 541/943-4479.

34 Corral Creek

4

Set along Corral Creek, this camp is adjacent to a trailhead that provides access into the Gearhart Mountain Wilderness, making it a prime base camp for a backpacking trip. Access is also available from camp to the Palisade Rocks, a worthwhile side trip. Another option is Quartz Mountain Snowpark, which is 14 miles east of the campground. The elevation is 6,000 feet.

Location: Near the Gearhart Mountain Wilderness in Fremont National Forest; Southeast Oregon map 6, grid e1.

Campsites, facilities: There are six sites for tents, trailers, or RVs up to 16 feet long. Picnic tables and fire grills are provided. Vault toilets are available. There is no drinking water, and all garbage must be packed out. Stock facilities include hitching posts, stalls, and corrals. Leashed pets are permitted.

Reservations, fees: No reservations; no fee. Open mid-May to late October.

Directions: From Klamath Falls drive east on Highway 140 for 53 miles to the town of Bly. Continue east on Highway 140 for another 13 miles to Forest Road 3660. Turn left and drive 13 miles to Forest Road 34. Turn right and drive about one-eighth mile to Forest Road 012 and continue to the campground.

Contact: Fremont National Forest, Bly Ranger District, P.O. Box 25, Bly, OR 97622; 541/353-2427.

35 Dairy Point

🎣 🐕 🚐 ⛺ 6

This campground, elevation 5,200 feet, is next to the Dairy Creek Bridge in a stand of ponderosa pine and white fir at the edge of a large and open meadow. The setting is beautiful and peaceful, with a towering backdrop of mountains. In the spring, bird-watching and wildflowers are a sight to behold. Fishing and inner tubing are popular activities at Dairy Creek. Warning: this campground is suitable for large groups and is often full on holidays and most weekends.

Location: On Dairy Creek in Fremont National Forest; Southeast Oregon map 6, grid e2.

Campsites, facilities: There are four sites for tents or small, self-contained trailers or RVs. Picnic tables, fire grills, a vault toilet, and drinking water are provided. All garbage must be packed out. Leashed pets are permitted.

Reservations, fees: No reservations; no fee. Open mid-May through October.

Directions: From Lakeview drive north on U.S. 395 for 23 miles to Highway 31. Turn northwest and drive 22 miles to Paisley. Continue on Highway 31 for one-half mile to Mill Street. Turn west on Mill Street and drive 20 miles (the road becomes Forest Road 33) and continue to the T intersection with Forest Road 28. Turn left and drive two miles (crossing the Dairy Creek Bridge) to Forest Road 3428. Turn left and drive to the campground (just past the intersection on the left).

Contact: Fremont National Forest, Paisley Ranger District, P.O. Box 67, Paisley, OR 97636; 541/943-3114; fax 541/943-4479.

36 Happy Camp

🎣 🐕 🚐 ⛺ 6

Here's a pleasant spot at 5,289 feet elevation, with open sites along Dairy Creek, though only one site is close to the water. The camp houses some old Depression-era Civilian Conservation Corps shelters, preserved in their original state. There are three 1930s-era picnic shelters. Horseshoe pits are provided. Fishing is available here for rainbow trout, though the creek is no longer stocked.

Location: On Dairy Creek in Fremont National Forest; Southeast Oregon map 6, grid e2.

Campsites, facilities: There are nine sites for tents, trailers, or RVs up to 16 feet long. Picnic tables and fire grills are provided. Vault toilets are available, but there is no drinking water. All garbage must be packed out. Leashed pets are permitted.

Reservations, fees: No reservations; no fee. Open mid-May to late October.

Directions: From Lakeview drive north on U.S. 395 for 23 miles to Highway 31. Turn northwest and drive 22 miles to Paisley. Continue on Highway 31 for one-half mile to Mill Street. Turn west on Mill Street and drive 20 miles (the road becomes Forest Road 33) and continue to the T intersection with Forest Road 28. Turn left and drive two miles (just before Dairy Creek) to Forest Road 047. Turn right and drive two miles to the campground on the left.

Contact: Fremont National Forest, Paisley Ranger District, P.O. Box 67, Paisley, OR 97636; 541/943-3114; fax 541/943-4479.

37 Marster Spring

🥾 🎣 🐕 🚐 ⛺ 6

This pretty campground is set at an elevation of 4,845 feet on the banks of the Chewaucan River, a good fishing area. It's right on the river among ponderosa pine trees, yet close to the town of Paisley. It's the largest of several popular camps in this river corridor. The Fremont National Recreation Trail is accessible at the Chewaucan Crossing Trailhead one-quarter mile to the south.

Location: On the Chewaucan River in Fremont National Forest; Southeast Oregon map 6, grid d4.

Campsites, facilities: There are 11 sites for tents, trailers, or RVs up to 22 feet long. Picnic tables and fire grills are provided. Drinking water and vault toilets are available. Leashed pets are permitted.

Reservations, fees: No reservations; no fee. Open May to October.

Directions: From Lakeview drive north on U.S. 395 for 23 miles to Highway 31. Turn northwest and drive 22 miles to Paisley. Continue on Highway 31 for one-half mile to Mill Street. Turn west on Mill Street and drive seven miles (the road becomes Forest Road 33) to the campground on the left.

Contact: Fremont National Forest, Paisley Ranger District, P.O. Box 67, Paisley, OR 97636; 541/943-3114; fax 541/943-4479.

38 Lofton Reservoir

6

This remote campground is on the shore of Lofton Reservoir, a small lake that can provide the best trout fishing in this region. Other lakes are nearby and are accessible by forest roads. This area marks the beginning of the Great Basin, a high-desert area that extends to Idaho. A large fire burned much of the surrounding forest about 20 years ago, making this campground an oasis of sorts.

Location: On Lofton Reservoir in Fremont National Forest; Southeast Oregon map 6, grid f2.

Campsites, facilities: There are 26 sites for tents, trailers, or RVs up to 22 feet long. Picnic tables and fire grills are provided. Vault toilets are available. No drinking water is available. Boat docks and launching facilities are nearby. Leashed pets are permitted.

Reservations, fees: No reservations; no fee. Open mid-May to late October.

Directions: From Klamath Falls drive east on Highway 140 for 54 miles to Bly. Continue east on Highway 140 for 13 miles to Forest Road

3715. Turn right and drive seven miles to Forest Road 013. Turn left on Forest Road 013 and drive one mile to the campground.

Contact: Fremont National Forest, Bly Ranger District, P.O. Box 25, Bly, OR 97622; 541/353-2427; fax 541/353-2750.

39 Cottonwood Recreation Area

6

This campground along the shore of little Cottonwood Meadow Lake is one of the better spots in the vicinity for fishing and hiking. Boats with electric motors are allowed on the lake, but gas motors are prohibited. Three hiking trails wind around the lake, and facilities for horses include hitching posts, feeders, water, and corrals. It is set at an elevation of 6,130 feet. This is a forested setting with aspen and many huge ponderosa pines.

Location: On Cottonwood Meadow Lake in Fremont National Forest; Southeast Oregon map 6, grid f3.

Campsites, facilities: There are 21 sites for tents, small trailers, or RVs. Picnic tables and fire grills are provided. Drinking water and vault toilets are available, but all garbage must be packed out. Boat docks are nearby. Electric motors are allowed, but gasoline motors are prohibited on the lake. The boating speed limit is 5 mph. Leashed pets are permitted.

Reservations, fees: No reservations; no fee. Open early June to mid-October.

Directions: From Lakeview drive west on Highway 140 for 24 miles to Forest Road 3870. Turn right and drive about 10 miles to the campground.

Contact: Fremont National Forest, Lakeview Ranger District, HC 64, Box 60, Lakeview, OR 97630; 541/947-3334; fax 541/947-6375.

40 Dog Lake

5

This campground is on the west shore of Dog Lake at an elevation of 5,100 feet. Fishing and boats with motors are permitted, though limited to a speed of 5 mph. Dog Lake provides a popular fishery for bass, perch, and crappie. It was named by Native Americans for the lake's resemblance in shape to the hind leg of a dog. Prospects for seeing waterfowl and eagles are good, too.

Location: On Dog Lake in Fremont National Forest; Southeast Oregon map 6, grid h3.

Campsites, facilities: There are eight sites for tents, trailers, or RVs up to 16 feet long. Drinking water, picnic tables, and fire grills are provided. Vault toilets are available. A boat launch is nearby. Leashed pets are permitted.

Reservations, fees: No reservations; no fee. Open mid-April to mid-October.

Directions: From Lakeview drive west on Highway 140 for seven miles to County Road 1-13. Turn left on County Road 1-13 and drive four miles to County Road 1-11D (Dog Lake Road). Turn right and drive four miles (the road becomes Forest Road 4017) into national forest. Continue on Forest Road 4017 for 12 miles (two miles past Drew Reservoir), then to Dog Lake and the campground entrance on the left.

Contact: Fremont National Forest, Lakeview Ranger District, HC 64, Box 60, Lakeview, OR 97630; 541/947-3334; fax 541/947-6375.

41 Drews Creek

9

This is an exceptionally beautiful campground, set along Drews Creek at 4,900 feet. Wild roses grow near the creek, and there are several unmarked trails that lead to nearby hills where campers can enjoy scenic views. The wild roses are often gorgeous. This is a great spot for a family trip and is also popular with group campers, with horseshoe pits, an area for baseball, and a large group barbecue. Fishing is available in nearby Dog Lake, which also provides facilities for boating. Water-skiing is another option at Drews Reservoir, two miles to the west.

Location: Near Lakeview in Fremont National Forest; Southeast Oregon map 6, grid h4.

Campsites, facilities: There are five sites for tents, trailers, or RVs. Picnic tables, fire grills, vault toilets, and drinking water are provided. All garbage must be packed out. Leashed pets are permitted.

Reservations, fees: No reservations; no fee. Open early June to mid-October.

Directions: From Lakeview drive west on Highway 140 for 10 miles to County Road 1-13. Turn left and drive four miles to County Road 1-11D. Turn right and drive six miles (the road will become Forest Road 4017) to the bridge that provides access to the campground.

Contact: Fremont National Forest, Lakeview Ranger District, HC 64, Box 60, Lakeview, OR 97630; 541/947-3334; fax 541/947-6375.

42 Junipers Reservoir RV Resort

6

This resort on an 8,000-acre cattle ranch is in a designated Oregon Wildlife Viewing Area, and campers may catch glimpses of seldom-seen species. There are many nature-walking trails at the park, and driving tours are offered for guests. Fishing for catfish and trout can be good, and because it is a private lake, no fishing license is required. The summer climate is mild and pleasant. Antelope and elk can be spotted in this area.

Location: On Junipers Reservoir; Southeast Oregon map 6, grid g4.

Campsites, facilities: There are 15 tent sites and 40 sites for trailers or RVs. Drinking water, restrooms, showers, a sanitary dump station, a public phone, modem access, a laundry room, and ice are available. Recreational facilities include a recreation hall, a volleyball court, and horseshoe pits. Some of the facilities are wheelchair-accessible. Leashed pets are permitted.

Reservations, fees: Reservations are recommended. Sites are $18–24 per night. Senior discount available. Open May to mid-October.

Directions: From Lakeview drive west on Highway 140 for 10 miles to the resort (at milepost 86.5) on the right.

Contact: Junipers Reservoir RV Resort, HC 60, Box 1994A, Lakeview, OR 97630; 541/947-2050; website: www.junipersrv.com.

43 Mud Creek

4

This remote and quiet camp (at 6,600 feet) is in an isolated stand of lodgepole pines along the banks of Mud Creek. Drake Peak (8,405 feet) is nearby. There are no other camps in the immediate vicinity. Fishing in Mud Creek is surprisingly good.

Location: On Mud Creek in Fremont National Forest; Southeast Oregon map 6, grid f7.

Campsites, facilities: There are seven sites for tents, trailers, or RVs up to 16 feet long. Drinking water, picnic tables, fire grills, and vault toilets are available. Leashed pets are permitted.

Reservations, fees: No reservations; no fee. Open June to mid-October.

Directions: From Lakeview drive five miles north on U.S. 395 to Highway 140. Turn right on Highway 140 and drive eight miles to Forest Road 3615. Turn left and drive seven miles to the campground.

Contact: Fremont National Forest, Lakeview Ranger District, HC 64, Box 60, Lakeview, OR 97630; 541/947-3334; fax 541/947-6375.

44 Goose Lake State Park

7

This park is on the east shore of unusual Goose Lake, which lies half in Oregon and half in California. Waterfowl from the Pacific flyway frequent this out-of-the-way spot. It is home to many species of birds and other wildlife, including a large herd of mule deer that spend much of the time in the campground. When the lake is full of water, canoeing and personal watercraft riding are popular here.

Location: On Goose Lake; Southeast Oregon map 6, grid h6.

Campsites, facilities: There are 48 sites with partial hookups (water and electricity), for tents, trailers, or RVs up to 50 feet long. Picnic tables, fire grills, garbage bins, and drinking water are provided. Flush toilets, showers, a sanitary disposal station, telephone, and firewood are available. Boat-launching facilities are nearby. Leashed pets are permitted.

Reservations, fees: No reservations. Sites are $12–16 per night, $5 per night for an additional vehicle. Open from mid-April to late October.

Directions: From Lakeview drive south on U.S. 395 for 14 miles to the California border and Stateline Road. Turn right (west) and drive one mile to the campground.

Contact: Goose Lake State Park, P.O. Box 207, New Pine Creek, OR 97635; 800/551-6949 or 541/947-3111.

45 Willow Creek

4

This campground (at 5,800 feet elevation) is situated among tall pines and quaking aspen not far from the banks of Willow Creek, near a dirt road that heads north to Burnt Creek. Among the secluded campsites wildflowers bloom in the spring. The campground is set in a canyon, with campsites along the creek. A hiking trail offers access to the Crane Mountain Trail. Pick up a U.S. Forest Service map that details the back roads.

Location: Near Willow Creek in Fremont National Forest; Southeast Oregon map 6, grid h7.

Campsites, facilities: There are eight sites for tents, trailers, or RVs up to 22 feet long. Picnic tables and fire grills are provided. There is no drinking water, and all garbage must be packed out. Vault toilets are available. Leashed pets are permitted.

Reservations, fees: No reservations; no fee. Open June to mid-October.

Directions: From Lakeview drive five miles north on U.S. 395 to Highway 140. Turn right (east) on Highway 140 and drive seven miles to Forest Road 3915. Turn right and drive nine miles to Forest Road 4011. Turn right and drive one mile to the campground.

Contact: Fremont National Forest, Lakeview Ranger District, HC 64, Box 60, Lakeview, OR 97630; 541/947-3334; fax 541/947-6375.

46 Deep Creek
8

Shaded by huge ponderosa pine and cottonwoods, this pretty, little-used campground at an elevation of 5,600 feet on the banks of Deep Creek is the place if you're after privacy. Magnificent spring wildflowers are a highlight here.

Location: On Deep Creek in Fremont National Forest; Southeast Oregon map 6, grid h7.

Campsites, facilities: There are two sites for tents and four sites for trailers or RVs up to 22 feet long. Picnic tables and fire grills are provided. Vault toilets are available. There

is no drinking water, and all garbage must be packed out. Leashed pets are permitted.

Reservations, fees: No reservations; no fee. Open June to mid-October.

Directions: From Lakeview drive five miles north on U.S. 395 to Highway 140. Turn right (east) on Highway 140 and drive six miles to Forest Road 3915. Turn right on Forest Road 3915 and drive 14 miles to Deep Creek and the campground entrance road on the right (Forest Road 4015). Turn right and drive one mile to the campground.

Contact: Fremont National Forest, Lakeview Ranger District, HC 64, Box 60, Lakeview, OR 97630; 541/947-3334; fax 541/947-6375.

47 Hart Mountain Antelope Refuge
6

This unusual refuge offers canyons and hot springs in a high desert area. There is no drinking water at the campground, but it can be obtained at the headquarters, which you pass on the way in. Some of Oregon's largest antelope herds roam this large area. It is one of the few campgrounds managed by the U.S. Fish and Wildlife Service. The nearest place for supplies is in the town of Plush.

Location: Near Adel; Southeast Oregon map 7, grid d4.

Campsites, facilities: There are 12 primitive sites for tents, trailers, or RVs up to 20 feet long. Pit toilets are provided, but there is no drinking water. Leashed pets are permitted.

Reservations, fees: No reservations accepted. There is no fee. Open from May to November, with limited facilities in the winter.

Directions: From Lakeview drive north on U.S. 395 for five miles to Highway 140. Turn east on Highway 140 and drive 28 miles to Adel and the Plush-Hart Mountain Cutoff. Turn left (signed for Hart Antelope Refuge) and drive north for 43 miles (first paved, then gravel) to the refuge headquarters. Continue four miles to the campground (the road is often impassable in the winter).

Contact: Hart Mountain National Antelope Refuge, P.O. Box 111, Lakeview, OR 97630; 541/947-3315; fax 541/947-4414; website: www.fws.gov.

48 Adel Store and Park

5

This remote park is the only game in town, so you'd better grab it while you can. Recreation options in the area include hang gliding, rockhounding, or visiting Hart Mountain National Antelope Refuge, 40 miles north of Adel.

Location: In Adel; Southeast Oregon map 7, grid g1.

Campsites, facilities: There are eight sites for trailers or RVs of any length. Electricity, drinking water, and sewer hookups are provided. A store, a small café, and ice are available. Leashed pets and motorbikes are permitted.

Reservations, fees: Reservations accepted. Sites are $15 per night. Open year-round.

Directions: From Lakeview drive five miles north on U.S. 395 to Highway 140. Turn right (east) on Highway 140 and drive 28 miles to Adel (a very small town). The RV park is in town along Highway 140 on the right.

Contact: Adel Store and Park, P.O. Box 58, Adel, OR 97620; 541/947-3850.

49 Steens Mountain Resort

9

The self-proclaimed "gateway to the Steens Mountains," this resort is bordered by the Malheur National Wildlife Refuge on three sides, and it has great views. The mile-high mountain and surrounding gorges make an excellent photo opportunity. Hiking and hunting are other possibilities in the area. Fishing is available on the Blitzen River, with easy access from the camp.

Location: On the Blitzen River; Southeast Oregon map 8, grid b1.

Campsites, facilities: There are 99 sites for tents, trailers, or RVs, plus nine cabins. Drinking water, restrooms, showers, a sanitary dump station, a public phone, laundry facilities, and ice are available. Leashed pets are permitted.

Reservations, fees: Reservations recommended. Sites are $12–20 per night; cabins are $50–75 per night. Open year-round.

Directions: From Burns drive east on Highway 78 for two miles to Highway 205. Turn south on Highway 205 and drive 59 miles to Frenchglen and Steens Mountain Road. Turn east and drive three miles to the resort on the right.

Contact: Steens Mountain Resort, North Loop Road, Frenchglen, OR 97736; 541/493-2415.

50 Page Springs

7

This campground is adjacent to the Malheur National Wildlife Refuge. The Frenchglen Hotel (three miles away) is administered by the state parks department and offers overnight accommodations and meals. Activities include hiking on the trails in the area, plus bird-watching, fishing, hunting, and sight-seeing.

Location: Near Malheur National Wildlife Refuge; Southeast Oregon map 8, grid b2.

Campsites, facilities: There are 36 sites for tents, trailers, or RVs up to 35 feet long. Picnic tables, garbage service, and fire grills are provided. Drinking water and vault toilets are available. Some facilities are wheelchair-accessible. A day-use area with a shelter is available nearby. Leashed pets are permitted.

Reservations, fees: No reservations accepted. Sites are $8 per vehicle per night, with a 14-day stay limit. Senior discount available. Open year-round.

Directions: From Burns drive east on Highway 78 for two miles to Highway 205. Turn south on Highway 205 and drive 60 miles to Frenchglen and Steens Mountain Loop Road. Turn east and drive three miles to the campground.

Contact: Bureau of Land Management, Burns District, HC 74-12533, U.S. Highway 20 West, Hines, OR 97738; 541/573-4400; fax 541/573-4411; website: www.or.blm.gov/burns.

51 Fish Lake

 8

The shore of Fish Lake is the setting for this primitive but pretty camp among the aspens at elevation 7,400 feet. It can make an excellent weekend-getaway spot for sight-seeing. Trout fishing is an option, made easier by the boat ramp near camp.

Location: On Fish Lake; Southeast Oregon map 8, grid c3.

Campsites, facilities: There are 23 sites for tents, trailers, or RVs up to 35 feet long. Picnic tables, garbage bins, and fire grills are provided. Drinking water and vault toilets are available. Boat-launching facilities are nearby (nonmotorized boats only). Some facilities are wheelchair-accessible. Leashed pets are permitted.

Reservations, fees: No reservations accepted. Sites are $8 per vehicle per night, with a 14-day stay limit. Senior discount available. Open from June through October, weather permitting.

Directions: From Burns drive east on Highway 78 for two miles to Highway 205. Turn south on Highway 205 and drive 60 miles to Frenchglen and Steens Mountain Loop Road.

Turn east and drive 20 miles to the campground.

Contact: Bureau of Land Management, Burns District, HC 74-12533, U.S. Highway 20 West, Hines, OR 97738; 541/573-4400; fax 541/573-4411; website: www.or.blm.gov/burns.

52 Jackman Park

This camp is set at 7,800 feet in the eastern Oregon desert, one of four camps in the area. Fish Lake is 2.5 miles away. This scenic campground has aspen and willow trees. Jackman Park is known as the one of the best places in the fall to view the golden leaves of the aspens on Steens Mountain. Trailers and RVs are not recommended on the access road.

Location: Near Malheur National Wildlife Refuge; Southeast Oregon map 8, grid c3.

Campsites, facilities: There are six primitive sites for tents. Picnic tables are provided. Drinking water and pit toilets are available. Leashed pets are permitted.

Reservations, fees: No reservations accepted. Sites are $6 per vehicle a night, with a 14-day stay limit. Senior discount available. Open from July to late October, weather permitting.

Directions: From Burns drive east on Highway 78 for two miles to Highway 205. Turn south on Highway 205 and drive 60 miles to Frenchglen and Steens Mountain Loop Road. Turn east and drive 22 miles to the campground

Contact: Bureau of Land Management, Burns District, HC 74-12533, U.S. Highway 20 West, Hines, OR 97738; 541/573-4400; fax 541/573-4411; website: www.or.blm.gov/burns.

53 Mann Lake

 8

There are two small boat ramps and a 10 horsepower limit on motors. Fishing, including wintertime ice fishing, and wildlife viewing are popular here. Weather can be extreme. The campground sits at the base of Steens Mountains and is open, with sagebrush and no trees. The scenic, high desert camp is mainly used as a fishing camp; please respect private property on parcels of land next to the lake. Fishing can be very good for cutthroat trout. Nearby Alvord Desert is also an attraction.

Location: On Mann Lake; Southeast Oregon map 8, grid b5.

Campsites, facilities: There are dispersed sites for tents, trailers, or RVs of up to 35 feet; there are open areas on each side of the lake. No drinking water is available, but vault toilets with wheelchair access and boat ramps are. Pack out all garbage. Leashed pets are permitted.

Reservations, fees: No reservations accepted. There is a no fee. Open year-round.

Directions: From Burns drive southeast on Highway 78 for 65 miles to Fields/Denio Road (Folly Farm Road). Turn south (right) and drive 22 miles to the campground at Mann Lake.

Contact: Bureau of Land Management, Burns District, HC 74-12533, U.S. Highway 20 West, Hines, OR 97738; 541/573-4400; fax 541/573-4411; website: www.or.blm.gov/burns.

54 South Steens

 6

This campground is set on the edge of the Steens Mountain Wilderness. The area features deep, glacial-carved gorges, volcanic uplifts, stunning scenery, and a rare chance to see elk and bighorn sheep. Redband trout fishing is a mile away at Donner und Blitzen River and its tributaries, a new reserve. This campground is also good for horse campers, with the campground set up so that horse campers are in a separate area from the other campers. Trails are accessible from the campground.

Location: Steens Mountain Wilderness; Southeast Oregon map 8, grid c2.

Campsites, facilities: There are 36 sites for tents, trailers, or RVs of up to 35 feet; 15 of the sites are designated for horse campers. Picnic tables, hitching posts, and fire grills are provided. Drinking water, wheelchair-accessible vault toilets, two wheelchair-accessible sites, and garbage bins are available. Leashed pets are permitted.

Reservations, fees: No reservations accepted. There is a 14-day stay limit. Sites are $6 per vehicle per night. Senior discount available. Open May through October, weather permitting.

Directions: From Burns drive east on Highway 78 for two miles to Highway 205. Turn south on Highway 205 and drive 60 miles to Frenchglen. Continue south on Highway 205 for 10 miles to Steens South Loop Road. Turn left (east) and drive 18 miles to the campground on the right.

Contact: Bureau of Land Management, Burns District, HC 74-12533, U.S. Highway 20 West, Hines, OR 97738; 541/573-4400; fax 541/573-4411; website: www.or.blm.gov/burns.

55 Willow Creek Hot Springs

7

This campground can be difficult to find, and only the adventurous should attempt this trip. A very small campground with no privacy, its campsites are about 100 feet from the hot springs, which are two connected smaller pools. Despite its being out of the way, travelers from far and away find their way here. The surrounding scenery is rocky hills, not a flat expanse.

Location: Near Whitehorse Butte; Southeast Oregon map 8, grid f7.

Campsites, facilities: There are four sites for tents, small trailers, or RVs.

Fire rings are provided. Vault toilets are available. No drinking water is available, and all garbage must be packed out. Leashed pets are permitted.

Reservations, fees: No reservations. There is a no fee. Open year-round, weather permitting.

Directions: From Burns drive southeast on Highway 78 for 105 miles to Burns Junction and U.S. 95. Turn right (south) on U.S. 95 and drive 20 miles to Whitehorse Road. Turn right (southwest) and drive 21 miles (passing Whitehorse Ranch) and continue for 2.5 miles to a fork (look for the telephone pole). Bear left and drive two miles to the campground.

Contact: Bureau of Land Management, Vale District, 100 Oregon St., Vale, OR 97918-9630; 541/473-3144; fax 541/473-6213; website: www.or.blm.gov/vale.

56 Rome Launch

🏊 🎣 ⚓ 🚗 🐕 🚐 ⛺ 6

This campground is used mainly for people rafting the Owyhee River and overnighters passing through. A few cottonwood trees and sagebrush live in this campground. There are a few farms and ranches in the area. Campsites are adjacent to the Owyhee River. I have canoed most of the Owyhee from the headwaters in Nevada below the Jarbidge Mountains all the way through Idaho and into Oregon, and I would rate this river as one of the top canoeing destinations in North America. The Owyhee Canyon is quite dramatic, like a miniature Grand Canyon. This is also a good wildlife-viewing area; mountain lions and bobcats have been spotted.

Note: No motorized boats are allowed on the river.

Location: On the Owyhee River; Southeast Oregon map 9, grid b3.

Campsites, facilities: There are five sites for tents, small trailers, or RVs. Picnic

tables and fire rings are provided. Drinking water, vault toilets, and a boat launch are available. No firewood is available, and all garbage must be packed out. Leashed pets are permitted.

Reservations, fees: No reservations; no fee. Open March through November, weather permitting.

Directions: From Burns Junction, drive east on U.S. 95 for 15 miles to Jordan Valley and the signed turnoff for the Owyhee River and BLM-Rome boat launch. Turn south and drive one-quarter mile to the campground.

Contact: Bureau of Land Management, Vale District, 100 Oregon St., Vale, OR 97918-9630; 541/473-3144; fax 541/473-6213.

57 Antelope Reservoir

🎣 ⚓ 🐕 🚐 ⛺ 3

Water levels fluctuate at this shallow lake and it can dry up. There is no tree cover in this open area on a slope above the reservoir. Be prepared for extreme weather. The campground gets little use except during the hunting season.

Location: On the Antelope Reservoir; Southeast Oregon map 9, grid a6.

Campsites, facilities: There are four sites for tents, small trailers, or RVs. Picnic tables and fire rings are provided. Vault toilets and boat access are available. No drinking water is available and all garbage must be packed out. Leashed pets are permitted.

Reservations, fees: No reservations; no fee. Open year-round, weather permitting.

Directions: From Burns Junction, drive east on U.S. 95 for 36 miles to the signed turnoff for Antelope Reservoir. Turn south and drive one mile to the campground on the left.

Contact: Bureau of Land Management, Vale District, 100 Oregon St., Vale, OR 97918-9630; 541/473-3144; fax 541/473-6213.

RESOURCE GUIDE

©TOM STIENSTRA

Resource Guide

U.S. National Forests

U.S. Forest Service, Pacific Northwest Region 6: 333 S.W. 1st Ave., Portland, OR 97204-3440; or P.O. Box 3623, Portland, OR 97208-3623; 503/808-2651, fax 503/808-2229; website: www.fs.fed.us/r6.

Maps of national forests in Oregon are available from the district offices listed as a contact for each national forest campground. They are also available from an interpretive organization: Nature of the Northwest, 800 N.E. Oregon St., Suite 177, Portland, OR 97232; 503/872-2750; website: www.naturenw.org.

For further information on individual national forests, write, call, or visit the websites of the following forests:

- **Deschutes National Forest:** 1645 U.S. Hwy. 20 E, Bend, OR 97701; 541/383-5300, fax 541/383-5531; website: www.fs.fed.us/r6/centraloregon
- **Fremont National Forest:** HC 10 Box 337, 1300 S. G St., Lakeview, OR 97630; 541/947-2151, fax 541/947-6399; website: www.fs.fed.us/r6/fremont
- **Malheur National Forest:** 431 Patterson Bridge Rd., P.O. Box 909, John Day, OR 97845; 541/575-3000, fax 541/575-3001; website: www.fs.fed.us/r6/malheur
- **Mount Hood National Forest:** 16400 Champion Way, Sandy, OR 97055; 503/668-1700, fax 503/668-1794; website: www.fs.fed.us/r6/mthood
- **Ochoco National Forest:** 3160 N.E. 3rd St., Box 490, Prineville, OR 97754; 541/416-6500, fax 541/416-6695; website: www.fs.fed.us/r6/centraloregon
- **Rogue River National Forest:** P.O. Box 520, 333 W. 8th St., Medford, OR 97501-0209; 541/858-2200, fax 541/858-2220; website: www.fs.fed.us/r6/rogue
- **Siskiyou National Forest:** 200 N.E. Greenfield Rd., Box 440, Grants Pass, OR 97528-0242; 541/471-6500, fax 541/471-6514; website: www.fs.fed.us/r6/siskiyou
- **Siuslaw National Forest:** P.O. Box 1148, 4077 S.W. Research Way, Corvallis, OR 97333; 541/750-7000, fax 541/750-7234; website: www.fs.fed.us/r6/siuslaw
- **Umatilla National Forest:** 2517 S.W. Hailey Ave., Pendleton, OR 97801; 541/278-3716, fax 541/278-3730; website: www.fs.fed.us/r6/uma
- **Umpqua National Forest:** P.O. Box 1008, 2900 N.W. Stewart Pkwy., Roseburg, OR 97470; 541/672-6601, fax 541/957-3495; website: www.fs.fed.us/r6/umpqua
- **Wallowa-Whitman National Forest:** P.O. Box 907, 1550 Dewey Ave., Baker City, OR 97814; 541/523-6391, fax 541/523-1315; website: www.fs.fed.us/r6/w-w
- **Willamette National Forest:** P.O. Box 10607, Eugene, OR 97440 or 211 E. 7th Ave., Eugene, OR 97440-2607; 541/465-6521, fax 541/465-6488; website: www.fs.fed.us/r6/willamette
- **Winema National Forest:** 2819 Dahlia St., Klamath Falls, OR 97601; 541/883-6714, fax 541/883-6709; website: www.fs.fed.us/r6/winema

State Parks

Oregon Parks and Recreation Department: 1115 Commercial St. NE, Salem, OR 97301-1002; 800/551-6949, fax 503/872-5289; website: www.prd.state.or.us; **Oregon Parks and Recreation Department:** P.O. Box 500, 97207 Portland, OR; 800/551-6949; website: www.oregonstateparks.org.

Oregon State Parks systems provide many popular camping spots. Reservations are often a necessity during the summer. The campgrounds include drive-in numbered sites, tent spaces, and picnic tables, with showers and bathrooms provided nearby. Although some parks are well known, there are still some little-known gems in the state parks systems where campers can get seclusion, even in the summer.

Oregon now sponsors a central reservation system. Reservations can be made for 26 Oregon state parks through Reservations Northwest at 800/452-5687. Online reservations for Oregon State Parks can be made through the website: www.prd.state.or.us. A nonrefundable reservation fee of $6 and the first night's fee will be required as a deposit, charged to a MasterCard or Visa credit card (debit cards linked to MasterCard or Visa also accepted). Under this system, reservations can be made throughout the year, up to 11 months in advance.

General information regarding Oregon State Parks can be obtained by calling 800/551-6949.

Oregon's National Parks

The national parks in Oregon are natural wonders, varying from the spectacular Columbia River Gorge to the breathtaking Crater Lake National Park.

For information about each of the national parks in Oregon, contact the parks directly at the following numbers or addresses:

- **Crater Lake National Park:** P.O. Box 7, Crater Lake, OR 97604; 541/594-2211, fax 541/594-2299; website: www.nps.gov/crla
- **Columbia River Gorge National Scenic Area:** 902 Wasco Ave., Suite 200, Hood River, OR 97031; 541/386-2333, fax 541/386-1916; website: www.fs.fed.us/r6/Columbia
- **Crooked River National Grassland:** 813 S.W. U.S. Hwy. 97, Madras, OR 97741; 541/416-6640, fax 541/416-6694; website: www.fs.fed.us/r6/centraloregon
- **Hells Canyon National Recreation Area:** 88401 Hwy. 82, Enterprise, OR 97828; 541/426-5546 or 541/426-4978, fax 541/426-5520; website: www.fs.fed.us/r6/w-w
- **Oregon Dunes National Recreation Area:** 855 U.S. Hwy. 101, Reedsport, OR 97467; 541/271-3611, fax 541/271-6019; website: www.fs.fed.us/r6/siuslaw/oregondunes

Bureau of Land Management (BLM)

- **Oregon Office:** 1515 S.W. 5th Ave., Portland, OR 97201, or P.O. Box 2965, Portland, OR 97208; 503/952-6002, fax 503/952-6308; website: www.or.blm.gov
- **Burns District:** HC 74,12533 U.S. Hwy. 20 W, Hines, OR 97738; 541/573-4400, fax 541/573-4411; website: www.or.blm.gov/burns.
- **Coos Bay District:** 1300 Airport Ln., North Bend, OR 97459; 541/756-0100, fax 541/751-4303; website: www.or.blm.gov/coosbay
- **Eugene District:** 2890 Chad Dr., Eugene, OR 97440, or P.O. Box 10226, Eugene, OR 97440; 541/683-6600, fax 541/683-6981; website: www.edo.or.blm.gov
- **Lakeview District:** HC 10, Box 337, 1300 S. G St., Lakeview, OR 97630; 541/947-2177, fax 541/947-6399; www.or.blm.gov/lakeview
- **Medford District:** 3040 Biddle Rd., Medford, OR 97504; 541/618-2200, fax 541/770-2400; website: www.or.blm.gov/medford
- **Prineville District:** 3050 N.E. 3rd St., Prineville, OR 97754, or P.O. Box 550, Prineville, OR 97754; 541/416-6700, fax 541/416-6798; website: www.or.blm.gov/prineville
- **Roseburg District:** 777 N.W. Garden Valley Blvd., Roseburg, OR 97470; 541/440-4930, fax 541/440-4948; website: www.or.blm.gov/roseburg
- **Salem District:** 1717 Fabry Rd. SE, Salem, OR 97306; 503/375-5646, fax 503/375-5622; website: www.or.blm.gov/salem
- **Vale District:** 100 Oregon St., Vale, OR 97918-9630; 541/473-3144, fax 541/473-6213; website: www.or.blm.gov/vale

U.S. Army Corps of Engineers

- **Portland District:** 333 S.W. 1st Ave., Portland, OR 97208, or P.O. Box 2946, Portland, OR 97208-2946; 503/808-5150, fax 503/808-4515; website: www.nww.usace.army.mil

Oregon Department of Forestry

- **Oregon Department of Forestry:** 2600 State St., Salem, OR 97310; 503/945-7200, fax 503/945-7212; website: www.odf.state.or.us
- **Tillamook State Forest, Forest Grove District:** 801 Gales Creek Rd., Forest Grove, OR 97116-1199; 503/359-7041, fax 503/357-4548; website: www.odf.state.or.us/TSF
- **Tillamook State Forest, Tillamook District:** 4907 E. 3rd St., Tillamook, OR 97141-2999; 503/842-2545, fax 503/842-3143.

Nature of the Northwest Information Center

800 N.E. Oregon St., Suite 177, Portland, OR 97232; 503/872-2750, fax 503/731-4066; website: www.naturenw.org

Index

Canoeing, Rafting, and Kayaking

Festivals and Events

Horseback Riding

Winter Sports and Activities

Maps

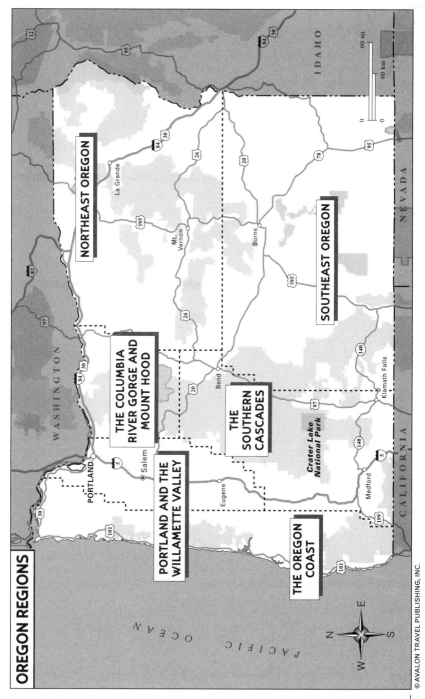

OREGON REGIONS

NORTHEAST OREGON

THE COLUMBIA RIVER GORGE AND MOUNT HOOD

PORTLAND AND THE WILLAMETTE VALLEY

THE SOUTHERN CASCADES

SOUTHEAST OREGON

THE OREGON COAST

Crater Lake National Park

WASHINGTON

IDAHO

NEVADA

CALIFORNIA

PACIFIC OCEAN

PORTLAND
Salem
Eugene
Medford
Klamath Falls
Bend
Burns
Mt. Vernon
La Grande

© AVALON TRAVEL PUBLISHING, INC.

AVALON
TRAVEL
publishing

How far will our travel guides take you? As far as you want.

Discover a rhumba-fueled nightspot in Old Havana, explore prehistoric tombs in Ireland, hike beneath California's centuries-old redwoods, or embark on a classic road trip along Route 66. Our guidebooks deliver solidly researched, trip-tested information—minus any generic froth—to help globetrotters or weekend warriors create an adventure uniquely their own.

And we're not just about the printed page. Public television viewers are tuning in to Rick Steves' new travel series, *Rick Steves' Europe*. On the Web, readers can cruise the virtual black top with *Road Trip USA* author Jamie Jensen and learn travel industry secrets from Edward Hasbrouck of *The Practical Nomad*.

In print. On TV. On the Internet.

We supply the information. The rest is up to you.

Avalon Travel Publishing

Something for everyone

www.travelmatters.com

Avalon Travel Publishing guides are available at your favorite book or travel store.

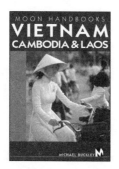

MOON HANDBOOKS provide comprehensive

coverage of a region's arts, history, land, people, and social issues in addition to detailed practical listings for accommodations, food, outdoor recreation, and entertainment. Moon Handbooks allow complete immersion in a region's culture—ideal for travelers who want to combine sightseeing with insight for an extraordinary travel experience in destinations throughout North America, Hawaii, Latin America, the Caribbean, Asia, and the Pacific.

WWW.MOON.COM

Rick Steves

shows you where to travel and how to travel—all while getting the most value for your dollar. His Back Door travel philosophy is about making friends, having fun, and avoiding tourist rip-offs.

Rick

has been traveling to Europe for more than 25 years and is the author of 22 guidebooks, which have sold more than a million copies. He also hosts the award-winning public television series *Rick Steves' Europe*.

WWW.RICKSTEVES.COM

ROAD TRIP USA

Getting there is half the fun, and Road Trip USA guides are your ticket to driving adventure. Taking you off the interstates and onto less-traveled, two-lane highways, each guide is filled with fascinating trivia, historical information, photographs, facts about regional writers, and details on where to sleep and eat—all contributing to your exploration of the American road.

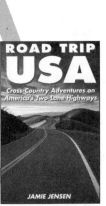

"[Books] so full of the pleasures of the American road, you can smell the upholstery."
~BBC radio

WWW.ROADTRIPUSA.COM

FOGHORN OUTDOORS

FOGHORN OUTDOORS guides are for campers, hikers, boaters, anglers, bikers, and golfers of all levels of daring and skill. Each guide focuses on a specific U.S. region and contains site descriptions and ratings, driving directions, facilities and fees information,and easy-to-read maps that leave only the task of deciding where to go.

"Foghorn Outdoors has established an ecological conservation standard unmatched by any other publisher." ~Sierra Club
WWW.FOGHORN.COM

TRAVEL SMART guidebooks are accessible, route-based driving guides focusing on regions throughout the United States and Canada. Special interest tours provide the most practical routes for family fun, outdoor activities, or regional history for a trip of anywhere from two to 22 days. Travel Smarts take the guesswork out of planning a trip by recommending only the most interesting places to eat, stay, and visit.

"One of the few travel series that rates sightseeing attractions. That's a handy feature. It helps to have some guidance so that every minute counts." ~San Diego Union-Tribune

CiTY·SMaRT™ guides are written by local authors with hometown perspectives who have personally selected the best places to eat, shop, sightsee, and simply hang out. The honest, lively, and opinionated advice is perfect for business travelers looking to relax with the locals or for longtime residents looking for something new to do Saturday night.